Time Out

Sydney

www.timeoutsydney.com.au

D1422312

90710 000 083 504

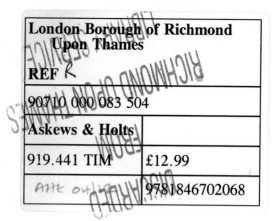

Guides

Time Out Guides Ltd
Universal House
251 Tottenham Court Road
London W1T 7AB
United Kingdom
Tel: +44 (0)20 7813 3000
Fax: +44 (0)20 7813 6001
Email: guides@timeout.com
www.timeout.com

Published by Time Out Guides Ltd, a wholly owned subsidiary of Time Out Group Ltd.
Time Out and the Time Out logo are trademarks of Time Out Group Ltd.

© Time Out Group Ltd 2011
Previous editions 1997, 2000, 2001, 2004, 2006, 2008.

10 9 8 7 6 5 4 3 2 1

This edition first published in Great Britain in 2011 by Ebury Publishing.
A Random House Group Company
20 Vauxhall Bridge Road, London SW1V 2SA

Random House Australia Pty Ltd 20 Alfred Street, Milsons Point, Sydney, New South Wales 2061, Australia

Random House New Zealand Ltd 18 Poland Road, Glenfield, Auckland 10, New Zealand

Random House South Africa (Pty) Ltd Isle of Houghton, Corner Boundary Road & Carse O'Gowrie, Houghton 2198, South Africa

Random House UK Limited Reg. No. 954009

Distributed in the US and Latin America by Publishers Group West (1-510-809-3700)
Distributed in Canada by Publishers Group Canada (1-800-747-8147)

For further distribution details, see www.timeout.com.

ISBN: 978-1-84670-206-8

A CIP catalogue record for this book is available from the British Library.

Printed and bound by Firmengruppe APPL, aprinta druck, Wemding, Germany.

The Random House Group Limited supports The Forest Stewardship Council (FSC), the leading international forest certification organisation. All our titles that are printed on Greenpeace approved FSC certified paper carry the FSC logo. Our paper procurement policy can be found at http://www.rbooks.co.uk/environment.

Time Out carbon-offsets its flights with Trees for Cities (www.treesforcities.org).

While every effort has been made by the author(s) and the publisher to ensure that the information contained in this guide is accurate and up to date as at the date of publication, they accept no responsibility or liability in contract, tort, negligence, breach of statutory duty or otherwise for any inconvenience, loss, damage, costs or expenses of any nature whatsoever incurred or suffered by anyone as a result of any advice or information contained in this guide (except to the extent that such liability may not be excluded or limited as a matter of law). Before travelling, it is advisable to check all information locally, including without limitation, information on transport, accommodation, shopping and eating out. Anyone using this guide is entirely responsible for their own health, well-being and belongings and care should always be exercised while travelling.

Contents

Introduction

In literature, cities are always female. So it is with Sydney, a hell-and-back starlet blessed with natural gifts so vast, every visitor wants to buy her a drink. Yet gorgeous as she is, Sydney's delinquent past is her most seductive charm. The city's origins as a convict settlement are omnipresent in the crazed sprawl of her suburbs and shires, the wildly different gusts of her architecture, the collision of nature and technology at her fringes and, most of all, in the happy-go-lucky egalitarianism of her people. Let it be known that Sydneysiders are the warmest of hosts – shout them a beer and you'll never walk alone.

Sydney has come further in the last two centuries than any city on the planet. The 18th-century criminal outpost for the British Empire ushered in the 21st century by hosting the greatest Olympics of the modern age in 2000, and has scarcely paused for breath since. Today, this insatiable city of 4.5 million people is the most international and electrifying of Australia's metropolises, with a food scene the envy of the world, cultural hubs attracting the best and brightest stars, a laid-back lifestyle nurturing athletes, artists and auteurs in equal measure, and a wild side everyone needs to walk before they die.

But Sydney is not a city that gives up her charms on the first (or even the second) date. Her harbour may bedazzle, her beaches may bare all, but beneath the glitter is grit. In Sydney, a visitor must dig to find real treasure. Scratch the surface here and amazing stories bubble up, not least those of the Gadigal tribes to whom Sydney belonged before the 'white invasion' of 1788. To them, Sydney was a living thing – breathing, seething, blessing, cursing – a spiritual land to whom they belonged, a mother and a master in one.

Some 40,000 years of dreaming later, Sydney retains an air of mystery. Be warned, humble traveller: this is not a city easily tamed. From the outset she has challenged and charmed her suitors. You must earn her favours with tribute, for hers has been a short life and a merry one and even from the gutter of her past, her gaze has never shifted from the stars.

So go well, Sydney visitor. Drink deep of supernatural harbours and skies and bask in the delights of food, nature, ancient lore and multiple cultures. Keep your tongue well oiled and your wits about you. Mark Twain observed that: 'God made the Harbour, but Satan made Sydney' and he was probably right. But now you've entered the Devil's playground, you might as well play.
Angus Fontaine, Editor

Sydney in Brief

IN CONTEXT

This introduction shines a light on Sydney's dark beginnings as
a prison for outlaws, misfits and soldiers from the far side of
the Earth. We explore the city's architecture, the buildings and
institutions carved from its natural sandstone heart and those
sparked from steel and glass. Finally, we confront the issues
facing the Sydney of tomorrow – transport, infrastructure, culture,
and, being the thirsty town it is, nightlife.

▶ For more, see pp13-40.

SIGHTS

Many of Sydney's main attractions are on the waterfront, with The
Rocks – birthplace of the nation – as ground zero. You can explore
the centre on foot or catch a bus, tram or train into the suburbs.
Better yet, jump on a ferry and chug the most beautiful harbour
in the world. Wherever you go, cultural hotspots jostle with
restaurants, cafés, museums and galleries in the 'optical
ecstasy' of Sydney's parks, bush, waterways and beaches.

▶ For more, see pp41-123.

CONSUME

Sydney is a gourmet's paradise teeming with fresh ingredients,
celebrity chefs and lots of markets and food stores. This is an
insatiable town, with vast clusters of cafés, buzzing eat streets
and a huge diversity of bars. In this section you'll find cheap
chow, top-flight kitchens and every type of belly fuel and neck oil
between, plus shops for purchases essential and frivolous – and
our selection of key hotels at key price points.

▶ For more, see pp125-216.

ARTS & ENTERTAINMENT

Culture vultures and art mavens rejoice! Sydney is alive with
amazing theatres, concert halls, art galleries, music venues and
comedy clubs. From orchestral manoeuvres at the Opera House to
laugh garages in the western suburbs, Sydney has something for
every age, taste and budget. This is also where to find our picks
from Sydney's rambunctious queer scene, commercial art
galleries, festivals and family destinations.

▶ For more, see pp217-274.

ESCAPES & EXCURSIONS

If there's not enough to fill your dance card in town, heading north,
west and south of the city by car, train or plane uncovers a seemingly
endless supply of off-the-beaten-track adventures. Small towns, blue
mountains, glorious bushland and secret coves are all within an
hour's drive of the big smoke. This section collects the best
destinations, hotels and eating and drinking venues.

▶ For more, see pp275-292.

Sydney in 48 Hours

Day 1 The Big Smoke

8am Kick the dew off the day with a stroll through Sydney's **Botanic Gardens** (*see p60*), visiting the **Art Gallery of NSW** (*see p58*) before looping left to dip your toe in the water at '**Boy' Pool** (*see p58*) or take in the view from **Lady Macquarie's Chair** (*see p57*) overlooking the working harbour. Curl around the coast to **Bennelong Point** (*see p30*), *taking in* the glory of the **Opera House** (*see p56*), and stroll through Circular Quay ferry terminal to enter The Rocks' cobblestone courtyards and higgledy-piggledy lanes. Head to ye olde **Lord Nelson Hotel** (*see p131*) for lunch and a pint brewed on-site.

1pm Head uptown along the main drag of George Street, stopping at the **GPO Building** (*see p64*) and either go up Martin Place to Macquarie Street's historic buildings or continue up George Street to **The Strand Arcade** (*see p196*) and **Queen Victoria Building** (*see p64*) for some retail therapy. Hyde Park connects both paths and leads you east past the **Anzac Memorial** (*see p58*) on to the 'pink mile' of Oxford Street, past Taylor Square to Paddington and its slick collection of cafés, bars, galleries, gardens and shops.

4pm A 380 bus at the top of Oxford Street will carry you past **Centennial Park** (*see p77*) and Bondi Junction to Bondi Road and – you guessed it – **Bondi Beach** (*see p79*). Slake the salt in your gullet with a 'sundowner' at **Drift** (*see p191*).

7pm Jump back on the 380 for the short trip to **Watsons Bay** (*see p84*). Here you can catch a ferry back to town for a lavish dinner.

10pm Still going strong? Whizz up New South Head Road and into the red light mayhem and magic of **Kings Cross** (*see p72*). If midnight chimes and you're hungry again, head to **Harry's Café de Wheels** (*see p80*) for a 'tiger' pie. Then cab it home – tomorrow's a big day.

NAVIGATING THE CITY
Sydney is a messy maze of suburbs fanning out from the harbour and city centre to the mountains of the west, the bushy shires in the south and the beaches and forests of the far north. Fear not. There are plenty of inexpensive public transport options and an abundance of taxis. Traffic is an issue in the city, so traverse the CBD and inner suburbs on foot and opt for buses and trains to go beyond the city limits.

Sydney has always been a land of many tribes and the legacy is a vast quantity of suburbs with their own identity. To help you absorb its topography, we've divided it into areas: Central Sydney, Eastern Suburbs, Inner West, North Shore, Northern Beaches, Parramatta & the West, and the South.

SEEING THE SIGHTS
There are some obvious traps for tourists in Sydney – weekend sightseeing for starters. Popular hubs like Bondi and Manly beach go into overdrive at weekends – far better to experience them as the locals do and visit midweek

Day 2 North by Northwest

9am Amble back down to **Circular Quay** (*see p54*) and take the Manly ferry ('seven miles from Sydney, a thousand miles from care') north for breakfast. Soak up the atmosphere of the Corso as you stroll to the beach then embark on the scenic walk to Spit Bridge, or picnic at Shelly Beach, scuba dive at Cabbage Tree Bay and keep your eyes peeled for the secret colony of Little Penguins at Fairy Bower.

Noon Back in the city, meander through the **Museum of Sydney** (*see p56*) or the nearby **Justice & Police Museum** (*see p56*) before grabbing a classic Sydney lunch overlooking the Harbour at **Café Sydney** (*see p150*) or a fast, classy pizza at Young Alfred, both in **Customs House** (*see p55*).

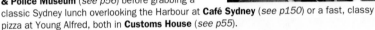

2pm Jump a RiverCat ferry for the trip north-west via the history-rich backwaters. This hour-long journey first takes you north to Milsons Point and kid-friendly Luna Park then pinballs you between the historic art colony of McMahons Point in the north and bohemian Birchgrove and Balmain in the west. You'll then chug to former prison turned culture hub Cockatoo Island and on out to Kissing Point, past Sydney Olympic Park and, after a moody snake upriver, into historic, multicultural Parramatta.

5pm Back on dry land at Darling Harbour, grab a waterfront drink at one of the King Street Wharf restaurants such as **Malaya** (*see p161*). As dusk falls, take an easy stroll around the controversial **Barangaroo** site to Dawes Point (named for the colony's first stargazer) and the theatre district of Walsh Bay. Grab a ticket to the Bangarra Dance Company or a Cate Blanchett co-production for the **Sydney Theatre Company** (*see p273*).

9pm Firefly (*see p185*) is great for a post-stage sip, tapas-style tidbit and debrief before you cab it south to the drinks strips of Surry Hills and Darlinghurst.

(though note that rush hour spans 8-9.30am and 5-7pm.)

Many of the city's attractions offer free (or token) admission, including several in the city centre. Opening times given are last-entry but many of the larger institutions stay open later, while smaller venues may shut up shop earlier if it's quiet. Public holidays are listed in the Directory section of the guide (*see p307*).

PACKAGE DEALS

Since April 2010, a new fare structure called **MyZone** has made travelling on Sydney public transport much easier. MyZone tickets are accepted on the entire CityRail, State Transit and Sydney ferries network, and some private services too. You can also get the SydneyPass, aimed specifically at tourists' needs. For more information, *see p295* **Getting Around**.

The **Sydney & Beyond Attractions Pass** (www.seesydneycard.com; $122 for two days) offers free admission to over 40 attractions in Sydney and out to the Blue Mountains. The **Sydney Explore4 Pass** (www.myfun.com.au; $49.99) gets you in for free at four landmark Sydney sights.

Sydney
in Profile

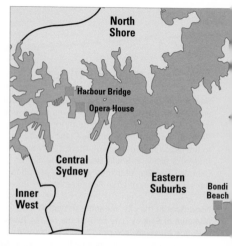

North Shore

Harbour Bridge

Opera House

Central Sydney

Eastern Suburbs

Bondi Beach

Inner West

CENTRAL SYDNEY
From the harbour to the first whiffs of suburbia, Central Sydney spans the city centre and its surrounding harbour ports (**Darling Harbour**, **Pyrmont**, **Potts Point**) extending into the buzzy drinks, dining and arts and entertainment hubs of **Surry Hills**, **Darlinghurst**, **Kings Cross**, **Redfern** and **Woolloomooloo**.
▶ For more, see pp51-73.

EASTERN SUBURBS
Sydney's east is where a lot of the hottest action is – in every sense. Beaches are catwalks in these parts. People are beautiful. Shopping is a high priority. Cycling in the parks and surfing, sailing and swimming in the sea are virtually compulsory here and there are picnic spots, walking trails and great gourmet adventures lurking around every corner.
▶ For more, see pp74-85.

INNER WEST
Edgier than its sun-kissed cousins to the east, Sydney's inner west thrives on indoor sports – restaurants, galleries, rock music and book shops. There are markets, beer gardens and bohemia galore around **Newtown**, **Leichardt**, **Enmore** and **Erskineville** and the multicultural fringe of the Sydney melting pot hits high boil the further west you head.
▶ For more, see pp86-92.

NORTH SHORE

Always leafy and ever more attractive for young families and the nouveau riche, the north shore is full of postcard views and quietly beautiful settings. Recently, the bar and restaurant scene has hit hyper-drive with quaint villages like **Neutral Bay**, **Kirribilli** and **Blues Point** now blossoming as nightlife nooks.
▶ *For more, see pp93-100.*

NORTHERN BEACHES

Laid-back and lovely, the northern beaches exist off the train line and far from the urban chaos of central Sydney. Yet these golden stretches of sandy beaches leave Bondi and Bronte for dead and are proving increasingly alluring to Sydneysiders seeking a sea change and tourists chasing paradise.
▶ *For more, see pp101-107.*

PARRAMATTA & THE GREATER WEST

The fastest growing area of Australia is a vibrant mix of history, natural beauty and delicious urban development. Sydney's sense of tribalism is never stronger than with 'westies' – they are fiercely proud of their food scene, their sporting teams, even their art and entertainment events. And, with festivals flourishing at this ferry-accessible area, it's easy to know why west is best.
▶ *For more, see pp108-113.*

THE SOUTH

Sun, sea and surf sparkle bright down south in the quaintly named 'Shire'. The townships dotting **Port Hacking** might be the perfect Sydney mix of national parks, ethnic cuisine, glorious beaches, art trails and indigenous roots. The south officially starts at Greek community hub **Brighton-le-Sands**. Full of rich secrets and quiet delights, the South's time has arrived.
▶ *For more, see pp114-116.*

Time Out Sydney

Editorial
Editor Angus Fontaine
Copy Editors Anna Norman, Jan Fuscoe
Proofreader Patrick Mulkern
Indexer Sally Davies

Managing Director Peter Fiennes
Editorial Director Ruth Jarvis
Business Manager Dan Allen
Editorial Manager Holly Pick
Assistant Management Accountant Ija Krasnikova

Design
Art Director Scott Moore
Art Editor Pinelope Kourmouzoglou
Senior Designer Kei Ishimaru
Group Commercial Designer Jodi Sher

Picture Desk
Picture Editor Jael Marschner
Acting Deputy Picture Editor Liz Leahy
Picture Research (Sydney) Phil Bunting
Picture Desk Assistant/Researcher Ben Rowe

Advertising
New Business & Commercial Director Mark Phillips
International Advertising Manager Kasimir Berger
International Sales Executive Charlie Sokol
Advertising Sales (Sydney) Ad Pack Australia
(colin.m@adpacau.com)

Marketing
**Sales & Marketing Director, North America
& Latin America** Lisa Levinson
Senior Publishing Brand Manager Luthfa Begum
Group Commercial Art Director Anthony Huggins
Marketing Co-ordinator Alana Benton

Production
Group Production Manager Brendan McKeown
Production Controller Katie Mulhern

Time Out Group
Director & Founder Tony Elliott
Chief Executive Officer David King
Group Financial Director Paul Rakkar
Group General Manager/Director Nichola Coulthard
Time Out Communications Ltd MD David Pepper
Time Out International Ltd MD Cathy Runciman
Time Out Magazine Ltd Publisher/MD Mark Elliott
Group Commercial Director Graeme Tottle
Group IT Director Simon Chappell

Contributors
Introduction Angus Fontaine. **History** Juliet Rieden (*The other history* Miranda Herron). **Siren City** Delia Falconer. **Sydney Today** Angus Fontaine. **Architecture** Angus Fontaine. **Hotels** James Wilkinson. **Sights** Angus Fontaine, Katie Ekberg, Ed Gibbs, Juliet Rieden, Prue Rushton. **Restaurants, Cafes, Bars & Pubs** Myffy Rigby, Erin Moy. **Shops & Services** Erin Moy. **Calendar** Angus Fontaine, Katie Ekberg. **Children** Karen Heinrich. **Classical & Jazz** Jason Catlett. **Comedy** Andrew P Street. **Dance** Darryn King. **Film** Nick Dent. **Galleries** Darryn King. **Gay & Lesbian** Andrew Georgiou. **Music** Andrew P Street. **Nightlife** Jonathon Valenzuela. **Sport & Fitness** Thomas Mitchell. **Theatre** Darryn King. **Escapes & Excursions** James Wilkinson. **Directory** Angus Fontaine, Katie Ekberg, Juliet Rieden. Thanks to Katie Ekberg, Juliet Rieden and all other previous contributors to this book.

Maps john@jsgraphics.co.uk. Map on p335 reproduced by kind permission of Sydney Ferries Corporation. Map on p336 reproduced with kind permission of CityRail.

Cover photograph: Emilio Suetone / Hemis / Axiom.
Back cover photography by Heloise Bergman; Hamilton Lund.

Photography by Michelle Grant except: page 3 HTU; page 4, 293 iofoto; pages 5 (top right), 13 Petronilo G Dangoy Jr; page 5 (top left) Tomas Pavelka; pages 5 (centre & bottom left), 7, 26, 30, 76, 91, 125, 148, 149, 150, 151, 155 (left), 179, 181, 184, 186, 189, 200, 236, 239, 250, 252, 255, 268 Daniel Boud; page 5 (bottom right) Yegor Korzh; page 6 Dan Breckwoldt; page 8 (top left) Ben Jeayes; page 9 (top right & left), 41, 53 (top), 54, 80, 81 (bottom), 89, 95 (top), 96 (right), 101, 108, 110, 113, 117, 121 Heloise Bergman; page 9 (bottom left) Jenna Lane Voigt; page 14, 18, 21 Getty Images; page 25 Mornee Sherry; page 29, 244 Hamilton Lund/Tourism NSW; pages 36, 51, 60 (bottom), 279 Chee-Onn Leong; page 39 Rorem; page 40 Rachelle Burnside; page 43 Jeff Schultes; page 96 (left) Rovenko Design; pages 106, 114, 259 Julie Lucht ; page 118 Kim Pin Tan; page 193 Craig Nye; page 218 Samantha Burns; page 245 (right) Morgan Carpenter / www.mardigras.org.au; page 245 (left), 247 Ann-Marie Calilhanna / www.mardigras.org.au; page 272 Wendy McDougall; page 277 Radim Spitzer; page 278 Sam D'Cruz; page 284 Adrian Matthiassen; pages 275, 287, 291 Christopher Meder; page 288 Ilya Genkin.

About the Guide

GETTING AROUND

The back of the book contains street maps of Sydney, as well as overview maps of the city and its surroundings, and transport maps. The maps start on page 320; on them are marked the specific locations of hotels, restaurants, cafés, pubs, bars and beaches. The majority of businesses listed in this guide are located in the areas we've mapped; the grid-square references in the listings refer to these maps.

THE ESSENTIALS

For practical information, including visas, disabled access, emergency numbers, lost property, useful websites and local transport, please see the Directory. It begins on page 294.

THE LISTINGS

Addresses, phone numbers, websites, transport information, hours and prices are all included in our listings, as are selected other facilities. All were checked and correct at press time. However, business owners can alter their arrangements at any time, and fluctuating economic conditions can cause prices to change rapidly.

The very best venues in the city, the must-sees and must-dos in every category, have been marked with a red star (★). In the Sights chapters, we've also marked venues with free admission with a FREE symbol.

PHONE NUMBERS

The area code for Sydney is 02, but you don't need to use this when calling from within Sydney and New South Wales: just dial the eight-digit number as listed in this guide.

From outside the UK, dial your country's international access code or a plus symbol (+), followed by the Australia country code (61), 2 for Sydney and the eight-digit number as listed in the guide. 1800 numbers are free when dialled within Australia but will be charged if called from abroad.

For more on phones, including information on calling abroad from Australia and details of local mobile-phone access, *see p304*.

FEEDBACK

We welcome feedback on this guide, both on the venues we've included and on any other locations that you'd like to see featured in future editions. Please email us at guides@timeout.com.

Time Out Guides

Founded in 1968, Time Out has grown from humble beginnings into the leading resource for anyone wanting to know what's happening in the world's greatest cities. Alongside our influential weeklies in London, New York and Chicago, we publish more than 20 magazines in cities as varied as Beijing and Beirut; a range of travel books, with the City Guides now joined by the newer Shortlist series; and an information-packed website. The company remains proudly independent, still owned by Tony Elliott four decades after he launched *Time Out London*.

Written by local experts and illustrated with original photography, our books also retain their independence. No business has been featured because it has advertised, and all restaurants and bars are visited and reviewed anonymously.

ABOUT TIME OUT SYDNEY

Time Out Sydney magazine was founded in 2007 and is available monthly from newsagents and by subscription. The companion website is at www.timeout sydney.com.au; find details here too of an iphone app and other Sydney offerings.

Sydney-born editor and publisher Angus Fontaine was a notorious tabloid journo, decorated magazine profiler and lifestyle TV presenter before launching TOS.

Unique wildlife in the heart of Sydney

Walk underwater and discover the world's largest collection of all-Australian aquatic life. Come face to face with sharks in the Great Barrier Reef habitat; marvel at giant rays; find Nemo in his coral home; look out for secretive platypus and get to know two of only six dugongs on display anywhere in the world!

Aquarium Pier • Darling Harbour, Sydney
Open daily 9am - 8pm

SYDNEY AQUARIUM

Discover an all-Aussie animal experience set in the heart of Sydney's Darling Harbour! Meet Rex, one of the world's largest crocodiles; get up close to iconic kangaroos; have your photo with a koala; meet wombats, reptiles, butterflies, bilbies, quolls, even a cassowary - it's one of the world's largest animal encounters under one roof!

Aquarium Pier
Darling Harbour, Sydney.
Open daily 9am - 5pm

Sydney WildlifeWorld

myfun.com.au

In Context

Monorail crossing Darling Harbour. *See p66.*

History

Reconciling the past.

TEXT: JULIET RIEDEN

People have inhabited the area now known as Sydney for tens of thousands of years. When Captain James Cook turned up in 1770 with orders that he should 'with the consent of the natives take possession of convenient situations in the name of the king', he noted that those natives 'appear to be the most wretched people on earth. But in reality they are far happier than we Europeans'. Not surprisingly, the first words the Europeans ever heard from the Aboriginal inhabitants of the Sydney area were 'Warra! Warra!' – meaning 'Go away!'

On 29 April 1770, Cook landed at Botany Bay, which he named after discovering scores of plants hitherto unknown to science. Turning northwards, he passed an entrance to a harbour where there appeared to be safe anchorage. Cook called it Port Jackson after the Secretary to the Admiralty, George Jackson. Back in Britain, King George III was convinced that the east coast of the island, which had been claimed for him and named New South Wales, would make a good colony. For one thing it would help reduce Britain's overflowing prison population. For another, a settlement in the region would be convenient both as a base for trading in the Far East and in case of a war with the French or Dutch.

STEPS TO SETTLEMENT

On 13 May 1787, Captain Arthur Phillip's ship, *Sirius*, along with three provisions ships, two warships and six vessels of convicts, set sail from Portsmouth. On board were some 300 merchant seamen, their wives, children and servants, and nearly 800 convicts. Thirty-six weeks later, on 18 January 1788, after stops in Tenerife, Rio de Janeiro and the Cape of Good Hope, the *Sirius* arrived at Botany Bay. The rest of the First Fleet arrived a couple of days later. Fewer than 50 passengers had perished en route – not a bad rate for the period.

At that time of year, Botany Bay turned out to be a grim site for the new colony: there was little fresh water and it was exposed to strong winds and swell. One plus was that the naked 'Indians' seen running up and down the beach 'shouting and making many uncouth signs and gestures' turned out to be relatively friendly. Eager to make a good impression, Phillip and a small party of frock coats took a rowing boat to meet their new subjects. The meeting went well: the British exchanged a looking glass and beads for a wooden club.

Probably relieved that his first contact with the locals had not gone awry – when William Jansz of the Dutch East India Company had met Aboriginal people in 1606 he reported back that they 'killed on sight' – Phillip decided to search for Port Jackson. He returned with glowing reports: it was 'one of the finest harbours in the world, in which a thousand sail of the line might ride in perfect security'. This is one of the earliest descriptions of Sydney Harbour.

That same day, Phillip's men caught the improbable sight of two ships approaching from the sea. These were the French frigates *La Boussole* and *L'Astrolabe*, commanded by Jean-François de Galaup, Count de la Pérouse, who was on a voyage of discovery through the southern hemisphere. Surprised by the old enemy, Phillip decided to up-anchor the whole fleet the following morning and lead it to Sydney Cove – named after Viscount Sydney, the minister responsible for the colony.

The First Fleeters set to as soon as they arrived. Trees were felled, marquees erected, convict shacks constructed from cabbage palms, garden plots dug and a blacksmith's forge set up. On 7 February, the settlers gathered to hear Phillip declared the first governor of the state of New South Wales and its dependencies. It wasn't long, though, before convicts started to disappear. Several were found clubbed or speared to death, probably in revenge for attacks on the locals. Food ran dangerously low, scurvy took hold and the settlers' small herd of cattle began to diminish.

During the next few weeks, the animosity between the settlers and the indigenous people came to a head, and the disappearance of several more convicts and a marine provoked Governor Phillip to try to capture some natives in a bid to force talks. Two boats were sent to Manly (named after the 'manly' nature of the undaunted Aborigines seen there). Following courteous overtures, the settlers suddenly grabbed an Aboriginal man, called Arabanoo, and rushed him to a boat under a hail of stones and spears. Arabanoo's hair was cut, his beard shaved and he was bathed and dressed in European clothes. But despite attempts by the settlers to persuade him to tell his compatriots that they meant no harm, no ground was gained on the path to friendship.

In those early days, capturing Aborigines to turn them into honorary white men was all the rage. Two such captives, Bennelong and Colbee, were rough-and-ready types, scarred from warfare and smallpox. Colbee soon bolted, but Bennelong stayed for five months and eventually, dressed in top hat and tails, travelled to London to have tea with the royal family. He gave his name to the point of land where a hut was built for him – and on which the Sydney Opera House now stands.

Early in 1789, the local Aborigines began to succumb to smallpox contracted from the British or from sailors on the French vessels that had put in at Botany Bay. Hundreds were soon dead, among them Arabanoo. The epidemics fuelled a belief among white settlers, then and later, that the Aboriginal peoples were ultimately doomed to extinction.

IN CONTEXT

RISE OF THE RUM CORPS

If conditions were bad for the settlers at first, they soon worsened. Two years and two months after the First Fleet sailed, Britain sent its first relief to Sydney. Carrying a small stock of provisions, the *Lady Juliana* arrived in 1790 with more than 200 convicts. Most were women, and almost all were too weak to work. This Second Fleet also brought a regiment known as the New South Wales Corps (NSWC), which had been formed to replace the marines. They found the settlement short of clothes, while rations had become so meagre that it was feared that everyone might starve to death.

The Other History

What happened to the people who were here first.

It's estimated that the first people arrived in Australia 50,000 to 70,000 years ago, travelling by foot from the north across land bridges and later by boat. Australian Aboriginals have one of the oldest continuous cultures in the world, but there was never a unified nation: instead, people grouped into an estimated 500 clans or tribes, speaking some 250 languages and living a mainly nomadic life.

One of the most difficult things for the individualist, capitalist Europeans to understand when they colonised Australia was the relation of land, spirituality and culture to Aboriginal people. According to indigenous laws, no individual can own, sell or give away land. Land belongs to all members of the community, and they in turn belong to the land. Ownership of a particular region was established during the Dreaming or Dreamtime – the time of creation. The thread of creation stories tells of spiritual ancestors who came from the sky or earth, creating the world, giving life to animals and people, and establishing laws.

As the settlement of Sydney staggered through its first years, the local indigenous population was almost wiped out by diseases such as smallpox. Those who survived were then caught in a cycle of dispossession, violence and armed resistance. The founding of the Commonwealth of Australia in 1901 ignored Aboriginal people, excluding them from the national census. This

was not an oversight: from the early days of settlement it was widely assumed that Aboriginal people were doomed as a race. By the 1930s, however, it became impossible to ignore that they were vigorously resisting extinction.

In 1939, assimilation became federal government policy. Indigenous people were expected to abandon their own culture and fit into white society. The most heartbreaking and controversial aspect of this brutal policy was the forcible removal of children – now known as the 'stolen generations' – from their parents. These children were placed in institutions or fostered out to white homes as part of what has since been described as 'a policy of cultural genocide'. It is thought that 100,000 people were affected from 1910 to the 1970s, when the policy was halted.

The 20th century was marked by the growth of political activism, which led in turn to a slow process of reconciliation. In 1967, more than 90 per cent of Australians voted in a national referendum to empower the federal government to make legislation in the interests of indigenous people and to count them as citizens in the census.

On top of this, the Mabo and subsequent Wik court cases in the 1990s sent shock waves through Australian society. The British had claimed Australia without treaty or payment because they categorised it as *terra nullius* – that is, as land that

Both soldiers and convicts were so frail through lack of food that the working day had to be shortened. Thefts became commonplace, and penalties for stealing increased. Meanwhile, the Aboriginal peoples were prospering on the food that grew, leaped or swam all around them, but the first settlers were so bound by the diet of the mother country that they would rather have starved than 'eaten native'.

By the end of June 1790, four more ships had sailed into Port Jackson, carrying with them a stock of convicts who were transported in abominable conditions. Some 267 people had died en route, and of the 759 who landed, 488 suffered from scurvy,

belonged to nobody. The court rulings recognised that indigenous Australians were in fact the original inhabitants of the land, and that British settlement did not necessarily extinguish their native title. Fear and uncertainty about potential land claims resulting from this decision grew until ultimately the Howard government stepped in and watered down the ownership rights, tying potential claims cases up in courts for years to come.

In 1997, an enquiry into the stolen generations produced a controversial report that shamed white Australians, but Prime Minister Howard refused to apologise (instead, he issued a statement of 'regret'). Nevertheless, a wave of reconciliatory activity ensued. In 2000, the People's Walk for Reconciliation saw an unprecedented 300,000 march across Sydney Harbour Bridge. In February 2008, Prime Minister Kevin Rudd delivered a formal official apology to Aborigines for 'past injustices', stating that the aim was 'to build a bridge of respect with indigenous Australia'.

It was a start, but Rudd's replacement Prime Minister Julia Gillard faces a long road ahead. The cold facts on the First Australians are positively chilling. Aboriginal people on average live 20 to 25 years less than the rest of the population. They suffer persistent problems of economic disadvantage, substance abuse, domestic violence and discrimination, exacerbated by limited access to employment,

education and health facilities in the remote areas where so many live.

Within the indigenous community there are contradictory views on the way ahead. Passively accepting government hand-outs is seen by some as perpetuating the problems. The emphasis now is on targeting money and finding innovative long-term social solutions while involving the indigenous community fully in the decision-making process. Sydney is at the spearhead. In September 2010, it was announced that the 'Block', a controversial 1970 Aboriginal housing development/ slum in the inner-city heartland of Redfern, would be dismantled and the Pemulwuy Project built in its place. This $50 million development, named for the Bidjigal (Sydney) word for 'earth' and also that of a famous Gadigal warrior whose one-man war against the white invaders has since entered mythology, aims to restore a strong and healthy community to Redfern with the emphasis on traditional culture and spirituality. It's now usual to preface public events with an acknowledgement of the 'traditional owners' of the area; the red, black and yellow Aboriginal flag is flown on public buildings; important sites, such as Uluru, have been handed back to Aboriginal ownership; and more and more indigenous people are appearing in public life.

None of this can make up for the lost centuries of repression, but it's a giant leap forward on the long path towards social harmony.

IN CONTEXT

Convict settlers

dysentery or fever. Between 1791 and 1792, the death rate matched London's at the height of the Great Plague. Those remaining alive were forced to struggle on. Men faced a lashing from the cat-o'-nine-tails if they didn't work hard. The women had it little easier and were forced into long hours of domestic work or kept busy weaving in sweatshop conditions.

Finally, though, the arrival of yet more transports from England, bringing with them convicts, free settlers and supplies, meant that life in the colony began to pick up. In October 1792, Phillip reported that nearly 5,000 bushels of maize had been harvested and around 1,700 acres were under cultivation. In December that year, Phillip returned to England convinced the settlement would last.

It was almost three years before another governor arrived to take Phillip's place. The commanders of the NSWC used this interim period to their own advantage by granting officers rights to work the land and employ convicts to do it for them. Thanks to a shortage of money, rum rapidly became common currency, and as the NSWC ruled the rum trade it became known as the Rum Corps.

Things progressed slowly until 1808, when Governor William Bligh (of mutiny on the *Bounty* fame) was deposed in a military coup. Bligh's evil temper and his attempts to deal with the corruption of the NSWC, which had bullied his predecessors through their control of the colony's rum, led to his downfall. The Rum Corps arrested the governor and imprisoned him for a year – the only time in Australian history when an established government has been overthrown by force.

The Corps ruled until Bligh was sent back to England and a new governor, Lachlan Macquarie, arrived. Macquarie later wrote that on his arrival he found the colony 'barely emerging from a state of infantile imbecility, and suffering from various privations and disabilities: the country impenetrable beyond 40 miles from Sydney'. A great planner, Macquarie oversaw the building of new streets and the widening of others. He named three of the largest streets: George Street, after the king, Pitt Street, after the prime minister, and the grandest of all he named Macquarie Street, after himself. With the help of convict architect Francis Greenway, he set about building a city to be proud of, with a hospital, several churches, a sandstone barracks and Macquarie Lighthouse (still on South Head) to guide ships into the harbour.

TAKING ROOT

With the discovery of the fertile hinterland beyond the Blue Mountains in 1813, the colony advanced in earnest. The flow of migrants increased after the end of the Napoleonic Wars in 1815, and soon farms and settlements dotted the regions around Sydney and Parramatta. In 1822, Macquarie was forced from the colony by powerful landowners; he returned to Scotland and died in London in 1824.

There still remained the issue of defence: Sydney was seen as prey to any passing foe. The city's vulnerability and its isolation from the distant motherland were confirmed in 1830 when its citizens woke to find that, in the night, four American frigates had passed through the Heads and sailed up to Sydney Cove without anyone noticing. Since that day, Australia has been paranoid about attack, whether from the Russians during the Crimean War, Yankee privateers or the Spanish. Fear of an invasion from Asia has been a constant undertone of government policy in more recent times.

Finding transportation ruinously expensive, the British government sought to have the infant colony subsidise the cost. Convict labour was increasingly used to generate income. As in all slave societies, the workforce was inefficient, and the colony soon became the dumping ground for England's unemployed working classes rather than her criminals. Most of these free immigrants were bonded to their colonial employers, their passage paid for by the sale of land. In 1840, transportation of convicts to New South Wales was abolished. A total of 111,500 convicts – of whom just 16,000 were women – had arrived in NSW and Tasmania.

IN CONTEXT

How To Speak Convict: an A-Z

Sydney's not a messiah metropolis… it's just a very naughty city

Aggranoy – vulgar merger of aggravate and annoy.
Bunko – a confidence trick.
Chiseller – a swindler. Term used by crims when a person takes them down.
Dangler – a prisoner convicted of obscene exposure.
Equaliser – a revolver, pistol, cannon or squirt.
Fizgig – a police informer.
Gigglesuit – a straitjacket.
Heelie – the ballast in loaded dice, the brake on the crooked roulette wheel, the pea in the thimble game – any contrivance geared to give a pat result.
Ice – jewellery, particularly diamonds.
Jelly – gelignite for blowing a safe.
Kite – a forged or stolen cheque.
Lair – one who wears showy clothes and swaggers in them.
Motza – an abundance or excess of anything, particularly money.
Nod the nut – to plead guilty to a charge.
On the coat – to be on bad terms, a fact signalled by tugging the lapel as warning.
Pelideluxe – a superlative pelican (idiot).
Rat – a betrayer or informer.
Saddling paddock – a popular site for alfresco amours.
Tiddly – not quite drunk but decidedly mellow.
Unstuck – brought to ruin.
Vagged – to be imprisoned for vagrancy (lagged for vag).
Whack up – to divide the spoils prior to scarpering.
Yips – an affliction of nerves before a stick-up or other nefarious act.
Zac – money, gains, bunts, chaff.

'The Rocks was known as Sydney's worst den of iniquity. Prostitution, drunkenness, theft and street gangs were rife.'

By 1849, the population of convicts was outnumbered by free settlers. A new type of vessel, the clipper ship, had cut the sailing time from England to Australia by 49 days, to just 91. In the 1850s, gold was discovered in New South Wales and Victoria, and prospectors rushed to Australia from all over the world. During the 1880s more than 370,000 arrived, mostly of British or Irish descent. Rich British businessmen poured money into the country and mine owners and farmers profited. Governor Phillip had ensured as far back as 1790 that some physical distance was maintained between the government precinct to the east of what is now known as Circular Quay, and the barracks and convict quarters to the west. Built into the steep sandstone cliffs, this no man's land – now known as the Rocks – quickly became as degenerate as the worst of London's slums. Tiers of narrow streets and sandstone stairs crammed with makeshift shacks led up from waterfront pubs and cheap lodging houses to comfortable terraced houses inhabited by sea captains and stevedores. The massive influx of immigrants in the mid 1800s meant that housing was scarce, a problem exacerbated by many inner-city homes being converted into storehouses and offices.

By the late 19th century, the Rocks was known as Sydney's worst den of iniquity. Prostitution, drunkenness, theft and street gangs were rife. Sailors ashore after months at sea were robbed of everything they owned or press-ganged straight on to another vessel.

The increasingly squalid goings-on and the build-up of rubbish, silt and sewage made conditions in the Rocks perfect for rats and the bubonic plague carried by their fleas. In the first nine months of 1900, the plague killed 103 people. Crowds stormed the Board of Health's offices demanding a share of the colony's meagre supply of anti-plague medicine. The Rocks and Darling Harbour were quarantined and in 1902 the Sydney Harbour Trust was set up to clean up the harbour: it later announced that it had pulled from the water 2,524 rats, 1,068 cats, 283 bags of meat, 305 bags of fish, 1,467 fowl, 25 parrots, 23 sheep, 14 pigs, one bullock, nine calves and nine goats.

CIVILISING MISSIONS

In the 1880s, Sydney's remaining Aboriginal inhabitants were rounded up into a camp at Circular Quay and given government rations in a bid to keep them off the streets. In 1895, an Aboriginal reserve was set up at La Perouse, near Botany Bay – far from the centre of the city. By the end of the 19th century, most of the area's indigenous inhabitants were restricted to reserves or in missions, where they were introduced to the supposed benefits of Christianity and European civilisation.

By this time it was apparent that, though the Aboriginal population was in decline, the mixed-descent population was increasing. The fact that the latter group had some European blood meant that there was a place for them – albeit a lowly one – in society. Many children of mixed race were forcibly separated from their parents and placed in segregated 'training' institutions before being sent out to work. Girls were sent to be domestic servants to satisfy the nation's demand for cheap labour. It was also held that long hours and exhausting work would curb their supposed promiscuity.

The Commonwealth of Australia came into existence on 1 January 1901. The country had 3.8 million inhabitants, and more than half a million of them crowded on to the streets of Sydney to celebrate the inauguration of the nation. The Aboriginal peoples weren't recorded in the first census, however. They had to wait until 1967, when 90 per cent of the public voted to make new laws relating to Aboriginal people. This led the way for them to be recognised as Australian citizens, and to be included in the census of 1971.

POPULATE OR PERISH

After a lull following the 1890s depression, migration revived. In the years leading up to 1914, 300,000 mainly British migrants arrived, half of whom came on an assisted-passage scheme. In 1908, a Royal Commission set up to advise on the improvement of Sydney concluded that workers should be moved out of the slums to the suburbs. Six years later, however, World War I broke out. Around 10,000 volunteers in Sydney queued to go on the 'big adventure'. Most were sent to Gallipoli – a campaign that became synonymous in the Australian collective memory with British arrogance, callousness and incompetence. By the time the Allied forces were withdrawn in January 1916, the combination of lacklustre Allied leadership and stiff Turkish resistance meant that casualties were well above 50 per cent, with little to show for thousands of lost lives. After the disaster of Gallipoli, Australia was not going to return to a subservient colonial role: the nation had come of age.

With the end of World War I it was reasoned that to defend Australia properly the country needed more people. A further 300,000 migrants arrived in the 1920s, mostly from England and Scotland, a product of the policy known as 'White Australia'. The origins of the policy can be traced to the mid 19th century, when white miners' resentment towards Chinese diggers boiled over in violence. The 1901 Immigration Restriction Act placed 'certain restrictions on immigration' and provided 'for the removal from the Commonwealth of prohibited immigrants'. For example, applicants were required to pass a written test in a specific, usually European, language – with

IN CONTEXT

Migrants leaving Liverpool for Australia.

which they were not necessarily familiar. It was not until 1974 that Australia eliminated such official racial discrimination from its immigration policy.

Australia's vulnerability to attack came back to haunt it during World War II. On 31 May 1942, three Japanese midget submarines powered through the Heads and into Sydney Harbour. The first got tangled in a net across the harbour mouth, but the others slipped past. The third midget was spotted and attacked, but the second took the chance to fire two torpedoes at the US cruiser *Chicago*. Both missed, but one sank the depot ship HMAS *Kuttabul*, killing 19 Australian and two British naval ratings asleep on board. Except for Aborigines and settlers killed in early skirmishes, these 21 men have been the only victims of enemy action on home ground in Sydney's history.

After the war, Australia once again decided it needed to boost the size of its population. The slogan 'populate or perish' was coined, and a new immigration scheme organised. In 1948, 70,000 migrants arrived from Britain and Europe. By the late 1950s, most migrants were coming from Italy, Yugoslavia and Greece.

In 1951, the concept of assimilation was officially adopted as national policy, with the goal 'that all persons of Aboriginal descent will choose to attain a similar manner and standard of living to other Australians'. Eradication of Aboriginal culture was stepped up during the 1950s and '60s, when even greater numbers of Aboriginal children were removed from their families. Many Aboriginal babies were adopted at birth and later told that their true parents had died. The removal of children from their parents was halted in the 1970s, but the scars remain. The 'stolen generations' became the subject of fierce debate in Australia. Expat director Phillip Noyce's 2002 film *Rabbit-Proof Fence* – the story of three stolen children who run away from a camp and attempt to walk home over 1,000 miles of inhospitable country – brought the story to the world.

In 1964, Australian troops joined their US counterparts in action in Vietnam. As in the States, anti-Vietnam War sentiment became a hot issue, and tens of thousands of Australians blockaded the streets of the major cities. A new Labor government, led by Gough Whitlam, came to power in 1972 after promising a fairer society and an end to Australia's involvement in the war. Within months, the troops were brought home. Not long afterwards, 'Advance Australia Fair' replaced 'God Save the Queen' as the national anthem, the Queen's portrait was removed from post office walls and her insignia on mailboxes painted out. Land rights were granted to some Aboriginal groups, and in 1974 the government finally put an end to the White Australia policy that had largely restricted black and Asian immigration since 1901. Two years later, the official cord to Britain was cut when the Australian Constitution was separated from that of its motherland.

Ties with Britain loosened further in 1975 during a messy political wrangle, when the Conservative opposition moved to block the government's supply of money in the upper house. Without a budget, Gough Whitlam's government was unable to govern, so the Queen's representative, Governor-General John Kerr, sacked it and made opposition leader Malcolm Fraser prime minister. There was fury that an Australian-elected government could be dismissed by the monarch's appointee, and resentment towards Britain flared.

A THIRD CENTURY BEGINS

Immigration continued throughout the 1980s and '90s, but now there were quite a few new faces among the crowds hoping for a better life in the 'lucky country'. Hundreds of thousands of migrants began arriving from Asia. Today, on average, around 90,000 people emigrate to Australia each year, from more than 150 countries. Of settlers arriving in 2002/3, the biggest groups were those born in the UK (13.3 per cent), New Zealand (13.1 per cent), China (7.1 per cent), India (6.1 per cent), South Africa (4.9 per cent), the Philippines (3.4 per cent) and Indonesia (3 per cent). With such a multicultural mix you'd think it was time to reconsider the 'self-governing republic'

IN CONTEXT

'In 1999, 55 per cent of the electorate voted to keep the Queen as head of state; only the state of Victoria voted for a republic.'

option – but you'd be wrong. In a close-run national referendum in 1999, 55 per cent of the electorate voted to keep the Queen as head of state; of Australia's six states, only Victoria wanted a republic.

Some 460,000 Aborigines and the ethnically distinct people from the Torres Strait Islands off northern Queensland live in Australia today, but a rift still exists between them and the rest of the population. Aboriginal life expectancy is 20 years lower than that of other Australians; the infant mortality rate is higher; the ratio of Aboriginal people to other Australians in prisons is disproportionately high, and many are still restricted to the fringe of society.

In 1992, the 'Mabo decision' marked a breakthrough in Aboriginal affairs: the High Court declared that Australia was not *terra nullius* ('empty land') as it had been termed since the British 'invasion'. This decision resulted in the 1993 Native Title Act, which allowed Aboriginal groups and Torres Strait Islanders to claim government-owned land if they could prove continual association with it since 1788. Later, the Wik decision determined that Aboriginal people everywhere could make claims on government land that was leased to agriculturists. But Prime Minister John Howard's Liberal coalition government, under pressure from farming and mining interests, curtailed these rights.

In response, Aboriginal groups threatened (but did not mount) major demonstrations during the 2000 Sydney Olympics. The Olympic opening ceremony paid tribute to the country's Aboriginal origins, and the flame was lit by Aboriginal runner Cathy Freeman. To outsiders it seemed that Australia was embracing its past rather than marginalising it, but indigenous Australians themselves were less impressed. John Howard, in particular, has come in for harsh criticism for his refusal to apologise for the actions of past generations.

IHOWARD'S LAND

With the reconciliation issue bubbling in the background, Howard's government turned its attentions to stemming the influx of refugees. In the late 1990s, asylum seekers from Iraq and Afghanistan landed in Australia only to face a grim, prison-like existence in detention centres in the middle of the South Australian desert – most notoriously, at Woomera (now closed). Processing their cases has taken years, and many are still in virtual incarceration, with their future prospects unresolved.

In 1999, when victims of war-ravaged Kosovo came knocking, the Australian government was slow to respond. Eventually, local and international pressure forced Howard's hand and the refugees were admitted, but only for a short respite on newly created 'safe haven' (ie temporary) visas. In August 2001, Howard played tough guy once again, turning away a Norwegian cargo ship carrying 400 Afghan and Iraqi asylum seekers, whom the captain had rescued from a leaky ferry. As the ship neared Australian shores, Howard – with one eye firmly on the voters – steeled himself for a showdown. 'I believe it is in Australia's national interests that we draw a line on what is increasingly becoming an uncontrollable number of illegal arrivals in this country,' he asserted.

Much unseemly to-ing and fro-ing followed. At one point, the government claimed that the refugees were blackmailing the Australian navy into rescuing them by throwing their children overboard. Later – after Howard had won the 2001 election – it was revealed that the pictures that had been flashed across the news had been taken a

IN CONTEXT

day later and were actually shots showing the bona fide rescue of the asylum seekers after their boat had sunk. Ultimately, the refugees weren't allowed to set foot on Australian soil: most ended up on the tiny Pacific island of Nauru.

Although heavily criticised internationally, Howard's strong policies proved popular at the ballot box and he won a third term in office in 2001, sending the opposition Labor party into free fall. Howard's government was returned once more in 2003, although NSW has remained a Labor stronghold under Bob Carr, who lasted ten years as premier before retiring in 2005, to be replaced by Morris Iemma.

Australia may be geographically removed from the centres of world affairs, but it is increasingly involved in some of the 21st century's key military issues. Australian troops led the UN peacekeeping force in East Timor in 1999, and in 2006 led a force to put down rebellion in the Solomon Islands. More controversially, the Australian army has been heavily involved backing up US adventures in both Afghanistan and Iraq.

The nation has suffered for it: the 2002 Bali nightclub bombings killed 88 Australians (out of a death toll of 202), while another attack in Bali in 2005 killed four Australians. The Australian embassy in Jakarta, Indonesia, was also bombed in 2004, though none of the 11 dead was Australian. Jemaah Islamiah, a militant South-east Asian Muslim group, has been blamed for all three attacks. Perhaps to calm that perennial sense of national vulnerability, in 2004 the Howard government announced a cruise missile programme to give Australia the region's 'most lethal' air combat capacity.

Antagonism towards Australia's Muslim communities grew after the bombings, and fears of more violence were raised when 15 people were arrested in November 2005 for allegedly planning bomb attacks in Sydney and Melbourne. All this may or may not have helped stoke up race riots in Cronulla and other oceanside suburbs a month later.

The climate has been hotting up too: the worst bush fires for more than 20 years killed nine people in South Australia in 2005, and 1 January 2006 was Sydney's hottest day since 1939, with a high of 44.3°C (111°F).

RUDD'S BRAVE NEW NATION

At the end of 2007, Australia entered what promised to be a new and exciting political era with the landslide ('ruddslide') victory of the 'Kevin 07' Labor party that delivered the youthful, Mandarin-speaking Queensland farm boy Kevin Rudd to the leadership. Prime Minister Rudd wasted no time in righting what many considered to be Howard's errors, joining a host of other nations in ratification of the Kyoto Protocol for climate change and delivering a formal apology to the Aboriginal people for the historic injustices that go right back to the First Fleet.

The party enjoyed a period of high popularity in the opinion polls but cracks began to show in 2009 when Rudd proposed a controversial Resource Super Profits Tax and the Senate rejected his Carbon Pollution Reduction Scheme. Then leaks from within his own party portrayed him as a megalomaniac, whose centralist leadership style involved insulting treatment of staff and ignoring the counsel of his fellow ministers. By June, Rudd had lost the support of his party and he found himself deposed on 24 June by his deputy Julia Gillard. As Rudd stepped down as party leader and prime minister, the 49-year-old Welsh-born, flame-haired, proudly unmarried and avowedly atheist Julia Eileen Gillard became Australia's 27th prime minister and the first female to hold the office. Keen to vindicate her decision to depose Rudd and win public endorsement as PM, she went to the polls 23 days later. In a closely fought race against the Liberal leader, the 'mad monk' former boxer turned triathlete and volunteer firefighter Tony Abbott, the two won 72 seats each of the 150 seat House of Representatives resulting in Australia's first hung parliament since 1940. Australia hung in flux for weeks as the two leaders wooed the six independent crossbench MPs who held the balance, Gillard ultimately prevailing for a 76-74 minority government. She was sworn in on 14 September 2010 and, at time of print, had begun laying down her blueprint for the new Australia, with health, education, green technology and climate change the key issues on her agenda.

The Siren City

*Her Harbour dazzles, her beaches bare all,
but the key to Sydney's heart lies
somewhere much deeper.*
TEXT: DELIA FALCONER.

*Delia Falconer
is a Sydney-born
author who writes
regularly for
a variety of
Australian
newspapers.*

If I had to choose a single story to sum up my city, it would be this. It takes place during a sultry dusk in December, several years ago. The light on New South Head Road, a brute gold filtered through fumes, was horizontal, but still strong enough to almost knock me down. Sydney is hostile to walkers, and you would be hard-pressed to find a more difficult place to cross, over eight lanes of cars that pass on either side of the Eastern suburbs railway line, and in and out of the Cross City Tunnel. As I waited for the lights to go through their long cycle, I became aware that the traffic was heavier than usual; in fact, it was at a standstill. Through the glare I began to notice a long convoy, stretching up the hill as far as Edgecliff. The cars all had their headlights on. There were red styrofoam menorahs on the top of some, and 'Happy Hanukkah' banners on others. I realised there must be a celebration on the other side of town. As the lights still refused to change, and the cars idled across the intersection, I became aware of two young men now standing beside me. Tall, bleach-blond, lugging an esky, they radiated a lean sense of menace that might not have been out of place at the Cronulla riots. As the traffic boiled, they peered in at the nearest driver. Hatted, bearded, he nervously peered back. Slowly, they read out the banner on his car. Then their faces broke into grins, and they began to chant and pump their fists: 'Ha-nu-kkah! Ha-nu-kkah!' As the traffic started to move again, the drivers honked their horns back. 'Ha-nu-kkah!' Like most of the city's magnanimities, this was a moment that could have easily gone the other way.

The story reminds me of another. In the eighties, in Camperdown, there was a famous piece of graffiti on the car park at the corner of Parramatta and Missenden roads. On the blue wall someone had spray-painted God hates homos. Beneath it, another hand had added, but he loves tabouleh. It is this irreverence that I missed terribly in Melbourne, when we moved there at the turn of the nineties. It was good to come back to my hometown a decade later, where, as an editor once said to me, 'you can open up your chest and take a deep breath'. When I first agreed to write this book I made myself a promise that I would not play the cities off against each other, because their rivalry is a cliché, and because I wanted to reflect the truth: while Melbourne regards the northern city as a Gomorrah, Sydney rarely thinks of Melbourne. Yet the fact is that I can imagine neither of these moments occurring south of the border, and they seem to invite me to understand better Sydney's quicksilver wit and ease. A sense of confident inclusion radiates from both. Our city is so big, so golden, each infers, that we do not need to overthink things. This is Sydney at its best, as a joyful melting pot. Yet a veiled aggression underpins the boys' enthusiastic cries of 'Ha-nu-kkah'. Join our light-heartedness, they suggest, or be too serious at your peril. That is why the second graffito is brilliant in harnessing the powers of the city's enforced brittleness for good. It is the hate-filled spray-painter who is instead revealed as abnormal; as too intense.

'While Melbourne regards the northern city as a Gomorrah, Sydney rarely thinks of Melbourne.'

Sydney is allergic to earnestness, and this has many causes. Perhaps because of the higgledypiggledy organisation of the early city that made social divisions hard to enforce, the peanut gallery has always been installed closer to the centre of our public life than in any other Australian city. It is there in the delight the 1803 Sydney Gazette took in relating undignified accidents, and all the way through to the pre-tabloid days of the Sydney Morning Herald, whose back page used to run an annual survey on which streets were the most polluted by dog shit (I lived on two of the top three: Arundel Street, in Forest Lodge and Abercrombie Street, in Chippendale). Perhaps because the city started life in the less hide-bound 18th century it has had an abiding affection for the carnivalesque over the pious. Even today at the Art Gallery of New South Wales, gabbing crowds drown out the speakers as the annual Archibald Prize awards are handed out. The piecemeal, busy nature of our spaces also lends itself to loudness; no quiet hush on the footpaths here, like cloudy Brunswick Street, Fitzroy. But live here and you soon learn that showing-off is only allowed if it is tempered by flippancy. You can observe your own beliefs, celebrate your good fortune outrageously, only as long as you do not do it in a way that implies criticism of others. You do it in private, or you do it with exaggerated parody. The distinctions are subtle, but exist.

Geography contributes, and not only because Sydney's balminess allows a kind of theatre to flourish on its streets – though, certainly, the city has always loved its public 'characters', like Jamaican ferryman Billy Blue, who was an inventive abuser of colonial passersby, or the 'peculiar and vivacious' Flying Pieman, William King, who, top hat decorated with streamers, would sell his home-made pastries to passengers boarding the Parramatta steamer at Circular Quay, then sprint 18 miles overland to sell them the remainder as they disembarked.

In Melbourne, that flat, planned city, you can construct a perfectly ordered existence for yourself. There are starched tablecloths in the cafés; transport is predictable; you can even park in town. More than likely, the same pubs you have been visiting for years are relatively untouched by renovation, the same crowd greyer and paunchier beneath their short-sleeved shirts and little hats. The weather may be miserable, but it is more often neutral. It doesn't matter anyway, as many of the city's entertainments – and it still has a vital centre – are reliably indoors. People stay, their friends stay, in the same places. Melburnians structure their lives around the real possibility of satisfaction. In fact, if any new restaurant or pub is mooted, it can cause distress.

It is Sydney's wild mix of the stunning and unplanned, of glitz and rot, by contrast, that gives it its very distinct cultural and intellectual life. In Sydney we are shaped spiritually by damp abrasion and the democracy of grit. The sublime and ridiculous are never far apart. Our pleasures, though at their best beyond compare, are rarely unalloyed with disappointment. There is a high chance at a sunny outdoor café that a bogong moth will dive bomb your perfect cappuccino; or, as happened to me quite recently, it will drown in the cheese on your focaccia, and you will be relieved, at least, as you stop yourself from taking a bite just in time, that the black antennae are not pubic hair. A simple downpour will bring the roads to a standstill, or you will find yourself jammed on the F3 with everyone else heading north for Christmas, even while the dry bush to either side of you thrums with joyful heat, and the bays below turn into tender mirrors. As a result, Sydney may be impatient, pushy, volatile, aggressive – but it is rarely righteous, because it is never surprised. We don't engage in the ructions

IN CONTEXT

that split the cultural life of other cities; we are too busy, too engaged in getting by. Imperfection and making do are part of our aesthetic. Only Sydney would nickname one of its public artworks, with graphic precision, 'Poo on Sticks' (Ken Unsworth's Stones Against the Sky, outside the 'Elan' apartments in Darlinghurst); and only here would a body corporate deal with a heritage order that forbade it from removing the sculpture by repainting it from faecal brown to grey.

The Japanese have coined a word for the fifth taste beyond bitter, sour, salt and sweet: umami ('savouriness'). It is brothy, mushroomy, earthy: the smell of cheese, the deepest element of stock. This is the secret force in Sydney's freighted air. It is not just heavy with humidity, but with sulphury mangrove, kelp, the iodine of dead marine animals, humus, salt, and mould. Over the top of this base, made more profound and lingeringly sad by it, are the sweeter smells of eucalyptus and frangipani, jasmine on baking wooden fences, gardenias, and the sun-hot needles of pines. When it has been raining hard it is sometimes possible to smell the layer of fresh water on top of the salt brew of the harbour – although the brackishness is always beneath it, giving a funky body, a pulse almost, to the air.

Of course this is sexual. The whole city is loaded, palpably enlivened by this spunky, ancient and gamey under layer. Its air is both languorous and fervid, for it comes with an almost overwhelming awareness of the city's great forces of life and death. Christina Stead captures this mad tension in her 1944 novel For Love Alone, which drew on her Sydney childhood in Watson's Bay, then a tiny fishing village by the South Head. It is high tide as her heroine, Teresa Hawkins, walks the cliffs, filled with the yearning that will eventually drive her into the arms of the wrong man. The glassy black sea is too full and swollen to even lap in the coves; it is filled with 'moonstruck fish, restless, swarming, so thick in places that the water looked oily'. As if reflecting this strange ecstasy, courting couples in the bush around her clinch and writhe. Sydney's visual artists have also given themselves over to this moist languor. It may seem surprising to include Conrad Martens in their number, but you can almost feel the dense humidity in his paintings, as it thickens the air over St John's College at Sydney University, or presses down the bush in Sydney Cove. These oils are as sensual to me as Brett Whiteley's paintings of hot azure harbours, viewed from balconies that seem bent by sunlight; though these have a special place in my heart, depicting my childhood view from McMahons Point with paint so thick, so self-involved, that it seems to capture the polymorphous perversity of childhood itself. This bittersweet depth is there too, if you look for it, in convict artist Joseph Lycett's naïve pictures, sometimes criticised for looking European, which seem instead to me to accurately capture that moment when the trunks of the gums catch the last light and seem almost to become erotically self-aware, beneath their darkening branches. Looking at them, I can feel the hushing of the bush, in the soft pause before nightfall, when the landscape feels as if it longs to slip free of its skin of heat and light.

Even George Rayner Hoff 's AN ZAC War Memorial in Hyde Park – the only one in the world in which a soldier is depicted naked – has absorbed this extra flavour, though perversely. In the central bronze sculpture, 'Sacrifice', the soldier swoons back on his plinth, held aloft by three caryatids, offering himself to the earthly pleasures he can no longer have. The sadness of this delicate art deco temple is that he will remain forever young and burnished in his gold-lit chamber, protected from the city's salt and rot. For, to feel truly alive, Hoff intuits, is to be continually touched by decay. Sydney's hammocky air is the memento mori that drives our sex, our partying, our real estate. When it is at its most tender and lovely, its most beautiful, that is precisely when its umami touches our every sense – when we worry, wherever we are, that perhaps we should be somewhere else; that we should have more money, more time, more life, more love; be at a better party, have a better view, or be in another city entirely. *Extracted from* Sydney *by Delia Falconer*
Published by New South (Australia), 2010, $29.95.

Sydney Today

Still growing

TEXT: ANGUS FONTAINE

It is not possible to compare Sydney with Rome, Athens or even London, her mother city; they are centres of the Old World and Sydney is only three human lifetimes old. Sydney today is a city at a confluence of energies, with tidal flows of money and people warping and contorting the structure of space within her boundaries. Although only slightly more populated than sister city Melbourne, Sydney is light years faster, brighter, busier and more brilliant. It's the iconic gateway to Australia and a true global city.

Yet, this Sydney is a different one to the metropolis that showed itself off to the world with the 'best ever' Olympics in 2000. Since that pivotal moment, Sydney has boomed and busted, experiencing unprecedented growth yet exploding at its suburban seams, with housing shortages climbing in time with property values and public transport crumbling in the hands of a floundering state government grappling with a maelstrom of controversies relating to internal corruption.

But two centuries-plus since it winked into existence, this convict-founded city is still the jewel in Australia's crown, with the lifestyle of Sydney's 4.5 million denizens the envy of the world. Yet the convict ethos is set deep within the buttery sandstone of Sin City's buildings. Sydney bedazzles both locals and visitors every day and night but the front pages are forever kept busy with natural predilection for crises, scandals and epidemics. These contradictions are a source of constant tension but Sydney is a triumph of complexity.

Angus Fontaine is a Sydney-born editor, publisher and TV presenter. He launched Time Out Sydney *in 2007.*

Future Sydney

The mayor's plans for a greener city.

Sydney's Lord Mayor Clover Moore (*pictured*) has a dream… of creating 'a city where people are more important than cars, where the city is reconnected with its stunning harbour, and where sustainability underpins the way Sydney does business'. The following projects are in the pipeline:

GREEN SQUARE

Work is under way on Sydney's first eco-village, Green Square – a 278-hectare site between the CBD and Sydney Airport (on the borders of Beaconsfield, Zetland, Rosebery and Waterloo). Moore has committed $1.7 billion over the next ten years to create a commercial and cultural hub setting new benchmarks in green urban design and housing 33,000 people.

PADDINGTON RESERVOIR

Already the winner of the nation's highest architectural honours, this once-derelict hangout for graffiti artists on Paddington's Oxford Street is now a subterranean wonderland open to the public, with hanging gardens, a lake of contemplation and a très cool vibe.

SURRY HILLS LIBRARY

Who said the public library was dead? Designed by FJMT architects in collaboration with the City of Sydney, this stunning four-storey creation on Crown Street in Surry Hills set new standards in sustainable design when it opened in 2010, with sun-tracking louvres, a rooftop photovoltaic system and a thermal labyrinth of rock baskets cooling and cleansing the air within.

SYDNEY PARK

Central Sydney's biggest park isn't even 20 years old and yet the site of 44 hectares formerly used for clay extraction and waste disposal now boasts a boardwalk weaving through wetlands and mega children's playground with a bike track. Even the old brickworks have been put to use – as an arts hub and events space.

BARANGAROO

A bold benchmark in urban waterfront renewal? Or a money-grabbing corporate fun-park set to violate the harbour beyond repair? No other architectural issue polarises Sydney like Barangaroo – 22 hectares of prime harbour real estate that has mega-developers and greenies at loggerheads. The former shipping site once known as the 'Hungry Mile' was awarded to Lend Lease in December 2009 to develop a $6 billion site of residential office towers with a new headland park connecting culture hub Walsh Bay with the food and drinks strip of Cockle Bay and Darling Harbour. But mayhem has ensued, with employment and industry bodies in favour of creating a 'financial gateway' facing off against architects and conservationists appalled at the scale of the designs since tender was awarded and citing the risk of toxic waste in the harbour. At time of print, Lord Mayor Clover Moore had resigned from the Barangaroo board claiming the public was being 'railroaded' and the lack of transparency in plans spelled disaster. Premier Kristina Keneally, desperate to retain office at the March 2011 polls, stepped in to assume personal responsibility for the development. Across Sydney, the argument continues…

IN CONTEXT

'Embarrassed by revelations that Sydneysiders are among the world's worst climate change offenders, the city is making big strides to clean up its act.'

THE RENT SQUEEZE

As of September 2009, Sydney had the highest median house price of any city in Australia (AUS$569,000) and asked the most of renters too (a median of $450 a week). No wonder the city remains stricken by a 'rental drought', with vacancy rates in August 2010 as low as 1.5 per cent. Increasingly, this is starting to affect the city's frontline industries. Workers are being squeezed out of the city, and the trend to 'seachanges' and 'treechanges' is high, with more affordable fringe suburbs and country towns catching the outflow. For the thousands who keep alive the dream of finding a Sydney home, the prospect of cattle-call property inspections with up to 100 others is a constant challenge. What does the state government plan to do about it? No one is quite sure (least of all, the government itself), but the federal government's 'first home-buyers grant' of $7,000 helps... even when the average three-bedroom house in Sydney easily tops $1 million. Investors smile at the squeeze but renters are riled and the trend for thirtysomethings still living at home with their parents is growing.

GRIDLOCKED

An enduring grievance facing commuters in Sydney is getting to and from work. The creaking train system carries up to a million passengers every day, but services are often late, cancelled or – at best – unpredictable. There are plenty of bus routes operating centrally on Railway Square, at the top of the bustling George Street central precinct, but because 75 per cent of commuters drive their cars to work, the mix makes for a traffic-choked nightmare. Independent experts say the state government should spend $36 billion on capital investment in new rail, light rail, buses and just one metro over the next 30 years. Tired of waiting, Sydney's progressive Lord Mayor Clover Moore mooted a congestion tax like that implemented in London, and maintains her quest for an integrated public transport system with a light rail network servicing the CBD to help ease the strain and cope with the expected 20 per cent rise in population in inner Sydney by 2021. And at the time of writing, Moore was turning the toxic tide, having persuaded NSW premier Kristina to back plans for a light rail network in the CBD to improve the livability of the city's heart for pedestrians. But the biggest obstacle remains the Roads & Traffic Authority, a rogue agency who, for 20 years has kept the city gridlocked with ugly, noisy, inhospitable beasts of burden that slow traffic and put a handbrake on Sydney's development as a modern, sustainable city.

PEDAL POWER!

When it comes to the lie of the land, Sydney is an argument between architects, city planners and surveyors. The legacy is a city that sprawls into a maze of peaks, valleys, flatlands, superhighways and suburban villages. The gridlock and grinding of teeth that are public transport in Sydney recently bequeathed the city a 200-kilometre network of Cycleways, spanning the CBD and inner city suburbs Glebe, Camperdown, Erskineville, Pyrmont, Ultimo and Surry Hills. Brainchild of Lord Mayor Clover Moore, these green bike lanes have stripped some suburbs of parking spaces and car access but generally been embraced as the way to connect Sydneysiders with their places of employment and recreation, while cutting emissions and congestion and improving public health.

IN CONTEXT

BAR WARS

Since 2007, Sydney has enjoyed a nightlife revolution made possible by cheaper liquor licences, the abolition of public entertainment restrictions and council encouragement of smaller venues that offer a more diverse array of bar attractions other than just neck oiling. A key consequence of the new wave of small bars has been the brave attempts to reanimate the derelict alleys and laneways in the city centre. These 'forgotten spaces' are now hosting bars, urban art murals, regular street performers and, during Festival time, thought-provoking installations of lighting and sculpture. Again, the credit falls mainly to Lord Mayor Clover Moore, a wildly popular radical with spiked hair, an iron fist and a penchant for big dogs and neck choker accessories. A very Sydney girl she is. But Sydneysiders who now enjoy minstrel sounds, ping pong, alfresco dining and pop-up pubs and clubs in abundance are toasting her.

CULTURAL CAPITAL

Sydney has always been confident in its skin and proud of its carefree convict character. But a concerted campaign by its neighbouring states to portray Sydney as a shallow hedonistic town with too great a love of sloth on beaches and bushland and too little interest in art and culture has riled the city to strike out.

A bold new events calendar was developed in 2008, boasting three centrepiece festivals designed specifically to re-engage locals with their city and, through them, to attract the world to a new Sydney. So it is that January finds Vivacity Sydney incorporating New Year's Eve celebrations, the Sydney Festival arts, theatre and music extravaganza and the sports spectacles of the Sydney to Hobart Yacht Race and the Sydney Cricket Test Match.

In winter comes Vivid Sydney, an arts, light and performance festival centred around the harbour foreshore, with a guest curator pulling the strings (Brian Eno curated in 2009, Lou Reed and wife Laurie Anderson in 2010), and the sails of the Opera House illuminated 24/7 by transformative avant garde projections from afar. In October, Crave Sydney ignites as a feast of food festivals, public art displays, island hopping odysseys and the annual Breakfast on the Bridge, in which the iconic 'Coathanger' is closed to traffic, lain with turf and opened to over 6,000 Sydneysiders who lay down picnic rugs 134 metres above sea level.

THE SUSTAINABLE CITY

Embarrassed by revelations that Sydneysiders are among the world's worst climate change offenders, the city is making big strides to clean up its act. Earth Hour leads the charge for the sustainable Sydney of the future. This modest initiative began in 2007, when a passionate rabble of business and non-profit agencies persuaded 2.2 million people to turn off their lights for one hour as a stand against climate change. As usual, Sydney turned the occasion into a party, with candlelit dinners and moonlight events proliferating city-wide. The world noticed. On 27 March 27, a record 128 countries joined Sydney in a global display of energy efficiency. Rome's Colosseum, San Francisco's Golden Gate Bridge and Sydney's own Opera House and Harbour Bridge fell into darkness and illuminated themselves as symbols of hope.

But the real impact of Earth Hour locally has been to inspire Sydneysiders to embrace solar panelling, recycling, energy efficiency and water conservation at home and in their offices. The NSW government is pushing forward with plans for a $1.4 billion desalination plant powered by 100 per cent renewable energy supplied by a wind farm at Bungendore in rural NSW, which will supply a third of the city's drinking water (500 megalitres). Even Cate Blanchett has swung into action for the Sydney Theatre Company, with a $5.2 million Greening the Wharf project that includes rainwater harvesting, smart flush toilets and 1,906 solar panels (the second largest rooftop solar structure in Australia) on the Wharf venue's roof to generate over 70 per cent of the theatre's electricity.

Architecture

*Sydney's architecture is an
argument that never ends...*

TEXT: ANGUS FONTAINE

The fever to chop and change, scrap and scupper, redevelop and redux is a decidedly convict ethic. From the moment the ancient culture of the indigenous Gadigal collided with the modern world of the British settlers, Sydney has been a city set on carving bold new futures from humble beginnings with hard 'yakka', big vision and a whatever-it-takes mentality. Unlike the old days, though, 21st-century Sydney takes no prisoners when it comes to the fields of architecture and design.

Nature has been the defining factor in Sydney's physical development – the city has come a long way in its two centuries of modern settlement since trees blunted axes and so were dynamited to make way for the first homes. Ever since, Sydney has specialised in sledgehammer development of its public places – even the city's own view of its ethereal harbour is bisected by an ugly stretch of highway called the Cahill Expressway, which casts a shadow over the otherwise glorious hurly-burly of Circular Quay and the Rocks.

Yet, despite planners, builders and architects actively poisoning its roots, it is the big blues of water and sky splitting Sydney's heavens that continue to govern its design. In Sydney, you either build on the water or scrape the sky, and the frenzied tidal flows of real estate ebb and flow on this fact of nature.

The travel apps city lovers have been waiting for...

Apps and maps work offline with no roaming charges

Search for 'Time Out Guides' in the app store

timeout.com/iphonecityguides

When Harry Met Sydney

A man with a Modernist vision.

He's known as 'the father of modern Australian architecture' and his buildings can be seen commanding Sydney's skyline wherever you look. **Harry Seidler** died in 2006 aged 82, but his spirit most certainly lives on. The great man never got to see his last project, the **Ian Thorpe Aquatic Centre** in Ultimo (*see p260*), which opened to huge acclaim in late 2007. Its white wave-shaped roof – with echoes of Utzon's Opera House (*see p36* **Profile**) – is striking enough, but it's inside that the real wonder starts, with the Olympic-sized pool appearing to have been caught in the curve of a huge rolling wave.

It seems particularly fitting that Seidler's last gift to Sydney should be a public space for locals to enjoy, not to mention one that embraces the city's growing commitment to green initiatives: using hydraulic roof vents for natural ventilation and harnessing rainwater for internal amenities such as toilets and sprinkler systems.

The inspirational architect was born in Vienna in 1923 and fled to England in 1938 to escape persecution by the Nazis. After the war he studied architecture at Harvard and arrived in Sydney in 1948. The first building he designed in the city was his parents' home – the **Rose Seidler House** (*see p100*), now a Historic Houses Trust museum. With this building, Seidler started on an incredible journey that saw him creating ultra-modern architecture celebrating the optimism and energy of Australia and especially Sydney. This is most tellingly demonstrated in his **Horizon tower** in Forbes Street, Darlinghurst, a glitzy 42-storey apartment block with curved balconies jutting out from a central column. The tower can be seen from all over central Sydney gleaming in the sunlight, a streak of bright white against the blue sky, and needless to say the views from the apartments are breathtaking. Seidler's buildings, however, have divided opinion, with critics labelling his architectural vision as being too narrow and single-minded.

Other Seidler buildings include **Australia Square**, the **MLC Centre**, and the contentious **Blues Point Tower** at the bottom of Blues Point Road in McMahons Point. Seidler was known as a man of passion who took on bureaucrats and local councils with gusto, and his legacy to the city is a series of buildings pulsating with that same passion.

Horizon Tower.

IN CONTEXT

Profile Sydney Opera House

The city's most famous building is a tale of architectural alchemy.

Set in a heavenly harbour on a former Gadigal fishing site, its cream wings reminiscent of the sails of the First Fleet (or great white sharks devouring each other), the Sydney Opera House is the city's most famous asset. It took 14 troubled years and $102 million to build – a staggering $95 million more than was anticipated. In true Aussie style, the shortfall was met by lotteries. The cultural cathedral has never been visited by the man who conceived and largely built it, Danish architect Jørn Utzon, who resigned in 1966, halfway through the project, following a clash with the Minister of Public Works over rising construction costs. Despite a protest calling for his reinstatement, the government appointed three Australian architects – DS Littlemore, Peter Hall and Lionel Todd – to finish the job. On the Opera House's inauguration on 20 October 1973, an impromptu stage appearance was made by two small possums.

The building's originality lies in its referencing neither history nor classical architectural forms. Here, the roof is infinitely more important than the walls and all columns, divisions, windows and pediments are dispensed with.

In 2007, the Opera House received World Heritage recognition as an architectural wonder of the world. Try to attend one of the 2,400 performances held each year: everything from comedy to theatre and dance, symphony and cinema, or the and, for the annual Vivid Sydney festival every winter, with light installations flashed across its sails. ; otherwise, book one of the daily guided tours, which include a two-hour backstage tour and a one-hour 'essential' tour. It's not all performance, the building is also a wonderful place to while away a few hours: eateries range from the haute-cuisine (and haute-priced) Guillaume at Bennelong (*see p153*) to the very stylish Opera Bar (*see p186*), with indoor and outdoor seating and live entertainment, and the family-friendly Sidewalk Café.

For more information on concerts, *see p250*; for theatre events, *see p272*.

'It says much of Sydney that its first great architect was a convict and a forger.'

NATURAL LEANINGS

In many ways, Sydney's topography mirrors its god-given natural framework – wild, ragged, epic. The city plan is based on an ancient pattern of camp sites, protected from hot, dry westerly winds and chilly southern gales, yet capturing the fresh north-east breezes that sweep in from the same direction as the views and the mid-morning sun. Winding main roads such as King Street and Oxford Street lie on Aboriginal walking tracks.

The natural connection between land and sea is the essence of Sydney life, yet even water, the most forceful of the city's elemental powers, cannot be kept at bay by the coast. Surf beaches burst through bushland and feed into rivers, vast oceans snake deep into broken bays and western inlets, creeks trickle their contents into lake systems and swampy billabongs. Animals are everywhere – birds, insects, fish, beasts defying description – all cohabiting with mankind,.

FIRST WESTERN ARCHITECTURE

It says much of Sydney that its first great architect was a convict and a forger (a forger later celebrated with a portrait on Australia's $10 note). **Francis Greenway** was in private practice in Bristol, UK, in 1812 when he was found guilty of forging a document and sentenced to death, a penalty later commuted to 14 years hard labour in the penal colony of Sydney.

In a city battling for survival, even convicts enjoyed certain freedoms. Greenway soon caught the attention of the colony's great visionary and emancipist Lachlan Macquarie. In 1817, he was given a ticket-of-leave to build the **Macquarie Lighthouse** at South Head and Macquarie was so pleased with the result that he called upon Greenway to design a new **Government House**. It was the first of many historic buildings Greenway bequeathed to the city. Others include **Cadman's Cottage** (*see p51*), **Hyde Park Barracks** (*see p61*), **Windsor Courthouse**, the **Conservatorium of Music** (originally constructed in 1821 as the Government Stables) and, his masterpiece according to many, **St James Church**. Greenway's visions (and irascible temper) later saw him exiled by the colony. It was portent of the fates that would befall many of the city's architects.

Hyde Park Barracks was built in 1819 – a huge, walled prison compound to cure night crime by Sydney's roaming population of convicts. The three-storey main building included a cookhouse, bakery, cells and soldiers' quarters. Each floor had four large rooms divided by staircases, with rows of hammocks for 70 convicts per room, a total of 800 in the barracks.

In 1887, the interior was rebuilt to house the District Law Courts of New South Wales, but thereafter the barracks fell into gross decay for over a century. They were saved from demolition by Sydney's Historic Houses Trust, which sensitively blended glass and steel into the original fabric of stone. In summer, this convict spirit of old surfaces afresh with the wild knight recitals of music for Sydney Festival.

The **Sydney Town Hall**, possibly the city's only non-religious building to retain its original function and interior since it was built in 1868, is another modern landmark typical of the city's turbulent architectural history. Built on the site of an old cemetery next to **St Andrew's Cathedral** (*see p64*), the town hall was to be Sydney's riposte to the lavish hall built by Melbourne during the gold rush. But things went awry early. The competition held for its design was won by JH Willson, an unknown Tasmanian architect. Alas, his sudden death seemed to curse all who followed him.

IN CONTEXT

Whatever your carbon footprint, we can reduce it

For over a decade we've been leading the way in carbon offsetting and carbon management.

In that time we've purchased carbon credits from over 200 projects spread across 6 continents. We work with over 300 major commercial clients and thousands of small and medium sized businesses, which rely upon our market-leading quality assurance programme, our experience and absolute commitment to deliver the right solution for each client.

Why not give us a call?

T: London (020) 7833 6000

City architect Albert Bond designed the chamber now known as the vestibule (open to the public) that served as the meeting hall until the larger Centennial Hall was built. This magnificent space, referred to in its day as the Place of Democracy, was an engineering triumph, with a highly structured roof lined with Wunderlich metal panels to protect patrons from falling plaster dislodged by the vibration of the immense organ that still functions today. The building's large porte-cochere over the present (rebuilt) steps, and its own ring road inside a stone and iron palisade was destabilised in 1934 during tunnelling for the underground railway and had to be demolished.

Off shore sits **Fort Denison**, formerly known as Pinchgut Island. Built from 8,000 tonnes of sandstone quarried near Kurraba Point in Neutral Bay, it features one of the last Martello Towers built in the world. This Harbour battlement (and ration-scarce prison – hence 'Pinchgut') was built in 1841 to defend Sydney against an attack by Russian warships that never came. Ironically, when a Japanese submarine entered the Harbour in May 1942 (passing through anti-submarine nets), a salvo from the American cruiser *USS Chicago* hit the tower, causing still-visible damage. Today, tours reveal the tower's gunroom with its three eight-inch muzzle-loading cannons; weapons never fired and yet never to be removed without dismantling the stonework.

20TH-CENTURY CONTROVERSIES

The **Queen Victoria Building** remains one of the great retailing success stories of Sydney. It was originally designed as a fresh produce market, construction began in the economically disastrous year of 1893. Arguments raged from the get-go as to the style required. Renaissance? Gothic? 'American Romanesque' won out, but, beautiful as it was, the QVB fell into redundancy and by the 1980s was listed for demolition, with a car park slated to replace it. Saved by a restoration proposal, the building is now hailed as one of the city's greatest architectural and commercial marvels.

East of the QVB sits the **Anzac War Memorial** at the south end of Hyde Park. Ever egalitarian, Sydney's 1919 competition for tenders was won by C Bruce Dellit, a 29-year-old in his second year of practice with a radical anti-revivalist vision that caused uproar with civic fathers and venerated architects alike. Built in Bathurst granite, Delitt's building can be approached from four directions, with the north and south's grand staircases climbing to a Hall of Memory, home to a unique wreath-like balustrade. The east and west ebb down to a Hall of Silence and Sacrifice, a sculpture of a naked soldier, to whom visitors naturally bow in reverence.

The second half of the 20th century in Sydney is especially known for the architectural works of two men: **Harry Seidler** and **Jørn Utzon**. The former was one of

Fort Denison

the city's most prolific architects (*see p35* **When Harry Met Sydney**), whose Modernist design principles (seen in the Rose Seidler House and Horizon Tower, among others) were widely praised but failed to garner universal popularity. Jørn Utzon's **Sydney Opera House** (*see p56* and *p250* **Profile**), meanwhile, is the city's most famous building. Completed in 1973, it is remarkable for many reasons, including its controversial beginnings. How did a former Gadigal fishing site unite an ambitious state premier (Joseph J Cahill), a visiting American architect (Eero Saarinen) and a young Danish architect (Joern Utzon) in generating one of the world's most important modern buildings? And why did Utzon resign from the project halfway through completion?

MODERN ICONS

Utzon's influence on Sydney runs deep. Sitting on the site of the first Government House (the archaeological ruins of which are still visible through the glass flooring), the tall, dark and handsome **Governor Phillip Tower** and **Museum of Sydney** (*see p56*) twin-set was designed in 1995 by Richard Johnson who worked with Utzon in the ten years prior to his death on Opera House modifications.

Italian superstar Renzo Piano is one of the few architectural virtuosos to dare establish a dialogue with the 'grand old lady down the road'. The soaring ghost-white façades of his **Aurora Place** 44-level office (88 Phillip Street) and 17-storey apartment high-rise nearby (114 Macquarie Street) play mainsail to Utzon's billowing spinnakers. Italian-born Piano might be famous for a craftsman's sense of materials but he unveiled Aurora Place in 2000 as Australia's most expensive piece of real estate yet.

A more Aussie architectural icon is Sydney-boy Glenn Murcutt, a Pritzker Prize-winner whose motto is 'touch the earth lightly' and whose fame stems from simple yet complex homes built from timber, corrugated iron and louvred glass. One of his early works (circa 1976) is the **Berowra Waters Inn** (*see p 173*), a flourishing restaurant still in operation today. Murcutt's influence pervades the breathtaking **Walsh Bay Finger Wharves**, a family of timber wharves and shore sheds recently reworked into a modern residential and cultural precinct by Bates Smart with the help of renowned French architect Phillipe Robert. These romantic echoes of Sydney's maritime history were the first locations in Australia to be nominated as a World Heritage Site and today house the Sydney Theatre Company and Sydney Dance Company.

For details of upcoming architectural projects in Sydney, *see p29* **Sydney Today**.

IN CONTEXT

Anzac War Memorial. *See p39*

Sights

North Sydney Olympic Pool *See p98*

AMAZING VALUE FOR
SYDNEY'S BEST
ATTRACTIONS!

Ensure your time in Sydney is unforgettable with the great value Explore4 Pass which gives you entry to Sydney's must-see attractions Sydney Aquarium, Sydney Wildlife World, Sydney Tower and Oceanworld Manly!! The Explore4 Pass, is the only ticket that lets you see koalas and kangaroos, plus one of the world's largest crocodiles, walk underwater amongst sharks, visit a dugong, experience the best views of Sydney and if you're lucky, meet a mermaid at Manly.

Walk underwater and discover the world's largest collection of all-Australian aquatic life. Come face to face with sharks in the Great Barrier Reef habitat; marvel at giant rays; find Nemo in his coral home; look out for secretive platypus and get to know two of only six dugongs on display anywhere in the world!

Aquarium Pier
Darling Harbour, Sydney.
Open daily 9am - 8pm

Discover an all-Aussie animal experience set in the heart of Sydney's Darling Harbour! Meet Rex, one of the world's largest crocodiles; get up close to iconic kangaroos; have your photo with a koala; meet wombats, reptiles, butterflies, bilbies, quolls, even a cassowary - it's one of the world's largest animal encounters under one roof!

Aquarium Pier
Darling Harbour, Sydney.
Open daily 9am - 5pm

Sydney's iconic golden tower - standing 250 metres (820 feet) above the city streets, you can view breathtaking Sydney in all its glory, day or night! Experience OzTrek an amazing virtual reality ride across Australia; and step out onto Skywalk, Sydney's highest adventure, for unique 360 degree views over glittering Sydney and beyond.

Centrepoint Podium Level,
100 Market St, Sydney.
Open daily 9am - 10:30pm

Dive into Oceanworld Manly with huge sharks, giant turtles, rays, tropical fish and more, with interactive shows every day including shark and fish feeds, and tunnel tours. First time divers can take the plunge with a Shark Dive Xtreme experience, and look out for kids holiday programs including Mermaid Camps and Kids Snorkel Adventures.

West Esplanade, Manly,
Sydney
Open 10am to 5.30pm

myfun.com.au

Tour Sydney

Sydney's a crooked town – it pays to have a guide to lead the way.

Finding your way around Sydney can seem a daunting task: it's big, bold and water keeps on getting in the way. Fortunately, there are countless options for exploring the city's attractions, whether your pleasure is cycling, sailing through and between it, flying over it – with or without motor propulsion – or simply walking along, with or without a companion. For additional inspiration, refer to *Time Out Sydney* magazine (or its website: www.timeout sydney.com.au).

BY FOOT

I'm Free Walking Tour of Sydney

Meet *Town Hall Square, 483 George Street, Chinatown (imfree.com.au).* CityRail Town Hall. **Tours** 10.30am daily. **Cost** free (donations welcome). **Map** p329 E7.

There are several free walking tour operators in Sydney but this one is a cut-above. Justine and Ross are seasoned travellers and ex-architectural students who started this business in 2009 and who work solely for tips at tour's end. Their fun tour takes you through a smorgasbord of famous Sydney sights, bouncing between the culture and lifestyle belts of the town while delving into the history, stories and secrets of Australia's most popular city. It's a three-hour, easy walk and there's no need to book. Simply turn up at the anchor beside Sydney Town Hall any day of the week at 10.30am. *Photo p45.*

Secret Saturday City Walking Tour

Meet *GPO Building, 1 Martin Place, CBD (0404 463 664, www.secretsofsydney.com.au).* CityRail City Centre. **Tours** 2pm Sat. **Cost** $70; $40 13-16s. **No credit cards. Map** 327 F5.

The Secret Saturday City Walking Tour is a beauty, guiding you through some of the city's most stylish haunts – from olive oil tastings at Italian restaurants in the Rocks through to the historic GPO Building and a tour of its arcades of jewellery and precious metals. This tour includes cupcakes and tea and a glass of sparkling wine in an 1890s underground bar.

Self-Guided Historical Walking Tours

www.cityofsydney.nsw.gov.au/aboutsydney/ visitorguidesinformation/ historicalwalkingtours.asp.

The City of Sydney promotes a series of self-guided walking tours on its website with downloadable PDF maps and suggested detours, museum stops and diversions along the way. Each tour takes approximately one or two hours. Choices include: Rock 'n' Roll Walking Tours, of which there are three to choose from – Surry Hills to Kings Cross, Oxford Street, King Street & Enmore Road, and City to Pyrmont.

The Oxford Street Walk of Fame & Shame is our pick because it also comes as a podcast that transports you back to the cutting edge of Australia's emerging sound scene in the 1960s, '70s and '80s, an era that changed the face of artistic Sydney. Featuring seminal sound merchants such as Radio Birdman, Mental as Anything and the Missing Links, this cool tour visits the hot spots and the 'not spots' and allows you to hear the songs and listen to guest voices from Sydney's raucous rawk past.

Or try the the Walk on Water Tour, which guides you through 30 different water features, all identified on the map along with photographs and historical information.

Then there's the Strip on the Strip tour, telling the stories that inspired the bronze street plaques of poetry, philosophy and hedonist history set in the pavement of Darlinghurst Road and highlighting the colour, diversity and wit of Kings Cross: the bohemians and artists, entrepreneurs, residents and businesses.

BY BICYCLE

Bonza Bike Tours

9247 8800, www.bonzabiketours.com.

Bonza do some great bike tours – see the website for further options – but our favourite is Manly. The

Get the local experience

Over 50 of the world's top destinations available.

Manly Beach Cycle Tour & Sunset Cruise starts you aboard the ferry to Manly and from there, rolls you past Manly beach and out to stunning North Head. You'll skirt coastal cliffs, catch glimpses of fairy penguins or humpback whales and then head back to Circular Quay with the fireball sun setting behind the Opera House, Harbour Bridge and city skyline. The tour costs $129 ($109 for children) and leaves at 2.15pm on Mon, Fri, Sat.

Sydney Uncovered

9252 5505, http://sydneyuncovered.com.au.
Sydney Uncovered lead interesting walking and cycling tours, but for those partial to 'drinking and riding', the Urban Adventures Pub & Cycle Tour is for you. Led by your knowledgeable guide, you'll learn about Sydney's thirsty convict origins while cycling over centuries-old cobblestones past iconic buildings and places, occasionally pausing to reflect (and imbibe) at the great pubs scattered all over the Rocks.

BY AIR

Balloon Aloft

1800 028 568, www.balloonsaloft.com.
Ballooning offers a serenity of air travel no plane or helicopter can match. Balloon Aloft provides the chance to chase the sunrise 1,000 metres above Sydney on a variety of different flight routes, most of which finish with a champagne breakfast. Weekday trips meet at Old Government House, Parramatta Park while weekends you'll meet at Camden Valley Inn, Camden. All flights last an hour and include flight certificates with prices starting at $289 per person ($210 for children 7-12).

Blue Sky Helicopters

9700 7888, www.blueskyhelicopters.com.au.
Blue Sky Helicopters offer a deluxe private charter service for up to four passengers on one of their elite R44 or Jet Ranger choppers. A 'Harbour Discovery' flight spans just 15 minutes but buzzes you over the panorama that is the Harbour, taking in the Opera House, Harbour Bridge, Fort Denison, Watsons Bay and Manly Beach and costs $190 per person. Other flights will take you as far as the Blue Mountains in the west or on specialised whale watching or horse racing jaunts. And if you book all four seats for a flight of 45 minutes or more, they throw in a free transfer from the City to the Heliport in a Mercedes S Class chauffeured car and a DVD of your flight.

Sydney Seaplanes

1300 732 752, www.seaplanes.com.au
One of the most classically Sydney experiences is to fly to a seafood feast by the beach. Perhaps the most scenic of these airborne adventures is the seaplane to Jonah's acclaimed restaurant at Whale Beach. Taking flight at picturesque Rose Bay, you'll watch Sydney Harbour and the golden sandy strips of the

Walking tour of **the Rocks**. *See p43.*

northern beaches slide beneath you as you pass over Freshwater, Curl Curl, Newport and Palm Beach. Landing at Barrenjoey Headland, you'll then be collected by a small boat and whisked to where a car awaits for the final glide to Jonah's. It costs $480 per person, but that does include lunch at Jonah's.

BY WATER

Ferry trips

Manly Ferry

131 500, www.sydneyferries.info. **Fare** *return* $13.20; $6.60 children.
For 155 years, the Manly Ferry has been the classic Sydney adventure. Today, stepping aboard one of these noble crafts bound for lunching, walking, shopping or beaching experiences is to know why Manly is 'seven miles from Sydney, a thousand miles from care'. And whether you're a Sydneysider

Offset your
flight with
Trees for Cities
and make your
trip mean
something for
years to come

www.treesforcities.org/offset

Trees for Cities
Charity registration number 1032154

Wet and Wild

Mess about on the water.

Thrill seeking on the harbour is reaching fever pitch as rival companies bring out bigger, better and faster jet boats to circle the waters at high speeds, performing 360° spins and heart-stopping power brake stunts under the Harbour Bridge, around the Opera House and out into the blue. Alternatively, you can take to the water with a frisson of style in an Italian wooden speedboat, or make like a champion and cruise in a yacht built for the America's Cup. The mighty **Jetcruiser** (8296 7255, www.jetcruiser.com.au) is a 1,300 horsepower thrill machine. Trips are 40 to 45 minutes long, leave from Jetty 6 at Circular Quay and cost $50 ($25 reductions). When it's not speeding at 35 knots – the spin between the Heads is pretty dizzying – you get some gentler cruising. With its unmistakeable gnashing shark teeth logo painted on to the brow of its vessels, **Oz Jet Boating** (1300 556 111, 9808 3700, www.ozjetboating.com; photo below) prides itself on top-notch stops, spins and wave riding. Not for the faint-hearted, the rides peak at a ridiculous 45 knots. Go for broke with the 45-minute Sydney Spin ride at $80 ($55 reductions), leaving from the Eastern Pontoon at Circular Quay.

For more jet boat rides try **Harbour Jet** (1300 887 373, www.harbourjet.com),

Ocean Extreme (1300 887 373, www.oceanextreme.com.au), **Thunder Jet Down Under** (9299 0199, www.thunderjet boat.com.au), **Sydney Jet** (9807 4333, www.sydneyjet.com.au) and **Matilda Cruises'** WildCAT thrill rides (9264 7377, www.matilda.com.au).

For a more debonair take on the harbour spin, jump aboard *La Dolce Vita*, the perfectly named, handmade mahogany diesel-engine speedboat (complete with walnut dash), courtesy of the **Italian Wooden Speedboat Company** (0410 529 903, www.waterlimo.com.au). Prices start at $250 per hour and there's room for four on board. The boat is berthed at Woolloomooloo Finger Wharf and owned by jazz muso David Paquette, who will also put together gourmet packages – dropping passengers off at a nearby island with a picnic hamper or for a meal at a harbourside restaurant.

Finally, if you really want to sample some proper sailing, get on board the *Spirit* (8456 7777, www.adrenalin.com.au), a yacht built for the 1992 America's Cup. For $95 per person ($66 reductions) you can cruise the harbour for around three hours, with sandwiches and soft drinks provided. The Spirit leaves Pyrmont wharf at 1.30pm on Fridays and 9.30am and 1.30pm on Saturdays, subject to numbers.

SIGHTS

Oz Jet Boating.

making the trip for the umpteenth time or a visitor from interstate or overseas climbing aboard for the first time, the Manly Ferry voyage is a unique thrill – the soothing chug of the motors, the tranquil churn of the big blue beneath, the thrill of the vistas passing by, the smug serenity in knowing that only in Sydney can such a trip be made. Manly Ferries depart every half hour from Circular Quay and the 30-minute journey offers sensational views and whale-spotting opportunities.

Parramatta

131 500, www.sydneyferries.info. **Times** every 30mins daily. **Fare** *return* $13.20; $6.60 children.
Sydney's greater west is the fastest growing area in all Australia. And little wonder – Parramatta is a thriving maelstrom of eat streets, art galleries, theatres and band venues, old and new bars and, increasingly, major festivals drawing huge crowds. But when you consider the 23km of noisy, often-congested highway between Parramatta and the CBD there's really no smarter or sexy a way to get there than via Ferry. Leaving from Circular Quay and zooming through Sydney's backwaters by RiverCat catamaran over a relaxed one-hour journey, you'll swing by Cockatoo Island, Drummoyne, Bayview Park, Kissing Point, Meadowbank, Sydney Olympic Park (aka Hombush Bay) all the way to the pretty end of Parramatta. Parramatta Ferries depart Circular Quay 6.55am-9.40pm Mon-Fri; 8am-9.35pm Sat, Sun.

Mosman

131 500, www.sydneyferries.info. **Fare** *return* $10.40; $5.20 children.
Although the first ferry service offered on Sydney Harbour was the Rose Hill Packet (aka 'the Lump') which put-puttered to Parramatta from 1789, the first official (albeit privatised) Sydney Ferries route was that of the North Shore Ferry Company. Today, 21st-century Sydneysiders can recreate that historic trip and get up close to Sydney's inner northern suburbs while they do it. Gliding past Cremorne Point, Taronga Zoo, south Mosman, Old Cremorne and finally Mosman Bay, you'll see how the other half live as you gawp open-mouthed at some of the city's most expensive, sought-after and architecturally impressive harbourside homes (including the prime minister's residence Kirribilli House – currently vacant because of PM Julia Gillard's reluctance to move from her red-brick Altona home in suburban Melbourne). Mosman Ferries depart Circular Quay 5.40am-12.10am Mon-Fri; 6am-12.10am Sat, Sun.

Cockatoo Island

131 500, www.sydneyferries.info. **Fare** *return* $10.40; $5.20 children.
Named after the noisy sulphur-crested parrots who squawk their ownership at high decibels, this is the largest island in Sydney's harbour – 18 hectares in size and set at the intersection of the Parramatta and Lane Cove rivers – and was an Aboriginal fishing spot before settlement saw it become a prison built to house convicts from Norfolk Island. Later incarnations as an industrial school for girls and naval training ship for boys (abandoned after 'unseemly and unscheduled meetings' between the sexes) and a repair and building dock for the Royal Navy (Australia's first steel warship was built here during World War II), eventually gave way to its being opened to the public in 2007. Since then, Nick Cave has curated a music festival here, Sydney Biennale has made a home of it twice, the Island has opened to overnight camp-stays and guided historical walking tours and all manner of bizarre activation has taken place – all achieved after a glorious and utterly unique Ferry trip from Circular Quay. Pack a picnic (and an imagination). Cockatoo Island Ferries depart from wharves 4 & 5 Circular Quay, 5.45am-9.30pm Mon-Fri.

Darling Harbour

131 500, www.sydneyferries.info. **Fare** *return* $10.40; $5.20 children.
If you're after a bite-size taste of the beauty of the Sydney ferries experience, the trip to Darling Harbour from Circular Quay lasts about 20 minutes and scoots you under the Harbour Bridge and around the Opera House, often via the gourmet village of Balmain, with its nexus of bars, cafés and restaurants. Your end point of Darling Harbour is full of cool family attractions – the IMAX Theatre, Sydney Aquarium, Wildlife World, Chinese Gardens and Powerhouse Museum, not to mention an assortment of shops in the Harbourside complex and restaurants, bars and cafés at Cockle Bay and King Street Wharf. Darling Harbour return ferries run 6.45am-7.15pm Mon-Fri; 8am-7pm Sat, Sun.

Watsons Bay

131 500, www.sydneyferries.info. **Fare** *return* $10.40; $5.20 children.
Long lunchers rejoice! The ferry to Watsons Bay is one of the most nourishing Sydney offers, both in terms of the views along the way and the visual and culinary feast awaiting at the end of your journey. Leaving Circular Quay, your ferry goes to Garden Island, Darling Point, Double Bay and Rose Bay before arriving at Watsons Bay, named for Robert Watson, of HMS *Sirius* who was Sydney's harbourmaster in 1811. The fishing village he knew is now one of the most favoured picnic and family fun zones in Sydney, with a cluster of cool, cheap cafés and restaurants, a thriving beer garden in the Watsons Bay Hotel and a series of charming coastal walks. Don't miss the Signal Hill Battery (built in 1892 to defend Sydney from off-shore bombardment by pirates and enemies of state) and the cool Hornby Light House and cottages at South Head. Wowsers beware: nearby Lady Bay is a legal nude beach. Watsons Bay ferries depart Circular Quay 7am-3.50pm Mon-Fri; 9.20am-7.10pm Sat, Sun.

SIGHTS

Central Sydney

Supernatural beauty meets human ambition in Sydney's heart.

The emblematic **Circular Quay** is the (decidedly rectangular) magic circle at the heart of Central Sydney. Here, boats, buses, trains and trams ebb and flow on heaving tides of people 24/7. Overseeing these swirls and eddies of humanity are Sydney's two great man-made icons – the **Sydney Harbour Bridge**, with its solid iron struts, and the **Opera House**, characterised by its gentle, mesmeric 'sails'. Above and below are the twin blues of sea and sky that have met on the horizon for over 40,000 years. The power and beauty of this place will take your breath away every time.

Fuelled by a radical Lord Mayor, a small bar renaissance and some high-profile festival agendas, Sydney's **CBD** (Central Business District) has enjoyed a revival with locals in recent years. The historic **Rocks** is no longer the preserve of tourists – cool pubs, restaurants and galleries now dominate, and Circular Quay positively hums with alfresco drinkers and diners nightly.

Indeed, gentrification is spreading all over central Sydney – even city-fringe ruffians **Redfern** and **Waterloo** are in on the act thanks to an urban renewal programme and a wealth of slick new apartment blocks. While the established fun zones of **Kings Cross**, **Darlinghurst** and **Surry Hills** retain their bohemian edge, the CBD's elegant Macquarie Street and Martin Place segue into wild places like the **Royal Botanic Gardens** and **Hyde Park**.

Map p326	**Restaurants** p148
Hotels p126	**Cafés** p176
	Pubs & Bars p184

SIGHTS

GETTING YOUR BEARINGS

Just as it was for the 11 groaning galleys of human flotsam Britain transported across the world in 1788, Circular Quay is the modern visitor's starting point.

And as the First Fleet did, the best way to arrive is by sea, preferably on one of the city's much-loved green-and-cream ferries (*see p95* **Profile**). Looking landwards from the sea you'll see the two sides that have always split the city of Sydney – bigwigs in their grand sandstone buildings and steel and glass towers to the east, unruly youth, convicts and carousers in their tumbledown cottages and seedy drinking dens in the Rocks to the west.

THE CBD

Ferry Circular Quay/CityRail Circular Quay, Martin Place, Museum, St James, Town Hall or Wynyard/Monorail City Centre, Galeries Victoria, Paddy's Markets or World Square/ LightRail Capitol Square or Paddy's Markets.

The Rocks & around

In January 1788, after an eight-month voyage from Plymouth, England, the First Fleet stumbled ashore (after a short visit to Botany Bay) at Sydney Cove. Their brief was to 'build where you can, and build cheap'. Hence, the Rocks. Named after its rough terrain, the area survived as a working-class district for almost

World Class

Perfect places to stay, eat and explore.

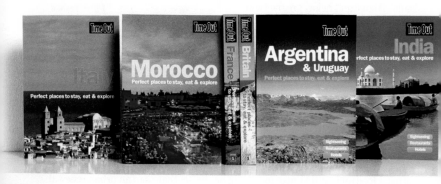

two centuries until the 1960s, when it was nearly demolished to create an Australian Manhattan. Civic protest saved the day, and the 'birthplace of the nation' was finally restored for posterity in the mid 1970s. Now safe under the wing of the Sydney Harbour Foreshore Authority, the Rocks still has to pay its own way, and many historic buildings have been turned to commercial use.

The resulting combination of period buildings, tourist shops, restaurants and pubs, along with harbourside vistas, has made the Rocks one of the city's major sightseeing attractions. As a result, locals used to shun the area, but a clutch of new pubs, some fine restaurants and the pull that in this part of town you can always get a cab home has changed all that. The slick development of the **Walsh Bay Finger Wharves**, home to the Sydney Dance Company and the Cate Blanchett-helmed Sydney Theatre Company, is another attraction. Head first for the excellent **Sydney Visitor Centre** in the **Rocks Centre** (corner of Argyle & Playfair Streets), where you'll also find the new **Rocks Discovery Museum** (*see p52*). Across George Street – the Rocks' central thoroughfare – is **Cadman's Cottage**, one of the nation's oldest houses. Now home to the **Sydney Harbour National Park Information Centre**, it's the place for information on getting to some of the harbour's islands (*see p67* **Island Hopping**). The **Rocks Market** (*see p199*) appears like magic every weekend, with souvenir stalls selling all manner of arts and crafts, puppeteers and swarms of street performers. Friday night Moonlight Markets emerge in the warmer months from November to February.

For a taste of Sydney's eastern cuisine, there's **Yoshii** (115 Harrington Street, 9247 2566), **Sake** (12 Argyle Street, 9259 5656) and David Thompson's **Sailors Thai** (106 George Street, 9251 2466). If you'd like a cocktail with your view, try the **Blue Horizon Bar** on the 36th floor of the Shangri-La Hotel on Cumberland Street (Level 36, no.176, 9250 6000). Historic buildings include the handsome sandstone **Garrison Church** (9247 1268, www.the garrisonchurch.org.au, open 9.30am-8pm daily), on the corner of Argyle and Lower Fort Streets. Officially named the Holy Trinity Church, this was the colony's first military church; regimental plaques hang on the walls and there's a brilliantly colourful stained glass window overlooking the pulpit. You can also take a peek at how 19th-century working-class families lived at the **Susannah Place Museum** (*see p54*), a row of four brick terraces on Gloucester Street.

Still, much has been lost. The site of Sydney's first hospital, which struggled to care for 500 convicts who disembarked from the Second Fleet in 1790 suffering from typhoid and dysentery, is now an unprepossessing row

INSIDE TRACK
GETTING AROUND

The CBD is easily walkable – virtually all its major thoroughfares are built on ancient Gadigal walking tracks. But if you want to save your feet, there are also CityRail trains travelling underground around the City Circle loop, covering Central, Town Hall, Wynyard, Circular Quay, St James and Museum stations.

of shops. Several galleries, including that of well-known Aussie artist Ken Done, now occupy the site of the **Customs Naval Office** (100 George Street), where one of the colony's most flamboyant customs officers, Captain John Piper, made money from mismanaging taxes. He went on to build Sydney's finest mansion of its day at Eliza Point – now **Point Piper** – where he held extravagant parties until his maladministration came to light. He then had his crew row him beyond the Heads and play a Highland lament as he threw himself overboard. To his embarrassment, they dragged him from the sea and he died, impoverished, in 1851.

Off the main drag, under the thundering Bradfield Highway that feeds the **Sydney Harbour Bridge** (*see p54* and *p53* **Profile**)

The Rocks

SIGHTS

SIGHTS

and towards Walsh Bay and Millers Point, the area has a quieter and gentler feel, with tiny cottages, working wharves and a few pubs vying for the honour of Sydney's oldest: the **Lord Nelson Brewery Hotel** (no.19, 9251 4044, www.lordnelsonbrewery.com) on Kent Street and the **Hero of Waterloo** (81 Lower Fort Street, 9252 4553, www.heroofwaterloo. com.au), which also has a fine restaurant favoured by visiting rock luminaries, such as U2. (Bono passed himself off as a backpacker here and Sydney-born rock legends AC/DC always stop in on tour.) **Glover Cottages** (124 Kent Street) – built by stonemason and surveyor Thomas Glover in the 1820s – were the first example of terraced housing in the colony. The charming Victorian **Sydney Observatory** (see p54), perched on the hill of the same name, offers views of the heavens above and the harbour below. Immediately below the observatory, **Argyle Place** has the air of an English village green and is one of the most picturesque and least touristy parts of the Rocks.

From Windmill Street, walk down the Windmill Steps past revered local artist Brett Whiteley's striking modern sculpture (originally planned for Bondi Beach) of a giant egg in a nest to Hickson Road and Walsh Bay, where the first wharves were built by a South Sea Islands trader in 1820. The area's grandest vision was realised by the Sydney Harbour Trust from 1901-22, when Hickson Road was carved through the sandstone, a massive sea wall was built and buildings and piers were erected. As shipping methods changed, however, the Walsh Bay wharves became obsolete and were finally abandoned in the 1970s. The area's revitalisation is now well under way, having kicked off back in the 1980s with the development of Piers 4/5 to house various cultural institutions, including the **Sydney Theatre Company** (see p269 and

p271). An additional 850-seat theatre for the company – the **Sydney Theatre** (see p273) – opened in 2004 in an artfully converted bond store on Hickson Road. All the piers have now been developed, and there's the chichi wine bar **Firefly** (see p185), the **Hickson Road Bistro** (no.20, 9250 1990), loosely attached to the theatre and serving the well-heeled residents of the swish waterside apartments, plus a number of restaurants, including the flamboyant **Ottoman** (see p154) and organic market-diner **Cafe Sopra** (see p165). A public boardwalk now stretches from Pier 1 – where the **Sebel Pier One** hotel (see 131) has prime position – to Piers 8/9. So you can walk along the foreshore from Circular Quay, past the Museum of Contemporary Art, behind the Overseas Passenger Terminal, in front of the celebrity-favoured **Park Hyatt Hotel** (see p128), under the Harbour Bridge, around Dawes Point Park, then past the piers all the way to Millers Point. Dawes Point Park contains the remains of Dawes Point Battery, Sydney's first permanent fortification. Built in 1790 against a feared Spanish invasion, it was rebuilt in 1820 by pioneer ex-convict architect Francis Greenway and renovated in the 1850s and '60s. The battery was demolished in 1925 when the Harbour Bridge was built, but excavation has uncovered some remains. These include the floor of the original powder magazine, the circular battery with evidence of four gun emplacements, underground magazines, a stone ramp and the footings of the officers' quarters.

FREE Rocks Discovery Museum

The Rocks Centre, Kendall Lane, at Argyle Street, The Rocks (9240 8680, www.rocks discoverymuseum.com). CityRail/ferry Circular Quay. **Open** 10am-5pm daily. **Admission** free. **Map** p327 F3.

Housed in a restored 1850s coach house, this museum covers the Rocks' history from the time of the indigenous Cadigal people to the 1970s demonstrations that saved many of the historic buildings from avaricious developers. It's a small space, but there's quite a bit packed in; amid the broken crockery and tarnished jewellery look out for a mummified rat with a curious collar of Chinese newsprint, a remnant of the Rocks' less sanitary past.

SH Ervin Gallery

National Trust Centre, Watson Road, next to the Observatory, The Rocks (9258 0173, www. nsw.nationaltrust.org.au/ervin.html). CityRail Circular Quay or Wynyard/ferry Circular Quay. **Open** 11am-5pm Tue-Sun. Closed mid Dec-mid Jan. **Admission** $7; $4 members/reductions. **Credit** AmEx, DC, MC, V. **Map** p327 E3.

A spectacular setting on Observatory Hill and an impressive line-up of annual exhibitions and themed

Profile Sydney Harbour Bridge

Sydney's original icon.

Long before the Opera House was built, Sydney had 'the coat hanger' as its icon. Locals had dreamed for decades of a bridge to link the north and south shores before construction of the 'All Australian Bridge' began in 1924, by which time Sydney's ferries were struggling to carry 40 million passengers a year.

The winning design came from English firm Dorman, Long & Co, but used Australian steel, stone, sand and labour. Families within the path of the new bridge and its highways were displaced without compensation, and 800 houses were demolished. A total

of 1,400 workers toiled on the structure, which is 134m (440ft) high and 1,149m (3,770ft) long, and was the world's largest single-span bridge when it was constructed. It took eight years to build, and workers grafting without safety rails took great risks: 16 died. The opening ceremony was held in 1932, and broadcast around the world.

The refurbished Pylon Lookout, in the south-east pylon, is well worth a visit. Climb 200 steps, past three levels of exhibits celebrating the history of the bridge and its builders. Stained-glass windows feature a painter, riveter, stonemason, rigger, concreter and surveyor. Original bridge memorabilia from the 1930s is also on display; more up-to-date souvenirs are available in the shop on level two. And the open-air views from the top are magnificent.

The bridge has been declared 'one of the seven wonders of the modern world' – though not everyone admires it. Writer James Michener commented in the 1950s that it was 'big, utilitarian and the symbol of Australia... But it is very ugly. No Australian will admit this.'

For the listing, *see p54.*

More intrepid visitors can take a guided tour to the top of the bridge itself, with only a harness between you and a plunge into the harbour.

SIGHTS

Circular Quay.

shows are the drawcards at the National Trust gallery. It specialises in Australian art (painting, sculpture and works on paper) both historical and contemporary in nature. Perhaps the gallery's strongest selling point is its popular annual shows: these include the 'Salon des Refusés', a selection of rejected works from the high-profile Archibald and Wynne art competitions. In March, the Gallery hosts Art Month Sydney, a vast showcase of works from more than 70 of Sydney's leading galleries.

Susannah Place Museum
58-64 Gloucester Street, at Cumberland Place Steps, The Rocks (9241 1893, www.hht.nsw. gov.au). CityRail/ferry Circular Quay. **Open** 10am-5pm Sat, Sun (daily in Jan). **Admission** $8; $4 reductions; $17 family. **Credit** (over $10) MC, V. **Map** p327 E4.
Built in 1844, this terrace of four houses – including a corner shop, original brick privies and open laundries – gives an idea of what 19th-century community living was really like. Entry to the museum is by guided tour only; tours leave every half hour from 10am, with no tour at 1.30pm; book ahead if possible. Note that steep, narrow stairs are involved.

★ Sydney Harbour Bridge & Pylon Lookout
Bridge & Pylon Lookout accessible via stairs on Cumberland Street (9240 1100, www.pylon lookout.com.au). CityRail/ferry Circular Quay. **Open** 10am-5pm Mon-Sat. **Admission** *Pylon*

Lookout $9.50; $4-$6.50 reductions; free under-7s. **Credit** AmEx, DC, MC, V. **Map** p327 F3. *See p153* **Profile**.

★ Sydney Observatory
Watson Road, off Argyle Street, Observatory Hill, The Rocks (9921 3485, www.sydneyobservatory. com.au). CityRail/ferry Circular Quay. **Open** *Museum* 10am-5pm daily. **Admission** *Museum & gardens* free. *Day tours* $7; $5 reductions; $20 family. *Night tours* $15; $10-$12 reductions; $45 family. **Credit** MC, V. **Map** p327 E3.
Built in 1858, Sydney Observatory gained international recognition under Henry Chamberlain Russell, government astronomer from 1870 to 1905, who involved Sydney in the International Astrographic Catalogue, the first complete atlas of the sky. The Sydney section alone took 80 years to complete and filled 53 volumes. Increasing air pollution made the observatory ineffective, and it became a museum in 1982. Interactive displays include a virtual-reality tour over the surfaces of Venus and Mars, and there are lessons on how telescopes work. Night tours (booking essential) include a talk and tour, 3-D Space Theatre session and viewing through a 40cm (16in) reflecting telescope.

Circular Quay

Circular Quay (more rectangular, in fact) is the hub of Sydney's ferry system, where the charming green-and-cream vessels putt-putt off for 39 wharves across 37km of harbour. Commuters and daytrippers board and disembark from a constant stream of ferries, JetCats, RiverCats and water taxis at the Quay's five wharves, while tourists and teenagers idle in the cafés drinking cappuccinos, listening to buskers and admiring the view. Fast-food kiosks abound, but you'll also find **City Extra** (9241 1422), one of the few 24-hour restaurants in town, and the delicious gelati of **Gelatissimo** (9241 1566). Information stands proffer free literature, and sightseeing cruises and tours leave from here. The view back to the city is blocked by the CityRail Circular Quay station and the much-reviled Cahill Expressway, but the view out over the harbour is particularly lovely at night, when the Opera House, the Harbour Bridge, the Overseas Passenger Terminal and Fort Denison are all lit up, often by cascading light installations linked to the many Festivals staged here.

On the west side of the Quay, with the Rocks stretching behind, is the grand façade of the **Museum of Contemporary Art** (*see p56*), housed in the deco-style former Maritime Services Board Building. Just beyond it is the striking Overseas Passenger Terminal, where cruise liners dock. Not only an award-winning piece of architecture, the terminal is also one of the city's coolest night-time hangouts with its clutch of restaurants and bars, including Mod Oz specialists **Quay** (*see p154*), **Ocean Room** (*see p153*), buzzy **Wildfire** (8273 1222,

SIGHTS

www.wildfiresydney.com) and **Cruise** (9251 1188, www.cruiserestaurant.com.au).

On the opposite side of the quay is East Circular Quay, a bland strip of modern buildings dubbed 'the Toaster' by wags during their construction phase several years ago. Nonetheless, it's a popular spot, not least because of its anchor tenant, the arty cinema **Dendy Opera Quays** (*see p231*), various shops and a string of popular restaurants including elegant **Aria** (*see p148*) and the high-rise **ECQ** (61 Maquarie Street, 9256 4000) on the third floor of the Quay Grand building. As you walk around the Quay, look out for a series of round metal plaques set into the promenade, each one dedicated to a famous writer. Forming Writers' Walk, these offer brief quotations on Sydney and human nature. Many (but not all) of the writers are Australian, including Germaine Greer, Peter Carey, Barry Humphries and Clive James. They share space with plaques marking the original Eora shoreline before white settlement.

Sydney Opera House (*see p56*), the city's pre-eminent modern icon, stands in lone majesty on Bennelong Point at the tip of the eastern side of Circular Quay. All the photos in the world cannot prepare you for how stunning it is. The site is where Governor Phillip provided a hut for an Aboriginal chieftain, Bennelong, in 1790. Phillip had captured Bennelong – one of the governor's rare foolish moves – and planned to use him as a mediator, but the two men from opposite sides of the earth struck up a close friendship and Bennelong accompanied Phillip back to London to meet King George III in 1793. Alas, the 'nobilised savage' found himself caught between two worlds on his return, with tragic results. Some of the key events in Bennelong's odyssey are depicted in a series of paintings by legendary draughtsman Donald Friend, on display in the Opera House.

From the steps in front, you can walk east along the harbour foreshore and into the Royal Botanic Gardens. Behind the Quay, across Alfred Street, is the city-owned **Customs House** (*see right*), which has a fantastic modern interior housing both Sydney's main public library and swish restaurant and cocktail bar **Café Sydney** (9251 8683, www.cafesydney.com.au) sitting majestically on the fifth floor. Two blocks over, on the corner of Albert and Phillip Streets, is the **Justice & Police Museum** (*see p56*). Look up and you'll spy the terracotta spine and wrapped-glass front of the 41-storey **Aurora Place**, designed by Italian architect Renzo Piano, and one of Sydney's most appealing modern buildings. Opposite Aurora Place is **Chifley Tower**, home to the sensational wine bunker **Bacco** (9223 9552 www.bacco.com.au), on one corner and **Governor Phillip Tower** on the other. Architecturally, these are three of the more

Justice & Police Museum. *See p56.*

interesting late 20th-century additions to the skyline and, sitting so close together, act as a reminder that this is the so-called 'big end' of town. Governor Phillip Tower stands on the site of the first Government House, and inside is Trevor Weeke's towering bust of Governor Macquarie. The excellent and informative **Museum of Sydney** (*see p56*), which also has a very good shop and café, is in front of it.

FREE Customs House

31 Alfred Street, between Loftus & Young Streets, Circular Quay (9242 8551, www.city ofsydney.nsw.gov.au/customshouse). CityRail/ ferry Circular Quay. **Open** 8am-midnight Mon-Fri; 10am-midnight Sat; 11am-5pm Sun. **Admission** free. **Map** p327 F4.

Built in 1885, Customs House was one of government architect James Barnet's finest works. Its double pillared colonnade, wrought-iron panels and long clean lines give it a feeling of space and majesty, underlined by the open area in front. The building is heritage-listed, but its use continually changes: today it houses a stylish public library – with decor slick enough to make boutique hotel junkies drool – and some local businesses. There's a fantastic scale model of the city under glass on the ground floor, as well the library's newspaper, magazine and computer room (including lots of foreign publications), and the tasty pizzeria and café Young Alfred (9251 5192, www.youngalfred.com.au). Fashionable eaterie Café Sydney retains its enviable location on level five, with amazing views.

SIGHTS

INSIDE TRACK
SIGN OF THE TIMES

Don't be offended by the symbols on the floor – the equilateral black cross with arms bent at right angles in both clockwise and anti-clockwise directions is not actually a Nazi swastika (which was clockwise). 'It is a fylfot, the universal positive symbol used since ancient times throughout many cultures and religions such Hinduism, Buddhism and Jainism as a blessing to bring wellbeing, luck and prosperity,' explains Shelly Fitzgerald, City of Sydney historian. 'When it was built in 1845, Customs House was the front door of Australia for all people and goods arriving at Circular Quay by boat. The fylfot was meant to be a welcoming sign to all who crossed the threshold into Sydney.'

★ Justice & Police Museum

Corner of Albert & Phillip Streets, Circular Quay (9252 1144, www.hht.net.au). CityRail/ ferry Circular Quay. **Open** 10am-5pm Sat, Sun (daily in Jan). **Admission** $8; $4 reductions; $17 family. **Credit** (over $10) MC, V. **Map** p327 G4.
Fittingly, the Justice & Police Museum has been a Water Police Court (1856), Water Police Station (1858) and plain old Police Court (1886). Death masks of some of Australia's more infamous crims are on display, as well as assorted deadly weapons and newspaper reports of sensational wrongdoings. Also on view is a recreated 1890s police charge room, a dark and damp remand cell, and a restored Court of Petty Sessions with its notorious communal dock, which could hold up to 15 prisoners at a time. Given Sydney's rich convict history and love for 'scallywags', underdogs and anti-authority figures, the Museum has taken on new appeal recently with the unearthing of a massive file of glass plate photography capturing police mug shots from Sydney's hardbitten 1920-50s era. These curiously mesmerising photos were brought together in Peter Doyle's *City of Shadows*, a book so charismatically villainous even Chanel designer Karl Lagerfeld drew sartorial inspiration from it.

★ FREE Museum of Contemporary Art

140 George Street, between Argyle & Alfred Streets, Circular Quay (9245 2400, 24hr recorded information 9245 2396, www.mca. com.au). CityRail/ferry Circular Quay. **Open** 10am-5pm daily. **Tours** 11am, 1pm Mon-Fri; noon, 1.30pm Sat, Sun. **Admission** free. **Credit** AmEx, DC, MC, V. **Map** p327 F4.
The MCA is the only major public gallery in Sydney with a serious interest in contemporary art. It has fared well under the directorship of Elizabeth Ann Macgregor, a feisty, flame-haired and inspirational Scot who has spearheaded the museum's renaissance. As well as the always interesting temporary shows, many from key overseas institutions and artists, the MCA has added a new gallery on level four to display its permanent collection. Macgregor's big 2010 coup was showcasing the work of Danish-born artist Olafur Eliasson, whose mist show mimicking the Earth's atmosphere wowed visitors at London's Tate Modern a few years back. The MCA Café (*see p177*), facing Circular Quay, is worth a look.

Museum of Sydney

Corner of Bridge & Phillip Streets, CBD (9251 5988, www.hht.net.au). CityRail/ferry Circular Quay. **Open** 9.30am-5pm daily. **Admission** $10; $5 reductions; $20 family. **Credit** AmEx, MC, V. **Map** p327 F4.
This modern building stands on one of the most historic spots in Sydney, site of the first Government House, built in 1788 by Governor Arthur Phillip and home to the first nine governors of NSW. In 1983, archaeologists unearthed the original footings of the house, which had survived since the building's 1846 demolition: these remains are now a feature at the museum. Run by the Historic Houses Trust and opened in 1995, the MOS offers a mix of state-of-the-art installations and nostalgic memorabilia – it's definitely worth a visit. A giant video spine spans the full height of the building and charts the physical development of the city; elsewhere a trade wall features goods on sale in Sydney in the 1830s. This area was the first point of contact for the indigenous Gadigal people and the First Fleet, so the museum also explores colonisation, invasion and contact. The Gadigal Place gallery honours the clan's history and culture, while outside the museum, the Edge of the Trees sculpture by Fiona Foley and Janet Laurence symbolises that first encounter as the Gadigal people hid behind trees and watched officers of the First Fleet struggle ashore (piggy-backed to dry land on the backs of convicts!).

★ Sydney Opera House

Bennelong Point, Circular Quay (box office 9250 7777, information 9250 7111, tours 9250 7250, www.sydneyoperahouse.com). CityRail/ferry Circular Quay. **Admission** $32; $23 reductions; $74 family. **Tours** every 30mins 9am-5pm daily. **Credit** AmEx, DC, MC, V. **Map** p327 G3.
See p36 **Profile** and *p250*.

Macquarie Street, Royal Botanic Gardens & Hyde Park

Tree-lined Macquarie Street – named after Lachlan Macquarie, the great reformist governor of NSW, who served from 1809 to 1821 and whose legacy was celebrated in 2010 with a series of festivals spanning the city to Parramatta – is the closest thing the CBD has to a boulevard. It fairly drips with old money and resonates with history: on one side you'll find Sydney's main public buildings, on the other, handsome apartment blocks belonging to medics, the well-heeled and the 'squatocracy' (a sarcastic term for Australia's 'landed gentry'). A notable addition is Norman Foster's Deutsche Bank Place on the corner of Hunter and Phillip Streets, a sleek, 39-storey tower that is instantly recognisable by the triangular-shaped lattice structure on top.

To the west of Macquarie Street, the 30 broad green hectares (74 acres) of the **Royal Botanic Gardens** (*see p61* and *p60* **Profile**) – site of **Government House** (*see p59*), the home of NSW governors – form a green and pleasant rump to the city, leading down to the water at **Farm Cove**. This was the site of Australia's first vegetable patch; you can still see the spot where, two centuries ago, Governor Arthur Phillip first planted his big yams. In summer, a huge screen rises from the water on the cove's eastern side, and seating is erected in the gardens so that locals can catch a movie at the **OpenAir Cinema** (*see p233*).

South of the Botanic Gardens, across Cahill Expressway, is another spacious green retreat, the **Domain**. Home to Sunday soap-box orators, the Domain has long been the place for civic protest: huge crowds gathered in 1917 to protest against World War I conscription, more than 100,000 demonstrated in 1931 against the governor's dismissal of Prime Minister Jack Lang, and in 2003, up to 50,000 demonstrated

against the invasion of Iraq. It is also the site of one of the key public events on the city's annual calendar, the free Festival First Night concert, the ignition switch for January's **Sydney Festival** (*see p219*). If you're in town at this time, don't miss these fabulous communal picnics and concerts, topped off by fireworks.

The Domain is also where you'll find the **Art Gallery of New South Wales** (*see p58*) and memorials to poets Robert Burns and Henry Lawson. The park itself, mainly open space, offers plenty of surprises, but hold your breath for the final sensational view: **Mrs Macquarie's Chair** overlooking the harbour. The Domain used to be Governor Macquarie's private park, and its tip was the favourite spot of his wife, Elizabeth. A seat has been shaped in the rock – hence the name – and the view is still one of Sydney's finest.

On the Woolloomooloo Bay side of the Domain is the **Andrew (Boy) Charlton Pool** (*see p58*), named for the youthful swim champ of the 1920s, and today a popular outdoor lap pool for city workers, and a favoured sunbaking spot for trim gay men. Heading south down Macquarie Street stands a row of impressive historical buildings: the **State Library of New South Wales** (*see p61*), **Parliament House** (*see p61*), **Sydney Hospital** (*see p62*), the **Mint** (*see p61*) and the **Hyde Park Barracks Museum** (*see p61*). Notable churches include **St James** (corner of King and Phillip Streets, 8227 1300, www.sjks.org.au), designed by Francis Greenway and the oldest church in Sydney (completed 1824), and **St Stephen's Uniting Church** (197 Macquarie Street, 9221 1688, www.ssms.org.au).

At Macquarie Street's southern end, between Elizabeth and College Streets, is gracious **Hyde Park**, named after its much larger London counterpart. It used to have a rowdy reputation, and was more a venue for sideshows, wrestling and boxing matches than a park; until the late 1820s it also served as Sydney's racecourse. Now it's a tranquil green space and fitting home to elegant Australian memorials, including the famous art deco **Anzac Memorial** (*see p58*), and the graceful **Archibald Fountain**, commemorating the Australian-French Alliance of 1914-18. During the Sydney Festival, the park erupts with free entertainment and, in summer, office workers flop down on the grass, while ibis pick their long-legged way around the supine bodies. Hyde Park is a fine sight at night, with fairy lights in the trees and possums scampering up trunks and foraging among the plants. The main avenue of Hills fig trees running north through the park is especially striking, particularly during Spring when its cathedral of trees transforms into a gallery for large-scale photography as part of the **Art & About**

SIGHTS

Museum of Contemporary Art.

In the 1920s, famous Aussie swimmer Andrew 'Boy' Charlton achieved many of his triumphs at the since-named Andrew (Boy) Charlton Pool (*see below*), including, aged 16, beating European champ Arne Borg in 1924, setting a new world record in the process and sparking cheers from a throng of 8,000.

festival and, in the same period, diverse culinary events and night markets as part of Sydney's International Food Festival through October. On the College Street side of the park are **St Mary's Cathedral** (*see p61*), the **Australian Museum** (*see below*), **Sydney Grammar School** and **Cook & Phillip Park** (*see p260*), an enormous subterranean aquatic and sports centre and, in winter, an ice rink in the Cathedral forecourt. Even if you don't fancy a dip, at least pop in to see Wendy Sharpe's wonderful murals above the 50-metre pool depicting the life of 19th-century swimming star Annette Kellerman, 'the Million Dollar Mermaid' who went on to become Australia's first Hollywood movie star (and a pioneer of the one-piece swimsuit we know today).

On Elizabeth Street, facing Hyde Park, sits the elaborate **Great Synagogue** (*see p59*). Opposite the south-eastern corner of Hyde Park on Liverpool Street is the block-long **Mark Foy's Building** (nos.143-147), with its distinctive gold trim and green turrets. Once a majestic department store, completed in 1917, it was converted to a court complex in 1991: you'll often see a huddle of lawyers, clients and, depending on the case, members of the Fourth Estate gathering outside. Francis Foy, one of the seven siblings who established the original store, took his architect to look at department stores around the world before settling on the design: the lower levels feature a special glazed brick shipped from Scotland. Unable to decide whose name the store should carry, the Foys settled the dispute by naming it after their father, Mark.

Andrew (Boy) Charlton Pool
Mrs Macquarie's Road, The Domain (9358 6686, www.abcpool.org). Bus 411. **Open** 6am-7pm daily (till 8pm daylight saving time). **Admission** $5.50; $3.60-$3.80 reductions; $15 family. **Map** p330 H5.
A $10 million refurbishment has made this harbourside pool the place for inner-city summer swimming. It was a popular bathing spot long before the British arrived, and public sea baths first opened here in 1860. Today, the baths offer an eight-lane, heated

50m pool, learners' and toddlers' pools, a sundeck and a great café. The pool's harbourside edges are glazed, allowing swimmers unparalleled views across the sparkling bay.

FREE Anzac Memorial
Hyde Park, between Park & Liverpool Streets, CBD (9267 7668). CityRail Museum. **Open** 9am-5pm daily. **Admission** free. **Map** p329 F7.
Sydney architect Bruce Dellit was only 31 when he won the 1930 competition to design this beautiful grey-pink granite memorial to the Australian and New Zealand troops who fell in World War I – and particularly those involved in the bloody battle for the Gallipoli peninsula. His art deco vision caused a sensation when it opened in 1934. The striking bas-reliefs are by Rayner Hoff, who also made the central bronze sculpture in the 'Well of Contemplation' of a Christ-like naked figure held aloft on a shield by three women, symbolising the sacrifices of war. Around $2.4 million was spent to shore up the monument in time for its 75th anniversary in 2009, and a series of 60m long cascades on the Liverpool Street side (part of Delitt's original vision) is part of a $5.6 million upgrade due soon. An act of remembrance is held here at 11am daily, and guided tours can be arranged at the reception desk in the monument's base, where you'll also find a small military museum.

★ FREE Art Gallery of New South Wales
Art Gallery Road, The Domain (9225 1700, www.artgallery.nsw.gov.au). CityRail Martin Place or St James then 10mins walk/bus 441. **Open** 10am-5pm Mon, Tue, Thur-Sun; 10am-9pm Wed. **Admission** free; charges for some exhibitions. **Credit** AmEx, MC, V. **Map** p327 H6.
NSW's main art gallery moved to its present site in 1885. It includes a solid collection of 19th- and 20th-century Australian artists, a wildly popular wing of Aboriginal and Torres Strait Islander art, big names in European art history and international contemporary artists, plus a fine Asian art collection. There are also regular blockbuster touring shows from overseas galleries. One of its most popular and controversial exhibitions is the annual Archibald Prize, a portraiture competition, which is complemented by the Wynne (landscape and sculpture) and Sir John Sulman (best 'subject/genre paintings' and murals) competitions. Wednesday is late-opening night (until 9pm), with free talks, debates and performances, and there are regular events for kids. Tours of the general collection are held two or three times a day.

Australian Museum
6 College Street, at William Street, CBD (9320 6000, www.austmus.gov.au). CityRail Museum or St James. **Open** 9.30am-5pm daily. **Admission** $10; $5 reductions; $25 family. **Credit** AmEx, MC, V. **Map** p329 G7.
The Australian Museum (established 1827) houses the nation's most important animal, mineral, fossil

Andrew (Boy) Charlton Pool.

and anthropological collections, and prides itself on its innovative research into Australia's environment and indigenous cultures. Displays cover the Pacific Islands, Asia, Africa and the Americas, with items ranging from Aboriginal kids' toys to a tattooed chalk head from the Solomon Islands. Any serious museum-tripper should see a few of the local stuffed animals, and the displays should answer all your questions about Australian mammals. If you're at all interested in Aboriginal culture and beliefs, visit the Indigenous Australia section, which tackles such contentious issues as the 'stolen generation', deaths in custody and problems facing indigenous people today. Around 1,000 Aboriginal objects of a secret and/or sacred nature are held separately from the main collection: access to these can be arranged through the Aboriginal Heritage Unit. In 2010, for the first time in its long history, the Museum commenced Behind-the-Scenes tours, allowing private access to the 95 per cent of their collection off-limits, such as a rug made entirely from platypus pelts and an arsenal of thousands of poison-tipped spears.

FREE Government House
Royal Botanic Gardens (9931 5222, www.hht. net.au). CityRail Circular Quay or Martin Place/ ferry Circular Quay. **Open** *House* guided tour only; every 30mins 10.30am-3pm Fri-Sun. *Garden* 10am-4pm daily. **Admission** free. **Map** p327 G3/4.

INSIDE TRACK
STARK REMINDER

The **Anzac Memorial** (*see 58*) is the only one of its kind in the world to depict a soldier completely naked, stripped of all life's garlands.

Designed in 1834 by William IV's architect, Edward Blore, the plans for Government House (the official residence of the NSW governor) had to be modified to take account of local conditions, such as the Australian sun being in the north rather than the south. However, the original Gothic Revival concept remained, and today's visitors can still enjoy the crenellated battlements and detailed interiors. Past governors have dabbled in redecorating and extensions with mixed results, but the marvellously restored State Rooms are now the best example of Victorian pomp in the country. The current governor doesn't live here, but it's still used for state and vice-regal functions. Don't miss the exotic gardens.

Great Synagogue
166 Castlereagh Street, between Park & Market Streets. Entry for services 187A Elizabeth Street, CBD (9267 2477, www.greatsynagogue.org.au). CityRail St James or Town Hall. **Open** *Services* 5.30pm (winter), 6.15pm (summer) Fri; 8.45am Sat. **Tours** noon Tue, Thur. **Admission** $8; $5 reductions. **Credit** MC, V. **Map** p329 F7.

Sydney's Jewish history dates back to convict times – there were around 16 Jews in the First Fleet – and the Great Synagogue, consecrated in 1878, is deemed the mother congregation of the Australian Jewry. Designed by Thomas Rowe, the building is a lavish confection of French Gothic with large amounts of Byzantine thrown in. The superb front wheel window, facing on to Hyde Park, repeats the design of the wrought-iron gates outside, while inside the cast-iron columns holding up the balcony where women sit are capped with intricate plaster designs. The ceiling depicts the Creation. Twice-weekly tours (entry from the back of the synagogue on Castlereagh Street) include a short video about the history of both the synagogue and Australia's Jewish community. A small museum is also open before and after tours.

SIGHTS

Profile Royal Botanic Gardens

With its flying foxes and rare cacti, this is more than just a place to rest.

SIGHTS

The beautiful Royal Botanic Gardens (*see p61*), established in 1816, make a sweeping green curve from the Opera House to Woollomooloo Bay. It's a gorgeous spot, full of majestic trees, spacious lawns, bird-filled ponds, statues, native wildlife and ornamental flowerbeds – all in the heart of a capital city. The Domain surrounds the gardens: in colonial times this land acted as a buffer between the governor's home and the penal colony, but by 1831 roads and paths had been built to allow public

access, and it has remained a people's place ever since. The Palm Grove area is a good place to start: there's a shop and visitor information counter, café, restaurant and toilets.

Highlights from the 30 hectares include the Tropical Centre, spectacular rose gardens, cacti collection, the large colony of fruit bats (aka flying foxes) near Palm Grove, possums and the 'living fossil' Wollemi pine, one of the world's rarest species, discovered in 1994 by a ranger in the Blue Mountains.

Controversial plans to relocate the Gardens' famous population of flying foxes (which number some 22,000 at their seasonal peak) have been proposed, as the bats' roosting habits are damaging important plants; when and how the relocation will take place remains to be seen.

The Fleet Steps provide a classic Opera House photo-op. There are free guided walks (10.30am daily), or you can take the 'trackless train' ($10, $5 reductions), which stops at areas of interest around the gardens, ending up at the Opera House.

Route maps can be downloaded from the website.

To learn more about Aboriginal life in the area, visit the Cadi Jam Ora garden or book a walk with an Aboriginal guide (9231 8134, $28; $15 reductions).

Hyde Park Barracks Museum

*Queens Square, corner of Macquarie Street &
Prince Albert Road, CBD (8239 2311, www.hht.
net.au). CityRail Martin Place or St James.* **Open**
9.30am-5pm daily. **Admission** $10; $5 reductions;
$20 family. **Credit** MC, V. **Map** p327 G6.

Designed by convict architect Francis Greenway,
the barracks were completed in 1819 to house 600
male convicts, who were in government employ
until 1848. Subsequently used as an immigration
depot and an asylum for women, they eventually
metamorphosed into a museum. On the top level
are recreated convict barracks: rough hammocks
hang side by side in the dormitories, while recorded
snippets of conversation surround you. A computer
database allows visitors to follow the official
records of convicts, from conviction via flogging to
rehabilitation. The women's section on level two is
no less fascinating – these (mostly Irish) women
were escaping an awful existence to start what
must have been an equally burdensome new life in
a harsh colony. The courtyard houses a pleasant
café for moments of quiet contemplation.

Mint

*10 Macquarie Street, between Queens Square &
Martin Place, CBD (8239 2288, www.hht.net.au).
CityRail Martin Place or St James.* **Open** 9am-
5pm Mon-Fri. **Admission** free. **Map** p327 G6.

This attractive building with its yellow façade and
two-storey, double-colonnaded veranda was built
between 1811 and 1816 as the southern wing of the
Sydney Hospital. It turned into a coin-making operation – the first branch of the Royal Mint outside
London – in the 1850s, following the discovery of
gold in NSW, and continued to churn out money
until 1926. There aren't any coins to gawp over, just
a small historical exhibit and an upstairs café overlooking Macquarie Street. The building also houses
the headquarters of the Historic Houses Trust.

FREE Parliament House

*6 Macquarie Street, opposite Hunter Street, CBD
(9230 2111, tours 9230 3444, www.parliament.
nsw.gov.au). CityRail Martin Place or St James.*
Open 9am-5pm Mon-Fri. **Tours** (groups)
9.30am, 11am, 12.30pm, 2pm, 3pm, 4pm non-
sitting days; 1.30pm Tue sitting days. Individual
tours available. **Admission** free. **Map** p327 G5.

Known to locals as the Bear Pit, the New South
Wales Parliament is said to be the roughest, tough-
est parliament in the country. Its impressive sandstone home was built between 1811 and 1814 as the
northern wing of the Rum Hospital, but was com-
mandeered in 1829 to house the new colony's decision makers. Only the Legislative Assembly (lower
house) existed until the 1850s, when the parliament
became bicameral. The Legislative Council (upper
house) meets in a building that was originally
intended for use as a church; the cast-iron prefab
was being shipped from Glasgow to Victoria when

it was diverted mid-voyage to Sydney. The parliament is largely modelled on its mother in London:
there's a Speaker and Black Rod, and even the colour
scheme follows the British tradition of green for the
lower chamber and red for the upper chamber.
Legislative sessions are open to the general public,
with viewing from a public gallery; booking is essential for the guided tours.

★ FREE Royal Botanic Gardens

*Mrs Macquarie's Road, CBD (9231 8111,
weekends 9231 8125, www.rbgsyd.nsw.gov.au).
CityRail Circular Quay, Martin Place or St
James/ferry Circular Quay.* **Open** *Gardens* 7am-
sunset daily. *Visitor Information* 9.30am-4.30pm
daily. *Tropical Centre* 10am-4pm daily. *Shop*
9.30am-5pm daily. **Admission** *Gardens* free.
Tropical Centre $4.40; $2.20 reductions. **Credit**
(shop only) AmEx, MC, V. **Map** p327 G/H3/5.
See left **Profile**.

FREE St Mary's Cathedral

*Corner of College Street & Cathedral Square,
CBD (9220 0400, www.stmaryscathedral.org.au).
CityRail St James.* **Open** 6.45am-6pm Mon-Fri;
9am-6.30pm Sat; 7am-6.30pm Sun. **Tours**
10.30am Sun; also by arrangement. **Admission**
free. **Map** p327 G6.

St Mary's Cathedral is the seat of the Roman Catholic
archbishop of Sydney (currently the controversial
Cardinal George Pell) and stands on the site of
Australia's first Catholic chapel. William Wilkinson
Wardell's design replaced the original cathedral,
ruined by fire in 1865. Constructed from local sandstone, it's the largest Gothic cathedral in the southern
hemisphere – 106m (348ft) long with a 46m (150ft) central tower – dwarfing many of the European models
from which it took inspiration. Wardell's original twin
spires, initially not erected due to funding problems,
were lowered into place by helicopter in 1999. Don't
miss the cathedral's crypt, which is decorated with a
beautifully designed terrazzo floor depicting the six
days of Creation. This was home and base camp for
Pope Benedict XVI when he came to Sydney for World
Youth Day in July 2008 and, in winter, the Sydney
Winter Festival ices the forecourt for a skating rink.

FREE State Library of New South Wales

*Corner of Macquarie Street & Cahill Expressway,
CBD (9273 1414, www.sl.nsw.gov.au). CityRail
Martin Place.* **Open** 9am-8pm Mon-Thur; 9am-
5pm Fri; 10am-5pm Sat, Sun. **Tours** 11am Tue;
2pm Thur. **Admission** free. **Map** p327 G5.

The State Library is essentially two libraries in one:
the modern General Reference Library (GRL) provides
access to five million books, CD-Roms and other media
stored over five floors below ground, while the 1910
Mitchell Wing (closed Sundays) holds the world's
greatest collection of Australiana, including James
Cook's original journals and the log book of Captain
Bligh. The latter wing has fine bronze bas-relief doors

SIGHTS

depicting Aboriginal peoples and European explorers, a grand mosaic and terrazzo vestibule, stained-glass windows and extensive amounts of Australian stone and timber. Its Shakespeare Room is a fine example of mock-Tudor style, with a ceiling modelled on Cardinal Wolsey's closet in Hampton Court and stained-glass windows depicting the 'seven ages of man'. Changing exhibitions highlight the library's large and fascinating collection of historic paintings, photos, manuscripts and rare books. There are free guided tours of both libraries.

FREE Sydney Hospital & Sydney Eye Hospital

8 Macquarie Street, opposite Martin Place, CBD (9382 7111, www.sesahs.nsw.gov.au/sydhosp). CityRail Martin Place. **Open** *Museum* 10am-3pm Tue. **Admission** *Museum tour* $5. *Historical tour* $10. **Map** p327 G5/6.

Originally known as the Rum Hospital because its construction was paid for by government-controlled rum sales, Sydney Hospital is the city's only early institutional building still performing its original function. The current structure is a grandiose, late Victorian edifice, which thoughtlessly replaced the centre of what was once an eye-catching trio; cast your eyes to Parliament House on one side and the Mint on the other to get an idea of what the hospital originally looked like. Outside stands *Il Porcellino* bronze boar sculpture, a copy of the famous original in Florence; its snout is shiny from people rubbing it for good luck. Inside, the marble floors, magnificent windows and colour scheme have been carefully restored. The lobby lists those who donated to its construction and the respective amounts – Dame Nellie Melba kicked in £100, as much as some of the business giants of the day. You can't just walk into the hospital itself, but you can book two weeks ahead for guided tours (groups only, minimum eight). The Lucy Osburn-Nightingale Foundation Museum is open to the public on Tuesdays, while the courtyard is open to all and has a very good café.

Martin Place, Centrepoint & Town Hall

Squashed between the green spaces of the Domain and Hyde Park and the waterside promenades of Darling Harbour is the CBD proper. Apart from walking, one of the best ways of getting around this central area, as well as to Darling Harbour and Chinatown, is on the elevated Monorail system.

The CBD's historic epicentre is **Martin Place**, a pedestrian boulevard lined with monumental buildings running west from **Macquarie Street** to **George Street**. The largest non-garden open space in the CBD, it houses the **Cenotaph** – which commemorates Australian lives lost in World War I – and, in December, a towering Christmas tree wilting in the scorching Sydney

sun. Lunchtime concerts and a fountain make this an outdoor mecca for office workers, and huge screens are often erected here during big sporting and cultural events. At the George Street end of Martin Place you'll find the grand **General Post Office** (*see p64*), outside which crowds gathered to celebrate the end of the two world wars. This fine Victorian building has been wonderfully renovated: in the basement you'll find several good restaurants, a sushi bar and an upmarket food court. The upper floors contain showy retail outlets and the formal luxury/ business hotel, the **Westin Sydney** (*see p128*).

The sandstone banks and office buildings erected along the southern edge of Martin Place during the economic boom of wool and wheat now jostle with the odd elegant skyscraper and modern monstrosities such as the MLC Centre, which houses designer shops, a huge electrical store and some great outdoor cafés. North of Martin Place, on the western side of George Street, is **Wynyard Station**, the main train and bus interchange for travelling across the Harbour Bridge to the north shore and northern beaches.

At night, the CBD sheds its grey veneer and twenty- and thirtysomethings shuck off suits to swarm in and sip until dawn. Many hit the Establishment complex – home of **Tank** nightclub (3 Bridge Lane, 9240 3000), **Hemmesphere** cocktail bar (252 George Street, 9240 3040) and **Bistrode CBD** (Level 1, 52 King Street, 8297 7010). Brash bar tzar Justin Hemmes is behind these enterprises, as well as the trendy bars and bistro of the **Hotel CBD** (corner of York and King Streets, 8297 7000), the **Slip Inn** (www.merivale.com.au) and wine bar and restaurant the **Ash Street Cellar** (*see p149*). His most ambitious venture, a pleasure complex of bars (one with a rooftop pool), restaurants and clubs called **Ivy** opened at 320-330 George Street and won *Time Out Sydney* magazine's 'Bar of the Year' in 2009. A competing hotspot is the newly renovated **Hilton Sydney** hotel (*see p127*), with its fashionable **Zeta Bar** (*see p187*), Luke Mangan-helmed **Glass** restaurant (Level 4, 488 George Street, 9265 6070) and opulent and ancient drinks den **Marble Bar** (*see p186*). A host of small bars in the surrounding laneways have introduced a fresh after-hours vigour. Look for **Grasshopper** (Temperance Lane, off George Street, 9947 9025) and **Small Bar** (48 Erskine Street, 9279 0782).

The main shopping district of the CBD – roughly bounded by Hunter, Elizabeth, George and Park Streets – orbits Sydney's two department stores, modern **Myer** (*see p195*) and majestic **David Jones** (*see p195*). Nearby are the grandiose **State Theatre** (*see p272*) and the stately **Queen Victoria Building** (*see p64*). Pedestrianised **Pitt Street Mall**

Martin Place.

is always jammed with shoppers and has lots of buskers (but never enough seats) and, as of October 2010, **Westfield Sydney**, a luxury complex of retail, leisure and dining venues. Make sure you take a turn through the elegant **Strand Arcade** (*see p196*), packed with designer fashion and gift shops, pre-eminent among them **Strand Hatters** (*see p208*) who are much sought-after by both urban hipsters, 'lid kids' and cinematic set designers. The **Sydney Tower** (*see p65*) – also known as Centrepoint after the shopping centre that it crowns, and as the AMP Tower after the ad sign on its turret – rises 305 metres (1,000 feet) between Pitt Street Mall and Castlereagh Street, making it the tallest structure in the city. Despite its spindly appearance, the tower, which is held in place by 56 cables, is capable of withstanding earthquakes and extreme wind conditions – as the publicity blurb goes, 'if the strands of these cables were laid end to end, they would reach from Sydney to New Zealand'. In 2005, the tower underwent a glitzy revamp, adding OzTrek, a virtual-reality adventure tour, and Skywalk, a heart-thumping open-air walk around the roof, with the base of the building stripped for rebuilding and connection to neighbouring arcades in 2009-10 by Westfield. The annual **Sydney Tower Run-up** is staged every year, with the first two to scale the 1,504 stairs eligible to compete in the Empire State Building Run-up.

The intersection of George, Park and Druitt Streets is a major crossroads surrounded by the QVB, the chic **Galeries Victoria** shopping mall (*see p196*) and **Sydney Town Hall** (*see p65*). Beneath them is bustling Town Hall train station and a warren of shopping alleys linking up the various above-ground buildings. It's a hectic area, particularly during the day when office workers and students gather on the Town Hall steps to chat, eat lunch and wait for buses. Next door is the Anglican **St Andrew's Cathedral** (*see p64*), where regular services take place and where INXS frontman and beloved Sydney son Michael Hutchence was farewelled in 1997. If Sydney's lord mayor Clover Moore has her way, this area will see striking changes in the coming decade: she is on a mission to buy up the George Street block facing the Town Hall so that it can eventually be demolished to create a grassy public square. Currently, it's a hyper-practical but far from pretty part of town. The multiplex cinema on George Street and the surrounding burger bars and late-night pubs keep folk hanging out well into the early hours: be prepared to jostle with teenagers streaming in to play video games at several louche amusement arcades, and rowdy backpackers and boozers heading for drinking dens such as the perpetually lively, round-the-clock Irish bar **Scruffy Murphy's Hotel** (43-49 Goulburn Street, 9211 2002, www.scruffymurphys.com.au).

One more authentic pocket is the '**Spanish Quarter**', the tiny stretch of Liverpool Street between George and Sussex Streets, where you can have tapas and a cerveza at the Spanish Club (no.88, 9267 8440, www.spanishclub.com.au) or take home some Spanish chorizo, olives and rioja from the **Torres Cellars & Delicatessen** (no.75, 9264 6862, www.torresdeli.com.au). The area was once quite down at heel, but a clean-up has encouraged previously lacklustre eateries to lift their game; best of the crop is the upmarket **Don Quixote** (545 Kent Street, 9264 5903), serving good Spanish food. A few doors down,

Tetsuya's (one of Sydney's star restaurants – see p158) hides behind the **Judges House** (531 Kent Street), built in 1827 and a rare example of a colonial Georgian bungalow with verandas. It's now occupied by an office, but you can admire it from the street. The area immediately south of Liverpool Street has been transformed by **World Square**, a mega shopping, office, residential and hotel complex that takes up a whole city block. Large-scale musicals such as *Wicked* and *Tap Dogs* play the glitzy **Capitol Theatre** (*see p270*) on Campbell Street. A block further south lies **Central Station**, Sydney's main train and bus nexus, surrounded by backpacker hostels and internet cafés.

General Post Office

1 Martin Place, between George & Pitt Streets, CBD (9229 7700, www.gposydney.com). CityRail Martin Place or Wynyard. **Map** p327 F5.

The GPO's foundations were laid in 1865, but workers' strikes and complications from building over the Tank Stream (the colony's first water supply) meant that it didn't open until 1874. The grand clocktower was added in 1891, its chimes based on London's Big Ben, with both the clock mechanism and bells made in England. The building's Italianate flourishes dominated the young city's skyline for decades before it fell into neglect; by 1989 the building was no longer adequate for the needs of Australia Post and in 1990 it was boarded up. A deal between the city authorities and the Westin Hotel group rescued the building, restoring the original cast-iron staircase, the clocktower and two ballrooms, and transforming the offices into hotel rooms. The GPO hall is now a light-drenched atrium that forms part of the hotel lobby and leads down to a classy food court and collection of restaurants. The colonnaded Martin Place entrance is flanked by upmarket shops. Much of the GPO's beauty is in the details: the stencilling on the walls, the moderne windows and the gold leaf ceiling patterned with leaves – spot the English rose and the Irish shamrock, as well as the Australian wattle and gum. The Tank Stream viewing room is open daily to visitors but tours of the Tank Stream itself run very rarely and are much sought-after (even dual-Booker Prize winner and ex-Sydney resident Peter Carey couldn't jump the queue!)

Queen Victoria Building (QVB)

455 George Street, between Market & Druitt Streets, CBD (9264 9209, www.qvb.com.au). CityRail Town Hall/Monorail Galeries Victoria. **Open** *Tours* 2.30pm daily. **Admission** $10. **Credit** AmEx, MC, V. **Map** p327 E6.

Designed by George McRae to resemble a Byzantine palace, the QVB occupies an entire block on George Street, and once dominated the Sydney skyline with its dramatic domed roof – an inner glass dome encased by a copper-sheathed outer one. Completed in 1898 to celebrate Queen Victoria's golden jubilee, it originally housed street markets. It has suffered (and gamely survived) long periods of neglect, and demolition threats were finally quashed in the 1980s when a $75 million budget restored the building to its former grandeur. It now houses 200 outlets, including shops, cafés and restaurants. Of particular note are the coloured lead-light wheel windows, the cast-iron circular staircase and the original floor tiles and lift. The ballroom on the third floor is now the Tearoom. On the hour, shoppers gather on gallery two to watch the Royal Automata Clock display a moving royal pageant. The execution of Charles I regularly goes down a storm with Sydney's many republicans.

FREE St Andrew's Cathedral

Sydney Square, corner of George & Bathurst Streets, CBD (9265 1661, www.cathedral. sydney.anglican.asn.au). CityRail Town Hall. **Open** 10am-3pm. **Tours** by arrangement daily. **Admission** free. **Map** p329 E7.

This huge late-Gothic edifice, the oldest cathedral in Australia, was started with astonishing confidence by Governor Macquarie (who named it after the patron saint of his native Scotland) when Sydney was still the size of a small village. The first stone was laid in 1819, and the cathedral was consecrated in 1868. Three architects contributed to it, the most notable being Edmund Blacket, city architect between 1849 and 1854. Special elements link the cathedral to the motherland, including intaglio tiles made by Mintons and two stones from the Palace of Westminster. Military commemorations honour the

Sydney Tower.

landings at Gallipoli and the prison camp at Changi
in Singapore. Recent conservation work has restored
the interior (altered in the 1950s) to its original glory.

Sydney Tower

*Centrepoint Podium Level, 100 Market Street,
between Castlereagh & Pitt Streets, CBD (9333
9222, www.sydneytoweroztrek.com.au, www.sky
walk.com.au). CityRail St James or Town Hall/
Monorail City Centre.* **Open** *Tower & OzTrek*
9am-10.30pm Mon-Fri, Sun; 9am-11.30pm Sat.
Skywalk 9.30am-8.45pm daily. **Admission** *Tower
& OzTrek* $24.50; $14.50-$18.50 reductions; $43-
$72 family; free under-4s. *Skywalk* $64.50; $44.50
reductions. **Credit** AmEx, MC, V. **Map** p327 F6.
Three high-speed lifts take approximately 40 sec-
onds to travel to the golden turret of this well-known
city symbol, which provides two levels of restaurants, a coffee lounge and an observation deck 250m
(820ft) above ground, with 360° views. Skywalk, the
latest of the city's thrill tours, opened in 2005, allowing visitors to wander around the outside of the turret. Harnessed to a range of skyways and viewing
platforms, participants have the whole of Sydney at
their feet: on a clear day you can see distant headlands up and down the coast, and as far west as the
Blue Mountains. You're only just above the observation deck and safe at all times, but being outside
is a definite buzz. Vertigo sufferers might prefer
OzTrek, a virtual-reality ride through Australia's
cultural history and geography, including climbing
Uluru and a tussle with a saltie (saltwater crocodile).

Sydney Town Hall

*Corner of George & Druitt Streets, CBD (9265
9189, concert information 9265 9007,
www.cityofsydney.nsw.gov.au). CityRail Town
Hall.* **Open** 8.30am-6pm Mon-Fri. **Map** p329 E7.
Built on a graveyard, completed in 1889 and given a
sustainability-driven overhaul in 2010, Sydney Town
Hall is an impressive High Victorian building, topped
by a clocktower with a two-ton bell. It has retained
its original function and interiors, including the council chamber and lord mayor's offices. The stunning
vestibule, its colourful domed ceiling hung with a
huge crystal chandelier, has some of the earliest
examples of Australian-made stained glass. Behind
this, Centennial Hall is dominated by a magnificent
8,000-pipe organ: with a capacity of 2,048, it was once
the largest concert hall in the world, and it is still used

for organ recitals and other musical events. A new
downstairs venue opened recently and in 2010 played
host to Sydney Fashion Festival and the lauded Da
Vinci Secrets: Anatomy to Robots exhibition.

Chinatown & Haymarket

Chinese people have been in Sydney since the
First Fleet landed in 1788: two of the ships' cooks
were said to be Chinese. By 1891, the Chinese
population had reached 14,000, but dwindled to
4,000 as the 'White Australia' policy peaked in
the 1950s. Today, Chinese migrants make up
the third-largest group of immigrants coming
to New South Wales. Vietnamese refugees
(including many of Chinese descent) arrived in
the wake of the Vietnam War, while dissident
students sought asylum after the 1989
Tiananmen Square debacle. In the years leading
to the handover of Hong Kong to China, many
Hong Kong Chinese also left for Australia.

When you hit **Chinatown**, the vitality of the
community is obvious. Sino-Sydneysiders do
not live in a ghetto – there are also established
surburban enclaves in Strathfield, Willoughby
and Ashfield, and many are simply integrated
into the community – but Chinatown is the
commercial and culinary hub. Once confined to
Dixon Street, a somewhat tacky pedestrianised
mall created in the 1980s, it continues to expand
and change at a phenomenal rate. It now
extends well into **Haymarket**, over Hay Street,
down Thomas and Ultimo Streets, and across
George Street. Three unremarkable little streets
in particular – Little Hay Street, Factory Street
and Kimber Lane – are in line for something of
a sprucing up in early 2011.

Around the ornate gates in Dixon Street, soil,
sand and rock from Guangdong province has
been buried. For the Chinese, it symbolises that
Australia is their home and they can be buried
there. Sussex Street has now taken over from
Dixon Street as the main strip; the brightly lit
section from Goulburn Street to Hay Street –
where **Paddy's Markets** (*see p197*) and the
Market City shopping centre reside – bustles
with activity day and nights. There are
restaurants, supermarkets, shops, Chinese-
language cinemas and some well-hidden
gambling spots, and this is one of the few
places in Sydney where you can get a meal
and a drink at 2am. In daylight hours, chic shops
sell (real and ersatz) designer gear: the Chinese
community is not only growing in size, it's also
increasingly affluent. The days of wall-to-wall
sweet-and-sour pork have been left far behind;
nowadays, little Chinatown diners serve Peking-
style dumplings. Others specialise in handmade
noodles and barbecued duck or seafood, and
grand Hong Kong-style dining rooms with over-
the-top chandeliers are always packed with

SIGHTS

Chinese and Anglos choosing delicacies from *yum cha* (dim sum) trolleys. For standout restaurants in the area, *see pp158-159*.

DARLING HARBOUR, PYRMONT & ULTIMO

Darling Harbour Ferry Darling Harbour/ CityRail Central or Town Hall/Monorail Convention, Darling Park or Harbourside/ LightRail Convention or Exhibition/bus 443. Pyrmont Ferry Pyrmont Bay/LightRail Fish Market, John St Square, Pyrmont Bay or Star City/bus 443, 449. Ultimo CityRail Central/Monorail/LightRail Exhibition or Paddy's Markets.

The reclaimed waterfront of **Darling Harbour**, on the western side of the CBD, boasts some acclaimed modern architecture (courtesy of architect Phillip Cox) and a huge retail complex (courtesy of global capitalism). The area is geared very much towards tourists, and can feel pretty soulless compared to the parts of town forged from convict stone. There are many attractions here – among them the **Sydney Aquarium** (*see p69*), the **Australian National Maritime Museum** (*see p68*), the **Chinese Garden of Friendship** (*see p68*), **Sydney Entertainment Centre** (*see p254*) and the **IMAX cinema** (*see p232*) – that it's easy to overlook the most basic one of all: the view of the western cityscape from the Pyrmont side of Darling Harbour, one of the best in Sydney. And it's free. There's also the **Harbourside shopping centre** (Darling Drive, 9281 3999, www.harbour side.com.au), a bit of a tourist trap, but good for souvenirs if you don't want to search too hard and, for the thrill seeker, boasting the **Flight Experience**, a Boeing 727 jet simulator on level three, and great ethical burgers at **Grill'd** on level two (9281 5121, www.grilld.com.au).

Darling Harbour hosts a stream of free festivals, concerts and other events at weekends and in school holidays throughout the year. New Year's Eve and Australia Day, in particular, are occasions for giant parties: call the **Darling Harbour Information Line** for details (1902 260 568, www.darlingharbour.com.au). There's also a branch of the **Sydney Visitor Centre** (*see p51*), behind the IMAX cinema. **Cockle Bay Wharf** (so named because of its original abundance of shellfish), on Darling Harbour's eastern shore, houses an array of cafés, restaurants and clubs spread across an epic space designed by populist American architect Eric Kuhne, who also designed the public areas in adjoining Darling Park (and the enormous Bluewater development in Kent, England). Initially written off by many as a failure, Cockle Bay has become a hugely successful

entertainment precinct and a fun place to dine and hang out. By day, it's a haven for teens and families; at night, tourists and twentysomethings move in, many heading for the sail-like glass building of superclub **Home** (*see p226*).

Further north, past the Sydney Aquarium, the party continues along the newly created **King Street Wharf** at yet more restaurants, cafés and a clutch of waterside apartments. A good place to be on a sweltering summer's night – if you're under 30, that is, is the **Cargo Bar** (21 Lime Street, 9262 1777), a rowdy outdoor venue with pumping music and great waterside views, or stylish bar **Loft** (3 Lime Street, 9299 4770) at the far end of the promenade. The iconic **Malaya** restaurant (39 Lime Street, 9279 1170), pioneers of the laksa in Sydney, is upstairs and always full.

Pyrmont, to the west of Darling Harbour (reached by the pedestrian Pyrmont Bridge, largest single steelspan bridge in the world), was once a mix of working-class cottages, refineries, quarries and engineering works. Now it is filling with apartment buildings and office blocks (including the Fairfax media empire and Channel Seven TV) as the city spreads ever westward. It is also home to **Star City** (*see p68*), Sydney's casino – a gaudy, vulgar, Las Vegas-like creation (also by Phillip Cox) with a deluxe hotel (*see p134*). Jones Bay Wharf, at the top end of the peninsula, has undergone a sleek renovation into classy offices, topped off with the fabulous seafood restaurant **Flying Fish** (*see p161*). Pyrmont's biggest draw is undoubtedly the **Sydney Fish Market** (*see p69*), widely regarded as one of the best in the world despite being desperately in need of renovation, on the edge of Blackwattle Bay. From its auction rooms premium-grade tuna goes to Japan, and a dozen or more outlets sell fresh-off-the-boat seafood. Browse among enticing mounds of salmon, snapper and yabbies (freshwater crustaceans), then pick up some rock oysters and find a sunny wharfside seat at which to picnic. But watch out for the pelicans: they're partial to seafood too.

Ultimo – south of Pyrmont and west of Chinatown, which is creeping towards it – has evolved into a strange meeting place of media, academic and museum life. Once notorious for some of Sydney's most squalid housing, and later the site of the municipal markets, it's now home to the sprawling University of Technology, the headquarters of the Australian Broadcasting Corporation and the masterfully converted **Powerhouse Museum** (*see p68*). The 2007 opening of the **Ian Thorpe Aquatic Centre** (*see p260*) has added to the growing chic of this area. Housing various pools, a fitness centre, sauna and café, the centre was one of the last works by top Sydney architect Harry Seidler (*see p35* **Profile**), who died in 2006.

Island Hopping

Exploring the Sydney Harbour peninsula.

Port Jackson, as Sydney Harbour is properly called, is sprinkled with islands. Some, such as tiny **Spectacle Island**, a domain of the Royal Australian Navy, and Goat Island, one-time nerve centre of port operations, are currently off limits to the general public. On others, however, you can cast yourself away, or take a historical tour.

The largest island, at 18 hectares (44 acres), is **Cockatoo Island**, managed by the Sydney Harbour Federation Trust (8969 2100, www.cockatooisland.gov.au). The trust runs informative one-and-a-half-hour walking tours on Sundays ($18; $14 reductions; $60 family), which depart from Circular Quay and must be pre-booked. Cockatoo Island was once a convict prison and later an enormous shipbuilding and repair operation: structures associated with both these eras still stand like ghostly sentinels to an alternately dark and industrious past. There's a spanking new camping ground with 135 sites for tents (bring your own or rent one on the island), eight electric BBQs, four sinks and seating and tables for 80 people, plus solar-powered hot showers, toilets, a laundry and internet access. Great for tourists is the full camping package ($75 per night), which includes site and tent hire, two self-inflating mattresses, two camp chairs and a lantern. All you need to bring is a sleeping bag. The site boasts amazing views across the Parramatta River to Hunters Hill, plus there's the Muster Station café and a bar.

The other islands that can be visited are under the auspices of the **National Parks & Wildlife Service** (NPWS; 9247 5033, www.nationalparks.nsw.gov.au), which has an office at Cadman's Cottage (*see p51*)

in the Rocks. **Fort Denison**, just off Mrs Macquarie's Point, served as an open-air prison and was once called Pinchgut Island thanks to the starvation rations – bread and water for a week – served to its inmates. Its first resident, Thomas Hill, was marooned here for seven days in 1788 as punishment for stealing biscuits. In 1862, a fort with a distinctive Martello tower was added and the island was renamed Fort Denison after then-governor William Denison. It's accessible by pre-booked tours ($17; $10-$16 reductions) on Matilda Cruises (9264 7377, www.matilda.com.au), leaving from Pier 26, Darling Harbour or no.6 Jetty, Circular Quay.

Shark Island, off Point Piper – named for its shape, not the creatures that lurk beneath – now has its own daily ferry service. It's great for picnics, as there are large grassy areas, lots of trees, picnic shelters, a gazebo and a wading beach. Toilets are on hand but there's no café, so bring your own tucker. Matilda Cruises (*see above*) leave from Pier 26, Darling Harbour or no.6 Jetty, Circular Quay ($16; $13.50-$14.50 reductions; $53 family), or you can hire your own water taxi.

Popular with wedding parties who like to hire their own island exclusively, **Clark Island**, near Darling Point, and **Rodd Island**, west of the Harbour Bridge in Iron Cove, are open to day-trippers year-round, with a $5 landing fee per person. Visitor numbers are limited, and you must book in advance with the NPWS and arrange your own transport by private boat, chartered ferry or water taxi from a NPWS list of licensed operators. Boats are allowed to drop off and pick up at the island wharfs, but not to tie up.

SIGHTS

Shark Island.

SIGHTS

FREE Australian National Maritime Museum

2 Murray Street, Harbourside, Darling Harbour (9298 3777, www.anmm.gov.au). Ferry Darling Harbour or Pyrmont Bay/LightRail Pyrmont Bay/Monorail Harbourside/bus 443. **Open** 9.30am-5pm daily (6pm Jan). **Admission** free; $12-$32 for special exhibits & vessels. **Credit** AmEx, MC, V. **Map** p326 D6.

For a city whose history has always been entwined with its harbour, the sea and water travel, it comes as no surprise that this museum is one of the finest when it comes to maritime treasures. An exhibition traces the history of the Royal Australian Navy, but the biggest exhibits are the vessels themselves, among them the 1888 racing yacht *Akarana*, 1950s naval destroyer *HMAS Vampire* and traditional Vietnamese junk *Tu Duo* ('Freedom'), which sailed into Darwin in 1977 with 39 refugees. A café offers seafood-oriented, open-air eating at the water's edge, while the shop sells books, nautical knick-knacks and sailing packages with qualified skippers.

★ Chinese Garden of Friendship

Corner of Pier & Harbour Streets, Darling Harbour (9281 6863, www.chinesegarden. com.au). CityRail Central or Town Hall/Monorail Paddy's Markets or World Square/LightRail Paddy's Markets. **Admission** $6; $3 reductions; $15 family. **No credit cards**. **Map** p329 E8.

Unless you're prepared to arm-wrestle for your share of tranquil spots, avoid this place at the weekend. Designed in Sydney's Chinese sister city, Guangzhou, to commemorate the 1988 bicentenary, the Garden of Friendship symbolises the bond between the two. The dragon wall features two dragon heads, one in gold for Guangzhou, one in blue for NSW, with a pearl in between. There are waterfalls, weeping willows, water lilies, 'wandering galleries' and wooden bridges. Head up to the tea room balcony, order a cup of tea and enjoy the best view of all: the entire park reflected in the Lake of Brightness. Not surprisingly, the garden is a big hit with wedding parties.

Powerhouse Museum

500 Harris Street, between William Henry & Macarthur Streets, Ultimo (9217 0111, www. powerhousemuseum.com). CityRail Central/ Monorail/LightRail Paddy's Markets. **Open** 10am-5pm daily. **Admission** $10; $5-$6 reductions; $25 family. **Credit** AmEx, DC, MC, V. **Map** p328 D8.

This former power station opened as a fun and funky museum in 1988 and is the largest in Australia, with a collection of 385,000 objects, 22 permanent and five temporary display spaces, and more than 250 inter-active exhibits, many pitched at the rock 'n' roll and fashion crowd. It covers science, technology, creativity, decorative arts and Australian popular culture, resulting in such diverse exhibitions as Tokyo street style and childhood memories of migration. Of late, it has hosted music-themed exhibitions. Also here is the Boulton & Watt steam engine (1785).

Star City

80 Pyrmont Street, at Foreshore Road, Pyrmont (9777 9000, www.starcity.com.au). LightRail Star City/Monorail Harbourside/bus 443, 449. **Open** 24hrs daily. **Map** p326 C6.

Opened in 1997, Star City is both slick and tacky – marble toilets, cocktails, champagne, fine dining, then fish and chips, beer and miles of pokies. There are

Chinese Garden of Friendship.

1,500 slot machines, a huge sports betting lounge and sports bar, and 200 gaming tables featuring everything from blackjack and roulette to Caribbean stud poker. Elsewhere are invitation-only private gaming rooms for the high-rollers, many of whom fly in from Asia. The Lyric Theatre (*see p270*) and Star Theatre stage glittery shows, Astral restaurant offers great views alongside its awesome food (although its famous founding chef Sean Connolly decamped in September 2010), and there's a luxury hotel with spa.

★ Sydney Aquarium & Sydney Wildlife World

Aquarium Pier, Wheat Road, Darling Harbour (8251 7800, www.sydneyaquarium.com.au). Ferry Darling Harbour/CityRail Town Hall/ Monorail Darling Park. **Open** 9am-10pm daily. *Seal sanctuary* 9.30am-sunset daily. **Admission** $28.50; $14.50-$19.50 reductions; $34-$80 family. **Credit** AmEx, DC, MC, V. **Map** p326 D6.
This fantastic aquarium comprises a main exhibition hall, two floating oceanariums – one dedicated to the Great Barrier Reef (and the largest collection of sharks in captivity), the other a sanctuary for Pig and Wuru, Australia's only captive dugongs and two of the only five on display anywhere in the world – and two touch pools. Gentler delights can be found via the elusive but ever-charming platypuses in the southern wing. Underwater viewing tunnels mean visitors can watch sharks and rays gliding past, or spot seals frolicking close up. Alternatively, the new glass-bottom boat Shark Explorer ride is another way to raise your heart beat.

Sydney Fish Market

Corner of Pyrmont Bridge Road & Bank Street, Pyrmont (9004 1100, www.sydneyfishmarket. com.au). LightRail Fish Market/bus 501. **Open** 7am-4pm daily. **No credit cards**. **Map** p326 C6.
This working fishing port – with trawlers in Blackwattle Bay, wholesale and retail fish markets, shops, a variety of indoor and outdoor eateries, and picnic tables on an outdoor deck – is well worth the trek to Pyrmont. Get up early and catch the stinky, messy, noisy wholesale fish auctions, from 7am. It's the largest market of its kind in the southern hemisphere, and you won't find more varieties of fish on sale anywhere outside Japan. The affiliated Sydney Seafood School (9004 1111) offers a wide range of classes in handling and cooking seafood (from $75).

Sydney Wildlife World

Aquarium Pier, Wheat Road, Darling Harbour (9333 9288, www.sydneywildlifeworld.com.au). Ferry Darling Harbour/CityRail Town Hall/ Monorail Darling Park. **Open** 9am-10pm daily. **Admission** $35; $18-23 reductions; $34-$80 family. **Credit** AmEx, DC, MC, V. **Map** p326 D6.
Opened in late 2006, this wildlife park on three levels is perfectly placed next to Sydney Aquarium (*see above*) for those families seeking an animal-oriented day out. There are over 100 Australian animal species on site and a huge variety of uniquely bizarre plant life. The ethos of the park is to tell each species' story on an evolutionary timeline within its own habitat, including elements of the Aboriginal dreamtime and conservation issues. Koalas naturally top the list, but the park is also home to wallabies, echidnas, reptiles, amphibians and more. The butterfly collection is truly amazing. Likewise, Rex, Wildlife World's five metre, 700kg saltwater crocodile, a beast whose taste for local dogs and crocodile co-habitants in far-north Kakadu saw him shipped to the city in 2009. A Combo Pass accessing Wildlife World, Sydney Aquarium, Oceanworld Manly and Sydney Tower was recently added to the ticket options for $50; $40 reductions.

EAST SYDNEY & DARLINGHURST

Kings Cross side CityRail Kings Cross/bus 311, 324, 325, 326, 327. Oxford Street side CityRail Museum/bus 333, 352, 378, 380, 382.

Stand with your back to Hyde Park at Whitlam Square facing down Oxford Street towards Paddington, and you're on the edge of the CBD and the inner city. The lower end of Oxford Street up to and around **Taylor Square** attracts a colourful crowd of down-and-outs and all-night hedonists. It's also the eastern-suburbs hub of gay Sydney, and as night falls, the street fills with perfectly pumped boys in regulation tight Ts, and high-haired drag queens flitting between shows in the huddle of pubs and clubs along the 'Pink Strip'. This area is lively from dusk to dawn and can get a little edgy when suburbia and bohemia collide in the wee hours. Sydney's gay community is fiercely protective of its own but if you're worried, your best bet is not to go out alone and to use the many safe houses of gay-friendly pubs, clubs and shops on Oxford Street if you feel under threat.

As with the rest of Sydney, apartment blocks are forever popping up between the trad Victorian terraces, and with them an influx of cashed-up DINKs (Double Income No Kids). Consequently, the previously drab retail options have perked up – the clothes shops are more innovative and there are even more coffee stores. Still, Darlinghurst and East Sydney are not yet a second Paddington or Double Bay

– the wonderfully queer-centric **Bookshop Darlinghurst** (*see p199*) proudly stamps its identity on the Strip, as do the wig and fetish-wear shops and tattoo parlours. Some consider Taylor Square the heart of gay Sydney and the epicentre of the Strip, though a slightly disappointing upgrade in 2003 left it as little more than a pocket patch of greenery (dubbed Gilligan's Island, after the US TV show), some arty bollards (several vandalised) containing local memorabilia and a lacklustre fountain. The adjoining Bourke Street cycleway and weekend Taylor Square Sustainability Markets amped the action in early 2010, with the reopening of infamous band bar venue **Kinselas** (no.383, www.kinselas.com.au) to adrenalise the area further. City planners have now turned their attention to the Oxford Street strip itself, widening the pavements and planting trees and introducing progressive stores such as **Reverse Garbage** (1-5 Flinders Street, 0413 508 636) and stylishly reduxed pubs such as the **Flinders Inn** (160a Flinders Street, 9331 0208).

Just beyond Taylor Square, on the north side of Oxford Street, Darlinghurst Road begins its downhill run to Kings Cross. The Victorian and art deco mansions here give a good idea of what the area used to be like, while the Harry Seidler-designed **Horizon** ('Horror Zone' to those who live in its shadow) residential tower, looming over it all, typifies the present face. Take the time to wander through the old Darlinghurst Gaol, a magnificent collection of sandstone buildings dating from the 1820s, where bushrangers such as Captain Moonlite were hanged, now a campus for the Sydney Institute of Technology and one of the city's best art schools. Incongruously, it also houses a butchery school, so don't be surprised to see arty types one minute and men in bloodied aprons the next.

The Darlinghurst ridge, where the Coca-Cola sign now stands at the top of William Street, was once the site of the city's windmills – walk past on a blustery August day and you'll see why. Another place worth visiting is the **Sydney Jewish Museum** (*see below*): Jewish immigrants have played a vital part in Australia's history and their story is told here. Running roughly parallel to Darlinghurst Road on its east side is **Victoria Street**, a lively mix of cafés, restaurants, shops and a few residential homes. The restaurants here and on Darlinghurst Road are generally better than those on Oxford Street. For a grand French night out, head to **Sel et Poivre** (no.263, 9361 6530); for ice-cream and sorbet, queue up at the popular **Gelato Messina** (no.241, 8354 1223) – one spoonful and you're hooked. To find the beautiful people, seek out the **Victoria Room** cocktail bar (*see p187*) or the stylish boutique hotels **Medusa** (no.267, 9331 1000) and

Kirketon (no.229, 9332 2011). Also nearby is that Sydney breakfast and lunch institution, **Bills** (*see p178*), famous for its scrambled eggs.

Sydney Jewish Museum

148 Darlinghurst Road, at Burton Street, Darlinghurst (9360 7999, www.sydneyjewish museum.com.au). CityRail Kings Cross/bus 311, 378, 380, 389. **Open** 10am-4pm Mon-Thur, Sun; 10am-2pm Fri. **Admission** $10; $6-$7 reductions; $22 family. **Credit** (shop only) MC, V. **Map** p330 H8.

After World War II, over 30,000 survivors of the Holocaust emigrated to Australia, settling mainly in Sydney and Melbourne. This museum opened in 1992 in Maccabean Hall, originally built to commemorate the Jews of NSW who had served in World War I. The hall has been the centre of Jewish life in Sydney ever since, so it seemed right to transform it into a permanent memorial to victims of both wars. There are two permanent displays – 'Culture and Continuity' and 'The Holocaust' – plus excellent touring exhibitions.

SURRY HILLS

CityRail/LightRail Central/bus 301, 302, 303.

South of Oxford Street is Surry Hills, an increasingly des-res area and nirvana for Sydney foodies and imbibers – a dozen new cafés, restaurants and revamped bars seem to open here every week. Its main thoroughfare is north–south Crown Street, an interesting mix of the very cool and the tatty. At night, the vibe is heady and laid-back, with watering holes to suit every taste and pocket. The Oxford Street end is a tad more chic; witness the **Dolphin** (no.412, 9331 4800, www.dolphinhotel.com.au). Opposite is **Medina on Crown** (no.359) a smart, serviced apartment block popular with short-stay business types, beneath which you'll find hip restaurants, such as **Billy Kwong** (*see p163*).

Moving a block further south, the very stylish **White Horse Hotel** (nos.381-385, 8333 9999, www.thewhitehorse.com.au) is providing strong competition to the long-established **Clock Hotel** (470 Crown Street, 9331 5333, www.clockhotel.com.au), with its dining room and wraparound balcony. The Shannon Reserve, a tiny park between these two hotels, hosts a lively flea market on the first Saturday of the month, but all through the week shoppers are well served by established premises such as the oriental curio shop **Mrs Red & Sons** (no.427, 9310 4860) and **Mondo Luce** (no.439, 9690 2667, www.mondoluce.com), one of a number of modish lighting shops. The **Book Kitchen** (*see p179*), one of Sydney's best combined book and café operations, and the **Bourke Street Bakery** (*see p179*), on the corner of Devonshire and Bourke Streets, are

INSIDE TRACK THE GADIGALS

Little remains of the Gadigal people, the cove's original inhabitants, save for displays at various museums. But their spirits still haunt central Sydney and their stories bubble up when you least expect it.

delicious and highly popular new additions, although success often translates into surly service at the latter.

Bourke Street itself, running parallel to Crown a block to the east, remains largely residential, but is also sprouting some interesting shops and restaurants, spurred on by the transformation of the old St Margaret's maternity hospital into a swanky apartment complex that also includes coffee shops and restaurants, the **Object Gallery** and its great shop **Collect** (no.417, 9361 4511, www.object. com.au), health point **Uclinic** (no.421, 9332 0400, www.uclinic.com.au), Ferdinando de Freitas's lush florists **Garlands** (9357 7900, www.garlands.net.au) and a rather chic **Woolworths** (no.417, 9326 0100). All this activity is gradually and inevitably gentrifying Surry Hills, as happened to previously funky Paddington, now almost too chichi for words. Bourke Street is also the site of the Brett **Whiteley Studio** (*see below*), a museum dedicated to the acclaimed Sydney-born artist.

FREE Brett Whiteley Studio

2 Raper Street, off Davies Street, Surry Hills (9225 1740, recorded info 9225 1790, 1800 679 278, www.brettwhiteley.org). CityRail Central then 10mins walk/bus 301, 302, 303, 352. **Open** 10am-4pm Sat, Sun. **Admission** free. **Credit** AmEx, MC, V. **Map** p329 G11.
Brett Whiteley was one of Australia's most exciting artists. In 1985, he bought a warehouse in Surry Hills and converted it into a studio, art gallery and home in which he lived from 1988. Following Whiteley's death in 1992 – in the motel room in which he often fell off the wagon to fuel his drug and alcohol habit – the studio was converted into a museum. Managed by the Art Gallery of NSW, it offers a singular insight into the artist through photos, personal effects, memorabilia and changing exhibitions of his work.

REDFERN & WATERLOO

Redfern CityRail Redfern/bus 305, 308, 309, 310, 352. Waterloo Bus 301, 302, 303, 343, 355.

The artfully ragged seams of Surry Hills extend west to Central Station (just beyond the rag-trade centre on and around Foveaux Street) and in

the south at Cleveland Street, the border with **Redfern**. Aboriginal people from rural areas started moving into Redfern in the 1920s because of its proximity to Central Station, cheap rents and local workshops offering regular work. More arrived during the Depression of the 1930s, and by the '40s the area had become synonymous with its indigenous population. Following the 1967 national referendum, which gave indigenous people citizenship rights, Redfern's Aboriginal population increased to 35,000, causing mass overcrowding.

In the decades that followed, government programmes (some helpful, some not) have disseminated the area's indigenous people, and today it is undergoing intensive reinvention, with some pockets hurtling upmarket. But the central patch of run-down terraces in a one-hectare area bounded by Eveleigh, Vine, Louis and Caroline Streets – which made up the Block, the beleaguered heart of a black-run Aboriginal housing co-operative – remains an indigenous enclave. Forty years after its inception, the last 75 residents of the Block were evicted on 19 November 2010 to allow for demolition and commencement of the Pemulwuy Project in 2011.

The area's problems – poverty, drugs and alcoholism – won't be bulldozed so fast, but there's an increasingly smarter edge to Redfern as artists' galleries take up residence, and those who can't quite afford Surry Hills turn their eyes south of the Cleveland Street border looking for residential bargains. The City of Sydney is pouring money in too, with a $50 million infrastructure programme for Redfern, Waterloo, Darlington and Eveleigh. This includes an $11 million revamp of **Prince Alfred Park**, between Central Station and Cleveland Street, with a 50-metre outdoor pool, the much-anticipated sequel to its acclaimed $19 million restoration of Redfern Park and its stadium, training ground of the South Sydney Rabbitohs rugby league team owned by Oscar-winning actor and dyed-in-the-wool Bunnies fan, Russell Crowe.

In neighbouring **Waterloo**, development is also running rife. Danks Street, at the heart of a previously industrial area, is now brimming over with a fine range of eateries and interior design shops, plus art gallery complex 2 Danks Street and top-quality Italian grocers Fratelli Fresh with its delicious **Café Sopra** (*see p165* and *p179*). Further south, in Zetland, if all goes to plan (and it's a 20-year plan), **Green Square** – focused around the Green Square train station and bordered by Botany Road and Bourke Street – is slated to house over 5,000 people in 2,800 new apartments and houses, plus parks, shops and recreation centres, all part of Australia's single largest development project.

KINGS CROSS, POTTS POINT & WOOLLOOMOOLOO

CityRail Kings Cross/bus 311, 324, 325, 326.

Kings Cross, formed by the intersection of Darlinghurst Road and Victoria Street as they cross William Street, has long been the city's red-light district, although today it's dominated as much by amazing bars and restaurants as drugs and prostitution. It remains Australia's most populated district per square mile, and it fairly bursts at the seams. The on-show seedy action is pretty much confined to 'the Strip', stretching along Darlinghurst Road from William Street to the picturesque El Alamein fountain, although visitors should stick to the main streets, especially at night when the winding roads leading back towards Potts Point and the Cross tend to become drug alleys. Along Darlinghurst Road you'll find Australia's first legal 'shooting gallery'; despite much controversy, the centre has remained open, and many in the know say it has reduced the number of heroin deaths in the area while providing support for the growing number of users. Alas, as heroin's grip loosened, so arrived the new scourge of Ice.

Community and local government efforts in recent years to clean up Kings Cross, spurred on by the influx of cashed-up residents to the swanky new apartments that have been created on the sites of several of the area's former hotels, have made a difference. Today's Cross is a pale hangover from the days of the Vietnam War, when thousands of US soldiers descended for R&R with fistfuls of dollars and the desire to party the horrors of war out of their systems. Their appetites tended towards the carnal, and the dreary parade of seedy strip clubs and massage parlours – now frequented mostly by suburbanites, out-of-towners and international sailors – is evidence of how they got their kicks. Nonetheless, the Cross's neon lights still pull in hordes of backpackers, sustained by a network of hostels, internet cafés and cheap restaurants.

The good news for tourists is that there are plenty of police on the beat, and when the night turns ugly, as it inevitably does for some, you needn't get caught in the trouble. The Cross officially starts from underneath the Coca-Cola sign at the intersection of William Street and Darlinghurst Road. Here you'll also find a cavernous underground Coles supermarket as well as perhaps the only bona fide straight sauna in the area – the **Body Inc Bathhouse & Spa**, formerly the Ginseng Bathhouse (Level 1, 224 Victoria Street, 9356 3477), a traditional Korean bathhouse with an impressive range of therapeutic treatments.

Victoria Street branches off Darlinghurst Road and it's here you'll find the **Holiday Inn** (no.203, 9368 4000, www.holidayinn.com) and, from 2008, the **Chifley Potts Point** (9358 2755, www.chifleyhotels.com), an upmarket refurb of the former Crest Hotel. Another smart new hotel sprucing up the area is the **Eight Hotels Group Diamant** (14 Kings Cross Road, 9295 8888, www.diamant.com.au). Beyond the El Alamein fountain you're into Potts Point proper. In contrast to the Kings Cross Strip's wall-to-wall neon lighting, Macleay Street, with its columns of cool plane trees, is made for slow strolling and offers architectural and culinary pleasures. Tall, impregnable apartment buildings such as the neo-Gothic **Franconia** (no.123) offer a glimpse of the grandeur of the old Cross. Orwell Street, running west off Macleay, houses one of Sydney's finest art deco buildings, the old Minerva theatre, now called the **Metro** (nos. 26-30), while at 3 Manning Street the **Royal Australian Institute of Architects** (RAIA; 9356 2955, www.architecture.com.au) was pivotal in helping rescue Tusculum, a grand villa dating from the 1830s.

Potts Point has many fine eateries and good coffee shops, and it's a far cry from the desperate world of the Strip. You seem to be on another planet: one populated by chic, wealthy Sydneysiders. If you turn off Macleay Street and into Challis Avenue (also dotted with cafés), you'll soon come to the northern end of Victoria Street and a handful of the grand 19th-century terraces that formerly made it one of the city's most elegant thoroughfares.

Victoria Street backs on to a cliff that drops down to Sydney's oldest suburb, **Woolloomooloo**, which stands partly on land filled with the remains of scuttled square-riggers, and is now a mix of public housing (incorporating many original buildings) and swish new developments. You can walk down from Victoria Street via Horderns, Butlers or McElhone Stairs. Alternatively, **Mezzaluna** (123 Victoria Street, 9357 1988, www.mezzaluna.com.au), serving Italian food, offers a spectacular view over Woolloomooloo Bay to the city skyline. **Embarkation Park**, atop a navy car park at the corner of Victoria Street and Challis Avenue, provides an equally magnificent vista, particularly midweek around twilight when the office towers are lit up. Macleay Street becomes Wylde Street, which runs out of puff at the **Garden Island Naval Base** on Woolloomooloo Bay, where you are greeted by the surreal sight of the Royal Australian Navy's fleet moored at the side of the road. The US Navy also regularly docks here. The newly opened **Royal Australian Navy Heritage Centre** (*see below*) is at the very tip of the base on Garden Island – although you can't access it on foot; instead you have to catch a ferry from Circular Quay.

SIGHTS

Woolloomooloo was named by the Womerah people who lived here before European colonisation and translates as 'place of plenty', a reference to the plethora of kangaroos that once inhabited the area. The area's Aboriginal roots are celebrated in several colourful street murals, although you should wander with care around this public housing estate: it doesn't have Sydney's best reputation for safety. Jutting into the bay is **Woolloomooloo Wharf** (also called Cowper Wharf), constructed in 1910 as a state-of-the-art wool and cargo handling facility. Over the years the wharf fell into disuse, and it seemed destined to crumble into the harbour until former Premier Bob Carr slapped a conservation order on the site. In 2000, a stylish mix of eateries, apartments, an upmarket hotel (formerly the W, now **Blue**; *see p137*) and private marinas opened. Those who can't afford to eat in the snazzy restaurants that line the finger wharf instead promenade up and down the boardwalk in the sun. And just up Cowper Wharf Road is **Harry's Café de Wheels** (*see p180*), Sydney's most famous pie cart, here since World War II and practically an obligatory fuel stop after a night's neck oiling in the Cross or 'Loo.

Opposite the wharf is **Artspace** (*see below*), an extraordinary government-run art gallery, and, on the corner of Bourke Street, the legendary **Woolloomooloo Bay Hotel** pub (no.2, 9357 1177, www.woolloomooloobayhotel.com.au), packed with old neighbourhood faces and rowdy youngsters who don't care for the Blue bar peacocks over the road. Around the corner on Nicholson Street the **Tilbury Hotel** has a great restaurant and a stylish bar (12-18 Nicholson Street, 9368 1955, www.tilburyhotel.com.au).

FREE Artspace

The Gunnery, 43-51 Cowper Wharf Road, between Forbes & Dowling Steets, Woolloomooloo (9356 0555, www.artspace.org.au). CityRail Kings Cross then 10mins walk/bus 311. **Open** 11am-5pm Tue-Sat. **Admission** free. **Credit** MC, V. **Map** p330 H6.

This government-funded contemporary art gallery presents edgy, experimental and challenging work. Five galleries and 12 studios (for local and international artists) are housed in the historic Gunnery building. Prepare to be 'shocked, stimulated, inspired and entertained' – or so the gallery claims.

FREE Royal Australian Navy Heritage Centre

Garden Island (9359 2003, www.navy.gov.au/ranhc). Ferry Garden Island. **Open** 9.30am-3.30pm daily. **Admission** free. *Special Exhibition Gallery* $5; free under-16s. **No credit cards. Map** p330 K3.

For close on a century Garden Island, home to the Royal Australian Navy (RAN), has been off-limits to the general public. In late 2005, the very tip of the one-time island, long since connected to Potts Point, was reopened, with the only access via a five-minute ferry ride from Circular Quay. It's worth a visit, if only to enjoy the relative quiet of the grounds and the odd collection of monuments and giant naval objects, including radars, a propeller and 21in torpedoes. The view from the former Main Signal Building is spectacular. The Heritage Centre, occupying what was the Gun Mounting Workshop (dating from 1922) and an ex-boat shed (1913), includes an oceanic range of items that provides plenty of insight into navy life. Bring a picnic or enjoy lunch or afternoon tea at the Salthorse Café with a lovely view across Elizabeth Bay.

SIGHTS

Woolloomooloo.

Eastern Suburbs

Life is more than just a beach for 'silvertails' living in the east.

Over the past 20 years, the eastern suburbs have been completely transformed by a young, go-getting moneyed set that want to live the high life close to the city. The east has always had a certain cachet – the back streets of **Woollahra**, **Double Bay**, **Vaucluse**, **Darling Point**, **Rose Bay** and **Centennial Park** are lined with grand colonial mansions that have housed generations of Sydney's wealthiest. But **Paddington**, **Bondi**, **Tamarama**, **Watsons Bay** and **Coogee** are where the nouveau riche are staking their claim.

The magnetism of the east lies with its easy proximity to the city and its natural beauty. The water – be it ocean or harbour – is never far away, and in

Map p330	Restaurants p148
Hotels p126	Cafés p176
	Bars & Pubs p184

many suburbs it's the main view. There is a host of pretty beaches with something for everyone, from family-centric **Nielsen Park** to sunbathers' haven Tamarama, surf paradise Bondi or peaceful **Parsley Bay**. Add to this great shops – Paddington is the appointed home of the city's fashion designers, many trading from terraced homes – plus enough restaurants, cafés and bars to keep locals busy, and, even if you're just spending a few hours here, it's pretty clear why the east has become the place to settle.

PADDINGTON

Transport Bus 333, 352, 378, 380, 389.

There's nowhere in Sydney quite like **Paddington** and it's not hard to see why the area has attracted a wealth of young, trendy professionals, all eager to pay high rents in exchange for the aspirational zip code. Unlike Darlinghurst and Surry Hills, its edgy neighbours to the west, Paddo has managed to create a fashionable chic without a seedy underside, but hasn't gone so far as its easterly neighbours Woollahra and Centennial Park in becoming so overpriced that the young and impressionable can't afford to live there.

Walking up the main drag of **Oxford Street**, with the city behind you, Paddington proper starts just after Taylor Square, the heart

of gay Sydney. The scene gets straighter (but no less fabulous) the further up the hill you go until you reach Centennial Park at the top. Banks, bottle shops, boutiques and beautiful boys and girls happily co-exist on Oxford Street, and it's a great place to spend a few hours just walking and taking in the buzzing atmosphere. Just past South Dowling Street are two of Sydney's best art-house cinemas, the **Palace Verona Cinema** (*see p232*) and **Chauvel** (*see p231*), the latter specialising in golden oldies and themed Friday night freak-outs for younger cinephiles.

Nearby are two of the city's finest bookshops, **Berkelouw Books** (*see p199*) and **Ariel** (*see p199*), open late for pre- and post-movie browsing.

Further along, on the south side of Oxford Street, is **Victoria Barracks** (*see p76*). Built

SIGHTS

by convicts to house soldiers and their officers, the complex predates most of Paddington, and its Georgian lines bring a sense of grandeur to the area's rows of terraces.

From the Barracks to Centennial Park, Paddington's best-dressed come out in force in the ever-changing mix of designer shoes, one-off boutiques and chain stores. The cafés, pubs, bars and gift shops get their fair share of trade too.

Paddington Town Hall & Library (1891) on the corner of Oatley Road and **Paddington Post Office** (1885) provide an elegant edge, and are reminders of the days when such grand Victorian buildings dominated the skyline and steam trams rattled up Oxford Street – the **Town Hall** is in typical Classical Revival style with a 32.5m (107ft) clock tower.

Next to the Post Office is the delightful **Juniper Hall** (1824), probably the oldest surviving villa in Australia. Built as a family home for gin distiller Robert Cooper, it was named after the berry used in making the drink. Cooper, nicknamed 'Robert the Large' for his size, was a colourful character, a convict who smuggled wine from France, fathered 28 children and founded Sydney College, which later became Sydney Grammar School. In 1984, the property was restored by the National Trust and is now privately leased to local businesses. Over the road is one of Sydney's newest success stories, the **Paddington Reservoir** (*see p76*). Opposite Juniper Hall is the amazing, not-to-be missed **Paddington Reservoir Gardens**.

The imposing **Paddington Inn** (338 Oxford Street, 9380 5913, www.paddingtoninn.com.au) is the area's best-known pub. It has good bar-bistro food and a heaving mix of locals, tourists and members of the transitory overseas population that washes through Paddo. For sensational pizza and rustic Italian food try **Love Supreme** (180 Oxford Street, 9331 1779, www.lovesupreme.com.au). The **Light Brigade** on the corner of Jersey Road (2A Oxford Street, 9331 2930, www.lightbrigade.com.au) is also worth checking out for its recently refurbished upstairs restaurant La Scala and cocktail lounge.

Each Saturday, you can sample the wares at the popular **Paddington Market** (*see p197*), on the corner of Oxford and Newcombe Streets. You'll find an assortment of local crafts and reasonably priced clothing (a number of Sydney designers started out here), plus fortune tellers, masseurs and purveyors of just about every other knick-knack you could hope for.

The streets off Oxford Street also hold much of interest. William Street, to the north just before the Paddington Inn, has a cluster of Sydney's best local fashion designers. Duck down and check out **Collette Dinnigan** (*see p201*), **Leona Edmiston** (*see p203*), the

Corner Shop (*see p205*) and **Sylvia Chan** (No.20, 9380 5981).

Back towards the city, opposite the Barracks, is Glenmore Road, flanked by the boudoir-style **Alannah Hill** boutique (*see p201*) on one corner and **Scanlan & Theodore** (*see p203*) on the other. You'll also find **Kirrily Johnston** (*see p203*) a few doors down and the super-trendy **Sass & Bide** (*see p203*) back around the corner on Oxford Street.

Further down Glenmore Road – past a few art galleries and yet more high-class boutiques – you'll find some of the area's most extravagantly and expensively refurbished Victorian terraces. Don't be fooled by the cramped exteriors: behind the front doors and delicate, iron-laced balconies so typical of Paddington, interior designers have gone to work creating bright, modern spaces with the use of the odd skylight or spiral staircase thrown in for good measure.

Over the roundabout on the left is the **Royal Hospital for Women Park**, a patch of green beloved by dog walkers because of its 'off-leash' status (there are only ten local parks where dogs are allowed to run free). The park sits behind the chi-chi Paddington Green housing development, a swanky conversion of the original Royal Hospital for Women buildings. There are a few benches and lots of sun (sunbathers catch the last rays of the day here), and the park also features some of the original sandstone blocks from the historic hospital.

SIGHTS

Paddington Market.

Five Ways – the junction of five roads at a mini-roundabout – is the popular villagey heart of the area and has recently benefitted from a pavement widening project. You're spoilt for choice for somewhere to eat here. There's the excellent Japanese restaurant **Wasavie** (*see p169*); terraced tapas spot **Tapenade** (corner of Broughton Street and Glenmore Road, 0488 198099); two French bistros, **Vamp's** (227 Glenmore Road, 9331 1032) and **L'Etoile** (*see p168*); upmarket fish 'n' chips den **A Fish Called Paddo** (No.239, 9326 9500); and **Plumer at Five Ways** (No.226, 9361 6131), a popular hangover stop where you can get your teeth into burgers and roast chook.

Overseeing the lot is the majestic **Royal Hotel** (*see p191*), built in 1888 in a grand classical style. On the ground floor is a busy pub with pokies and TV screens; upstairs there's a restaurant with a popular wrap-around balcony. If you carry on down Glenmore Road you'll find **White City Tennis Club** (9360 4113) on your left, and eventually **Trumper Park** with its cricket oval named for Sydney's 'prince of batsmen'. Behind is native bush, plus a steep walkway up to Edgecliff on the left and Woollahra – via the Palms Tennis Centre – on the right.

FREE ★ Paddington Reservoir

Corner of Oatley and Oxford streets. Bus 352, 378, 380, L82. **Open** sunrise-sunset daily. **Admission** free.

Built 144 years ago as a reservoir for billabong water pumped from the nearby Botany and Centennial Park swamplands, it was decommissioned in 1914 and later became a pub (bomb-blasted out of business) and then a garage whose roof collapsed in 1993. The site thereafter fell into a derelict state and became subterranean base for a shadowy graffiti movement who filled its 1,023 square metres (11,000 square feet) of walls and chambers with stunning murals and frescoes while feeding a growing colony of stray cats. In 2008, work began on a $10 million facelift and in 2009, Paddington Reservoir Gardens was unveiled as a stunning Romanesque sunken garden with a lake of contemplation at its centre and a hanging garden canopy around the perimeter and an eastern chamber left empty but for the wall art. Already the recipient of most of Australia's greatest architectural restoration prizes, the Reservoir's blank canvas is yet unrealised with a 'cultural precinct' mooted and markets, and festivals jousting for residency.

▶ *For more on the Reservoir and other Sydney design marvels see pp33-39 Architecture.*

FREE Victoria Barracks

Oxford Street, between Greens & Oatley roads (9339 3170). Bus 352, 378, 380, L82. **Open** *Museum* 10am-3pm Sun. *Tour with museum entry* 10am Thur. Closed Christmas holidays. **Admission** *Museum* $2 donation. *Tour* free. **Map** p332 J10.

Built with local sandstone between 1841 and 1849, the Regency-style Victoria Barracks were designed by Lieutenant-Colonel George Barney, who also built Fort Denison and reconstructed Circular Quay. Sydney's first barracks had been at Wynyard Square, where the soldiers of the 11th (North Devonshire) Regiment of Foot had been able to enjoy all the privileges of living in the city: the pubs, the eating houses and the brothels. So there were groans of despair when they were uprooted to the lonely

Paddington Reservoir.

outpost that was Paddington. The site was chosen because it had borehole water and was on the line an attacker from the east might use, but its main feature was scrub: heath, swamp and flying sand from the adjacent dunes, which caused conjunctivitis (known as 'Paddington pink-eye'). And while the main building and parade ground were (and still are) quite stunning, the soldiers' quarters were cramped, and British regiments dreaded being posted to Australia. Nowadays, the old barracks is used as a military planning and administration centre. The museum is housed in the former 25-cell jail, also home to a ghost, Charlie the Redcoat, who hanged himself while incarcerated for shooting his sergeant.

CENTENNIAL PARK & MOORE PARK

Transport Centennial Park Bus 333, 352, 355, 378, 380. Moore Park Bus 339, 373, 374, 376, 377, 392, 393.

Centennial Park.

If it's greenery you're after, head to the top of Oxford Street where **Centennial Park** (*see p77*) awaits. It's hard to believe that such a huge and lush expanse of breathing space and picnic spots lies so close to the inner city. Filled with artificial lakes, bridle paths and cycle tracks, the park attracts a mix of families looking for the perfect spot for a toddler's birthday party, outdoor fitness fanatics and casual strollers. Rolling all the way down to Randwick Racecourse and across to Queens Park and Moore Park (home to Sydney's first zoo), Centennial Park was created in the 1880s on the site of the Lachlan Swamps as part of the state celebrations to mark the centenary of the landing of the First Fleet. The three parks (Centennial, Moore and Queens) encompass 3.8 square kilometres (1.5 square miles) and are collectively known as Centennial Parklands.

The former Royal Agricultural Society Showground on the west side of Centennial Park has been controversially and expensively redeveloped by Fox Studios Australia into a film studio and entertainment complex, the **Entertainment Quarter** (*see p77*). Next to the complex (approached from Moore Park Road or Driver Avenue), the huge white doughnuts that form **Sydney Cricket Ground (SCG)** and **Sydney Football Stadium (SFS)** (for both, *see p263*) light up the skyline for miles around at night. South of the cricket ground, **Moore Park Golf Course** (*see p259*) is one of the best and most popular public courses in the city.

FREE Centennial Park
Between Oxford Street, York, Darley, Alison & Lang roads (9339 6699, www.cp.nsw.gov.au). Bus 333, 352, 355, 378, 380. **Open** *Pedestrians*

24hrs daily. *Vehicles* sunrise-sunset daily. Car-free days last Sun in Mar, May, Aug, Nov. **Admission** free. **Map** pp332-333.
A weekend trip to Centennial Park, especially in summer, reveals Aussies at their leisurely best. There's an outdoor fitness station, and you can hire in-line skates and bikes or even go horse riding. Cyclists used to be a bit of a menace, but these days most adhere to the 30km/hr (18.6mph) speed limit and will dodge a pedestrian if at all possible. But don't be scared off by all this activity: the park is also teeming with those just looking for a shady spot to snooze or read a good book. Even in peak season, when it seems every Sydneysider wants a piece of the park, the vast lawns mean that there's always a secluded spot to claim as your own. Statues, ponds and native Australian flowers make it one of the prettiest places to spend a day, and there's a great restaurant and café. Ranger-led walks include Tree Tours, Frog Pond Workshops and the night-time Spotlight Prowl, and keep your eyes peeled for the Moonlight Cinema (*see p233*) from December to March.

Entertainment Quarter
Driver Avenue, Moore Park (8117 6700, www. entertainmentquarter.com.au). Bus 355, 373, 374, 376, 377, 391, 392, 396. **Map** p332 J/K12.
Fox Studios Australia (www.foxstudiosaustralia. com) opened in May 1998. Since then, Sydneysiders have become used to seeing US movie stars in their city; some, such as Keanu Reeves and Kate Bosworth, have become regular visitors. Regrettably, Australia's first (and only) Hollywood-style film studios are not open to the public any more, even for tours. What the public gets instead is the super-slick Entertainment Quarter complex, with cinemas, shops, a barrage of eateries and some huge entertainment spaces. There's a weekend

crafts market and a farmers' market on Wednesdays and Saturdays (both open 10am-4pm). Kids will have a ball at the two state-of-the-art playgrounds, seasonal ice-rink, ten-pin bowling centre, crazy golf course and the popular Bungy Trampoline. The Forum music venue is also found here as is the popular Comedy Store (Building 207, 9357 1419, www.comedystore.com.au).

▶ For more great Sydney comedy venues see pp268-274 Theatre.

WOOLLAHRA

Transport Bus 200, 389.

If a long day of being fashionable on Oxford Street proves too much, you'll find a welcome escape opposite the Paddington Gates of Centennial Park. **Queen Street** is the closest thing in eastern Sydney to an old-fashioned English high street, and the villagey feel will make you think the city is hours rather than minutes away. Pricey antique shops, galleries, delis, homeware stores and boutiques line the first stretch, leading down to the upmarket village of Woollahra. The antique shops are not for the bargain hunter, but are surprisingly rich in wares.

Walking along Queen Street, turn left at the traffic lights onto Moncur Street at French restaurant **Bistro Moncur** (116 Queen Street, 9363 2519, www.woollahrahotel.com.au), past posh deli **Jones the Grocer** (68 Moncur Street, 9362 1222, www.jonesthegrocer.com), round to the right into Jersey Road and you'll come to the **Lord Dudley Hotel** (No.236, 9327 5399, www.lorddudley.com.au). The Dudley is an oasis for nostalgic Poms looking for a touch of home; it positively screams English pubdom, from its ivy-clad exterior down to its cosy bar with British beers on tap. It's also popular with mature moneyed locals and revellers from the nearby **Palms Tennis Centre** (Quarry Street, Trumper Park, 9363 4955) and **Paddington Bowling Club** (2 Quarry Street, 9363 1150), who meet at the pub for a post-match tipple.

A walk from the east end of Queen Street via Greycairn Place and Attunga Street to Cooper Park – which runs east into the suburb of Bellevue Hill – is a pleasure in the jacaranda season (late November to December), when the streets are flooded with vivid purple blossoms.

At the east end of Cooper Park, across Victoria Road, you'll find small **Bellevue Park**, which has some unbeatable views of the harbour. The eastern suburbs, from Woollahra to Double Bay, Bellevue Hill, Bondi Junction and Bondi, are home to Sydney's Jewish community. On Friday evenings and Saturday mornings, the streets are alive with the devout walking to and from the various synagogues dotted throughout the area,

including the liberal **Temple Emanuel** in Woollahra (7 Ocean Street, 9328 7833, www.emanuel.org.au) and the beautifully designed, light-filled **Central Synagogue** in Bondi Junction (15 Bon Accord Avenue, 9389 5622, www.centralsynagogue.com.au).

BONDI JUNCTION

Transport CityRail Bondi Junction/bus 200, 333, 352, 378, 380.

While the almost mythical appeal of Bondi Beach is what draws the crowds to this part of Sydney, Bondi is in fact its own sprawling suburb, made up of four distinct and individual areas. **Bondi Junction** is the buzzing shopping and transport hub bordering Paddington, Woollahra and Queen's Park to the west. Bondi proper is really just Bondi Road, the suburban and commercial road that links the Junction to Bondi Beach. That famous beach heads north by way of its main drag, Campbell Parade, and leads straight into the quieter area of North Bondi, home of many an expat veteran Sydneysider and the Bondi Golf Course.

While it's the beach that is the focus for most, the Junction, with its monster mall – the **Westfield Bondi Junction** (*see p197*) – has become the place to shop in eastern Sydney, if you don't mind crowds. It boasts every brand-name shop from Oxford Street and the city, plus supermarkets, restaurants, a multi-screen cinema and even a state-of-the-art gym with great views over Sydney.

The proximity of the city by train or bus has turned Bondi Junction into a booming residential and commercial hub, and although the older parts look relatively shabby in the shadow of the Westfield, on the whole the place has finally come into its own.

From the Junction, there are two roads that lead to Bondi Beach. **Old South Head Road** turns away from the ocean and winds north to Watsons Bay, so take the turn-off at O'Brien Street or Curlewis Street. It tends to be quieter than the other route, **Bondi Road**, which can be thick with buses; in summer, when the crowded vehicles trundle at a snail's pace, it's often quicker to walk (about 30 minutes).

Snaking through Waverley into Bondi (increasingly called 'Bondi Heights' by estate agents keen to exploit its trendiness), Bondi Road is a mixed bag of alternative shops and international restaurants. **Kemeny's Food & Liquor** (Nos.137-147, 13 8881, www.kemenys.com.au) is the best place to buy fine wine on the cheap, and you can take your pick from a variety of casual eateries, including well-known fish restaurant **The One That Got Away** (No.163, 9389 4227).

BONDI BEACH TO COOGEE BEACH

Transport Bondi Beach CityRail Bondi Junction then bus 333, 380, 381, 382, 389/bus 333, 380, 389. Coogee Beach CityRail Bondi Junction then bus 313, 314/bus 372, 373, 374, X73.

Bondi Beach is anything but a romantic, stroll-in-the-moonlight strand. It's the closest ocean beach to the city and at first glance could easily be dismissed as a tacky tourist trap. But don't be fooled: there's a reason that some die-hard Sydneysiders wouldn't live anywhere else.

The main thoroughfare is noisy, four-lane **Campbell Parade**, which runs parallel to the beach and is lined with restaurants, cafés and souvenir shops, all of them usually packed at weekends. Below that is dinky **Bondi Park** – housing the 1928 Bondi Pavilion and the **Bondi Surf Bathers' Life Saving Club** (claiming to be the first of its kind in the world, although that boast is hotly contested by rival clubs) – and after that the sand itself.

Bondi is a good surfing beach, and there are plenty of places to hire wetsuits and boards along Campbell Parade; check out **Bondi Surf Co** (No.80, 9365 0870) for info on lessons too.

Summer nights bring in punters by the carload, particularly around Christmas and on New Year's Eve, when Bondi is best given a wide berth. Campbell Parade thumps and pumps for interlopers and blow-ins on weekends and offers more languorous delights for locals during the

Bondi Explorer bus, **Bondi Beach**.

week but to get a feel for why some people live and die in Bondi, you need to look around the corners and head inland.

Hall Street is the villagey heart of Bondi Beach, with such everyday necessities as banks, a post office and travel agents, as well as a gaggle of cafés and restaurants that have changed it from a daytime strolling location to a funky nightlife strip. The new vibe has spread to the surrounding streets: visit **Hurricanes** (126 Roscoe Street, 9130 7101, www.hurricanesgrill.com.au) for steaks, and **Brown Sugar** (106 Curlewis Street, 9130 1566) for its famous breakfast eggs blackstone.

The linking Gould Street has a small but significant collection of designer shops, many of whose keepers started selling their wares at the famous **Bondi Market** (*see p197*), which takes place in the vacant school playground every Sunday.

Bondi is popular with backpackers for good reason: it's loud, crowded and anything goes. Most of the budget accommodation is on or around Campbell Parade, Hall Street and nearby Lamrock Avenue and Roscoe Street. Further north is the favourite drinking spot of all out-of-towners, **Hotel Bondi** (178 Campbell Parade, 9130 3271, www.hotelbondi.com.au). It has guest rooms and is a fun spot for watching sport, dancing into the wee hours or enjoying a mid-afternoon beer, but give it a miss if you're hoping to meet locals. Australians prefer the **Beach Road Hotel** (71 Beach Road, 9130 7247, www.beachroadbondi.com.au).

On the corner of Hall Street, hotel **Ravesi's** (*see p141*), with its cocktail bar Drift, is still a fashionable flame drawing the pretty people in from the suburbs to drink and get merry. Sydney's small bar boom has flared in Bondi too with the small but perfectly formed **Shop and Wine Bar** (78 Curlewis Street, 9365 2600) and **Roy's Seafood & Tapas Bar** (141 Curlewis Street, 0450 955 987) offering respite from the bigger beer barns. Mid-range elbow-bending palaces **White Revolver** (Curlewis & Campbell Parade) and the adjoining **Cream Tangerine** (02 9300 8471) are upmarket and so cool as to be chilly to anyone but the most beautiful.

The north end of the beach has blossomed with its share of cafés and eating establishments – including **Sean's Panaroma** (270 Campbell Parade, 9365 4924, www.seanspanaroma.com.au), and **North Bondi Italian** on the north-end of the sand (118-120 Campbell Parade, 9300 4400, www.irdb.com). The outdoor gym, which is really just a collection of bars set up for pull-ups, is now generally acknowledged as the number one spot for tanning, posing and mutual admiration among Sydney's gay men.

Further on is the pricey Ben Buckler headland and the shops of North Bondi. Beyond

SIGHTS

Walk 1: Bondi to Coogee

Surfing, swimming, sculpture – and superb views.

Bondi Beach.

Character Dramatic ocean views.
Length 5km (3 miles) one way.
Difficulty Easy, some uphill climbs and steps.
Transport CityRail Bondi Junction then bus 333, 380, 381, 382.

This coastal walk through some of the prettiest beaches in suburban Sydney takes about two-and-a-quarter hours. You don't have to go all the way to Coogee – you can stop at any of the beaches en route – and you can, of course, do the walk in reverse. Start at the southern end of Bondi Beach, where steps take you up to Notts Avenue and past the stylish **Icebergs** clubhouse and outdoor pool (*see p82*). The path starts to the left of Notts Avenue, dropping down then up some steep steps to Marks Park on the spectacular cliff-top Mackenzies Point, with its 180° views along miles of coastline. This first stretch – as far as Tamarama Beach – is the site of the annual **Sculpture by the Sea** festival in November (*see p219*). It's a fantastic sight but attracts occasionally overwhelming crowds. After another headland the path drops down to Tamarama, which has a park, a little café next to the beach and plenty of surfers. At the southern end of Tamarama, steps lead up to the road, which after a few hundred coast-skirting metres takes you to Bronte Beach. Bronte is popular with surfers and families (especially the southern end, around the outdoor pool), and good for picnics and barbecues. There are also shower and toilet blocks and a kiosk (prices go up on Sundays), plus a cluster of cafés

and restaurants on the road just behind the beach. Walk through the car park and take the road uphill via steps through Calga Reserve to Waverley Cemetery. Spreading over the cliffs, the cemetery is a tranquil, well-kept area, and the view out to sea makes this a fitting resting place. Take the oceanside path through the adjoining Burrows Park to the warm welcome of Clovelly Beach. Equipped with a café and a pub just up the hill, this is one of the prettiest of the walk's beaches and a great place to stop for a bite to eat or a swim. It's at the end of a long, narrow inlet, meaning that the waves are small and manageable, making it popular with families.

As you continue around the next headland, the last patch of sand before Coogee is Gordon's Bay; there's not much of a beach, but the view over the water is stunning. Then comes Dunningham Reserve, where a sculpture commemorates those who died in the 2002 Bali bombings. Two plaques nearby list the victims from Sydney: six from the local Dolphins rugby league club and 20 from the eastern suburbs. Then it's down to Coogee Beach. At the far end is South Coogee, where you'll find Wylie's Baths, a pretty nature walk and dog park. To get back to the city, take the 372, 373, 374 or X73 bus from Arden Street.

A word to the wise. Avoid the walk at all costs if it's a windy day, as the cliffs are exposed. If you insist on going in the midday sun, take plenty of water and a hat. Oh, and watch out for the joggers – they brake for no one!

is the small but pretty **Bondi Golf Course**, site of some Aboriginal rock carvings, and **Williams Park**, a favourite spot with North Bondi residents hoping to watch the sunset or the New Year fireworks. Watch out, though: civilised North Bondi has an occasional unpleasant side when the smell from the sewage treatment plant – visible as a large chimney on the headland – drifts down. Gunk from the plant runs via a network of tunnels to an outlet five kilometres (three-and-a-half miles) into the ocean.

Bondi is also home to the famous **Bondi Icebergs Club** (*see below*), housed in a strikingly modern, four-storey building at the southern end of the cove. Throughout the winter, members of the club (formed in 1929) gather every Sunday morning for their ritual plunge into the icy waters of the outdoor pool.

The club also houses the upmarket **Icebergs Dining Room** (*see p168*) and its bar on the third floor – both ideal for panoramic views over the beach.

Past the Icebergs complex is the start of a stunning walk along the cliffs to **Tamarama Beach**, **Bronte Beach** and beyond (*see p80* **Walk 1: Bondi to Coogee**). The views are fabulous from Bondi's southern headland, which turns inwards to show off Bondi Beach in all its glory. Past Waverley Cemetery, the coastal walk continues south to lovely **Clovelly Beach** and then on to dramatic **Coogee Beach**, with its historic **Wylie's Baths** and the deservedly popular women's pool.

Generally acknowledged to be Bondi's poorer cousin in terms of fashion, restaurants, bars and even its beach, **Coogee** has raised its game in the past few years. Although still littered with backpackers – who find the cheaper rates preferable to overpriced Bondi – it's answered a need for more palatable eating and drinking spots. The travellers' faves, the **Coogee Bay Hotel** (*see p140*) with its vast beer garden overlooking the beach and the **Beach Palace Hotel** (169 Dolphin Street, 9664 2900, www.beachpalacehotel.com.au), are still thumping every weekend, but trendy **Cushion Bar** (corner of Carr and Arden Street, 9315 9130) provides a slightly swankier spot for a drink. **A Fish Called Coogee** (229 Coogee Bay Road, 9664 7700) is a casual-looking gem, and there are also Indian, Thai and Japanese restaurants, plus breakfast spots aplenty.

★ Bondi Icebergs Club

1 Notts Avenue, Bondi Beach (café 9130 3120, gym 9365 0423, pool 9130 4804, www.icebergs. com.au). CityRail Bondi Junction then bus 333, 380, 381, 382. **Open** *Bar* 10am-late daily. *Café* 10am-10pm Mon-Fri; 8am-10pm Sat, Sun. *Gym* 6am-8.30pm Mon-Fri; 8am-5pm Sat, Sun. *Pool*

6am-6.30pm Mon-Fri; 6.30am-6.30pm Sat, Sun. **Admission** *Gym* $15. *Pool* $5; $3 reductions; $13 family. **Map** p334.

Although most famous for its all-weather swimming club, Icebergs houses a number of other attractions. There's a pool, gym, sauna and deck on the ground floor, all open to the public, plus the national head-quarters of Surf Life Saving Australia and a small museum on the first floor. The stunning Italian restaurant and cocktail bar are on the top floor, but you can get equally good views (and cheaper booze and nosh) from the Icebergs Club bar and Sundeck Café on the second floor.

ELIZABETH BAY & RUSHCUTTERS BAY

Transport CityRail Kings Cross/bus 200, 311, 323, 325.

Back on Sydney Harbour, **Elizabeth Bay** begins beyond Fitzroy Gardens at the southern end of Macleay Street. Gone are the backpackers and crowded streets: here the calm, quiet roads are lined with residences that date from the 1930s. Worth a peek are **Elizabeth Bay House** (*see p83*) and **Boomerang** (corner of Ithaca Road and Billyard Avenue), a 1930s Alhambra-esque fantasy that has been home to some of Sydney's highest flyers – and fastest fallers. On the edge of Elizabeth Bay is **Beare Park**, one of many little green Edens that dot the harbourside.

The next inlet east is the romantically named **Rushcutters Bay**, so called because of the convicts who really did cut rushes here: two of them were the first Europeans to be killed by the local Aboriginal inhabitants, in May 1778. There's now a large and peaceful park lined by huge Moreton Bay figs.

The bay is also home to the **Cruising Yacht Club of Australia (CYCA)** on New Beach Road: its marinas are a frenzy of activity every December when the club is the starting point for the Sydney Hobart Yacht Race. If you fancy trying your hand at some sailing, or simply want to sit back, glass of wine in hand, while someone else steers you around the harbour, **Eastsail** (d'Albora Marinas, New Beach Road, 9327 1166, www.eastsail.com.au), close to the CYCA, will make life easy for you.

Elizabeth Bay House

7 Onslow Avenue, Elizabeth Bay (9356 3022, www.hht.net.au). CityRail Kings Cross/bus 311, 312. **Open** 9.30am-4pm Fri-Sun. **Admission** $8; $4 reductions; $17 family. **Credit** (over $10) MC, V. **Map** p330 K6.

No expense was spared on this handsome Greek Revival villa, designed by John Verge for NSW colo-nial secretary Alexander Macleay in 1839: it

Rushcutters Bay Park.

and still de rigueur for flash society, showbiz and celebrity weddings.

The next suburb to the east is **Double Bay**, also known as 'Double Pay' as it is home to Sydney's luxury shopping precinct. Migration after World War II turned 'the Bay' into a sophisticated European-style village of cafés, restaurants, delicatessens and ritzy boutiques. Don't wander through here unless you look the part: you'll feel out of place in less than a well-put-together outfit and will have to cope with scathing looks and bad service in cafés. It's no surprise that cosmetic surgeons prosper in the area – take a look at the ladies who lunch and you'll see the results. Despite the snob quota being fairly high, it's still a good place to grab a coffee or a bite to eat amid the pretty streets and lanes.

The stunning purple blooms of the jacaranda tree set Double Bay ablaze in springtime, and for good reason: Michael Guilfoyle, one of the area's earliest professional gardeners, whose own nursery of exotic plants could be found on the corner of Ocean Avenue in the mid 1800s, was responsible for first acclimatising the Brazilian species to Australia.

New South Head Road is the main thoroughfare through the Bay. The **Golden Sheaf Hotel** (429 New South Head Road, 9327 5877, www.goldensheaf.com.au) is a popular watering hole with four bars catering to drinkers of all ages and tastes. The bistro is exceptional, and the busy beer garden is especially fun on Sunday afternoons when bands perform. At the western end of New South Head Road you'll find real estate agents, upmarket tea specialist **Taka Tea Garden** (No.320, 9362 1777, www.takateagarden.com.au) and the **Sharon-Lee Studios** (Nos.308-310, 1300 769 011, www.sharon-lee.com.au), base of Sydney's eyebrow plucker to the stars.

There are also two beaches at Double Bay, but only one of them is suitable for swimming. The beach next to **Steyne Park** sadly isn't, but it's a nice place to wander and is always bustling with yachties. On summer weekends, you can see the famous 18-foot sailing boats that compete in the annual Sydney-to-Hobart race rigging up and practising their moves, ready for battle. The **Australian 18 Footers League club** (77 Bay Street, 9363 2995, www.18footers.com.au), located just to the left of the beach, is something of a local secret. From October to the end of March, 25 or so skiffs race on the harbour every Sunday, with the club running a spectators' ferry, leaving the wharf at 2.15pm ($20, under-14s free, 9363 2995). It's a thrilling outing and you can kick back and indulge in an iconic Aussie pie served on board, or dine in style beforehand at Alruth, the club restaurant, which overlooks the water.

boasted the first two flushing toilets in the country, the finest staircase in Australian colonial architecture, and breathtaking views of Elizabeth Bay and the harbour. But Macleay's extravagance proved fatal, and his debt-ridden family were forced to move out. Over the years the grand old house was vandalised, partly demolished and finally divided into 15 studio flats, garrets for the artists who flocked to Kings Cross. From 1928 until 1935, it acted as a kind of cheap boarding house for the Sydney 'Charm School' artists, who included Wallace Thornton, Rex Julius and Donald Friend. The gardens, on which Macleay lavished so much love, have long since gone to property developers, but the beautiful house (now run by the Historic Houses Trust) still breathes noblesse, wealth and good taste. Rooms are furnished as they would have been in its heyday, 1839-45.

DARLING POINT & DOUBLE BAY

Transport Darling Point Ferry Darling Point/bus 324, 325, 326, 327. Double Bay Ferry Double Bay/bus 324, 325, 326, 327.

Bordered by Rushcutters Bay Park to the west and Edgecliff to the south, **Darling Point** is another of Sydney's most salubrious suburbs, with spectacular views as standard – the best of these can be sampled free from **McKell Park** at the northern tip of Darling Point Road. Head south down the street to the corner of Greenoaks Avenue to see **St Mark's Church**, designed by the acclaimed Gothic Revival architect Edmund Blacket, consecrated in 1864

SIGHTS

If you do want to swim in Double Bay, continue east for ten minutes on New South Head Road to **Redleaf Pool** (a shark-netted swimming area) and **Seven Shillings Beach**. This adorable little harbour beach is well hidden from the road, has a lovely garden setting and welcomes everyone. Behind the beach, next to Blackburn Gardens, is the attractive Woollahra municipal council building. On the other side of the gardens is **Woollahra Library** (548 New South Head Road, 9391 7100), undeniably the quaintest library in Sydney: it's a good place to read the newspapers for free.

POINT PIPER, ROSE BAY, VAUCLUSE & WATSONS BAY

Transport Point Piper Bus 323, 324, 325. Rose Bay Ferry Rose Bay/bus 323, 324, 325. Vaucluse & Watsons Bay Ferry Watsons Bay/bus 323, 324, 325, 380, 386, 387.

Even if you can't match the hefty wallets of the people who live in these stunning harbourside suburbs, they are still easily enjoyed on the cheap. By ferry from Circular Quay you can take in Darling Point, Rose Bay and Watsons Bay – though not every ferry stops at every destination, and there's no service to Darling Point at weekends.

From Double Bay, small harbour beaches dot the shore up to **Point Piper**, which is full of stunning high-walled mansions. You can enjoy the multi-million-dollar views for free from the tiny Duff Reserve on the edge of the harbour, a good picnic spot if you can beat the crowds. Lyne Park in Rose Bay is where the city's seaplanes land. You can watch them in more comfortable

surroundings at the bayside restaurants **Catalina** (Lyne Park, 9371 0555, www.catalin arosebay.com.au) and **Pier** (*see p169*) – both great (and expensive) places to eat.

On the other side of New South Head Road is **Woollahra Golf Course**, which is very charitably open to the general public, unlike the snooty Royal Sydney Golf Course right next door. The streets from Rose Bay to Vaucluse feature yet more millionaire mansions: for the jealously inclined, the hidden jewels of the **Hermitage Foreshore Reserve** and an arm of **Sydney Harbour National Park**, which run around the peninsula, come as compensation. They are reached by a walking track that starts at Bayview Hill Road, below the imposing stone edifice of Rose Bay Convent, and offer fine views of the Harbour Bridge, as well as picnic spots aplenty and glimpses of the lifestyles of the rich and comfortable. The walk emerges at **Nielsen Park** (*see p85*), off Vaucluse Road, where there is an enclosed bay, **Shark Beach** – particularly beautiful on a summer evening – and the popular **Nielsen Park Café & Restaurant** (9337 7333, www.nielsenpark.com.au).

Further along, on Wentworth Road, the estate that became **Vaucluse House** (*see p85*) was bought by newspaperman and politician William Charles Wentworth in 1827. It's open to the public, along with its fine tearooms. Next to Vaucluse Bay, **Parsley Bay** is a lesser-known, verdant picnic spot popular with families.

It is claimed that **Watsons Bay** was the country's first fishing village. Now largely the province of **Doyles on the Beach** seafood restaurant (11 Marine Parade, 9337 2007, www.doyles.com.au) and rowdy weekend pub

Watsons Bay.

the **Watsons Bay Hotel** (1 Military Road, 9337 5444, www.watsonsbayhotel.com.au) – it has stunning views back across the harbour to the city, particularly at night, and retains vestiges of its old charm, including original weatherboard houses and terraces. These are best seen by walking north to the First Fleet landing spot at Green Point Reserve and on to Camp Cove and Lady Bay beaches, and the Hornby lighthouse on the tip of South Head.

On the other (ocean) side of the peninsula from Watsons Bay back is the bite in the sheer cliffs that gives the **Gap** its name – and from which many have jumped to their doom. **Gap Park** is the start of a spectacular cliff walk that runs south back into Vaucluse. Along the way, hidden high above the approach to Watsons Bay at the fork of the Old South Head Road, is another fine Blacket church, **St Peter's** (331 Old South Head Road, 9337 6545, www.stpeterswb.org.au), home to Australia's oldest pipe organ, which dates from 1796 and was once loaned to the exiled Napoleon. The church gates commemorate the Greycliffe ferry disaster of 1927 when 40 people (including many schoolchildren) died in a collision at sea.

FREE Nielsen Park

Greycliffe Avenue, Vaucluse (9337 5511, www.nationalparks.nsw.gov.au). Bus 325.
Open 5am-10pm daily. **Admission** free,
Generations of Sydneysiders have been flocking to Nielsen Park for family get-togethers since the early 1900s. They sit on Shark Beach or the grassy slopes behind or climb the headlands either side for a great view across the harbour. With its abundance of shady trees, gentle waters, panoramic views and excellent Nielsen Park Café & Restaurant (9337 7333, www.nielsenpark.com.au), it's the perfect picnic spot. It's also a favourite New Year's Eve viewing point for the harbour fireworks. Nestled in the grounds to the rear of the grassy slopes lies Greycliffe House, a Gothic-style mansion built in 1862 as a wedding gift from the co-founder and first editor of the *Australian* newspaper, William Charles Wentworth, for his daughter Fanny and her husband John Reeve. In 1913, it became a baby hospital, then a home for new mothers. Nowadays, it's a NSW National Parks & Wildlife Service office, providing information on parks in the state. Watch out for the seaplanes that take off in neighbouring Rose Bay and begin their ascent over the waters of Shark Bay.

Vaucluse House

Vaucluse Park, Wentworth Road, Vaucluse (9388 7922, www.hht.net.au). Bus 325. **Open** *House* 9.30am-4pm Fri-Sun. *Grounds* 10am-5pm Tue-Sun. **Admission** $8; $4 reductions; $17 family. **Credit** (over $10) MC, V.
The oldest 'house museum' in Australia nestles prettily in a moated 19th-century estate, surrounded by ten hectares (28 acres) of prime land, with its own sheltered beach on Vaucluse Bay. From 1827-53 and 1861-62, this was the opulent home of William Charles Wentworth. The house originally stood in a much larger estate, and 26 servants were required to look after the master's seven daughters and three sons, not to mention his vineyards, orchards and beloved racehorses. The Historic Homes Trust has endeavoured to keep the place as it was when the Wentworths were in residence. In the kitchen a fire burns in the large grate and hefty copper pans line the walls; a tin bath, taken on European travels, still displays its sticker from London's Victoria Station; the drawing room is sumptuously furnished, and has a door that hides a secret (just ask a guide to open it for you).

RANDWICK & KENSINGTON

Transport Randwick Bus 314, 316, 317, 371, 372, 373, 374, 376, 377. Kensington Bus 391, 392, 393, 394, 395, 396, 397, 399.

For a flutter on the horses or just an excuse to get dressed up for a day, head to the **Royal Randwick Racecourse** (*see p266*). It's on Alison Road bordering Centennial Park, and the Spring Carnival in November is especially popular, giving all the fillies – on and off the track – a chance to show off their finery. Check www.ajc.org.au for race dates. In November 2007, the course was famously shut down because of the devastating bout of equine flu that broke out in Sydney, but was quickly back up and running once the bans were lifted later in the year. In 2010, the prohibitive walls of the Racecourse were torn down and replaced by gardens and pathways, symbolising the allure of 'the sport of kings' to Sydney's punt-hungry public.

The **University of NSW** campus lies south of the racecourse, while, across the road, the **National Institute of Dramatic Art (NIDA)** – alma mater of such stars as Nicole Kidman, Mel Gibson and Sam Worthington – has its headquarters and theatre.

Anzac Parade is one long highway, but will lead you to **Grotta Capri Seafood Restaurant** (Nos.97-101, 9662 7111, http://grottacapri.com.au). Hardly convenient for the city, the only reason to make the trip out is to gaze in wonder at the decor of this bizarre but wonderful eaterie that has featured in films such as *Muriel's Wedding* and various iconic Aussie TV series. Decked out like an undersea fantasy with over a million oyster shells on the walls and roof, it's well worth the taxi ride. Just up the road is the pinkest department store you'd ever hope to see, **Peter's of Kensington** (*see p196*). Avoid it like the plague at Christmas or during sale season, unless you like to queue.

SIGHTS

Inner West

A mix of grunge and glamour beyond the centre.

Despite regular attempts to clean up and gentrify the more fashionable suburbs in this underrated area, the inner west is still defined by its mix of bohemian and chic. At one extreme are the alternative hub of **Newtown** – home to goths, punks, musos, artists, writers, gays and lesbians – and the university student hangout of **Glebe**; at the other end, the cafés and restaurants of harbourside **Balmain** and trendy **Leichhardt** attract yuppie out-of-towners. Foodies also flock to **Rozelle**, **Haberfield** and **Petersham** to pick up delicacies from multicultural delis and bakeries, many of which remain local secrets.

Property prices are almost as high here as in the eastern suburbs, and

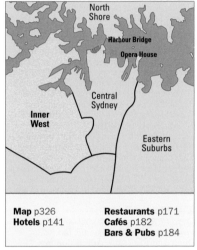

Map p326	Restaurants p171
Hotels p141	Cafés p182
	Bars & Pubs p184

there's plenty of modernisation, but much of the inner west likes to pretend it's still down-to-earth and 'real' by comparison. Overall it holds on to its status as an intriguing urban village, but you have to look a bit harder than you once did to find the cheap and quirky gems that make it so special.

BALMAIN, BIRCHGROVE & ROZELLE

Balmain Ferry Balmain, Balmain West or East Balmain/bus 442, 434. Birchgrove Ferry Birchgrove/bus 441. Rozelle Bus 432, 433, 434, 440, 441, 442, 500.

Snuggled in the inner west's harbour, a six-minute ferry ride from Circular Quay or a 20-minute bus trip from the city centre, **Balmain** was settled in the 1830s by boatbuilders; today, it's increasingly home to on-the-make moneyed types. **Darling Street** – the spine of the area – starts at Balmain East Wharf and curves uphill past the sandstone Watch House (built in 1854, it was once the police lock-up and is now the HQ of the Balmain Historical Society). For an easy ferry-and-food experience, walk a couple of minutes up from the wharf to **Relish at Balmain Bug** (55 Darling Street, 9810 5510). Housed in a cute stone cottage, this restaurant concocts traditional Australian food with an Asian edge.

Further up in central Balmain, Darling Street is lined with yet more food options interspersed with homeware and clothing shops, all winding along in a pleasingly low-key, two-storey way. A cluster of impressive Victorian buildings – the **Post Office**, **Court House**, **Town Hall** and **Fire Station** – are testament to Balmain's prosperity in the 1880s. **Balmain Market** held on Saturdays in the grounds of St Andrew's Church, opposite Gladstone Park, is worth a browse, as is **Bray Books** (No.268, 9810 5613).

Pockets of urban cool include **Chopsticks** (No.264, 9818 3551), a dark, devil's-lair dining spot that serves pho, laksa and noodles at good prices. **Kazbah on Darling** (No.379, 9555 7067, www.kazbah.com.au) transports you to Morocco, while **Tuk Tuk Real Thai** (No.350, 9555 5899) offers fast and funky Thai food. **Blue Ginger** (No.241, 9818 4662) specialises in modern Asian cuisine, and newcomer **Efendy**, just off the main drag (79 Elliott Street, 9810 5466, www. efendy.com.au), serves modern Turkish food in

SIGHTS

a contemporary setting. **Dockside Seafood** (No.314, 9810 6587) is the place to order mandarin scallops or spicy prawns.

Cafés abound too, including the modern and spacious **Canteen Café** (No.332, 9818 1521) and fashion hotspot **Bertoni Casalinga** (No.281, 9818 5845, www.bertoni.com.au), with its crates-on-the-footpath seating and high-quality Italian food. **Circle Café** (No.344, 9555 9755) recalls Balmain's simpler 1970s period: it houses a Uniting Church service on Sunday mornings. To create your own meal, head to French bakery **Victoire** (No.285, 9818 5529), a 25-year-old institution with a loyal following, for sourdough baguettes, outrageously good pastries and fresh cheeses.

The patissier on all Sydney's lips in 2010 was **Adriano Zumbo**, whose patisserie stands at 296 Street Balmain (9810 7318) and whose goal in life is, he says, to 'caramelise the nation'. After an appearance on the all-time ratings hit *Masterchef*, Zumbo sold 6,000 macaroons in a single day, with hundreds queueing all day.

Pubs are still the lifeblood of Balmain. Glamour couples head for the refined surroundings of the **London Hotel** (234 Darling Street, 9555 1377), or the **Exchange Hotel** (corner of Beattie and Mullens streets, 9810 1171) – never mind the incongruity of a ping pong tournament and Martini club on Thursday nights. Ageing funsters patronise the **Unity Hall Hotel** (292 Darling Street, 9810 1331), while the **Town Hall Hotel** (No.366, 9818 8950) hovers oddly between pleasing pool sharks and house music lovers. Meanwhile, a variety of bands play the ever-popular **Cat & Fiddle Hotel** (456 Darling Street, 9810 7931).

On the northern side of Darling Street is **Birchgrove**, flanked on three sides by water. The somewhat ramshackle **Sir William Wallace Hotel** (31 Cameron Street, 9555 8570) features a large autographed poster of a kilted Mel Gibson in *Braveheart* mode. On Sundays, the owners throw a free barbecue lunch. There's also the **Riverview Hotel** (29 Birchgrove Road, 9810 1151), for years owned by legendary Olympic gold medal-winning swimmer Dawn Fraser and now another of Balmain's gentrified bloodhouses – their mulligatawny soup is as close to liquid nirvana as it gets hereabouts (outside the latest drop from the newly-relaunched Balmain Brewing Company, that is).

Fraser's name lives on at the carefully restored harbourside pool at the edge of

The Best Quiz Nights

Pitch your wits against the locals.

Pub trivia quizzes are big in Sydney, and some of the best are in the Inner West. To see a different side of the city, and to prove yourself a right clever clogs, match up against the local regulars at the following quiz nights.

AB Hotel
225 Glebe Point Road, Glebe (9660 1417). **When** *World trivia* 7.30pm Mon; *music trivia* 7.30pm Wed. **Prize** $50 bar credit, plus monthly Cooper's Trivia: win a keg party for 20 people.

Australian Youth Hotel
63 Bay Street, Glebe (9692 0414, www.australianyouthhotel.com.au). **When** 8pm Wed. **Prize** $50 bar credit.

Bald Rock Hotel
15 Mansfield Street, Rozelle (9818 4792). **When** 7.30pm Thur. **Prize** Cash jackpot.

Carlisle Castle
19 Albermarle Street, Newtown (9557 4852). **When** 7pm Mon. **Prize** Bistro meal.

Cooper's Hotel
221 King Street, Newtown (9550 3461). **When** 7.30pm Tue. **Prize** $100 bar credit.

Dicks Hotel
89 Beattie Street, Balmain (9818 2828). **When** 7.30pm Mon. **Prize** $80 bar credit plus cash jackpot.

Duke of Edinburgh
148 Enmore Road, Enmore (9519 1935). **When** 8pm Tue. **Prize** $75 bar credit.

Erskineville Hotel
102 Erskineville Road, Erskineville (9565 1608). **When** *General trivia* 7.30pm Tue; *music trivia* 7.30pm first Thur of the month. **Prize** *General* $70 bar credit; *music* CDs.

Friend in Hand
58 Cowper Street, Glebe (9660 2326). **When** 7pm last three Tue of month. **Prize** $60 bar credit.

Gladstone Park Hotel
140 Marion Street, Leichhardt (9569 4057). **When** 7.30pm Thur. **Prize** Bar credit.

SIGHTS

INSIDE TRACK MEL GIBSON

Regulars at the **Sir William Wallace Hotel** (31 Cameron Street, 9555 8570, www.sir williamwallacehotel.com.au) claim that Mel Gibson was first inspired by the Scottish patriot – the original *Braveheart* – while drinking at their bar.

---

charming **Elkington Park**. The park overlooks **Cockatoo Island**, the largest of the harbour's islands and a former prison and shipyard.

Another park can be found at the tip of the narrow finger of **Louisa Road**, which is lined with half-hidden, multi-million-dollar homes. The peninsula was originally an abattoir of sorts, where Aboriginal people used to kill kangaroos. Its name was officially changed from **Long Nose Point** to **Yurulbin Point** in 1994 to reflect its indigenous heritage, but most people still use its former name. The wharf at its end is where the Birchgrove ferries arrive.

To reach **Rozelle**, simply continue west along Darling Street. If you're driving, let the overall-clad lads fill 'er up at Balmain's oldest service station, **Bill's Garage** (418 Darling Street, 9810 2611), established in 1915 and still featuring its original fixtures.

For years, the weekend **Rozelle Market** (Rozelle Public School) was about the only thing that brought people here, with bargain stalls selling CDs, plants, ceramics and collectibles. That was, of course, until food became such an integral part of Sydney life.

The first figure to make local folk think beyond lentils was Tetsuya Wakuda, the internationally renowned Japanese chef, who opened his first restaurant (now closed) in the area. These days there are two hulking hangars that have become monuments to modern cuisine. First to arrive was **Barn Café & Grocery** (731 Darling Street, 9810 1633), mixing a restaurant, a café and a 'supermarket' of hard-to-find, beautifully packaged and rather pricey ingredients. Next came **About Life** (No.605, 8755 1333), a self-styled 'natural marketplace' – a posh mix of café, caterer and naturopath. Across the road, the **Organic Trading Company** (No.584, 9555 9991) is a toned-down rival selling yet more organic lotions and funky home clothes.

The rest of this stretch of Darling Street is a smattering of cafés, nurseries, antique stores and gift shops. Chocolatier **Belle Fleur** (658 Darling Street, 9810 2690, www.bellefleur.com. au) injects some wicked indulgence into the somewhat earnest, upmarket-hippie scene. But it's **Orange Grove Farmers' Market**, held on Saturdays at Orange Grove Public School (at

the junction of Darling Street and Balmain Road) that has the last word, with its organic produce and multinational cuisines (Ethiopian, Japanese, Dutch), all of them good (and cheap) enough to lure even Bondi dwellers across town.

Back out along Victoria Road to the north, the **Balmain Leagues Club** (138-152 Victoria Road, 9556 0400), one of two venues belonging to local rugby legends the Wests Tigers, is a good place for a cheap steak and beer, rivalled only by the **Red Lion Hotel** (726 Darling Street, 9555 7933), which caters to travelling backpackers.

Bringing back a smidge of Tetsuya glamour to this part of the strip is **La Grande Bouffe** (758 Darling Street, 9818 4333), a modern take on the classic French bistro. Back down Victoria Road towards the city is the **Restaurant at Three Weeds** (197 Evans Street, 9818 2788), serving modern European flavours. Housed in the Three Weeds Hotel, a former rock haven, it's a revamped, remodelled testimony to redemption.

GLEBE

LightRail Glebe/bus 431, 432, 433, 434.

Directly to the west of central Sydney and shaped by its proximity to Sydney University on Parramatta Road, **Glebe** is an incongruous but atmospheric mix of grand, turn-of-the-20th-century mansions flanking quaint terraces and drab 1970s flat lets, with most streets still sporting their original rusty street signs. There are probably more cheap takeaway joints per square mile than anywhere else in Sydney – Glebe is the land of the $5 pad Thai.

The main drag is **Glebe Point Road**. Walking along it you find yourself weaving in and out of students and travellers, who are well catered for by several budget hotels, including the **Alishan International Guesthouse** (100 Glebe Point Road, 9566 4048, www.alishan.com.au) and the large and leafy hostel **Glebe Village Backpackers** (256 Glebe Point Road, 9660 8133). Become as one with them at the **Toxteth Hotel** (no.345, 9660 2370) or bond with Brits at **British Sweets & Treats** (no.85, 9660 9912), which has helpfully collected together all the faves needed to console homesick Poms.

You will never go hungry in Glebe, with its overwhelming array of Indian, Chinese, Thai and Vietnamese eateries – expect quick-fill, rather than gourmet. But the retail landscape is changing, home to the likes of the **Sonoma Baking Company** (no.215, 9660 2116), which offers brilliant baked-on-the-premises spelt breads. For organic takeaway, try Moby's favourite Sydney haunt **Iku** (25A Glebe Point Road, 9692 8720, www.ikuwholefood.com) –

Glebe.

think brown rice, miso, tofu and tahini-type offerings wrapped up in little paper parcels. And it's worth opening your wallet to try out modern European hit **Restaurant Atelier** (22 Glebe Point Road, 9566 2112, www.restaurantatelier.com.au) and oyster specialist the **Boathouse on Blackwattle Bay** (Ferry Road, 9518 9011, www.boathouse. net.au), where Sydney's cinema godfather Bryan Brown often hosts epic liquid lunches for the likes of Sam Neill, Tom Cruise and co.

For bestsellers and books to impress, head to **Gleebooks** (*see p199*), something of a literary institution, with user-friendly extended opening hours and two branches. Duck next door for a cheaper browse in **Sappho Books** (51 Glebe Point Road, 9552 4498, www.sapphobooks. com.au), which peddles second-hand tomes and has the added lure of fresh coffee.

You'll probably find cheaper still across the road on Saturdays at **Glebe Market** (*see p197*); sprawling out through school grounds, it deals in everything from clothes to CDs, with a small army of Asian food stalls to keep you going.

Traditional pubs include the British-style **Nag's Head Hotel** (162 St John's Road, 9660 1591), and Irish pub the **Friend in Hand Hotel** (58 Cowper Street, 9660 2326), which is stuffed with street signs, number plates and even a surfboat hanging from the ceiling, and hosts live crab races every Wednesday night.

For a feel of what Sydney used to be like before the money took over, visit **Wentworth Park Greyhound Track** (*see p265*), Sydney's premier dog-racing venue, which has meets every Monday and Saturday night. It's a great

night out – there are bars and a bistro and, if you're lucky, a dog racing solely because his trainer awaits at the finishing line with an ice cream for him – and the betting ring here is about the only place where you'll still see pork-pie hats worn without a trace of irony.

At the Rozelle Bay end of Glebe Point Road are **Jubilee Park**, **Bicentennial Park** and **Harold Park Raceway** (Wigram Road, Glebe, 9660 3688, www.haroldpark.com.au), home of 'the trots'; The park area has undergone a major facelift to become a pleasantly marshy play zone with canoes and watercraft at its edge.

Pirrama Park is the latest sustainable green space built on this waterfront, with $20 million spent in 2010 to change an old Water Police site into playgrounds, native plantings, walking trails and community squares, much of it themed in tribute to the peninsula's original Gadigal inhabitants and the stevedores who toiled here in the 19th century.

ANNANDALE

Bus 436, 437, 438, 440, 470.

Annandale was once earmarked as a model township, hence the look of its main throughfare: broad, tree-lined **Johnston Street** (named after Lieutenant George Johnston, the first man to step ashore from the First Fleet in 1788 – albeit on the back of a convict). Located between Glebe and Leichhardt, it soon became a predominantly working-class district. These days it's gradually upping its foodie quotient on Booth Street to cope with the growing influx of residents decamping from the east.

Opened in late 2007, the rustic Italian **Vicini** (No.37, 9660 6600) is run by locals Natalie and George, who previously owned the Palace restaurant in Darlinghurst and Mars Lounge in Surry Hills, while head chef Massimiliano Borsato hails most recently from the central Summit restaurant. Providing a quick fix for those seeking sustenance in its red-chair

**INSIDE TRACK
GLEBE STREET FAIR**

If you're in town in November, look out for the one-day **Glebe Street Fair** (*see p219*), the city's longest-running street party.

SIGHTS

Italian Forum.

surrounds is **Bar Asia** (no.101, 9571 9919), where it's noodles, rice and curry in a box to eat in or take away. **Bar Sirocco** (no.60, 9660 3930) picks up the pieces with brilliant breakfasts after a night out at the **North Annandale Hotel** (corner of Booth and Johnston streets, 9660 7452).

Relaxed to the point of being horizontal, Annandale has a gentle vibe that smacks of parents with two-point-five kids. However, at the Parramatta Road end of the district, the **Annandale Hotel** (*see p255*) punks up the atmosphere with some of Australia's best rock bands, plus low-budget 16mm movie screenings on Tuesday nights and Pub Cha (dim sum) on weekends and public holidays from 11am.

LEICHHARDT

Bus 436, 437, 438, 440.

Further west still lies **Leichhardt**. Formerly known as the 'Little Italy' of the west, it's long outgrown that title, and the suburb's main thoroughfare, Norton Street, now pumps with a whole new nightlife vibe, although with young, slick Italians still having a firm grip on the area.

Two stalwarts of the Italian dining scene are the recently revamped **Elio** (159 Norton Street, 9560 9129), which offers an elegant modern take on old favourites, and **Grappa** (267-277 Norton Street, 9560 6090), with its barn-like proportions, would happily house the entire crew from *The Sopranos* – proper big-night-out stuff.

Get down with old Med boys at **Bar Italia** (*see p182*) to snap up cheap focaccia, great ice-cream and gutsy rustic pasta dishes. For a friendly trattoria (replete with a '*rompipalle*'

charge incurred by '*ballbreakers*') try **Osvaldo Polletti** (148 Norton Street, 9560 4525) or drive the kids into **Café Gioia & Pizzeria** (no.126, 9564 6245), housed in a renovated service station, or visit the **Italian Forum** shopping mall: the architecture isn't to everyone's taste, but the enclosed piazza is a blessing for parents with wandering offspring – they can eat and watch at the same time. **La Cremeria Sorbetteria** (no.106, 9564 1127), still shifts great *gelati*, while **Glace** around the corner (27 Marion Street, 9569 3444) sexes it up with champagne sorbet. For a serious caffeine hit, you can always rely on **Bar Sport** (2A Norton Street, 9569 2397).

A cluster of Australian heritage buildings on Norton Street includes the two-storey **Leichhardt Town Hall** (no.107), built in 1888, which often hosts visiting art exhibitions, the former **Post Office** (no.109) and **All Souls Anglican Church** (no.126). But it's the **Palace Norton Street Cinema** (no.99), a four-screen art-house specialist with a licensed bar, a restaurant, a café and even a CD shop that pulls the crowds. Readers, meanwhile, should look to **Berkelouw Books** (70 Norton Street, 9560 3200) across the road for a great selection of titles and a decent café to read them in.

HABERFIELD

Bus 436, 437, 438, 440.

Situated to the west of Leichhardt, **Haberfield** is the more recently discovered 'Little Italy' of the west – 'little' being the operative word. Yet despite its size, Haberfield remains the true heartland of homeland authenticity.

Foodies make a beeline for the main thoroughfare, **Ramsay Street**, where you'll find delicatessen **Paesanella** (no.88, 9799 8483), offering arguably the best antipasti and cheeses in Sydney; **Haberfield Bakery** (no.153, 9797 7715) with its staggering array of bread; and **A&P Sulfaro Pasticceria** (no.119, 9797 0001) boasting ice-cream, biscotti and handmade chocolates.

Trattoria Il Locale (no.94A, 9797 8966) is a newcomer to the scene. A simple tiled shell with wooden tables, its pizza is proving popular with the masses – book ahead or prepare to queue. Also good is **Dolcissimo** (nos.96-98, 9716 4444); choose from the bright café or the smarter, low-lit restaurant, although it's something of a bloodsport trying to get a seat in either. And still going strong is old favourite **Napoli in Bocca** (73 Dalhousie Street, 9798 4096): the red-checked tablecloths and pizza and pasta menu are as much of an institution as the bustling, old-style service.

NEWTOWN, ERSKINEVILLE & ENMORE

Newtown CityRail Newtown/bus 422, 423, 426, 428, 352. Erskineville CityRail Erskineville. Enmore CityRail Newtown/bus 426, 428.

You can throttle it with renovators and young families, you can tart up the rough edges with smart shops, but **Newtown** somehow manages to remain stubbornly and comfortably down-at-heel, like an old drag queen in her glitter rags. Lying to the south of Annandale and Glebe, Newtown has it all: few other areas accommodate so many subcultures – grungy students from the nearby University of Sydney, young professional couples, goths, spiky punks, gays and lesbians – and in such apparent harmony. See the community in all its glory during the **Newtown Festival** (*see p219*) in November.

You could easily spend a day wandering along the main drag, **King Street** (and it's faster to stroll than drive, since the traffic can be horrendous). Intriguing and often eccentric specialist shops include one dedicated solely to buttons, another to ribbons and braids. A major player in the area is the **Dendy Newtown** four-screen cinema (nos.261-263); next door is a good dance and alternative music shop, **Fish Records** (*see p216*), which opens late, as does bookshop **Better Read Than Dead** (no.265, 9557 8700). There's also **Goulds** (*see p200*), one of the largest and most popular second-hand bookshops in the city.

Maybe it's because of the wild mix of humanity that makes up Newtown, but it's the perfect place to find anything for anyone.

Café 2042.

Pentimento (no.249, 9565 5591) has an exquisite range of books, homewares and handbags, while **Eastern Flair** (no.319, 9565 1499) offers exotic jewellery and furnishings. For divine teas, visit **T2** (no.173, 9550 3044), and for funky bags of all kinds stop in on **Crumpler** (no.305, 9565 1611).

You'll have no trouble finding somewhere to linger over a cappuccino – every second shopfront houses a café, and new places seem to open every week. Try **Astino's** (no.284, 9565 5238) for organic coffee, **El Basha Café** (no.233, 9557 3886) for top-notch Lebanese sweets and pastries and **Café 2042** (nos.403-405, 9550 2500) for its 28 types of cured meat and 33 varieties of cheese.

The restaurants on the strip have, in the past, veered towards pan-Asian bland, but are satisfying for the price. **Thanh Binh** (no.111, 9557 1175) is a stand-out Vietnamese, while funky **Simply Noodles** (no.273, 9557 4453) or **Italian Bowl** (no.255, 9516 0857), offers a nifty, choose-your-own selection of pastas and sauces. For a contemporary take on Australian cuisine, book well in advance for **Oscillate Wildly** (*see p172*), just off King. Even better, try **Bloodwood** (no.416, *see p192*) which burns brightest on a warm night when you can bag a seat on the open balcony and gorge on fried chicken wings, garlic prawns and polenta chips.

Newtown also has no shortage of pubs, each with its own distinctive slant. Check out bands at the **Sandringham Hotel** (*see p256*), still adorned with its original green and yellow tiles. New on the block for jazz and blues is the **Vanguard** (*see p256*) – more of a moody club than a pub, with sit-down dining during performances. Then there's the tarted-up **Marlborough Hotel** (no.145, 9519 6500), which has a wide art deco balcony upstairs. For near-24-hour comfort, try **Zanzibar** (no.323, 9519 1511): with a rooftop bar, pool downstairs and a cushion room upstairs, it relies on low lighting and beads to fulfil its name's exotic promise. New bars to seek out include **Madame Fling Flong** (no.169, 9565 2471) with its cushy couches, board games and imported beer list, and **Kuletos** (no.157, 9519 6369) with its 2-for-1 cocktails Monday to Friday and rooftop sausage sizzle every arvo.

The bottom end of King Street, south of the railway station, has always been heaven for fans of antiques, junk and second-hand clothes, but edgy fashion shops are now beginning to predominate – look for **Dragstar** (no.535A, 9550 1243) and **Zukini** (no.483, 9519 9188), while kids get the star treatment at **Shorties** (no.537, 9550 5003). **Fiji Market** (no.591, 9517 2054) offers Indian and Pacific Islander produce as well as cheap sari fabrics and fabulously kitsch Hindu icons and posters.

SIGHTS

For a coffee break, locals head to the grungily hip **Chocolate Dog Café** (no.549, 9565 2526). Get the total Lebanese experience at **Arabella's** (nos.489-491, 9550 1119), where a small clutch of Beirutians seem to be in permanent celebration mode; on Friday and Saturdays, there's also bellydancing.

While in Newtown it's also worth ducking off King Street to the two 'E' suburbs, **Erskineville** and **Enmore**. To reach the former – which is rapidly expanding into a crowd-puller in its own right – turn off King Street at Erskineville Road and keep walking. You may recognise the landmark art deco **Imperial Hotel** (35 Erskineville Road) from *Priscilla, Queen of the Desert*. If drag shows are your thing, head here on Thursday to Saturday nights to see one of the best. If your tastes veer more to music and micro-brew head to **Hive Bar** (no.93, 9519 9911) where it's BYO mug, coffee cup and vinyl for discounts, local beers (try the local drop E'ville) and DJs on Wednesday night.

On **Swanson Street** – a continuation of Erskineville Road – is music club the **Rose of Australia** (no.1, 9565 1441), which has been revved up to become a bar and restaurant with pavement seating. Across the road, **Stir Crazy** (128 Erskineville Road, 9519 0044) is creating its own noise with tasty twists like pumpkin stir-fry and chilli jam seafood. For well-priced, good all-round grub, try the **Tart Café** (106 Erskineville Road, 9557 9448) before heading down for a seriously strong espresso at **Café Sofia** (7 Swanson Street, 9519 1565). It's worth walking a little further down the road (which changes its name again, to Copeland Street) for the gourmet **Bitton Café** (36-37A Copeland Street, 9519 5111). Despite its somewhat out-of-the-way location, Bitton has thrived under French-born chef David Bitton and his Indian wife, Sohani. You can buy sauces, dressings and oils to take home, and David also offers cookery classes.

To get to Enmore, return to Newtown and then turn off King Street onto Enmore Road. Bands and DJs occupy the renovated **@Newtown RSL** (no.52, 9557 5044), two levels of slink with beads, funky wallpaper and chandeliers. Also check out the **Enmore Theatre** (*see p254*), a renovated deco-style theatre popular with local and international rock bands and stand-up comedy acts. For a pre-gig dinner, try out any of the Thai restaurants – **Banks Thai** (91 Enmore Road, 9550 6840) is one of the best. The best post-gig kebabs in the inner-west can be found at late-opening **Saray Turkish Pizza** (no.18, 9557 5310), and there are plenty of high-quality Lebanese restaurants on the street too, namely **Emma's** on Liberty.

Perhaps one of the oddest yet coolest additions to the Sydney nightlife scene is the **Sly Fox** (199 Enmore Road, 9557 1016); the music varies nightly, alternating between house, electro, techno, drum 'n' bass, rock and goth, while Wednesday brings Sydney's lesbians and drag kings out in force.

PETERSHAM

CityRail Petersham/bus 428.

Petersham lies north-west of Enmore; if you're driving, turn right off Enmore Road into Stanmore Road, which becomes New Canterbury Road, the main thoroughfare. Until very recently the neighbourhood was home to the Oxford Tavern that hulks at its gateway, flashing '24 hour lingerie waitresses' in screaming neon. It took some time to see that within the cloud of choking fumes of the main road, a 'Little Portugal' had already been born. It's a tiny strip that lacks the glamour of Leichhardt or the more villagey vibe of Haberfield, both just over Parramatta Road to the north, but makes up for it with authenticity.

A fleet of excellent traditional Portuguese restaurants and patisseries line the few blocks of New Canterbury Road from Audley Street to West Street. There's often a trail of prettily dressed Portuguese families heading into **Silvas Portuguese Traditional Charcoal Chicken** (82-86 New Canterbury Road, 9572 9911). At first glance it looks like a Portuguese McDonald's with alcohol, but scratch the surface and you'll find seafood specialities (salt cod croquettes, *espetada*) and table service alongside the tender-as-hell chook and chips. Other Portugese chicken meccas are **O Pescador** (102 New Canterbury Road, 9564 1163), with its *chourico* (spicy sausage) grilled and served with pickles) and pork *alentejana*, in which little chunks of potato are tossed with *pipis* and pieces of pork. At the sweetly named **Honeymoon Patisserie & Coffee Lounge** (no.96, 9564 2389) elderly Iberian gents gather for Portuguese snacks, while the barn-like **Petersham Liquor Mart** (no.41, 9560 2414) offers shelves of red, white and rosé wines imported from Portugal.

To experience the full flavour of the area's cuisine and culture, be sure to visit during Audley Street's annual **Bairro Português festival**, which is held on a Sunday in March. Finally, don't miss Petersham's main claim to fame on the food front – even though it's Greek, not Portuguese. Modern taverna **Perama** (88 Audley Street, 9569 7534) has soaked its way so completely into the touchy taste buds of Sydney's foodie elite that they don't mind the trek out to plane-traffic territory. Its signature dish of crisp *kataifi* pastry with *bastourma*, warm ricotta and figs is regularly eulogised on critics' lists of the best eats in Sydney.

SIGHTS

North Shore

Safe, comfortable and family friendly – not to mention stunning.

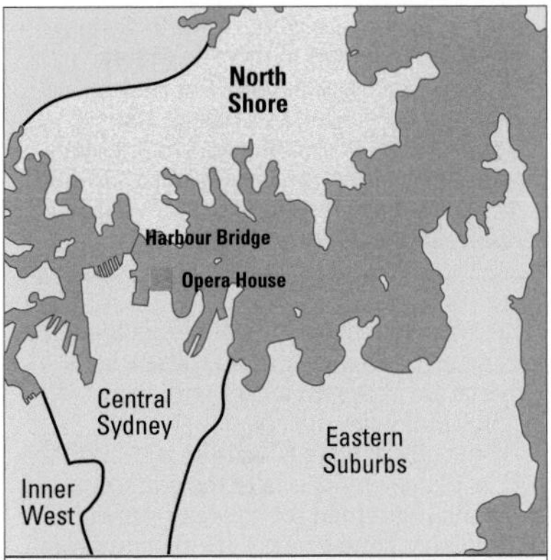

Crossing the bridge to the north side of Sydney has always meant joining the comfortable set. Since 1932, anyway. Until the construction of the Harbour Bridge that year, the north shore was largely undeveloped and the rugged coastline was thick with bushland and fauna and, of course, the first north shore tribes – the Gorualgal (Mosman and Willoughby tribe), Cammeraygal (North Sydney and eastern Lane Cove) and Wallumedegal (Turramurra to Parramatta) – who have long since been squeezed out.

Today, with the surge of suburbia and the advent of train and car travel, the 'leafy' north shore is both the most urbane and strangely wild of Sydney's shires. Second only to the CBD for

North Shore

Harbour Bridge
Opera House

Central Sydney

Eastern Suburbs

Inner West

Hotels p126   **Cafés** p176
Restaurants p148   **Bars & Pubs** p184

business activity, North Sydney itself is a frenzied fiscal centre for insurance, publishing and especially advertising, so it's no surprise that many of the homes in the surrounding area are middle-class family mansions. Such a community has shaped the landscape here, establishing quaint villagey hubs hugging the jaw-dropping waterways. This makes it a good place to visit – there's always a café, restaurant, deli or ice-cream parlour nearby, and most of them are on or close to the water.

Another pull here is the child-friendly double whammy of funfair **Luna Park Sydney** and **Taronga Zoo**, both on the family must-do list.

WHAT'S IN A NAME?

Note that the 'north shore' is not an officially designated area: rather, it's a term to lump together the suburbs on the north side of the harbour that are south and/or west of the northern beaches. Many of these suburbs are not actually on the shore, nor are they especially interesting to tourists, being suburban enclaves. Those that are worth visiting – Kirribilli, North Sydney, McMahons Point, Milsons Point, Mosman, Balmoral and Cremorne – are all on the water.

Getting around the north isn't easy. Its size and sprawl mean that you're best off in a car, and many of its hidden beaches can only be reached by car, on foot (if you're prepared for the

hills) or by charter boat (if you're not). But there is public transport available in the form of the north shore CityRail train line from North Sydney to Hornsby, a wide range of buses and the green-and-cream ferries from Circular Quay (*see p95* **Profile**). The ferries offer the most picturesque way to travel and really capture the area's vibe as they visit the lower north shore suburbs.

KIRRIBILLI

Ferry Kirribilli.

The north shore starts at **Kirribilli** and **Milsons Point**, tiny suburbs nestled on either side of the Harbour Bridge and boasting sweeping vistas of the city and the Opera

SIGHTS

INSIDE TRACK NICOLE KIDMAN

She may have played an Englishwoman out of her depth in the Baz Luhrman blockbuster *Australia*, but the Oscar-winning lass from Lane Cove is Sydney royalty – she grew up here on the North Shore, where she went to North Sydney Girls High School, married in **Manly** (*see p101*) and still calls the Harbour City home. Marriage to Tom Cruise, participation in the longest continuous shoot in history (for *Eyes Wide Shut*) and 14 years' ambassadorship to UNICEF Australia make her a local hero.

House. Despite the apartment blocks that have sprung up in between the old houses, both suburbs are Victorian in feel, with many original buildings still standing.

The southern tip of **Kirribilli** is home to the official Sydney residences of the prime minister (Kirribilli House) and the governor-general (**Admiralty House**), where British royals and other foreign dignitaries also stay. The latter is the most impressive, a classic colonial mansion built in 1844 to 1845 by the collector of customs, Lieutenant-Colonel Gibbes. Originally called Wotonga, it was bought in 1885 by the NSW government to house admirals of the fleet, hence its name today. Next door, **Kirribilli House**, with its rolling, manicured lawns, was built in 1855 in a Gothic Revival style by a rich local merchant. It was acquired by the government in 1956 for use by the prime minister, his family and important guests. Unlike her Sydney-born Liberal predecessor in the PM job, John Howard, the current prime minister Julia Gillard only lives in Kirribilli House to entertain foreign dignitaries when in Sydney, residing in Canberra during the week, and in her red-brick suburban bunker in Altona when in Melbourne. To get the best views of Kirribilli House and Admiralty House (neither are open to the public), hop on a ferry from Circular Quay (*see p95* **Profile**).

There's a distinctly villagey feel to Kirribilli, and its good-life residents continue to fill the cafés and restaurants around the hub of Fitzroy, Burton and Broughton Streets. Try sitting down to a meal of excellent seafood at **Garfish** (9922 4322, 2/21 Broughton Street) or great Thai noodles at **Stir Crazy** (1 Broughton Street, 9922 6620). There's also laid-back **Freckle Face** (32 Burton Street, 9957 2116), the justly renowned **Kirribilli Hotel** (35 Broughton Street, 9955 1415) with its lovely outdoor terrace and the sweet-as-pie café **Epi D'Or** with its French vibe, multiple bread baskets of artisan loaves and earthy Toby's Estate coffee.

Once bodily needs are catered to, turn your mind to cultural pursuits at the famous and well-patronised **Ensemble Theatre Company** (*see p269*), built over the water at Careening Cove, which serves up dramatic treats both contemporary and classic. A particularly good time to visit Kirribilli is on the fourth Saturday of the month, when one of Sydney's oldest bric-a-brac, fashion and antiques markets is held in Bradfield Park, on the corner of Burton and Alfred Streets.

MILSONS POINT, MCMAHONS POINT & NORTH SYDNEY

Milsons Point *CityRail/ferry Milsons Point.*
McMahons Point *Ferry McMahons Point.*
North Sydney *CityRail North Sydney.*

On a sunny day, treat yourself to a ferry trip from Circular Quay wharf 4 (*see p95* **Profile**), gliding past the Opera House to Milsons Point wharf (Alfred Street South). From here, you can take the harbourside walk in either direction. The ferry pulls up right in front of the grinning face and huge staring eyes of the **Luna Park Sydney** funfair (*see p97*). To the right (with your back to the water) is the historic **North Sydney Olympic Pool** (*see p98*), which must be the top contender for the 'most stunningly located swimming pool in the world' award: it's on the water's edge, beneath the northern pylon of the Harbour Bridge. The pool also houses a couple of snazzy eateries that are popular with the media and advertising crowd that works in North Sydney. The less formal restaurant **Ripples** (corner of Alfred Street and Olympic Drive, 9929 7722) is right next to the pool and has outdoor tables. On the other side, in a glass box overlooking the pool, is the pricey **Aqua Dining** (*see p172*). The same people run both restaurants, and both are open for lunch and dinner. Cheaper (and closer to the water) is the **Deck** (9033 7670, 1 Olympic Drive) with awesome cocktails and legendary paella.

Walking along the boardwalk in front of the pool, it's possible to peek in through the bay windows at the swimmers and sunbathers, while the colourful art deco façade has fabulous mouldings of frogs and cockatoos. Carry on under the bridge and continue past the green lawns of Bradfield Park with its rather ugly Australian Angel, the Swiss cultural contribution to an exhibition of sculpture and graphic art at the 2000 Olympics. There's also a plaque commemorating the deaths of 51 people from typhus aboard the quarantined ship the Surry, which was anchored here in 1814. Third Mate Thomas Raine was the only officer to survive, and his grandson Tom Raine founded the wealthy Sydney estate agents Raine & Horne

Profile Sydney Ferries

Sydney's water transport is the source of one of its most emblematic icons.

No trip to Sydney would be complete without clambering aboard one of the picture-postcard green-and-yellow ferries that ply the harbour (all depart from Circular Quay ferry terminal) and which are used daily by hundreds of commuters. These stately vessels – a key feature of Sydney's tourism industry – are a great way to explore the harbour and further afield: there's plenty of room to take pictures from the decks or just to sit in the sun and enjoy the ride.

Although the first ferry service offered on Sydney Harbour was the Rose Hill Packet (aka 'The Lump') which put-puttered to Parramatta from 1789, the first official (albeit privatised) Sydney Ferries route was that of the North Shore Ferry Company, in operation since 1878 (the company changed its name in 1899). Today, 21st-century Sydneysiders can recreate that historic trip and get up close to Sydney's inner northern suburbs while they do it. Gliding past Cremorne Point, Taronga Zoo, south Mosman, Old Cremorne

and finally Mosman Bay, you'll see how the other half live as you gawp at some of the city's most expensive, sought-after and architecturally impressive harbourside homes (including the prime minister's residence Kirribilli House – currently vacant because of PM Julia Gillard's reluctance to move from her red-brick Altona home in suburban Melbourne).

If you're after a bite-size taste of the beauty of the Sydney Ferries experience, the trip to Darling Harbour from Circular Quay lasts about 20 minutes and scoots you under the Harbour Bridge and around the Opera House, often via the gourmet village of Balmain, with its nexus of bars, cafés and restaurants. Your end point of Darling Harbour is full of cool family attractions – the IMAX Theatre, Sydney Aquarium, Wildlife World, Chinese Gardens and Powerhouse Museum, not to mention an assortment of shops in the Harbourside complex and restaurants, bars and cafes at Cockle Bay and King Street Wharf.

For more information, visit www.sydneyferries.info.

For more great ferry rides, *see p45.*

SIGHTS

Luna Park Sydney.

SIGHTS

– a fitting north shore tale. The foreshore walk ends at **Mary Booth Lookout**, a patch of green with a great view that's perfect for picnics.

In the other direction from Luna Park the foreshore walk winds around **Lavender Bay**: it's especially dazzling at sunset when the city lights shimmer in the golden glow. Walk up the Lavender Bay Wharf steps to Lavender Street, turn left and after a few minutes you'll reach Blues Point Road, which slices down from North Sydney through the heart of McMahons Point. It's one of Sydney's great people-watching strips, and there are numerous cafés, pubs, delis and restaurants from which you can take in the view; try **Blues Point Café** (No.135, 9922 2064), which serves Italian food, or the **Commodore Hotel** (No.206, 9922 5098, www.commodore hotel.com.au), a rowdy after-work haunt with a

---

INSIDE TRACK **VIEWPOINTS**

From this side of the city you get postcard views of the Harbour Bridge and the Opera House – the best, of course, is from the prime minister's home in **Kirribilli** (*see p93*). Other dreamy spots include **Cremorne** foreshore (*see p98*), where laughing kookaburras and sweetly screeching rainbow lorikeets nestle in weeping figs, and **Balmoral** beach (*see p99*), Sydney's most sophisticated oceanside suburb.

---

large outdoor terrace. Allow time to walk down to Blues Point Reserve, a swathe of parkland at the southern tip of Blues Point, for a photo op for the obligatory Sydney Harbour holiday snap.

The northern end of Blues Point Road merges into Miller Street, dominated by North Sydney office blocks and constituting Sydney's main business district after the CBD. A little way up on the left-hand side of Miller Street is Mount Street and the bizarre **Mary MacKillop Place** (*see p98*). This homage to Australia's only saint stands on the site of her former convent and is worth a visit if only for its zany exhibition. To get a sense of the history of the area, visit the nearby **Don Bank Museum** (*see right*), located inside one of North Sydney's oldest houses. Further up Miller Street is **North Sydney Oval** one of the oldest and prettiest cricket grounds in Australia (established 1867), now used for rugby (league and union) as well as cricket matches and, on summer evenings, the alfresco **Starlight Cinema** (*see p233*).

The main commercial centre of the lower north shore is Military Road, a seemingly endless strip of shops, cafés and restaurants that heads east through Neutral Bay to Balmoral. At No.118, in Neutral Bay, is the popular **Oaks** pub (*see p193*) with its tree-covered courtyard, a hangout for local movers and shakers who order steaks and fish by the kilo and then make for the outdoor barbecue to cook up a storm. Further up the road is the unmissable **Pickled Possum pub** (No.254, 9909 2091), a tiny outback-style boozer in the centre of the city where stubbies are served straight from an ice box. In between you'll find a host of new diners – the **Blue Plate Bar & Grill** (24 Young Street, 9953 2942) with its Americana-style food and fancy cocktails, next door's **Firefly Neutral Bay** (24 Young Street, 9909 0193), a tapas and wine bar with a twist, and **Neutral Bay Bar & Dining** (132 Military Road, 9953 5853), the new restaurant from the team behind Glebe Point Diner.

Don Bank Museum
6 Napier Street, off Berry Street, North Sydney (9955 6279). CityRail North Sydney. **Open** *Museum* 1-4pm Wed, Sun. *Garden* 7am-7pm daily. **Admission** $1; 50¢ reductions. **No credit cards**.
It's not known exactly when this house was built, but parts are thought to date from the 1820s. Originally called St Leonards Cottage (most of North Sydney as it is now was once called St Leonards), it was part of the Wollstonecraft Estate granted to Edward Wollstonecraft in 1825. The house was bought by North Sydney Council in the 1970s and restored with assistance from heritage groups: it is now a community museum. As well as visiting exhibitions, its permanent displays include kitchen objects from the times of the early settlers and other historical items. The building itself is significant: it's one of the few surviving examples of an early timber-slab house.

Luna Park Sydney
1 Olympic Drive, at the foreshore, Milsons Point (9033 7676, www.lunaparksydney.com). CityRail/ferry Milsons Point. **Open** 11am-6pm Mon-Thur; 11am-11pm Fri; 10am-11pm Sat; 10am-6pm Sun (later in school holidays). **Admission** *Entry* free. *Rides* individual rides vary. Unlimited ride pass $20-$43; free children under 85cm (3ft). **Credit** AmEx, DC, MC, V. **Map** p327 F1.
The huge laughing clown's mouth that marks the entrance to Luna Park is visible from Circular Quay. Walk through that mouth and you'll find Sydney's venerable funfair back in full stomach-churning swing after a few troubled decades. The park opened in 1935 on the site of the Dorman Long workshops used to build the Harbour Bridge, and its heyday lasted until well into the 1950s. A slow decline during the 1970s ended in sudden closure in 1979 following a fatal fire on the ghost train. But an uprising from Sydney's artist community revitalized the park for new generations – Sydney painters Martin Sharp, Peter Kingston and Garry Shead installed a new psychedelic energy to the old funfair via massive murals, metal-flaking mind trickery and cartoon comic strip heroes soon bursting over the walls while restoring classic elements of the original park to their former glories. Lovingly referred to as 'Sydney's heartbeat' by Sydneysider Clive James, Luna Park's smile lit up afresh in 2004 as a 1930s-style fun park and performance venue. Some of the park's original rides and sideshows are still around, and there's no shortage of fixes for addicts of high speeds and vertigo.

INSIDE TRACK EARLY SETTLERS

The north shore settlers of the early 1800s were land dealers, and its development into a place of white estates and family homes stems from that time. The Cammeraygal, Gorualgal and Wallumedegal tribes who inhabited the area when the First Fleet arrived at Sydney Cove in 1788 had largely been driven out of the region by the 1860s. The Cammeraygal, recorded as being a powerful and numerous tribe, 'most robust and muscular', lived along the foreshore, in the bushland and cliffs, and in rock shelters. Places such as Berry Island, Balls Head, Kirribilli, Cremorne and Cammeray are dotted with cultural remnants of the tribe's heyday.

More recently the area has become increasingly multicultural, with first and second-generation immigrants from Japan, China, Korea and South Africa all settling in and now calling the area home.

North Sydney Olympic Pool. *See p98.*

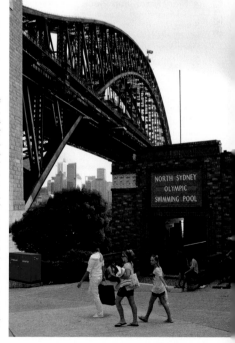

SIGHTS

Cremorne Point Lighthouse.

★ Mary MacKillop Place
7-11 Mount Street, between Edward & William Streets, North Sydney (8912 4878, www.mary mackillopplace.org.au). CityRail North Sydney. **Open** 10am-4pm daily. **Admission** $8; $6 reductions; $21 family. **Credit** MC, V.
Mary MacKillop (1842-1909) was the founder of the Sisters of St Joseph, an order initially devoted to educating poor Australian children. Often referred to as 'the people's saint', MacKillop's pioneering work lead to her beatification in 1995 when the Pope visited and blessed the site, giving Australia its first – and only – saint to date. She died on 8 August 1909, and the eighth day of each month has become one of pilgrimage to the museum for devout Catholics. It includes MacKillop's home, Alma Cottage, and the chapel housing her tomb. A curious mix of humble 19th-century artefacts and high-tech wizardry, the displays of MacKillop's possessions – including crucifixes, rosary beads, figurines and scraps of her habits – are jazzed up with talking dioramas, videos and other surprisingly cool special effects.

★ North Sydney Olympic Pool
4 Alfred Street South, at the foreshore, Milsons Point (9955 2309, www.northsydney.nsw.gov.au). CityRail/ferry Milsons Point. **Open** 5.30am-9pm Mon-Fri; 7am-7pm Sat, Sun. **Admission** *Pool* $6.50; $3.20 reductions. *Sauna, spa & swim* $11. **Credit** AmEx, DC, MC, V. **Map** p327 F1.
This unique outdoor swimming pool, between Harbour Bridge and Luna Park, holds a special place

in the hearts of many a Sydneysider. Built on the site where much of the construction work for the bridge was carried out, it opened in 1936. Hailed as 'the wonder pool of Australasia' because of the high standard of its facilities and sophisticated filtration system – at the time one of the most advanced in the world – the building has wonderful art deco stylings and decorative plasterwork, most of it still intact. Art aside, a total of 86 world records have been set here by such swimming greats as Jon Konrads, Shane Gould and Michelle Ford. Today a slick 25m indoor pool, state-of-the-art gym, spa and sauna have been added to the famed 50m heated outdoor pool. Views from the pool and from the terraced concrete seating above it are stupendous. There are two onsite eateries to provide post-swim sustenance. *Photo p97.*

CREMORNE, MOSMAN, BALMORAL & THE SPIT BRIDGE

Cremorne *Ferry Cremorne Point then bus 225/ bus 247, L88 to Neutral Bay then bus 225.* **Mosman** *Ferry South Mosman, Old Cremorne or Mosman Bay/CityRail Milsons Point then bus 228, 229, 230.* **Balmoral** *Ferry Taronga Zoo then bus 238.*

If you continue east along Military Road (an extension of the busy main route that links the suburbs of the lower north shore), you will arrive at some of Sydney's richest suburbs: **Cremorne**, **Mosman** and **Balmoral**, where the heavily moneyed live in conspicuous splendour.

Cremorne Point, a sliver of a peninsula, offers one of the finest panoramas of Sydney Harbour. It's the perfect setting for a scenic harbourside stroll down to the whitewashed 1904 lighthouse. You can then hop back on the ferry to **Mosman Bay** wharf, where an uphill walk or bus will take you into Mosman village. Further east lies **Taronga Zoo** (*see right*), which occupies a splendid vantage point overlooking Bradleys Head. North of the zoo, Mosman's commercial centre runs along Military Road – a good place to people-watch

INSIDE TRACK
BALMORAL GAZEBO

The Gazebo at Balmoral was built by the Order of the Star of the East, in 1923. This mysterious sect believed Jesus himself was coming through the Heads. They built a marble ampitheatre for the occasion but when JC never showed up, the Rotunda was hastily redefined as 'a monument to happiness' and today hosts weddings and alfresco theatre.

and shop, if your wallet can cope. But there's
more to Mosman than shopping. **Sydney
Harbour National Park** is a local secret
that is winning new fans thanks to the opening
of **Ripples Chowder Bay** (Chowder Bay Rd,
Mosman, 9960 3000). This sister restaurant to
Ripples at Milsons Point (Olympic Drive,
Milsons Point, 9929 7722) is in one of the city's
most divine locations and so is packed for
breakfast, lunch and dinner. Surrounded by the
rugged green slopes of the National Park (a
favourite jogging spot), and with views over
Chowder Bay wharf and way out to Port
Jackson, the place feels a million miles from
suburban Mosman. If walking to it seems like
an unfair hike, go on a weekday when the 244
bus runs down Chowder Bay Road.

Over on the 'Middle Harbour' side of Mosman
is **Balmoral**, one of Sydney's prettiest harbour
suburbs. Boasting not one but two beaches,
lots of green space and a curiously Romanesque
bandstand (the venue for many local events),
this is also a good dining spot, with a few
excellent restaurants; **Watermark** (2A
The Esplanade, 9968 3433, www.watermark
restaurant.com.au) and **Bathers' Pavilion** (4
The Esplanade, 9969 5050) are among the best
to be found in the city, while **Bottom of the
Harbour** (21 The Esplanade, 9969 7911) is an
excellent promenade fish and chip shop. Watch
out for the seagulls, however – they are a
particularly robust flock here and will steal the
chips from out of your mouth given half a chance.

The two arcs of sand, **Edwards Beach** and
Balmoral Beach, are separated by **Rocky
Point**, and part of Edwards is protected by a
shark net. If you come on a Saturday before 10am
you're likely to spy members of the Balmoral
Beach Club pounding the water. This family-
friendly club is a local institution and has been
using Balmoral's outdoor baths since 1914. Head
further north and you hit Spit Bridge, the lovely
bottleneck faced by those wanting to head
towards Manly and the northern beaches (*see
p102*). The view driving down Spit Road from
Military Road is one of Sydney's most amazing,
with boats bobbing in the marina both sides of
the narrow causeway and swanky mansions
clinging to the rocky cliffs. Traffic stops when
the bridge lifts to let boats pass beneath.

★ Taronga Zoo

*Bradleys Head Road, Mosman (9969 2777,
www.zoo.nsw.gov.au). Ferry Taronga Zoo/bus
247.* **Open** 9am-5pm daily. **Admission** $43;
$21-30 reductions; $108.80 family; free under-4s.
Credit AmEx, DC, MC, V.
Only 12 minutes by ferry from Circular Quay, the
'zoo with a view' covers 17.5 hectares (43 acres) on
the western side of Bradleys Head. The zoo contains
2,600 animals of more than 340 species: best of all,

Taronga Zoo.

SIGHTS

especially for foreigners, are the native ones, including koalas, kangaroos, platypuses, echidnas, Tasmanian devils and lots of colourful, screechy birds (follow the Wild Australia Walk to see them all). Visitors are no longer allowed to cuddle koalas, but a 'koala encounter' (11am-2.45pm) lets you have your photo taken beside one of the sleepy critters. Other highlights at Taronga include the Free Flight Bird Show, the Seal Show, Giraffes in Focus – where you can meet the giraffes face to face, listen to a keeper talk and grab a close-up photo – the huge Komodo Dragon, named Tuka, in the Serpentaria exhibit, and the Gorilla Forest. Backyard to Bush is a journey from an Aussie back garden through an adventure-packed farmyard and into a bush wilderness, while the new Asian Elephant Rainforest is a sight to behold with its deep swimming pool waterfall and mud wallows. The elephant exhibit is part of a new area called Wild Asia, which includes a 2.3km (1.4-mile) stretch where the elephants interact with other species including gorillas, penguins and kodiak bears. Taronga's elephants have been particularly busy of late, with the first ever elephant births in Australia falling within nine months of each. The first baby was Luk Chai, born 4 July 2009 to Thong Dee and Gung. The second baby was thought to have died in labour on 8 March 2010 but two days later was born alive. He was named Pathi Harn, a Thai word expression for 'miracle'. In recent years, the zoo also offers sleepovers ('Roar and Snore' packages – $120/ $88 reductions) and classes aimed at addressing phobias of spiders and snakes. All in all? A truly delightful place. *Photo p99.*

WAVERTON

CityRail Waverton.

While it's true that the north shore's most spectacular vistas are found on the harbour foreshore, there are a couple of areas worth visiting for something a little different. A train ride across the Harbour Bridge to Waverton (one stop past North Sydney) will deliver you to **Balls Head Reserve**, a thickly wooded headland overlooking the start of the Parramatta River. Turn left out of the station down Bay Road, which runs into Balls Head Road; it's a five- to ten-minute walk. From here you can look west to Gladesville, south to the city, Balmain and Goat Island, and east to McMahons Point and beyond. Until 1916 this area was the home of a local Aboriginal community – a carving of a six-metre (20-foot) whale with a man inside is still preserved – but during World War I the Australian army claimed the land, and a Quarantine Depot (still standing) was established. Wildlife is abundant, and on summer nights you might see flying foxes feeding on the Port Jackson fig trees, dragon lizards, geckos, brush-tailed possums and around 70 bird species.

There are free barbecues, so you can take your own steak or prawns and dine out at one of the finest window seats in Sydney. (Check there isn't a fire ban first though, especially in summer.)

West of Balls Head, around the next cove, **Berry Island Reserve** is the best place to see remnants of the north shore's Aboriginal heritage. The island was originally a camping area for Aboriginal communities, and evidence of their way of life – including shell middens, axe grindings and a rock hole that would have stored water – are still visible. In the early 19th century, Edward Wollstonecraft attached the island to his land by building a stone causeway over mud flats (now reclaimed as lawns); the area became a public nature reserve in 1926.

WAHROONGA

Wahroonga CityRail Wahroonga.

Wahroonga is a quiet, leafy suburb on the northwest fringe of the north shore, and where you'll find **Rose Seidler House** (*see below*), the first building that the late Viennese-born architect Harry Seidler designed in Australia. He became one of Sydney's most celebrated architects, and his unusual buildings around the city continue to provoke admiration and controversy in equal measure. The house is impressive enough on its own, but check out the amazing panoramic views of Ku-ring-gai Chase National Park from every window – you'll see why Seidler chose this spot.

★ Rose Seidler House

71 Clissold Road, at Devon Street, Wahroonga (9989 8020, www.hht.nsw.gov.au). CityRail Wahroonga. **Open** 10am-5pm Sun; also by appointment. **Admission** $8; $4 reductions; $17 family. **No credit cards**.
Harry Seidler built this house, his first commission, between 1948 and 1950 for his parents, Rose and Max. The ambitious architect came over from New York, where he had been working for Bauhaus guru Marcel Breuer, specifically to build the house; it was the first local instance of 'mid-century modern' domestic architecture. In basic terms, the house is a flat single-storey box resting on a smaller box, with a section cut out to form a sun deck and floor-to-ceiling windows. The open-plan interior is divided into two distinct zones: the living or public areas, and the sleeping or private areas. The original 1950s colour scheme has been restored, and the furnishings are by important post-war designers such as Charles Eames and Eero Saarinen. The kitchen had all mod cons – the latest refrigerator, stove and dishwasher, plus a waste-disposal unit and exhaust fan – which were then utterly new to Australia and added to the house's allure locally. Max and Rose Seidler lived in the house until 1967. It's now run by the Historic Houses Trust. Guided tours are available on request.

Northern Beaches

Surfer's paradise (and easy-living for everyone else).

Beyond the environs of the city lies Sydney's secret – the seemingly endless stretch of surf beaches that line the north coast like a string of pearls. This is a wonderful place and the locals know it – which is why they have fiercely protected the northern beaches from tourist overload. It's not for nothing that this area is dubbed 'the insular peninsula'.

The northern beaches start over the Spit Bridge, which crosses Middle Harbour and connects Mosman to Seaforth and Manly. Busy, touristy **Manly**, where there is a plethora of hotels, kicks off the run of beaches, but it's the more distant suburbs such as **Collaroy**, **Narrabeen**, **Newport**, **Avalon**, **Whale Beach** and **Palm Beach** that set the tone for the area, which is lush, laid-back and totally devoted to living well in the great outdoors.

MANLY

Ferry Manly.

A summery explosion of shops, restaurants, cafés, surfboards, people and colour, this famous beachside suburb nestles on its own peninsula, boasting both ocean and harbour beaches, plus views from every corner. Since its first days as a resort in the 1920s, **Manly**'s catchphrase has been 'seven miles from Sydney and a thousand miles from care' – actually an advertising slogan coined by the once-famous Port Jackson & Manly Steamship Company. Hearing it might cause the locals to cringe a little these days, but the sentiment still stands.

The suburb also gives its name by Arthur Phillip, the first governor of New South Wales, when he saw a number of 'manly' Aboriginal men of the Kay-ye-my clan on the shore of what he later called Manly Cove. Now it's a centre for such macho pursuits as surf lifesaving, bodysurfing, kayaking and the Australian Ironman Championships, so the name still fits. Just a few years ago, Manly was slipping into decline and had the feel of a fading British seaside resort, but it has since rejuvenated itself and is now a vibrant and dynamic suburb with a bevy of amenities and some good festivals that attract major crowds. For all that, Sydneysiders have mixed feelings about Manly, but its perennial holiday atmosphere and one-and-a-half kilometres (one mile) of tree-lined

ocean beach are irresistible to visitors. The tourists who head to Manly are a curious mix of the well-heeled (who stay at the area's expensive hotels), a burgeoning (predominantly British) backpacker brigade holing up in cheap hostels and pubs, and day-trippers delivered by ferry from the Sydney suburbs.

To get to Manly, take one of the large Manly ferries (30 minutes) from Circular Quay to the slickly refurbished **Manly Wharf**, with its cafés, pubs and restaurants on **Manly Cove**. Here you'll also find a peaceful patch of harbourside sand (though no surf, and the water is a tad murky for swimming). Stop in at the **Visitor Information Centre** (*see p103*) in front of the wharf for maps and brochures. The **Manly Wharf Hotel** (Manly Wharf East Esplanade, 9977 1266) is one of Sydney's finest waterside eating and drinking spots, but it does get extremely busy. Try **Hugos Manly** (Manly Wharf East Esplanade, 8116 8555) instead – chef Monica Cannataci won 'Best Pizza in Australia' at the 2010 Australian Fine Food Show.

Nearby, at the western end of the cove, is popular **Oceanworld Manly** (*see p104*), **Manly Art Gallery & Museum** (*see p103*) and **Manly Waterworks** (9949 1088, www.manlywaterworks.com), a small water park that's open from September to April. Further west is the start of a fine ten-kilometre (6.2-mile) walk through bushland and along clifftops to **Spit Bridge** (pick up a self-guided walk leaflet at the Visitor Information Centre).

SIGHTS

INSIDE TRACK MANLY PINES

The pines were planted in the 1850s by Henry Gilbert Smith, a wealthy English immigrant who decided to turn Manly from a tiny fishing village into a holiday resort for Sydneysiders.

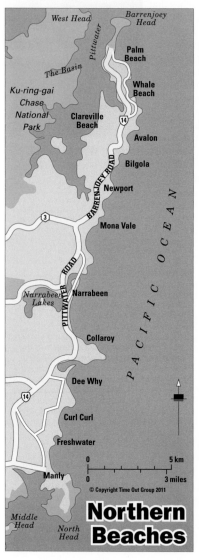

West Head

Barrenjoey Head

Pittwater

The Basin

Palm Beach

Whale Beach

Ku-ring-gai Chase National Park

Clareville Beach

14

Avalon

Bilgola

BARRENJOEY ROAD

Newport

3

Mona Vale

PITTWATER ROAD

Narrabeen Lakes

Narrabeen

Collaroy

Dee Why

14

Curl Curl

Freshwater

0   5 km

0   3 miles

© Copyright Time Out Group 2011

Manly

Middle Head

North Head

PACIFIC OCEAN

Northern Beaches

SIGHTS

The main pedestrian precinct, the **Corso**, links Manly Wharf with Manly Beach, and is lined with restaurants, surf shops, fast-food joints and tourist shops. Here you'll find a clutch of high-street chains, plus cool clothing and footwear stores amid a myriad of cafés and restaurants; **Bacino** (no.1A, 9977 8889) is a corner coffee spot popular first thing in the morning but **Das Kaffeehaus** (5B Market Lane, 9976 5099) and **Max Brenner Chocolate Bar** (East Esplanade, 9977 4931) have their fans too, with good reason.

The Corso's amphitheatre is used regularly for live entertainment and has been known to draw enormous crowds, particularly for the **Manly Jazz Festival** (*see p218*) in October and the **Food & Wine Festival** in June. The **Manly Arts & Crafts Market**, worth a browse for handmade jewellery and souvenirs, is held every weekend on the lower end of Sydney Road, just off the Corso. The **Manly Farmers Markets** (Short Street Plaza, 9315 7011) are another magnet for green gourmets on Saturdays.

The suburb's main attraction, though, is **Manly Beach** itself, a long crescent of sand and ocean surf, fringed by a promenade lined with giant Norfolk pines that is a magnet for surfers, sunbathers, cyclists, in-line skaters and beach volleyball enthusiasts. The pines inspired local microbrewery and restaurant **Four Pines Brewing Co** (29/43-45 East Esplanade, 9976 2300). The services of Eddie and Joe Sly, the first lifesavers to patrol the beach, were soon needed, as the holidaymaking crowds failed to understand the danger of the surf. Today, surfboards, wetsuits and beach umbrellas are available for hire on the beach, and novice surfers can hone their skills with the **Manly Surf School** (9977 6977, www.manlysurfschool.com).

Head south along the beachfront road to find a row of laid-back bars and cafés with lovely ocean views on **South Steyne** – busy most of the time, they are perfect spots in which to enjoy a meal or a coffee, or just watch the world cruise by. Some of the most popular spots include **Blue Water Café** (no.28, 9976 2051), **Manly Fish Café** (no. 25, 9976 3777), with its sublime grilled octopus, and **Rouge Mediterranean Café** (no.33, 8966 9872). There's also the chic **Manly Ocean Beach House** (Ocean Promenade, North Steyne, 9977 0566) slap bang in the middle of the promenade.

A must is the 15-minute walk to **Shelly Beach**. Potter south along the beachfront from Manly Beach to Marine Parade and follow the winding path around the headland known as **Fairy Bower**, passing magnificent cliff-top homes along the way. Watch out for the beautiful and carefully hidden sea-themed artworks of the **Sculpture Walk** sited en

Manly Beach.

collection of beach memorabilia, including vintage swimming costumes. The shop sells leaflets describing two Heritage Walks around Manly.

Manly Visitor Information Centre
Manly Wharf (9976 1430, www.manlytourism. com). Ferry Manly. **Open** 9am-5pm Mon-Fri; 10am-4pm Sat, Sun (5pm summer). **Map** p334.
At the front of the wharf, this is the place to find brochures, timetables, maps and information.

North Fort
North Fort Road, off North Head Scenic Drive (9976 6102, www.northfort.org.au). Ferry Manly then bus 135. **Open** 9am-4pm Wed-Sun. **Admission** $11; $5-$8 reductions; $25 family. **Credit** MC, V.
The remote location of North Fort means its landscape has changed little since early colonial paintings of the spot. Wind-blown sand dunes cover the headland, with hillside 'hanging' swamps among the coastal shrub. Today, it is home to the Royal Australian Artillery National Museum, once part of the School of Artillery, constructed between 1935 and 1938 in the shadow of war and the need to defend Sydney Harbour from naval attack. You can still tour the fortifications and underground tunnels. A memorial walkway undergoes continual upgrades as more and more inscribed paving stones are added, honouring nationals who have served in the defence of Australia.

★ North Head Quarantine Station
North Head Scenic Drive (9976 6220, www. q-station.com.au). Ferry Manly then bus 135. **Open** (pre-booked tours only) *Day tour* 3-5pm Sat; 10am-noon, 3-5pm Sun. *Adults' ghost tour* 8-11pm Wed-Sun. *Family ghost tour* 6.30-8.30pm Thur, Sun. **Admission** *Day tour* $25; $19 reductions; $70 family. *Adults' ghost tour* $34; $32 reductions. *Family ghost tour* $25; $19 reductions; $70 family. **Credit** MC, V.
The ghost tours at North Head Quarantine Station are possibly the creepiest sightseeing you'll ever do. Built in 1828, the station was the prison – and burial place – of scores of unfortunate souls, who were quarantined here for a minimum of 30 days if their ship was suspected of carrying an infectious disease

route, and feel free to stop in at a couple of decent eateries: the **Bower Restaurant** (7 Marine Parade, 9977 5451) is a good spot for breakfast, lunch or an early dinner, while the sandstone **Le Kiosk** at Shelly Beach (1 Marine Parade, 9977 4122) is a smart restaurant with a cheaper takeaway booth next door.

Also unmissable is the spectacular view from **North Head**, the northern of the two Heads that form the gateway to Sydney Harbour. It's a five- to ten-minute drive via Darley Road (running south-east from the middle of the Corso) and North Head Scenic Drive.

North Head is also home to the historic **North Head Quarantine Station** (*see right*) and **North Fort** (*see right*). You can take bus 135 from Wentworth Street, but be aware that the service operates in the daytime only. Keep your eyes peeled on the walk down towards the harbourside: you might spot some of Sydney's famous fairy penguins, tiny versions of their Antarctic cousins, living in the heart – and the heat – of the city. Don't approach them, though, as they're a protected species.

FREE Manly Art Gallery & Museum
West Esplanade (9976 1420, www.manly australia.com.au/manlyartgallery). Ferry Manly. **Open** 10am-5pm Tue-Sun. Closed public holidays. **Admission** free. **Map** p334.
Manly isn't exactly synonymous with high culture, but you can pop into this small gallery/museum if all that surfer lingo starts to curdle your brain. Opened in 1930, it has an 845-strong collection of paintings by Australian artists, more than 2,000 historic photographs of the northern beaches area, and some impressive ceramics and exhibitions by local students and photographers. The museum is devoted to the history of Manly and has a marvellously kitsch

SIGHTS

INSIDE TRACK PIE BREAK

Sylvia and Fran's legendary **Upper Crust** (*see p104*) meat pies have amassed a devoted following since opening on this site in 1948 so there's always a jostle for a parking spot outside: be prepared to fight for your place in the queue with barefooted surfers who dash across the busy street for a bite between waves.

such as smallpox, bubonic plague or influenza. The station was overcrowded, the treatment often degrading and many who died were buried in unmarked graves. Closed in 1972 (though, incredibly, it was used as emergency housing for Vietnamese orphans in 1975), the station is currently a top attraction for ghoulish tourists. They are led through its black streets, old fumigation rooms, shower blocks and cemetery by a guide with a kerosene lamp. Several visitors claim to have seen the resident ghosts – a moustachioed man in a three-piece suit and a stern matron – and others have reported feeling nauseous after getting a whiff of putrid and inexplicable smells. If you take a night tour, bring a torch and wear flat shoes.

Oceanworld Manly

West Esplanade (8251 7877, www.oceanworld. com.au). Ferry Manly. **Open** 10am-5.30pm daily. **Admission** $20; $10 reductions; $46 family; 15% discount after 3.30pm. **Credit** AmEx, MC, V. **Map** p334.

Located a couple of hundred metres from Manly's ferry terminal, Oceanworld is about as good as aquaria get. The three-level attraction has a floor devoted to dangerous Australian creatures (poisonous snakes, funnel-web spiders, giant monitor lizards, crocodiles) and another to tropical fish, corals and venomous sea creatures. The main attraction, on the lower level, is the oceanarium, which holds the largest sharks in captivity in Australia, plus giant rays and sea turtles – all seen via a 110m

Collaroy Beach.

> ## INSIDE TRACK AVALON BEACH
>
> This beautiful surf spot was once considered as a possible location by the makers of *Baywatch*, but Avalon Beach's territorial locals weren't having any of it.

(360ft) underwater viewing tunnel. Fish and sharks are fed at 11am on Mondays, Wednesdays and Fridays, and there's a Dangerous Australian Animals show at noon daily. Other attractions include the 'touch pool', where you can get up close and personal with hermit crabs and starfish. For the really adventurous there's Shark Dive Xtreme ($185-$250), a chance to dive with huge grey nurse sharks.

FRESHWATER TO WHALE BEACH

Dee Why, Collaroy, Narrabeen & Mona Vale *Bus 188, 190, E83, E84, E86, E87, E88, E89, L88, L90. Newport & Avalon Bus 188, 190, E88, E89, L88, L90. Whale Beach Bus 190, L90 then bus 193.*

From Manly, the beaches get less crowded and more spectacular, with names like Collaroy, **Freshwater, Curl Curl, Narrabeen, Dee Why**, Newport and Avalon slipping off the tongue like a surfer off the crest of a wave. You are now entering serious surfing territory, with Sydney's pros limbering up along the coast on a daily basis. Here the air smells of sea salt and coconut oil, and it seems as if every second teenager hides under a mop of matted bleached blond hair, surfboard in tow.

The best way to explore is by car, allowing you to stop, take in the view, and swim at leisure at whichever beach you fancy. Otherwise, the L90 bus from Wynyard will take you all the way to Palm Beach – the journey takes about 90 minutes if you don't stop – calling in at various beaches (but not Manly) en route. The road becomes steeper and more winding after you've passed Newport and the views get increasingly breathtaking.

You can pick up the useful and informative Sydney's Northern Beaches Map, produced by the Northern Beaches Visitors Association, from **Sydney Beachhouse YHA** (*see p145*), located on Collaroy beach; much of the same information is on the association's website, www.sydneybeaches.com.au. Also useful is www.sydneynorthernbeaches.com.au. If you want to try one of the best meat pies in Sydney head for **Upper Crust** (1003 Pittwater Road, 9971 5182) at the crest of the hill in **Collaroy**. And for a cool beer in spectacular surroundings pop into the **Surf Rock Hotel** (1062 Pittwater

Avalon Sea Pool.

Road, 9982 3924), with its balcony overlooking the seashore and sensational interior design.

Visitors with a car can take a detour to **Garigal National Park** (9451 3479, www. nationalparks.nsw.gov.au), which links Sydney's north shore suburbs with the northern beaches. Covering more than 20 square kilometres (nearly eight square miles) of rugged bush, sandstone outcrops and waterways, it's divided into sections. The western section hugs **Middle Harbour Creek**, which leads into Sydney Harbour; a walking track by the creek offers much historical interest (and four picnic areas), plus some rare native ash and stringybark trees.

Further north is the much larger **Ku-ring-gai Chase National Park** (*see p107*), on the south-eastern edge of which, inland from **Mona Vale**, is a striking domed white building. This is the **Bahá'í House of Worship** (173 Mona Vale Road, Ingleside, 9998 9221, www.bahai. org.au), a temple for members of the Bahá'í faith, a religion founded in the 19th century that has five million members worldwide. The temple's design, with nine sides and nine entrances, represents the unification of the human race under one God. Whatever your religious views, it's a lovely spot, with beautiful grounds and great views of the ocean.

North of Mona Vale is **Newport**, worth a stop for its great delicatessen, **Tongue Teasers** (339 Barrenjoey Road, 9997 3557) – a top spot to load up for a picnic – and the **Newport Arms Hotel** (*see p193*), a much-loved pub with a fantastic beer garden overlooking the tranquil ocean inlet of Pittwater.

The final community before Palm Beach is **Avalon**, once something of a secret but now a thriving shopping centre and booming

residential village, and getting bigger by the year. It's approached via an unnervingly steep and winding road, which offers dramatic ocean views for whoever is in the passenger seat but one hairy ride for the driver. On the right you'll pass the shockingly steep decline that leads to **Bilgola Beach**: take time to turn off, follow signs for the beach and drive around the breathtaking bends – the road's not called the Serpentine for nothing – that lead you down and then back up the hillside. Just before you rejoin the main road, the lookout point on **Bilgola Head** is well worth a stop – it offers unique views down the coastline towards Bondi and up to Barrenjoey Lighthouse at Palm Beach. On the upward ascent into Avalon, look out for the traditional birthday and anniversary greetings that locals pin to the trees. **Avalon Beach** is down the hill on the right. Avalon surfers jealously guard their waters; they're in their combies from dawn until dusk, waiting for that perfect wave. The town itself has two main strips: **Avalon Parade**, which runs from the beach up towards the Pittwater side of the peninsula, and the **Old Barrenjoey Road**, which crosses Avalon Parade and leads to Palm Beach in one direction and Sydney in the other.

On Avalon Parade, chic new licensed café, deli and gelateria **'Allo 'Allo** (no.24, 9973 4785) is popular with locals who sit outside on the bentwood furniture, while on Old Barrenjoey Road there's a longstanding favourite, the **Ibiza Café** (no.47, 9918 3965), which does a roaring trade: it's got an open pavement area for the summer and a warm, friendly feel in winter. **Bookoccino** (no.37A, 9973 1244) is one of the best bookshops on the northern beaches, with an excellent range of children's books, cookery books, biographies, history, Australiana and more; as the name suggests, there's a café too.

To get to the idyllic stretches of **Clareville Beach** on the calm shore of Pittwater, sheltered from the ocean waves, head up Avalon Parade with the post office on your left. Avalon Parade becomes Hudson Parade and hooks left to run parallel to Pittwater; when you reach the bottom of the hill, turn right into Delecta Avenue – 20 minutes' walk from Avalon, or a few minutes by

SIGHTS

INSIDE TRACK SUMMER BAY

When the 'Summer Bay SLSC' sign is hanging on the side of the **North Palm Beach Surf Club** building, the Seven Network crew are in business for *Home and Away*, and you may well spot wily old Alf Stewart (aka actor Ray Meagher) ordering a latte from the kiosk, or younger cast members learning their lines.

Whale Beach.

car. The sandy beach, one of Sydney's 'secret beaches', is not good for swimming, but it's popular with locals for meet-and-greet Sunday barbecues; many also moor their boats here. **Clareville Kiosk** (27 Delecta Avenue, 9918 2727, www.clarevillekiosk.com), a delightful beach-house-style restaurant, is open from Wednesday to Sunday for dinner, and Saturday and Sunday for lunch. Be sure to book ahead.

There's one more treasure to be seen before you reach Palm Beach, the end of the northern beaches road. For many locals, **Whale Beach** is closer to paradise than glitzier Palm. Its inaccessibility helps, making it a definite 'those in the know' bolt-hole. You can get there by bus – the 193 from Avalon Parade in Avalon – or by walking from the L90 bus stop on Careel Head Road. From there, turn left on to Whale Beach Road and continue until you reach the beach itself; it's a roughly half-hour and suitably hilly trek through roads lined with wonderful beach houses, but it's worth the effort. The pink sand, rugged surf and rocky headland have a quality all of their own, and there's an oceanside swimming pool. The **Whale Beach Kiosk** (corner of Surf Road and The Strand) serves up freshly-made rolls, antipasti plates, fish and chips, and much more. If you want something more substantial and you're feeling flush, then stop in at the lovely **Jonah's** (69 Byna Road, 9974 5599), where the area's swankier denizens enjoy five-star food on a coastal hilltop; there are guest rooms too (*see p143*). You might want to bring a change of clothes, though – beachside gear won't cut it here.

PALM BEACH & AROUND

Bus 190, L90.

Finally to **Palm Beach**, the well-heeled tip of the northern beaches, where you'll find more multi-million-dollar mansions than seagulls. The area is a luxurious home to a high concentration of the rich and famous keen on living outside of Sydney's glaring limelight, including tennis star Lleyton Hewitt, rugby league champion turned TV star Matthew Johns. And soon, if rumours are right, Cronulla's favourite swimsuit model Elle 'The Body' Macpherson.

It wasn't always thus. In 1900, all the land except Barrenjoey Headland (which had been purchased by the government in 1881) was divided into 18 large blocks and offered for sale. None sold. Today, the average price of a Palm Beach property is a cool $3 million and every ocean view is taken; as a result, there aren't as many cabbage tree palms around as there were when they gave the place its name.

Palm Beach is worth at least a day's exploration. The community itself is reserved and somewhat haughty, but there are lots of restaurants and cafés worth stopping in at and masses of watersports on offer. If you haven't time for the road trip from the city, splash out and do it in style by seaplane. Planes fly from Rose Bay to Pittwater on the sheltered western side of the Palm Beach peninsula and companies offer sightseeing and gourmet tours.

Don't mistake Palm Beach Wharf on the western side of the peninsula for the main beach. **Palm Beach** proper is on the eastern, ocean side. At the southern end of the beach – the safest place to swim – the colonial-style buildings of the **Palm Beach Surf Club** and private **Palm Beach Pacific Club** sit majestically, their picturesque wooden balconies surrounded by stately palms. It was this beautiful corner of Australia that Governor Arthur Phillip first passed in his cutter before entering Broken Bay in 1788; a plaque commemorates his voyage. Now Palm Beach Surf Club is the club to join for wannabe

SIGHTS

Walk 2: Barrenjoey Lighthouse

Take a walk on the wild side.

Character Rugged bushland and incredible ocean views.
Length 700m (2,300ft) one way.
Difficulty Moderate.
The starting point, at the northern end of Barrenjoey Beach (on the Pittwater side), is marked by a sign next to a rust-coloured shed. There's a choice of routes to the top: the left-hand one, the Service Road, is the less steep of the two and has the best views back over Palm Beach. But don't let the short distance mislead you – you'll work up a sweat climbing to the grassy summit; a panoramic vista takes in the Pacific Ocean, Pittwater, Palm Beach and Lion Island, a deserted rocky outcrop that guards the entrance to Broken Bay. The lighthouse, built from Hawkesbury sandstone in 1881, is 113 metres (370 feet) above sea level and visible from 35 kilometres (22 miles) out at sea. It's open on Sundays (11am-3pm) for guided tours, weather permitting (9472 8949, $3; $2 reductions). Downhill takes less puff, but it's hard on the knees.

socialites in Sydney – and as a result one of the pickiest, with half the applicants turned down every year and more failing to get through the first year's strict initiation. The reason is that membership also grants you access to the prestigious **Cabbage Tree Club** and **Palm Beach Pacific Club** next door, the hangouts of Sydney's real movers and shakers, where Krug is the resident tipple and banking is the common profession. Soap fans might want to head further up to **North Palm Beach**, where, if you're lucky, the kids from *Home and Away* will be filming by the **North Palm Beach Surf Club** (ironically, one of the easiest surf clubs to join, as it's at the unfashionable end of Palmy). Right at the top of the peninsula is **Barrenjoey Head** and its historic lighthouse, which can be reached by a short but steep walk (*see above* **Walk 2**).

If the sun gets too hot – there's not much shade, particularly at the southern end of the beach – head to the wharf and take a boat trip instead. The **Palm Beach Ferry Service** (9947 2411, www.palmbeachferry.com.au) runs every day (including Christmas Day) across Pittwater to the Basin, an area within Ku-ring-gai Chase National Park (*see below*) where you can ponder some excellent Aboriginal rock carvings. Cool off afterwards with a swim in the spookily dark and seriously deep bay that gave the Basin area its name thanks to its shape.
Palm Beach & Hawkesbury River Cruises (0414 466 635, www.sydneyscenicruises.com) offers a trip that crosses Pittwater into Broken Bay, stopping at **Patonga** (a pleasant beach village) and then cruising up the beautiful lower Hawkesbury River into Cowan Waters, stopping at **Bobbin Head** for lunch. The boat leaves Palm Beach daily at 11am, returning at 3.30pm, with more cruises on weekends and during school holidays. Alternatively, splash out with **Peninsula Water Taxi** (0415 408 831), which offers bespoke cruises for up to six people.

★ Ku-ring-gai Chase National Park
NPWS office 9472 8949, www.nationalparks. nsw.gov.au. **Open** sunrise-sunset daily. **Admission** $3 arriving by boat/ferry; $2 reductions; $11 per vehicle. **Map** p321. Occupying nearly 15,000 hectares (37,000 acres) of dense forest, hidden coves and sheltered beaches where the Hawkesbury River meets the sea, Ku-ring-gai Chase National Park was awarded its designated status in 1894. It is located in one of Sydney's wealthiest municipalities, stretching from the suburbs of St Ives North and Wahroonga in the south to Broken Bay in the north. Every visitor to Sydney should take in the West Head lookout, with its views over the mouth of the Hawkesbury, the beginning of the Central Coast, Barrenjoey Lighthouse (*see above*) and Palm Beach. Walking tracks lead to significant examples of Aboriginal rock art. Guided walks and canoe and boat tours can also be arranged.

Ku-ring-gai Chase National Park.

SIGHTS

Parramatta & the West

Bursting with great stories from all over the world.

If you want to get to Sydney's multicultural heart you'll need to head west. **Parramatta** – the 'capital' of the west – boasts a historic importance that rivals any area in Sydney, and also lays claim to the city's second business district. Closer in to town, the **Sydney Olympic Park** in **Homebush Bay** was where the Aussies proudly held their 2000 Olympic Games, and they haven't forgotten it. The area has since been turned into a family-oriented sports complex, with adjacent **Newington** feeding the facilities with people, cash and the retail outlets to go with it. Further west is the Asian centre of **Cabramatta**, a food and clothes shopper's delight that draws visitors with its vibrant market life.

SIGHTS

PARRAMATTA

CityRail/RiverCat Parramatta.

Parramatta may be the gateway to the west, but it's also the geographic centre of the Sydney sprawl. There are various ways of getting here: the nicest is by RiverCat ferry from Circular Quay along the pristine Parramatta River (a laidback and very beautiful journey taking just under an hour). Those in more of a hurry can travel by train (25 to 30 minutes) or car (35 to 40 minutes).

Historically, western Sydney belonged to the Dharug, Dharawal and Gandangara people before the white settlers moved in, and the word Parramatta is, like many Sydney place names, Aboriginal in origin. At the last census of the Parramatta population just 1,201 Aboriginal

INSIDE TRACK
NOT WITHOUT A FIGHT

The Aboriginal warrior Pemulwuy kept the white people of Parramatta in fear of their lives for more than a decade before he was eventually killed in 1802 and his head sent to England.

---

and Torres Strait Islanders were counted – that's 0.8 per cent of the city's inhabitants – and the majority of these were under 50, thanks to the low life expectancy of the Aboriginal community. And while 86 per cent of the city's population was comprised of Australian citizens, English was spoken in just under 50 per cent of Parramatta homes, with Arabic, Cantonese, Mandarin, Korean and Hindi being the next most common languages.

It wasn't always like this, and Parramatta's heritage as Australia's second-oldest white settlement makes it a popular stop for historically-minded tourists. You can learn more about the area at the **Parramatta Heritage & Visitor Information Centre** (*see p110*), on the north bank of the river next to **Lennox Bridge**, which was built by convict labour in the 1830s. The centre is a short stroll from the ferry wharf via the **Riverside Walk**, designed by Aboriginal artist Jamie Eastwood and exploring the story of the Parramatta River and the traditions of the Burramatta people, Parramatta's first inhabitants.

Once known as the 'cradle city', Parramatta is the site of many Australian firsts: its first jail, land grant, successful farm (which saved the First Fleet from starvation in 1788), orchard, train line to Sydney and wool mill. Many of the first settlers were buried in **St John's**

Cemetery, on O'Connell Street between **St John's Cathedral** and **Parramatta Park**.

Parramatta also contains New South Wales' second-largest business district (after the CBD to the east), itself a dynamic mix of old and new, with towering skyscrapers next door to heritage-listed huts. **Elizabeth Farm** (*see below*), built in 1793 by wool pioneer John Macarthur and named after his wife, is the oldest colonial home still standing in Australia. Nearby is **Experiment Farm Cottage** (*see p110*), a beautiful colonial cottage built on the site of Australia's first land grant. Also open for viewing is **Old Government House** (*see p110*), the oldest public building in Australia. Standing in the grounds of spacious Parramatta Park, the spot was chosen by the colony's founding governor, Arthur Phillip, within months of the establishment of the penal settlement at Sydney Cove in January 1788, and was used by NSW governors until the new residence opened in the centre of Sydney in 1845. Old Government House and Experiment Farm Cottage are both run by the National Trust (www.nationaltrust.org.au); buy a combined admission to both and you'll also get a ten per cent discount in the visitor shops and restaurant.

Parramatta was also the site of Australia's first recorded race meeting and its first legal brewery – and Westies still love a beer and a bet. **Rosehill Gardens Racecourse** (*see p266*) on Grand Avenue is a citadel of both pursuits, particularly during the **Autumn Carnival**, when the $3.5 million Golden Slipper – the world's richest race for two-year-olds – is held. Cultural attractions include the **Parramatta Riverside Theatres** (*see p270*), three well-patronised venues that host stand-up comedy, various arts events and part of the Sydney Festival each January, as well as local plays from all over Australia. The **Roxy** (69 George Street, 9687 4219) is a hip hangout for local DJs and their fans. **PJ Gallagher's Irish Pub** (74 Church Street, 9635 8811) prides itself on being the finest drinking hole in the west (it's not, but it's not bad), while other old Parramatta pubs with character include the **Woolpack** (19 George Street, 9635 8043), which is said to be Australia's oldest licensed hotel and dating back to 1796 (though it was on a different site until 1821), the **Commercial Hotel** (2 Hassall Street, 9635 8342) and the **Albion Hotel** (135 George Street, 9891 3288), which boasts an enormous garden bar. Those seeking retail therapy during their tour of the west should head to the gargantuan mall **Westfield Parramatta** on Church Street, near the station. Pretty much everything is here – there are 528 outlets – including an 11-cinema complex popular with local teens.

Elizabeth Farm

70 Alice Street, between Arthur & Alfred streets, Rosehill (9635 9488, www.hht.net.au). CityRail Parramatta then 15min walk. **Open** 9.30am-4pm Fri-Sun. **Admission** $8; $4 reductions; $17 family. **Credit** MC, V.

Elizabeth Farm is notable both for being the birthplace of the Australian wool industry – John Macarthur imported merino sheep for breeding at the site – and for the farm's main building. With its deep, shady verandas and stone-flagged floors, it became the prototype for the Australian homestead, and parts of the original 1793 construction – the oldest surviving European building in Australia – remain. The interior has been restored to its 1830s

Ferry at **Elizabeth Farm**.

Experiment Farm Cottage.

SIGHTS

condition, with a recreated Victorian garden to match, while the museum's genteel tearooms are open from 11am to 3pm. The farm is run by the Historic Houses Trust, which looks after various museums and historic sites in Sydney.

★ Experiment Farm Cottage

9 Ruse Street, Harris Park (9635 5655, www. nsw.nationaltrust.org.au). CityRail Harris Park then 10min walk/RiverCat Parramatta then 20min walk. **Open** 10.30am-3.30pm Tue-Fri; 11am-3.30pm Sat, Sun. **Admission** $6; $4 reductions; $14 family. *Joint admission with Old Government House* $10; $7 reductions; $25 family. **Credit** (over $20) MC, V.

In 1789, Governor Phillip set up an experiment 'to know in what time a man might be able to support himself'. The guinea pig was convict James Ruse, who became wholly self-sufficient in two years and was given the colony's first land grant here as a reward, thereby becoming Australia's first private farmer. He then sold the land to a surgeon, John Harris, who built this modest cottage in 1793.

Old Government House

Parramatta Park, Parramatta (9635 8149, www.nsw.nationaltrust.org.au). CityRail/RiverCat Parramatta then 15min walk. **Open** 10am-4pm Mon-Fri; 10.30am-4pm Sat, Sun. **Admission** $9; $6 reductions; $24 family. *Joint admission with Experiment Farm Cottage* $13; $9 reductions; $35 family. **Credit** MC, V.

Set in 105 hectares (260 acres) of parkland, Old Government House was built between 1799 and 1818 on the foundations of Governor Phillip's 1790 thatched cottage, which had collapsed, and is Australia's oldest public building. At times serving as everything from a vice-regal residence to a boarding house for local schoolboys, the building has been restored to its former glory by a multi-million-dollar revamp. It also boasts the nation's most important collection of Australian colonial furniture, while the ghost tours on the third Friday evening of every month are a hoot.

Parramatta Heritage & Visitor Information Centre

346A Church Street, next to Lennox Bridge, Parramatta (8839 3311, www.parracity.nsw. gov.au). CityRail/RiverCat Parramatta then 10min walk. **Open** 9am-5pm daily.

HOMEBUSH BAY

CityRail Olympic Park/RiverCat Sydney Olympic Park.

If you've got even the tiniest sporting spark in your body, be sure to visit the site of the triumphant 2000 Olympic Games. **Sydney Olympic Park** (*see p111*) is in **Homebush Bay**, eight kilometres (five miles) east of Parramatta. The site features a huge range of sporting and entertainment facilities, including the mammoth **Acer Arena** (*see p253*) and the **Sydney Showground** (9704 1111, www.sydneyshowground.com.au), which plays host to the annual **Big Day Out** music festival (*see p253*) and other major events.

An arm of the **Parramatta River**, the bay is surrounded by 1.8 square kilometres (0.7 square miles) of wetlands, woodland and grassland, which provide sanctuary for 160 bird species. **Bicentennial Park** (open sunrise to sunset daily), the largest of the bay's five main parkland areas, is one of the best places to go for specialist birdwatching excursions. A waterbird refuge and salt marsh are out on the water, with a fine viewing tower at their north-easterly tip. You may recognise the **Brickpit**, at the park's heart,

---

INSIDE TRACK CAR CULTURE

Public transport is generally poorer in the west than in the east, so Westies tend to have a special attachment to their cars. Rev-heads love **Eastern Creek Raceway** (Brabham Drive, Eastern Creek, 9672 1000, www.eastern-creek-raceway.com), which regularly hosts touring car, motorbike and drag races.

---

as Mad Max's Thunderdome. There's a café and restaurant, and it's a pleasant spot for picnics.

Sydney Olympic Park
Visitor Centre, 1 Showground Road, at Murray Rose Avenue (9714 7888, www.sydneyolympic park.com.au). CityRail Olympic Park/RiverCat Sydney Olympic Park then bus 401. **Open** 9am-5pm daily.

If you're time-rich, hop on the most scenic route to Olympic Park: the RiverCat ferry from Circular Quay to Sydney Olympic Park (50 minutes). Bus No.401 meets the boat and takes you to the visitor centre. If you prefer to travel by train, the station you want is Olympic Park, bang in the middle of the complex – but be warned: frustratingly, there are few direct CityRail services (even when an event is being staged); your best bet is to go to Lidcombe and pick up the Sprint train from there.

To see the stadia rising out of the flat landscape as you approach is awe-inspiring. The size and scope of the biggest – ANZ Stadium – dwarfs everything else in the vicinity. The park is big but easily walkable if the weather isn't too hot; even better, you can explore by bike (for hire at the visitor centre). At the Aquatic Centre you can go for a dip, marvel at the indoor water slides and get a faint tingle of what it must be like to perform before thousands of cheering spectators (swim meets continue to be held here). It's free to visit the Sports Centre and stroll down the gallery's Hall of Champions, covering athletes from the 1890s to the present. To get into the other key venues, you'll need to take an organised tour (there are many – ask at the visitor centre). The one-hour ANZ Stadium 'Explore' tours are particularly good, including the new interactive tour, in which you follow in the footsteps of heroes of the 2000 games. Check out the website before you go; it's packed with information.

BLACKTOWN & AROUND
CityRail Blacktown.

Blacktown, located 11 kilometres (seven miles) north-west of Parramatta, earned its name from being home to the Native Institution, established by the early colonial authorities to educate Aboriginal children. Today, 2.3 per cent of the local population is Aboriginal – just over 7,000.

For a unique insight into Australian taste through the years, head north of Blacktown to historic **Rouse Hill House & Farm** (*see p112*). You can only visit the house as part of a guided tour (which don't run if the weather's bad) – it's wise to book in advance. And if you want to see native wildlife, including a face-to-face encounter with a koala, visit the excellent, family-run **Featherdale Wildlife Park** (*see p112*), home to strange-looking cassowaries and scary-looking owls.

Experiment Farm Cottage.

SIGHTS

In keeping with local tastes, western Sydney boasts more social clubs than any other suburb. League clubs, golf clubs, bowling clubs, workers' clubs, returned servicemen's clubs – they're absolutely everywhere, providing community services, cheap food and drink, and live entertainment, subsidised by row upon row of poker machines. Two of the biggest and best around here are **Blacktown Workers Club** on Campbell Street (9830 0600, www.bwcl.com.au) and **Rooty Hill RSL Club** (9625 5500, www.rootyhillrsl.com.au) on the corner of Sherbrooke and Railway Streets, in Rooty Hill.

★ Featherdale Wildlife Park

217-229 Kildare Road, Doonside (9622 1644, www.featherdale.com.au). CityRail Blacktown then bus 725. **Open** 9am-5pm daily. **Admission** $23; $12.50 reductions; $68 family; free under-3s. **Credit** AmEx, DC, MC, V.

Kangaroos, koalas and Tasmanian devils all feature in this well-kept wildlife park, which houses one of Australia's largest collections of native animals. The huge diversity of birds includes the bizarre cassowary (which lives in the rainforests in the tropical far north, but is rarely spotted by locals).

Rouse Hill House & Farm

Guntawong Road, off Windsor Road, Rouse Hill (9627 6777, www.hht.net.au). CityRail Riverstone then bus 741R or taxi. **Tours** 9.30am-4.30pm Wed-Sun. Closed in bad weather. **Admission** $8; $4 reductions; $17 family. **Credit** MC, V.

This two-storey Georgian sandstone house, set in a 15 hectare (37 acre) estate, was the home of the Rouse family for six generations. Free settler Richard Rouse built the original house between 1813 and 1818, and his last direct descendant left in 1993. There are also some 20 outbuildings, ranging from a pretty Victorian summerhouse to a corrugated iron cottage annex, and a very early 'dry weather' garden.

CABRAMATTA & BANKSTOWN

Bankstown CityRail Bankstown. Cabramatta CityRail Cabramatta.

INSIDE TRACK GRITTY FILMS

For a grittily honest portrayal of the lives of the homeless and disadvantaged in the Asian centre of Sydney, check out local director Khoa Do's no-holds-barred film *The Finished People* (2003), star-studded, downbeat drama *Little Fish* (2005), starring Cate Blanchett and Hugo Weaving and *Cedar Boys* and *The Combination* (2009, both dealing in youthful Lebanese gang life in the west).

Cabramatta, **Bankstown** and their neighbours comprise the country's multicultural heartland. Given Sydney's dominance over Australia's other state capitals, it's hardly surprising that it remains the most popular destination for immigrants entering Australia, and the vast majority of them go to live in the western suburbs. In some south-western suburbs, more than half the population was born overseas, with residents hailing from Italy, Greece, Vietnam, Cambodia, the Philippines, China, Serbia, Croatia, Poland, Latin America, Lebanon and the Pacific Islands.

One of the consequences of this multicultural mix is that there's high-quality, inexpensive dining to be had – Cabramatta in particular has developed a name for itself as the culinary centre of the western suburbs. It also suffers from a reputation as heroin central in Sydney thanks to the proliferation of Asian gangs, and tends to hit the headlines for drug- and gang-related deaths. For all that, it's important to keep things in perspective when visiting Cabramatta. True, as a casual tourist, you should remain vigilant and savvy when wandering about – it's better to visit during the day than after dark – but don't let the negative press affect your opinion. If you like dining and shopping, don't miss the area's exotic mix of Aussie suburbia. From Cabramatta CityRail station, cross over the road to Arthur Street and pass through the ornate Pai Lau Gate into **Freedom Plaza**, the main marketplace. It's like stepping into Asia itself, with the authentic flavours of Thai, Laotian, Cambodian, Filipino and Chinese cuisines on offer at numerous stalls. There are plenty of discount fabric, clothing and jewellery dealers too: on Park Road, John Street, Hughes Street and around the main plaza, direct importers and wholesalers ply their wares in typical Asian bazaar fashion (haggling is the norm). Other attractions are the nearby **Tien Hau** and **Kwan Zin** Buddhist temples.

The best time to visit is when the Chinese and Vietnamese communities hold their **New Year** celebrations (around February), with wild dragon parades and more firecrackers than you can shake a match at. Some lucky visitors may experience the annual **Moon Festival**, held on the 15th day of the eighth lunar month – August or September, depending on the year.

Sport is a key feature of life in the west too. It's thanks to the high number of immigrants that soccer is a bigger sport than rugby in this part of the city. Sydney soccer fans follow their teams with a fiery passion based along ethnic lines, and the games can be boisterous and spectacular affairs. Local teams in the NSW premier league include the Parramatta Eagles, Marconi Stallions, Blacktown City Demons and Bankstown City Lions. Bankstown is also the

Cabramatta.

home town of the famous cricketing Waugh brothers, and boasts an impressive cricket team, which you can catch on summer weekends at the **Bankstown Oval** (corner of Chapel Road South and Macauley Avenue).

PENRITH

CityRail Penrith.

At the foot of the Blue Mountains and perched on the banks of the Nepean River, **Penrith** lies 50 kilometres (31 miles) west of central Sydney. It's a sprawling modern suburb distinguished by beautiful rural and bushland scenery as well as history and modern culture.

At its heart is Panthers, Australia's largest licensed club, and the rugby league team it supports. The huge **Panthers World of Entertainment** on Mulgoa Road (4720 5555, www.panthersworld.com.au) resembles an Antipodean Butlins resort; you'll find a vast array of 24-hour bars, restaurants, nightclubs, gaming facilities and music performances as well as a motel, swimming pools, water-skiing, water slides, tennis courts, beach volleyball, a driving range and more. This staggering creation rakes in more than $100 million a year, with profits being ploughed back into the rugby club and the community. You might catch the Panthers training at winter weekends in **Penrith Park**, just opposite the club centre. Or try to attend one of their home games in **Penrith Stadium** against one of the western suburbs' other first-class rugby league teams, the Parramatta Eels, the Bulldogs or the Wests Tigers.

Penrith also offers dogs and trots at **Penrith Paceway** (corner of Ransley and Station Streets, 4721 2375, www.harness.org.au/ penrith). On a more cultural note, there's the long-running and well-respected **Q Theatre Company** (www.railwaystreet.com.au), with which Toni Colette made her professional stage debut in 1990; the company moved into its new home, the striking, glass-fronted **Joan Sutherland Performing Arts Centre** (597 High Street, 4723 7611, www.jspac.com.au), at the end of 2005. Also worthy of your time is the beautiful **Penrith Regional Art Gallery** (86 River Road, Emu Plains, 4735 1100, www.penrithregionalgallery.org).

If you want to get away from urban life for a bit, you'll find a waterborne solution in the form of the historic paddle-wheeler **Nepean Belle** (The Jetty, Tench Avenue, 4733 1274, www.nepeanbelle.com.au), which offers lunch and dinner cruises up the spectacular **Nepean Gorge**. The Penrith area is also home to several vineyards, among them **Vicary's Winery** in Luddenham (The Northern Road, 4773 4161, www.vicaryswinery.com.au): Sydney's oldest working winery, it runs wine tastings (9am-5pm Tue-Fri, 11am-5pm Sat, Sun) and uses a converted woolshed for weekend bush dances ($48-$57, book well in advance). North of Penrith, the Nepean River becomes the **Hawkesbury River**, which forms the lifeline of another unique part of western Sydney. For the historic towns of Richmond and Windsor, the **Ku-ring-gai Chase National Park**, and more on the delights of the Hawkesbury, *see p106.*

SIGHTS

The South

Broad beaches, bright cars, blonde hair.

As Sydneysiders search for their own piece of beachside paradise, the south is coming into its own. Here houses are bigger, prices are lower and there's more of a family vibe. The south starts at Greek community hub **Brighton-le-Sands** in the district of Rockdale before extending into a very cliquey district known as 'the Shire' and inhabited by people who call themselves 'the locals'. **Cronulla** is the stronghold of the Shire, championing a lifestyle of sun, sea, surf and anything (preferably motorised) that allows you to travel on water. Across Port Hacking from Cronulla is the former pirate's grotto turned artists' colony of **Bundeena**. Here, inside the **Royal National Park**, life carries on as normal – with private picnics, swimming spots and much home- and pool-building.

BRIGHTON-LE-SANDS

Kurnell *CityRail Cronulla then bus 987.*
Brighton-le-Sands *CityRail Rockdale then bus 475, 478, 479.*

From the air, the first thing you notice about Brighton-le-Sands is the oversized pyramid of the **Novotel** (*see p145*). Set on the west side of **Botany Bay**, just below the airport, this hulking hotel doesn't look much prettier from the ground. Fortunately, the swankier end of the Greek community is bent on transforming the car-laden beachfront drag of **Grand Parade** into, well, a grand parade, and has lined it with sleek cafés – anyone familiar with the coastline near Athens will have some idea what they're aiming for. On Friday and Saturday evenings and all day Sunday, Grand Parade is bumper to bumper with traffic and crowds visiting the

eating and drinking establishments of 'Little Athens'. The stretch starts at the north end with **Gecko** (no.18, 9567 3344), a chic indoor and outdoor café. Nearby is **Mezes** (no.36, 9567 2865), equal parts café, restaurant and ice-cream bar and understandably popular with a young crowd. Further down, **Eurobay** (no.86, 9597 3300) goes for an ultra-smooth, Greco-Italian blend of food and style, while nearby restaurant and café **Kamari** (no.82, 9556 2533) is more rustic, with whitewashed walls and sleek terracotta floors.

The cafés and restaurants along Bay Street around the corner attract a slightly older and more glamorous Greek crowd. There's **One Bay** (Shop 1, 376 Bay Street, 9599 5775) and **Zande Brasserie** (Shop 2, 376 Bay Street, 9567 6475). The most upmarket restaurant (price-wise, if not style-wise) is **Le Sands** (Grand Parade, 9599 2128) with its panoramic views of Botany Bay – never mind the planes landing to the left and the pipes and towers of the oil refinery to the right. To learn more about the beginnings of colonial Australia, head south around the bay to the tip of **Kurnell Peninsula**, where the British first landed in 1770. Under the command of James Cook, and with botanist Joseph Banks leading a party of scientists, the crew of HMS *Endeavour* spent a week exploring the area and recording information on the flora and fauna they found (hence the bay's name). **Captain Cook's Landing Place** is now a regular school excursion: on weekdays, it's crowded with children visiting the **Cook Obelisk**, **Cook's Well** and **Landing Rock**. To find out more about the history of the area and the young colony, visit the **Discovery Centre** (Captain Cook Drive, Botany Bay National Park, 9668 9111, 11am-3pm Mon-Fri, 10am-4.30pm Sat, Sun, $7 per car).

CRONULLA

CityRail Cronulla.

It helps to have 'the look' when you're visiting **Cronulla Beach**. This largely revolves around a tan, blonde hair and as little clothing as modesty will allow – imagine the love children of Jessica Simpson and David Hasselhoff. Alternatively, you might prefer to hang with the multicultural Sunday crowd picnicking beneath the trees. And don't let the legacy of the 2005 riots put you off – the locals are friendly.

Cronulla is a much longer beach than its more famous city counterparts Bondi, Coogee, Clovelly and Maroubra. It takes at least four hours to walk its length from South Cronulla northwards to Green Hills and beyond. There's also a walking track that starts at the end of South Cronulla and wends its way southwards around the cliff of **Port Hacking**, past sea pools to **Darook Park**, where you can swim in calm, clear water. Halfway along the track is **Bass and Flinders Point**: from here you can stare across the water to **Jibbon Beach** in Bundeena on the edge of the Royal National Park (*see p116*).

Serious surfers like to head to the northern end, to **Eloura**, **Wanda** and **Green Hills** beaches, where there's often the background churn of 4WDs playing on the sand dunes behind the beach. Revs are big in these parts – especially on the water. Jet skis, speedboats and waterskiers create chaos in the otherwise sleepy arms of the Port Hacking river every weekend. For more water action, contact **Cronulla Surf School** (9544 0895, www.cronullasurf.com.au) for surfing lessons, or **Pro Dive** (9544 2200, www.prodivecronulla.com) to discover what lies beneath the waves.

In Cronulla itself, the pedestrianised strip of **Cronulla Street** is jammed with surf shops. For great coffee and corn cakes, duck into gourmet deli **Surfeit** (2 Surf Road, 9523 3873) – you might even see swimming supremo Ian Thorpe having breakfast here. Better coffee still can be found closer to the beach at **Grind** (20-26 the Kingsway, 9527 3100) or at **HAM** (8521 7219, 3/17 Gerrale Street), a friendly café owned by brothers Harry and Mario Kapoulas and fuelled by their mum, Kitty, whose fruit-studded muffins are second only to her home-country *spanakopita* and baklava.

If your wallet stretches to city prices, head to **Summer Salt** (Elouera Surf Club, 66 Mitchell Road, 9523 2366) for uninterrupted beach views and a mix of tapas and seafood. More city chic can be found at Mod Oz mecca the **Nun's Pool** (103 Ewos Parade, 9523 3395), named after a little rock pool across the road through Shelley Park. On the Kingsway, views can be found at mid-market prices at **Stonefish** (Nos.8-18, 9544 3046), which offers a mix of stir-fries, steaks and

SIGHTS

Wattamolla Beach, Royal National Park, Bundeena. *See p116.*

seafood, while **Bella Costa** (9544 3223), in the same complex, specialises in modern Italian. The **Naked Grape** on Gerrale Street just off the Kingsway (Nos.59-65, 9527 7729) has become a hit with local foodies who come for its swish contemporary cuisine. It's also worth hiking up the road to **Peter Michael's Seafood** (no.47, 9544 0033) for first-rate seafood kebabs and grills; if you're in the mood for Lebanese food, opposite the train station is the top-notch **Cedars Corner** (138 Cronulla Street, 9527 0488).

On summer nights, the electric-coloured interiors of **Northies Cronulla Hotel** (corner of Elouera Road and the Kingsway, 9523 6866, www.northies.com.au) spill over with energy. For a slower vibe, try **Brass Monkey** (115A Cronulla Street, 9544 3844), which hosts live jazz and blues bands.

BUNDEENA & AROUND

CityRail Cronulla then ferry Bundeena.

A 20-minute ferry ride from Cronulla's Tonkin Street wharf across Port Hacking delivers you to **Bundeena**, a small township (population 2,300, of which about a quarter is under 18 years old) that spreads out along the top of the north-eastern section of the **Royal National Park** (*see below*). Established in 1879, this was Australia's first national park – and only the second in the world after Yellowstone in the US. Covering 150 square kilometres (58 square miles) on the southern boundary of the Sydney metropolitan area, it offers stunning coastline, rainforest, open wetlands, estuaries and heath.

Bundeena, which means 'noise like thunder' in the local Aboriginal language, was named after the sound of the surf pounding on the east coast. The Aboriginal Dharawal people used the area as a camping ground, and were sometimes joined by other large clans for feasting and ceremonies. In the 1820s, white settlers arrived in 'the Village', as locals call Bundeena, to build a few fishing shacks. More came during the 1930s Depression, but it was only after World War II that a substantial number of permanent houses and holiday homes began to appear.

There are three main beaches, two of which fall within the national park. The main strip of sand is **Hordens Beach**, which you'll see to your right as you approach by ferry. If you walk up the hill from the wharf you'll find a small supermarket, a newsagent, a couple of inexpensive cafés and a fish and chip shop, the best of which is **Passionfruit Café** (48 Brighton Street, 9527 6555) – its pies are the duck's nuts.

To reach **Jibbon Beach**, walk left from the ferry, past a toilet block and the **RSL club**, which serves very cheap drinks with brilliant

views and where head chef Wayne Walsh serves up Med fare in the rather civilised restaurant **SaltBush** (open noon-4pm, 6-10pm Fri-Sun) and equally tasty treats in the accompanying brasserie (open noon-9pm daily; both 9527 7850). Follow the road to its end, turn downhill and go through a cutting to the magnificent orange-sand beach. At the far end, hop up the rocks and take the track through the bush to **Jibbon Head**, about 20 minutes away, where there are awe-inspiring views out to sea. A sign en route points to Aboriginal rock carvings of whales and fish. From Jibbon Head you can walk further down the coast on a well-worn track; it's about a three-hour return walk to **Marley Beach**, or six hours to **Wattamolla**. Take plenty of water, sunscreen and insect repellent in summer. The third beach, **Bonnie Vale**, is to the right just before you leave the village; you can walk to it in about 15 minutes via Bundeena Drive. Edged by swamp and ponds, it's an exceptionally long and pristine beach, with shallow water that's ideal for kids.

The ferry to Bundeena leaves Cronulla every hour on the half-hour between 5.30am and 6.30pm on weekdays (there's no 12.30pm service), returning on the hour from 6am to 7pm. On weekends, the first ferry leaves at 8.30am and the last returns at 7pm. It costs $5.70 ($2.85 reductions; $17 family) each way. It's around a 20-minute drive to Bundeena through the national park if you come by road – about an hour in total from the city.

★ Royal National Park
9542 0648, www2.nationalparks.nsw.gov.au. **Open** *Park* 7am-8.30pm daily. *Visitor centre* 9.30am-4.30pm Mon-Fri; 8.30am-4.30pm Sat, Sun. **Admission** $11 per vehicle (free if you're visiting Bundeena and Maianbar).
You can get to the Royal by following walking paths from various nearby CityRail stations – Engadine, Heathcote, Loftus, Otford, Waterfall – but driving is the easiest way to explore its vast expanse. The park's nerve centre is at Audley, on the Hacking River, once the heart of the park's Victorian 'pleasure gardens'. There you'll find the main visitor centre, spacious lawns, an old-fashioned dance hall and a causeway. You can hire a canoe or rowing boat from the Audley boathouse and head upstream to picnic spots at Ironbark Flat or Wattle Forest. If you're a surfer, Garie Beach provides the waves, while further south is Werrong Beach, which is located among littoral rainforest and is the park's only authorised nude bathing spot. At secluded Wattamolla Beach you can often see migrating whales. Walking trails include Lady Carrington Drive, an easy 10km (six-mile) track along the Hacking River, and the more arduous 26km (16-mile) Coast Track, which hugs the coastline from Bundeena to Otford.

Sydney's Best Beaches

Surf City, here we come...

Summer, winter, after school, after work, with a bunch of mates or just plain solo, beaches are where Sydneysiders head to cool off and get zen. And with more than 50 beaches along Sydney's coastline, from flash-as-a-rat-with-a-gold-tooth **Palm Beach** in the north to family-magnet **Cronulla** in the south, each one has its own character. The protected harbour beaches inside the **Heads** are smaller and have no surf, but are great for views and picnics – after heavy rain they're not ideal for swimming though, as pollution floats in through the storm pipes. Instead, locals

often take their daily dip in the outdoor seawater pools cut into the rocks on many beaches – both harbour and ocean. The bigger, bolder ocean beaches attract hordes of surfers and serious swimmers.

BEACH BASICS

From September to May, nearly all Sydney's ocean beaches are patrolled at weekends by local volunteer lifesavers and during the week by lifeguards – hours vary with the beach. The famous surf lifesavers wear red and yellow uniforms and an unmistakeable skullcap. The council-paid lifeguards wear different colours – usually a more sober blue or green – and in surfing hot spots work 365 days a year; their exploits frequently the subject of reality television shows like *Bondi Rescue*.

Locals love to fish but these days you need a licence and there are catch ankd size limits. Dropping rubbish is also an offence – 'Don't be a tosser, take your rubbish with you!' is the motto – and recycling encouraged. Don't expect to find deckchair touts, donkeys or even ice-cream sellers. Sydneysiders are protective of their unspoilt beaches and intend to keep them that way.

WATER TEMPERATURES

The water at Sydney beaches can turn icy without warning, so take the following as a guide only. As a general rule, the water temperature lags a few months behind the air temperature. So when the weather is warming up in October and

November, the ocean is still holding its winter chill of 16-17°C (61-63°F). Only in December does the sea become a nicely swimmable 18-19°C (64-66°F). The ocean is a balmy 20-21°C (68-70°F) from February to April, sometimes until May. It can even reach 23-24°C (73-75°F) if there's a warm current running from the north.

Below are Sydney's best beaches: the harbour beaches are listed from east to west; the northern ocean beaches heading north; and the southern ocean beaches heading south. Orange numbers given in this chapter correspond to the location of each beach as marked on the Greater Sydney map on p321 or the Sydney Harbour map on pp322-323. There's also a more detailed map of the northern beaches on p334.

For more information on many of the beaches listed here, see the relevant Sightseeing chapters. For information on the latest surfing conditions, visit www.coastalwatch.com.

HARBOUR BEACHES

South

Shark Beach
Nielsen Park, Vaucluse Road, Vaucluse. Bus 325.
Map p323 ③④

Bondi Beach.

Locals swim in the smooth warm waters of this sheltered harbour inlet all year round. In summer, it's as packed as an Australian beach can get, with families swarming on the narrow 300m beach or picnicking in the shade of the Moreton Bay fig trees on the grassy slopes. Part of leafy Nielsen Park, the beach also boasts fabulous views of Manly, Shark Island (hence its name) and, from the upper parklands, the Harbour Bridge. If you don't swim, you can watch the ferries, yachts, kayakers, seaplanes and oil tankers vie for space in the harbour, or you could just grab a bite to eat. Nielsen Park (9337 7333), an Italian restaurant that's been serving since 1914, offers trattoria fare when it's not booked out for a wedding. More informal is its licensed café next door, which serves pizzas, wraps, ice-creams and excellent coffee – just be prepared to queue.
Services *Café. Changing rooms. Child-friendly. No dogs. Parking. Picnic area. Restaurant. Shade. Shark net (Sept-May). Showers. Toilets.*

★ **Parsley Bay**
Horler Avenue, Vaucluse. Bus 325. **Map** p323 ㉙
It's the grass, not the tiny beach, that is the big draw here. Nestled at the foot of a steep (and sometimes treacherous) road of million-dollar mansions, the bay is part of a 5.7-hectare (14-acre) nature reserve with its own ranger and an abundance of birds, fish and insects. It's great for small children, who can play safely on the lawns and in the well-equipped recreation area, and there are excellent walks through the bush and even across a rickety suspension bridge over the water. The small crescent-shaped beach (roughly 70m long) leads into what are often murky waters: after heavy rain, rubbish floats into the bay from storm pipes. Nevertheless, the millpond-like swimming area is popular with snorkellers and scuba divers thanks to its array of tropical fish.
Services *Café (closes 4pm). Changing rooms. Child-friendly (play area). No dogs. Parking. Picnic area. Shade. Shark net (removed for repairs 1mth winter). Showers. Toilets.*

Camp Cove
Victoria Street, Watsons Bay. Ferry Watsons Bay/bus 324, 325, 380, L24. **Map** p323 ❹
Serious sun-seekers love this 200m strip of bright yellow sand, which runs in a thin curve against a backdrop of designer cottages. The beach is not particularly great for surfing, but it's a fine place for a dip and provides fabulous views of the city's skyscrapers. At the southern end of the upper grasslands is the start of the South Head Heritage Trail. Camp Cove has one small kiosk serving sandwiches, coffee and ice-creams. Although the beach does have a dedicated parking area, spaces are at a huge premium; far better to come by ferry to Watsons Bay and walk around the corner.
Services *Café (Oct-May). Lifesavers (Oct-May). No dogs. Parking. Toilets.*

Lady Bay Beach
Victoria & Cliff Streets, Watsons Bay. Ferry Watsons Bay/bus 324, 325, 380, L24. **Map** p323 ㉒
Sydney's first nudist beach, Lady Bay is just below South Head and a short walk along the South Head Heritage Trail from Camp Cove. Steep iron steps lead down to the 100m beach, which is reduced to virtually nothing when the tide comes in: you're better off sunbathing on one of the rocks. It's popular as a pick-up place for gay men, but Lady Bay offers scenic as well as sexual thrills, including spectacular views of the city and, if you walk around the headland to Hornby Lighthouse, the open sea to the east (it's actually the last southern beach inside the harbour).
Services *No dogs. Toilets (located on the clifftop above beach).*

North

★ **Balmoral Beach**
The Esplanade, Balmoral. Ferry South Mosman (Musgrave Street) then bus 233/ferry Taronga Zoo then bus 238. **Map** p323 ❶

SIGHTS

Home to Sydney's seriously rich, Balmoral has been a popular bathing spot since the late 1900s. Its beach promenade and Bathers' Pavilion (now one of Sydney's most sought-after eateries, *see p173*) were both built in the late 1920s and retain a genteel air from that era. Hundreds of families flock here at weekends to enjoy the sheltered waters of its two large sandy beaches, which together stretch for about a mile. The beaches are separated by Rocky Point, a tree-covered picnicking island accessible by a footbridge. To the south, Balmoral Beach has an enclosed swimming area surrounded by boardwalks and is excellent for children; to the north, Edwards Beach is bigger and less protected, but has interesting rock pools with shells, fish and anemones. You can hire boats from Balmoral Boathouse. The white rotunda, which is often used for weddings, also acts as a stage for Shakespeare by the Sea, a short season of the Bard's work performed on summer evenings (www.shakespeare-by-the-sea.com).
Services *Boat hire. Cafés. Changing rooms. Child-friendly (play area). Danger: underwater rocks. No dogs. Parking. Picnic areas. Restaurants. Shade. Shark nets. Shops. Showers. Toilets.*

★ Chinamans Beach
McLean Crescent, Mosman. Bus 175, 178, 185, 229, 249. **Map** p323 ❻
A real Sydney secret, Chinamans Beach in Middle Harbour is stumbled upon through dunes on the edge of the Rosherville bushland reserve. It's a quiet paradise, with 300m of beautiful sand, gently lapping waters and huge, strikingly designed homes perched on the hills above. Located right opposite busier Clontarf Beach, Chinamans has plenty of recreational facilities – a play area, picnic tables nestled under pepper trees, and rolling lawns where you can play ball games – but no shop, café or restaurant. Children love the mass of barnacle-encrusted rock pools at the southern end, but there's a $500 fine for taking any crustaceans home.
Services *Changing rooms. Child-friendly (play area). No dogs. Parking. Picnic area. Shade. Showers. Toilets.*

Clontarf Beach
Sandy Bay Road, Clontarf. Bus 171, E71. **Map** p323 ❽
With around 600m of sand, a large grassy picnic area, an excellent playground, an outdoor netted pool and all the facilities you might need, Clontarf is a very popular beach location for families. It's situated right opposite the Middle Harbour Yacht Club, so there are good views of the Spit Bridge with boats sailing underneath and cars racing over the top. It's worth stopping at Balgowlah Heights en route to pick up a picnic – the fantastic Balgowlah Heights Deli on Beatrice Street (No.122, 9949 3969) is open from 7am to 7pm daily.
Services *Barbecues. Café. Changing rooms. Child-friendly (play area). No dogs. Parking.*

Picnic area. Pool. Restaurant (closed July). Shade. Shark net (Sept-May). Showers. Toilets.

OCEAN BEACHES
East

Bondi Beach
Campbell Parade, Bondi Beach. CityRail Bondi Junction then bus 380, 381, 382, 333, X84/bus 222, 380, 389, 333. **Map** p323 ❷
Australia's most famous beach, Bondi is believed to have been named after an Aboriginal word meaning 'the sound of breaking waves'. Today, its crashing breakers attract a huge fraternity of urban surfies as well as ubiquitous Britpackers and new-generation hippies strumming guitars on the sand. At the height of summer, the beach draws up to 40,000 people per day, but, and you'll be hard put to believe this if you arrive when it's crowded, there are times in the week when it's relatively empty. The elegant Bondi Pavilion, built in 1929 as a changing area, houses showers, toilets, a community centre and cafés. Two lifesaving clubs patrol the half-mile beach – 'Ready Aye Ready' is the motto of the North Bondi Surf Life Saving Club. The central area near the Pavilion is the safest swimming area; surfers favour the southern end, with its strong rips. Also at this end is a skateboard ramp and the famous Bondi Icebergs' pool and club. Be vigilant: 'Thieves go to the beach too', warn big NSW police signs. Lockers are available in the Pavilion – use them. For a local area map, *see p334.*
Services *Barbecues. Cafés. Changing rooms. Child-friendly (play area). Lifeguards/savers. No dogs. Parking. Picnic area. Pool. Restaurants. Shark net (Sept-May). Shops. Showers. Toilets.*

Tamarama Beach
Pacific Avenue, Tamarama. CityRail Bondi Junction then bus 361. **Map** p323 ❿
A 100m sheltered cove, Tamarama Beach is neither easy to get to by public transport nor to park at should you decide to drive there. Not only that, once you arrive, it's not particularly accessible either: you have to climb down 40 steep steps to reach the water. And with its tricky surf and deep rip, it's not a swimming spot. That said, it's got a serious fan base of

---

INSIDE TRACK AUSSIE RULES

Rules on Sydney's beaches are stringent: no alcohol or fires, and on many beaches ball games, skateboards, in-line skaters, kites and frisbees are also illegal. There's no Smoking, either, on many beaches, including Bondi. That said, rules are regularly flouted by 'no worries, she'll be right' regulars, especially off-season.

SIGHTS

macho surfers who like to live dangerously and equally dedicated sun-seekers (there's absolutely no shade to be found on the sand). Britpackers play Sunday soccer matches on the large grassy picnic area and volleyball is the sport on the beach itself. The small children's play area with swings and a slide is within eyeshot of the excellent Tama Café (9130 2419), which serves wonderful gourmet vegetarian and non-vegetarian sandwiches as well as refreshing power juices and coffee.

Services *Barbecue. Café. Changing rooms. Child-friendly (play area). Danger: underwater rocks. Lifeguards/savers (Sept-May). No dogs. Parking. Picnic area. Shark net (Sept-May). Showers. Toilets.*

Bronte Beach

Bronte Road, Bronte. CityRail Bondi Junction then bus 378. **Map** p323 ❸

Bronte is absolute bliss for parents – pack the kids, the swimsuits and the boogie boards, and this 300m stretch of sand (complete with cute kids' train) will babysit all day long. Though the water has a strong rip and is great for surfing, the outdoor Bronte Baths at the southern end – and the adjacent community centre – are the preserve of kids. There's plenty of shade under the sandstone rocks and scores of covered picnic benches (some with inlaid chessboards) on which to enjoy the Aussie tucker served at the Bronte Kiosk on the beach – meat pies and hot chips aplenty. For more sophisticated dining options try Bronte Road for anything from from sushi to gourmet salads, and from fish and chips to Mediterranean treats.

Services *Barbecues. Cafés. Changing rooms. Child-friendly (play area). Danger: underwater rocks. Lifeguards/savers (Sept-May). No dogs. Parking. Picnic area. Pool. Restaurants. Shade. Shark net (Sept-May). Shops. Showers. Toilets.*

★ Clovelly Beach

Clovelly Road, Clovelly. CityRail Bondi Junction then bus 360/bus 339, X39. **Map** p323 ❾

Once known as Little Coogee, tucked as it is around the corner from the more famous Big Coogee (which is now simply Coogee Beach; *see below*), Clovelly is an idyllic spot, swathed in natural beauty. The tiny square of sand slopes into a long inlet of calm water, surrounded by a boardwalk and a concrete promenade with chic barbecue pavilions and picnic tables. It's a favourite with scuba divers and snorkellers, but it's the wheelchair access that weaves the real magic. The Clovelly Bay boardwalk boasts specific entry points to the water with locking devices for a submersible wheelchair, on loan from the Beach Inspector's office (weekdays) or the SLSC (weekends). On the south promenade sits a chic 25m three-lane lap pool, built in 1962 and nicely revamped in 2002. There's also a good café, Seasalt (9664 5344), which serves fish and chips at the takeaway kiosk and more exotic fare at the tables.

Services *Barbecues. Café. Changing rooms. Child-friendly. Lifeguards/savers (Sept-May). No dogs. Parking. Picnic area. Pool. Restaurant. Shade. Showers. Toilets. Wheelchair access.*

South

Coogee Beach

Beach Street, Coogee. CityRail Bondi Junction then bus 313, 314/bus 372, 373, 374, X73, X74. **Map** p323 ⓬

This excellent family swimming beach is 400m long, with old-fashioned pools carved into the rocks at both ends. In 1929, it was declared Australia's first shark-proof beach when nets were introduced. It's not great for surfing, but at least you don't have to worry about getting hit by boards. There are fast-food restaurants aplenty, cafés and places to picnic, and it's very much a tourist attraction. In 2003, the northern headland was renamed Dolphin Point in memory of the six Coogee Dolphins rugby league players who were killed in the Bali bombings. Two memorial plaques, plastered with photographs, list the 26 victims from the local community (from a total Australian death toll of 88).

Services *Barbecues. Cafés. Changing rooms. Child-friendly. Lifeguards/savers. No dogs. Parking. Picnic area. Pools. Restaurants. Shade. Shark net (Sept-May). Shops. Showers. Toilets.*

★ Maroubra Beach

Marine Parade, Maroubra. CityRail Bondi Junction then bus 317, 353. Bus 376, 377, 395, 396, X77, X96. **Map** p323 ❾

Maroubra Beach was chosen as the new headquarters for Surfing NSW in 2003 – which didn't come as much of a surprise, since the waves are huge here and it's long been a top surf spot. All the outfit's coaching, judging, educational and safety programmes are conducted at the 1.1km (0.7-mile) beach. The Safe Surf School (9365 4370, www.safesurfschools.com.au) is a perfect place for children to learn how to surf away from all the crowds. Much less touristy than neighbouring Coogee, it's also a favourite with beach sprinters who run through the shallows in their Speedos. There are a few local shops, showers and toilets, a well-equipped kids' play area and a sizeable skatepark (which is packed when school's out) located next to the beach's windswept dunes.

Services *Barbecues. Cafés. Changing rooms. Child-friendly (play area). Lifeguards/savers. No dogs. Parking. Picnic area. Pool. Restaurants. Shark net (Sept-May). Shops. Showers. Toilets.*

Cronulla Beach

Mitchell Road, Cronulla. CityRail Cronulla. **Map** p321 ❺

A vast sandy beach more than 6km (3.75 miles) long, Cronulla had a flash of worldwide notoriety in December 2005 as a battleground between groups

Sea Safety

It's best to admire Sydney's lifeguards from a distance.

TO THE RESCUE

Each year Sydney's famed surf lifesavers carry out countless rescue operations. A disproportionate number of these rescues are of foreigners who have underestimated the 'rips' (currents) in the surf. Waves at Sydney's ocean beaches can be up to four metres (13 feet) high and conceal powerful rips. More often, they are less than one metre; at Bondi and Manly, they're somewhere in between. To be safe, always swim between the red and yellow flags that the lifesavers plant in the sand each day. If you stray outside the flags, the lifesavers will blow whistles and scream through megaphones at you. And don't think shallow water is completely safe. 'Dumpers' are waves that break with force, usually at low tide in shallow water, and can cause serious injury. Waves that don't break at all (surging waves) can knock swimmers over too and drag them out to sea. Finally, remember that alcohol and water don't mix – most of the adults who drown in NSW are under the influence. If you do get caught by a rip and you're a confident swimmer, try to swim diagonally across the rip. Otherwise, stay calm, stick your hand in the air to signal to a lifeguard and float until you're rescued: don't fight the current by swimming toward shore.

SHARK THINKING

Shark attacks are very rare. In the past 20 years only one person in all NSW has been killed by a shark attack, and the last fatal attack in Sydney harbour was way back in 1963. It's true there have been more sharks seen in recent years, but this is because better sewage methods have made the beaches much cleaner and so more palatable to sharks. That said, the closest most people get to a shark is in an aquarium: since beach swimming became popular, sharks have tended to shy away. A lot of Sydney's beaches are shark-netted. The nets are usually around 150 metres long, seven deep and are anchored to the sea floor within 500 metres of the shore. You won't spot them because they are always dropped in ten metre-deep water ensuring three metres (ten feet) of clearance for swimmers and surfers.

The nets are meant not so much as a physical block to sharks but to prevent them establishing a habitat close to shore. If you do see a shark while swimming, try not to panic: just swim calmly to shore. Easier said than done, yes, but keep in mind that sharks are attracted to jerky movements. 'However,' say the experts at Taronga Zoo, 'if a shark gets close then any action you take may disrupt the attack pattern, such as hitting the shark's nose, gouging at its eyes, making sudden movements and blowing bubbles.' Scared? Honestly, it hardly ever happens.

STINGERS

Two kinds of jellyfish are common on Sydney's beaches in summer. The jimble (a less potent southern relative of the deadly box jellyfish) is box-shaped with four pink tentacles. It is often found at the harbour beaches. On the ocean beaches you're more likely to come across bluebottle jellyfish (aka Portuguese man-of-war), which has long blue tentacles and tends to appear only when an onshore wind is blowing. Jimbles can deliver a painful sting but are not dangerous; bluebottles are nastier, causing an intense, longer-lasting pain, red, whip-like lesions and, occasionally, respiratory problems. Even dead bluebottles on the beach can sting, so don't touch them.

Treatment for each is different. If stung by a jimble, wash the affected area with vinegar (lifeguards and lifesavers keep stocks of it) – or, if you can, pee on it – gently remove any tentacles with tweezers or gloves, and apply ice to relieve the pain. If stung by a bluebottle, leave the water immediately, don't rub the skin and don't apply vinegar; instead use an ice pack or anaesthetic spray. The tentacles should be wiped off with a towel not pulled off with your fingers.

of white and Middle Eastern Australians. To Sydneysiders, though, it has long been the south's most popular surfing and swimming spot. Cronulla isn't actually one beach but a whole series, running from Kurnell on Botany Bay at the northern end through Wanda, Elouera, North Cronulla, South Cronulla and on down to Shelly and Port Hacking in the south. On the surfing front Cronulla Point has lots of breaks off three reef ledges and pros like to attempt Shark Island, the area's most notorious break. The southern end, a half-moon patch of sand around 100m long, patrolled by a lifeguard all year round, has less of a rip and is family territory for bathing, fossicking in the rock pools or swimming indoors at the Cronulla Sports Complex (located next to the lifesavers' hut). The much longer northern end of the beach has a fiercer undertow and views of a not-so-pretty oil refinery. There's a huge grassy picnic area with plenty of tables and an esplanade walkway. Getting to Cronulla from the city takes about 50 minutes by train or an hour by car.

Services *Cafés. Changing rooms. Child-friendly (play area). Lifeguards/savers (south all year round; north Sept-May). No dogs. Parking. Picnic area. Pools. Restaurants. Shade. Shark net (Sept-May). Shops. Showers. Toilets.*

North

★ Shelly Beach
Marine Parade, Manly. Ferry Manly.
Map p323 ⑥
A ten-minute stroll south of Manly, small Shelly Beach is a family delight with yellow sand, gentle waters and a grassy picnic area. As you stroll south along the promenade from Manly, don't miss the Fairy Bower ocean pool, an excellent outdoor rock pool with spectacular views of the coastline and its famous sculptures (*Sea Nymphs* by artist Helen Leete). Set in Cabbage Tree Bay, Shelly Beach is best known for its good swimming conditions, but it is also popular with novice scuba divers testing the deep and for seekers of quality surf; Shelly is the paddle out spot for the Bower – one of Australia's better big wave locations.

Services *Barbecue. Café. Changing rooms. Child-friendly. No dogs. Parking. Picnic area. Restaurant (closed winter Sun-Mon). Shade. Showers. Toilets.*

Manly Beach
Manly. Ferry Manly. **Map** p323 ㉖
Jumping aboard a Sydney ferry is a must and a trip to Manly is the perfect excuse. Take the ferry from Circular Quay to Manly Wharf in Manly Cove, where there's a small harbour beach (about 250m long) and a netted swimming area. To reach the open sea, head across the busy pedestrianised street, the Corso, to the 1.5km (mile-long) crescent of sand known as Manly Surf Beach, but actually comprising Queenscliff in the north, followed by North Steyne, South Steyne and Manly Beaches. Manly has all the facilities of a big resort and can attract up to 50,000 visitors a day. It also has plenty of history: in 1903, it was one of the first beaches to permit daylight swimming, but due to the rips along the entire length of the beach fishermen Eddie and Joe Sly set up Manly's first lifesaving patrol. It's not all about surfing, though, you can snorkel, dive, sail, fish and play beach volleyball. Cyclists and in-line skaters can also enjoy the bike lane along the shore, from Burnt Bridge Creek to Shelly Beach. For a local area map, *see p334*.

Services *Cafés. Changing rooms. Child-friendly. Lifeguards/savers. No dogs. Parking. Picnic area. Pool (at Queenscliff). Restaurants. Shade. Shark net (Sept-May.) Shops. Showers. Toilets.*

★ Collaroy Beach
Pittwater Road, Collaroy. Bus 188, 190, E83, E84, E86, E87, E88, E89, L88, L90. **Map** p321 ❹
North of Manly lies a stretch of magnificent surfing beaches with wonderfully ludicrous names such as: Curl Curl, Dee Why, Long Reef, Narrabeen. At Collaroy, which lies directly south of Narrabeen, there's a 1km (half-mile) stretch of honey-coloured sand pounded by huge waves. It's also got an excellent, large ocean pool, plus a toddler pool at its southern end. The Bruce Bartlett Memorial Playground to the rear is shaded and has masses of fun equipment. The Surf Rock Hotel is right on the beach. The Deck is the place to be for alfresco beers and light meals, right on the sand. This is a true local hangout; it gets thumping at night.

Services *Barbecues. Cafés. Changing rooms. Child-friendly (play area). Danger: underwater rocks. Lifeguards/savers (Sept-May). Parking. Picnic area. Pools. Restaurants. Shark net (Sept-May). Shops. Showers. Toilets.*

Newport Beach
Barrenjoey Road, Newport. Bus 188, 190, E88, E89, L88, L90. **Map** p321 ⑫
This half-mile of windswept beach offers good surf with easy access to a busy main road of shops, cafés and restaurants. Its accessibility makes it very popular with locals keen to catch a quick wave. There's a well-equipped, fenced-off play area in the grassland to the rear, but at dusk the beach can get rowdy and is no place for youngsters.

Services *Barbecues. Cafés. Changing rooms. Children's play area. Danger: underwater rocks. Lifeguards/savers (Sept-May). No dogs. Parking. Picnic area. Pool (south end). Restaurants. Shark net (Sept-May). Shops. Showers. Toilets.*

Avalon Beach
Barrenjoey Road, Avalon. Bus 188, 190, E88, E89, L88, L90. **Map** p321 ❶
This sandy and sophisticated half-mile beach gets pretty busy in the summer, especially with surfers, who arrive by the carload to tackle the generous waves. There's also good swimming and an excellent ocean pool at the southern end, and the whole beach is backed by grassy sand dunes.
Services *Barbecues. Changing rooms. Children's play area. Lifeguards/savers (Sept-May). Parking. Picnic area. Pool. Shark net (Sept-May). Showers. Toilets.*

Whale Beach
The Strand, Whale Beach. Bus 190, L90 to Avalon then bus 193. **Map** p321 ⓯
Approached via a precariously steep road, this 700m stretch of salmon-pink sand offers big surf and a rugged coastline. There's a 25m ocean pool at the southern end: take care when the tide comes in as the waves crash over the pool and surrounding rocks. Unlike nearby Palm Beach, Whale tends to remain crowd free and is something of a local hideaway. There's a kiosk on the beach serving freshly made rolls, juices and hot food, while more elaborate cafés and restaurants turn a trade back up Whale Beach Road: the Olive and Rose café (9974 1383, open Wednesday to Sunday) is worth a visit.
Services *Barbecues. Café (closed July). Changing rooms. Child-friendly (play area). Danger:*

underwater rocks. Lifeguards/savers (Sept-May). Parking. Picnic area. Pool. Restaurants. Shade. Shark net (Sept-May). Showers. Toilets.

Palm Beach
Barrenjoey Road, Palm Beach. Bus 190, L90. **Map** p321 ⓭
Situated at the northernmost tip of the northern beaches peninsula, Palm Beach is a local paradise. Don't be fooled by Palm Beach Wharf, a busier beach on the west side that you come to first. Keep on driving up the hill and around the bend to get to the real deal on the east side: you won't be disappointed. Palm Beach is home to Sydney's rich and famous; colonial-style mansions set on the hillside possess breathtaking views of foaming ocean and more than a mile of caramel-coloured sand. The southern end, known as Cabbage Tree Boat Harbour, is the safest spot to swim and surf. If you find the sea too daunting, there's the excellent Jack 'Johnny' Carter outdoor pool, named after the man who spent 50 years teaching local kids to swim. The Sugar Palm Restaurant on Ocean Road (No.24, 9974 4410), right in the heart of Palm Beach proper, is a very popular addition to the many eateries here: try to catch the evening wine and tapas served from 4pm to 9pm for a taste of the local high life. If you want to swap some D-list celebs, further back on North Palm Beach, keep an eye out for young Aussie actors on a tea break– you're in *Summer Bay*: this is where the hit soap *Home and Away* is filmed.
Services *Barbecues (in the play area). Café. Changing rooms. Child-friendly (play area is in the adjacent Governor Phillip Park). Lifeguards/savers (Sept-May). Parking. Picnic area. Pool. Restaurant. Shade. Shark net (Sept-May). Shops. Showers. Toilets.*

SIGHTS

Shelly Beach.

EXPERIENCE THE CHARM

Located in upmarket Paddington, at the heart of Sydney's art and fashion scene, the Arts Hotel is the perfect base from which to explore Sydney. Within walking distance of City shops, with direct buses to Circular Quay and Bondi Beach.

- Unique location
- Garden courtyard
- Swimming pool
- Free wi-fi in public areas

- Personal service
- Free bicycles
- Fitness room
- Family rooms

arts HOTEL

21 Oxford Street, Paddington, Sydney 2021
T +61 2 9361 0211   res@artshotel.com.au

www.artshotel.com.au

Consume

Bloodwood Newtown. *See p192*.

Hotels

Sydney's hotel scene is as varied as its scenery.

The Harbour City offers everything from great backpacker digs to five-star suites, from the CBD to Bondi and all suburbs in between.

The range of hotels, serviced apartments, backpacker hangouts and boutique havens can be quite dazzling, but at least it means there's something for everyone. Hotels at the top end compete with those you'll find in any top world city. The secret is to peek behind the glass palaces, look outside the city centre and seek out the many unusual, independently-run establishments. Standards are pretty high, wherever you go: Sydneysiders are used to their spaces being spick and span and this is reflected in their hotels.

CONSUME

WHERE TO STAY

In the centre, you'll find the four- and five-star establishments in prime positions, many with fantastic harbour views. The 3.5-star-plus hotels are strung around the central sightseeing areas: the Rocks, Circular Quay, George Street, Hyde Park and Darling Harbour. Meanwhile, a swag of backpacker joints congregate around Kings Cross, nearby Potts Point and Darlinghurst, and Elizabeth Bay. Staying in these areas means you'll have access to plenty of restaurants and bars, but if you want to see the tourist sights you'll need to catch a CityRail train back into town.

The inner-west suburbs, such as Newtown and Glebe, are likewise a short train or bus ride from the city centre, but have the advantage of good pubs and a student atmosphere, if that's more your scene. Newtown's bustling King Street can be noisy and traffic-polluted, but that's just part of its charm.

If you fancy staying near the beach, you can't go wrong with Bondi, Coogee or Manly.

INSIDE TRACK ROOM PRICES

Room prices vary greatly, but in general Sydney is less expensive than many European cities, and you should be able to get a decent double room in the city for under $200 a night.

If you stay in Manly (a popular option with British visitors), you're limited by the (picturesque) ferry service from the city, which stops around midnight. For the full seaside experience, head for the northern beaches, such as Newport, Collaroy or the stunning but pricey A-listers playground Palm Beach.

In the end, though, where you stay may depend on when you come. The busiest tourist times are between November and May. The beach areas are packed from mid December to late January, when the school holidays are in full swing. If you want a room during Mardi Gras (February/March) or a harbour view at New Year, you'll have to book well in advance.

Serviced apartments, listed at the end of this chapter, are often a good option for long stays.

ABOUT THE LISTINGS

Most hotels are air-conditioned, but not all – check first if this is an important requirement. Rates quoted below are 'rack' rates, standard prices that are often higher than what you'll pay. It's always worth asking for standby prices, weekly rates or special deals – you may well get them, even in the peak season. Top hotels also often offer discounts at weekends, when business people with a life are sleeping in their own beds. A ten per cent Goods & Services Tax (GST) applies to all hotels and hostels (as well as tours, internal air fares and restaurant meals), and by law it has to be part of the advertised price.

Note that 1800 telephone numbers are toll-free, and 1300 numbers are always charged at a local rate – but these only work within Australia, not if you're dialling from abroad.

THE CBD & THE ROCKS

Deluxe

Four Seasons Hotel Sydney

199 George Street, at Essex Street, CBD, NSW 2000 (1800 142 163, 9238 0000, www.fourseasons.com). CityRail/ferry Circular Quay. **Rates** $240-$1,150 double. **Rooms** 531. **Credit** AmEx, DC, MC, V. **Map** p327 F4 **❶**
The former Regent Hotel (some taxi drivers still know it by that name) was taken over by Canadian chain Four Seasons in the early 1990s and since then has been quietly delivering an extremely high level of service within very plush surroundings indeed, as evidenced by the fact that it was the official Olympic headquarters in 2000 and Olympic officials certainly don't sleep rough. The decor is expensive looking in a modern way, with a pared-down opulence. All the rooms are spacious and have marble bathrooms; some overlook Walsh Bay, the Harbour Bridge and the Opera House, while the rest have city views. The 32nd-floor Executive Club caters to high-flying business types with its corporate concierge, separate check-in and added goodies such as meetings facilities and complimentary refreshments. *Bar. Business centre. Concierge. Disabled-adapted rooms. Gym. Internet (high-speed/wireless pay terminal). No-smoking floors. Parking ($33). Pool (outdoor). Restaurants (2). Room service. Spa. TV (cable).*

Hilton Sydney

488 George Street, between Park & Market Streets, CBD, NSW 2000 (9266 2000, reservations 9265 6045, www.hiltonsydney.com.au). CityRail Town Hall. **Rates** $320-$2,850 double. **Rooms** 577. **Credit** AmEx, DC, MC, V. **Map** p327 F6 **❷**
Since its refurbishment in 2005, the Hilton has reinstated itself as one of the city's premier five-star hotels – quite an achievement as it's done that despite being without the otherwise obligatory harbour view. From the light-filled, four-storey-high lobby with its spiralling aluminium sculpture to the 31 'relaxation' rooms and suites, it is an undeniably classy experience. The design throughout is impeccable, with limestone flooring, plush fabrics, mood lighting and (in the suites) open-plan spa bathrooms. Eating and drinking spots include Luke Mangan's Glass brasserie (*see p153*) and wine bar, the Zeta cocktail bar (*see p187*) and the historic Marble Bar (established 1893) in the basement, left untouched during the refurbishment. There are also extensive conference and business facilities, and a top-end health club with gym, indoor pool, saunas and steam rooms. Great views, too, from the higher floors over nearby Sydney Tower. *Bars (3). Business centre. Concierge. Disabled-adapted rooms. Gym. Internet (high-speed/wireless). No smoking. Parking ($40). Pool (indoor). Restaurant. Room service. Spa. TV (cable/DVD).*

InterContinental Sydney

Corner of Bridge & Phillip Streets, CBD, NSW 2000 (1800 221 335/9253 9000, www.sydney.intercontinental.com). CityRail/ferry Circular Quay. **Rates** $290-$4,825 double. **Rooms** 509. **Credit** AmEx, MC, V. **Map** p327 G4
Set in a building that dates all the way from 1851, the InterContinental now features such modern extras as high-speed internet access and digital TV in all rooms, plus two TV broadcast and video conferencing studios. Rooms have a classic-contemporary feel and come with either harbour or city views. Sleek restaurant/lounge bar Etch serves contemporary cuisine, the sandstone-arcaded Cortile café dispenses traditional high tea, and Café Opera offers a seafood buffet. The luxurious rooftop lounge, with its uninterrupted harbour views, is only accessible to Club InterContinental members, who pay extra for such privileges as a personal concierge service. The vistas from the top over Sydney Harbour are spectacular, and available to all guests from the indoor swimming pool on the 31st floor.

Park Hyatt Sydney. *See p128.*

CONSUME

Bars (2). Business centre. Concierge. Disabled-adapted rooms. Gym. Internet (high-speed). No-smoking floors. Parking ($30). Pool (indoor). Restaurants (2). Room service. Spa. TV (cable/ pay movies).

Observatory Hotel

89-113 Kent Street, between Argyle & High Streets, Millers Point, NSW 2000 (9256 2222, www.observatoryhotel.com.au). CityRail/ferry Circular Quay. **Rates** $315-$650 double. **Rooms** 100. **Credit** AmEx, DC, MC, V. **Map** p327 E4 ❸

A consistent favourite among the more well-heeled visitors to the city, the service-oriented Observatory has the feel, and indeed some of the looks, of a typical European grand hotel. Tones are hushed as the army of staff attend to every need and desire of the guest. The furniture is mainly rich mahogany with a mass of antiques and lush drapes, and there is almost a gentleman's club feel to some of the public rooms. The hotel is owned by Orient-Express and its refined elegance has garnered a mass of awards. Rooms boast original artworks, plus marble bathrooms, CD players hidden away in antique armoires and high-speed internet points. Most rooms have views of Walsh Bay or Observatory Hill. The Observatory's renowned spa, which comes with an indoor pool complete with a sparkling night-sky ceiling, is quite something; it offers deluxe treatments by Payot and La Prairie.

Bar. Business centre. Concierge. Disabled-adapted rooms. Gym. Internet (high-speed). No-smoking floors. Parking ($40). Pool (indoor). Restaurant. Room service. Spa. TV (cable/pay movies/DVD).

Park Hyatt Sydney

7 Hickson Road, The Rocks, NSW 2000 (9241 1234, www.sydney.park.hyatt.com). CityRail/ferry Circular Quay. **Rates** $705-$1180 double. **Rooms** 158. **Credit** AmEx, DC, MC, V. **Map** p327 F3 ❹

Since opening in 1990, the Park Hyatt has played host to a steady stream of celebrities, heads of state and international jet-setters with money to burn. The jaw-dropping, close-up vista of both the Opera House and the Harbour Bridge is a major selling point, but you get what you pay (a lot) for – the cheaper rooms offer just glimpses of what the more expensive suites have framed through their windows. A recent refurbishment has transformed the top-end suites into über-minimalist apartment-style hangouts. Extras include a rooftop swimming pool, deluxe spa and much-vaunted 24-hour butler service. There are also LCD TVs, CD/DVD players, high-speed internet connections and marble bathrooms. The chic harbourkitchen&bar restaurant provides yet more amazing views (through floor-to-ceiling glass doors) and excellent food, while the harbourbar offers cocktails and tapas. The Club Bar caters to whisky fans, but anti-smoking laws mean that it's no longer a cigar haven. *Photo p127.*

Bars (2). Business centre. Concierge. Gym. Internet (high-speed/wireless). No smoking. Parking ($26). Pool (outdoor). Restaurant. Room service. Spa. TV (cable/DVD/pay movies/satellite).

Shangri-La Hotel

176 Cumberland Street, between Essex & Argyle Streets, The Rocks, NSW 2000 (9250 6000, www.shangri-la.com). CityRail/ferry Circular Quay. **Rates** $355-$650 double. **Rooms** 563. **Credit** AmEx, DC, MC, V. **Map** p327 E4 ❺

Ideally located between the Opera House and the Harbour Bridge, this is another five-star spot with undeniably breathtaking views. And, what's more, the views are there from every room, which is one reason for its popularity. Rooms here are some of the largest in the city and service remains a major priority, with lots of extra touches designed to maintain a loyal base of regulars. The Horizon Club executive lounge on the 30th floor, with its towering 18m (60ft) glass atrium, comes at a premium but with complimentary breakfast and snacks and business facilities it's worth it. The swanky Blu Horizon cocktail bar is popular with city boys, while Altitude restaurant on the 36th floor offers unbeatable picture-postcard views of the the harbour, the bridge and the Opera House. Decor is a mix of modern eastern with classic hotel chic, but really you don't look at the furniture with views like these. There's also a gym and indoor swimming pool.

Bar. Business centre. Concierge. Disabled-adapted rooms. Gym. Internet (high-speed). No-smoking floors. Pool (indoor). Restaurants (2). Room service. Spa. TV (cable/DVD).

Sheraton on the Park

161 Elizabeth Street, between Market & Park Streets, CBD, NSW 2000 (1800 073 535, 9286 6000, www.sheraton.com). CityRail St James. **Rates** $345-$980 double. **Rooms** 557. **Credit** AmEx, DC, MC, V. **Map** p327 F6 ❻

Overlooking bucolic Hyde Park, this huge award-winning hotel occupies a prime location in the central business and shopping district. The grand lobby screams luxury with its massive black marble pillars and curved staircase, and the rooms have a refined, modern and quasi-nautical design theme (all stripes and circles), and feature black marble bathrooms. There's a spacious pool and fitness centre on level 22, the revamped Conservatory Bar on level one and a tea lounge off the lobby, which offers 'contemporary' high tea served by stylish black-clad waiters.

Bar. Business centre. Concierge. Disabled-adapted rooms. Gym. Internet (high-speed). No-smoking floors. Parking ($40). Pool (indoor). Restaurant. Room service. Spa. TV (cable).

Westin Sydney

1 Martin Place, between Pitt & George Streets, CBD, NSW 2000 (1800 656 535/8223 1111, www.westin.com). CityRail Martin Place.

Rates $340-$765 double. **Rooms** 416.
Credit AmEx, DC, MC, V. **Map** p327 F5 **❼**
Here you get the best of both worlds – a sense of history married to some very contemporary design and deluxe service. Located in pedestrianised Martin Place, smack-dab in the middle of the CBD, the Westin is partly housed in what used to be the General Post Office, built in 1887. Rooms in the heritage-listed building feature high ceilings and period details, while tower rooms have floor-to-ceiling city views and a more contemporary look (think stainless steel and pale wood). There is a renowned spa and a spectacular atrium as well as a selection of restaurants and bars in the GPO building. Exercise addicts take note: the 'Workout Rooms' come with treadmill, weights, a yoga mat and other fitness paraphernalia. *Bar. Business centre. Concierge. Disabled-adapted rooms. Gym. No-smoking floors. Internet (high-speed). Parking ($35). Pool (indoor). Restaurant. Room service. Spa. TV (cable/pay movies).*

Expensive

Establishment

5 Bridge Lane, at George Street, CBD, NSW 2000 (9240 3100, www.merivale.com). CityRail Circular Quay or Wynyard/ferry Circular Quay.

THE BEST HOTELS

For beach chic
Enjoy cool beachside lodgings at Coogee's **Dive Hotel** (*see p141*), Bondi's **Ravesi's** (*see p141*), Whale Beach's **Jonah's** (*see p143*) or **Manly Pacific Sydney** (*see p144*).

For designer touches
Sleep in style-mag splendour at **Diamant Hotel** (*see p137*), **Blue, Woolloomooloo Bay** (*see p137*), **Establishment** (*see p129*), **Medusa** (*see p135*) or the **Sebel Pier One** (*see p131*).

For families on a budget
Save money for ice-creams at **Hotel Altamont** (*see p135*), **Novotel Darling Harbour** (*see p134*) or **Y Hotel City South** (*see p142*).

For five-star glamour
Spot a celeb at **Park Hyatt Sydney** (*see p128*), **Shangri-La Hotel** (*see p128*) or **Hilton Sydney** (*see p127*).

For old-fashioned charm
Step back in time at **Hughenden Hotel** (*see p138*), **Lord Nelson Brewery Hotel** (*see p131*), **Observatory Hotel** (*see p128*) or **Simpsons of Potts Point** (*see p137*).

Rates $249-$1,050 double. **Rooms** 31. **Credit** AmEx, DC, MC, V. **Map** p327 F4 **❽**
Although it only has 31 rooms, including two penthouse suites, the Establishment's cool clout far outweighs its capacity. Exceedingly stylish, this place would be perfectly at home in the smarter districts of London or New York. Catering to celebrities, fashionistas and those with deep pockets, the complex incorporates two critically acclaimed restaurants, Sushi e and est., three bars, including Hemmesphere, and a popular nightclub, Tank. As for the guest rooms, half are all sharp angles, minimalist Japanese elements and flashes of bright colour, while the others are more subdued – choose which suits your mood. Expect luxurious touches at every turn (Philippe Starck taps, Bulgari toiletries, Bose stereo systems). *Bars (3). Business centre. Concierge. Gym. Internet (high-speed). No-smoking floors. Restaurants (2). Room service. TV (cable/DVD).*

Four Points by Sheraton Darling Harbour

161 Sussex Street, at Market Street, CBD, NSW 2000 (1800 074 545, 9290 4000, www.fourpoints.com). CityRail Town Hall/ferry Darling Harbour/ Monorail Darling Park.
Rates $310-$2,075 double. **Rooms** 630.
Credit AmEx, DC, MC, V. **Map** p327 E6 **❾**
With 630 rooms including 45 suites, this place caters to large tour groups, executives and the international conference crowd: the Sydney Convention & Exhibition Centre is a stone's throw away, and the hotel is within walking distance of several museums as well as Chinatown and the central business and shopping districts. All mod cons are provided, such as high-speed wireless internet, large work desks and cable TV. Some rooms have balconies overlooking Darling Harbour. There are high-tech conferencing facilities, a fitness centre and a sprawling shopping centre with a food court. The glassed-in Corn Exchange restaurant offers an elaborate seafood buffet, the historic Dundee Arms pub specialises in barbecued pub grub, and locally brewed beer and cocktails are served in the Lobby Lounge. *Bars (2). Business centre. Concierge. Disabled-adapted rooms. Gym. Internet (wireless). No-smoking floors. Parking ($35). Restaurant. Room service. TV (cable/pay movies).*

Grace Hotel

77 York Street, at King Street, CBD, NSW 2000 (9272 6888, www.gracehotel.com.au). CityRail Martin Place or Wynyard. **Rates** $280-$305 double. **Rooms** 382. **Credit** AmEx, DC, MC, V. **Map** p327 E6 **❿**
This charming hotel is housed in an 11-storey corner block – a loose copy of the Tribune Tower in Chicago – that began life in 1930 as the headquarters of department store giant Grace Brothers. During World War II, General MacArthur directed South Pacific operations from here. A total refur-

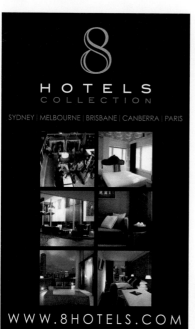

bishment was completed in 2005, but many of the original features, such as the lifts, stairwells, marble floors and ornate ironwork, have been retained and restored to great effect. Rooms, however, are modern, large and comfortable, and all have bathtubs. The indoor heated lap pool is small, but there's also a sauna and a steam room, plus a sun-filled fitness centre and rooftop terrace. While the rack rate here seems high, there are usually much more reasonable internet offers to be had. Bar77Grace serves cocktails and innovative bar food.

Bars (2). Concierge. Disabled-adapted rooms. Gym. Internet (high-speed). No smoking. Parking ($30). Pool (indoor). Restaurant. Room service. Spa. TV (cable/pay movies).

Rydges World Square

389 Pitt Street, at Liverpool Street, CBD, NSW 2000 (1800 838 830, 8268 1888, www.rydges.com). CityRail Central or Town Hall/Monorail World Square/LightRail Central. **Rates** $367-$739 double. **Rooms** 443. **Credit** AmEx, DC, MC, V. **Map** p329 F8 ⑪

Located in the new shopping and entertainment precinct known as World Square, the Rydges (which was converted from the previous Avillion hotel) was still a work in progress at the time of writing. The restaurant had just completed its refurbishment and the bar was waiting for an upgrade; the guest rooms, meanwhile, had been completed to a comfortable (albeit rather blandly furnished) standard. Since it is within easy walking distance of Darling Harbour, Chinatown and the Queen Victoria Building, this hotel is popular with business people and those seeking cheaper (relatively speaking), good-quality rooms. There's also a large fitness centre and a retail plaza that connects to the lower lobby.

Bar. Business centre. Concierge. Disabled-adapted rooms. Gym. Internet (high-speed). No-smoking floors. Parking ($35). Restaurant. Room service. TV (cable/pay movies/satellite).

Sebel Pier One

11 Hickson Road, on Dawes Point, Walsh Bay, NSW 2000 (1800 780 485, 8298 9999, www.sebelpierone.com.au). CityRail/ferry Circular Quay then 15min walk. **Rates** $309-$549 double. **Rooms** 160. **Credit** AmEx, DC, MC, V. **Map** p327 F2 ⑫

Another successful marriage of historic architecture and contemporary design, this sleek, chic boutique hotel has water views in the most unexpected places, including beneath your feet: the glass floor in the lobby is quite the showpiece. Located in a converted warehouse at the quiet end of the Rocks, the rooms feature much of the original timber and ironwork. Some rooms have telescopes, some have Walsh Bay or partial Bridge views, and all have wireless internet connection and slick modern furnishings. The Front restaurant and wine bar

offers alfresco dining and cocktails on the water, while the private pontoon is convenient for those travelling by water taxi or private yacht.

Bar. Business centre. Concierge. Disabled-adapted rooms. Gym. Internet (high-speed). No smoking. Parking ($25). Restaurant. Room service. TV (cable/pay movies).

Moderate

Central Park Hotel

185 Castlereagh Street, at Park Street, CBD, NSW 2000 (9283 5000, www.central park.com.au). CityRail Town Hall/Monorail Galeries Victoria. **Rates** $150-$210 double. **Rooms** 35. **Credit** AmEx, DC, MC, V. **Map** p329 F7 ⑬

With its motto 'hip on a budget', the less-expensive little sister of Blacket's is perfect for those who love to be in the heart of the action. Located on a busy city corner, this compact urban hotel has standard en suite rooms, 'studios' with an additional double sofa bed and a spa bath, and seven airy, two-storey loft apartments that can sleep up to four people. Some rooms overlook Hyde Park. Perched above a busy bar, restaurant and gaming room complex, the noise is kept to a minimum with efficient soundproofing and window seals.

Concierge. Disabled-adapted rooms. Internet (dataport). No smoking. Parking ($40). TV (cable/DVD).

Lord Nelson Brewery Hotel

19 Kent Street, at Argyle Street, Millers Point, NSW 2000 (9251 4044, www.lordnelson. com.au). CityRail/ferry Circular Quay. **Rates** $130-$190 double. **Rooms** 9. **Credit** AmEx, DC, MC, V. **Map** p327 E3 ⑭

Time marches on, but you wouldn't know it at the Lord Nelson, whose motto is 'You've been praying, the Lord has delivered'. The clean and relatively spacious Victorian-style rooms with plantation shutters are air-conditioned, but the look and feel of the place is pure 19th-century colonial – the pub opened in 1841 and claims to be the oldest in the city. There are only nine guest rooms, all with original bare sandstone walls, and, despite the antique feel, most come with en suite bathrooms. The laid-back downstairs brasserie hewn from the convict quarried sandstone serves contemporary Australian cuisine, while the bar, serving ploughman's lunches, and the microbrewery (*see p186*) draw a lively crowd.

Bar. No smoking. Internet (dataport). Restaurant. TV.

Russell

143A George Street, at Globe Street, The Rocks, NSW 2000 (9241 3543, www.therussell.com.au). CityRail/ferry Circular Quay. **Rates** $150-$290 double. **Rooms** 29. **Credit** AmEx, DC, MC, V. **Map** p327 F4 ⑮

With a great location in the middle of the Rocks, the Russell still somehow manages to feel more like a cosy country B&B than a city-centre hotel. Housed in a turreted 1887 building, rooms feature such period flourishes as ornate fireplaces, antique brass beds, marble washbasins, pine dressers and floral bedspreads and wallpapers. Some rooms are en suite, and some have portable air-conditioners and TVs. There's also the pleasant Acacia breakfast room on the ground floor, the historic Fortune of War pub and a tiny rooftop garden.

Bar. Internet (shared terminal). No smoking. Parking ($30). Restaurant. TV.

Budget

Legend Has It... Westend
412 Pitt Street, between Goulburn & Campbell Streets, CBD, NSW 2000 (1800 013 186,

---

Blingpackers

A new breed of traveller.

They wear designer shades, customised Birkenstocks and smart jeans, and they wouldn't be seen dead with a koala hanging off their backpack: meet the blingpackers, a growing tribe of urban travellers who are shaping the future of the budget hotel industry in the Emerald City. The 'BPs', as they're known to the hostels and boutique hotels who are falling over themselves to win their custom, are an eclectic group. More than just your average gap-year backpacker, BPs are twenty- and thirtysomethings taking a career sabbatical, couples with children who want to put a 'travelling' spin on the school hols, new partners cementing their relationship with a few months on the road... the list goes on.

And in response to this new breed of tourist comes a more enloved species of low-rent accommodation. Exit bed bugs, rickety towering bunks, swirly carpets and bobbly blankets; enter a new era of slick, spotless hostels jostling for design kudos with modern furniture, up-to-the-minute bathrooms, kitchens, plush pillows, freshly ground coffee and perfectly mixed cocktails.
To name a few names, you might want to swap peeling wallpaper for textbook *Wallpaper** at: **Legend Has It... Westend** (*see above*), **Pensione** (*see right*), **Railway Square YHA** (*see right*), **Wake up!** (*see p133*), **Hotel Altamont** (*see p135*) and **Y Hotel City South** (*see p142*).

9211 4588, www.legendhasitwestend.com.au). CityRail Central or Museum/LightRail Central. **Rates** $30 dorm; $80 double. **Rooms** 90. **Credit** MC, V. **Map** p329 F8 ⑯
Who says backpackers have it rough? Located just around the corner from Central Station, this clean and modern hotel is rightly popular with anyone on a budget, including families. There are laundry facilities, a commercial-grade kitchen, a café, plus extras geared toward working holidaymakers, such as an in-house travel agency and jobs board. There's always something going on here, making it the perfect option for travellers on their own – at the time of writing Friday is wine and cheese night and Saturday is barbie night. Rooms (most do come with air-conditioning) are either en suite or have a private bathroom adjacent. The reception is open 24 hours daily, breakfast is astonishingly good value at just two dollars and airport transfers are offered to guests staying for three or more nights.
Disabled-adapted room. Internet (high-speed pay terminal). No smoking. TV (TV room).

Pensione
631-635 George Street, between Goulburn & Campbell Streets, CBD, NSW 2000 (1800 885 886; 9265 8888, www.pensione.com.au). CityRail Central/Monorail World Square. **Rates** $135-$275 double. **Rooms** 72. **Credit** AmEx, DC, MC, V. **Map** p329 E8 ⑰
The Pensione is part of the Eight Hotels group of affordable, stylish hotels in central Sydney. On the edge of Chinatown opposite World Square, budget accommodation really doesn't come much better than this (although, as a result, you should choose your rooms wisely as it can get noisy). Yes, some rooms are very small, but they're all kitted out with a mini fridge, TV, air-con and phone, and feature modern tiled bathroooms that wouldn't look out of place in a glossy homes mag. There are around 15 family rooms, the largest sleeping up to six, so it's a good option for young families who want something urban and edgy. Other facilities include internet kiosks and wireless internet in the guest lounge, a kitchenette and a coin-operated laundry.
Bar. Disabled-adapted rooms. No smoking. Internet (wireless in guest lounge). Parking ($23). Restaurant. TV (cable).

Railway Square YHA
8-10 Lee Street, at Railway Square, Haymarket, NSW 2000 (9281 9666, www.yha.com.au). City Rail/LightRail Central. **Rates** $29.50-$33 dorm; $86-$107 double. **Rooms** 65. **Credit** MC, V. **Map** p329 E9 ⑱
This YHA hostel, built in a former parcels shed, is very near its Central counterpart (*see p133*). The design incorporates a real disused railway platform, with some dorms housed in replicas of train carriages (very Harry Potter); bathrooms in the main building adjacent. Most dorms have between four

and eight beds, and there are a couple of ensuite double rooms. It's clean and bright, with a large open-plan communal area dotted with sofas, a sizeable kitchen, laundry facilities and an internet café. Mod cons include a fun small spa pool and air-conditioning. It's very popular, so book ahead.
Disabled-adapted rooms. Internet (high-speed pay terminals). No smoking. Pool (outdoor). Restaurant. TV (DVD/TV room).

Sydney Central YHA
11 Rawson Place, at Pitt Street, CBD, NSW 2000 (9218 9000, www.yha.com.au). CityRail/LightRail Central. **Rates** $35-$41.50 dorm; $100-$123 double/twin. **Rooms** 155. **Credit** MC, V. **Map** p329 E9 ⑲
The largest of the YHA properties in Sydney, this place has it all. Deep breath: kitchen, laundry, separate games, dining and TV rooms, high-speed internet terminals, mini supermarket, café, underground bar and a rooftop pool, sauna and barbecue area with panoramic city views. Popular activities include pub crawls, big-screen movie nights and walking tours. All of this is housed in an imposing, heritage-listed building opposite Central Station. There are around 50 twin rooms, some en suite, and dorms that sleep up to eight.
Bar. Disabled-adapted rooms. Internet (high-speed pay terminals). No smoking. Parking ($14). Pool (indoor). Restaurant. TV (TV rooms).

Wake up!
509 Pitt Street, at George Street, Haymarket, NSW 2000 (1800 800 945/9288 7888, www. wakeup.com.au). CityRail/LightRail Central. **Rates** $28-$36 dorm; $98-$108 double; $115 triple. **Rooms** 500 beds. **Credit** MC, V. **Map** p329 E9 ⑳
Located opposite Central Station, this award-winning hostel is part of that new breed – big, clean, efficiently run and with very proactive security, despite the party atmosphere. A major refurbishment in 2006 has made it better than ever. The common areas are like a twentysomething's dream, with circular sofas, a funky TV lounge, endless banks of computers for internet use, a street café, kitchen, laundry, ATMs and a travel agent to organise your trips and help with finding work locally. The air-conditioned dorms sleep four, six, eight or ten, and some are women-only. There are also double and twin rooms, some with private showers. Bedlinen is provided and check-in is 24 hours.
Bar. Disabled-adapted rooms. Internet (high-speed pay terminals). No smoking. Restaurant. TV (DVD/TV room).

Y Hotel Hyde Park
5-11 Wentworth Avenue, at Liverpool Street, CBD, NSW 2010 (1800 994 994/9264 2451, www.yhotel.com.au). CityRail Museum.

Pensione.

CONSUME

Medusa.

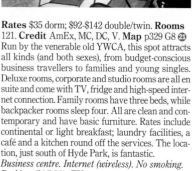

Rates $35 dorm; $92-$142 double/twin. **Rooms** 121. **Credit** AmEx, MC, DC, V. **Map** p329 G8 ㉑
Run by the venerable old YWCA, this spot attracts all kinds (and both sexes), from budget-conscious business travellers to families and young singles. Deluxe rooms, corporate and studio rooms are all en suite and come with TV, fridge and high-speed internet connection. Family rooms have three beds, while backpacker rooms sleep four. All are clean and contemporary and have basic furniture. Rates include continental or light breakfast; laundry facilities, a café and a kitchen round off the services. The location, just south of Hyde Park, is fantastic.
Business centre. Internet (wireless). No smoking. Parking ($17.50). TV.

DARLING HARBOUR & PYRMONT

Deluxe

Star City Hotel & Serviced Apartments
80 Pyrmont Street, between Jones Bay Road & Union Street, Pyrmont, NSW 2000 (1800 700 700/9657 8393, www.starcity.com.au). LightRail Star City/ Monorail Harbourside/bus 443, 449. **Rates** $224-$550 double. **Rooms** 482. **Credit** AmEx, DC, MC, V. **Map** p326 C6 ㉒
Gambling is big business in Australia. And nowhere is it bigger than at this little slice of Las Vegas, Oz-style. The numbers are dizzying: 306 standard rooms, 43 suites with 24-hour butler service, two

penthouses, 131 fully serviced apartments (rates from $550), 11 restaurants and bars, two theatres and – of course – a casino that's open 24 hours a day. Facilities include a spa and health club and an indoor-outdoor pool with panoramic views of the city. The Astral bar on the 17th floor has a large outdoor terrace with fantastic views.
Bars (6). Business centre. Concierge. Disabled-adapted rooms. Gym. Internet (high-speed). No-smoking floors. Parking ($26). Pool (outdoor). Restaurants (11). Room service. Spa. TV (cable/pay movies/satellite).

Expensive

Novotel Sydney on Darling Harbour
100 Murray Street, at Allen Street, Darling Harbour, NSW 2000 (1300 656 565/9934 0000, www.noveldarlingharbour.com.au). CityRail Town Hall/Monorail/LightRail Convention. **Rates** $269-$329 double. **Rooms** 525. **Credit** AmEx, DC, MC, V. **Map** p326 D6 ㉓
Next door to the Sydney Convention & Exhibition Centre, the Novotel is aimed mainly at business travellers. As a result, all the rooms come stuffed with communication gizmos such as LCD TVs, broadband and wireless internet access, and mobile phone- and laptop-charging stations. The panoramic harbour and city views are lovely, and there's also a swimming pool, tennis court, gym and sauna. The hotel is home to Liquid – an average cocktail bar with a good outdoor terrace – and a restaurant, Dish.

Bar. Business centre. Concierge. Disabled-adapted rooms. Gym. Internet (high-speed/wireless). No-smoking floors. Parking ($30). Pool (outdoor). Restaurant. Room service. TV (cable/pay movies).

Moderate

Ibis Sydney Darling Harbour
70 Murray Street, at Allen Street, Darling Harbour, NSW 2000 (1300 656 565, 9563 0888, www.accorhotels.com.au). CityRail Town Hall/Monorail/LightRail Convention. **Rates** $166-$213 double. **Rooms** 256. **Credit** AmEx, DC, MC, V. **Map** p326 D6 **24**
This is a no-frills, get-what-you-pay-for option in a good location. The rooms are on the small side, but were refurbished with a cool new look in late 2007. For location alone it's still good value for your money, especially if you manage to get a cheap internet rate. Some rooms have views of Darling Harbour and the city, while others look over Pyrmont. The Ibistro bar and restaurant has an outdoor terrace.
Bar. Disabled-adapted rooms. Internet (high-speed). No-smoking floors. Parking ($25). Restaurant. TV (cable).

DARLINGHURST & SURRY HILLS
Expensive

Medusa
267 Darlinghurst Road, between Liverpool & William Streets, Darlinghurst, NSW 2010 (9331 1000, www.medusa.com.au). CityRail Kings Cross. **Rates** $210-$420 double. **Rooms** 18. **Credit** AmEx, DC, MC, V. **Map** p329 H8 **25**
What's not to love about a heritage-listed Victorian mansion that's been painted pink? Embodying a very Darlinghurst sense of urban chic, the Medusa is an ode to colour and design, all interesting angles and bright flourishes of imagination. The lobby is pink, too, with bulging floral mouldings and an over-sized paper chandelier. All rooms have luxe touches like Aveda toiletries and fluffy bathrobes, plus a kitchenette and CD player. The expansive Grand Rooms feature period fireplaces, groovy chaises longues and a sitting area. The recently added business suite, including generous desk space and wireless internet, can be rented hourly, while rooms around the diminutive courtyard are pet friendly.
Business centre. Internet (wireless). No smoking. Room service. TV (cable/DVD).

Moderate

Crown Hotel
589 Crown Street, at Cleveland Street, Surry Hills, NSW 2010 (9699 3460, www.crownhotel.com.au). Bus 352, 372, 393, 395. **Rates** $160-$200 double. **Rooms** 8. **Credit** MC, V. **Map** 329 G11 **26**

This very hip yet thoroughly unpretentious complex opened in 2005, and there's nothing quite like it in Surry Hills, land of fab restaurants but very few hotels. On the ground floor is Players, an airy pub converted from an 1880s hotel, plus an upscale wine shop. Level two features Dome, a sexy cocktail bar complete with chandeliers, a glass bar and a huge mural based on François Boucher's baroque painting *Girl Reclining*. Last but not least are the hotel rooms, equally stylish and featuring deluxe extras such as L'Occitane bath products, Egyptian cotton bedlinen and wall-mounted 42-inch plasma screen TVs.
Bars (3). Disabled-adapted rooms. Internet (high-speed). No smoking. TV (cable/DVD).

Kirketon
229 Darlinghurst Road, between Farrell & Tewkesbury Avenues, Darlinghurst (1800 332 920/ 9332 2011, www.kirketon.com.au). CityRail Kings Cross. **Rates** $145-$199 double. **Rooms** 40. **Credit** AmEx, DC, MC, V. **Map** p330 H8 **27**
Originally built in the late 1930s and now one of the Eight Hotels group, owner of various budget boutique operations in Sydney, the Kirketon had a major refurbishment in 2007. Rooms today come with nice touches such as chocolates and Kevin Murphy toiletries, and the overall design is contemporary minimalist, with rich colours and slick bathrooms with showers. The dining room and bar – where chef Eric Tan serves ultra-modern international cuisine – remain popular with locals.
Bar. Concierge. Internet (wireless). No smoking. Parking ($25). Restaurant. TV (cable/DVD/VCR).

Budget

Hotel Altamont
207 Darlinghurst Road, between Liverpool & William Streets, Darlinghurst, NSW 2010 (1800 991 110/ 9360 6000, www.altamont.com.au). CityRail Kings Cross. **Rates** $109-$129 double. **Rooms** 15. **Credit** AmEx, MC, V. **Map** p330 H8 **28**
This is the hotel equivalent of Stella McCartney designing a collection for H&M – luxury on a sensible budget. The Altamont (part of the Eight Hotels stable) is housed in a colonial Georgian mansion that has been given an elegant, thoroughly contemporary makeover. There are skylights throughout the hotel, a glass-fronted, light-filled lobby and lounge, heavy custom-built wooden beds and dressers in the very

INSIDE TRACK
ONLINE BOOKINGS

On prices, the key is to work the internet. Booking online can save you hundreds of dollars, with prices often as low as half the rack rate.

CONSUME

spacious bedrooms, and a lovely, ornate Tuscan roof terrace. The loft suite was once the VIP room of the famous Cauldron nightclub, frequented by the likes of Mick Jagger and accessed by a stairway hidden away from the lenses of roving paparazzi. Rooms range from the said airy suite with its soaring ceilings and walk-in wardrobe to family rooms suitable for six with a combination of bunk beds and king or queen beds. Unsurprisingly, it's hugely popular, so it's best to book well in advance.

Bar. Internet (wireless high-speed). No smoking. Parking ($15). TV (cable/DVD).

KINGS CROSS, POTTS POINT & WOOLLOOMOOLOO

Deluxe

Blue, Woolloomooloo Bay

Woolloomooloo Wharf, 6 Cowper Wharf Road, opposite Forbes Street, Woolloomooloo, NSW 2011 (9331 9000, www.tajhotels.com). CityRail Kings Cross then 10 min walk or bus 311. **Rates** $225-$1,080 double. **Rooms** 100. **Credit** AmEx, DC, MC, V. **Map** p330 H6 ㉙
The former W hotel in the historic Woolloomooloo Wharf is now owned by Taj, India's luxury hotel and resort chain. While the edge may have been blunted a little, it's still a funky, alternative hotel with lots to offer those who like something a bit different from their five-star hangout. The plush rooms feature original elements from the old wharf building, and there's a fitness centre, indoor pool and the very popular Water Bar (*see p191*). The hotel has no restaurant, but there's an array of high-class, high-priced eateries along the marina edge of the wharf (rooms on this side have the best views). The hotel occupies only part of the swanky wharf development; there's also a complex of exclusive apartments and the deluxe Spa Chakra, which is pricey but divine.
Bar. Business centre. Concierge. Disabled-adapted room. Gym. Internet (high-speed). No-smoking floors. Parking ($40). Pool (indoor). Room service. Spa. TV (cable/DVD/pay movies).

Expensive

Diamant Hotel

14 Kings Cross Road, at Penny's Lane, Potts Point, NSW 2011 (1800 816 168, 9295 8888/8899, www.diamant.com.au). CityRail Kings Cross. **Rates** $165-$305 double. **Rooms** 76. **Credit** AmEx, DC, MC, V. **Map** p330 J7 ㉚
This new boutique hotel features the best accommodation in the area. It's part of the Eight Hotels group (which also owns the Altamont and Kirkton in Darlinghurst and the Pensione in the CBD) and is undoubtedly the swishest addition to the set. A major feature is that all rooms have opening windows – this may not sound revolutionary, but in a city of air-conditioned high-rise towers, it's quite a

boast. Bells and whistles include 42-inch plasma-screen TVs, iPod docks and DVD and CD players. Some rooms have private courtyards with comfortable furniture, while the Harbour View Room has just that, with the bridge bang centre. The Penny's Lane restaurant is already a local favourite.
Bar. Business centre. Concierge. Internet (high-speed wireless). Parking ($35). Restaurant. Room service. TV.

Moderate

Simpsons of Potts Point

8 Challis Avenue, at Victoria Street, Potts Point, NSW 2011 (9356 2199, www.simpsonshotel. com). CityRail Kings Cross. **Rates** $235-$325 double. **Rooms** 12. **Credit** AmEx, DC, MC, V. **Map** p330 J6 ㉛
A very elegant and charming place, combining the stylishness and comforts of a boutique hotel with the informal sociability of a B&B. Located at the quieter end of a tree-lined street, the lovingly restored mansion was built in 1892 and still retains many of its original Arts and Crafts details. The high-ceilinged guest rooms are old-fashioned, but elegantly so, and by no means dowdy. This is the life: sipping a free port and sherry by an open hearth in winter (OK, the fires are gas-powered imitations), tucking into a continental breakfast in the conservatory, thumbing through the hardbacks in the library… Book well in advance as Simpsons gets a lot of repeat business, and note that it doesn't have a licence to sell alcohol.
Internet (wireless). No smoking. Parking (free). TV.

Victoria Court Hotel

122 Victoria Street, between Orwell & Hughes Streets, Potts Point, NSW 2011 (1800 630 505, 9357 3200, www.victoriacourt.com.au). CityRail Kings Cross. **Rates** $88-$250 double. **Rooms** 22. **Credit** AmEx, DC, MC, V. **Map** p330 J6 ㉜
Leafy Victoria Street is an interesting mix of posh restaurants, ramshackle youth hostels and converted Victorian mansions – all just around the corner from the strip clubs and general sleaze of Kings Cross. This small hotel, formed from two 1881 terraced houses, is a celebration of Victorian extravagance, from the four-poster beds to the floral-printed everything (carpeting, curtains, wallpaper). All rooms are air-conditioned and have private bathrooms; some have marble fireplaces and wrought-iron balconies. Breakfast is served in the gorgeous plant-filled courtyard around a bubbling fountain.
Internet (dataport/high-speed pay terminal). No smoking. Parking ($11). TV.

Budget

Eva's Backpackers

6-8 Orwell Street, at Victoria Street, Kings Cross, NSW 2011 (1800 802 517/9358 2185,

INSIDE TRACK PUB OR HOTEL?

In Australia pubs are also called 'hotels'. Many pubs do have rooms at reasonable prices, but standards are mixed, so ask to see the accommodation first. Also check that there is adequate soundproofing.

www.evasbackpackers.com.au). CityRail Kings Cross. **Rates** $30 dorm; $80 double. **Rooms** 28. **Credit** MC, V. **Map** p330 J6 **⑬**

With its friendly, laid-back atmosphere and reputation for being very clean and quiet (rare for a backpackers' hostel in this neighbourhood), Eva's has rightfully gained a following. There are twin, double and dorm rooms, some en suite, some with air-conditioning. Extras include free breakfast, a kitchen, a laundry room with free washing powder, wake-up calls, luggage storage facilities, broadband internet access and a rooftop terrace and barbecue area with fabulous views over Sydney. Located at the (less dodgy) Potts Point end of Kings Cross, it's on a quiet street, but close to everything.
Internet (shared terminal). No smoking. TV (DVD/TV room).

Hotel Formule 1 Kings Cross

191-201 William Street, between Forbes Street & Kirketon Road, Kings Cross, NSW 2011 (9326 0300, www.formule1.com.au). CityRail Kings Cross. **Rates** $89 double. **Rooms** 115. **Credit** AmEx, DC, MC, V. **Map** p330 H7 **㉞**

The Accor Group budget hotel with a chequered flag logo – the idea is you're having a pitstop, get it? – is basic, but clean and very functional with bunk, twin or double beds, en suite bathroom and in-room TVs. Set on the busy part of William Street, it can feel like you're on a race track at times, and don't expect any special comforts, but everything you need is here. There's no restaurant, but with Kings Cross and Darlinghurst on your doorstep you won't starve.
Disabled-adapted rooms. No smoking. Internet (shared terminal). Parking ($20). TV (pay movies).

O'Malley's Hotel

228 William Street, at Brougham Street, Kings Cross, NSW 2011 (9357 2211, www.omalleys hotel. com.au). CityRail Kings Cross. **Rates** $79 double. **Rooms** 15. **Credit** MC, V. **Map** p330 H7 **㉟**

It may be attached to a popular Irish pub and music venue, and, yes, it's dangerously close to everything that's wrong with Kings Cross, but don't write off O'Malley's. The 1907 building's rooms are all en suite and feature lovely period touches along with old-fashioned charm. The location is quite convenient, too: just two minutes from the rail station. The Harbour View suite has a kitchen.
Bar. No smoking. TV.

Original Backpackers Lodge

160-162 Victoria Street, between Darlinghurst Road & Orwell Street, Kings Cross, NSW 2011 (9356 3232, www.originalbackpackers.com.au). CityRail Kings Cross. **Rates** $30 dorm; $75-$95 double/twin. **Rooms** 35. **Credit** MC, V. **Map** p330 J7 **㊲**

Established in 1980, this sprawling hostel in a Victorian mansion may look a little on the lived-in side, but it has plenty of character – not to mention lots of extras such as a lovely spacious courtyard, free bedlinen and towels, 24-hour check-in and complimentary airport pick-up (very welcome after spending a day on an aeroplane). There are single, double and family rooms as well as ten-person dorms, some of which are women-only. All rooms have televisions and fridges, and some have balconies, although most bathroom facilities are shared. There's usually something going on in the courtyard, whether it's karaoke or an Aussie barbie. The kitchen is big and modern, with food lockers, and there are laundry facilities available as well.
Internet (high-speed, pay terminals). No smoking. TV (cable/DVD/TV room).

PADDINGTON, WOOLLAHRA & DOUBLE BAY

Moderate

Hughenden Hotel

14 Queen Street, at Oxford Street, Woollahra, NSW 2025 (9363 4863, 1800 642 432, www.hughendenhotel.com.au). Bus 333, 352, 378, 380. **Rates** $158-$268 double. **Rooms** 36. **Credit** AmEx, DC, MC, V. **Map** p332 L11 **㊲**

This four-star boutique hotel was thought to be a lost cause when sisters Elizabeth and Susanne Gervay bought it back in 1992. But instead they set about transforming the crumbling, grand 1870s mansion into what it is today: an award-winning hotel offering sophisticated modern accommodation in comfortable old-world surroundings. All rooms are en suite, and there's also an attached four-bed terraced house that can be rented in its entirety. Elizabeth is an artist and Susanne an author, so literary events and art exhibitions take place regularly. There's a cosy lounge, an old-fashioned bar with a baby grand piano (played once a month by talented night porter Victor) and a sun terrace. Quaife's restaurant is named after the original owner, founder of the colony's medical association, and serves bistro-style dishes in generous portions. Three rooms are designated as pet friendly.
Bar. Disabled-adapted rooms. Internet (wireless). No smoking. Parking (free). Restaurant. Room service. TV.

Sullivans Hotel

21 Oxford Street, between Greens Road & Verona Street, Paddington, NSW 2021

(9361 0211, www.sullivans.com.au). Bus 352, 378, 380, L82. **Rates** *$165-$180 double.* **Rooms** *64.* **Credit** AmEx, DC, MC, V. **Map** p332 H9
This exceedingly friendly, family-run hotel has a great location in Paddington, with fabulous independent cinemas and bookshops virtually outside the door. The central business and shopping districts, as well as the eastern suburbs' beaches, are also just a short bus ride away. All rooms have private bathrooms, and there are some interconnecting family rooms available as well. You can make the most of the weather with the solar-heated pool and garden courtyard, or just relax in the ground-floor breakfast room overlooking busy Oxford Street. The hotel's owners also rent out their alpine chalet (three beds, two baths) in the Blue Mountains.
Disabled-adapted rooms. Gym. Internet (high-speed wireless). No smoking. Parking (free). Pool (outdoor). TV.

Vibe Rushcutters

100 Bayswater Road, next to Rushcutters Bay Park, Rushcutters Bay, NSW 2011 (13 8423, 8353 8988, www.vibehotels.com.au). CityRail Edgecliff or Kings Cross. **Rates** *$170-$290 double.* **Rooms** *245.* **Credit** AmEx, DC, MC, V. **Map** p330 K7
The Vibe hotel chain tries to be many things at once – stylish, affordable, young – and, by and large, it succeeds in achieving these goals. Rooms may be on the small side but they get lots of light, and facilities here include a spacious fitness centre with steam room. While the rooftop pool is a little exposed on windy days, its panoramic vista of Rushcutters Bay Park (great for jogging), the water and the city is superb. There's a cocktail bar, and a restaurant with a pleasant covered terrace. There are two other Vibes in town: one in North Sydney and one on Goulburn Street in the city.
Bar. Business Centre. Concierge. Disabled-adapted rooms. Gym. Internet (high-speed/wireless). No-smoking floors. Parking ($16.50). Pool (outdoor). Restaurant. Room service. TV (cable/pay movies).

Budget

Golden Sheaf Hotel

429 New South Head Road, at Knox Street, Double Bay, NSW 2023 (9327 5877, www.golden sheaf.com.au). Ferry Double Bay/bus 323, 324, 325, 326, 327. **Rates** *$90 double.* **Rooms** *9.* **Credit** AmEx, MC, V. **Map** p331 N8
This art deco pub (a long-time meeting spot for posh young eastern-suburbs types) has always been known for its lovely, leafy beer garden. But a refurbishment a few years ago saw the creation of nine handsome and large en suite rooms, all pared down and modern in design, though some original details were allowed to remain. Such cheap accommodation is a rare find in fancy Double Bay, but be warned: don't expect much peace and quiet, especially in

CONSUME

Hughenden Hotel.

summer – the pub hosts DJs and and various music performances nearly every night of the week.
Bars (5). No smoking. Parking (free). Restaurant. TV (cable).

BONDI & COOGEE BEACHES
Expensive

Swiss-Grand Resort & Spa
180-186 Campbell Parade, Bondi Beach, NSW 2026 (1800 655 252/9365 5666, www.swissgrand.com.au). CityRail Bondi Junction then bus 333, 380, 381, 382/bus 333, 380. **Rates** $260-$386 double. **Rooms** 202. **Credit** AmEx, DC, MC, V. **Map** p334 ⑪

The Swiss-Grand Resort & Spa may do a mean imitation of a wedding cake (all gleaming white columns and tiered levels), but it's still the classiest hotel to be found in Bondi – which says something about the state of the area's accommodation, since parts of the building are starting to look a little on tired side. But change is in the air: seven private courtyard suites (with their own barbecues) are now open, along with six family suites. Rooms are spacious, with two TVs, separate bath and shower, minibar and bathrobes. There's a rooftop pool and an indoor lap pool, a very good fitness centre, and the renowned Samsara Day Spa, offering Balinese treatments. The Epic Brasserie serves decent seafood, while the classiest of the three bars (the outdoor Deck Bar) rustles up tasty barbecue.

Bars (3). Business centre. Concierge. Disabled-adapted rooms. Gym. Internet (high-speed shared terminal). No smoking. Parking ($15). Pools (1 indoor, 1 outdoor). Restaurants (2). Spa. Room service. TV (cable/pay movies).

Moderate

Coogee Bay Hotel
Corner of Arden Street & Coogee Bay Road, Coogee Beach, NSW 2034 (9665 0000, www.coogeebayhotel.com.au). Bus 372, 373, 374. **Rates** $130-$330 double. **Rooms** 74. **Credit** AmEx, DC, MC, V.

The award-winning Coogee Bay Hotel has been operating on the same site since 1873 – though it's had a few face-lifts in that time. Not exactly a quiet beachside retreat, this complex is very big and very busy. The brasserie serves hearty fare for breakfast (included in the room price), lunch and dinner seven days a week, and there are several different bars (*see p191*) including a spectacular 'sports bar' whose big-screen aesthetic is offset with a tapas menu ('to attract a female crowd'). The Boutique wing has spacious and modern rooms with marble bathrooms, balconies and, in some rooms, kitchenettes. The Heritage wing is more basic. Rooms have been recently refurbished throughout with a crisp white, blue and natural timber beachside effect.

Bars (6). Disabled-adapted rooms. Internet (high-speed). No smoking. Parking (free). Restaurant. TV (cable/VCR/in-house movies).

Jonah's. *See p143.*

CONSUME

Dive Hotel

234 Arden Street, opposite the beach, Coogee Beach, NSW 2034 (9665 5538, www.divehotel. com.au). Bus 372, 373, 374. **Rates** $165-$280 double. **Rooms** 16. **Credit** MC, V.

A smart and elegant guesthouse, the Dive Hotel's contemporary design centres on bold colours, polished wood and clean, crisp bedlinen. Its cosy, sun-filled breakfast room looks out on to a bamboo-bordered garden, while views of the ocean from some of the rooms are equally wonderful. All rooms are en suite, with a microwave, fridge, TV and VCR, and while the bathrooms may be small, they are stylishly fitted out with mosaic tiles and stainless steel sinks. The annex – a three-bed house two blocks from the beach – accommodates families. Dive is a disarmingly welcoming place, thanks to its gracious owners Terry Bunton and Mercedes Mariano and their poodle (Babe), retriever (George) and cat (Bob) who help take the sharpness off the style.

Internet (wireless/high-speed). No smoking. Parking ($20). TV (cable).

Ravesi's

118 Campbell Parade, at Hall Street, Bondi Beach, NSW 2026 (9365 4422, www.ravesis. com.au). CityRail Bondi Junction then bus 333, 380, 381, 382/bus 333, 380. **Rates** $240-$350 double. **Rooms** 12. **Credit** AmEx, DC, MC, V. **Map** p334 ⓯

Ravesi's is known primarily for its noisy street-level bar, but upstairs you'll also find this chic boutique hotel. All rooms have private bathrooms and are

impeccably furnished: the designs, courtesy of renowned abstract artist Dane van Bree, use a palette of Aboriginal colours – mainly black, copper and bronze. The split-level suites have private terraces and superb sea views.

Bars (2). Internet (high-speed/wireless). No smoking. Parking ($8 per 24hrs). Restaurant. Room service. TV (cable/DVD).

Budget

Lamrock Lodge

19 Lamrock Avenue, at Consett Avenue, Bondi Beach, NSW 2026 (9130 5063, www.lamrocklodge.com). CityRail Bondi Junction then bus 333, 380, 381, 382/bus 333, 380. **Rates** $23-$45 dorm; $54-$80 double/twin. **Rooms** 55. **Credit** AmEx, MC, V. **Map** p334 ⓰

A good bet for the more mature backpacker looking for somewhere cheap and not too raucous to stay. The Lamrock is located on a quiet street 100m from Bondi Beach, and it's a very clean, well-maintained place, now sporting funky new bamboo flooring. All rooms have TVs, microwaves and fridges, and there are four-bed dorms with rates that get better the longer you stay. Furniture and decor are in typical hostel style (bedlinen, quilts and pillows are supplied), and there are plenty of vending machines (in addition to the kitchen and laundry). Friendly, helpful staff and 24-hour security help to create a genuinely relaxed and easy-going vibe.

Internet (pay terminal, wireless). No smoking. TV.

INNER WEST
Moderate

Tricketts Luxury B&B

270 Glebe Point Road, opposite Leichhardt Street, Glebe, NSW 2037 (9552 1141, www.tricketts. com.au). LightRail Jubilee Park/bus 431, 434. **Rates** $198-$245 double. **Rooms** 7. **Credit** AmEx, DC, MC, V.

A haven for antiques lovers, Tricketts has spared no detail – from the ornate moulded ceilings and imposing original cedar staircase to the cut-crystal glassware in the bedrooms and persian rugs – to establish its periods credentials. Practically everything you can see is a collectable. A wealthy merchant's house in the 1880s, a boys' home in the 1920s and then a children's courthouse, 270 Glebe Point Road has been many things to many people, but as a B&B it may have finally found its ultimate role. The seven guest rooms (one king-, five queen- and one twin-bedded room) are decorated in different styles, but all are en suite, and two are aimed at honeymooners (that is, they have four-poster beds). In summer, breakfast is served on the rear deck; in the cooler months, it is in the conservatory.

Internet (high-speed/wireless). No smoking. Parking (free). TV.

Budget

Alishan International Guesthouse
100 Glebe Point Road, between Mitchell Street
& St Johns Road, Glebe, NSW 2037 (9566 4048,
www.alishan.com.au). LightRail Glebe/bus 370,
431, 432, 433, 434. **Rates** $25-$33 dorm; $99-
$115 double. **Rooms** 19. **Credit** AmEx, MC, V.
Map p328 B9 ㊹
Conveniently located among the cafés, bookshops
and restaurants that line Glebe Point Road, this converted century-old mansion is a good Inner West
option for those on a budget. The spacious lounge-
diner sports a smart stone floor and rattan furnishings, and the very large commercial-grade kitchen
is for guests to use (no meals are provided). There
are dorms, simple single, double and family rooms,
plus a Japanese-style twin room with low beds and
tatami mats. Some of the rooms do come with private bathrooms but note that none of them have air-
conditioning or an in-room phone.
Disabled-adapted rooms. Internet (pay terminal/
high-speed wireless). No smoking. Parking ($5 dorm
guests; free other guests). TV (DVD/TV room).

Australian Sunrise Lodge
485 King Street, between Camden & Alice
Streets, Newtown, NSW 2042 (9550 4999,
www.australiansunriselodge.com). CityRail
Newtown. **Rates** $99-$119 double. **Rooms** 22.
Credit AmEx, DC, MC, V. **Map** p334 ㊺
Established in 1990, this friendly, family-run inn is
cosy and surprisingly quiet (given its location on King
Street – Newtown's main drag). A much-needed renovation spruced the place up a couple of years ago,
with a new reception, leather sofas in the lounge, new
carpet throughout and a new kitchen. Guest rooms
have a TV, fridge, microwave, tea and coffee facilities,
and kitchen utensils. Some have balconies overlooking a courtyard and are ensuite, but none have a telephone or air-con (though there are ceiling fans). The
lodge is recommended by Sydney University for off-
campus accommodation, so expect a student vibe.

INSIDE TRACK
ILLEGAL HOSTELS

Despite increased government
intervention, there are still a number of
illegal backpacker hostels operating all
over Australia. Their flyers are pasted
on lamp-posts or pinned to backpacker
bulletin boards. While the prices may be
tempting, these places can be cramped
fire traps that flout accommodation laws.
For an up-to-date list of recommended
legal hostels, see www.hostelaustralia.
com, www.visitnsw.com.au or
www.yha.com.au.

Disabled-adapted rooms. No smoking. Parking
(free). TV.

Billabong Gardens
5-11 Egan Street, at King Street, Newtown,
NSW 2042 (9550 3236, www.billabonggardens.
com.au). CityRail Newtown. **Rates** $23-$25
dorm; $69-$89 double. **Rooms** 36. **Credit** MC,
V. **Map** p334 ㊻
Bohemian, bright and arty, the decor at this
Newtown hostel-motel is a patchwork of bright
colours, exposed brick and crazy patterns. Set just
off the bustling environs of King Street, it attracts
artists and musos, even offering special deals for visiting bands, including space to store their equipment. The place is clean and all rooms have ceiling
fans and wireless internet. Some rooms have TVs
and fridges, but note that none of them have air-
conditioning. Other pluses include a large modern
kitchen, laundry, solar-heated pool, TV room and a
lovely, leafy courtyard. Staff are extremely friendly
and more than willing to help guests with everything from organising tours to finding work on an
organic farm via the World Wide Opportunities on
Organic Farms association.
Internet (wireless). No smoking. Parking ($5).
Pool (outdoor). TV (TV room).

Y Hotel City South
179 Cleveland Street, at Regent Street,
Chippendale (1800 300 882/8303 1303,
www.yhotel.com.au). CityRail Central/LightRail
Central. **Rates** $30 dorm; $118-$125 double.
Rooms 60. **Credit** AmEx, DC, MC, V.
Map p334 ㊼
Close to Sydney University, Prince Alfred Park (with
its great pool), Broadway, Glebe and Newtown,
this architect-designed new boutique hotel is quite
a find. It's run by the YWCA and is a joy to stay in,
as evidenced by its diverse clientele – everyone
from low-key backpackers and families through
to business people. In-room broadband, air-
conditioning and chic contemporary decor make for
comfortable surroundings, while a decent gym, outdoor terrace, rooftop garden, secure on-site parking
and the usual laundry and kitchen facilities are
added bonuses. If you're feeling flush (or have up to
five in your party), the tranquil and very comfortable apartment, with two large bedrooms, two bathrooms, courtyards, fully equipped kitchen, living
and dining area, is wonderful.
Gym. Internet (kiosk/wireless broadband).
No smoking. Parking ($7). TV.

NORTH SHORE
Expensive

Rydges North Sydney
54 McLaren Street, between Miller & Walker
Streets, North Sydney, NSW 2060 (1300 857

Periwinkle Guest House. *See p145.*

922/9922 1311, www.rydges.com). *CityRail North Sydney.* **Rates** $188-$304 double. **Rooms** 166. **Credit** AmEx, DC, MC, V.

North Sydney, with all its office towers and corporate headquarters, means business. So it's no surprise that the Rydges caters mostly to business travellers. All rooms have a private bath and shower, and many of the deluxe rooms and suites have beautiful views over the harbour. There are also 18 'iRooms' with a computer and unlimited internet access, as well as executive boardrooms, video-conferencing facilities and even a conference concierge service. The hotel has spent millions of dollars on its back-friendly 'dream beds', so at least there's a good night's kip to look forward to after a hard day at the office.

Bar. Business centre. Internet (high-speed). No-smoking floors. Parking ($15). Restaurant. Room service. TV (cable/pay movies).

Budget

Glenferrie Lodge

12A Carabella Street, between Peel Street & Kirribilli Avenue, Kirribilli, NSW 2061 (9955 1685, www.glenferrielodge.com). Ferry Kirribilli. **Rates** $40-$60 dorm; $109-$189 double. **Rooms** 70. **Credit** MC, V. **Map** p334 ⑭

A swish, three-star, harbour-front B&B just seven minutes by ferry from Circular Quay, this pretty, rambling house boasts spotless facilities and ample bathrooms. Air-conditioning may not be installed in

the guest rooms – at least that means your sinuses won't dry out – but they do have ceiling fans and there's a lovely harbour breeze to ensure that the nights never get too stuffy. The guest lounge offers cable TV and wireless internet access, and the dining room serves dinner five nights a week. The pet-friendly policy means the critters can come too. *Internet (wireless/high-speed). No smoking. TV (cable).*

NORTHERN BEACHES
Deluxe

Jonah's

69 Bynya Road, between Norma & Surf Road, Palm Beach, NSW 2108 (9974 5599, www.jonahs.com.au). Bus 190, L90. **Rates** $449-$799 double. **Rooms** 12. **Credit** AmEx, DC, MC, V.

You'll have a whale of a time at Jonah's – provided, that is, you can afford room rates that verge on the leviathan. Everything here is geared to the big spenders – the hotel was incorporated into the exclusive Relais & Chateaux group at the end of 2007. All of the dozen suites (including the particularly luxurious penthouse) are plushly furnished in contemporary style and have stunning views over Whale Beach from their private balconies. King-sized beds, limestone bathrooms with whirlpool spas and Bulgari toiletries are just some of the pampering touches you can expect. Friday and Saturday rates

Pittwater YHA.

include the unmissable dinner and breakfast at the renowned restaurant (*see p174*), and if you really want to put the rubber stamp of luxury on the whole experience, why not skip the car journey and fly up by seaplane from Rose Bay? *Photo p140*.
Bar. No smoking. Parking (free). Pool (outdoor). Restaurant. Room service. TV (cable/DVD).

Expensive

Manly Pacific Sydney

55 North Steyne, between Raglan & Denison Streets, Manly, NSW 2095 (9977 7666, www.accorhotels.com.au). Ferry Manly. **Rates** $199-$309 double. **Rooms** 214. **Credit** AmEx, DC, MC, V. **Map** p334 ㊾
Formerly known as the Manly Pacific Parkroyal, this four-star hotel that's run by Novotel and over-looks Manly Beach was taken over by the multi-national Accor chain in 2003. Since then, 52 court-yard rooms have been added, and various refurbishments undertaken. A heated outdoor pool, a rooftop fitness centre, sauna and spa ensure that guests get plenty of opportunities to burn off any of the calories they might have gained at the hotel's restaurant, Zali's, which provides an upmarket café menu in the evenings and a Mediterranean buffet on Saturday evening and Sunday lunch. Alternatively, the Corso, Manly's pedestrian shopping and café strip, is within easy walking distance, and central Sydney is only a half-hour ferry ride away.
Bars (2). Business Centre. Concierge. Disabled-adapted rooms. Gym. Internet (high-speed/wireless). No smoking. Parking ($18-$25). Pool (outdoor). Restaurant. Room service. Spa. TV (cable/in- house movies).

Moderate

Barrenjoey House

1108 Barrenjoey Road, opposite Palm Beach Wharf, Palm Beach, NSW 2108 (9974 4001, www.barrenjoeyhouse.com.au). Bus 190, L90. **Rates** $130-$220 double. **Rooms** 7. **Credit** AmEx, DC, MC, V.

The atmosphere at the Barrenjoey is relaxed and beachy, with white-painted walls, white furniture and the odd touch of rattan or bamboo, all punctuated by colourful sprays of fresh-cut flowers. A guesthouse since 1923, it has three en suite rooms and four with shared bathrooms – all are spotless and comfortable. The front rooms are best, as they overlook sparkling Pittwater. The café-restaurant, with its convivial terrace in summer and roaring fire in colder months, is a perennial meeting spot for both locals and tourists drawn to the sights of Palm Beach. Unsurprisingly, given the decor of the hotel, the restaurant's speciality is seafood.
Bar. No smoking. Restaurant. TV (TV room).

Newport Arms Hotel

Corner of Beaconsfield & Kalinya Streets, Newport, NSW 2106 (9997 4900, www. newportarms.com.au). Bus 188, L88, 190, L90. **Rates** $160-$170 double. **Rooms** 9. **Credit** AmEx, DC, MC, V.

To mark its 127th birthday, the Newport Arms was given a complete facelift in 2007, but despite its swish new look, it remains a firm favourite with local families for its child-friendly restaurant and playgrounds. On the shores of Pittwater, which is about a 40-minute drive from the CBD or 15 minutes from Palm Beach, the Newport is close, but thankfully not too close, to the action. There are eight doubles, all with basic furniture and private bathrooms, and one family room that sleeps six. The hotel also houses a very popular pub (*see p193*), with cheap drinks and live music. The waterfront beer garden features the new Garden Bistro, two new bars and an all-weather dining area.
Bars (5). No smoking. Parking (free). Restaurants (3). TV.

Periwinkle Guest House

18-19 East Esplanade, at Ashburner Street, Manly, NSW 2095 (9977 4668, www.periwinkle. citysearch.com.au). Ferry Manly. **Rates** $137-$195 double. **Rooms** 18. **Credit** MC, V. **Map** p334 ⑩
Perched above the waters of tranquil Manly Cove, within walking distance of the ferry wharf, this 1895 Federation building has iron-lace verandas and lots of period charm without feeling in any way stuffy. The 18 colourful bedrooms have ceiling fans, fireplaces and cane furniture; 12 of them are en suite. Heaters and electric blankets are provided in the winter. Guests can use the kitchen and laundry, and there's a courtyard with seating.
No smoking. Parking (free). TV (TV room).

Budget

Pittwater YHA

Morning Bay, Pittwater, NSW 2105 (9999 5748, www.yha.com.au). Reception open 8-11am, 5-8pm daily. Ferry/water taxi Halls Wharf then 15min walk. **Rates** $25-$28 dorm; $65-$72 double. **Rooms** 8. **Credit** MC, V.

If you're looking for a real Australian bush experience within the city limits of Sydney, then head here. Overlooking pretty Morning Bay, this recently refurbished stone-and-wood hillside lodge is hidden in the trees in Ku-ring-gai Chase National Park. You can't get here by car, but it's worth the arduous journey – an hour's bus to Church Point, a ferry to Halls Wharf, then a steep, 15-minute climb through the bush – because the wildlife all around is breathtaking. Red and green rosellas, laughing kookaburras, wallabies, possums and goannas are just a few of the native Aussie animals you're likely to spot here. Guests can hire canoes and kayaks or swim in the bay, and there are women-only massage workshops once or twice a year. It's BYO food (there are no shops) and bedlinen, or you can hire the latter subject to water availability; no sleeping bags are allowed. It's incredibly popular, so advance bookings are essential. There are also kitchen and laundry facilities and, of course, a barbie.
No smoking.

Sydney Beachhouse YHA

4 Collaroy Street, at Pittwater Road, Collaroy, NSW 2097 (9981 1177, www.yha.com.au). Bus 188, L88, 190, L90. **Rates** $23-$39 dorm; $63-$100 double. **Rooms** 60. **Credit** MC, V.
Who needs the glamour and glitz of Palm Beach when Collaroy's got charm to burn and much, much lower prices? This YHA hostel is one of the best budget options in the northern beaches, with bright, clean rooms and plenty of extras (check out the hilarious inflatable surf machine). There are four-person dormitories, twins and family rooms, free surfboards, boogie boards and bicycles to borrow, and a compact, solar-heated outdoor pool. You won't be bored – other facilities include a kitchen, a barbecue area, arcade games, pool table and internet café.
Disabled-adapted room (family). Internet (pay terminals). No smoking. Parking (free). Pool (outdoor). TV (cable/DVD/free movies/TV room).

THE SOUTH

Expensive

Novotel Brighton Beach

Corner of Grand Parade & Princess Street, Brighton-le-Sands, NSW 2216 (1300 656 565, 9556 5111, www.novotelbrightonbeach.com.au). CityRail Rockdale then bus 475, 478, 479/ bus 303, X03. **Rates** $209-$319 double. **Rooms** 296. **Credit** AmEx, DC, MC, V.

CONSUME

The family-friendly Novotel Brighton Beach is full of extras that help to make up for its rather uninspiring decor – an overhead walkway to the beach, a pool with outdoor slide for the kiddies, tennis court, fitness centre and a spa offering all the usual treatments. The Baygarden restaurant, on the third floor with a swanky terrace, has views over the bay and serves modern Australian cuisine, and the cocktail bar also has a fine prospect. The hotel is five minutes from Sydney International Airport (25 minutes from downtown), thus making it a convenient option for stopover travellers. All rooms have private bathrooms and balconies with views inland or over Botany Bay.
Bar. Business centre. Concierge. Disabled-adapted rooms. Gym. Internet (high-speed/wireless). No smoking. Parking ($20). Pool (1 indoor, 1 outdoor). Restaurant. Room service. Spa. TV (pay movies).

Rydges Cronulla
20-26 Kingsway, at Gerrale Street, Cronulla, NSW 2230 (1300 857 922/9527 3100, www.rydges.com). CityRail Cronulla. **Rates** $198-$360 double. **Rooms** 84. **Credit** AmEx, DC, MC, V.
Overlooking Cronulla Beach and the picturesque sweep of Gunnamatta Bay, this mid-range option is good for the naturalist, being close to the great bushwalking trails and wildlife of Royal National Park. All rooms have en suite bathrooms and at least one balcony, plus a desk and TV. Other facilities available include a pool, sauna, spa and beauty salon. At the time of writing, the hotel's restaurant was undergoing a large-scale refurbishment.
Bar. Business Centre. Disabled-adapted rooms. Internet (dataport/wireless). No-smoking floors. Parking (free). Pool (outdoor). Restaurant. Room service. Spa. TV (in-house movies/cable).

Serviced apartments

Somewhere between a hotel suite and a rented apartment, these used to be strictly the domain of the business traveller. But no more. These days, many holidaymakers can't get enough of the comforts of home – more space, more flexibility, in-built kitchens and other conveniences, such as washing machines.

Apartment One
297 Liverpool Street, Darlinghurst, NSW 2010 (9331 2881, www.contemporaryhotels.com.au). Bus 311, 333, 352, 373, 377, 378, 380, 392, 394, 396. **Rates** $385-$485. **Apartments** 1. **Credit** AmEx, DC, MC, V. **Map** p329 H8 ⑤1
This gloriously hip two-level apartment is part of the Contemporary Hotels group. There are three outdoor terraces and lovely designer touches everywhere you look. Long-stay rates are available.
Internet (dataport). Parking (free). TV (DVD).

Clarion Southern Cross Harbour Suites
Corner of Harbour & Goulburn Streets, Darling Harbour, NSW 2000 (1800 888 116, 9268 5888, www.southerncrosssuites.com.au). CityRail Central/ LightRail Paddy's Markets/ Monorail Paddy's Markets. **Rates** $185-$345. **Apartments** 67. **Credit** AmEx, DC, MC, V. **Map** p329 E8 ⑤2
The immediate location may not be very inspiring, but this block is conveniently sandwiched between Darling Harbour and Chinatown. The complex includes two restaurants, a nightclub and karaoke bar, an outdoor pool and a volcano-shaped jacuzzi.
Concierge. Disabled-adapted apartments. Gym. Internet (broadband). No-smoking apartments. Parking ($36). Pool (outdoor). Restaurants (2). Room service. Spa. TV (VCR).

Harbourside Apartments
2A Henry Lawson Avenue, McMahons Point, NSW 2060 (9963 4300, www.harbourside apartments. com.au). Ferry McMahons Point. **Rates** $275-$495. **Apartments** 82. **Credit** AmEx, DC, MC, V. **Map** p327 E1 ⑤3
The Harbourside's sweeping views of the Bridge and Opera House are fantastic (so be sure to ask for an apartment overlooking the water). The apartments themselves are now looking much slicker than in previous years, with white walls, modern furniture and fully equipped kitchens.
Internet (high-speed). No-smoking apartments. Parking (free). Pool (outdoor). Restaurant. TV (cable).

Mantra 2 Bond Street
Corner of George & Bond Streets, CBD, NSW 2000 (1800 222 226/9250 9555, www.savillesuites.com.au). CityRail Wynyard. **Rates** $340-$1,300. **Apartments** 170. **Credit** AmEx, DC, MC, V. **Map** p327 F5 ⑤4
Located in the heart of the financial district, these apartments have full business services and well-equipped kitchens. There are three penthouses and a small rooftop pool.
Concierge. Gym. Internet (high-speed/wireless). No-smoking floors. Parking ($35). Pool (outdoor). Room service. Spa. TV (cable/in-house movies).

Medina Executive Sydney Central
2 Lee Street, at George Street, Haymarket, NSW 2000 (8396 9800, www.medina apartments.com.au). CityRail/LightRail Central. **Rates** $300-$540. **Apartments** 98. **Credit** AmEx, DC, MC, V. **Map** p329 E9 ⑤5
Choose from one- and two-bed apartments, lofts and studios, most with full kitchens, housed in the Parcel Post building. There's a grocery delivery service and a new bar and café. Laundry facilities too.
Bar. Gym. Internet (high-speed broadband). Parking (indoor). Pool (indoor). TV (cable/DVD).

CONSUME

Meriton World Tower.

Meriton World Tower

*World Tower, 91-95 Liverpool Street, at George
Streets, CBD, NSW 2000 (1800 214 822,
8263 7500, www.meritonapartments.com.au).
CityRail Central or Town Hall/Monorail World
Square/ LightRail Central.* **Rates** $178-$1,000.
Apartments 152. **Credit** AmEx, DC, MC, V.
Map p329 E/F8 🏨
World Tower, part of the new World Square devel-
opment, is the tallest residential building in the city.
Studios and one-bed apartments are on levels 18-36,
and two- and three-bed apartments on levels 62-74;
the higher you go, the better the views.
*Business centre. Concierge. Disabled-adapted
apartments. Gym. Internet (high-speed).
No-smoking apartments. Parking ($35). Pool
(indoor). Room service. Spa. TV (cable/DVD).*

Quay Grand Suites Sydney

*61 Macquarie Street, East Circular Quay, NSW
2000 (9256 4000, www.mirvachotels.com.au).
CityRail/ferry Circular Quay.* **Rates** $550-$800.
Apartments 68. **Credit** AmEx, DC, MC, V.
Map p327 G4 🏨
Near the Opera House, this five-star complex of one-
and two-bedroom apartments delivers the goods –
spacious suites (twice the usual size) with balconies
and views over the harbour, en suite bathrooms,
well-equipped kitchens, two TVs and plenty more.
Bar. Business Centre. Gym. Internet (high-speed

*broadband/wireless). No-smoking suites. Parking
($30). Pool (indoor). Restaurant. Room service.
TV (cable/DVD).*

Regents Court Hotel

*18 Springfield Avenue, off Victoria Street,
Potts Point, NSW 2011 (9358 1533, www.
regentscourt.com.au). CityRail Kings Cross.*
Rates $275-$385. **Apartments** 30. **Credit**
AmEx, DC, MC, V. **Map** p330 J7 🏨
This swish boutique hotel of studio suites is
favoured by film and arty types – they even have a
writer/artist-in-residence programme. The rooftop
terrace has great skyline views and there's free tea,
coffee and *biscotti* at reception.
*Bar. Internet (high-speed/wireless). No-smoking
apartments. Parking ($15). TV (cable/DVD).*

Wyndham Vacation Resort

*Corner of Wentworth Avenue & Goulburn
Streets, Surry Hills, NSW 2000 (9277 3388,
www.wyndhamvrap.com). CityRail Museum.*
Rates $180-$300. **Apartments** 120. **Credit**
AmEx, DC, MC, V. **Map** p329 F8 🏨
Just south of Hyde Park, apartments on offer vary in
size (taking from two to six people) but all are well
equipped and furnished in smart contemporary style.
*Disabled-adapted rooms. Gym. Internet
(dataport). No-smoking apartments. Parking
($30). Restaurant. TV (cable/DVD).*

Restaurants

The best food in the southern hemisphere.

Sydney is one of the greatest cities of the world when it comes to dining, with superb seafood restaurants and a plethora of creative and international (particularly Asian) cuisine – not to mention a plentiful supply of waterside views. Not that that's breaking news to its residents who sleep, breathe and yes, eat food. Restaurants such as **Quay** combine world-class fine dining with snap happy harbour views taking in both Opera House and Harbour Bridge, while **Rockpool** relies on what's on the plate to tell the story.

But Sydney can also be a notoriously fickle city, with locals crowding to a restaurant for the first few months then leaving it for dead. This isn't the case everywhere, of course. **Bodega**, the coolest tapas restaurant you'll come across in the southern hemisphere, still has queues out the door and has done so every night since opening in 2006. But up until very recently, Sydney has had the reputation for being too flashy, with little going on at ground level. That's changing, however, with restaurants and bars opening up that speak to Sydney's daily restaurant habit, not its monthly one – venues the likes of Argentinian grill **Porteño**, and Italian wine bar/restaurant **Berta**.

While Sydney restaurants make the best of local produce, they belong to that light, inventive, produce-driven cuisine common to the Western world's finest, albeit with a keener understanding of the flavours of Asia and fewer ties to French technique. Native ingredients appear on some menus and indeed are the focus of some restaurants, but they're regarded in much the same terms as, say, Native American foods in the States or Welsh food in the UK: more a diversion than a serious component of contemporary dining. You can eat crocodile and kangaroo and wattleseed in Sydney, but the native ingredients you'll see in the city's better restaurants tend to run more along the lines of Coffin Bay scallops, Yamba prawns, West Australian crayfish and Tasmanian oysters than Skippy and co.

And there lies one of Sydney's great strengths: seafood. It's diverse, plentiful, fresh and of excellent quality. Just as importantly, perhaps, people know how to cook it: that is, not very much – or at all. Minimal interference between hook and plate keeps the natural qualities of the fish to the fore.

Many of the city's best seafood restaurants happen to make the most of the city's other great asset, the harbour. It's another distinctive facet of Sydney dining: true, there is no shortage of waterside places that will strip your wallet in return for food and service distinguished only by their ordinariness, but a significant fraction of the view-restaurants are worth visiting for more than the eye candy – in some instances grandly so.

In the restaurant listings that start below we've given the price range for main courses at dinner, and have also indicated whether or not the restaurant is licensed and/or operates a BYO policy (*see right* **Inside Track**).

CENTRAL SYDNEY
The CBD & the Rocks

Aria
1 Macquarie Street, East Circular Quay (9252 2555, www.ariarestaurant.com.au). CityRail/ferry Circular Quay. **Open** noon-2.30pm, 5.30-11pm Mon-Fri; 5-11.30pm Sat; 6-10.30pm Sun. **Main courses** $44-$56. **Licensed**. **Credit** AmEx, DC, MC, V. Map p327 G3 ❶ **Modern Australian**
TV's Matt Moran is much more than just another celebrity chef. He really can cook. Few compare to

the service, the wine list is multi-award winning and the stylish room makes for a special evening. The five-spice duck consommé is a highlight, as is the slow-roasted pork belly. And that's before you even mention the view of the Opera House.

★ Ash St Cellar
1 Ash Street, CBD (9240 3000, www.merivale.com). CityRail/Wynyard. **Open** noon-late Mon-Fri. **Share plates** $16-$32. **Licensed. Credit** AmEx, DC, MC, V. **Map** p327 F5 ❷ **European**
This little laneway wine and tapas bar is the jewel of megaclub complex Ivy. It caters for everyone from wine Luddites to the more adventurous types, who head straight for the tongue twisters. Head over on Monday for movie night – $35 gets you the flick, a glass of wine and tapas. The Ivy's other offerings, Mad Cow, Sushi Choo and Sailors Thai, are worth a visit, too.

Azuma
Level 1, Chifley Plaza, 2 Chifley Square, corner of Phillip & Hunter Streets, CBD (9222 9960, www.azuma.com.au). CityRail Martin Place. **Open** noon-2.30pm, 6-10pm Mon-Fri; 6-10pm Sat. **Main courses** $13-$66. **Licensed/BYO. Credit** AmEx, MC, V. **Map** p327 F5 ❸ **Japanese**
The deluxe skyscraper setting will have you squinting and pretending you're in Roppongi Hills or some other moneyed Tokyo setting, but the lightness and boldness of the kitchen's way with traditional Japanese flavours will tell you otherwise. When Azuma-san suggests you try sashimi with a squeeze of lemon rather than the ubiquitous soy, follow his advice and experience raw fish perfection.

INSIDE TRACK BYO BOOZE

The bring-your-own (BYO) tradition is alive and kicking in Sydney; even some of the more high-flying establishments allow it. But it often extends only to bottled wine, so call ahead if you plan to bring a few bottles of beer. Some restaurants offer BYO in the week, but go in-house-only on busier nights. A small corkage fee is usually charged, either by the head or bottle. In the listings in this chapter we've indicated whether the restaurant is licensed, BYO, both or doesn't allow alcohol at all.

★ Bacco
Level 1, Chifley Plaza, 2 Chifley Square, CBD (9223 9552, www.bacco.com.au). CityRail Town Hall. **Open** noon-10.30pm Mon-Fri. **Main courses** $29-$32. **Licensed. Credit** AmEx, DC, MC, V. **Map** p327 F5 ❹ **Italian**
Bacco is located in Chifley Tower, but before you discount it as shopping mall fodder be assured: this is a very good bar. The space, designed by Michael McCann, is all warm wood, low, long booths and tinkling, grape-shaped purple lights. Sit up at the bar, admire the huge booze selection, marvel at the cold larder filled with cured meats and raise a glass to Bacchus – the guy that loved a drink. *Photo p150.*
▶ *A brand new Bacco opened in the Queen Victoria Building in the CBD in late 2010. For more on the food, design and retail smörgåsbord on offer at the QVB, see p196.*

CONSUME

Ash St Cellar.

Baroque Bistro

88 George Street, The Rocks (9241 4811,
www.baroquebistro.com.au). CityRail Wynyard.
Open 9am-late Mon-Sat; 9am-3pm Sun. Main
courses $25-$29. **Licensed. Credit** AmEx, DC,
MC, V. **Map** p327 F3 **❺** French
This French bistro is brought to you by the Charkos
family, owners of the Rocks patisserie La
Renaissance – makers of some of the best macarons
in town. The macarons at Baroque are worth the trip
alone and their savoury offerings impress in equal
measure. The food is classic bistro fare with some
dishes wandering a little farther afield and their $25
plats du jour are perfect for easy, no-fuss dining.

Bécasse

204 Clarence Street, between Druitt & Market
Streets, CBD (9283 3440, www.becasse.com.au).
CityRail Town Hall. **Open** noon-2.30pm, 6-
10.30pm Mon-Fri; 6-10.30pm Sat. **Main courses**
$42-$49. **Licensed. Credit** AmEx, DC, MC, V.
Map p327 E6 **❻** French
Justin North is one of the city's brightest young chefs,
and with a French-based menu bursting at the seams
with delights such as john dory with scallops or the
seriously protein-punched rib-eye, it's especially big
with the lunchtime business crowd. The stunning
room is decked out in muted mushrooms, heavy curtains and hula hoop chandeliers. *Photo p153.*
▶ *See p162* **Where's the Beef** *to find out why
Plan B's burgers are the 'duck's guts'.*

Bilson's

Radisson Plaza Hotel, 27 O'Connell Street,
at Hunter Street, CBD (8214 0496,
www.bilsonsrestaurant.com). CityRail Wynyard.
Open 6-10pm Mon-Sat; noon-2.30pm Mon-Fri.

Set menu $130-$185. **Main courses** $45.
Licensed. Credit AmEx, DC, MC, V. **Map**
p327 F5 **❼** French
Tony Bilson is something of a legend in these parts,
having cooked in Australian kitchens for over 30
years. The unashamedly francophile elder states-
man of Sydney dining creates marvels, whether
turning his hand to spanner crab with chilled
almond gazpacho or an assiette of Angus beef. Order
the dégustation for the full Bilson's experience. The
wine list is pretty spectacular.

Bistrode CBD

Level 1, CBD Hotel, 52 King Street, at York
Street, CBD (8297 7010, www.merivale.com).
CityRail Wynyard. **Open** noon-3pm, 6-10pm
Mon-Fri. **Main courses** $31-$40. **Licensed.**
Credit AmEx, DC, MC, V. **Map** p327 E6 **❽**
Modern European
Bistrode CBD offers classic British stylings in a
stunning city dining room. You'll fall in love with
'Hearts and Minds' – probably the best-named dish
the world has ever seen. The perfect bite combines
tender brains, sweet lamb's heart and bitter greens
all in the one forkful. Or opt for the homely and com-
forting corned wagyu beef with brown bread
dumplings, mustard and horseradish. It's simple,
elegant food made and served with skill and finesse.
▶ *Jeremy Bistrode and his wife Jane also run an
elegant diner out of a converted butcher shop in
Surry Hills; see p163.*

Café Sydney

5th Floor, Customs House, 31 Alfred
Street, Circular Quay (9251 8683,
www.cafesydney.com). CityRail/ferry Circular
Quay. **Open** noon-11pm Mon-Fri; 5-11pm Sat;

CONSUME

Bacco. *See p149.*

noon-4pm Sun. **Main courses** $32-$39. **Licensed**. **Credit** AmEx, DC, MC, V. **Map** p327 F4 **9** Modern Australian
The setting is the draw here. Stepping out of the glass elevator, you enter a light-filled room with a dreamy vista over the harbour. There's a cool cocktail bar and a restaurant (where the view depends on the table you get). The menu is dominated by fresh fish and seafood, which are the highlights – meat dishes can be a little pedestrian for the price.
▶ *For illumination on the mystery of the 'swastikas' on Custom House's floor, see p55.*

$ Chat Thai
Galeries Victoria Shop 5, Lower Ground Floor, 500 George Street, between Market & Park Streets, CBD (9264 7109, www.chatthai.com.au). CityRail Town Hall/Monorail City Centre. **Open** 9am-8pm Mon-Wed, Fri-Sun; 9am-9pm Thur. **Main courses** $7-$9. **BYO. No credit cards.** Map p329 F7 **10** Thai

The queues wind halfway down the street and nearly everybody dining in the restaurant is Thai. With a stylish room and dishes like redfish mousse fritters and an excellent version of chicken rice with bitter melon soup, you can see why.

★ DeVine
Corner of Clarence & Market Streets, CBD (9262 6906, www.devinefoodandwine.com.au). CityRail Town Hall. **Open** 11am-10pm Mon-Fri; 6pm-10pm Sat. **Main courses** $32-$35. **Licensed**. **Credit** AmEx, DC, MC, V. **Map** p327 E6 **11** Italian
With a stylish interior within a heritage sandstone building, we'd happily whittle away more than a few hours in DeVine. It makes for a great long lunch/ Make your way through the sensational wine list in the front bar area or head out the back for simple and sophisticated modern Italian food.

Etch
62 Bridge Street, CBD (9247 4777, www.etchdining.com). CityRail/ferry Circular Quay. **Open** noon-11pm Mon-Fri; 5-11pm Sat. **Main courses** $29-$38. **Licensed**. **Credit** AmEx, DC, MC, V. **Map** p327 G4 **12** Modern Australian
Justin North's Becasse follow-up is a classic bistro with a Spanish twist and a focus on local produce. Be sure to sample the incredibly floral sweetcorn and blue swimmer crab soup enriched with sherry cream – a marvel from first spoonful till last. Once down from your soup high, try one of the daily specials like Monday's lobster omelette or Wednesday's roast rib of beef served with super silky mash. Great food, reasonable prices and top notch service. Get there now.

Est.
Level 1, Establishment Hotel, 252 George Street, between Bridge Street & Abercrombie Lane, CBD (9240 3010, www.merivale.com.au). CityRail Circular Quay or Wynyard/ferry Circular Quay. **Open** noon-2.30pm, 6-10pm Mon-Fri; 6-10.30pm Sat. **Main courses** $43-$52. **Licensed**. **Credit** AmEx, DC, MC, V. **Map** p327 F5 **13** Modern Australian
To step out of the lift and into the bright, colonnaded Est. dining room is to enter a bubble of total assurance. Peter Doyle's menu is flawlessly presented, skilfully cooked and hits its mark every time. And what you'll lose in pocket change, you'll gain in pure joy per bite. Amateur botanists, take note: manager Frank Moreau can tell you the name of every flower in the restaurant.

Glass
2nd Floor, Hilton Sydney, 488 George Street, between Park & Market Streets, CBD (9265 6068, www.glassbrasserie.com.au). CityRail Town Hall/Monorail City Centre. **Open** 6am-3pm, 6pm-

CONSUME

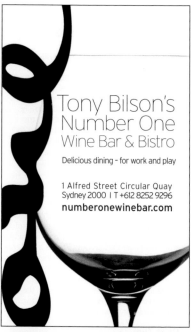

late Mon-Fri; 7-11am, 6pm-late Sat, Sun.
Main courses $30.50-$59. **Licensed**.
Credit AmEx, DC, MC, V. **Map** p327 F6
⑭ **Modern Australian**
Yes, it's one of those hotel dining rooms dreamed up
by the damned. The same panel may have also
thought that yoking culinary whizz Luke Mangan
to a steak-frites-and-soufflés brasserie-by-numbers
menu was a good idea. Sadly, the schismatic result
does little service to either, but the room is seriously
splashy and real effort has been made in the wine
department. The wine bar (see p186) is nice too.
▶ *As well as owning Glass, Luke Mangan is also
the consulting chef for Richard Branson's Virgin
Airways and in 2009 launched Salt Grill on the
P&O superliner Pacific Jewel.*

Guillaume at Bennelong
*Sydney Opera House, Bennelong Point, Circular
Quay (9241 1999, www.guillaumeatbennelong.
com.au). CityRail/ferry Circular Quay.* **Open**
5.30-11.30pm Mon-Wed, Sat; noon-3pm, 5.30-
11.30pm Thur, Fri. **Main courses** $38-$90.
Licensed. **Credit** AmEx, DC, MC, V. **Map**
p327 G3 ⑮ **French**
Given the following that Guillaume Brahimi picked
up while working with Joël Robuchon in Paris, it's
tempting to call his food French (not least his rendition of the great Robuchon's Paris mash). But there's
a lightness that is pure Sydney to his signature dish
of tuna infused with basil, for example, or the crab
sandwiches that are the mainstays of the bar menu.
Wine and service are of a similarly high order, and
the Opera House is a nonpareil setting.

Gumshara
*25-29 Dixon Street, Haymarket. CityRail
TownHall or Central.* **Open** 10am-10pm Tue-
Sun. **Main courses** $9.50. **BYO**. **Map** p329 E8
⑯ **Japanese**
You'll find the stall at the far end of the Eating
World. There's no phone number, no menu except
what's on the board. It takes seven days to make the
pork stock for the tonkotsu ramen and three ingredients: water, miso and 120kg of pork bones. This
incredibly collagen enriched noodle soup is so thick,
rich and porky that one between two is usually more
than enough. Yowza.

Ocean Room
*Ground Level, Overseas Passenger
Terminal, West Circular Quay (9252 9585,
www.oceanroomsydney.com). CityRail/ferry
Circular Quay.* **Open** noon-3pm, 6-11pm Mon-
Thur; noon-3pm, 6pm-midnight Fri, Sat. **Main
courses** $36-$50. **Licensed**. **Credit** AmEx, DC,
MC, V. **Map** p327 F3 ⑰ **Japanese**
Executive chef Raita Noda creates dishes that blur
the line between bar food and dinner – a casual, graz-
ing-style menu running to more substantial fare.
With a new look thanks to designer Yasumichi

Bécasse. *See p150*.

CONSUME

Morita, a relaxed menu style and great service, Ocean Room is high end without the hushed tones and bottom-clenching tension you may experience at other Japanese fine diners and worth a look-in.

▶ *Ocean Room features a colossal chandelier made from 42,458 beads of Asiatic timber, which shimmers over the room like a vast wooden tsunami symbolising wind and water.*

Ottoman

Pier 2, 13 Hickson Road, Dawes Point (9252 0054). CityRail/ferry Circular Quay. **Open** 6-10pm Mon; noon-3pm, 6-10pm Tue-Fri; 6-10pm Sat; noon-3pm Sun. **Main courses** $25-$33. **Set menu** $80. **Licensed**. **Credit** AmEx, DC, MC, V. **Map** p327 E2 ⓲ **Turkish**

Sister restaurant to Ottoman Cuisine in Canberra, this restaurant opened with a few coughs and splutters. Service was slow and faltering, and prices seemed high. But matters have improved since then, and the food here is worth the wait. Don't overdo the dips or you'll have no room for the signature dish – salmon dolma (salmon, minced prawns and crayfish wrapped in vine leaves). The setting on a deck of a finger wharf at Dawes Point is sublime too.

Prime

Lower Ground Floor, GPO Sydney, 1 Martin Place, between George & Pitt Streets, CBD (9229 7777, www.gposydney.com). CityRail Martin Place or Wynyard. **Open** noon-3pm, 6-10pm Mon-Fri; 6-10pm Sat. **Main courses** $32-$62. **Licensed**. **Credit** AmEx, DC, MC, V. **Map** p327 F5 ⓳ **European**

This designer basement in the old GPO building is all about the blokey business of heavy stone, big-dollar blockbuster reds, and meat – thick slabs and quivering haunches of the stuff. The red wine sauces are finger-lickin' great, and the knives are made from German surgical steel.

★ Quay

Upper Level, Overseas Passenger Terminal, Circular Quay West (9251 5600, www.quay.com.au). CityRail/ferry Circular Quay. **Open** 6-10pm Mon, Sat, Sun; noon-2.30pm, 6-10pm Tue-Fri. **Set menu** $155. **Credit** AmEx, DC, MC, V. **Map** p327 F3 ⓴ **Modern Australian**

Peter Gilmore's food roves the world, making this one of Sydney's greatest dining experiences. Try the mud crab congee or ravioli of slow-cooked rabbit, rare-breed pig belly with green-lipped abalone or the eight-hour slow-braised Flinders Island milk-fed lamb. What's more, there's not a bad seat in the house – they all offer beautiful views of the harbour. Such perfection comes at a price, naturally.

★ Rockpool

107 George Street, between Alfred & Argyle Streets, The Rocks (9252 1888, www.rockpool.com.au). CityRail/ferry Circular Quay. **Open** noon-3pm, 6-11pm Mon-Fri; 6-10pm Sat. **Main courses** $29-$140. **Licensed**. **Credit** AmEx, DC, MC, V. **Map** p327 F4 ㉑ **Modern Australian**

You won't find a restaurant in Sydney so burdened with the expectations of diners as Rockpool; there's something particularly special about the flagship restaurant. Maybe it's the thick white tablecloths; the plushly carpeted catwalk up the middle of the restaurant; the rubbernecking to see who's dining around you; or the incredibly professional service. Or maybe it's the food. Rockpool briefly changed course in 2007, becoming a more laid-back seafood spot for a couple of years; but now it's back to business as normal as a fine dining establishment (and the seafood is still top notch). The menu is offered over five small courses or as an eight-course grand tasting and while it isn't an everyday restaurant, it is an absolute must for every self-respecting food-loving Sydneysider. *See also right* **Profile**. *Photo p157.*

Sailors Thai Canteen & Restaurant

106 George Street, opposite Mill Lane, The Rocks (9251 2466). CityRail/ferry Circular Quay. **Open** *Canteen* noon-10pm Mon-Sat. *Restaurant* noon-2.30pm, 6-10pm Mon-Fri; 6-10pm Sat. **Main courses** *Canteen* $10-$28. *Restaurant* $19.50-$39.50. **Licensed**. **Credit** AmEx, DC, MC, V. **Map** p327 F3 ㉒ **Thai**

CONSUME

THE BEST RESTAURANTS

For relaxed dining
Bodega (*see p163*); **Fratelli Paradiso** (*see p166*); **Lotus** (*see p166*).

For water views
Berowra Waters Inn (*see p173*); **Guillaume at Bennelong** (*see p153*); **Manly Pavilion** (*see p174*).

For bistro fare
Ad Lib (*see p172*); **Bistro Moncur** (*see p166*); **Tabou** (*see p165*).

For vegetarians
Bentley Restaurant & Bar (*see p163*); **Glebe Point Diner** (*see p171*); **Manly Pavilion** (*see p174*).

For amazing bar food
Rockpool Bar & Grill (*see p154*); **Berta** (*see p163*).

For great service
Buzo (*see p166*); **Bilson's** (*see p150*); **Est.** (*see p151*); **Sean's Panaroma** (*see p169*).

Profile Neil Perry

The chef behind Rockpool is also one of Australia's best food ambassadors.

The year 2009 was a big one for Sydney chef and restaurant owner Neil Perry. Not only did his world-renowned **Rockpool** (*see p154*) restaurant celebrate its 20th anniversary in style, but he also opened not one but two new multi-million-dollar venues… in the same building and in the middle of a global financial crisis. People said he was crazy, but he can now give all those naysayers the two-fingered salute, for **Rockpool Bar & Grill** (sister to the eponymous Melbourne venue) and the modern Chinese **Spice Temple** (*see p157*) have both been packed since opening.

This is testament to Perry's pedigree and reputation, with a Sydney cheffing career that started in the 1980s. At the age of 29, he opened his first restaurant. Rockpool followed suit three years later – within six months of opening, it had been voted Sydney's best new restaurant by the *Good Food Guide*, and has gone on to garner a host of accolades for its fine Modern Australian cuisine.

Perry is now one of Sydney's foremost 'celebrity' chefs; he's authored several cookbooks (including *Good Food*, *Simply Asian*, and *Balance & Harmony*), created a range of Neil Perry fresh food products (in conjunction with Woolworth's Supermarkets), is a television presenter on Australia's LifeStyle Channel and a consultant to Quantas Airways. His emphasis on the freshest and finest local ingredients (seafood and beef in particular) has led to him becoming one of the country's best and most high-profile food ambassadors.

The venues that make up the Rockpool stable are all classy affairs that play on the senses; Rockpool Bar & Grill, located in one of Australia's finest art deco palaces (the 1936 City Mutual Building) impresses with its display of 6,500 stacked Riedel wine glasses and installations, while fellow newcomer Spice Temple, his modern Chinese venture, is all about 'light, sound and food'. 'Right from the beginning I wanted to give people a unique, multi-layered experience…', he told *Time Out Sydney* magazine – all the more impressive considering that the basement restaurant has no windows to draw from Sydney's emblematic views.

For despite the stylishness of his venues, it's Perry's passion for quality produce, evident in all his dishes, that ensures his loyal customers keep returning.

CONSUME

Chef David Thompson now spends most of his time running Nahm, his Michelin-starred Thai restaurant in London. Here you can eat food every bit as dynamic and thrilling, but for a fraction of the cost. Upstairs is more casual, serving the usuals like pad thai and som tum, while the ground-floor restaurant is a little more fancy (and expensive). The Thai sweets are particularly special – try the coconut custard.

★ Spice Temple
10 Bligh Street, at Hunter Street, CBD (8078 1888, www.rockpool.com.au). **Open** noon to 3pm, 6pm-late Mon-Fri; 6pm-late Sat. **Main courses** $12-$55. **Licensed. Credit** AmEx, DC, MC, V. **Map** p327 F5 ㉓ **Modern Chinese**
Neil Perry's first Chinese restaurant opened to much fanfare in 2009, in the basement of the art deco City Mutual Building, also home to the Rockpool Bar & Grill (*see p154*).While the latter is a go-to for prime-quality beef, Spice Temple showcases Neil's passion for Asian cuisine via the unique and spicy regional Chinese flavours that make up its menu. The inspirations behind the food are drawn from various Chinese provinces (with a distinct avoidance of Cantonese cuisine) and the dishes delight the senses with their contrasting tastes and textures. Spice Temple's food is designed for the shared table and is cooked to excite, yet the balance and harmony is never lost. *See also p155* **Profile.**

Summit
Level 47, Australia Square, 264 George Street, between Bond Street & Curtain Place, CBD (9247 9777, www.summitrestaurant.com.au). CityRail Wynyard. **Open** noon-3pm, 5-10pm Mon-Fri; 6-10pm Sat, Sun. **Set menu** $85. **Licensed. Credit** AmEx, DC, MC, V. **Map** p327 F5 ㉔ **Modern Australian**
Generally the revolving restaurant is the one to avoid, but Summit lifted its game with a fantastic relaunch in 2007. Chef Michael Moore worked at Bluebird in London, as well as a clutch of top-notch eateries in Sydney, and his experience is paying off. He uses plenty of local fresh fish and seafood, and gives an Asian frisson to dishes like blue swimmer crab with red chilli salt and coriander. Heartier fare such as pork with thick crackling keeps the traditionalists happy. The view is a further reason to visit – Sydney in its glory, from every angle.

Sushi Tei
1 Chifley Square, corner of Phillip & Hunter Streets, CBD (9232 7288). CityRail Martin Place. **Open** 11.30am-2.30pm, 5.30-9.30pm Mon-Sat. **Main courses** $9-$20. **Licensed. Credit** AmEx, DC, MC, V. **Map** p327 F5. ㉕ **Japanese**
For inexpensive Japanese food in the middle of the city, look no further than this newcomer, which rather cheekily mushroomed apparently overnight across the road from the smooth operators and

Japanese restaurant to the stars, Azuma (*see p149*). Order the edamame and gyoza and don't miss the sea urchin roe – it's spectacular.

$ Sydney Madang
371A Pitt Street, between Bathurst & Liverpool Streets, CBD (9264 7010). CityRail Museum. **Open** 11.30am-midnight daily. **Main courses** $13-$25. **Licensed. Credit** MC, V. **Map** p329 F8 ㉖ **Korean**
Korean food is taking over the world. Well, Pitt Street, at least. The service here is outstanding, and the kim chi pancake tasty as hell. The fried dumplings with rice vinegar are other must-orders, while the little sides of pickle, fish cake and tofu will leave you feeling virtuous from the inside out.

★ Tetsuya's
529 Kent Street, between Bathurst & Liverpool Streets, CBD (9267 2900, www.tetsuyas.com). CityRail Town Hall/Monorail Galeries Victoria. **Open** 6-10pm Tue-Fri; noon-3pm, 6-10pm Sat. **Tasting menu** $200. **Licensed/BYO. Credit** AmEx, DC, MC, V. **Map** p329 E7 ㉗ **Modern Australian**
You must eat here. No, no arguments. Yes, it's a lot of money to hand over for a meal. But, given that Tetsuya Wakuda is a culinary Olympian of the order of France's Alain Ducasse and the USA's Thomas Keller, it's actually a bargain of sorts. Don't be put off by the numerous (ten) courses in the fixed menu: each is so light and small you're guaranteed

Rockpool. See p154.

CONSUME

Marigold Citymark.

to leave groaning only with pleasure. And, fear not: everyone ends up eating the entire dish of butter whipped with black truffle and parmesan that accompanies the bread. They'd worry if you didn't.

Yoshii
115 Harrington Street, between Essex & Argyle Streets, CBD (9247 2566, www.yoshii.com.au). CityRail/ferry Circular Quay. **Open** 6-9.30pm Mon, Sat; noon-2pm, 6-9.30pm Tue-Fri. **Set menu** $80; $130 tasting menu. **Licensed**. **Credit** AmEx, DC, MC, V. **Map** p327 E4 **㉘** Japanese
Ryuichi Yoshii's father was a sushi chef, and the genes have run true in his offspring, with young Yoshii-san offering the finest sashimi in the land. Sit at the bar and watch him at his work or take a table for exquisitely cooked treats like the chaud-froid of egg and sea urchin roe. This is culinary inventiveness at the bleeding edge, presented in cosy but utterly civilised surrounds.

Chinatown & Haymarket

East Ocean Restaurant
88 Dixon Street, at Liverpool Street, entrance at 421-429 Sussex Street, Haymarket (9212 4198, www.eastocean.com.au). CityRail Central/ Monorail Paddy's Markets. **Open** 10am-2am Mon-Fri; 9am-2am Sat, Sun. **Main courses** $15-$35. **Licensed/BYO**. **Credit** AmEx, DC, MC, V. **Map** p329 E8 **㉙** Cantonese

East Ocean Restaurant comes across as a slick Hong Kong-style eaterie. The salt and pepper squid is particularly good, as are the baby abalone steamed with ginger and spring onion. The yum cha, meanwhile, is among the city's finest, with impressive diversity and freshness. The downside of this is that the news has spread, so be prepared to queue at weekends.

Emperor's Garden BBQ & Noodles
213 Thomas Street, between Ultimo Road & Quay Street, Haymarket (9281 9899). CityRail Central/Monorail Paddy's Markets/LightRail Capitol Square or Paddy's Markets. **Open** 9.30am-11pm daily. **Main courses** $9.50-$25. **Licensed/BYO**. **Credit** AmEx, DC, MC, V. **Map** p329 E9 **㉚** Cantonese
There are other establishments in Chinatown that dispense barbecue that's nearly as good as the Emperor's, but for the hardcore of roast and barbecue pork fanciers (and their pigeon and soy chicken loving brethren), Westerners and Cantonese alike, there is only one place to go for their regular fix. The Garden also does faithful renditions of stir-fried asparagus with garlic, ma po bean curd and the usual classic Cantonese dishes.
Other locations 96-100 Haymarket, CBD (9211 2135).

★ Golden Century
393-399 Sussex Street, between Goulburn & Hay Streets, Haymarket (9212 3901). CityRail Central/Monorail World Square/LightRail Capitol

Square. **Open** noon-4am daily. **Main courses** $15-$30. **Licensed/BYO. Credit** AmEx, DC, MC, V. **Map** p329 E8 ❸ **Cantonese**
Although the printed menu is fine, many regulars bypass it completely and flag down a member of the famously surly staff for steamed fish with ginger and spring onion, salt and pepper prawns and the restaurant's top-notch signature Peking duck. After 10pm the restaurant switches down a gear, offering cheaper, one-bowl meals for owls, drunks, waiters, chefs and other miscreants.

▶ *For more of the best 'after midnight' destinations in Sydney, see p225.*

Marigold Citymark
Level 4 & 5, 683 George Street, between Hay Street & Ultimo Road, Haymarket (9281 8988, www.marigold.com.au). CityRail Central/LightRail Capitol Square. **Open** 10am-3pm, 5.30pm-midnight daily. **Set menu** $33-$48. **Licensed. Credit** AmEx, DC, MC, V. **Map** p329 E8 ❷ **Cantonese**
Some argue that this is the best yum cha in Sydney. You'll be swayed by the dumplings (their har gau can't be beaten) as well as the flat rice noodles fried and served with dark and light sesame sauce.

$ Pho Gia Hoi
711 George Street, Haymarket (9211 0221). CityRail/LightRail Central. **Open** 9am-midnight daily. **Main courses** $6-$10. **BYO. No credit cards.** **Map** p329 E9 ❸ **Vietnamese**
Pho – the classic Vietnamese beef noodle soup – is the one to order here. Their vermicelli rice salads with bits of chopped up spring roll, pickled carrot, grilled pork, lettuce and green onion are also worth a look.

Red Chilli
51 Dixon Street, entrance on Little Hay Street, Haymarket (9211 8122). CityRail Central/Monorail Paddy's Markets/LightRail Paddy's Markets. **Open** 11.30am-3pm, 5-11pm daily. **Main courses** $10.80-$68.80. **Licensed/BYO. Credit** AmEx, DC, MC, V. **Map** p329 E8 ❸ **Sichuan**
Abandon hope all ye who fear spice, for this is not the place for thee: Red Chilli is one of only a handful of Sichuan restaurants in the whole of Australia – and one of the best. The signature deep-fried chicken served with its weight in chilli (balanced in the mouth by the cool burn of Sichuan pepper, of course) is famous for good reason.

Zilver
Level 1, 477 Pitt Street, entrance on Hay Street, Haymarket (9211 2232, www.zilver.com.au). CityRail Central/LightRail Capitol Square. **Open** 10am-3.30pm, 5.30-11pm Mon-Fri; 9am-3.30pm, 5.30-11pm Sat, Sun. **Main courses** $16.80-$180. **Licensed/BYO. Credit** AmEx, DC, MC, V. **Map** p329 E8 ❸ **Cantonese**

With its crisply uniformed staff and attractive dark tones, this place is just about impossible to get into around Chinese New Year. The yum cha here is a notch above the usual, but be sure to try the flat rice rolls or the congee. It's best to arrive around noon.

Darling Harbour & Pyrmont

Bar Zini
78 Harris Street, Pyrmont (9660 5718). CityRail Central/Monorail John Street Square. **Open** 7am-3pm Mon-Fri; 9am-3pm Sat; 5-10.30pm Wed-Fri. **Main courses** $15. **Licensed. Credit** AmEx, DC, MC, V. **Map** p326 C5 ❸ **Italian**
Gianni Chicco and Charlie Bruyere focus on fresh produce with an eye to simple Italian dishes. The housemade pasta is a standout and the salads are dazzling too. Want to eat honest Italian food, made from scratch in a tiny neighbourhood restaurant? Head to Zini.

Coast
Roof Terrace, Cockle Bay Wharf, Darling Harbour (9267 6700, www.coastrestaurant.com.au). CityRail Town Hall/ferry Darling Harbour/Monorail Darling Park. **Open** noon-midnight Mon-Fri; 5-midnight Sat. **Main courses** $29-$41. **Licensed. Credit** AmEx, DC, MC, V. **Map** p326 D6 ❸ **Italian**
Traditional Italian food in stunning, breezy surrounds high above Darling Harbour, with timber decking and slanting glass windows. The menu is slick, with deluxe salumi (cured meats), oysters, pastas, meat and fish, plus a 'market menu' that showcases seasonal ingredients. The wine list has some interesting by-the-glass options.

Fisherman's Wharf
Level 1, Bank Street, Pyrmont (9660 9888, www.fishermanswharf.com.au). CityRail Central/Monorail Wentworth Park. **Open** 11am-

---

INSIDE TRACK ASIAN CUISINE

Nowhere else in Australia is the country's proximity to Asia better expressed on the plate. While good and authentic Cantonese, Thai, Vietnamese, Japanese, Korean and Malaysian food is readily available (truly outstanding Indian, Pakistani and Sri Lankan is another matter, however), the modern Asian restaurants make a much better fist of things than their Western counterparts, dispensing with the ugly forced unions of 'fusion' food in favour of dishes that remain true to their ethnic roots even while dressing them up for the cocktail-and-couture set at the same time.

CONSUME

HARD ROCK ROCK SHOP® NOW OPEN
HARD ROCK CAFE OPENING MID 2011
Rock Shop® located on ground floor • Hard Rock Cafe on 1st floor

Hard Rock CAFE® SEE THE SHOW SYDNEY

HARBOURSIDE • DARLING HARBOUR
+612-9280-0077 • HARDROCK.COM

3pm Mon-Fri; 10am-3pm Sat, Sun. **Main courses** $21-$37. **Licensed**. **Credit** AmEx, DC, MC, V. **Map** p326 A6 ⑬ **Cantonese**
Fisherman's Wharf is one of the better locations in town for yum cha with spectacular views of Blackwattle Bay and the most impressive fish tank in town. It has the best range of seafood you're likely to find from pipis and scallops to coral trout and yabbies. And it'd want to – it's right above the Sydney Fish Market.

Flying Fish
Lower Deck, Jones Bay Wharf, 19-21 Pirrama Road, Pyrmont (9518 6677, www.flyingfish.com.au). LightRail Star City/bus 443. **Open** 6.30-10.30pm Mon; noon-2.30pm, 6.30-10.30pm Tue-Fri; 6-10.30pm Sat; noon-3.30pm Sun. **Main courses** $40-$48. **Tasting menu** $130. **Licensed**. **Credit** AmEx, DC, MC, V. **Map** p326 D4 ⑬ **Seafood**
Seafood from the tank is the forte here, with Tasmanian scallops and mighty Queensland mud crabs. Peter Kuruvita's menu also features Sri Lankan curries, raw fish dishes, chargrilled wagyu beef and some of the best chips in town.

★ Malaya
39 Lime Street, King Street Wharf, Darling Harbour (9279 1170, www.themalaya.com.au). CityRail Town Hall/ferry Darling Harbour/Monorail Darling Park. **Open** noon-2.30pm, 6pm-late Mon-Sat; 6-8.30pm Sun. **Main courses** $20-$34. **Licensed**. **Credit** AmEx, DC, MC, V. **Map** p326 D6 ⑩ **Malaysian**
The Malaya looms large in the recent history of Sydney restaurants, having been responsible, over the course of 30-odd years and several changes of location, for introducing local palates to galangal, lemongrass and other Asian flavours of which the locals had been unaware before. It might not be the cutting edge for Malaysian food any more, but the laksa and fish curry still delight in this airy establishment boasting water views.

East Sydney & Darlinghurst

A Tavola
348 Victoria Street, between Liverpool & Surrey Streets, Darlinghurst (9331 7871, www.atavola.com.au). **Open** 6pm-late Mon-Sat; noon-3pm, 6pm-late Fri. **Main courses** $22-$37. **Licensed/BYO**. **Credit** AmEx, MC, V. **Map** p330 J8 ⑪ **Italian**
Pasta is the speciality here. The communal marble table packs in around 25 people – just enough to serve comfortably with everyone getting the right attention from the very cool waitresses. The olive all'ascolana (olives wrapped in pork mince then deep fried – a bit like Italian Scotch egg) are spectacular, while orecchiette with broccoli is a stunning rendition of a homey Italian classic.

La Brasserie
118 Crown Street, Darlinghurst (9358 1222, www.labrasserie.com.au). Bus 324, 325, 326, 327. **Open** noon-3pm, 6-10pm Wed-Sat; 6-10pm Mon, Tue, Sun. **Main courses** $27-$49. **Licensed**. **Credit** AmEx, MC, V. **Map** p329 G7 ⑫ **French**
La Brasserie is, you guessed it, a classic Parisian brasserie serving rich French fare such as escargots, tripe, confit of duck and cassoulet in the perfect Gallic environs – La Vache Qui Rit poster on the wall and long bar at the front. Normandy-born co-owner Philippe Valet's grandfather once owned famous Parisian brasserie and nightclub Chez Castel, there's something of that sparkle here. The chef is an Aussie – David Bransgrove – but his cooking is Gallic through and through.

Omerta
235 Victoria Street, Darlinghurst (9360 1011, www.omerta.com.au). CityRail Kings Cross. **Open** 5pm-late Tue-Sun. **Main courses** $36-$38. **Licensed**. **Credit** AmEx, DC, MC, V. **Map** p330 J7 ⑬ **Italian**
This Darlinghurst gem is by the people that brought you the incredibly-hard-to-get-into Italian restaurant, A Tavola, across the street. The wine list is thick with tasty beverages and the food menu is also worth a nudge. It's not cheap at Omertà, but it is an offer you can't refuse.

Onde
346 Liverpool Street, between Womerah Avenue & Victoria Street, Darlinghurst (9331 8749, www.onderestaurant.com). CityRail Kings Cross. **Open** 5-11pm Mon-Thur; 5-11.30pm Fri, Sat; 5-10pm Sun. **Main courses** $17.50-$26. **Licensed**. **Credit** AmEx, DC, MC, V. **Map** p330 J8 ⑭ **French**
At times this seems not so much a restaurant as the part-time dining room of half of swinging Darlinghurst. Thankfully, Onde is unpretentious, buzzy, well priced and friendly. Think classic bistro food in space-age environs: you'll find yourself in the large polished concrete room faced with choices such as fried lamb's brains or duck pâté.

Rambutan
96 Oxford Street, between Crown & Palmer Street, Darlinghurst (9360 7772, www.rambutan.com.au). Bus 311, 333, 352, 373, 377, 378, 380, 392, 394, 396. **Open** 6pm-late Tue-Sat. **Main courses** $18-$36. **Licensed**. **Credit** AmEx, MC, V. **Map** p329 G8 ⑮ **Thai**
Rambutan is one of the most promising establishments to have opened on the Pink Strip for what seems like ages. The highlights are the wagyu shin with rice noodles, and the tea-smoked quail. Make sure you head to the downstairs bar for a cocktail before going on to hit the nosh pit.

CONSUME

★ Rise

23 Craigend Street, at Royston Street, Darlinghurst (9357 1755, www.rise restaurant.com.au). CityRail Kings Cross. **Open** 6-10pm Tue-Sun. **Main courses** $20-$35. **Tasting menu** $42; $60. **Licensed**. **Credit** AmEx, DC, MC, V. **Map** p330 J8 ⑯ **Japanese**
Deep-fried soft-shell crab tacos? Chicken teriyaki with potato salad? Fasten your seatbelt and make sure you've got a firm grip on your chopsticks: Rise's Japanese chefs take the food of their homeland as their departure point and then proceed deftly to interweave international influences at a fierce rate of knots. Plump for one of the great-value seven-course tasting menus.

$ Xage

333 Crown Street, Surry Hills (9332 3344, www.xage.com.au). CityRail Central. **Open** 6-10pm daily. **Main courses** $7.50-$10. **BYO**. **Credit** AmEx, DC, MC, V. **Map** p329 G9 ⑰ **Vietnamese**
This streetside Vietnamese joint does huge trade thanks to incredibly cheap prices for super tasty food. Make sure to try some of their signature dishes such as the slow cooked pork kho – a sweet melt-in-the-mouth braise of pork bits topped with fresh chilli and a nest of bean shoots.

Universal

Republic, 2 Courtyard, Palmer Street, between Burton & Liverpool Streets, Darlinghurst (9331 0709, www.universalrestaurant.com). **Open** 6-10pm Mon-Thur, Sat; noon-3pm, 6-10pm Fri. **Main courses** $24-$30. **Licensed**. **Credit** AmEx, MC, V. **Map** p329 H8 ⑱ **Modern Australian**
Sydney star chef Christine Manfield is back after a stint in London, and she has come back with all guns blazing. Universal is a small-plates-only establishment with a technicolour fit-out to match the food. The flavours are big and often Asian-inspired (jasmine tea-soaked duck, turmeric lemongrass broth), the crowd is cool and the cocktails are potent.

Where's the beef?

The new wave in burgers.

Australian hamburgers, served from milk bars all over the nation, traditionally come with rebel additions such as beetroot and even pineapple. And we still love 'em, occasionally. But Sydney is welcoming a new era of burgers. Locals now seek an authentic American style burger, where the cheese is melted on the patty, the patty is made of great quality meat and the most outrageous set dressing is a slice of tomato and (maybe) lettuce.

Below is a mix of our favourite new wave burgers... and a sprinkling of some of the old school classics.

Burger Joint
393 Liverpool Street, Darlinghurst (9380 2575, www.theburgerjoint.com.au). **Open** 11am-10pm daily. **Credit** AmEx, DC, MC, V.
These burgers are bloody good. It's all about the beetroot, barbecue sauce and pineapple.

Paul's Burgers
12 Princes Highway, Sylvania (9522 5632, www.paulsfamoushamburgers.com.au). CityRail. **Open** 11.30am-9pm Wed-Fri; 11.30am-7pm Sat, Sun. **Credit** AmEx, DC, MC, V.
You're right under the overpass but it's worth it for oldest-skool burgers and chips in a paper bag.

Plan B by Becasse
204 Clarence Street, CBD (9283 3450, www.becasse.com.au). CityRail Town Hall. **Open** 8am-4pm Mon-Fri. **Unlicensed**. **Credit** AmEx, DC, MC, V.
Grade nine wagyu patty, onion confitted in duck fat, pickled beetroot and cheddar on a brioche bun.

Ruby's Diner
Shop 1, 173-179 Bronte Road, Waverley (9386 5964). CityRail Bondi Junction. **Open** 6.30am-3.30pm Mon-Fri; 8am-3.30pm Sat, Sun. **Credit** AmEx, DC, MC, V.
Ruby D's does an excellent burger with pickled beetroot and fried baby chats.

Rockpool Bar & Grill
66 Hunter Street, CBD (8078 1900, www.rockpool.com.au). CityRail Martin Place. **Open** 12.30pm-3pm, 6pm-11pm Mon-Sat; 6pm-11pm Sat. **Licensed**. **Credit** AmEx, DC, MC, V.
The slickest of the pack is Rockpool Bar & Grill, Neil Perry's opulent city dining room. Perch at the bar and lay down $22 for the wagyu burger. Served on a fist-sized brioche bun, it's a juicy wagyu patty, pickles à la Zuni Café, Gruyere, tomato and lettuce. You could order chips on the side but the potato gratin is better. For more on Neil Perry, *see p155* **Profile**.

CONSUME

Surry Hills

Bentley Restaurant & Bar

320 Crown Street, at Campbell Street (9332 2344, www.thebentley.com.au). Bus 311, 333, 352, 373, 377, 378, 380, 392, 394, 396. **Open** noon-midnight Tue-Sat. **Main courses** $33-$40. **Tasting menu** $120. **Licensed. Credit** AmEx, DC, MC, V. **Map** p329 G9 ❹ **Modern Australian**

This popular restaurant in a heritage pub is the work of chef Brent Savage and sommelier Nick Hildebrandt, who complements the food with matching wines from an unbelievably comprehensive list (including lots by the glass). Try some of the progressive tapas, or go the whole hog and do the tasting menu. The dishes here are always surprising, which keeps regulars coming back for more.

Berta

17-19 Alberta Street, Surry Hills (9264 6133). CityRail Town Hall or Central. **Open** 6pm-late daily. $12-$24. **Licensed. Credit** AmEx, DC, MC, V. **Map** p329 F8 ❺ **Italian**

Berta has an industrial aesthetic, dim lights, chalkboard menus and a strict no-bookings policy, but any wait is more than worth it. The menu is broken into fairly share-worthy propositions. Try the likes of cuttlefish and zucchini – fingers of pan fried cuttlefish enriched with extra squid ink and accompanied by rounds of zucchini. Or a big ol' plate of mixed suckling pig bits (leg, loin, belly, wiggly little tail) with crisp, scorched golden skin.

Billy Kwong

355 Crown Street, between Albion & Foveaux Streets (9332 3300, www.kyliekwong.org). CityRail/LightRail Central then 10min walk/bus 301, 302, 303, 374, 376, 391. **Open** 6-10pm Mon-Thur; 6-11pm Fri, Sat; 6-9pm Sun. **Main courses** $27-$48. **Licensed/BYO** (wine only). **Credit** AmEx, MC, V. **Map** p329 G9 ❺ **Modern Chinese**

It's loud, you can't book, you eat elbow-to-chopstick with other diners on three-legged stools – and it's utterly fabulous. Celebrity chef Kylie Kwong takes the food of her Cantonese ancestry and sexes it up, keeping the emphasis on freshness, flavour and lightness. The stir-fries rock, the kingfish sashimi sings with sweet crispness and the crisp duck with blood plums has a well-deserved following.

Bistrode

478 Bourke Street, between Foveaux & Phelps Streets (9380 7333, www.bistrode.com). Bus 301, 302, 303. **Open** 6-10.30pm Tue-Thur, Sat; noon-3pm, 6-10.30pm Fri. **Main courses** $23-$34.50. **Licensed. Credit** AmEx, DC, MC, V. **Map** p329 G10 ❺ **European**

Don't let the bistro setting in a heritage butcher's shop put you off. To some, Jeremy and Jane Strode's

food may seem simple, but this is real art on the plate. Dishes like fried duck egg with sourdough crumbs and pine mushrooms show why three things on a plate are better than six. There's a French inspiration to some dishes, plus a well-priced wine list.

★ Bodega

216 Commonwealth Street, Surry Hills (9212 7766, www.bodegatapas.com). CityRail Central. **Open** noon-late Thur, Fri; 6pm-late Sat-Wed. **Tapas** $8-$32. **Licensed. Credit** AmEx, DC, MC, V. **Map** p329 F9 ❺ **Spanish**

The walls of Bodega Bar are adorned with a tripped out graffiti-cum-pop art mural of the sexiest bullfighter you'll ever see and the girls on the floor are all red lips and pin-up girl hair. The menu pleases as much as the aesthetics, with classic cocktails tweaked with a Spanish rock 'n' roll streak and the some of Sydney's best tapas dishes.

▶ *For the Bodega boys' latest opening, the excellent Porteño, see p164.*

Café Mint

579 Crown Street, between Devonshire & Cleveland Streets (9319 0848, www.cafemint.com.au). CityRail/LightRail Central then 10min walk/bus 301, 302, 303. **Open** 7am-4pm Mon, Sat; 7am-9.30pm Tue, Wed; 7am-10.30pm Thur, Fri. **Main courses** $21.50-$28.50. **BYO. No credit cards. Map** p329 G11 ❺ **Mediterranean**

A cool yet inexpensive caff-cum-restaurant, Café Mint is tucked away down at the uncool end of Crown Street. The food from chef/owner Hugh Foster is great – try the spicy lamb with houmous – and the almond and grapefruit frappé is an exceptional hangover-buster. It's a tiny space, note.

★ Erciyes

409 Cleveland Street, between Crown & Bourke Streets (9319 1309, www.erciyesrestaurant.com.au). Bus 372, 393, 395. **Open** 11am-midnight daily. **Main courses** $13-$29. **Licensed/BYO. Credit** AmEx, MC, V. **Map** p329 G11 ❺ **Turkish**

'Err-chee-ehs'. It's really not that hard to pronounce, but it seems to elude most non-Turkish speakers for some reason. But no one seems to have a problem wrapping their tongue around the spicy sausage-topped Turkish pizzas, the cabbage rolls or smoky kebabs. Hit the dips and breads hard and don't leave without a Turkish coffee. Saturdays see the ante upped by gyrating belly dancers.

$ House

202 Elizabeth Street, Surry Hills (9280 0364). CityRail Central. **Open** midday-2am daily. **Main courses** $5-$18. **Licensed. Credit** AmEx, DC, MC, V. **Map** p329 F9 ❺ **Thai**

If you're among the some who like it hot, this is the restaurant you'll want to run, nay, sprint to because at House the team from Spice I Am are delivering the authentic (and spicy) street food of northeast Thailand. The restaurant lives in the massive lantern-lit courtyard adjoining Triple Ace Bar, which is well stocked with Tiger, Kirin and Tsingtao – perfect to take the edge off the heat.

Longrain

85 Commonwealth Street, at Hunt Street (9280 2888, www.longrain.com). CityRail Central or Museum/LightRail Central. **Open** 6-11pm Mon-Wed, Sat; noon-2.30pm,6-11pm Thur, Fri; 5.30-10pm Sun. **Main courses** $27-$39. **Licensed**. **Credit** AmEx, DC, MC, V. **Map** p329 F8 ⑤ **Thai**

The restaurant is hip and gorgeous and so is the crowd along its communal tables. Think the food's going to have less depth and integrity than your waiter's lipgloss? Think again. Witness big, mostly Thai flavours dressed up for a big night out. Peanut curry of braised wagyu beef with chilli and thai basil is curry gone glam, and the betel leaves with prawn, peanuts and pomelo are frequently imitated but seldom bettered. The bar is a must-visit too (*see p188*).

Marque

Shops 4-5, 355 Crown Street, between Albion & Foveaux Streets (9332 2225, www.marquerestaurant.com.au). CityRail/LightRail Central then 10min walk/bus 301, 302, 303, 374, 376, 391. **Open** 6.30-10.30pm Mon-Thur, Sat; noon-3pm, 6.30-10.30pm Fri. **Set menu** $95. **Licensed/BYO. Credit** AmEx, DC, MC, V. **Map** p329 G9 ⑤ **Modern Australian**

Chef Mark Best trained in some of France's finest kitchens and has one eye on the pioneering work done by Spain's gastronomic wizards, yet the food at his quietly luxurious restaurant manages to be at once at the bleeding edge and utterly his own. Beetroot tarte (almost a tatin) with horseradish foam sits cheek-by-jowl with sweetbreads paired with sea urchin roe and samphire on one of the country's most exciting menus. The outstanding – and out-there – wine list rolls with every punch.

Maya Da Dhaba

431 Cleveland Street, between Baptist & Bourke Streets (8399 3785, www.maya masala.com.au). Bus 301, 302, 303, 372, 393, 395. **Open** 6-11pm Mon-Wed, Sat; noon-2.30pm, 6-11pm Thur, Fri; 5.30-10pm Sun. **Main courses** $10.90-$16.90. **Licensed/BYO. Credit** DC, MC, V. **Map** p329 G11 ⑤ **South Indian**

Spawn of the city's increasingly common Maya Indian sweet shops. But where the other Maya outlets typically only augment their dessert sales with the odd masala dosai and other vegetarian snacks, Dhaba has a full – and very attractive – menu of meaty delights from the subcontinent's south.

★ Pizza Mario

417-421 Bourke Street (9332 3633, www.pizzamario.com.au). Bus 311, 333, 352, 373, 377, 378, 380, 392, 394, 396. **Open** 6pm-late daily. **Main courses** $11-$25. **Licensed**. **Credit** AmEx, MC, V. **Map** p329 H9 ⑥ **Pizza**

These guys have the Verace Pizza Napoletana stamp of approval, which is a licence to say that they make pizza properly. Pretty much everything they do is done the way it is in the old country. Try the killer potato, sea salt and rosemary pizza and don't neglect the excellent antipasto.

Porteño

358 Cleveland Street, Surry Hills (8399 1440, www.porteno.com.au). CityRail Central/LightRail Central. **Open** 6pm-late Tue-Sat. **Main courses** $16-$38. **Licensed. Credit** AmEx, DC, MC, V. **Map** p329 F11 ⑥ **Argentinian**

This Argentinean bar and restaurant from the Bodega crew is a mix of local retro and items shipped straight from South America. Start upstairs with a cocktail. Try the Aereolineas Argentina's (their take on the classic Aviation) or the Pepe's Piña (rye, pineapple juice, honey and ginger syrup, oloroso sherry and bitters). Downstairs, watch as Ben Millgate and Elvis Abrahanowicz play with fire, lowering entire beasts over it for your delectation.

Restaurant Assiette

48 Albion Street, at Mary Street (9212 7979, www.restaurantassiette.com.au). CityRail/LightRail Central. **Open** noon-3pm Fri; 6-10.30pm Tue-Sat. **Main courses** $25-$37. **Licensed. Credit** AmEx, DC, MC, V. **Map** p329 F9 ⑥ **French**

Marco Pierre White-trained chef Warren Turnbull may dabble a little in the dark arts of progressive cuisine, but for the most part it's solid cooking with some lovely French flavours at excellent prices. Restaurant Assiette really is the place where you'll find Sydney's best-value fine dining.

★ Spice I Am

90 Wentworth Avenue, between Campbell & Commonwealth Streets (9280 0928, www.spice iam.com). CityRail Central or Museum/LightRail Central. **Open** 11.30am-3.30pm, 6-10pm Tue-Sun. **Main courses** $13.90-$25.90. **BYO. Credit** AmEx, DC, MC, V. **Map** p329 F8 ⑥ **Thai**

INSIDE TRACK SMOKE SIGNAL

It's illegal to smoke in any restaurant in Sydney. You may be allowed to smoke outdoors – the decision rests with individual establishments – but even then there may be a no-smoking policy early in the evening to allow alfresco diners to enjoy their meals smoke-free.

Spice they certainly are: this unremarkable-looking bolt-hole on a fume- and backpacker-loaded street serves the most authentic Thai food in Sydney. If you want to dice with some serious chilli, just ask your waitress to take down your order in Thai. That way the kitchen will do your green mango salad, your mussel and chilli pancakes and sour curries without concession to local tastes. Be warned – food this good is addictive, and so is the value: witness the queue of would-be diners waiting for a table.

Tabou
527 Crown Street, between Devonshire & Lansdowne Streets (9319 5682, www.tabou restaurant.com.au). Bus 301, 302, 303. **Open** noon-2.30pm, 6.30-10pm Mon-Fri; 6-10.30pm Sat, Sun. **Main courses** $28-$36. **Licensed/BYO** (wine only, Mon-Thur, Sun only). **Credit** AmEx, DC, MC, V. **Map** p329 G11 ❻❹ **French**
Tabou is, to all appearances, a classic French bistro with all the trimmings – glass mirrors with the menu scribbled on them, wooden chairs, the works. And the menu is what you'd expect, too, from steak-frites to brains and brawn. However, sufferers of noise fatigue should be wary – it may be a comfy, sweet little space but it's also loud as they come.

Uchi Lounge
15 Brisbane Street, between Goulburn & Oxford Streets (9261 3524, www.uchilounge.com.au). CityRail Museum. **Open** 6.30-11pm Mon-Sat. **Main courses** $12-$24. **Licensed/BYO (wine only). Credit** AmEx, MC, V. **Map** p329 G8 ❻❺ **Japanese**
Downstairs will get you some edamame or spiced almonds and a sake cocktail, upstairs will get you the likes of lightly seared salmon sushi blocks and aubergine with sweet soy paste topped with parmesan. For dessert, you can't look past the green tea and cinnamon crème brûlée. The food is fairly priced and it's plenty of fun on a Friday night.

Vini
Shop 3, 118 Devonshire Street, at Holt Street (9698 5131, www.vini.com.au). CityRail/LightRail Central. **Open** noon-midnight Tue-Fri; 5pm-midnight Sat. **Main courses** $24-$28. **Licensed. Credit** AmEx, DC, MC, V. **Map** p329 F10 ❻❻ **Italian**
A tiny restaurant with a whole lotta style, Vini plays off the brevity of its excellent Italian menu – two starters, two mains, two desserts and some snacks – with the richness and variety of its blackboard of Italian wines. The value on both counts is bang-on.

Kings Cross, Potts Point & Woolloomooloo

Aki's
1 Woolloomooloo Wharf, Cowper Wharf Road, opposite Forbes Street, Woolloomooloo (9332 4600, www.akisindian.com.au). CityRail Kings Cross then 10min walk or bus 311. **Open** noon-3pm, 6-10pm Mon-Fri, Sun; 6-10pm Sat. **Main courses** $25-$29. **Licensed. Credit** AmEx, DC, MC, V. **Map** p330 H5 ❻❼ **Indian**
Sydney's Indian dining scene doesn't have the sophistication of London or Manchester, let alone the old country. But it does have Sydney Harbour, as seen from Aki's – and that's got to count for something. Enjoy artfully presented (mostly Southern) Indian food while the water laps gently at the edge of Woolloomooloo Wharf.

Cafe Sopra
81 Macleay Street, Potts Point (9368 6666, www.fratellifresh.com.au). CityRail Kings Cross. **Open** noon-3pm, 6-10pm Mon-Sat; 6-9pm Sun. **Main courses** $15-$25. **Licensed. Credit** AmEx, DC, MC, V. **Map** p330 J6 ❻❽ **Italian**
This great establishment opens at brunch time and stays open for dinner (for those who can't drag themselves out of bed before Saturday arvo, this is a major blessing). The menu is constantly changing depending on produce, but is always simple, fresh and perfectly executed Italian fare.
▶ *There's a Cafe Sopra at Walsh Bay too, a favoured hang for actors from the Sydney Theatre Company over the road.*

China Doll
3/6 Cowper Wharf Road, Woolloomooloo (9380 6744, www.chinadoll.com.au). **Open** noon-3pm, 6-10.30pm Mon-Sat; noon-8.30pm Sun. **Main courses** $26-$44. **Licensed. Credit** AmEx, DC, MC, V. **Map** p330 H5 ❻❾ **pan-Asian**
Contrary to what you might imagine China Doll is not just a Chinese restaurant, serving a pan-Asian menu including some great dumplings and our favourite, Penang curry. And it's one of Russell Crowe's favourite eating spots.

$ Fei Jai
31 Challis Avenue, Potts Point (8668 4424, www.feijai.com). CityRail Kings Cross. **Open** 6pm-late Mon, Wed-Fri; noon-late Sat, Sun. **Main courses** $10-19. **Licensed. Credit** AmEx, DC, MC, V. **Map** p330 J6 ❼⓿ **Chinese**
The idea here is Chinese comfort eating, wrapped up in a slick package with friendly service and fruity beverages, and it's done well. Grab a few dumplings (they're best with chilli sauce) and some lamb-rich spring rolls and then check out the specials.

★ Fish Face
132 Darlinghurst Road, between Liverpool & Burton Streets, Darlinghurst (9332 4803, www.fishface.com.au). CityRail Kings Cross/bus 389. **Open** 6-10pm Tue-Sat; 6-9pm Sun. **Main courses** $28.50-$38. **Licensed/BYO. Credit** AmEx, MC, V. **Map** p330 H8 ❼❶ **Seafood**

CONSUME

Restaurants

Steve Hodges and fish go together like milk and honey. He has a more in-depth knowledge of seafood than just about anyone in town and boy can he cook it. He does so in every which way, but keep it simple and opt for the fish and chips.

Fratelli Paradiso
12-16 Challis Avenue, at Macleay Street, Potts Point (9357 1744, www.fratelliparadiso.com). CityRail Kings Cross. **Open** 7am-11pm Mon-Fri; 7am-6pm Sat, Sun. **Main courses** $21-$32. **Licensed. Credit** AmEx, DC, MC, V. **Map** p330 J6 ⓻ Italian
All-Italian menu, all-Italian wine list, all-Italian waiting staff. If the restaurant's packed (it invariably is), the waiter will stand out front and recite the menu. Take ten mates and order everything.

Jimmy Liks
186-188 Victoria Street, between Darlinghurst Road & Orwell Street, Potts Point (8354 1400, www.jimmyliks.com). CityRail Kings Cross. **Open** 5-11pm daily. **Main courses** $27-$35. **Licensed. Credit** AmEx, DC, MC, V. **Map** p330 J7 ⓻ South-east Asian
Jimmy Liks has copped some flak in the past for not treating its customers particularly well. And in terms of service, it's a fair cop. But don't let that keep you from the good cocktails, nor, for that matter, the full-flavoured takes on the street food of South-east Asia. The mussaman curry of veal shank with peanut betel leaf and ar-jard dipping sauce is inspired.

Lotus
22 Challis Avenue, at Mcleay Street, Potts Point (9326 9000, www.merivale.com). CityRail Kings Cross. **Open** 6-10.30pm Tue-Sat. **Main courses** $20-$26. **Licensed. Credit** AmEx, DC, MC, V. **Map** p330 J6 ⓻ Modern Australian
Beware: the cocktails here are the stuff of legend, and with good reason. But Dan Hong's smart, upbeat, well-executed Mod Oz menu is another reason to stay the course. The restaurant proper is insanely loud, so try to bag a seat outside if you can, but don't miss a glimpse of the stunning Florence Broadhurst wallpaper lining the walls of the bar.

Otto
8 Woolloomooloo Wharf, Cowper Wharf Road, Woolloomooloo (9368 7488, www.otto.net.au). CityRail Kings Cross then 10min walk/bus 311. **Open** noon-3pm, 6pm-late daily. **Main courses** $29-$110. **Licensed. Credit** AmEx, DC, MC, V. **Map** p330 H5 ⓻ Italian
Don't ask to speak to Otto – it's Italian for 'eight', the address of this celebrity magnet. If you can fight your way through the air-kissing and attract the attention of the charming but wildly inconsistent waiters, you might be in for some outstanding *cucina moderna*. Or you might not – it's that sort of place. But you'll have fun either way.

Velero
2/6 Cowper Wharf Road, Woolloomooloo (9356 2222, www.valero.com.au). CityRail Kings Cross then 10min walk/bus 311. **Open** noon-3pm, 6-late daily. **Main courses** $38-$68. **Licensed. Credit** AmEx, DC, MC, V. **Map** p330 H5 ⓻ Spanish
Velero is chic and relaxed. The open bar runs the length of the back wall, but the real attraction is the outside area. The mod-Oz menu has a strong Spanish tilt and the cocktail list is best enjoyed in the sun.

EASTERN SUBURBS
Bistro Moncur
Woollahra Hotel, 116 Queen Street, corner of Moncur & Queen Streets, Woollahra (9327 9713, www.woollahrahotel.com.au). Bus 378, 380, 389. **Open** 6-10.30pm Mon; noon-3pm, 6-10.30pm Tue-Sun. **Main courses** $29-$43. **Licensed. Credit** AmEx, DC, MC, V. **Map** p333 M10 ⓻ French
Bistro Moncur isn't as cheap as its name might suggest, but then it's been a long time since anyone went into a bistro expecting a cheap meal. However, Bistro Moncur is one of the finest examples of a smart-casual restaurant in Sydney that really gets it right, balancing near-boisterous conviviality with food that is as satisfying as it is seductive. Damien Pignolet is the god of (seemingly) simple culinary things done exceptionally well. Bistro classics such as provençal fish soup with rouille, pork sausages with lyonnaise onions and sirloin steak with Café de Paris butter are near-perfect every time.

Buon Ricordo
108 Boundary Street, at Liverpool Street, Paddington (9360 6729, www.buonricordo.com.au). CityRail Kings Cross/bus 389. **Open** 6-10.30pm Tue-Thur; noon-2.30pm, 6.30-10.30pm Fri, Sat. **Main courses** $31.50-$58.50. **Tasting menu** $125. **Licensed. Credit** AmEx, DC, MC, V. **Map** p330 J9 ⓻ Italian
You might think Armando Percuoco a chef, but he's actually hospitality on two legs. Watch him: clapping a back here, kissing a hand there, his big sandpaper voice booming one minute, confidential the next. And yet he somehow runs a tight kitchen too, with Buon Ricordo's luxe fare earning it a swag of best-Italian awards over the past decade. Go all out with the *fettuccine al tartufovo*, a rich explosion of house-made pasta with soft-poached truffled egg, or spare your arteries and delight your palate with the excellent seared beef carpaccio.

Buzo
3 Jersey Road, at Oxford Street, Woollahra (9328 1600, www.buzorestaurant.com.au). Bus 333, 352, 378, 380, 389. **Open** 6pm-late Mon-Sat. **Main courses** $27-$32. **Licensed. Credit** AmEx, DC, MC, V. **Map** p332 L10 ⓻ Italian

Icebergs Dining Room. *See p168.*

The atmosphere of this classy osteria in Woollahra is fostered by the rustic simplicity of the blackboard menu, pricing that is relatively modest for the area. Antipasti are a highlight – the salad of celery, white anchovy and parsley for example – as are faves such as the Sicilian roast lamb and the *vincisgrassi*, which interleaves porcini mushrooms, prosciutto, pasta and truffle oil in a luxurious lasagne.

Catalina

Lyne Park, off New South Head Road, Rose Bay (9371 0555, www.catalinarosebay.com.au). Ferry Rose Bay/bus 323, 324, 325. **Open** noon-10pm Mon-Sat; noon-4pm Sun. **Main courses** $35-$99. **Licensed**. **Credit** AmEx, DC, MC, V. **Modern Australian**

Arriving by boat has a certain cachet, yes, but to really nail the sense of occasion there's really nothing that beats pulling up in a seaplane. Catalina is pricey, showy and not immune to occasional attitude attacks. That said, the juxtaposition of so-Sydney water views and superb wine is pretty special, and the food itself is slick. You won't go wrong by ordering gutsy classics like pig's head with sauce gribiche or Whitebait fritters with fried duck egg.

★ Churrasco

240 Coogee Bay Road, between Arden & Brook Streets, Coogee (9665 6535, www.churrasco.com. au). Bus 372, 373, X73. **Open** 6-10.30pm Mon-Sat; noon-4pm, 6-10.30pm Sun. **Set menu** $35. **Licensed**. **Credit** MC, V. **Brazilian**

Six words: All. You. Can. Eat. Brazilian. Barbecue. Churrasco serves much that once walked or trotted, from sausages to hunks of lamb, all skewered on giant sword-like things and cooked over hot coals. It's TOO LOUD for conversation, unfortunately.

Claude's

10 Oxford Street, between Queen Street & Jersey Road, Woollahra (9331 2325, www.claudes.com.au). Bus 333, 352, 378, 380, 389. **Open** 7-10pm Tue-Sat. **Set menu** $135. **Tasting menu** $165. **Licensed/BYO. Credit** AmEx, DC, MC, V. **Map** p332 L11 ❻⓿ **French**
The room is classic and beautiful. The location is a terrace in Paddington. The service is attentive and the dishes are intriguing – caramel roasted Aylesbury duck, and sour sweet quail. Chui Lee Luk does wonderful things with food. No surprise therefore that it is a stalwart of the Sydney dining scene.

L'Etoile

211 Glenmore Road, Paddington (9332 1577, www.letoilerestaurant.com.au). Bus 389. **Open** 6pm-late Mon-Thur; noon-3pm, 6pm-late Fri; 10am-3pm, 6pm-late Sat, Sun. **Main courses** $28-$35. **Licensed. Credit** AmEx, MC, V. **Map** p332 K9 **French**
Classic, ultra-French food brought to hungry Sydnesiders from within the civilised surrounds of Paddington. Scallops with *boudin noir* (blood sausage) sees plump, bouncy scallops perched on rounds of rich sausage, while the roast garlic and hazelnut soup is creamy, smooth and soothing.

$ Flying Squirrel Tapas Parlour

249 Bondi Road, Bondi (9130 1033, www.flyingsquirreltapasparlour.com.au). CityRail Bondi Junction then bus 333, 380, 381, 382/bus 333, 380. **Open** 6pm-midnight Mon-Fri; 2pm-midnight Sat; 2pm-10pm Sun. **Tapas** $8-$18. **Licensed. Credit** MC, V. **Spanish**

INSIDE TRACK PERFECT PIZZA

INSIDE TRACK PERFECT PIZZA

Pizza wasn't the food of choice for the glamour crowd until Chef Peter Evans's super-trendy **Hugo's Pizza**. The seafood broth and meatballs at this Italian are outstanding but it's the pizzas that are gourmet, with toppings including belly pork and baked aubergine. The chef was even a finalist in the World's Best Pizza championship in 2010.
Level 1, 33 Bayswater Road, Kings Cross (9357 4411, www.hugos.com.au). CityRail Kings Cross. **Open** 5pm-late Tue-Sat; 3pm-late Sun. **Main courses** $22-$35. Licensed. **Credit** AmEx, DC, MC, V. **Map** p330 J7 ❻❶

The Flying Squirrel Tapas Parlour is the place to hang with the über-trendy Bondi-ites. Try the salt and pepper squid and chargrilled beef tenderloin, or stay old-school with the chorizo. And why not throw in a bloody caesar on the side (they import their own Clamato juice from Canada).

Icebergs Dining Room

1 Notts Avenue, at Campbell Parade, Bondi Beach (9365 9000, www.idrb.com). CityRail Bondi Junction then bus 333, 380, 381, 382/ bus 333, 380. **Open** noon-3pm, 6.30-10.30pm Tue-Sat; noon-3pm, 6.30-9pm Sun. **Main courses** $38-$48. **Licensed. Credit** AmEx, DC, MC, V. **Map** p334 ❻❷ **Mediterranean**
Bondi Beach-flavoured eye candy and visiting celebs are the order of the day here. Fortunately, the food more than matches the location. Salt-crusted suckling lamb, melt-in the mouth ox fillet, light crab and soft polenta – it's all excellent. The adjoining bar (*see p191*) is fabulous at dusk, and it's also home to the Icebergs winter swimming club. *Photo p167.*

La Cocina Peruana

103 Avoca Street, between Alison Road & Francis Street, Randwick (9326 4344, www.lacocinaperu.com.au). Bus 371, 372, 373, 376, 377, X73, X77. **Open** noon-3pm, 6-10pm Mon-Fri; noon-4pm, 6pm-late Sat, Sun. **Main courses** $12.50-$20. **BYO. Credit** AmEx, MC, V. **Peruvian**
La Cocina Peruana is a bright Peruvian restaurant that serves up meat platters alongside purple corn drinks and Incan cola. Try the platter with a mix of deep-fried pork, chicken, sweet potato served with a battery of sauces and cured onions.

La Scala

Above the Light Brigade Hotel, corner of Jersey Road and Melrose Lane, Paddington (9357 0815, www.lascalaonjersey.com.au). Bus 333, 380. **Open** 5.30pm-late Tue-Sat. **Main courses** $28-$39. **Licensed. Credit** AmEx, DC, MC, V. **Map** p332 L10 ❻❸ **Italian**
Darren Simpson's La Scala very much resembles his old, similarly named, haunt La Sala. Just as the name is only very slightly different, the menu is very nearly identical. But if it ain't broke, folks, why fix it? Simpson seems content to keep doing what he does best. Dates stuffed with almonds and fried crisp in batter; roasted bone marrow with parsley salad; *vitello tonnato* 'my way': winning dishes all. And be sure to try his chocolate nemesis cake.

Lucio's

Corner of Windsor & Elizabeth Streets, Paddington (9380 5996, www.lucios.com.au). Bus 380, 382, 389. **Open** 12.30-3pm, 6.30-11pm Mon-Sat. **Main courses** $39-$45. **Licensed. Credit** AmEx, DC, MC, V. **Map** p332 L9 ❻❹ **Italian**

CONSUME

Love art and food? Lucio's – where the myth of the starving artist is exploded – is the answer. The walls are festooned with works by many of Australia's foremost painters of the past 50 years, while the plates come adorned with two decades' worth of modish Italian eats. Head chef Logan Campbell cooks up traditional Ligurian fare such as duck neck filled with its own liver. It ain't cheap, but, rest assured, it certainly is tasty.

North Bondi Italian Food

118-120 Ramsgate Avenue, at Campbell Parade, North Bondi (9300 4400, www.idrb.com). CityRail Bondi Junction then bus 333, 380, 381, 382/bus 333, 380. **Open** 6-10pm Mon-Thur, Sun; noon-4pm, 6-10pm Fri, Sat. **Main courses** $24-$29. **Licensed**. **Credit** AmEx, DC, MC, V. **Map** p334 ❻❺ **Italian**

Yes, it can get a bit noisy; no, you can't book; and, no, it isn't as cheap as menus printed on disposable paper place mats may suggest. But this place, run by Icebergs' Maurice Terzini (*see p168*), is fabulous – fabulously busy, fabulously simple, a fabulously stylish osteria by the beach, with Coopers Pale Ale and red wine on tap, and tripe with cotechino sausage, borlotti beans and peas in its own tripe section on the menu. Be sure to taste the spaghetti arrabiatta with crab cooked in a paper bag. *Photo p170.*

Pier

594 New South Head Road, opposite Cranbrook Road, Rose Bay (9327 6561, www.pierrestaurant.com.au). Bus 323, 324, 325. **Open** noon-3pm, 6-10pm Mon-Sat; noon-3pm, 6-9pm Sun. **Main courses** $24-$45. **Licensed**. **Credit** AmEx, DC, MC, V. **Seafood**

Pier offers sheer delight on a plate, with smooth service and a waterside setting to boot. Floor-to-ceiling windows produce great views looking out over Rose Bay. Greg Doyle's menu is centred on seafood, with the odd meat dish on the side; the pan-roasted barramundi is poetry. The verdict? Far from cheap, but close to perfect. For smaller, less expensive offerings, try the adjoining Tasting Room.

Pompei's

Corner of Roscoe & Gould Streets, Bondi Beach (9365 1233, www.pompeis.com.au). CityRail Bondi Junction then bus 333, 380, 381, 382/bus 333, 380. **Open** 3-11pm Tue-Thur; 11am-11pm Fri-Sun. **Main courses** $17-$33. **Licensed/BYO** (wine only). **Credit** AmEx, MC, V. **Map** p334 ❻❻ **Pizza**

It's a matter of fierce debate: is the greatest thing about Pompei the creamy, all-natural gelato that comes in a range of drool-worthy flavours – or is it the pizza, Neapolitan-thin and available topped with everything from seasonal delights, like the pizza bianco with fresh artichoke, to the timeless margherita? It's a question that is probably best examined in person, as frequently as possible.

Restaurant Balzac

141 Belmore Road, at Avoca Street, Randwick (9399 9660, www.restaurantbalzac.com.au). Bus 371, 372, 373, 376, 377, X73, X77. **Open** 6-10pm Tue-Thur, Sat; noon-2.30pm, 6-10pm Fri. **Main courses** $32-$42. **Licensed/BYO**. **Credit** AmEx, DC, MC, V. **Modern French**

Matt Kemp does the Franglais thing (mixing up French and British cuisine) better than anyone in town. The saddle of lamb with olive crust is a standout. And there's a special dégustation menu ($95) on the last Sunday of every month. The value is sound, and that's before you try the famous pre-Ritz special – two courses for $50. C'est magnifique, innit?

★ Sean's Panaroma

270 Campbell Parade, at Ramsgate Avenue, Bondi Beach (9365 4924, www.seanspanaroma.com.au). CityRail Bondi Junction then bus 333, 380, 381, 382/bus 380, 333. **Open** 6.30-9.30pm Wed, Thur; noon-3pm, 6.30-9.30pm Fri, Sat; noon-3pm Sun. **Main courses** $32-$48. **Licensed/BYO**. **Credit** MC, V. **Map** p334 ❻❼ **Modern Australian**

Sean's Panorama is pure Sydney – if you can handle forking out top dollar for three (sometimes two) elements on a plate (perhaps you're paying for what they have the good sense to leave off). Chef Sean Moran waxes herbal at times, but his baseline is good-quality, local ingredients treated with maximum integrity. And with the new addition of a tasting menu (fantastic Queensland mud crab), there's even more reason to make your way to Bondi.

$ Wasavie

8 Heeley Street, at Glenmore Road, Paddington (9380 8838, www.wasavie.com.au). Bus 333, 352, 378, 380, 389. **Open** 6-10pm Tue-Thur; noon-3pm, 6-10pm Fri-Sun. **Main courses** $18-$36. **BYO**. **Credit** AmEx, MC, V. **Map** p332 K9 ❻❽ **Japanese**

INSIDE TRACK
TIME OUT SYDNEY
FOOD AWARDS

The *Time Out Sydney* Food Awards is an annual celebration of all things delicious. We at *Time Out* think of great food as one big package, celebrating quality wherever we find it. From down and dirty Thai restaurants where buckets of beers ride side by side with charcoal chickens rubbed in chilli to prog-French where shaved frozen foie gras meets crab custard to easy neighbourhood dining. Every year we celebrate the best of Sydney dining and every year, it's our biggest selling issue. Tuck in.

CONSUME

North Bondi Italian Food. *See p169.*

This minimal little local is living proof that good, cheap Japanese food isn't a paradox. You can sear your slices of raw fish on a hot stone for a bit of theatre, abandon yourself to the pleasures of the flesh in the form of the sumptuously sticky braised pork belly with hot mustard, or walk on the wilder side with Japanese/Mod Oz experiments.

INNER WEST

Bistro Ortolan

134 Marion Street, between Flood & Edith Streets, Leichhardt (9568 4610, www.bistro ortolan.com.au). Bus 436, 437, 438, L38, L39. **Open** 6-10pm Tue-Sat. **Main courses** $32-$45. **Licensed** (Fri, Sat)/**BYO** (wine only, Tue-Thur). **Credit** AmEx, DC, MC, V. French

This sweet little restaurant gets plenty right, with straight bistro food in stylish surrounds and smart service. Try the steak tartare served with a teeny weeny quail's egg nested in the raw mince. Capers, tomato and wasabi are arranged on the plate like little accoutrement soldiers.

★ Boathouse on Blackwattle Bay

Blackwattle Bay end of Ferry Road, Glebe (9518 9011, www.boathouse.net.au). Bus 431, 432, 433, 434, 370. **Open** 6-10pm Tue-Wed; noon-3pm, 6-10pm Thur-Sun. **Main courses** $36-$48. **Licensed. Credit** AmEx, DC, MC, V. **Map** p328 B7 ❻❾ Seafood

At Boathouse on Blackwattle Bay – and how about that for a name – it's all about the oysters. Order lots of them – there are typically at least six kinds – and lash out on some quality bubbles. Now marvel at the oysters' freshness, their diverse tastes and textures, how well they go with brown bread and champagne – and at the unique glory of this most relaxing of top-tier Sydney restaurants.

▶ *Several big names regularly dine here, including local acting star Bryan Brown.*

Ecco

2 St George's Crescent, corner of Park Avenue, Drummoyne (9719 9394, www.ecco.com.au). Bus 500, 501, 502, 503, 504, 505, 506, 507, 508, 509. **Open** 6-10pm Tue-Wed, Sat; noon-3pm, 6-10pm Thur, Fri, Sun. **Main courses** $32-$34. **Licensed. Credit** AmEx, DC, MC, V. Italian

The views are extraordinary, the staff are all incredibly friendly and the food is smart Italian. What else can we ask for? The orecchiette with peas and pancetta is a winner, while the zabaglione with tiny sugared doughnut balls is sensational.

$ Faheem's Fast Food

196 Enmore Road, between Metropolitan & Edgware Roads, Enmore (9550 4850). CityRail Newtown. **Open** 5pm-midnight daily. **Main courses** $12-$20. **Unlicensed. No credit cards.** Indian/Pakistani

Faheem may be the man, but we reckon that *haleem* is responsible for all the repeat business. In a menu of brilliant halal and vegetarian subcontinental cheap treats, *haleem* – a Pakistani curry of four different kinds of lentils and boneless beef cooked to seriously flavoursome mush – still stands out. How many dishes earn a subtitle, much less one as highfalutin' as 'the king of curries'? Super cheap too.

Fifi's

158 Enmore Road, between Metropolitan & Simmons Roads, Enmore (9550 4665). CityRail Newtown. **Open** 5.30am-midnight Tue-Sun. **Main courses** $11-$25. **Licensed/BYO** (wine only). **Credit** AmEx, DC, MC, V. Lebanese

The best falafels outside Lakemba can be found at this Enmore restaurant. The little room is packed every night and waitresses barge through the throng with plates heaving with houmous, tabouleh and rice. They also have Lebanese cola, which tastes a lot like plum juice, and some pretty tasty baklava.

★ Glebe Point Diner

407 Glebe Point Road, between Cook & Forsyth Streets, Glebe (9660 2646, www.glebepointdiner. com.au). Bus 431, 434. **Open** 6pm-late Mon-Thur; noon-3pm, 6pm-late Fri, Sat; noon-3pm Sun. **Main courses** $18-$30. **Licensed. Credit** MC, V. Modern Australian

Organic roast chicken, house-made pasta and Scharer's lager on tap. And we'll be damned if that isn't a suckling pig. This is the best Glebe has on offer – and the most crowd-pleasing place to have opened in recent years.

▶ *The GPD team opened Neutral Bay Bar & Dining (132 Military Road, 9953 5853, www.nbbaranddining.com.au) in 2010.*

Grappa Ristorante e Bar

267-277 Norton Street, at City West Link, Leichhardt (9560 6090, www.grappa.com.au). Bus 440, 445, L40. **Open** 6-10pm Mon; noon-3pm, 6-10pm Tue-Fri; 6-10pm Sat; noon-3pm, 6-9.30pm Sun. **Main courses** $28-$39. **Licensed/BYO** (wine only). **Credit** AmEx, DC, MC, V. Italian

From toddlers sucking on strands of linguine with chilli and roasted tomato to couples exchanging looks over slices of pizza to tables of old whippersnappers hoeing into the whole salt-baked snapper, punters of all ages and stripes find something to tempt on this barn-like restaurant's menu.

$ Guzman y Gomez

175 King Street, corner of O'Connell Street, Newtown (9517 1533, www.guzmanygomez.com). CityRail Newtown. **Open** 11am-11pm Mon-Sat; 11am-10pm Sun. **Main courses** $7.90-$10.00. BYO. **Credit** AmEx, MC, V. **Map** p334 ❺❶ Mexican

It may look like little more than a fast-food joint, but, in this case, it ain't necessarily so. This is the most authentic Mexican food to be found in the city: the corn chips are legendary and the pork adobado burrito is the bomb.

Other locations throughout the city.

Iku Wholefood Kitchen

25A Glebe Point Road, between Parramatta Road & Francis Street, Glebe (9692 8720, www.ikuwholefood.com). Bus 370, 431, 432, 433, 434. **Open** 11am-9pm Mon-Fri; 11am-8pm Sat; noon-7.30pm Sun. **Main courses** $7-$9.50. **BYO. No credit cards. Map** p328 C10 ㉜ Vegan

Vegetarians, vegans, macro-eaters and diet-conscious individuals flock to Iku's sharp-looking establishments in search of nourishment that is entirely vegetable. Pleasing tastes and textures don't always rule, but specialities such as the lime leaf curry laksa and the rice balls have dedicated followings.

Other locations throughout the city.

Il Piave

639 Darling Street, between Merton Street & Victoria Road, Rozelle (9810 6204). Bus 432, 433, 434, 442, 445. **Open** 6.30-10pm Tue-Sat. **Main courses** $30-$36. **Licensed/BYO** (wine only, Tue-Thur). **Credit** AmEx, DC, MC, V. Italian

Rozelle and Balmain have more than their fair share of Italian restaurants, but this one is a cut above. It's the fresh pastas like the ravioli that pull in the crowds, not to mention the pork belly.

Oscillate Wildly

275 Australia Street, between King Street & Hoffman Lane, Newtown (9517 4700). CityRail Newtown. **Open** 6-10pm Tue-Sat. **Set menu** $100. **BYO** (wine only). **Credit** AmEx, MC, V. **Map** p334 ㉝ Modern Australian

Eating at Oscillate is an experience as much as it is dinner. It's just the one degustation and, dietary restrictions aside, everyone has the same thing. Eight wild and wacky courses are dished up for $95, there's a great wine list and you can BYO.

Pomegranate

191 Darling Street, between Ann & Stephen Street, Balmain (9555 5693). Bus 434, 442. **Open** 5.30-10pm Tue-Thur; 12.30-3pm, 5.30-10pm Fri-Sun. **Main courses** $17.50-$32.50. **Licensed/BYO. Credit** AmEx, DC, MC, V. **Map** p326 A3 ㉞ Thai

The best Thai in Balmain. Betel leaves with whitebait and soft-shell crab with a side of pomegranate salad are the best choices, but save room for the salty-sweet Thai desserts.

Peasant's Feast

121A King Street, between Missenden Road & Elizabeth Street, Newtown (9516 5998, www.peasantsfeast.com.au). CityRail Newtown.

Open 6-10pm Tue-Sat. **Main courses** $18-$29.50. **BYO. Credit** AmEx, MC, V. **Map** p334 ㉟ Pan-European

King Street's dining scene is a bit of a sham: restaurants, restaurants everywhere, but nothing good to eat. So dining at the Feast comes as a pleasant surprise. Organic produce is brought to the fore, but flavour and presentation are strong too. Check out the gnocchi with a ragoût of aubergine and mushrooms, or the organic cassoulet. The good prices also help.

Perama

88 Audley Street, between New Canterbury Road & Trafalgar Street, Petersham (9569 7534, www.perama.com.au). CityRail Petersham. **Open** 6-10.30pm Tue-Sat. **Main courses** $28-$32. **Licensed/BYO** (wine only). **Credit** MC, V. Greek

The whitewash and retsina are in place, yes, but there's something unusual about this Greek restaurant. That's right, it's the food: from favourites such as falling-off-the-bone lamb or rabbit pie to adventures in food such as honey-peppered figs – it's really interesting, and really good. Super-warm service, as well as superb baklava ice-cream, seal the deal.

Restaurant Atelier

22 Glebe Point Road, between Parramatta Road & Francis Street, Glebe (9566 2112, www.restaurantatelier.com.au). Bus 431, 432, 433. **Open** 6-10pm Tue-Sat. **Main courses** $30-$36. **Licensed/BYO** (wine only). **Credit** MC, V. **Map** p328 B/C10 ㊱ Modern European

Glebe Point Road has a knack for killing off restaurants, so let's hope the curse passes here. Darren Templeman cut his teeth in the Michelin-starred restaurants of the UK, and his command of technique is clear in everything from Berkshire pork rillettes with pickles to a 'lasagne' of blue swimmer crab, shellfish oil, basil and olives.

NORTH SHORE

Ad Lib

1047 Pacific Highway, Pymble (9988 0120, www.adlibbistro.com). **Open** noon-2.30pm, 5-10pm Mon-Fri; 5-10pm Sat. **Main courses** $28-$42. **Licensed. Credit** AmEx, DC, MC, V. **French**

While Ad Lib is set in a fairly nondescript space, it has all the hustle and bustle of a proper French bistro. The food is made with exceptional skill and great produce. Onion soup, thick with tendrils of melted gruyere is brown, glossy and, well, oniony, while porky pucks of ear, trotter and tail are fried and served with a runny sauce gribiche and a couple of fresh-shucked oysters on the side. Bring it on.

Aqua Dining

North Sydney Pool, corner of Paul & Northcliff Streets, North Sydney (9964 9998, www.aquadining.com.au). CityRail/ferry Milsons

Bathers' Pavilion.

Point. **Open** noon-2.30pm, 6.30-10.30pm Mon-Sat; noon-2.30pm, 6-10pm Sun. **Main courses** $48-$49. **Licensed**. **Credit** AmEx, DC, MC, V. **Map** p327 F1⑨ **Modern Australian**
Aussies with childhood memories of standing barefoot and dripping by the deep end while clutching a meat pie slathered in tomato sauce may be thrown by the setting of this hip diner. But there's something very appealing about looking out over North Sydney's lovely Olympic pool and across the harbour as you dine. The food isn't amazing or cheap, but that view is something else.

Bathers' Pavilion

4 The Esplanade, between Awaba Street & Mandolong Road, Balmoral Beach (9969 5050, www.batherspavilion.com.au). Ferry Taronga Zoo, then bus 238/ferry Mosman South then bus 233. **Open** *Café* 7am-late daily. *Restaurant* noon-2.30pm, 6.30-9.30pm daily. **Main courses** *Café* $15.50-$33.50. **Set menu** *Restaurant* $95-$115. **Licensed**. **Credit** AmEx, DC, MC, V. **Modern Australian**
Serge Dansereau is one of the big men of Australian cuisine. Big, that is, in terms of his contribution to Sydney dining, helping to usher in the idea of seasonality (witness his chestnut soup) and an Australian style of cooking. This beautiful beachside restaurant highlights the best of his philosophy. The prices may send you out the back to wash up the plates, but this is a popular choice with locals and tourists.
▶ *For more information on Sydney's favourite beaches, see pp117-123.*

★ Berowra Waters Inn

Via east or west public wharves, Berowra Waters (9456 1027, www.berowrawatersinn.com). Deck C, Chowder Bay Road, Mosman (9960 3000, www.aquadining.com.au). **Open** noon-5pm Fri-Sun; 6.30pm-late Thur-Sat. **Main courses** $150 for 5 courses. **Licensed**. **Credit** AmEx, DC, MC, V. **French**
There's no land access to the actual restaurant but the waiting for the restaurant's own ferryman to take you for a ride from the wharf is part of the adventure. Chef Dietmar Sawyere's food is as much about being simple as it is studied, artful and styled and the whole idea with this menu is to make a Choose Your Own Adventure dégustation with a choice between four, five or six courses with the dishes travelling from lighter to heavier proteins. Happy travels!

Garfish

Corner of Burton & Broughton Streets, Kirribilli (9922 4322, www.garfish.com.au). CityRail/ferry Milsons Point. **Open** 7.30-11am, noon-3pm, 6-9.30pm Mon-Sun. **Main courses** $25.50-$35.50. **Licensed/BYO** (wine only). **Credit** AmEx, MC, V. **Seafood**

CONSUME

These guys are really into their fish. Working hand-in-fin with one of Sydney's leading seafood suppliers, they focus on freshness. And it's great to see the fish choice going beyond the usual clichés of salmon and tuna. Try the likes of aromatic kingfish curry with aubergine pickle or choose one of the day's catch from the blackboard.

Ju Ge Mu/Shimbashi
246-248 Military Road, between Waters Road & Winnie Street, Neutral Bay (9904 3011). Bus 169, 175, 178, 180, 247. **Open** noon-2pm, 6-9.30pm Tue-Sat; 6-9.30pm Sun. **Main courses** $12-$28. **Licensed**. **Credit** MC, V. **Japanese**
One half of the restaurant (Ju Ge Mu) is an *okonomiyaki* (a kind of Japanese pancake) and teppanyaki house, whereas the other half (Shimbashi) is all about the handmade soba noodles.

Mino
521 Military Road, between Gurrigal & Harbour Streets, Mosman (9960 3351). Bus 169, 175, 178, 180, 247. **Open** 6-10pm Tue-Sun. **Main courses** $18-$55. **Licensed/BYO** (wine only). **Credit** AmEx, MC, V. **Japanese**
Military Road's many Japanese eateries range from very ordinary mass-market sushi joints to the well-hidden charms of this little restaurant. Not much to look at from the outside, Mino is quite nice once you're through the door and regulars all seem happy to put their faith in the chef's kaiseki menu.

Shinju Teppanyaki
51 Berry Street, North Sydney (9957 6511, www.shinju.com.au). CityRail North Sydney. **Open** 6-10pm Mon-Sun. **Set menus** $33-$72. **Licensed**. **Credit** AmEx, DC, MC, V. **Japanese**
This restaurant is a North Sydney stalwart on the teppanyaki circuit. It provides the whole kit and caboodle, with flying fried eggs, fish and rice, and punters trying their very best to catch it all, with varying degrees of success.

Vera Cruz
314 Military Road, between Winnie Street & Langley Avenue, Cremorne (9904 5818). Bus 169, 175, 178, 180, 247. **Open** 6-10pm Mon-Sat. **Main courses** $18-$30. **Licensed/BYO**. **Credit** AmEx, MC, V. **Mexican**
'True Cross', maybe, but it's not true Mexican cuisine – that great gap in the Australian culinary landscape. Nonetheless, the food on offer at this very designer boîte isn't aiming for authenticity so much as a crowd-pleasing lightness and clarity of flavour.

NORTHERN BEACHES

Alhambra Cafe & Tapas Bar
54 West Esplanade, opposite Manly Wharf, Manly (9976 2975). Ferry Manly. **Open** 6-10.30pm Tue; noon-2pm, 6-10pm Wed-Sun.

Main courses $23-$54. **Licensed/BYO** (wine only). **Credit** AmEx, DC, MC, V. **Map** p334 ⓮
Moroccan/Spanish
Moorish by theme, moreish by nature, this loud, fun restaurant does a kickin' line in tapas, as well as spiced tagines, fluffy jewelled couscous and luscious pastilla. The outdoor seating and wild flamenco on Saturday nights up the ante.

Jonah's
69 Bynya Road, between Norma & Surf Roads, Palm Beach (9974 5599, www.jonahs.com.au). Bus 190, L90. **Open** 8-9.30am, noon-3pm, 6.30-9.30pm Mon-Sun. **Main courses** $27-$35. **Licensed**. **Credit** AmEx, DC, MC, V. **Modern Australian**
California-born but now an Aussie maestro, George Francisco cooks up roasted marrow bone with garlic croûtons and Murray cod in this lovely setting, but the snow crab is a highlight, as is the soufflé with mixed berries. For a complete blow-out, catch the seaplane over from Rose Bay.

★ Manly Pavilion
West Esplanade, Manly (9949 9011, www.manlypavilion.com.au). Ferry Manly. **Open** noon-3pm, 6pm-late daily. **Main courses** $26-$39. **Licensed**. **Credit** AmEx, DC, MC, V. **Map** p334 ⓯ **Modern Australian**
This flash mod-Italian restaurant is perched above the waters of Manly, but it's not the views that make this restaurant, it's the chef – Jonathan Barthelmess. He has a real gift when it comes to packing a lot of flavour and guts into such elegant looking dishes. And while you can pick and choose from the modern Italian menu, Manly Pavilion recommends you try the five-course menu at a fixed price of $88. It's advice worth heeding.

Pilu at Freshwater
Freshwater Beach, Moore Road, Harbord (9938 3331, www.piluatfreshwater.com.au). Ferry Manly then bus 136, 139. **Open** noon-3pm, 6-10pm Tue-Sat; noon-3pm Sun. **Main courses** $29-$45. **Licensed**. **Credit** AmEx, DC, MC, V. **Sardinian**
The Freshwater in question is the beach of the same name, while the Pilu is talented Sardinian-born chef Giovanni Pilu. For eastern feasters it's a bit of a mission to get to, but the gnochetti sardi with goat ragoût, the sweet honey and ricotta ravioli, and the roast suckling pig are worth the trip.

PARRAMATTA & THE WEST

$ Pho An
27 Greenfield Parade, between Chapel Road & Neville Lane, Bankstown (9796 7826). CityRail Bankstown. **Open** 7am-9pm daily. **Main courses** $10.70-$12.80. **Unlicensed**. **No credit cards**. **Vietnamese**

There's plenty of dissent over who does what best in Sydney's Vietnamese restaurants. But not when it comes to phô. The beef noodle soup (and the chicken version too) dispensed at this Bankstown landmark is the very coriander-accented nectar of the gods, and the toppings, from steak slices (prosaic) to wobbly bits (exciting), are without peer.

Sofra

35-39 Auburn Road, at Queen Street, Auburn (9649 9167). CityRail Auburn. **Open** 7am-midnight daily. **Unlicensed. No credit cards. Turkish**
In the very Turkish suburb of Auburn is this very Turkish eaterie. Forget rugs on the walls and belly dancers – the look here is tiles and fluoro strips – Sofra's cred is down to its very good charcoal-grilled kebabs and fluffy pide. And the baklava rocks.

$ Summerland

457 Chapel Street, between Ricard & French Streets, Bankstown (9708 5107). CityRail Bankstown. **Open** 6-10.30pm Mon-Sun. **Banquet** $35. **Licensed/BYO** (wine only). **Credit** AmEx, MC, V. **Lebanese**
Thirty-five bucks and a big appetite will take you far at this most hospitable of Lebanese restaurants. One of its many drawcards is a focus on seafood. It goes well beyond the usual whitebait – a breadth not common in Lebanese eateries in Australia.

Tan Viet

100 John Street, between Railway Parade & Hill Street, Cabramatta (9727 6853). CityRail Cabramatta. **Open** 9am-7pm daily. **Main courses** $10-$19. **BYO. No credit cards. Vietnamese**
The poultry versions of phô, the great Vietnamese soup, tend to be overshadowed by the beef style that is the nation's lifeblood. But not here: chicken gets celebrated in soup as well as some very fine fried incarnations, while the duck phô is a rare treat.

★ Temasek

71 George Street, between Church & Smith Street, Parramatta (9633 9926). CityRail Parramatta. **Open** 11.30am-2.30pm, 5.30-10pm Tue-Sun. **Main courses** $11.80-$30.80. **BYO. Credit** AmEx, DC, MC, V. **Malaysian**
Long held to be the purveyor of Sydney's finest curry laksa, this plastic-tableclothed palace also takes top honours in the beef rendang and Hainan chicken stakes. Call ahead for house specialities such as fishhead curry and chilli crab.

Thanh Binh

52 John Street, between Railway Parade & Smith Street, Cabramatta (9727 9729, www.thanhbinh. com.au). CityRail Cabramatta. **Open** 9am-9pm daily. **Main courses** $2-$20. **BYO. No credit cards. Vietnamese**

John Street is full of buzzy Vietnamese restaurants, but Angie Hong's Thanh Binh is pretty much universally accepted as the mothership. The choice is typically broad, but, atypically, almost everything on the menu is interesting, with many dishes unique to this establishment.

Woodland's

238 George Street, Liverpool (9734 9949). CityRail Liverpool. **Open** 11.30am-2.30pm, 6-9.30pm Tue-Sun. **Main courses** $9.50-$18. **BYO. Credit** AmEx, MC, V. **South Indian**
Consider the masala dosai: is there a bigger commonly available foodstuff? You may not find the answer here, but you will find blissfully light examples of the dosai genre.

SOUTH

Blackwater

Shop 1, 8 Water Street, Sans Souci (9529 4893, www.blackwaterrestaurant.com.au). CityRail Rockdale then bus 477/bus 303. **Open** 6-9.30pm Tue; noon-2.30pm, 6-9.30pm Wed-Fri; 6-9.30pm Sat; noon-2.30pm Sun. **Main courses** $17-$55. **Licensed/BYO. Credit** AmEx, MC, V. **Italian**
Traditional Italian food hits Sans Souci with the help of chef Riccardo Roberti who dishes up firm, thumb-sized gnocchi with hand-pounded pesto and light-as-a-feather pear sorbet in stylish surrounds.

Chez Pascal

250 Rocky Point Road, at Robert Street, Sans Souci (9529 5444). Bus 476. **Open** 7-9.30pm Tue-Sat. **Main courses** $21.50-$23.50. **BYO** (wine only). **Credit** DC, MC, V. **French**
Hankering for some old-school French fun? Make a beeline for Chez Pascal: in a room decorated with murals of a can-can chorus line you can indulge in gloriously unreconstructed coq au vin.

$ Ocean King House

247 Princes Highway, at English Street, Kogarah (9587 3511, www.oceankinghouse.com.au). CityRail Carlton. **Open** 11am-3pm, 5.30-10pm Mon-Fri; 10am-3pm, 5.30-10pm Sat, Sun. **Main courses** $18.50-$50. **Licensed/BYO. Credit** AmEx, DC, MC, V. **Cantonese**
It may be a rickety old house on the edge of the highway, but it's also the place of places to spend Chinese New Year. Don't miss the legendary yum cha.

Shanghai Yangzhou House

177 Forest Road, at Rose Street, Hurstville (9580 9188). CityRail Hurstville. **Open** 11am-3.30pm, 5.30-10pm daily. **Main courses** $9.50-$38.50. **BYO. No credit cards. Shanghainese**
'The number one dish in the world' – which happens to be fried rice squares with vegetable and tomato sauce – may have the coolest name, but the soup filled dumplings are our favourites.

CONSUME

Cafés

The finest city for 'doing shots'.

Coffee is an elemental force in Sydney and the city's baristas are all charged up for battle: who can craft the best design in your froth, who knows most about the beans and who will go the extra mile and give you a free biscuit or double shot with your black magic?

Starbucks was all but run out of town in 2009, admitting it had underestimated Sydney's passion for good espresso with pedigree, but the heart of the café scene is still in the independent establishments that abound along caffeine arteries such as Darlinghurst's Victoria Street, Paddington's Oxford Street, King Street in Newtown, Norton Street in Leichardt and Glebe Point Road in Glebe and, increasingly, wending their way into the veins of outer suburbia too. Baristas have now replaced bartenders as Sydney's sin doctors – they weigh the city's mood and tot up a shot to match, as pure a service as could be. Time to get back in black...

CENTRAL SYDNEY
The CBD & the Rocks

Bambini Trust Restaurant & Café
185-187 Elizabeth Street, between Park & Market Streets, CBD (9283 7098, www.bambini trust.com.au). CityRail Museum or St James/ Monorail City Centre. **Open** 7am-11pm Mon-Fri; 5.30-11pm Sat. **Licensed**. **Credit** AmEx, DC, MC, V. **Map** p327 F6 ❶
Designed with echoes of Milan in its wooden Venetian blinds and dark timber against crisp linen

INSIDE TRACK
COFFEE CULTURE

There are short blacks, flat whites and long blacks, but Italianate terms and style still pervade – you can't go wrong ordering an espresso, a latte or, more contemporarily, a macchiato or a retro-credible cappuccino. Unlike Italy, however, prices remain the same whether you stand, sit inside or sit outside. Table service is the norm and, contrary to other Australian states, many cafés here aren't licensed to sell or serve alcohol.

and white tiles, this is the canteen for Sydney's media elite, not least the editors of the Australian Consolidated Press stable, whose building it adjoins and who can usually be seen monopolising the back corner banquettes. The coffee is great, the food is fine, but the buzz is the real deal.

★ Klink
Gaffa Gallery, 281 Clarence Street, CBD (www.gaffa.com.au). CityRail Town Hall or Wynyard. **Open** 7am-4pm Mon-Fri. **Unlicensed**. **Credit** AmEx, DC, MC, V. **Map** p327 E6 ❷
This hot-to-trot hole-in-the-wall café adjoins a gallery but truth is, it's out front where the real art is happening. Although Botany-roasted Golden Cobra LHLH (named for a 1994 song by Sydney punk band Crow) is the house blend, you're as likely to be offered an under-the-counter bootleg like Ethiopian Lima or Harra, or a blueberry-hued Monte Allegre from Brazil. Contraband coffee? Or best connected café in town? Think Klink.

La Renaissance Pâtisserie
47 Argyle Street, off George Street, The Rocks (9241 4878, www.larenaissance.com.au). CityRail/ferry Circular Quay. **Open** 8.30am-6pm daily. **Unlicensed**. **Credit** AmEx, MC, V. **Map** p327 F3 ❸
This family business established in 1974 is highly recommended for its gateaux made daily by a team

of pastry chefs, which can be savoured in the lovely courtyard. Afterwards, check out the aboriginal and contemporary art in the Gannon House Gallery located just down the street.

MCA Café
Museum of Contemporary Art, 140 George Street, between Argyle & Alfred Streets, The Rocks (9245 2458, www.mca.com.au). CityRail/ferry Circular Quay. **Open** noon-3pm Mon-Fri; 10am-11.30pm Sat, Sun. **Licensed**. **Credit** AmEx, DC, MC, V. **Map** p327 F3 ❹
Not for the MCA the glam stylings of the eateries at the Guggenheim in Bilbao, say, or New York's MOMA. The deco design takes its cues more from the building's days when it housed the Maritime Services Board, while the food is light Mod Oz fare. There's also a nice deck at the front of the museum.

MoS Café
Museum of Sydney, 27 Phillip Street, corner of Bridge Street, CBD (9241 3636, www.mos cafe.com.au). CityRail/ferry Circular Quay. **Open** 7am-9pm Mon-Fri; 8.30am-5pm Sat, Sun. **Licensed**. **Credit** AmEx, DC, MC, V. **Map** p327 F4 ❺
The trad porridge with thick slices of poached apricots and peaches is a favourite with the money men, while lunch sees tourists move in for Grant Gordon's set menus of a decent main, a side of chips, salad, bread and a coffee.

Plan B
204 Clarence Street, CBD (9283 3450). CityRail Town Hall/Monorail Galeries Victoria. **Open** 8am-4pm Mon-Fri. **Unlicensed**. **No credit cards**. **Map** p327 E6 ❻
This cute hole-in-the-wall café next to its big brother, fine-dining restaurant, Bécasse (*see p150*), is a great place for a mouth-watering lunch. The wagyu burger is a no-nonsense deal of beef, fresh roasted beetroot, cheddar and tomato, although the coronation chicken sandwich is an excellent second choice.

Tea Room
Level 3, Queen Victoria Building, 455 George Street, between Market & Druitt Streets, CBD (9283 7279, www.thetearoom.com.au). CityRail Town Hall/Monorail Galeries Victoria. **Open** 11am-5pm Mon-Fri, Sun; 10am-3pm Sat. **Licensed**. **Credit** AmEx, DC, MC, V. **Map** p327 E6 ❼
Grandmothers sip single-estate Darjeelings and attack three-tiered platters of pretty cakes and finger sandwiches, while the CBD business set takes advantage of the widely spaced tables to talk shop over white tea, pinot noir and Mark Holmes's light, contemporary food.
Other locations Gunners' Barracks, Suakin Drive, off Middle Head Road, Mosman (8962 5900).

La Renaissance Pâtisserie.

CONSUME

THE BEST CAFES

For art-isans
Book Kitchen (*see p179*), **MCA Café** (*see left*), **Klink** (*see left*), **MoS Café** (*see left*) and **Tropicana** (*see p179*).

For a beaut brunch
Bills (*see p178*), **Café Sopra** (*see p179*), **Danks Street Depot** (*see p179*), **Flat White** (*see p181*) and **Plan B** (*see left*).

For coffee & cake
Bourke Street Bakery (*see p179*), **La Renaissance Pâtisserie** (*see left*) and **Tea Room** (*see left*).

For a classic Italian vibe
Bacino Bar (*see p183*), **Bar Coluzzi** (*see p178*), **Bar Italia** (*see p182*) and **Café Sopra** (*see p179*).

For people watching
Dee Bee's (*see p181*), **Jackie's** (*see p181*) and **Lumiere** (*see p180*).

Pyrmont

Blackwattle Deli
*Sydney Fish Markets, Bank Street, Pyrmont
(9660 6998, www.sydneyfishmarket.com.au).
LightRail Fish Market.* **Open** 7am-4pm daily.
Unlicensed. Credit AmEx, DC, MC, V. **Map**
p326 B6
From boutique Australian cheeses to meats of the
world, this little deli holds a fine range of eats, not
to mention the best coffee in the area. It's the perfect
respite to a morning at the Fish Market.

East Sydney & Darlinghurst

★ Bar Coluzzi
*322 Victoria Street, between Surrey & William
Streets, Darlinghurst (9380 5420). CityRail
Kings Cross.* **Open** 5am-7pm daily. **Unlicensed.**
No credit cards. Map p330 J8
Decorated with old boxing memorabilia, Bar Coluzzi
is one of Sydney's oldest coffee shops. The macchiato is excellent, but they also make a mean chocolate milkshake. You'll see lots of old Italian men
sitting on the squat wooden stools outside, smoking
and eyeing up the ladies.
▶ *Coluzzi's regulars include Oscar-winner Russell
Crowe, former prime minister Gough Whitlam,
and Sydney's Lord Mayor Clover Moore.*

Bills
*433 Liverpool Street, at West Street, Darlinghurst
(9360 9631, www.bills.com.au). CityRail Kings
Cross/bus 389.* **Open** 7.30am-3pm, 6-10.30pm
Mon-Sat; 8.30am-3pm Sun. **Licensed. Credit**
AmEx, MC, V. **Map** p330 J8
Chef Bill Granger has an expanding empire of cookbooks and TV appearances, but this café is still the
finest of his achievements. Its communal table plays
host to his famous creamy scrambled eggs, sunrise
drink and toasted own-made coconut bread at breakfast, while lunch sees the simplicity of steak sandwiches with garlic cream and chicken club
sandwiches with roasted tomatoes. If you want
(slightly) shorter queues, try the sister cafés.
Other locations 359 Crown Street, Surry Hills
(9360 4762); Queen's Court, 118 Queen Street,
Woollahra (9328 7997).

Bunker
*399 Liverpool Street, Darlinghurst (0440 7349).
CityRail Kings Cross/bus 389.* **Open** 6.30am-
5pm Mon-Fri; 7.30am-5pm Sat; 8am-5pm Sun.
Unlicensed. Credit AmEx, DC, MC, V. **Map**
p330 H8
In name and nature, the Bunker is a place to hunker
down. Here, it's home cooking par excellence with
immaculate espressos and, served on the side, gooey
eggs and hot buttered toast soldiers, house-styled
baked beans and muffins... plus a banana bread with
lemon butter fast becoming Sydney legend.

Bourke Street Bakery.

Ecabar
*2/128 Darlinghurst Road, at Liverpool Street,
Darlinghurst (9332 1433). CityRail Kings Cross.*
Open 7am-3pm Tue-Fri; 7.30am-4pm Sat;
8.30am-4pm Sun. **Unlicensed. Credit** AmEx,
MC, V. **Map** p330 H8
It's all about the coffee. Not that the scrambled eggs
with pesto or the sliced boiled egg with tomato and
avocado on rye aren't great. And not to make light
of the brilliant fresh pear, apple and lime juice. It's
just that the joe at this popular, sunny sliver of a
venue is really, really outstanding.

Kings Lane Sandwiches
*28 Kings Lane, between Palmer & Bourke
Streets, Darlinghurst (9360 8007, www.kings
lanesandwiches.com.au). CityRail Museum/
bus 311, 373, 377, 378, 380, 392, 394, 396,
399.* **Open** 8am-2.30pm Mon-Fri; 10am-2pm
Sat. **Unlicensed. No credit cards.**
Map p330 H8
King's Lane Sandwiches is a long-time favourite ,
with lunchtime queues waiting for the gigantic con-
structions the inevitable result. Top-quality ingredients, great bread and inventive condiments make for
Sydney's best sandwiches, including a vegetarian
offering of walnut humous that's good enough to
tempt any carnivore.

Latteria
*320 Victoria Street, between Surry & William
Streets, Darlinghurst (9331 2914). CityRail
Kings Cross.* **Open** 5.30am-7.30pm daily.
Unlicensed. No credit cards. Map p330 J8

Want a *caffè* just like mamma used to make? Check out Latteria, next door to Bar Coluzzi (*see p178*). The coffee and panini are pure Italian, sure, but it's the incredible efficiency with which the limited space is used that really makes you think you're just off the Via Tornabuoni.

Le Petit Crème

116-118 Darlinghurst Road, between Farrell Avenue & Liverpool Street, Darlinghurst (9361 4738). CityRail Kings Cross. **Open** 7am-2.30pm Mon-Sat; 8am-2.30pm Sun. **Unlicensed. No credit cards. Map** p330 J8 ⓯
Everything here, from the crêpes to the coffee to the 1980s film posters, is pure Paris. Pull up a bentwood chair and dive into an enormous Gallic breakfast. The milkshakes, made with French-style chocolat chaud as their base, can't be beaten.

Ten Buck Alley

185A Bourke Street, corner of William Street, East Sydney (9356 3000). CityRail Kings Cross/bus 389. **Open** 6.30am–6.30pm Mon-Fri. **BYO. Credit** AmEx, MC, V. **Map** p330 H7 ⓰
This hall-in-the-wall café is named for the rather shady street out back where anything's yours for a price. However, inside your money buys you what might be the best java in the city. When it comes to food, keep it simple with a sandwich or salad. Iced coffee is a speciality in summer.

Tropicana

227 Victoria Street, between Surrey & William Streets, Darlinghurst (9360 9809, www.tropicanacaffe.com). CityRail Kings Cross. **Open** 5am-11pm daily. **Licensed/BYO. No credit cards. Map** p330 J8 ⓱
Forget agents and casting calls: this is where the real business of Sydney's film and theatre industries takes place. Against a background of reasonable coffee, adequate café food and capable service, deals are done and names are made. Immortalised in the name of Tropfest, the country's leading short film showcase, the Tropicana has an energy – and a clientele – like no other.

Una's

338-340 Victoria Street, at Surrey Street, Darlinghurst (9360 6885, www.unas.com.au). CityRail Kings Cross. **Open** 7.30am-10.30pm Mon-Sat; 8am-10.30pm Sun. **Licensed/BYO** (wine only). **No credit cards. Map** p330 J8 ⓲
It's Heidi meets *Queer as Folk* at this wood-panelled Victoria Street stayer. Lederhosen-wearing waiters flit between tables of guys fuelling up on the menu's big, meaty mainstays of schnitzel, stews, rösti, wurst and sauerkraut. Una's is cheap, no one leaves hungry and the upstairs bar is worth its weight in weird. **Other locations** 135 Broadway, Ultimo (9211 3805); 372 New South Head Road, Double Bay (9327 7287).

Surry Hills & Waterloo

Book Kitchen

255 Devonshire Street, at Bourke Street, Surry Hills (9310 1003, www.thebookkitchen.com.au). CityRail/LightRail Central then 10min walk/bus 301 303, 355. **Open** 8am-3pm Mon-Fri; 6am-9.30pm Sat-Sun. **Licensed/BYO. Credit** AmEx, MC, V. **Map** p329 G11 ⓳
The idea of a bookshop as a café has currency, so why not a café selling books? Better yet, why not a café selling cookbooks? You can browse shelves of new, imported and second-hand cooking titles here while you wait for excellent hand-cut chips or own-made baked beans cooked with ham hock.

Bourke Street Bakery

633 Bourke Street, at Devonshire Street, Surry Hills (9699 1011). CityRail/LightRail Central then 10min walk/bus 301, 303, 355. **Open** 7am-6pm Mon-Fri; 8am-5pm Sat, Sun. **Unlicensed. No credit cards. Map** p329 G11 ⓴
It's hard to swing a ciabatta here, let alone a cat. Yet this slightly scruffy corner bakery still finds room to pack shelves with ace chocolate cookies, pork and fennel sausage rolls, pastries rich with tomato and olive, and all sorts of great bread. Only food and coffee this good could condone surliness this pronounced. **Other location** 130 Broadway, Ultimo (9281 3113).

★ Café Sopra

1st Floor, Fratelli Fresh, 7 Danks Street, between Young & Bourke Streets, Waterloo (9699 3174, www.fratellifresh.com.au). Bus 301, 302, 303, 355. **Open** 10am-3pm Mon-Fri; 8am-4pm Sat; 10am-3pm Sun. **Licensed/BYO. Credit** AmEx, MC, V.
Italian for 'upstairs', Sopra is above Fratelli Fresh, the warehouse HQ of one of Sydney's top importers of Italian foodstuffs. Simplicity is the watchword, and sparkling fresh produce and the warehouse's peerless dry goods are at the fore in dishes such as *papa al pomodoro*, the luscious peasant soup. *Photo p181.*

Danks Street Depot

2 Danks Street, at Young Street, Waterloo (9698 2201, www.danksstreetdepot.com.au). Bus 301, 302, 303, 355. **Open** 9am-3pm Mon-Thur, Sun; 9am-3pm, 6-11pm Fri; 8am-3pm, 6-11pm Sat. **Licensed. Credit** AmEx, MC, V.

INSIDE TRACK TROPFEST

The first **Tropfest**, now the biggest small film festival on the planet, was staged at **Tropicana** (*see above*) in 1993 with creator John Polson projecting the films on to the café walls.

CONSUME

Jared Ingersoll's laid-back café/bar is where you want to be on a lazy weekend. Go for breakfast and have the sardines on toast or slow-cooked broccoli and eggs. Or sit back in the evening on Friday and Saturday with a kir royale and some salt and vinegar potatoes. From 6pm on those days it shifts to full dinner mode.

Lumiere

Shop 13, 425 Bourke Street, Surry Hills (9331 6184). Bus 311, 333, 373, 377, 378, 380, 392, 394, 396, 397, 399, L94. **Open** 7.30am-5pm Mon-Fri; 8am-5pm Sat, Sun. **Unlicensed. Credit** AmEx, MC, V. **Map** p329 G9 ㉑

This smart pâtisserie/coffee/lunch joint is located in the St Margarets development. Sit outside for Sunday brunch with your paper amid the cool crowd in designer T-shirts. Lunch options include a mammoth ribeye beef baguette for hearty appetites, plus plenty of healthy snacks for waistline watchers.

Single Origin

60-64 Reservoir Street, between Elizabeth & Mary Streets, Surry Hills (9211 0665, www.singleorigin.com.au). CityRail Central/ LightRail Central. **Open** 6.30am-4pm Mon-Fri. **Unlicensed. No credit cards. Map** p329 F9 ㉒

The guys who work the bean at Single O are trippers. On caffeine, that is. You may come for cakes and muffins, but you stay for the coffee (beans are roasted in the behemoth they call Boris the Roaster). Have a heart-starting ristretto and follow with a calming flat white to get a grip on the magic these fellas weave.

Wah Wah Lounge

1 Danks Street, at Young Street, Waterloo (9699 3456). Bus 301, 302, 303, 355. **Open** 7.30am-4pm daily. **Licensed/no BYO. Credit** MC, V.

Comfortable banquettes and a wealth of smoothies and frappés make this a popular healthy morning treat for Waterloo's smooth set. At lunch the menu opens up with everything from sandwiches to salads to salmon and mash.

Kings Cross, Potts Point & Woolloomooloo

Café Hernandez

60 Kings Cross Road, between Ward Avenue & Roslyn Street, Kings Cross (9331 2343, www.cafehernandez.com.au). CityRail Kings Cross. **Open** 7am-11.59pm daily. **Unlicensed. Credit** MC, V. **Map** p330 J7 ㉓

A favourite among strong-coffee drinkers, this Spanish-inflected establishment just off the Kings Cross strip is one of the few places where you'll find non-alcoholic entertainment up to the witching hour.

★ Harry's Café de Wheels

Cowper Wharf Road, opposite Brougham Street, Woolloomooloo (9357 3074, www.harryscafede wheels.com.au). CityRail Kings Cross/bus 222,

311. **Open** 8.30am-2am Mon-Thur; 8.30am-4am Fri; 9am-4am Sat; 9am-12.30am Sun. **Unlicensed. No credit cards. Map** p330 H6 ㉔

This shiny snack van has been supplying late-night meat pies with gravy, mash and mushy peas to locals, visitors, sailors, cab drivers and drunks for more than 50 years. The 3am stagger to Harry's is almost a Sydneyside rite of passage.

Toby's Estate

129 Cathedral Street, at Palmer Street, Woolloomooloo (9358 1196, www.tobysestate.com. au). CityRail Kings Cross. **Open** 7am-5.30pm Mon-Fri; 8am-4pm Sat; 9am-4pm Sun. **Unlicensed. Credit** AmEx, DC, MC, V. **Map** p330 H7 ㉕

Although Toby's beans are widely available, coffee obsessives come to this Cathedral Street roastery-cum-espresso bar to worship at the scant few tables that surround the roasting machinery. Textbook espresso is guaranteed, and there are some nice teas. **Other locations** 32-36 City Road, Chippendale (9211 1459); corner of Manning & Macleay Streets, Potts Point (8356 9264).

Uliveto

33 Bayswater Road, between Kellett Street & Ward Avenue, Kings Cross (9357 7331). CityRail Kings Cross. **Open** 7am-5pm Mon-Sat; 8am-5pm Sun. **Licensed. Credit** AmEx, MC, V. **Map** p330 J7 ㉖

This indoor/outdoor slice of Bayswater Road between a gym and a strip club is handy for both crowds as, in addition to fine breakfast staples, it does a wonderful heart-starter smoothie.

Zinc

77 Macleay Street, corner of Rockwall Crescent, Potts Point (9358 6777). CityRail Kings Cross. **Open** 7am-4pm Mon; 7am-4pm, 6.30-10pm Tue-Sat; 8am-4pm Sun. **Licensed/BYO. Credit** DC. **Map** p330 J6 ㉗

Perhaps Zinc's popularity with the beautiful folk is to do with the big role that mirrors play in its design. Or the city's lovelies love just-squeezed blood orange juice, good coffee and fresh Italian-style salads.

EASTERN SUBURBS

Alimentari

2 Hopetoun Street, at William Street, Paddington (9358 2142). Bus 333, 352, 378, 380. **Open**

INSIDE TRACK ELTON'S CAFE

Elton John re-consummates his long-time love affair with Sydney by making **Harry's Café** (*see left*) his first stop whenever he tours. Harry's other famous fans are plastered in photos all over his caravan.

Café Sopra. *See p179.*

7am-6pm Mon-Fri; 8am-5pm Sat. **Unlicensed.**
Credit AmEx, MC, V. **Map** p332 L9
Tucked away at the end of fashion central William
Street under the frangipani trees is this little piece
of Italy in Paddo. A slick revamp has made it the
hangout for locals in the know as they feast on handmade Italian delicacies, rich coffee and paninis.

Blue Orange

49 Hall Street, between Jacques & Consett
Avenues, Bondi Beach (9300 9885, www.blue
orangerestaurant.com.au). CityRail Bondi Junction
then bus 380, 381, 382, 333/bus 380, 333. **Open**
6.30am-10.30pm Tue; 7am-5pm, 6.30-10.30pm
Wed-Sat; 7am-5pm Sun. **Licensed/BYO** (wine
only). **Credit** AmEx, MC,V. **Map** p334
Intimate and woody, Blue Orange is a sultry restaurant by night, but its daytime incarnation as a café
offers the most mileage, particularly since a
November 2010 refurb. If a ricotta and passion fruit
soufflé somehow isn't your cup of tea first thing, try
the smoked salmon pancakes.

Dee Bee's

27 Knox Street, Double Bay (9327 6696). Bus
324, 325, 326. **Open** 7.30am-1.30am Mon-Thur,
Sun; 7.30am-2am Fri, Sat. **Licensed** (wine only).
Credit AmEx, MC,V. **Map** p331 N8
Dee Bee's is always packed with Double Bay's own
versions of Paris Hilton and paps trying to catch a shot
of celebs staying at the Stamford around the corner.
Service is friendly and sandwiches above average.

Flat White

98 Holdsworth Street, at Jersey Road, Woollahra
(9328 9922). Bus 200, 389. **Open** 7am-3pm
Mon-Sat; 8am-3pm Sun. **BYO. Credit** AmEx,
DC, MC, V. **Map** p333 M10
Gruyère and ham brioche toastie? Yes please. The
space isn't huge (nor are the portions), but everything here is skewed towards the perfectly formed
– including the clientele. European is the slant, eggs
are a favourite, and the milk coffees are as good as
you'd hope with a name like this. *Photo p183.*

Gusto Deli Café

2A Heeley Street, corner of Broughton Street,
Paddington (9361 5640). Bus 389. **Open** 7am-
11pm Thur-Sat. **Licensed. Credit** AmEx, DC,
MC, V. **Map** p332 K9
A Paddington institution with limited seating inside
but a number of tables outside. The coffee is excellent but most people come for the healthy range of
spicy salads, substantial rolls and sandwiches.
There's deli food to go, plus cold cuts and fresh bread.

Jackie's

122 Oxford Street, corner Glenmore Road,
Paddington (9380 9818). Bus 333, 352, 378, 380.
Open 8am-3.30pm Mon, Tue, Sun; 8am-8pm Wed-
Sat. **Licensed. Credit** MC, V. **Map** p332 J9
This café diner in the designer fashion hub collecting
around the corner of Glenmore Road and Oxford
Street is a great spot for breakfast before shopping –
vanilla ricotta pancakes with maple syrup are the go
– and popular with ladies who lunch.

Micky's Café

268 Oxford Street, Paddington (9361 5157,
www.mickyscafe.com.au). Bus 333, 352, 378,
380. **Open** 8am-midnight daily. **BYO. Credit**
AmEx, MC, V. **Map** p332 K10
It's all about the ambience here. Paddo's fun young
crowd chow down on BLTs, nachos, big hangover
breakfasts with fresh frappés and shakes, and coffee with a biscuit or Mars Bar cheesecake on the side.

Parc

30 Clovelly Road, between Darley Road & Avoca
Street, Randwick (9398 9222). Bus 339, X39.
Open 7am-3pm Mon-Fri; 8am-3pm Sat, Sun. **BYO.**
Credit AmEx, DC, MC, V. **Map** p333 N14
Toast made with bread from the Infinity Sourdough
Bakery is just the beginning. The set menu is revered,
particularly the salad of smoked trout with orange,
baby cos lettuce and fried capers. Daily specials such
as tomato and smoked ham soup thickened with arbo-
rio rice also draw a crowd. Popular with cyclists from
nearby Centennial Park and the yummy mummies.

CONSUME

INNER WEST

★ Bar Italia

169 Norton Street, at Macauley Street, Leichhardt (9560 9981). Bus 436, 437, 438, 440, 445, L40. **Open** *9am-midnight Mon-Thur, Sun; 9am-1am Fri, Sat.* **BYO. No credit cards.**
Many Sydneysiders got their first taste of gelato within these walls, and more still make the pilgrimage as soon as the weather warms up. The savoury stuff is nothing special – Bar Italia is all about the coffee, the vibe and the double scoop of pistachio and tiramisu that's slowly trickling down your fingers.

Bitton Café

36-37 Copeland Street, between Newton Street & Mitchell Road, Alexandria (9519 5111, www.bittongourmet.com.au). CityRail Erskineville. **Open** *7am-5pm Mon, Tue, Sat, Sun; 7am-9pm Wed-Fri.* **Licensed/BYO. Credit** *AmEx, MC, V.*
A liberal splash of Gallic charm colours everything in this friendly café, from the repartee of the waiters and kitchen staff to the divine crêpes with orange jelly. Bitton also trades in jams, sauces, oils and anything else that can be bottled or put in a jar.

★ Campos

193 Missenden Road, at Longdown Street, Newtown (9516 3361, www.camposcoffee.com). Bus 352, 370, 422, 423, 426, 428, L23, L28. **Open** *7am-4pm Mon-Fri; 8am-5pm Sat.* **Unlicensed. Credit** *MC, V.* **Map** *p334* ㊱
These guys are serious about their coffee, but it is bloody good and they don't even cringe when you ask for a flat white. There are a couple of seats, but you're probably better off taking your coffee away and sitting somewhere in the park.

Clipper Cafe

16 Glebe Point Road, at Broadway, Glebe (0411 800 063). Bus 431, 432, 433, 434. **Open** *6am-6pm daily.* **Unlicensed. Credit** *AmEx, DC, MC, V.* **Map** *p328 B10* ㊲
Adriano Matteoni has got his café blend spot on with Clipper – a shabby-chic terrace full of character and characters. The tasty menu is heavy on the likes of spinach, eggplant and halloumi; they have their own blend of coffee roasted for them; and their juices will perk you up with a five-a-day sense of wellbeing.

Flint & Steel

24 Addison Street, corner of Cook Road & Addison Road, Marrickville (9516 1997, www.coffeealchemy.com.au). Bus 428. **Open** *9am-2pm Tue-Sat.* **Unlicensed. Credit** *MC, V.*
This cutting-edge café cranks out some of the most gorgeous espresso in Sydney. F&S roast on demand and specialise in single origin beans, with owner Hazel de los Reyes on a mission to make Aasca Demitasse, Kenyan Gethumbwini and Yirgacheffe part of Sydney's coffee vocab. It's black magic.

Giulia Café

92 Abercrombie Street, between Meagher & Little Queen Streets, Chippendale (9698 4424, www.cafegiulia.com). CityRail Central/bus 352. **Open** *6.30am-4pm Tue-Fri; 8am-3pm Sat, Sun.* **Licensed. Credit** *AmEx, DC, MC, V.* **Map** *p328 D10* ㊳
Set in a 100-year-old butchery, Giulia is packed every Saturday morning with people queuing out the door for breakfasts, shakes, juices and bagels. The long counter groans with breads, pastries and glossy mags, plus a huge espresso machine.

Sonoma Café

215 Glebe Point Road, between Bridge Street & St Johns Road, Glebe (9660 2116, www.sonoma.com.au). Bus 370, 431, 432, 433, 434. **Open** *8am-4pm Mon-Fri; 8am-3pm Sat; 8am-2pm Sun.* **Unlicensed. No credit cards. Map** *p328 A9* ㊴
If you haven't tried the organic sourdough bread from these guys, you're missing out on some of the best buns this side of San Francisco. They also do decent coffee and pastries, and sell delicious breads such as walnut and raisin and soy and linseed.

Vargabarespresso

Corner of Wilson Street & Erskineville Road, Newtown (9517 1932). CityRail Newtown. **Open** *7am-6pm Mon-Fri; 8am-5pm Sat, Sun.* **BYO. No credit cards. Map** *p334* ㊵
Forget café-laden King Street, the coolest coffee in Newtown is just off the beaten track. Friendly staff serve thoughtful, interesting eats in the mould of American diner-style meatball sandwiches with grilled cheese, and hangover-helpers such as iced liquorice tea or Berocca frappé.

NORTH SHORE

Awaba

67 The Esplanade, at Awaba Street, Balmoral (9969 2104, www.awabacafe.com.au). Bus 233, 238, 247, 257. **Open** *7.30am-3pm Mon-Wed, Sun; 7.30am-3pm, 6-9.30pm Thur-Sat.* **Licensed/BYO. Credit** *AmEx, MC, V.*
This white-on-white sunny space makes sunglasses a necessity. No need to shield your eyes from the menu, however: what's on offer is pretty upmarket fare. The buttermilk flapjacks with maple syrup and berry compote are a winner.

Delicado Foods

134 Blues Point Road, McMahons Point (9955 9399, www.delicadofoods.com.au). CityRail North Sydney. **Open** *7am-11pm Tue-Sun.* **Licensed. Credit** *AmEx, MC, V.*
Ben Moechtar was the star sommelier at Wildfire but now imports the city's finest Spanish *jamón* and lots of fine South American fare. The coffee is good and strong, and lunchtime treats include

Flat White. *See p181.*

freshly-made soup served inside or on the street-side tables under the shade of the trees.

★ Forsyth Cafe
284 Willoughby Road, Naremburn (9906 7388, www.forsythcoffee.com.au). CityRail St Leonards. Bus 273. **Open** 7am-10am, noon-2pm daily. **Unlicensed. Credit** AmEx, MC, V.
This awesome cafe is run by Rob Forsyth, a man at the vanguard of Sydney coffee for 25 years as barista, coach, master roaster and international judge. However, he's most famous for serving monkey parchment coffee – beans chewed and spat out by rhesus apes at Merthi Mountain in India ($9 a plunger).

NORTHERN BEACHES

Bacino Bar
Shop 1A, The Corso, at Darley Road, Manly (9977 8889, www.bacinobar.com). Ferry Manly. **Open** 6am-6pm Mon-Fri, Sat; 7am-5pm Sun. **Licensed/BYO. No credit cards.** **Map** p334 ④
People line up for their morning fix from this Italian corner café. The Little Italy blend coffee is rich and addictive, and there's a selection of well-stuffed paninis and *tramezzini* too.

Cook's Larder
Shop 1, 21-23 Old Barrenjoey Road, near Avalon Parade, Avalon (9973 4370, www.thecooks larder.com.au). Bus 188, 190, E88, L88, L90. **Open** 8am-4pm Mon-Thur, Sat; 8am-4pm, 6.30pm-late Fri; 8am-3.30pm Sun. **BYO. Credit** AmEx, MC, V.
The cake here is legendary. But that's not all: there's also a delicious menu stuffed with goodies from buttermilk pancakes to house-made baked beans to

chargrilled lamb. There are deli items to go, and the people who run the place also host cookery classes. And to top it all, it's just two minutes from the beach.

Ground Zero
18 Sydney Road, at Central Avenue, Manly (9977 6996). Ferry Manly. **Open** 8am-5pm daily. **BYO. Credit** AmEx, MC, V. **Map** p334 ④
Sun, sand, surf and… short black espressos? The coffee at Ground Zero – a loungey establishment just a hop and a skip from the sand of Manly Beach – is among the best in Sydney. The fresh salmon is always succulent too.

Tea Room, Gunner's Barracks
Suakin Drive, Georges Heights (8962 5900, www.thetearoom.com.au). **Open** 11am-5pm daily. **Licensed. Credit** AmEx, DC, MC, V.
Enjoy high tea with a view inside and out. The view over the bay is superb, while within tea is served with chicken and egg finger sandwiches, scones and cakes, set against a backdrop of Florence Broadhurst wallpaper.

THE SOUTH

★ Allpress Espresso
58 Epsom Road, between Dunning & Mentmore Avenues, Rosebery (9662 8288, www.allpress espresso.com.au). CityRail Green Square/bus 309, 310, 343, 345, 370. **Open** 7am-3pm Mon-Fri; 8am-2pm Sat. **Unlicensed. Credit** MC, V.
Allpress reflects the evolution of this neighbourhood, with industrial machinery juxtaposed with gentrified customers and the swish look of the café itself. The coffee is outstanding, while the breads and pastries, from sister company Brasserie Bread, are a must. Try a *vitello tonnato* roll to go.

Nuns' Pool
103 Ewos Parade, Cronulla (9523 3395, www. thenunspool.com). CityRail Cronulla then bus 985. **Open** 8am-4pm Tue-Sun. **Licensed. Credit** AmEx, MC, V.
Walking in to the Nun's Pool is like entering a sun-drenched living room. Breakfasts include modern takes on fry-ups, such as poached eggs with asparagus, while the lunch menu features the likes of sautéed mushrooms with prosciutto and thyme, and grilled scampi with angel hair pasta.

> ## INSIDE TRACK CRAPUCCINOS
>
> Ask **Forsyth Café** (*see above*) owner Rob nicely and he might even offer you a Kopi Luwak – beans eaten and excreted by wild Asian civet cats. This one-off 'crapuccino' costs $120 per 100 grams and tastes a helluva lot better than it sounds!

CONSUME

Bars & Pubs

Sydneys's sophisticated cocktail scene (and stubbies for the die-hards).

Sydney's a thirsty town. Always has been, always will be. Most of that neck oiling goes on in big pubs (known also as 'hotels') and clubs in the company of gambling, but change is afoot. New laws spearheaded by Lord Mayor Clover Moore have changed the landscape of the city's pubs and bars, and the future looks good. Now, small hole-in-the-wall venues can afford the previously exorbitant liquor licences, and the aim of creating a sophisticated, European-style bar culture is looking realistic. In truth, the change had already started happening when the indoor smoking ban

kicked in in mid 2007. This forced those drinkers to smoke outdoors, and resulted in pub and bar owners all over town creating glorious under-the-stars drinking spots, enjoyed by smokers and non-smokers alike.

Sydneysiders love a cocktail, but the primary trade is in beer. Cold draught beer is bought in either middies (a 285ml glass, close to a half-pint) or, more commonly, 425ml schooners.

CENTRAL SYDNEY
The CBD & the Rocks

Argyle
12-18 Argyle Street, at Playfair Street, The Rocks (9247 5500, www.theargyle.biz). CityRail/ferry Circular Quay. **Open** 11am-late daily. **Credit** AmEx, DC, MC, V. **Map** p327 F3 ❶
This 1826 wool store built around a grand sandstone outdoor courtyard has become the chosen place for smart drinkers on a weekday night. There are many levels here and it's easy to get separated from your bunch, but seek out the cocktail quarter with fab red daybeds and you can't go wrong.

★ Australian Hotel
100 Cumberland Street, at Gloucester Street, The Rocks (9247 2229, www.australianheritage hotel.com). CityRail/ferry Circular Quay. **Open** 11am-midnight Mon-Sat; 11am-10pm Sun. **Credit** AmEx, DC, MC, V. **Map** p327 E4 ❷
Locals and tourists flock to this old-school pub just by the Harbour Bridge. There's no view to speak of, but the neighbourhood is very much olde Sydney towne, yet happily a step away from backpacker ground zero. It's a great place to play two-up on Anzac Day, or to tuck into the superior pizzas. It also provides accommodation.

Bennelong Bar
Sydney Opera House, Bennelong Point, Circular Quay (9241 1999, www.guillaumeatbennelong. com.au). CityRail/ferry Circular Quay. **Open** 5.30pm-late Mon-Sat. **Credit** AmEx, DC, MC, V. **Map** p327 G3 ❸
Being situated in the smallest sail of the Sydney Opera House does give the Bennelong Bar something of an edge. The soaring ceiling is stunning, the harbour views rock, the superb wine list and service make you feel grown-up and sexy, and the Saarinen chairs are God's gift to lounging. The bar is in the top level of classy restaurant Guillaume at Bennelong (*see p153*).
▶ *For the inside story on the design marvel that is the Opera House, see p36* **Profile**.

Ember
Overseas Passenger Terminal, Circular Quay West, The Rocks (8273 1222, www.wildfire sydney.com). CityRail/ferry Circular Quay. **Open** noon-11pm Mon-Thur, Sun; 6pm-midnight Fri; 6pm-midnight Sat. **Credit** AmEx, DC, MC, V. **Map** p327 F3 ❹
If there's one drink that defines Ember, it's the manhattan. Settle back, admire the view of the bridge and the Opera House, and crunch some popcorn shrimp while you peruse the selection of infused bourbons and the other cocktails on the list.

CONSUME

Firefly

Pier 7, 17 Hickson Road, Walsh Bay (9241 2031, www.fireflybar.net). CityRail/ferry Circular Quay then 10min walk/bus 343, 431, 432, 433, 434. **Open** *Apr-Nov* noon-11pm Mon-Sat. *Dec-Mar* noon-10pm Mon-Sat; 3-10pm Sun. **Credit** AmEx, MC, V. **Map** p327 E3 **5**

This bar's name perhaps reflects the fact that it's so small and shiny. Not the sort of place you'd want to be kicking back at during, say, a gale or one of Sydney's rare snap frosts, Firefly's indoors-outdoors shtick runs to fine coffee all day and good cocktails and small, smart, snacky plates of an upmarket order after dark. It's absolutely sublime on a balmy evening.

★ Grasshopper

Temperance Lane, CBD (9947 9025, www.the grasshopper.com.au). CityRail Town Hall or Wynyard. **Open** noon-1am Mon-Fri. **Credit** AmEx, DC, MC, V. **Map** p327 E6 **6**

Grasshopper is a collection of mismatched furniture picked up at various auctions around town, from kidney tables to a television permanently stuck on static. The drinks are served in olive jars and just to add a little more spice, the music is as eclectic as the furniture. *Photo p189.*

▶ *Grasshopper was Time Out Sydney magazine's Best Small Bar in 2010. For more on the city's nightlife revolution, see p29* **Sydney Today**.

Hemmesphere

Level 4, Establishment Hotel, 252 George Street, between Bridge Street & Abercrombie Lane, CBD (9240 3104, www.merivale.com). CityRail Wynyard or Circular Quay/ferry Circular Quay. **Open** 5.30pm-late Mon-Fri; 6pm-late Sat. **Credit** AmEx, DC, MC, V. **Map** p327 F5 **7**

On the ground floor of the enormous Establishment building, lots of guys and girls in near-identical suits shout orders for pricey beers and stare blankly at the talent. Upstairs sees a much rosier picture: couples lounge around a high-ceilinged bar, sipping luxe cocktails. Celeb-spotting is a bonus; the downside is that you may need to book in advance. Sushi e, adjoining the lounge, serves fabulous modern Australian fare.

Ivy

320-330 George Street, at Angel Place, CBD (9240 3000, www.merivale.com.au). CityRail Wynard. **Open** 11am-late Mon-Sat. **Credit** AmEx, DC, MC, V. **Map** p327 F5 **8**

A little bit lShoreditch House (London), a little bit Miami, Justin Hemmes' multi-level venue holds countless bars and restaurants, and a ballroom, with cool music piped through the entire complex. No wonder there are lines snaking down George Street Thursday to Saturday. Hell, there's even a swimming pool on the roof complete with lifeguard and cabanas. If you can be arsed with lining up, getting checked off lists by the door girls and generally leaping through hoops to get in, Ivy assures you a brilliant time.

THE BEST BARS

For quirky styling
Bloodwood (*see p192*), **Grasshopper** (*see left*), **Flinders Hotel** (*see p188*) and **Shady Pines Saloon** (*see p188*).

For celeb spotting
The **Ivy** (*see p185*), **Kit & Kaboodle** (*see p189*), **Hemmesphere** (*see left*), **Zeta Bar** (*see p186*) and **Icebergs Bar** (*see p191*).

For old-fashioned pub style
Australian Hotel (*see p184*), **Lord Nelson Brewery Hotel** (*see p186*), **Hollywood Hotel** (*see p188*), **Cricketers Arms** (*see p187*) and **East Sydney Hotel** (*see p189*).

For smart bar food
Café Pacifico (*see p187*), **Victoria Room** (*see p187*), **Courthouse Hotel** (*see p192*), **Bennelong Bar** (*see left*), **Lincoln** (*see p190*) and the **Red Door** (*see p188*).

For water views
The **Opera Bar** (*see p186*), **Bennelong Bar** (*see left*), **Watsons Bay Hotel** (*see p192*), **Drift** (*see p191*) and the **Loft** (*see p187*).

Argyle.

CONSUME

Firefly. *See p185.*

Lord Nelson Brewery Hotel

Corner of Argyle & Kent Streets, Millers Point (9251 4044, www.lordnelson.com.au). CityRail/ ferry Circular Quay. **Open** 11am-11pm Mon-Sat; noon-10pm Sun. **Credit** AmEx, DC, MC, V. **Map** p327 E3 **9**

Real ale fans, rejoice – the Lord Nello is one of the best places to explore Sydney's microbrews. Anyone else can admire the pub's colonial stonework and tuck into a hearty bar plate – pickled onions, cheese, pickles, doorstop wedge of bread and all. Keep an eye out for Nelson's Blood, the pub's signature beer.

Marble Bar

Sydney Hilton, Level B1, 488 George Street, CBD (9266 2000, www.marblebarsydney.com.au). CityRail Wynyard or Town Hall. **Open** 5pm-late Mon-Thur; 2pm-late Fri, Sat. **Credit** AmEx, DC, MC, V. **Map** p327 E6 **10**

Built in 1893 by George Adams, this is one of Sydney's most beautiful bars. Miles of marble, carved wood and stained glass makes it an almost holy drinking experience. Drinks-wise, stick to beer or simple mixers as partners for soul, jazz and R'n'B nights and a unbeatable venue for getting your groove on.

INSIDE TRACK ANDREW CIBEJ

Andrew Cibej is the chef/owner of the wildly successful Vini (see *p165*) – a wine bar/diner so successful, he ended up buying the café next door in order to expand the business (and you still have to leave your number and have a beer at the pub while you wait for one of the much-coveted tables). Now with follow-up **Berta** (see *p163*) turning away just as many keen diners, it seems that Cibej has something of a monopoly on the city's middle-tier bar scene.

▶ *The beloved Sydney band Cold Chisel shot the cover of their 1979 album Breakfast at Sweethearts here. See p309 of* **Further Reference** *for more great Sydney bands.*

Opera Bar

Lower Concourse Level, Sydney Opera House, Bennelong Point, Circular Quay (9247 1666, www.operabar.com.au). CityRail/ferry Circular Quay. **Open** 11.30am-late daily. **Credit** AmEx, DC, MC, V. **Map** p327 G3 **11**

The Opera Bar is one of those multi-purpose venues that gets it right. It offers better-than-it-needs-to-be lunch for quayside rubberneckers; a lovely environment for an afternoon beer; quick, reasonably priced dinners for the pre-theatre crowd; and live music (see *p257*) and cocktails most nights for people looking to shake a little booty. The views are particularly pretty at dusk, and the prices are reasonable.

Rockpool Bar & Grill

66 Hunter Street, CBD (8078 1900, www.rockpool.com.au). CityRail Martin Place. **Open** 12.30-3pm, 6-11pm Mon-Sat; 6-11pm Sat. **Credit** AmEx, DC, MC, V. **Map** p327 F5 **12**

Situated in a 1936 City Mutual Building – perhaps the finest art deco building in Australia – Rockpool Bar and Grill is straight out of *Mad Men*. Riedel glasses – 6,500 of them – are stacked in backlit metal brackets like working art installations. The table and chairs are heavy wood and leather. The cocktail list is short and classic.

▶ *Neil Perry's renowned Rockpool (see p154) and Spice Temple (see p157) restaurants are also well worth a visit. See p155* **Profile**.

Zeta Bar

4th Floor, Hilton Sydney, 488 George Street, between Park & Market Streets, CBD (9265 6070, www.zetabar.com.au). CityRail Town Hall/Monorail City Centre. **Open** 5pm-late Mon-Sat. **Credit** AmEx, DC, MC, V. **Map** p327 F6 **13**

CONSUME

Kin to London's Zeta by virtue not only of its Hilton connection and Tony Chi design, but also the handful of London bar geezers who run the place, the Sydney Zeta has 'bright lights, big city' written all over it. It's a large space, running from glam VIP areas (yours too for a hefty minimum spend) past acres of bar to a tree-shaded terrace overlooking George Street many storeys below.

Darling Harbour

Loft
3 Lime Street, King Street Wharf (9299 4770, www.theloftsydney.com). CityRail Wynyard/ferry Darling Harbour/Monorail Darling Park. **Open** 4pm-1am Mon-Wed; 4pm-3am Thur; noon-3am Fri, Sat; noon-1am Sun. **Credit** AmEx, DC, MC, V. **Map** p326 D5 ⓴
The Baghdad Iced Tea – cucumber Smirnoff Blue vodka, Plymouth gin, apple, mint, lime and jasmine tea – is the perfect early-evening refresher. There's much to love about the Loft in general, even if bridge-and-tunnel types pack the place out on weekends. Carved Moorish-styled ceilings, lots of squishy leather loungers, verandas opening onto water views across Darling Harbour and great tapas served late will all conspire to keep you smiling.

East Sydney & Darlinghurst

The heart of gay Sydney (and therefore gay Australia), the 'Golden Mile' of **Oxford Street** stretches from mixed, occasionally sleazy business down at the Hyde Park end, becoming noticeably flasher as it goes art house with cinemas and bookshops between **Taylor Square** and the **Paddington Town Hall**, and then much straighter and glossier in the land of moneyed boutiques and collar-up pubs for private-school kids between there and Centennial Park.

The area around Taylor Square can be a bit of a zoo on weekends, as it's the meeting point for Surry Hills cool kids, Darlinghurst hipsters, suburbanites up for a lark, bottom-feeding eastern suburbs wannabes and every flavour of homosexuality. The bars cater for all types and are, by and large, quite mixed and open. Thirst and a willingness to pay to cater to it are the common denominators.

For more gay bars, *see pp242-244.*

Burdekin Hotel
Corner of Oxford & Liverpool Streets, Darlinghurst (9331 3066, www.burdekin.com. au). CityRail Museum/bus 333, 378, 380. **Open** noon-2am Tue-Thur; noon-4am Fri; 4pm-midnight Sun. **Credit** AmEx, DC, MC, V. **Map** p329 G8 ⓯
One of the best Sydney bars of the early 1990s, the Burdekin Hotel may have aged, but it still has a

great bone structure. A range of upstairs rooms offers a world of dance options at the weekend, while the ground-floor bar feels like an upmarket pub. The tiny tiled art deco Dugout Bar in the basement, with its speakeasy cred, is the coolest bet.

Café Pacifico
1st Floor, 95 Riley Street, between Stanley & William Streets, East Sydney (9360 3811, www.cafepacifico.com.au). CityRail Kings Cross/bus 389. **Open** 6pm-late Tue-Sat. **Credit** AmEx, DC, MC, V. **Map** p329 G7 ⓰
Yes, it's part of the same chain that operates Café Pacificos in London, Paris and Amsterdam; no, the Tex-Mexican food here isn't far above Sydney's relatively low standard – but Pacifico has a rockin' bar scene and the kind of random crowd mix on any given evening that makes it pleasingly unpredictable. Or maybe that's just the nation's broadest range of tequilas talking. Muy bien.

★ Darlo Bar
Corner of Liverpool Street & Darlinghurst Road, Darlinghurst (9331 3672, www.darlobar.com.au). CityRail Kings Cross/bus 389. **Open** 10am-midnight Mon-Sat; noon-midnight Sun. **Credit** AmEx, DC, MC, V. **Map** p330 H8 ⓱
More properly known as the Royal Sovereign Hotel, the Darlo Bar has been a local institution for the past decade: in gay-friendly Darlinghurst it's distinguished by its reputation for being the number-one straight pick-up joint. Sure, there's plenty of boy-boy, girl-girl action to be had over its pool tables, mismatched second-hand furniture and adequate drinks, but the ease with which happy young heteros hook up here is almost freakish.

Victoria Room
Level 1, 235 Victoria Street, between Liverpool & William streets, Darlinghurst (9357 4488, www.thevictoriaroom.com). CityRail Kings Cross. **Open** 6pm-midnight Tue-Thur; 6pm-2am Fri; noon-2am Sat; 1pm-midnight Sun. **Credit** AmEx, DC, MC, V. **Map** p330 J8 ⓲
Victoria Street goes truly Victorian with this dim and sexy space harking back to the Raj, with much in the way of heavy baroque furnishings and classic cocktails. There's plenty to like in the way of tom collinses and old fashioneds, but no shortage of ginger and vanilla martinis and their ilk should you wish to travel back to the future. There's a Mediterranean/Middle East-inflected restaurant too.

Surry Hills

★ Cricketers Arms
106 Fitzroy Street, at Hutchinson Street (9212 4192). CityRail Central then 10min walk/bus 339, 374, 376, 391. **Open** noon-midnight Mon-Sat; noon-10pm Sun. **No credit cards. Map** p332 H10 ⓳

One of the finest places in the city to down beers, the Cricketers is everything that's good about Surry Hills in microcosm, remaining poised between unreconstructed flavour (read grime and the occasional thug) and moving with the times (read decent grub, a good range of beers and quality tracks issuing from the decks by the bar). The beer garden is the ideal place for mounting a late-afternoon assault on sobriety.
▶ *This is a favoured stop-off for those en route to the SCG (see p263) for cricket and AFL games.*

Flinders Hotel
63 Flinders Street, Darlinghurst (9356 3622, www.theflindershotel.com.au). Bus 311, 333, 352, 373, 377, 378, 380, 392, 394, 396. **Open** 5pm-3am Tue-Thur; 5pm-5am Fri, Sat; 5pm-midnight Sun. **Credit** AmEx, DC, MC, V. **Map** p329 H9 ㉓
Every inch of the Flinders is covered in tat – old signs, beer cans, bits of animal skeletons, you name it. There are no fancy cocktail glasses, the service is as casual as it comes (but still professional and personable) and they serve straight-up great cocktails. Be sure to try a pickleback – a shot of whiskey followed by a shot of pickle juice – or a backscratch – a shot of whiskey and a side of pork scratchings – while you're there.

Gaslight Inn
278 Crown Street, between Oxford & Campbell Streets (9360 6746). Bus 311, 333, 352, 373, 377, 378, 380, 392, 394, 396. **Open** noon-midnight Mon, Tue; noon-1am Wed; noon-2am Thur; noon-3am Fri, Sat; noon-10pm Sun. **No credit cards**. **Map** p329 G8 ㉑
Prop up the bar downstairs for some peace and quiet and a well-poured schooner, or stake a claim at one of the tables in the little-known courtyard upstairs.

★ Hotel Hollywood
Corner of Foster & Hunt Streets (9281 2765, www.hotelhollywood.com.au). CityRail Central or Museum/bus 301, 302. **Open** 11am-midnight Mon-Wed; 11am-3am Thur, Fri; 6pm-3am Sat. **No credit cards**. **Map** p329 F8 ㉒
This Surry Hills stalwart has outlived, out-shone and out-sung half the pubs in the area and with bags more style and all the original fittings still in place. It also does a decent cheese plate and, of late, pizzas.

Longrain
85 Commonwealth Street, at Hunt Street (9280 2888, www.longrain.com.au). CityRail Central or Museum/bus 301, 302. **Open** 5.30pm-midnight Mon-Sat; 5pm-midnight Sun. **Credit** AmEx, DC, MC, V. **Map** p329 F8 ㉓
Now this is a bar. It's also a restaurant, for that matter, but the bar is so much part of the leading edge of Sydney nightlife that it commands equal footing with the famed Thai diner (*see p164*). Taste the greatness in the Bloody Longrain – a mix of vodka, red chilli, *nahm jim*, cucumber and coriander – and

then settle back on a low stool to contemplate the beauty of the century-old converted warehouse.

Red Door at Foveaux
65-67 Foveaux Street, between Commonwealth & Belmore streets (9211 0664, www.foveaux.com. au). Bus 339, 374, 376, 391. **Open** 5pm-late Tue-Sat. **Credit** AmEx, DC, MC, V. **Map** p329 F10 ㉔
Darrell Felstead makes mean snacks upstairs while bartenders mix it up in the dungeon-like downstairs. Try the Señor Papa cocktail or maybe the Ode to Van Gogh. The menu constantly changes as Felstead experiments with miniature toffee apples, popcorn and pork in all its guises.

★ Shady Pines Saloon
Shop 5, 256 Crown Street, Darlinghurst. Bus 311, 333, 352, 373, 377, 378, 380, 392, 394, 396. **Open** 4pm-midnight daily. **Credit** AmEx, DC, MC, V. **Map** p329 G8 ㉕
While Brooklyn and New York's Lower East Side may have their fair share of pioneer-style dive bars, it's a first for Sydney. So what makes Shady Pines the place you should be drinking in right now? A number of things, from the excellent booze (get 'em to make you an Old Pal while you're there – equal parts whiskey, sweet vermouth and Campari), friendly vibe and expert bartenders. Win.

Kings Cross, Potts Point & Woolloomooloo

Aperitif
7 Kellett Street, at Bayswater Avenue, Kings Cross (9357 4729). CityRail Kings Cross. **Open** 6pm-3am Mon, Wed-Sat; 6pm-midnight Sun. **Credit** AmEx, DC, MC, V. **Map** p330 J7 ㉖
With a courtyard set under a massive old fig free and dotted with rickety tables lit by candles, this is balmy summer sipping at its finest. The bar is at the back end of an old terrace, boasting an all-French wine and champagne list, great martinis and doing a mean trade in, you guessed it, wonderful aperitifs.

INSIDE TRACK ANTON FORTE

The owner and bartender at the popular Surry Hills bar **Shady Pines Saloon** (*see above*) is as laid-back as they come. And yet, behind the shoot-from-the-hip attitude, cheeky grin and mop of curls is a highly skilled bartender who has worked at the likes of Lotus and the Oxford Art Factory. His cocktail skills are superb but he can also rip the top off a stubby with incredible panache.

Grasshopper. *See p185.*

Bourbon

24 Darlinghurst Road, at Macleay Street, Kings Cross (9358 1144, www.thebourbon.com.au). CityRail Kings Cross. **Open** 10am-6am Mon-Fri; 9am-6am Sat, Sun. **Credit** AmEx, DC, MC, V. **Map** p330 J7 ㉗

The former Bourbon & Beefsteak opened in the 1960s to cater to visiting US sailors on leave during the Vietnam war. It stayed decidedly idiosyncratic until a makeover a few years ago rendered it designer-bland cookie-cutter contemporary. It remains, however, very broad in the scope of drinkers it attracts, and is a fine last resort for a night out in the area. It also has its own club, the Cross.

East Sydney Hotel

Corner of Cathedral & Crown Streets, Woolloomooloo (9358 1975, www.the-eastsydneyhotel.com.au). CityRail Kings Cross/bus 200. **Open** 10am-late Mon-Sat; noon-midnight Sun. **Credit** MC, V. **Map** p330 H7 ㉘

With signs proudly bearing the news that it's an establishment free of poker machines, the East Sydney Hotel marks itself out as a breed apart. And if the friendly bar staff, roaring darts tournaments and generally genial air of this old-fashioned pub, complete with pressed-tin ceilings, are any guide, it's a breed that should really be encouraged.

Goldfish

111 Darlinghurst Road, Kings Cross (8354 6630, www.thegoldfish.com.au). CityRail Kings Cross. **Open** 6pm-late daily. **Credit** AmEx, DC, MC, V. **Map** p330 J7 ㉙

The Goldfish Bowl was once the spot where teenage junkies, grizzled old men clutching their form guides and slobbering drunks all gathered for 24-hour beers, but it's gone from house of seed to house of great drinks. Get to the bar and grab a cocktail list – one for each hand. What you'll find is a mix of classics, punches, fizzes, mules and the like.

Hugos Lounge

Level 1, 33 Bayswater Road, between Ward Avenue & Kellett Street, Kings Cross (9357 4411, www.hugos.com.au). CityRail Kings Cross. **Open** 8am-3pm Thur-Sun. **Credit** AmEx, DC, MC, V. **Map** p330 J7 ㉚

As well as the drinks, most people come here for the babes; male and female, they tend towards the blonde, corn-fed, moneyed (or money-hungry) end of the spectrum and prowl the Lounge's broken-glass bar and canopied veranda. Mere mortals come for the peerless fresh mango daiquiris or to gaze at the blonde-dom on display. Downstairs is Hugo's pizzeria.

Jimmy Liks

186-188 Victoria Street, between Darlinghurst Road & Orwell Street, Potts Point (8354 1400, www.jimmyliks.com). CityRail Kings Cross. **Open** 5pm-midnight daily. **Credit** AmEx, DC, MC, V. **Map** p330 J7 ㉛

As well as a drink called the Kyoto Protocol, Jimmy Liks' list features some of the finer Asian-accented cocktails in town, incorporating the likes of chilli, saké, *nahm jim*, ginger and more. Service is famously uneven, so arrive early, pull up a pew on the street or slide on to a stool at the long, elegant bar, and bat those lashes extra hard.

★ Kit and Kaboodle

33-37 Darlinghurst Road, Kings Cross (9368 7333, www.kitkaboodle.com.au). CityRail Kings Cross. **Open** 7pm-5am Tue; 8pm-5am Wed, Thur; 6pm-5am Fri 5.30pm-5am Sat. **Credit** AmEx, DC, MC, V. **Map** p330 J7 ㉜

Sydney's best 'club in a pub' sits atop Keystone's cool Sugarmill hotel in the heart of Kings Cross. Climb the stairwell where pretty much everyone is checking each other out, and you'll find plush furniture lounged on by everyone from Swannies players to *Home and Away* delinquents. The beauty is that the bar staff really can make a great drink at three in the morning.

Lincoln
36 Bayswater Road, at Ward Avenue, Kings Cross (9331 2311, www.thelincoln.com.au). CityRail Kings Cross. **Open** 5pm-late Mon; 6pm-late Thur; 5pm-3am Fri; 6pm-3am Sat, Sun. **Credit** AmEx, DC, MC, V. **Map** p330 J7 ㉝

Bar manager George Nemec is mixing it up. Take a classic (say a tom collins) give it a bit of a twist like adding watermelon juice and kaffir lime leaves and you have yourself a cocktail, Lincoln style. There's also a great line in bar snacks like Welsh rarebit.

Lotus
22 Challis Avenue, at Macleay Street, Potts Point (9326 9000, www.merivale.com). CityRail Kings Cross. **Open** 6pm-1am Tue-Sat. **Credit** AmEx, DC, MC, V. **Map** p330 J6 ㉞

Alfresco addicts

Sydney's outdoor bar scene is still smokin'.

Smokers in Sydney may feel like social pariahs thanks to the stringent NSW laws that ban puffing in their traditional haunt of pubs, bars and clubs, but they don't have to give up the habit just yet. Keen to hang on to this lucrative sector of their business, drinking holes are falling over themselves to provide enticing outdoor settings to lure smokers in, and keep on the right side of the law. Here are a few of best.

In the east is the hugely popular **Moncur Terrace** (116 Queen Street, Woollahra, 9327 9777), on the first floor of the Woollahra Hotel. Chow down on one of the most expensive wagyu burgers in town, then puff away on the classy indoor terrace. In fine weather, the retractable roof is pulled back and the blue skies or twinkling stars revealed. When the roof is closed, smokers can retreat to the front balcony. Eastern 'burbers also flock to **Icebergs Bar** (*see p191*), where the outdoor terraces at the front and the side of this square glass establishment often prove to be the most windswept smoking spots in the city. Still, at least you get to watch the surfers as you puff. And there's the glorious, if pricey, **Gazebo Wine Garden** (2 Elizabeth Bay Road, Elizabeth Bay, 9357 5333, www.gazebowinegarden.com.au), a wine bar at the foot of one of the city's more flashy apartment blocks. In Darlinghurst, the refurbished **Beauchamp Hotel** (267 Oxford Street, 9331 2575, www.thebeauchamp.com.au) is in the heart of the gay strip and has a lovely private courtyard on the first floor. Heaters and awnings keep the place open and useable in winter, and thanks to the latter you can even smoke in a downpour. In the CBD, the Hilton's **Zeta Bar** (*see p186*) has a large outdoor smoking terrace complete with trees and great views of the city and the Queen Victoria Building. And let's not forget the **Opera Bar** (*see p186*), where you can smoke under the sails of the grand lady.

Get a little more edgy at Surry Hills' **Café Lounge** (277 Goulburn Street, 9356 8888). On the northern beaches, meanwhile, you can't beat the cavernous garden at the **Newport Arms Hotel** (*see p193*) where you can chain smoke all night.

Moncur Terrace.

You'll probably be bouncing off the snakeskin-padded walls here, the cocktails are so good. It's a small and perfectly formed place, and with the oriental decor and comfy ottomans, you think you've died and gone to some sort of Susie Wong heaven.

Melt Bar

Level 3, 12 Kellett Street, at Bayswater Road, Kings Cross (9380 6060, www.meltbar.com.au). CityRail Kings Cross. **Open** 9pm-late Thur-Sat. **Credit** AmEx, MC, V. **Map** p330 J7 ㉟

Here, the walls are covered in murals, the lighting is virtually nonexistent, tatty couches and milk crates make up the furnishings, and DJs mix everything they can get their grubby little hands on.

Old Fitzroy Hotel

129 Dowling Street, at Cathedral Street, Woolloomooloo (9356 3848, www.oldfitzroy.com.au). CityRail Kings Cross/bus 200. **Open** 11am-midnight Mon-Fri; noon-midnight Sat; 3-10pm Sun. **Credit** AmEx, DC, MC, V. **Map** p330 H7 ㊱

Theatre, laksa, beer, all under one roof. Even without the cheap and reasonable Asian noodle soups and the talents of the Tamarama Rock Surfers, one of the city's more daring theatre troupes, the pub has a rollicking charm rare for this neck of the woods.

▶ *For more on the Old Fitzroy's stage play, see p270* **Theatre**.

Water Bar @ Blue

Blue Hotel, Woolloomooloo Wharf, 6 Cowper Bay Road, opposite Forbes Street, Woolloomooloo (9331 9000). CityRail Kings Cross then 10min walk or bus 311. **Open** 5-10.30pm Mon, Sun; 5-11.30pm Tue-Sat. **Credit** AmEx, DC, MC, V. **Map** p330 H6 ㊲

The guys at this trendy, dark hangout in the Blue Hotel know how to mix a drink. Let them show you what they can do, or just muddle your way through the way-too-extensive list and hope for the best.

EASTERN SUBURBS

Coogee Bay Hotel

Corner of Arden Street & Bay Road, Coogee (9665 0000, www.coogeebayhotel.com.au). Bus 372, 373, 374. **Open** *Beach Bar* 10am-late daily. *Sports Bar* 9am-4am Mon-Thur; 9am-6am Fri, Sat; 9am-10pm Sun. *Arden Bar & Arden Lounge* noon-1am daily (summer only). *Nightclub* 9pm-late Thur-Sat. **No credit cards.**

Seating 500 people, the Coogee Bay's beer garden is a sight to behold, and with a cool ocean breeze waving the palms, and Coogee Beach before you, it's a contender for the best of its ilk. Other bars within the pub offer sports, DJs, a pool, a brasserie and music.

Drift

Ravesi's, 118 Campbell Parade, at Hall Street, Bondi Beach (9365 4422, www.ravesis.com.au). CityRail Bondi Junction then bus 333, 380, 381, 382/bus 333, 380. **Open** 6pm-late Thur, Fri; 3pm-late Sat; 2pm-late Sun. **Credit** AmEx, MC, V. **Map** p334 ㊳

This incredibly popular drinking haunt opened in late 2007 and has been overflowing with prettysomethings ever since. Upstairs at Ravesi's hotel, slap bang on Campbell Parade, it's a chic glass-and-soft-furnishings hangout, and guests fight for the seats at the front with views across to the beach.

Icebergs Bar

1 Notts Avenue, at Campbell Parade, Bondi Beach (9365 9000, www.idrb.com). CityRail Bondi Junction then bus 333, 380, 381, 382/bus 333, 380. **Open** noon-midnight Mon-Sat; noon-10pm Sun. **Credit** AmEx, DC, MC, V. **Map** p334 ㊴

Carved into the Bondi rockface and with stunning ocean views, Icebergs is a natural wonder, but the extra yard comes in the form of dashingly dressed bartenders schooled in the art of giving customers what they need before they know it. So whether it's a soul-soothing glass of Fernet-Branca or a heroic local beer, Icebergs has you covered.

★ Light Brigade

2A Oxford Street, at Jersey Road, Woollahra (9357 0888, www.lightbrigade.com.au). Bus 333, 352, 378, 380, 389. **Open** *Downstairs* 11am-midnight daily. *Upstairs* 6pm-late Tue-Sat. **Credit** AmEx, DC, MC, V. **Map** p332 L10 ㊵

On the one hand a beautiful old pub, on the other – as its name suggests – something of a battleground. In the trenches (ie downstairs), owner Dean Haritos is going more for a blaring sports bar than a lounge bar. But over the top (upstairs) it's all about plush privacy and original features and cocktails. Head bartender Percy Small mixes playful concoctions like his Apple and Grapefruit Sling. Chaaarge!

Royal Hotel

237 Glenmore Road, at Five Ways, Paddington (9331 2604, www.royalhotel.com.au). Bus 389.

INSIDE TRACK JUSTIN HEMMES

The king of Sydney drinking built his $160 million **Ivy** (*see p185*) complex a few years back and the result is like nothing Sydney had ever seen before – both in terms of scale and quality. He's answered detractors who wrote him off as a playboy by proving himself the city's premier bar tsar and businessman. It now reigns supreme alongside the rest of his Merivale portfolio, which includes **Lotus** (*see p190*), **Establishment**, **Hemmesphere** (*see p185*) and **Chinese Laundry** (*see p225*).

INSIDE TRACK BEER BRANDS

Boutique Australian beers, such as
Coopers, James Boag's, Cascade and
James Squire, are increasingly popular,
and imported brands are widely available,
but the bulk of beer drunk tends to be the
big domestic names. They once divided
fiercely down state lines, with Reschs and
Tooheys beers being the big deal in Sydney
and NSW, but lately Foster's VB (Victoria
Bitter) has become ubiquitous. Foster's
Lager itself, it should be mentioned, rarely
gets a look-in at Sydney bars – except
when tourists order it.

Open 11am-midnight Mon-Sat; 10am-midnight
Sun. **Credit** AmEx, DC, MC, V. **Map** p332 K9 ⑤
Paddington is ground zero for strapping lads and
lasses who love their rugby. Three levels of well-
heeled conviviality are divided between the ground-
floor bar, the quite reasonable Mod Oz restaurant on
the first floor, and the top floor's Elephant Bar, which
is stuffed with pachyderm knick-knacks and young
upwardly mobiles enjoying cosmos and caipiroskas.

Watsons Bay Hotel

*1 Military Road, at Cliff Street, Watsons Bay
(9337 5444, www.watsonsbayhotel.com.au).
Ferry Watsons Bay/bus 324, 325, 380.* **Open**
10am-midnight daily. **Credit** AmEx, DC, MC, V.
The fish and chips are so-so. The drinks aren't
thrilling or cheap. But the Watto, as it's known, is
an eastern suburbs institution, and still on most
Sydneysiders' list of top pubs. There really is something to be said for watching the sun sink over the
harbour from the comfort of its capacious veranda,
surrounded by other beer-swilling day trippers.
▶ *Watsons Bay Hotel is a favourite stop for those
travelling by ferry (see p95* **Profile***).*

INNER WEST

★ Bloodwood

*416 King Street, Newtown (9557 7699,
www.bloodwoodnewtown.com). CityRail Newtown.*
Open 5pm-late Mon, Wed, Thur; noon-late Fri,
Sat; noon-late Sun. **Credit** AmEx, DC, MC, V.
Map p334 ㊷
Designed by local architect Matt Woods, the majority of the space at Bloodwood has been built using
recycled and reclaimed materials, from the vintage
chairs upstairs to the massive sleepers framing parts
of the open kitchen downstairs. The cocktail list is
short, sweet and simple (bloody marys, manhattans,
martinis) and the wine list is reasonably priced. It's
not that much of a mission digging up something
you'll be happy drinking and did we mention they
serve longies of Coopers?

Clare Hotel

*20 Broadway, between Regent & Abercrombie
Streets, Ultimo (9211 2839). CityRail Central.*
Open 9.30am-midnight Mon-Wed; 9.30am-1am
Thur, Fri; 6.30pm-3am Sat. **No credit cards.**
Map p328 D10 ㊸
It was the bike couriers who first colonised this place
anew a few years back. Soon their Lycra-clad bums
were being crowded off the shared-house couches
by students from the nearby University of
Technology, and now the Clare Hotel runs the gamut
from blow-ins here for the music to late teens to beer-
loving twentysomethings.

Corridor

*153A King Street, Newtown (0422 873 879,
www.corridorbar.com.au). CityRail Newtown.*
Open 7.30am-midnight Mon-Fri; 8.30am-
midnight Sat; 8.30am-10pm Sun. **Credit** AmEx,
DC, MC, V. **Map** p334 ㊹
Corridor used to be a fairly average tapas bar but
has since turned into this cool little local. What we
like about the folks at Corridor is that they're
friendly and down to earth. They're just doing what
they do and they're doing it well: long necks of
Coopers pale for $12, simple mixers (get 'em to do
you a ginger beer with rum and limes) and local
wines by the glass. It's very easy to lose an evening
here on the upstairs deck, which houses relaxed punters shooting the breeze.

Courthouse Hotel

*Corner of Australia & Lennox Streets, Newtown
(9519 8273). CityRail Newtown.* **Open** 10am-
midnight Mon-Sat; 10am-10pm Sun. **No credit
cards.** **Map** p334 ㊺
Counter meals are on offer to go with your fine
schooner of beer (the stout is especially good) plus
there's one of the nicest courtyards in Sydney, popular in fair weather but never unpleasantly crowded
thanks to the pub's relative seclusion from the hustle and bustle of King Street.

Madame Fling Flong

*Level 1, 169 King Street, at O'Connell Street,
Newtown (9565 2471, www.madameflingflong.
com.au). CityRail Newtown or Macdonaldtown.*
Open 4pm-late daily. **No credit cards.** **Map**
p334 ㊻
In a cosy room, perched above a restaurant you
wouldn't cross the street for, hides a bar space kitted out with retro furnishings and tatty chaises
longues accommodating a big corner bar. It's easy
to see why MFF has become the bar du jour for
renaissance slackers in the inner west, as it keeps
things eclectic with vintage movie nights, smooth
Sunday sounds and crackerjack cocktails all night.

Town Hall Hotel

*326 King Street, between Newman & Wilson
Streets, Newtown (9557 1206, www.townhall*

hotel.com.au). CityRail Newtown. **Open** 9am-2.30am Mon; 9am-3.30am Tue-Thur; 9am-4.30am Fri, Sat; 10am-midnight Sun. **No credit cards**. **Map** p334 ⑰

Along with the Zanzibar (née Oxford) and Bank Hotel, the Town Hall forms what the locals affectionately refer to as the Devil's Triangle of pubs near the junction of King Street and Enmore Road. All three are popular with students, the pierced, tattooed, dyed and branded, as well as the just plain reckless, but there's a kind of mojo at work at the Townie that sees its two floors of undistinguished wooden furniture and framed train-wreck photos play host to the sort of two-fisted drinking mayhem that make it a thing of beauty unto itself.

NORTH SHORE

★ Oaks

Corner of Military & Ben Boyd Roads, Neutral Bay (9953 5515, www.oakshotel.com.au). Bus 175, 178, 180, 243, 246, 247, 249, 263. **Open** 10am-midnight Mon-Wed; 10am-1.30am Thur-Sat; noon-midnight Sun. **Credit** AmEx, DC, MC, V.

Sydney's biggest pub? Quite possibly. The Oaks is a North Shore institution, beloved of locals young and old. The cook-your-own barbie may or may not be regarded as a plus, but the huge spreading namesake tree in the beer garden is lovely, and the fireplaces, bistro, pizzeria, innumerable bars and various other nooks are put to good use.

NORTHERN BEACHES

Manly Wharf Hotel

Manly Wharf, East Esplanade, Manly (9977 1266, www.manlywharfhotel.com.au). Ferry Manly. **Open** *Main bar* 11.30am-midnight Mon-Fri; 11am-midnight Sat; 11am-10pm Sun. *Harbour bar* noon-midnight Mon-Sat; noon-10pm Sun. *Jetty bar* noon-10pm daily. *Lounge bar* 5pm-midnight Thur-Sat; 3-10pm Sun. **Credit** AmEx, DC, MC, V. **Map** p334 ㊽

From the bamboo-screened cocktail bar to the main bar opening on to the large timber deck and the open-air jetty bar, the Manly Wharf Hotel is all about light, water and a fresh, contemporary look. There's a good range of well-priced margarita variants, summery stick drinks and classics. The Mod Oz restaurant is worth a gander too.

Newport Arms Hotel

Corner of Beaconsfield & Kalinya Streets, Newport (9997 4900, www.newportarms. com.au). Bus 188, 190, L88, L90. **Open** 10am-midnight Mon-Sat; 10am-10pm Sun. **Credit** AmEx, DC, MC, V.

This Newport landmark (est. 1880) has a mammoth beer garden out the back with a spectacular view over Pittwater and the eucalyptus-clad hills of Ku-ring-gai Chase National Park. It's the perfect spot for a post-beach beer and to contemplate your sunburn. Three restaurants, a vast outdoor screen and guest rooms are further attractions.

Shore Club

36-38 South Steyne, between the Corso and Wentworth Street, Manly (9977 6322, www. shoreclub.com.au). Ferry Manly. **Open** *Sand bar* 11.30am-midnight Mon-Wed; 11.30am-2am Thur-Sat; noon-midnight Sun. *Sound bar* 8pm-2am Fri, Sat; 7pm-midnight Sun. *Sun deck* 4pm-midnight Mon-Wed; 4pm-2am Thur, Fri; noon-2am Sat; noon-midnight Sun. **Credit** AmEx, MC, V. **Map** p334 ㊾

The sun deck is as breezy, laidback and cool a place as you can drink in. Get the Pimm's jug for $28 – bargain – or, if you're feeling serious and need a lift, the Mexican Pony Ride (tequila, orange blossom and chilli). Musical guests keep the weeknights interesting, and with enough variation across the bars there's usually a space to suit any taste.

CONSUME

Madame Fling Flong.

Shops & Services

Join in Sydney's shopping revolution.

Shopping is the latest leisure pursuit to take hold in Sydney: gone are the days when the entire city shifted to the beach at the weekend. Sydneysiders are getting the style smarts: sophisticated urbanites fill the streets and malls in search of chic new threads, accessories and homewares – and there are plenty of shops to provide them.

Fortunately, the backbone of this burgeoning shopping boom is not the blood-sucking chain store, but a host of local talents prepared to put themselves on the line. Their lights shine most brightly in the rag trade, where old favourites like **Collette Dinnigan**, **Lisa Ho** and **Akira Isogawa** have paved the way for daring young designers such as **Kirrily Johnston**, **Josh Goot** and the super-successful Sarah-Jane Clarke and Heidi Middleton of **Sass & Bide**.

WHERE TO SHOP

The CBD is where visitors gravitate on their first visit, and where you'll find the biggest concentration of shops. A labyrinth of arcades and malls snakes around the centre via the corner of Bathurst and Kent Streets through to Town Hall Square, connecting George, Pitt and Market Streets. Pedestrianised Pitt Street Mall (the section of Pitt Street between Market and King Streets) is a focal point, and leading department stores David Jones (*see p195*) and Myer (formerly Grace Bros; *see p195*) battle for supremacy on Market Street, while a shiny new Westfield complex now occupies the prime shopping real estate bound by Pitt Street Mall and Market and Castlereagh Streets.

INSIDE TRACK
OPENING HOURS

Shops open between 9am and 10am and close between 5.30pm and 7pm Monday to Friday, except for Thursday, when most mainstream shopping areas stay open until around 9pm. On Saturday most places tend to shut pretty sharply between 5pm and 6pm. Sunday trading is the norm, with most shops open between 11am and 4pm, or 5pm in the summer – though hours can vary quite a bit.

If it's traditional souvenirs and duty-free you're after, head to the historic but touristy Rocks district, where upmarket fashion labels and didgeridoo shops line up for 21st-century tourist dollars – a far cry from the original slums and sluice of the 19th-century immigrants who used to live in the area.

City insiders make for Oxford Street, an epically long road that acts as a spine to surrounding Darlinghurst, Surry Hills and Paddington. The city end of Oxford Street, in Darlinghurst, is queer Sydney central with fetish and wig shops and music shops. In the Paddington area you'll find the flagships of the fashion chain stores, and at Glenmore Road and William Street, pretty boutiques harbouring smaller designers who have escaped being swallowed up by bigger brands. On Crown Street, heading south towards Surry Hills, offbeat clothing stores sit among the numerous restaurants and arty cafés.

In Double Bay, the ladies who lunch browse middle-of-the-road designer fashion in between leisurely stops at the area's many good restaurants. Woollahra's Queen Street boasts some excellent antique shops, upmarket clothes shops and delicatessens, the high prices reflecting the privilege of living in the postcode. Across the Harbour Bridge, Neutral Bay and Mosman have pretty well everything a middle-class family could possibly need, including homewares, high-end fabric shops, kids' clothes and fashion.

On the west side of the CBD lie the suburbs of Balmain, Rozelle, Leichhardt and Glebe, all of which have seen a yuppie influx in recent years as families move out of the eastern suburbs in the hunt for reasonably priced property. Darling Street is Balmain's main drag and caters for the area's funky, upwardly mobile young families. Further up Darling Street in Rozelle, the spending changes gear with interesting bric-a-brac stores and organic produce. In Leichhardt, revel in Italian delis on Norton Street and at the Italian Forum (see p196).

Backpacker-friendly Glebe Point Road in Glebe has numerous second-hand booksellers amid cafés, pubs and health-food shops. Further south, King Street is the main thoroughfare in studenty, multicultural Newtown, and home to well-priced furniture shops, great vinyl outlets and loads of vintage clothing stores.

For the best swim- and surfwear head over to Bondi Beach and North Bondi, where you can also find good vintage clothing shops and ultra-trendy boutiques. Nearby Bondi Junction offers an entirely different vibe, centred around the massive Westfield Bondi Junction mall (see p197). It's got the major brands and a few exclusives, plus a multi-screen cinema and an excellent food court with sensational views of the Harbour. The Westfield overshadows the shops that were here before the development, but some are still worth checking out – there's a good cobbler on Oxford Street and other stores geared towards budget-conscious families. Look out for cheap second-hand furniture and electrical goods in the area too.

General

DEPARTMENT STORES

David Jones
Market Street, at Castlereagh Street; Elizabeth Street, at Market Street, CBD (9266 5544, www.davidjones.com.au). CityRail St James or Town Hall/Monorail City Centre. **Open** 9.30am-7pm Mon-Wed; 9.30am-9pm Thur, Fri; 9am-7pm Sat; 10am-7pm Sun. **Credit** AmEx, DC, MC, V. **Map** p327 F6.
Opened in 1838 by its Welsh-born namesake, David Jones is the oldest department store in the world still to be trading under its original name. The flagship city-centre store is on two sites at the junction of Market and Castlereagh Streets, linked by a first-floor walkway, and has long been the city's leader in opulent window dressings. The Market Street store has three floors of menswear, plus furniture, homewares and electrical goods. There's a gourmet food hall with an excellent noodle bar, a champagne and oyster bar, a sushi bar and much more on the

THE BEST SHOPS

For all-in-one shopping
David Jones (*see below*), **Queen Victoria Building** (*see p196*) and **Westfield Bondi Junction** (*see p197*).

For cool cossies
Tuchuzy (*see p207*), **Tigerlily** (*see p207*) and **Zimmermann** (*see p204*).

For foodies
David Jones' food hall (*see below*), **Fratelli Fresh** (*see p210*) and **Simon Johnson Quality Foods** (*see p211*).

For funky jewellery
Dinosaur Designs (*see p212*), **South West Trader** (*see p208*) and **Paddington Markets** (*see p197*).

For the latest international mags, comics and newspapers
Mag Nation (*see p200*) and **Kinokuniya** (*see p200*).

lower ground floor as well as a stationer's and a cosmetics section (although the main one is on the ground floor, along with jewellery and accessories). More cosmetics, perfumes, jewellery and accessories are on the ground floor of the Elizabeth Street store. Above them are four floors of women's fashion, including a good range of international designers.
Other locations Westfield Bondi Junction (9619 1111); see website for other suburban locations.

★ Myer
436 George Street, at Market Street, CBD (9238 9111, www.myer.com.au). CityRail St James or Town Hall/Monorail City Centre. **Open** 9am-7pm Mon-Wed, Sat; 9am-10pm Thur; 9am-8pm Fri; 10am-6pm Sun. **Credit** AmEx, DC, MC, V. **Map** p327 F6.
In 2004, Sydney institution Grace Bros changed its name to Myer in one of the biggest rebrandings in Australian history, although it had been owned by Coles Myer since 1983. Sidney Myer was a penniless Russian immigrant who opened his first store in Bendigo, Victoria. Now, along with David Jones (*see left*), Myer is one of the two leading department stores in the country. It positions itself as providing something for everyone, stocking a good range of clothes, homewares, electrical goods and cosmetics. Every year, David Jones and Myer battle it out on the runway, attempting to win over Sydney's fickle fashion set in the style stakes.
Other locations Westfield Bondi Junction (9300 1100); Westfield Parramatta (8831 3100); see website for other suburban locations.

CONSUME

Peter's of Kensington

*57 Anzac Parade, between Todman Avenue
& Alison Road, Kensington (9662 1099,
www.petersofkensington.com.au). Bus 390, 391,
392, 393, 394, 395, 396, 397, 398, 399.* **Open**
9.30am-5.30pm Mon-Fri; 9.30am-5pm Sat. **Credit**
AmEx, DC, MC, V.

This suburban emporium in a bubblegum-pink
building first opened its doors in 1977 and has been
winning fans ever since. Step inside and you'll see
it's packed to the rafters (literally) with homewares,
collectibles, luggage, high-end cookware, traditional
children's toys, stationery and a good cosmetics section. Everything is at highly competitive prices, giving big guns David Jones and Myer a run for their
money.

► *To meet Peter's boyfriend, Ken, sweat on a
visit to Ken's at Kensington, where you can work
up an indecent amount of steam – especially when
DJ Seymour Butts is spinning the music on the
decks. See p249.*

MALLS

Chatswood Chase

*345 Victoria Avenue, Chatswood (9422 5316,
www.chatswoodchaseshopping.com.au). CityRail
Chatswood.*

This North shore mall has everything you could possibly need from home wares to fashion and a great
food court to combat shoppers' fatigue. Don't go
without visiting Alannah Hill for a frilly frock or
That Store for the perfect pair of jeans.

Chifley Plaza

*2 Chifley Square, corner of Hunter &
Phillip Streets, CBD (9221 6111,
www.chifleyplaza.com.au). CityRail Martin
Place.* **Map** p327 F5.

Chic business workers shop at this New York-style
tower complex, which sells designer labels such as
MaxMara, Pierucci and Leona Edmiston. There's
also a food court, not to mention the excellent
Japanese restaurant Azuma (a favourite of Tetsuya
Wakuda – *see p149*).

★ Galeries Victoria

*500 George Street, at Park Street, CBD
(9265 6888, www.tgv.com.au). CityRail Town
Hall/Monorail Galeries Victoria.* **Map** p329 F7.

Designed by the award-winning firm of Sydney
architects, Crone Associates, the Tokyo-esque four-
level Galeries Victoria is a welcome relief from the
nearby identikit Pitt Street malls. Here you'll find
Mooks, Incu and Graniph, as well as cosmetics boutique Mecca Cosmetica and cheap and cheerful laksa
joint Jimmy's. Worth the trip alone is Kinokuniya,
on Level 2, Sydney's largest cross-cultural bookshop, with titles in English, Japanese, Chinese,
French and German alongside a very impressive
selection of comics, graphic novels and manga.

Italian Forum

*23 Norton Street, between Parramatta Road
& Marion Street, Leichhardt (9518 3396,
www.theitalianforum.com). Bus 435, 436,
437, 438, 440, 445, L38, L40.*

A mall modelled on an Italian village complete with
Romanesque piazza? Not as bad as it sounds, in fact.
This suburban square of upmarket shops, restaurants, cafés and apartments does a good job of con-
juring up an authentic taste of Italy. Check out the
Merchant of Venice, where everything, from carnival masks to Murano glass, is imported from Venice,
and Marles Jewellers, with Italian white and yellow
gold pieces and Zoppini stainless steel jewellery
from Florence. For the cultural consumer, there's a
statue of Dante in the main piazza.

MLC Centre

*Corner of King Street, Castlereagh Street
and Martin Place, CBD (9224 8333,
www.destinationfashion.mlccentre.com.au).
CityRail Martin Place or Wynyard.*

This Harry Seidler designed building is a great
Aussie architectural specimen and the shops inside
are just as impressive. Jimmy Choo, Salvatore
Ferragamo, Gucci, Longchamp and Cartier are all
residents.

★ Queen Victoria Building (QVB)

*455 George Street, between Market & Druitt
Streets, CBD (9264 9209, www.qvb.com.au).
CityRail Town Hall/Monorail Galeries Victoria.*
Map p327 E6.

The elegant, airy Victorian halls of this historic
building pull in the tourist dollars, but there are
plenty of places for Sydneysiders to shop as well.
You'll find designer labels, fashion chain stores, shoe
shops, florists and chocolate shops on the ground
floor, and arts, antiques and Australiana on level
two. The lower ground level links through to the
Town Hall Square shops and station, along with the
Galeries Victoria shopping centre.

Strand Arcade

*412-414 George Street, between King
& Market Streets, CBD (9232 4199, www.
strandarcade.com.au). CityRail MartinPlace,
St James or Town Hall/Monorail City Centre.*
Map p327 F6.

This beautiful arcade is as historic as the Queen
Victoria Building, but a hundred times cooler. There
are the all-but obligatory touristy shops, such as the
Haigh's Chocolates and Strand Hatters, on the
ground floor, but if you venture on upwards you'll
discover the current darlings of the flourishing
Australian fashion scene, including Akira, Lisa Ho,
Alannah Hill, Bettina Liano, Zimmermann, Little Joe
by Gail Elliott, Terry Biviano and Dinosaur Designs.
The prices continue to escalate as you move up
again – check out the divine Alex Perry and sleek
Jayson Brunsdon.

INSIDE TRACK SALES

Sale time is usually at the end of summer and of winter, but department stores also hold sales to coincide with public holidays. The big ones to watch out for are David Jones's twice-yearly clearances at the end of June and after Christmas, and Myer's Boxing Day sale.

Westfield Bondi Junction

500 Oxford Street, at Grosvenor Street, Bondi Junction (9947 8000, www.westfield.com.au). CityRail Bondi Junction/bus 333, 352, 378, 380. **Map** p311 P11.
Love it or hate it, you can't ignore the Westfield Bondi Junction (popularly known as the WBJ, of course), Sydney's largest and chicest shopping centre. Its roster of shops includes department stores Myer and David Jones, supermarkets Coles and Woolworths, chain stores Target, Country Road, Borders and the Body Shop, plus around 450 speciality shops, an 11-screen cinema, 3,300 car parking spaces and a food court with some of the best views of Sydney Harbour. Phew!

Westfield Sydney

Corner of Pitt Street Mall and Market Street, CBD (8236 9200, www.westfield.com.au). CityRail Town Hall. **Map** p327 F6.
The behemoth CBD mall has everything. There's a huge range of men's and women's fashion stores, shoes, accessories, home wares and more. And it's super central!

World Square

Corner of Liverpool, George, Goulburn & Pitt Streets, CBD (8669 6900, www.worldsquare.com.au). CityRail Central or Town Hall/LightRail Central. **Map** p329 E/F8.
This office, residential, hotel and retail development, which covers an entire block at the Central Station end of the CBD, has more than 90 fashion, lifestyle and homeware shops, medical centres, travel agents, bars and restaurants, and a big Coles supermarket. The emphasis here is generally on commercial affordability rather than top-of-the-range designer chic, so there's Pulp Footwear, Hype DC teenage fashion, Rebel Sport and some mid-range furniture stores like Dare Gallery. You'll also find a Toni & Guy hairdressers and Napoleon Perdis Cosmetics. It might not be cool, but it's complete.

MARKETS

On the weekend, Sydney comes alive with fashion, design, art, craft and produce markets, but leave your credit cards at home – they're a cash only affair.

Bondi

Bondi Beach Public School, corner of Campbell Parade & Warners Avenue, Bondi Beach (9315 8988, www.bondimarkets.com.au). CityRail Bondi Junction then bus 333, 380, 381, 382/bus 380, 333. **Open** 10am-4pm Sun. **Map** p334.
Bondi Markets, aside from being one of the city's ultimate treasure trove markets, is a great place to track down the next big thing in Sydney street fashion. Having provided the original rack space for Ksubi, Lover and Pete Vs Toby, these stall spots are sure to be trodden by future Fashion week stars.

★ Eveleigh Farmers Market

243 Wilson Street, Eveleigh (9209 4220, www.eveleighmarket.com.au). Cityrail Redfern. **Open** 8am-1pm Sat.
A traditional weekly undercover farmers' market in the renovated market space at Eveleigh Railyards (also home to CarriageWorks), the market houses over 80 stalls and have become a firm favourite of Sydneysiders in search of guilt-free culinary treats.

Glebe

Glebe Public School, Glebe Point Road, between Mitchell Street & Parramatta Road, Glebe (4237 7499). Bus 370, 431, 432, 433, 434. **Open** 10am-4pm Sat. **Map** p328 B9.
One of Sydney's favourite outdoor markets is a community event. Browse second-hand clothing, accessories, books, recordings, arts, crafts, and furniture to the sounds of live music. And don't leave without snacking on a Turkish Gozleme.

Kirribilli

Bradfield Park, Alfred Street, Milsons Point (9922 4428, www.kncsydney.org). CityRail/ferry Milsons Point. **Open** 7am-3pm 4th Sat of the mth; extra markets on 1st & 3rd Sat in Dec.
This monthly market is all about fashion. There's always ample vintage and Aussie designers are often selling off samples. Get there early.

Paddington

Paddington Uniting Church, 395 Oxford Street, at Newcombe Street, Paddington (9331 2923, www.paddingtonmarkets.com.au). Bus 333, 352, 378, 380. **Open** 10am-5pm Sat. **Map** p332 L10.
This is the centre of Paddo shopping activity on a Saturday. Many a big-name fashion designer began by selling here. There are also masses of jewellery makers, artisans selling their wares and multicultural food stalls. A little further down Oxford Street Fringe Bar holds a Saturday market (10am-5pm Sat). And yes, that means beer-in-hand shopping.

Paddy's

Market City, at Thomas Street, Haymarket (1300 361589, www.paddysmarkets.com.au). CityRail Central or Town Hall/Monorail/LightRail Paddy's Markets. **Open** 9am-5pm Wed-Sun. **Map** p329 E8.

CONSUME

Paddy's covered labyrinth of more than 1,000 stalls caters to bargain-hunting families and backpackers. Expect kooky Asian clothing, shoes, CDs, electronics and fruit and veg – all at cheap, cheap prices.

Rocks

North Precinct, George Street & Playfair Street, The Rocks (Sydney Harbour Foreshore Authority 1300 655995, www.rocksmarket.com). CityRail/ferry Circular Quay. **Open** 10am-5pm Sat, Sun. **Map** p327 F3.

Mainly quality arts, crafts, home wares, antiques and collectibles, with lots of stalls selling indigenous craft and souvenirs. On Friday night in summer the historic laneways come alive with fairy lights, market stalls and entertainment courtesy of on-the-up local musos.

★ Surry Hills

Shannon Reserve, corner of Crown Street & Foveaux Street, Surry Hills (9310 2888). CityRail/Light Rail Central. **Open** 7am-4pm 1st Sat of mth. **Map** p329 G10.

Still the hippest of all of the city's many weekend markets. There's lots to catch the eye in the form of clothes, accessories and good junk. This is also where you'll find retro revivals before anyone else realises they are fashionable.

Specialist

BOOKS & MAGAZINES

Dymocks (www.dymocks.com.au) is Sydney's best-established bookshop chain, and also features excellent stationery and travel sections. It has branches all over town, including a big one at 424 George Street (between King & Market Streets, CBD, 9235 0155).

Ariel

42 Oxford Street, between Barcom Avenue & West Street, Paddington (9332 4581, www.arielbooks.com.au). Bus 333, 352, 378, 380. **Open** 9am-midnight daily. **Credit** AmEx, DC, MC, V. **Map** p329 H9.

Situated opposite NSW University College of Fine Art, Ariel stocks gorgeous hardback art, design, photography, fashion and contemporary culture books, most of which come with price tags to match their high production values. However, the laid-back staff are happy for you to leaf through for as long as you like.

Berkelouw Books

19 Oxford Street, between South Dowling Street & Greens Road, Paddington (9360 3200, www. berkelouw.com.au). Bus 333, 352, 378, 380. **Open** 9am-11pm Mon-Thur, Sun; 9am-midnight Fri, Sat. **Credit** AmEx, DC, MC, V. **Map** p329 H9.

More or less opposite Ariel, which is also worth a visit, Berkelouw Books has an intriguing selection of new and antique Australiana and assorted rare books. It's also right next to the Palace art-house cinemas and has a café upstairs, both of which go towards making it a great place to grab a soy latte and a yummy slice of orga-nic toasted banana bread before the movie. Note that the other branches have shorter opening hours.

Other locations 70 Norton Street, Leichhardt (9560 3200); 708 New South Head Road, Rose Bay (9371 5500); 12-14 Park Street, Mona Vale (9979 2112).

Bookshop Darlinghurst

207 Oxford Street, between Flinders & South Dowling Streets, Darlinghurst (9331 1103, www.thebookshop.com.au). Bus 352, 378, 380. **Open** 10am-9pm Mon; 10am-9.30pm Tue, Wed; 10am-10.30pm Thur; 10am-11pm Fri, Sat; 11am-11pm Sun. **Credit** AmEx, DC, MC, V. **Map** p329 H9.

The Bookshop Darlinghurst specialises in gay and lesbian literature, but apart from that it also stocks a range of rare imported books, as well as mainstream books that cater for hip inner-city dwellers. The staff are exceptionally knowledgeable in their particular subject areas.

Borders

Westfield Shoppingtown, 500 Oxford Street, Bondi Junction (9389 2200, www.borders.com.au). CityRail Bondi Junction. **Open** 9.30am-10pm Mon-Sat; 10am-10pm Sun. **Credit** AmEx, DC, MC, V. **Map** p327 E6.

The US monster book chain is well represented in Sydney with huge stores in Bondi Junction, Parramatta, Chatswood and the 'burbs. The shops are typically capacious, and many have coffee shops, not to mention a very comprehensive selection of international magazines.

Other locations Westfield Parramatta (9687 3388); Westfield Chatswood (9415 4800); see website for other suburban locations.

★ Gleebooks

49 Glebe Point Road, between Cowper & Francis Streets, Glebe (9660 2333, www. gleebooks.com.au). Bus 370, 431, 432, 433 434. **Open** 9am-9pm daily. **Credit** AmEx, DC, MC, V. **Map** p328 B9.

Highly rated Gleebooks has two branches on Glebe Point Road alone. No.191 specialises in second-hand and children's books, as well as more esoteric works on the humanities. No.49 sells everything else. The theatre shop in Walsh Bay opens around performance times to catch the luvvies. A key location for Sydney's bibliophiles.

Other locations 191 Glebe Point Road, Glebe (9552 2526); Sydney Theatre, 22 Hickson Road, Opposite Pier 6/7, Walsh Bay (9250 1930).

CONSUME

Shops & Services

Kinokuniya
*Level 2, The Galleries Victoria, 500
George Street, CBD (9262 7996,
bookweb.kinokuniya.co.jp). CityRail Town Hall.*
Open 10am-7pm Mon-Wed, Fri, Sat; 10am-9pm
Thur; 10am-6pm Sun. **Credit** AmEx, D, MC, V.
Map p329 F7.
This CBD bookstore's got everything – classics, art
books, pulp, textbooks, children's and loads more –
but the thing that sets this mighty store apart is their
huge rage of comics, manga and graphic novels.

Mag Nation
*155 King Street, Newtown (9516 0202,
www.magnation.com). CityRail Newtown or
Central.* **Open** 10am-6pm Mon, Tue, Sun;
10am-9pm Wed-Fri. **Credit** AmEx, MC, V.
Map p334.
Calling all quirky mag lovers. This is a store that
you must check out. It has over 4000 magazines,
including mainstream selections, freshly brewed coffee while you browse and free wireless internet.

Map World
*280 Pitt Street, between Park & Bathurst Streets,
CBD (9261 3601, www.mapworld.net.au).
CityRail Town Hall/Monorail Galeries Victoria.*
Open 9am-5.30pm Mon-Fri; 10am-3.45pm Sat.
Credit AmEx, MC, V. **Map** p329 F7.
As you might have guessed, Map World sells road
maps for the whole of Australia, as well as travel
guides, atlases and books about such outdoor activ-
ities as four-wheel-driving and rock climbing.

Used & antiquarian

See also p199 **Berkelouw Books** and
Gleebooks.

★ Goulds
*32 King Street, between Queen & Fitzroy Streets,
Newtown (9519 8947, www.gouldsbooks.com.au).
Bus 352, 422, 423, 426, 428.* **Open** 9am-11pm
daily. **Credit** AmEx, MC, V. **Map** p334.
Around 3,000m (9,000ft) of bookshelves make this
the largest second-hand bookshop in Sydney. It's a
librarian's nightmare, but worth the rummage; you
never know what serendipity might reveal. And it's
open until midnight. It specialises in Australian history and politics, plus general Australiana.

Sappho Books
*51 Glebe Point Road, between Cowper & Francis
Streets, Glebe (9552 4498,
www.sapphobooks.com.au). Bus 370, 431, 432,
433, 434.* **Open** 8.30am-7pm Mon, Tue, Sun;
8.30am-10pm Wed-Sat. **Credit** AmEx, DC, MC,
V. **Map** p329 B9.
A popular, friendly and immaculately catalogued
second-hand bookshop that offers something for
every bookworm – from Australian first editions

Kinokuniya.

and leather-bound tomes to art books and the latest
kiddie's classic. There's also a comfortable café at
the rear, with a lovely big courtyard.

CHILDREN
Fashion

Bonds (www.bonds.com.au), **Gumboots**
(www.gumboots.com.au) and **Fred Bare**
(www.fredbare.com) are good Australian brands;
look for them at **David Jones** (*see p195*) and
Myer (*see p195*). **Cotton On** (www.cottonon.
com.au) also has very cute children's clothes at
great prices and Sydney's tiniest fashionistas are
outfitted at the sophisticated **Manon et
Gwenaelle** (www.manonetgwenaelle.com) in
Darlinghurst. Or try the markets (*see p197*) for
something more original – Bondi, Balmain and
Paddington markets are particularly good while
Billycart Markets (www.billycartmarkets.
com) at Narrabeen sells only handmade kids
clothes and toys.

Toys

Both **David Jones** (*see p195*) and **Myer** (*see
p195*) have good toy departments.

Kidstuff
*126A Queen Street, between Moncur &
Ocean Streets, Woollahra (9363 2838,
www.kidstuff.com.au). Bus 389.* **Open** 9am-
5.30pm Mon-Sat; 9am-5pm Sun. **Credit**
AmEx, MC, V. **Map** p333 M10.
Wooden toys and doll's houses that are likely to last
considerably longer than today's plastic tat, as well
as educational toys for children of all ages.

Other locations 774-776 Military Road, Mosman (9960 3222).

ELECTRONICS & PHOTOGRAPHY
Cameras & photo developing

Paxtons
285 George Street, at Hunter Street, CBD (9299 2999, www.paxtons.com.au). CityRail Wynyard. **Open** 9am-6pm Mon-Wed, Fri; 9am-9pm Thur; 9am-6pm Sat, Sun. **Credit** AmEx, DC, MC, V. **Map** p327 F5.
Sydney's largest independent camera retailer stocks a fine range of digital cameras, SLRs, video cameras, lenses, audio gear and more. Don't be shy about asking for a discount: staff are keen to outprice competitors. Processing also available.
Other locations Westfield Bondi Junction (9389 6100); Westfield Chatswood (9413 1144); Westfield Parramatta (9635 9696); see website for other suburban locations.

Electronics

Dick Smith (www.dicksmith.com.au) and **JB Hi Fi** (www.jbhifi.com.au) are Australia's leading electronics retailers are well represented both in Sydney's CBD and in the suburbs.

FASHION
Australian designers

For the latest Aussie fashion names, *see p204* **From Rags to Riches**.

★ Akira Isogawa
12A Queen Street, at Oxford Street, Woollahra (9361 5221, www.akira.com.au). Bus 333, 352, 378, 380. **Open** 10.30am-6pm Mon-Wed, Fri; 10.30am-7pm Thur; 10am-6pm Sat; 11am-4pm Sun. **Credit** AmEx, MC, V. **Map** p332 L11.
Akira is known for his romantic, other-worldy multi-layering of transparent fabrics and bold colours. The shop has been in Woollahra since 1993, and his garments are now sold in fashion epicentres across the globe. If you're a follower of original and high-end designs, he's well worth checking out.
Other locations Strand Arcade, CBD (9232 1078).

Alannah Hill
118-120 Oxford Street, at Glenmore Road, Paddington (9380 9147, www.alannahhill.com. au). Bus 333, 352, 378, 380. **Open** 10am-6pm Mon-Wed, Fri, Sat; 10am-8pm Thur; 11am-6pm Sun. **Credit** AmEx, DC, MC, V. **Map** p332 J9.
Melbourne designer Alannah Hill has cornered the market in flirty feminine styles. The vintage-doll-like shop assistants look like they're having as much fun trying on the rich fabrics, velvet trims, lace and feathered hats as the customers. A good place to buy race-day accessories. *Photo p205.*
Other locations Strand Arcade, CBD (9221 1251); Westfield Bondi Junction (9389 3066); Chatswood Chase Shopping Centre, Chatswood (9413 2755).

Bassike
26 Glenmore Road, Paddington (9360 3606, www.bassike.com). Bus 380, 378, 389, 333. **Open** 10am-6pm Mon-Wed, Fri, Sat; 10am-7pm Thur; 11am-5pm Sun. **Credit** call for details. **Map** p332 J9.
You can't go past good quality basics and this Sydney duo has got them in spades. Stock up on simple bikinis, singlets, jeans and dresses in great cuts and made with great fabrics. You can't go wrong!

Collette Dinnigan
33 William Street, off Oxford Street, Paddington (9360 6691, www.collettedinnigan.com.au). Bus 333, 352, 378, 380. **Open** 10am-6pm Mon-Sat; noon-5pm Sun. **Credit** AmEx, DC, MC, V. **Map** p332 K10.
Models about to get married and celebs in need of a sensational gown to wear on the red carpet love Dinnigan's exquisite beading and sensual embroidery. Collette has also launched a children's range, which is very cute if money is no object.

Easton Pearson
18 Elizabeth Street, between Oxford & Underwood Streets, Paddington (9331 4433, www.eastonpearson.com). Bus 333, 352, 378, 380. **Open** 10am-5pm Mon-Sat. **Credit** AmEx, MC, V. **Map** p332 L10.
Beautiful fabrics and unusual textiles are the go with dynamic design duo Pamela Eston and Lydia Pearson, who take their influences – and a lot of their materials – from India, Africa, Mexico and Polynesia. Their attention to the smallest details – buttons, stitching – is what defines their special style. You can wear one of their shirts or skirts for years and it will always look new and surprising.

Gorman
30 Oxford Street, Paddington (9331 7099, www.gorman.ws). Bus 333, 352, 378, 380. **Open** 8am-6pm Mon-Wed, Fri, Sat; 10am-8pm Thur; 11am-5pm Sun. **Credit** call for details. **Map** p332 H9.
Melbourne born, Gorman's label is bright, bold and fun. On top of working with Fair Trade manufacturers, she is striving to make all aspects of her business planet-conscious from the office to the factory.

Jayson Brunsdon
Strand Arcade, 412-414 George Street, between King & Market Streets, CBD (9233 8891,

CONSUME

Discover the city from your back pocket

Essential for your weekend break, over 30 top cities available.

www.jaysonbrunsdon.com). CityRail MartinPlace, St James or Town Hall/Monorail City Centre.
Open 9.30am-5.30pm Mon-Wed, Fri; 9.30am-8pm Thur; 9.30am-4pm Sat. **Credit** AmEx, DC, MC, V. **Map** p327 F6.

Brunsdon has been in the fashion industry for 20 years, first as an illustrator and fashion editor, then as creative director of Morrissey; he then went on to launch his own label. He likes to work with bold colours and shapes that accentuate a woman's figure and stand out in a crowd – the resulting creations are real event pieces.

Kirrily Johnston

6 Glenmore Road, at Hopewell Lane, Paddington (9380 7775, www.kirrilyjohnston.com). Bus 333, 352, 378, 380. **Open** 10am-6pm Mon-Wed, Fri, Sat; 10am-7pm Thur; 11am-5pm Sun. **Credit** AmEx, MC, V. **Map** p332 J9.

Kirrily Johnston stormed onto the Australian fashion scene a few years back. Her bold sassy use of colour and lush fabrics blend with genuinely comfortable designs meaning you don't have to be a stick model to wear her clothes. But watch out: the price tag can carry quite a sting.

★ Ksubi

82 Gould Street, between Hall & Curlewis Streets, Bondi Beach (9300 8233, www.ksubi.com). CityRail Bondi Junction then bus 380, 381, 382, 333/bus 222, 380, 333. **Open** 10am-6pm Mon-Sat; 11am-6pm Sun. **Credit** AmEx, MC, V. **Map** p334.

Sydney surfer boys Dan Single, George Gorrow and Gareth Moody launched their brand (then called Tsubi) at Australian Fashion Week 2001. Since then they've made a name with ultra-cool jeans and Ts, while making headlines with quirky shows.
Other locations 16 Glenmore Road, Paddington (9361 6291).

Leona Edmiston

88 William Street, off Oxford Street, Paddington (9331 7033, www.leonaedmiston.com.au). Bus 333, 352, 378, 380. **Open** 10am-6pm Mon-Fri; 10am-5pm Sat; noon-4pm Sun. **Credit** AmEx, DC, MC, V. **Map** p332 K10.

Sydneysider Leona Edmiston once teamed up with Morrissey, but she set up on her own in 2001. Now her designs couldn't be more different, with a fun and flirty collection of pretty frocks and fabulous accessories. Chic and cheeky femininity is the thing here, with delicate prints and flattering cuts a particular speciality.

Lisa Ho

Corner of Oxford & Queen Streets, Woollahra (9360 2345, www.lisaho.com.au). Bus 333, 352, 378, 380. **Open** 10am-6pm Mon-Wed, Fri; 10am-7pm Thur; 10am-5pm Sat; 11am-5pm Sun. **Credit** AmEx, MC, V. **Map** p332 L11.

If the prices at Collette Dinnigan seem a little steep, try equally luxurious Lisa Ho. When Australian actress Sarah Wynter wore one of Ho's creations to the Emmy awards ceremony back in 2004, regard for the designs became international. Stretch fabrics, silk and sheer chiffon are beaded and pleated with gorgeous results. Great swimwear too.
Other locations Strand Arcade, CBD (9222 9711); Chatswood Chase Shopping Centre, Chatswood (9411 8442); Castle Towers Shopping Centre, Castle Hill (9659 9459).

RM Williams

389 George Street, between King & Market Streets, CBD (9262 2228, www.rmwilliams.com.au). CityRail Martin Place, St James or Town Hall/Monorail City Centre. **Open** 9am-6pm Mon-Wed, Fri; 9am-9pm Thur; 9am-5pm Sat; 11am-5pm Sun. **Credit** AmEx, DC, MC, V. **Map** p327 E/F6.

Reginald Murray Williams and his pardner Dollar Mick started out as a 'bush outfitters' in South Australia in the early 1930s. Now their clothes are more likely to be seen on urban cowboys than the hard-riding jackaroos they were first designed for. Boots and moleskins are the staple, but you can also get good-quality shirts, knits and shorts for men.
Other locations throughout the city.
► *If you're an urban cowboy who fancies cutting a dash with a class Australian hat with less of a Dundee vibe, then head to Strand Hatters (see p208) in the CBD's Strand Arcade.*

Sass & Bide

132 Oxford Street, between Glenmore & Shadforth Streets, Paddington (9360 3900, www.sassandbide.com.au). Bus 333, 352, 378, 380. **Open** 10am-6pm Mon-Wed, Fri, Sat; 10am-8pm Thur; 11am-5pm Sun. **Credit** AmEx, DC, MC, V. **Map** p332 J9.

Sarah-Jane 'Sass' Clarke and Heidi 'Bide' Middleton started selling clothes on London's Portobello Road, but struck gold when they made international headlines with their sexy, skinny low-rise jeans. This concept store is one of two in the world devoted to their label (the other is in Brisbane), though you'll find their clothes in department stores and boutiques.

Scanlan & Theodore

122 Oxford Street, at Glenmore Street, Paddington (9380 9388, www.scanlantheodore.com.au). Bus 352, 378, 380, L82. **Open** 10am-6pm Mon-Wed, Fri; 10am-8pm Thur; 10am-5.30pm Sat; noon-5pm Sun. **Credit** AmEx, DC, MC, V. **Map** p332 J9.

If you love fashion and can only make it to one Aussie designer, make it Scanlan & Theodore. Gary Theodore and Fiona Scanlan use outrageously luxurious fabrics with creative but classy colours.
Other location Chatswood Chase Shopping Centre, Chatswood (9410 1711).

CONSUME

★ Wheels & Doll Baby

259 Crown Street, at Goulburn Street, Darlinghurst (9361 3286, www.wheelsand dollbaby.com). CityRail Museum/bus 373, 374, 377, 378, 380. **Open** 10am-6pm Mon-Wed, Fri, Sat; 10am-8pm Thur; 11am-5pm Sun. **Credit** AmEx, DC, MC, V. **Map** p329 G8.

Melanie Greensmith started her vampy fashion label in 1987. Her clothes became synonymous with all things rock when Michael Jackson came in browsing for a customised leather jacket for his Bad tour. Now rockers such as Debbie Harry and the Black Crowes wear her styles and burlesque queen Dita Von Teese is a W&DB postergirl.

▶ *Melanie's boyfriend is the songwriter and guitarist in legendary Sydney band Divinyls. See p309 in Further Reference.*

Zimmermann

387 Oxford Street, opposite William Street, Paddington (9357 4700, www.zimmermann wear.com). Bus 333, 352, 378, 380. **Open** 10am-6pm Mon-Wed, Fri, Sat; 10am-8pm Thur; 10am-5pm Sun. **Credit** AmEx, DC, MC, V. **Map** p332 K10.

Sisters Nicole and Simone Zimmermann launched this label in the early 1990s. Swimwear is their calling card – bright, bold, contemporary designs for hip bodies – but they have cute dresses and tops too. **Other locations** Strand Arcade, CBD (9221 9558); Westfield Bondi Junction (9387 5111).

Boutiques

Belinda

8 Transvaal Avenue, off Cross Street, Double Bay (9328 6288, www.belinda.com.au). Ferry Double Bay/bus 323, 324, 325, 326. **Open** 10am-6pm Mon-Fri; 10am-5pm Sat. **Credit** AmEx, DC, MC, V. **Map** p331 N7.

The pick of the crop of exquisite fashion and beautiful accessories, both local and overseas, selected

From Rags to Riches

Sydney's designers are increasingly visible on the global scene.

More than anything else, it's the fashion industry that's booming in Australia. It's not due to cheap imports, but rather a groundswell of inspirational local talent. Australian designers like **Collette Dinnigan** (*see p201*) and **Lisa Ho** (*see p203*) have been creating a buzz in the front rows of global fashion shows for a while now, and Dinnigan even has her own London boutique in Chelsea. But it's in the high streets that these stars of the southern hem are really making their mark, with ultra-trendy stores such as London's Harvey Nichols and New York's Bloomingdale's stocking up on Sydney's **Wheels & Doll Baby** (*see above*), **Sass & Bide** (*see p203*) and **Ksubi** (*see p203*). Then there's **Alex Perry** (*see p196*) following in the footsteps of **Akira Isogawa** (*see p201*), cutting a swathe through Kuwait, Saudi Arabia, Hong Kong and Indonesia. Of course, international recognition (and a lucrative global market) is what every young designer dreams of, but on their way to the top it's also exciting for Sydneysiders (and visitors) to be the first to snap up their designs. So start talent-spotting!

The heart of Australian fashion beats in Melbourne, but label lovers visiting Sydney for the first time are often surprised at the diversity of home-grown designers found here too. The CBD's **Strand Arcade** (*see p196*) is home to many of these names.

For high-high-end party frocks, head to Alex Perry or **Jayson Brunsdon** (*see p201*), whose Audrey Hepburn-esque eveningwear is already a staple. Also in the arcade are some of the coolest names, including quirky **Leona Edmiston** (*see p203*), jeans goddess Bettina Liano and super-sexy **Zimmermann** (*see above*).

Newer to the scene are a clutch of designers who are on the brink of global recognition, but are still driving the fashion industry forward in their home country. The Corner Shop in Paddington is a good starting point as it specialises in emerging Australian designers: it stocks Marnie Skillings' ladylike creations and Josh Goot's slinky jersey knits for men and women and the out-there looks from Sydney hipsters Romance was Born. The interesting textures and shapes of Gareth Moody's Chronicles of Never can be found at **South West Trader** (*see p208*). Alice McCall's hippy-dippy floaty numbers and fab jeans and Dion Lee's structured feminine creations are stocked at David Jones (*see p195*).

The annual Rosemount Australian Fashion Week trade shows (Spring/Summer, held in April/May, and the Transseasonal shows in October) are key events for new designers. If you're in town, check the fashion columns in newpapers to discover new hot young things.

CONSUME

by the store's stylish namesake Belinda Seper, who was a model and is now an Australian fashion queen. Marni, Lanvin, Stella McCartney, Jimmy Choo, Dries Van Noten all feature.
Other locations 39 William Street, Paddington (9380 8728); MLC Centre, CBD (9233 0781); Shoe Salon, 14 Transvaal Avenue, Double Bay (9327 8199).

Blood Orange
35 Elizabeth Bay Road, Elizabeth Bay (9357 2424, www.bloodorange.com.au). CityRail Kings Cross. **Open** 11am-6.30pm Tue-Fri; 10.30am-5.30pm Sat; 11am-4pm Sun. **Credit** AmEx, MC, V. **Map** p330 K6/7.
This small store bursts at the seams with stylishly pared-back offerings from APC, Filippa K and Alexander Wang. Well-priced goodies such as K Jacques sandals and Lover swimsuits are the answer to recession shopping blues.

Corner Shop
43 William Street, off Oxford Street, Paddington (9380 9828). Bus 333, 352, 378, 380. **Open** 10am-6pm Mon-Sat; noon-5pm Sun. **Credit** AmEx, DC, MC, V. **Map** p332 K10.
For this eclectic fashion venture, the Belinda team (see above) scours the world's international fashion fairs to bring back the hippest and brightest of the up-and-coming designers. It's also a good place to catch the newest Aussie names.
Other locations Strand Arcade, CBD (9221 1788).

Incu
256 Oxford Street, Paddington (9331 6070, www.incuclothing.com). Bus 333, 352, 378, 380. **Open** 10am-6pm Mon-Wed, Fri, Sat; 10am-8pm Thur; 11am-5pm Sun. **Credit** call for details. **Map** p333 K10.
Brian and Vincent Wu, aside from bringing London's Topshop to the Sydney streets, have long been giving ample rack space to great local brands like Lover, Something Else and TV.
Other location The Galleries Victoria, 500 George Street, CBD (9266 0244).

★ Mint
Shop 8, 9-15 Central Avenue, Manly (9976 6468, www.mintshop.com.au). Ferru Manly. **Open** 10am-5.30pm Mon-Wed, Sat; 10am-7pm Thur, Fri; 11am-5pm Sun. **Credit** call for details. **Map** p334.
Mint was founded as a men's and women's boutique and has quickly became a household name in the local area and grown in popularity. Mint showcases some of the best Australian and International labels around including Cheap Monday, Chronicles Of Never, Dr Denim, Karen Walker, Ksubi and Lonely Hearts Club, Vanishing Elephant, Thousand Reasons, Alice McCall, Bec & Bridge, Sass & Bide,

Alannah Hill. *See p201.*

Elke Kramer and Seventh Wonderland, but is also very willing to give fresh young designers ample rack space.

One of a Kind
114 Burton Street, Darlinghurst (0414 617 450, www.oneofakindsydney.com). Bus M10, 373, 396, 377, L94, 380, 394, M40. **Open** 11am-6pm Tue-Fri; 11am-5pm Sat. **Credit** call for details. **Map** p330 H8.
Dion Kovac's unique eye fills this little menswear shop with classic garments to suit all tastes, so this is the place to go to pick up old-school understated pieces by Three Over One, lively prints by Rittenhouse and super-cool textured black looks by Melbourne designer Claude Maus.

Pretty Dog
5 Brown Street, Newtown (9519 7839, www.prettydog.com.au). **Open** 11am-6pm Tue, Wed, Fri, Sat; 11am-8pm Thur; noon-5pm Sun. **Credit** call for details. **Map** p334.
Tanya Stevanovic, having moved her Newtown fashion temple up the road to a larger abode a few years back, now has plenty of extra rack space for local lovelies Friedrich Gray, Material by Product, Romance Was Born and loads more. And did we mention that she stocks Tristan Blair shoes?

Chain stores

Sydney has large branches of womenswear chain stores like **Country Road** (142 Pitt Street, CBD, 9394 1818, www.countryroad. com.au), which is excellent for basics; cheap and cheerful **Dotti** (356 Oxford Street, Paddington, 9332 1659, www.dotti.com.au); popular street wear chain **General Pants** (Westfield Bondi

Junction, 9389 7905, www.generalpants.com.au); **Cue** (323 George Street, CBD, 9299 9933, www.cue.cc), stocking reliable work clothes, and **Sportsgirl** (Skygarden, 77 Castlereagh Street, CBD, 9223 8255, www.sportsgirl.com.au), where many girls spend their first pay cheque before graduating to the more grown-up **David Lawrence** (Westfield Bondi Junction, 9386 5583, www.david lawrence.com.au). **Witchery** (332 Oxford Street, Paddington, 9360 6934, www.witchery.com.au) offers well-priced runway copies in a Zara vain.

Fetish

House of Fetish
93 Oxford Street, between Crown & Riley Streets, Darlinghurst (9380 9042, www.houseoffetish.com.au). Bus 222, 311, 373, 377, 378, 380, 392, 394, 396, 397, 399. **Open** 10am-7pm Mon-Wed, Fri; 10am-9pm Thur; noon-5pm Sun. **Credit** AmEx, DC, MC, V. **Map** p329 G8.
For purist goths and S&M dabblers. Here you'll find a great array of corsetry, latex, hosiery, men and women's clothing, plus spiky shoes and jewellery.

★ Tool Shed
81 Oxford Street, between Crown & Riley Streets, Darlinghurst (9332 2792, www.toolshed.com.au). Bus 222, 311, 373, 377, 378, 380, 392, 394, 396, 397, 399. **Open** 9am-midnight Mon-Thur; 9am-2am Fri, Sat. **Credit** AmEx, DC, MC, V. **Map** p329 G9.
Should you feel the need for an extra-sexual accessory, head for Tool Shed, which stocks a vast range of appliances, protuberances and fetish wear. Other locations Basement, 191 Oxford Street, at

Taylor Square, Darlinghurst (9360 1100).
▶ *The Gay & Lesbian section (pp241-249) has plenty of suggestions for where to test your Tool Shed purchases.*

Surfwear & swimwear

Aussie Boys
102 Oxford Street, between Crown & Palmer Streets, Darlinghurst (9360 7011, www.aussieboys.com.au). Bus 333, 352, 378, 380. **Open** 10am-6pm Mon-Wed, Fri, Sat; 10am-9pm Thur; 11am-5pm Sun. **Credit** AmEx, DC, MC, V. **Map** p329 G8.
A fun, friendly store selling beach towels from the cute Aussie Boys label, Dolce & Gabbana bathers and Bonds T-shirts; there's even a hair stylist downstairs. It's a one-stop shop for all that the smart gay man needs at the beach, and there are all sorts of underwear and jockstraps to investigate too.

Big Swim
74 Campbell Parade, between Lamrock Avenue & Hall Street, Bondi Beach (9365 4457, www.bigswim.com.au). CityRail Bondi Junction then bus 333, 380, 381, 382/bus 222, 333, 380. **Open** *Summer* 9.30am-6pm daily. *Winter* 9.30am-5pm daily. **Credit** AmEx, DC, MC, V. **Map** p334.
An Aladdin's cave of bikinis, tankinis, one-pieces, G-strings and bandeau tops. It's perhaps the best place in Sydney for women to buy swimwear: rack after rack of well-priced stuff in loads of different styles and cup sizes, plus bags, towels, sarongs and footwear. The shop is across the road from the beach.
Other locations 51 The Corso, Manly (9977 8961); Warringah Mall, Brookvale (9907 3352).

Grandma Takes a Trip.

★ Mambo

80 The Corso, Manly (9977 9178, www.mambo. com.au). Ferry Manly. **Open** 9.30am-6pm daily. **Credit** AmEx, MC, V. **Map** p334.

Launched in 1984, this flamboyant surf/skatewear label has become an institution. Founder Dare Jennings employed radical artist Reg Mombassa of the band Mental As Anything to create his trademark gnarly designs. Pick up shorts, T-shirts, swimwear, sunnies, caps and wallets.

▶ *Dare also owns Deus Ex Machina, one of Camperdown's favourite cafés.*

Surf Dive 'n' Ski

Lower Ground Level, 197 Pitt Street Mall, CBD (8275 5141, www.sds.com.au). CityRail Town Hall or Wynyard. **Open** 9am-5pm Mon-Fri; 9am-9pm Thur; 9am-5pm Sat, Sun. **Credit** AmEx, DC, MC, V. **Map** p327 F6.

This is a one-stop shop for surf equipment. Along with your wetsuit and board you can pick up cute bikinis, tees, shorts, jeans, shoes and bags as the shop carries some great surf fashion labels. Local favourites Insight, Billabong, Roxy, Seafolly, and Rusty are all well represented, as are internationals like Levis, Havaianas and Converse.

Other locations throughout the city.

Tigerlilly

37 William Street, Paddington (8354 1832, www.tigerlilyswimwear.com.au). **Open** 10am-6pm Mon-Sat; 11am-5pm Sun. **Credit** call for details. **Map** p332 K10.

Founded by Jodhi Meares in 2000, Tigerlilly has become a summer staple for Australian women. They have a huge selection of well priced, well made and on-trend swimwear that often uses interesting cuts and fabrics as well as towels, kaftans, bags and a beach inspired fashion line.

Other location Westfield Miranda, 600 Kingsway, Miranda (9531 7682).

Tuchuzy

90 Gould Street, Bondi Beach (9365 5371, www.tuchuzymag.blogspot.com). Bus 333, 380. **Open** 9am-6pm Mon-Wed, Fri, Sat; 9am-7pm Thur; 10am-6pm Sun. **Credit** AmEx, DC, MC, V. **Map** p334.

Tuchuzy amps up the style factor in beachwear, stocking expertly selected cult labels. We love the Fairground and We Are Handsome swimsuits, muted, floaty wraps from KJ by Kirrily Johnston and of course finishing the look like a true Bondi local with a pair of Graz shades.

Used & vintage

Blue Spinach Recycled Designer Clothing

348 Liverpool Street, at Womerah Avenue, Darlinghurst (9331 3904, www.bluespinach.

INSIDE TRACK TEMPE TIP

Sydney's vintage capital is Tempe Tip (7 Bellevue Street, St Peters, 9519 1513), where you can battle it out with style kids for shoes, bikes and endless glad rags. It has one of the largest and oldest Salvation Army stores in NSW, hence the best of badly kept secrets.

---

com.au). CityRail Kings Cross/bus 389. **Open** 10am-6pm Mon-Wed, Fri, Sat; 10am-7pm Thur. **Credit** AmEx, DC, MC, V. **Map** p330 J8.

If your idea of recycled clothing is more about last season's Missoni than musty-smelling cast-offs, head down to this fashion-insider spot. Run by Mark and Jayne Thompson, it's the most innovative and upmarket recycled clothing joint in town. The building is bright blue, so you can't miss it.

★ Grandma Takes a Trip

263 Crown Street, Surry Hills (9356 3322, www.grandmatakesatrip.com.au). Bus 339, 376, 391, 174. **Open** 10am-6pm Mon-Wed, Fri, Sat; 10am-8pm Thur; 11am-5pm Sun. **Credit** call for details. **Map** p329 G8.

Firmly established as one of Sydney's pre-eminent vintage and retro boutiques, Grandma is where you go for the funkiest 50s, 60s, 70s and 80s threads. A magnet for hip cats, international celebrities and Sydney's most retro-active locals, this emporium of cool lovingly selects each individual piece and reluctantly parts with those that take your fancy. And plenty do.

Pelle

90 William Street, Paddington (9331 8100, www.pelleshoes.com.au). Bus 378, 352. **Open** 10am-6pm Mon-Fri; 10am-5pm Sat; noon-4pm Sun. **Credit** call for details. **Map** p332 K9/10.

Fancy a pair of Yves St Laurent sandals, once thrown over the shoulder of a free spirit delighting from the feeling of the San-Franciscan park grass beneath her feet? This William Street destination is the perfect store for finding said rare gems, and the bohemian earrings to match. Pelle is known for its exquisite selection – with labels to boot.

Puf'n Stuff

96 Glenayr Avenue, at Blair Street, North Bondi (9130 8471). CityRail Bondi Junction then bus 333, 380, 381, 382/bus 333, 380. **Open** 11am-6pm Mon-Fri; 10am-6pm Sat, Sun. **Credit** DC, MC, V.

If you want to fit in with the hip Bondi crowd, you need to make the short walk from the beach to this shop, which sells cowboys boots, floaty dresses and envy-inducing vintage accessories. If you're quick you can snap up a 1950s or '70s original.

CONSUME

CONSUME

FASHION ACCESSORIES & SERVICES

Bags & hats

Mimco
436 Oxford Street, between Elizabeth Street
& George Street, Paddington (9357 6884,
www.mimco.com.au). Bus 333, 352, 378, 380.
Open 9am-6pm Mon-Wed, Fri; 9am-7pm Thur;
11am-4pm Sat; 11am-5pm Sun. **Credit** AmEx,
MC, V. **Map** p332 L10.
Highly original funky bags, luggage, fantastic sun-
hats and up-to-the-minute jewellery and wallets.
Owner Amanda 'Mim' Briskin is an Aussie success
story, and her gear sells all over the world.
Other locations throughout the city.

★ Strand Hatters
*Strand Arcade, 412-414 George Street, between
King & Market Streets, CBD (9231 688,
www.strandhatters.com.au). CityRail Martin
Place, St James or Town Hall/Monorail City
Centre.* **Open** 9am-5.30pm Mon-Fri; 9.30am-
4.30pm Sat; 11am-4pm Sun. **Credit** AmEx, MC,
V. **Map** p327 F6.
While Akubras pull the crowds in, you can also top
off your look with an authentic panama or fedora,
or even a replica of the pith helmet worn by dapper
soldiers at Rorke's Drift in 1879. *Mad Men* fans
should definitely drop in and dip their lid.

Jewellery

Apart from the establishment listed below, it's
also worth making a stop at **South West
Trader** (36 Oxford Street, Paddington, 9332
2311, www.southwesttrader.com.au), which has
most out-there local accessories, or the jewellery
sold at gift shop **Dinosaur Designs** (*see
p212*). If you're in the market for opals – a
popular Australian souvenir, as 95 per cent of
the world's supply comes from here – be sure to
check that the retailer is a certified member of
the **Jewellers' Assocation of Australia**
(www.jaa.com.au): look for the JAA 'pink
diamond' in the shop.

Harlequin Markets
*94a Oxford Street, Paddington (9357 4433,
www.harlequinmarket.com). Bus 333, 380, M40.*
Open 10am-6pm Mon-Wed, Fri, Sat; 10am-7pm
Thur; noon-5pm Sun. **Map** p332 J9.
You'll find it all here from snakeskin gloves to cat-
shaped bangles alongside a huge range of vintage
gear, costume jewellery and their own house range.

Lingerie & underwear

Some department stores also have excellent
lingerie sections: try **David Jones** (*see p195*)

and **Myer** (*see p195*). For sexy sleepwear, visit
Peter Alexander (Pitt Street Mall, 9223 3440,
www.peteralexander.com.au).

★ Arianne on Oxford
*310 Oxford Street, between Perry Lane &
William Street, Paddington (9331 4820). Bus
333, 352, 378, 380.* **Open** 10am-6pm Mon-Wed,
Fri, Sat; 10am-8pm Thur; 11am-5pm Sun. **Credit**
AmEx, MC, V. **Map** p332 K10.
High-end, handmade underwear that has obviously
been crafted with seduction in mind. There's a good
selection of nightwear too.
▶ *For saucy lessons in Burlesque, head to Q
Bar's exclusive 34B club nearby (34 Oxford
Street, Darlinghurst), gyrating its way into hearts
on Saturdays since 2005.*

Dress Me Darling
*305 Darling Street, between College &
Mort Streets, Balmain (9810 8818,
www.dressmedarling.com.au). Bus 433, 434,
442, 445.* **Open** 10am-5pm Mon-Sat; 11am-5pm
Sun. **Credit** AmEx, MC, V.
As its name suggests, this boutique is basically an
enormous walk-in wardrobe full of decadent buys.
There's a well-picked selection of undies veering on
the cutesy side, making it perfect for girlie girls.

Shoes

Apart from the shops listed below, *see also
p195* **Department stores**.

Andrew McDonald
*58 William Street, Paddington (9358 6793,
www.andrewmcdonald.com.au). Bus 333, 380.*
Open 10am-6pm Mon-Fri; 10am-5pm Sat.
Credit AmEx, DC, MC, V. **Map** p332 K10.
Bespoke shoemaker Andrew McDonald handcrafts
beautiful leather shoes for Sydney's seriously stylish set.

Cosmopolitan Shoes
*Shop 1, 22 Knox Street, Double Bay (9362
0515). Bus 324, 325, 326.* **Open** 10am-6pm
Mon-Wed, Fri, Sat; 10am-7pm Thur; noon-5pm
Sun. **Credit** AmEx, DC, MC, V. **Map** p331 N7.
This is hands down the best designer shoe store in
Sydney. With Jimmy Choo, Sonia Rykiel, Dolce &
Gabbana, Azzedine Alaia, YSL, Bottega Veneta and
Balenciaga sitting pretty on the shelves, you'll need
to exercise a bit of restraint when you visit.

Funkis
*Shop 19, Ground Floor, The Strand Arcade,
412-414 George Street, CBD (9221 9370,
www.funkis.com). CityRail Town Hall or
Wynyard.* **Open** 9am-5.30pm Mon-Wed, Fri;
9am-8pm Thur; 9am-5pm Sat; 11am-4pm Sun.
Credit AmEx, MC, V. **Map** p327 E/F 6.

Those in need of a clog fix should visit The Strand Arcades Funkis store. The Swedish label stocks all manner or colours, shapes and designs for these super comfortable and chic wooden wonders. There are hip brands, like Diesel, Onitsuka Tiger, Crocs, Vans and Birkenstock, all available at fairly reasonable prices.

Gary Castles
Strand Arcade, 412-414 George Street, between King & Market Streets, CBD (9232 6544, www.garycastlessydney.com). CityRail Martin Place, St James or Town Hall/Monorail City Centre. **Open** 9.30am-6pm Mon-Wed, Fri, Sat; 9.30am-8pm Thur; 11am-5pm Sun. **Credit** AmEx, MC, V. **Map** p327 F6.
Smart, gorgeous, sophisticated styles in great colour combinations. Wait for the sales if you find the prices too close to international designer levels.
Other locations 45A Bay Street, Double Bay (9327 5077); 112 Queen Street, Woollahra (9327 5611).

Mollini
302 Oxford Street, between Underwood & William Streets, Paddington (9331 1732, www.mollini.com.au). Bus 333, 352, 378, 380. **Open** 10am-6pm Mon-Wed, Fri; 10am-8.30pm Thur (8pm in winter); 9.30am-6pm Sat; 11am-5pm Sun. **Credit** AmEx, DC, MC, V. **Map** p332 K10.
Wedges, flats, round-toes, point-toes, boots, kitten heels, mid-heels, sandals, stilettos and platforms, plus bags and belts from around the world – phew. They come in fashionable shapes and designs, in various finishes (plaited leather, ponyskin, sequins, metallic). A fix for shoe addicts.
Other locations throughout the city.

Victor Churchill.

FOOD & DRINK
Asian

Pontip
78a Campbell Street, Surry Hills (9211 2208). Bus 309, 501, M20, 310. **Open** 9am-10pm daily. **Credit** AmEx, DC, MC, V. **Map** p329 F8/9.
All the major Thai chefs in town get their ingredients here and it's no wonder: you'll find everything you need to make a Thai feast from longans to those tiny little red hot chillies and dried baby shrimp.

TQC Burlington Supermarket
Corner of Thomas & Quay Streets, Haymarket (9281 2777, www.tqc-burlington.com.au). CityRail Central/Monorail Paddy's Markets/LightRail Capitol Square, Central or Paddy's Markets. **Open** 9am-7pm daily. **Credit** AmEx, MC, V. **Map** p329 E9.
A huge emporium of Chinese and other Asian groceries, including fruit and veg, and a butcher.
Other location 285-289 Penshurst Street, Willoughby (9417 2588).

Butchers

Sam the Butcher
129 Bondi Road, Bondi (9389 1420, www.samthebutcher.com.au). Bus 333, 380. **Open** 8am-6pm Mon-Fri; 8am-4pm Sat; 8am-3pm Sun. **Credit** AmEx, DC, MC, V.
Sam likes meat like plentiful, varied in origin and all-natural. Organic and free range is the directive here, and Sam Diasinos delivers an impressive array of meats from ten suppliers in three states. If you don't know the difference between a spatchcock and a quail, the helpful staff can help.
Other location 371 Rocky Point Road, Sans Souci (9583 1144).

★ Victor Churchill
132 Queen Street, Woollahra (9328 0402, www.victorchurchill.com.au). Bus 352, 378. **Open** 9am-7pm Mon-Fri; 8am-6pm Sat; 9am-4pm Sun. **Credit** AmEx, DC, MC, V. **Map** p333 M10.
Victor Churchill is a shrine to meat. If Salvador Dali and Elton John got together to open the world's fanciest butcher, it'd look very much like this. An entire wall is inlaid with bricks made from Himalayan rock salt where whole sides of cow dry age. Rows and rows of chickens roast on a rotisserie. In the fridge rest every type of terrine imaginable in proper ceramic moulds, along with confit duck legs, sausages and patés.

Chocolates

Belle Fleur
658 Darling Street, off Victoria Road, Rozelle (9810 2690, www.bellefleur.com.au). Bus 432,

CONSUME

CONSUME

433, 434, 440, 445. **Open** 9am-6pm Mon-Fri; 9am-4.30pm Sat; 10am-4pm Sun. **Credit** AmEx, MC, V.

Where confectionery meets art. Jan and Lynne ter Heerdt are third-generation chocolatiers from Belgium who set up in Sydney 20 years ago. The chocolates are made fresh every day.
Other location 584 Parramatta Road, Petersham (9550 0650).

Just William
4 William Street, at Oxford Street, Paddington (9331 5468, www.justwilliam.com.au). Bus 333, 352, 378, 380. **Open** 10am-6pm daily. **Credit** AmEx, MC, V. **Map** p332 K10.
This diminutive store, filled to the rafters with chocolate-covered delights, is a chocoholic's fantasy. The glass cabinets boast beautifully-presented trays of dark, milk and white chocolates with every filling imaginable, as well as glistening pyramids of jellies and nut-encrusted morsels.

Max Brenner
437 Oxford Street, between Centennial Park & Elizabeth Street, Paddington (9357 5055, www.maxbrenner.com). Bus 333, 352, 378, 380. **Open** 8.30am-9pm Mon-Thur; 8.30am-10pm Fri; 9am-10pm Sat; 9am-9pm Sun. **Credit** AmEx, DC, MC, V. **Map** p332 L10/11.
There's a café at the front and a shop at the back of this branch of the international chain. Drink frozen chocolate cocktails or steaming cups of hot choc, or gorge on strawberries dipped in melted chocolate.
Other locations throughout the city.

Delis & gourmet foods

★ Adriano Zumbo
296 Darling Street, Balmain (9810 7318, www.adrianozumbo.com). Bus 433. **Open** 8am-6pm Mon-Sat; 8am-4pm Sun. **Credit** MC, V.
The standard of product coming out of Zumbo's kitchen is punching so crazily above its weight that any restaurant in town could serve one of these desserts and be proud of what they're putting on the plate. Layers of fine pastry hold a gooey custard and dulce de leche cream centre, topped with South American caramel. There's also a seriously killer selection of chocolate goodness.

Fratelli Fresh
7 Danks Street, between Young & Bourke Streets, Waterloo (1300 552 119, www.fratellifresh.com.au). Bus 301, 302, 303. **Open** 9am-6pm Mon-Fri; 8am-4pm Sat; 9am-4pm Sun. **Credit** AmEx, MC, V.
Sydney's top restaurants have long benefitted from Fratelli Fresh's produce, so when the owners opened a store for the public the response from the locals was rightfully enthusiastic. Foodies from all over make the pilgrimage to Danks Street for its ware-

Adriano Zumbo.

house market full of top-quality Italian and Australian produce – fruit, veg, meat, salami, poultry, dry goods, dairy, bread – even flowers.
▶ *Fratelli Fresh is the gateway to Café Sopra upstairs. See also p179.*

Formaggi Ocello
Shop 16, 425 Bourke Street, Surry Hills (www.ocello.com.au). Bus 393, 372, 395. **Open** 9am-7.30pm Mon-Fri; 9am-6pm Sat; 10am-6pm Sun. **Credit** AmEx, DC, MC. **Map** p329 G9.
If cheese was porn then Formaggi Ocello would be triple-X rated. Scratch that: cheese is porn, and this is the place that foodies in Sydney go to obtain the quality European stuff. One comes not only to find extraordinary imported Italian, French and Spanish cheeses, but also to ogle and press against the glass cabinets with maximum voyeurism in mind.

Jones the Grocer
68 Moncur Street, at Queen Street, Woollahra (9362 1222, www.jonesthegrocer.com). Bus 389. **Open** 7.30am-5.30pm Mon-Sat; 9am-5pm Sun. **Credit** AmEx, MC, V. **Map** p333 M10.
Known for fine cheeses, sausages, cakes and high-quality grocery, Jones the Grocer is also a great place to just hang out and have a coffee.
Other locations 91-93 Macleay Street, Potts Point (9358 3343); 166 Military Road, Neutral Bay (8905 0150).

Provedore Pelagios
235 Victoria Street, between Liverpool & Surrey Streets, Darlinghurst (9360 1011). CityRail Kings Cross/bus 311, 389. **Open** 6am-10pm Mon-Fri; 6am-9.30pm Sat; 6am-10.30pm Sun. **Credit** AmEx, DC, MC, V. **Map** p330 J8.

Established in 1926, this traditional Italian grocer prides itself on its knowledgeable and enthusiastic staff. The bread is divine and there are also salads, cold cuts, cheeses, organic veg and gourmet pasta. The chocolate counter at the checkout is especially tempting at Easter. You can also have a coffee in the small lounge area at the front.

Simon Johnson Quality Foods
55 Queen Street, between Oxford & Moncur Streets, Woollahra (9328 6888, www.simonjohnson.com). Bus 389. **Open** 10am-6.30pm Mon-Fri; 9am-5pm Sat; 10am-4pm Sun. **Credit** AmEx, MC, V. **Map** p333 M10.
Esteemed foodie Simon Johnson has set himself up as the nation's leading provider of Australian and imported gourmet foods. His produce comes from more than 50 key sources, all vetted for quality. This shop has a great kitchenware section, a pleasingly odorous cheese room and plenty of sweet offerings. **Other locations** 181 Harris Street, Pyrmont (9552 2522); 24A Ralph Street, Alexandria (8244 8220).

Health foods

About Life Natural Marketplace
31-37 Oxford Street, at Ruthven Street, Bondi Junction (9389 7611). CityRail Bondi Junction, then bus 333, 378, 380, 389. **Open** 7am-8pm Mon-Fri; 7am-7pm Sat; 8am-7pm Sun. **Credit** AmEx, MC, V. **Map** p329 G8.
About Life Natural Marketplace is the mecca for macrobiotic, vegan, vegetarian and organic food. These people are serious about their natural, clean, fresh produce, and the prices aren't bad either. You can even buy organic pet food here.

Bayside Natural Health Centre
30-36 Bay Street, between Cooper & Cross Streets, Double Bay (9327 8002). Ferry Double Bay/bus 323, 324, 325, 326. **Open** 9am-6pm Mon-Sat; 11.30am-5pm Sun. **Credit** AmEx, DC, MC, V. **Map** p331 N7/8.
Lots of organic fresh and dried produce, including bread and a small deli section. A few well-placed stone buddhas and oil burners create a calming ambience in which to splurge on the herbal remedies, natural skincare cosmetics and therapeutic massages (book in advance) on offer.

Health Emporium
263 Bondi Road, between Denham & Castlefield Streets, Bondi (9365 6008). CityRail Bondi Junction then bus 333, 380, 381, 382/bus 333, 380. **Open** 8.30am-7pm Mon-Fri; 8.30am-6pm Sat, Sun. **Credit** AmEx MC, V.
As well as stocking earth-friendly cosmetics including Jurlique, Dr Hauschka and Weleda, this shop also has a good organic and grocery section and as many vitamins and supplements a vegan could need. You can also buy eco-safe detergents and 'ethical' coffee from the small takeaway deli.

GIFTS & SOUVENIRS

There is an unsettling whiff of Disneyland about the historic Rocks area near Circular Quay, but it is still a quaint and interesting place to spend a day. There's plenty of kitsch Australiana for sale, but also genuinely decent souvenirs in stores large and small, at a reasonable range of prices.
Didj Beat Didjeridoos (corner of Argyle & Harrington Streets, 9251 4289,

CONSUME

Tasteful Takeways
Another kind of Australiana to bring home.

It doesn't have to be a koala in a can or a boomerang that doesn't come back. Here are a few suggestions of genuinely Australian-made gifts that will raise a smile rather than a groan.
• A Robert Foster jug, cup and bowl from the Sydney Opera House Shop (*see 56*). Foster's F!nk Water Jug became an immediate design classic in 1994, and since then he has exhibited and sold all over the world. His homewares are minimalist gems.
• A piece of Elke Kramer's bold, geometric jewellery. Kramer is one of Sydney's hottest young designers – with one of her pieces on your neck/wrist/finger the complements will just keep on coming.

• A resin platter or vase, a jug or a plate from Dinosaur Designs (*see p212*). This trio of artists uses organic colours and shapes inspired by land- and seascapes. The results are soothing.
• A Florence Broadhurst overnight bag. The flamboyant portfolio of the late Sydney grande dame of lush wallpaper and prints has been resurrected by local entrepreneurs David and Helen Lennie. Head to Signature Prints, Unit 2, 3 Hayes Road, Rosebery (8338 8400, www.signatureprints.com.au).
• Mambo board shorts and tees from their Manly store (*see p207*). These are the must-have attire for beach, beer and board lubbers. Pure Australiana – and drip-dry too!

CONSUME

www.didjbeat.com) sells didgeridoos, Aboriginal art and artefacts from all over Australia. Staff can teach you how to play a didgeridoo and tell you about the Aboriginal artists the shop buys from. **Naturally Australian** (43 Circular Quay West, 9247 1531, www.naturallyaust.com.au) specialises in native timber furniture and craft, while **Craft NSW** (104 George Street, 9241 5825) is operated by the **Society of Arts & Crafts NSW** (www.artsandcraftsnsw.com.au) and has a wide selection of ceramics, handwoven, hand-spun and hand-knitted garments, as well as glass and woodwork. **Natural Selection Souvenirs** (Metcalfe Arcade, 82-84 George Street, 9247 9174) sells Driza-Bone coats and Ugg boots. Head to **Flame Opals** (119 George Street, 9247 3446, www.flameopals.com.au) for opal jewellery. Check www.therocks.com for more options.

The **Museum of Contemporary Art** (*see p56*) has a good gift shop, as does the **Museum of Sydney** (*see p56*), the **Powerhouse Museum** (*see p68*) and the **Sydney Opera House** (*see p56*). The latter has shops in the foyer and a new separate store with funky artefacts on the Lower Concourse.

Collect

Object Gallery, St Margarets, 417 Bourke Street, Surry Hills (9361 4511, www.object.com.au). Bus 371, 373, 377, 380, 396. **Open** 11am-5pm Tue-Fri; 10am-5pm Sat, Sun. **Credit** AmEx, MC, V. **Map** p329 H9.

Located beneath Object Gallery (which shows the work of Australian designers), this shop sells collectable glass and ceramics, plus Australia-made homewares and jewellery. A not-for-profit organisation, it supports the local artistic community.

★ Dinosaur Designs

Strand Arcade, 412-414 George Street, between King & Market Streets, CBD (9223 2953, www.dinosaurdesigns.com.au). CityRail Martin Place, St James or Town Hall/Monorail City Centre. **Open** 9.30am-5.30pm Mon-Wed, Fri; 9.30am-8pm Thur; 10am-4pm Sat; noon-4pm Sun. **Credit** AmEx, MC, V. Map p327 F6.

Founded in 1985 by three former art students, Dinosaur Designs makes bright, glowing resin bowls, vases, jugs, plates and other household items, as well as chunky jewellery, with ranges inspired by artists as well as by natural forms. **Other location** 339 Oxford Street, Paddington (9361 3776).

Gaffa Gallery

281 Clarence Street, CBD (9281 1103, www.gaffa.com.au). CityRail Town Hall. **Open** 10am-6pm Mon-Fri; 11am-5pm Sat. **Credit** AmEx, DC, MC, V. **Map** p329 E7.

Gaffa is a hub for emerging art, craft and design practitioners and has the works – four gallery spaces, a bright cafe serving fine coffee and treats, and workshops in object and jewellery design. Peruse the work of local designers and then purchase some to take with you.

▶ *The gateway to Gaffa sees you pass Klink (see p177), one of Sydney's best new cafés… and soon-to-be small bars.*

Gavala Aboriginal Cultural Centre

Harbourside Centre, Darling Drive, Darling Harbour (9212 7232, www.gavala.com.au). CityRail Town Hall/ferry Darling Harbour/Monorail Harbourside. **Open** 10am-9pm daily. **Credit** AmEx, MC, V. **Map** p327 D6.

Established in 1995, Gavala Aboriginal Cultural Centre is Aboriginal-owned and staffed, and is a top spot to buy arts, crafts and souvenirs made by Aboriginal artists. Expect clothes, jewellery, boomerangs, didgeridoos and more, including paintings in the separate art gallery.

HEALTH & BEAUTY
Complementary medicine

Complete City Health

Level 14, National Mutual Building, 44 Market Street, at York Street, CBD (9299 1661, www.completecityhealth.com.au). CityRail St James or Town Hall/Monorail City Centre. **Open** 8am-6pm Mon-Fri. **Credit** MC, V. **Map** p327 E6.

One of the first centres in Sydney to bring together all major healthcare professions, with the philosophy that the body only works when it is well as a whole. You'll find a GP and dentist, as well as chiropractors, naturopaths, massage therapists, reflexologists and more.

A Natural Practice

161A Glebe Point Road, between Mitchell Street & St Johns Road, Glebe (9660 7308, www.anaturalpractice.com.au). Bus 431, 432, 433. **Open** 9am-7pm Mon-Sat; also by appointment. **Credit** MC, V. **Map** p328 B9.

A Natural Practice has been running for 20 years and has experts in acupuncture, homeopathy, iridology, shiatsu, reflexology, reiki, remedial massage, naturopathy, osteopathy, psychotherapy and more. Detox programmes are also on offer.

Uclinic

Level 1, 421 Bourke Street, between Church Lane & Albion Street, Surry Hills (9332 0400, www.uclinic.com.au). Bus 371, 373, 377, 392, 394, 396, 397, 399, 890, L94. **Open** 8am-6pm Mon-Fri; 8am-1pm Sat. **Credit** AmEx, DC, MC, V. **Map** p329 G9.

Professor Kerryn Phelps, former chairman of the
Australian Medical Association, has done a brave
thing stepping outside the confines of her western
medicine training to set up this fully complementary
health clinic. All are welcome here and the emphasis is on achieving a healthy body and lifestyle.
Practitioners include acupuncturists, naturopaths
and Chinese medicine specialists, and there's a 24-
hour physio service available.

Cosmetics

★ Aesop
*Shop 20, The Strand Arcade, 412-414 George
Street, CBD (9235 2353, www.aesop.net.au).
CityRail Town Hall and Wynyard.* **Open** 9am-
5.30pm Mon-Wed, Fri; 9am-8pm Thur; 9am-5pm
Sat; 11am-4pm Sun. **Credit** AmEx, DC, MC, V.
Map p327 F6.
Go natural with Aesop's bath and body products at
this one-of-a-kind Sydney store (a local designer creates each store individually, so no two look the
same). Want more? The Sydney store offers facial
treatments using Aesop products – and that's no
fable.

Jurlique
*Shop 33, Strand Arcade, 412-414 George Street,
between King & Market Streets, CBD (9231
0626, www.jurlique.com.au). CityRail Martin
Place, St James or Town Hall/Monorail City
Centre.* **Open** 9am-6pm Mon-Wed, Fri; 9am-9pm
Thur; 9am-5.30pm Sat; 11am-5pm Sun. **Credit**
AmEx, DC, MC, V. **Map** p327 F6.
This small company based in South Australia is
making big news at home and overseas. It might not
be cheap, but this is the real deal when it comes to
gorgeous 'aromatherapeutic' natural toiletries.
Other locations throughout the city.

Kiehl's
*396 Oxford Street, Paddington (9326 9980,
www.kiehls.com). Bus 333, 380.* **Open** 9.30am-
6pm Mon-Wed, Fri, Sat; 9.30am-7pm Thur;
9.30am-5pm Sun. **Credit** AmEx, DC, MC, V.
Map p332 K/L10.
Kiehl's natural skin and hair products cater to every
member of the family, selling cleansers and mois-
turisers for women, babies, men, and even pets. And
pooches can really enjoy their shampoo, because
nothing is tested on animals.

Mecca Cosmetica
*126 Oxford Street, opposite Victoria
Barracks, Paddington (9361 4488,
www.meccacosmetica.com.au). Bus 333, 352,
378, 380.* **Open** 10am-6pm Mon-Wed, Fri, Sat;
10am-8pm Thur; 11am-5pm Sun. **Credit** AmEx,
DC, MC, V. **Map** p332 J9/10.
A chic cosmetic boutique with overseas brands such
as Nars, Stila and Philosophy. Some branches have
pedicure and make-up services too.
Other locations David Jones, Westfield Bondi
Junction (9389 4406); Galeries Victoria, CBD (9261
4911).

Hairdressers & barbers

Brad Ngata
*273-275 Goulburn Street, Surry Hills (9281
1220, www.bradngata.com). Bus 308, 309, 310,
320, 343.* **Open** 10am-6pm Tue; 9am-7pm Wed;
10am-9pm Thur, Fri; 9am-6pm Sat. **Credit** DC,
MC, V. **Map** p329 G8.
Sydney's favourite hairdresser is edgy, slick and
chic. A visit might break the bank, but it will be one
of the best hairdos you'll ever get. Ngata now also
has a salon in the plush Justin Hemmes Ivy complex,
so you can get primped before cocktail hour.
Other location Shop 2, Palings Lane, 320-348
George Street, CBD (9235 2723).

★ Grand Royal Barbers
*397 Liverpool Street, Darlinghurst (9360 3063,
www.grandroyalbarbers.com.au). Bus 309, 310,
343, M20.* **Open** 10am-6pm Mon; 10am-7pm
Tue-Fri; 9am-5pm Sat. **Credit** AmEx, DC, MC, V.
Map p329 H8.
Grab a fine brew while you're clipped, trimmed and
shaved at this traditional grooming house. Grand
Royal Barbers is a staple salon for men, located in
the heart of Sydney– and it's bringing the longstanding barber tradition to the 21st century.

Opticians

George Skoufis Optometrist
*38A Oxford Street, Paddington (9360 7487,
www.gso.net.au). Bus 333, 352, 378, 380.* **Open**
10am-6pm Mon-Fri; 10am-8pm Thur; 10am-5pm
Sat. **Credit** AmEx, DC, MC, V. **Map** p329 H9.
A great optometrist that stocks an impressive range
of spectacles and shades such as Colab and Isson.

OPSM
*183 Maquarie Street, corner of Chifley Square,
CBD (9232 7995, www.opsm.com). CityRail
Martin Place.* **Open** 7.30am-5pm Mon-Wed, Fri;
8am-5pm Thur. **Credit** AmEx, DC, MC, V. **Map**
p327 F5.
One of the country's biggest chains, with a good
selection of designer frames.
Other locations throughout the city.

CONSUME

Sydney Style Council

Two hip locals spill their cool beans.

The Sydney surfer boys behind Ksubi, **Dan Single** and **George Gorrow** name their hometown haute spots.

If Sydney was a bloke, what would he look like?
'A scruffy guy, great looking, always welcoming, always listening, always got a story or a joke to tell and always funny to be around.'

What inspires you?
Shop
Dan: If I was to buy something fancy I would head to Assin in Paddington. There is a great record shop in Marrickville called Mint Condition. Assin 2 Verona St, Paddington 2021 (www.assin.com.au). Mint Condition 403 Illawarra Rd, Marrickville 2204 (www.mintcondition.com.au).

Gallery
George: The Monster Children Gallery is great for young up and coming art. Monster Children, 6/12 Chester St, Camperdown 1450. (www.monsterchildren.com).

Magazine
Dan: My favourite magazine store is Taylor Square Newsagency. My magazines are: *Purple* magazine, *Another Magazine*, music mags and girly mags. (Taylor Square Newsagency, 163 Oxford Street Darlinghurst 2010.)

Website
Dan: I browse music blogs like fluokids, the hype machine, discobelle, bigstereo… geeky stuff like that. (fluokids.blogspot.com, hypem.com, www.discobelle.net, this.bigstereo.net/)

Creative space
George: Our office in Surry Hills is a great creative space. It is pretty shambolic but there are enough things lying around to keep you entertained for days. www.ksubi.com

What element of style does Sydney have that the rest of the world needs?
It needs to be more carefree and not so serious, like Sydney is.

Who's a Sydneysider to watch?
Music-wise Beni, Gus da Hoodrat, Spruce Lee, the Hoops. In fashion: Therese Rawsthorne, Romance was Born.

Pharmacies

There are very few 24-hour pharmacies in Sydney, but many are open into the evening.

CBD Pharmacies
92 Pitt Street, at Martin Place, CBD (9221 0091). CityRail Martin Place or Wynyard. **Open** 7.45am-6.45pm Mon-Fri. **Credit** AmEx, DC, MC, V. **Map** p327 F5.
Centrally located chemist open weekdays for troubled city staff, with an affiliated medical centre just up the road (open 8am-5pm Monday to Friday).

Spas & salons

Detail For Men
6 O'Connell Street, between Hunter & Bent Streets, CBD (9231 5999, www.detailformen.com). CityRail Wynyard. **Open** 9am-7pm Mon-Wed, Fri; 9am-8.30pm Thur; 9am-6pm Sat. **Credit** AmEx, DC, MC, V. **Map** p327 F5.
Aimed at city boys, Detail For Men is a salon that provides a premium hairdressing and day spa service designed for 'today's modern man'. The services that are provided include waxing, facials, haircuts, shaves and massages.

★ Miss Frou Frou
20-22 Elizabeth Street, Paddington (9360 2444, www.valonz.com.au). Bus 525, 378, 380, 333. **Open** 8.30am-6pm Mon-Wed, Fri; 8.30am-7pm Thur; 8.30am-6pm Sat. **Credit** AmEx, DC, MC, V. **Map** p332 L10.
Rub shoulders with Sydney's elite, and the odd Hollywood starlet, while you get your phalanges buffed, polished and lacquered in custom colours such as Pink Venus, Green Envy and Red Hot.

Observatory Day Spa
Observatory Hotel, 89-113 Kent Street, Sydney (8248 5250, www.observatoryhotel.com.au). CityRail Wynyard. **Open** 5.45am-9pm Mon-Fri; 6.45am-9pm Sat, Sun. **Credit** AmEx, DC, MC, V.
If spending a day in the manner of a Russian oligarch appeals to you then head to the Observatory Day Spa where you can, and will, be treated like royalty with caviar facials, or perhaps a full body treatment with crushed diamonds and pearls.

Zen Day Spa
116-118 Darlinghurst Road, between William &
Liverpool Streets, Darlinghurst (9361 4200,
www.zendayspa.com.au). CityRail Kings Cross.
Open 9am-9pm Mon-Fri; 8am-8pm Sat; 10am-
7pm Sun. **Credit** AmEx, MC, V. **Map** p329 H8.
Serenity is the name of the game at this day spa, a
sanctuary in the heart of bustling Darlinghurst.
Options include massage, aromatherapy sessions,
and skincare treatments.
Other location 118-122 Queen Street,
Woollahra (9328 1656).

Tattoos & piercing

Inner Vision Tattoo
334 Crown Street, at Campbell Street, Surry Hills
(9361 4376/www.innervisiontattoo.com.au). Bus
301, 302, 303. **Open** 11am-7pm daily. **No
credit cards**. **Map** p329 G9.
A clean and smart place offering top-quality service
(including great follow-up advice). The other branch
has a wider range of options, such as full body, facial
and genital piercing, and also sells jewellery.

Steel Lotus Body Arts
174 Crown Street, at Chapel Street, Darlinghurst
(9326 0555, www.steellotus.com). Bus 324, 325,
326, 327. **Open** 11am-7pm Tue, Wed, Fri, Sat;
11am-8pm Thur. **Credit** AmEx, DC, MC, V. **Map**
p329 G7.
The five tattooists and one body piercer here take
time and care to create custom-made work for their
clients. Not surprisingly, they're all booked well in
advance by a broad clientele of body-art devotees.
Jewellery is also stocked.

HOUSE & HOME

Circa C20 (9212 2557, www.circa-c20.com.au)
is the authority in Sydney on 20th-century
glass, carrying products from elegant teacups
to funky Italian lamps to clean-lined
Scandinavian vases, while **Space** (8339 7588,
www.spacefurniture.com.au), the purveyor of
all things ultra cool for the home, carries
leading names such as Edra, Giorgetti, Ingo
Maurer and Kartell. Space is by no means
cheap, but then again fabulous things never are.
For smaller items head to **Top 3 by Design**
(9388 9699, www.top3.com.au) where aesthetics
meet seamless functionality. True to name, the
shop carries up to three products for each
category, chosen according to design values.

There are heaps of second-hand furniture
emporiums that sell buy and sell all types of
furniture, from lamps to sofas, beds to washing
machines. Two reliable outlets are **Mitchell
Road Auction House** (9310 7200,
www.mitchellroadauctions.com) and the
Bower (9568 6280, www.bower.org.au).

MUSIC & ENTERTAINMENT

Sydney's megastores are **Virgin** (343 George
Street, CBD, 9347 0300) and **Sanity** (Imperial
Arcade, Pitt Street Mall, 9239 0050,
www.sanity.com.au).

★ Ashwood's Music & Books
129 York Street, at Market Street, CBD (9267
7745). CityRail Town Hall/Monorail Galeries
Victoria. **Open** 9.30am-6pm Mon-Wed, Fri;
9.30am-8pm Thur; 9.30am-5pm Sat; noon-4pm
Sun. **Credit** MC, V. **Map** p327 E6.
This basement music emporium opposite the QVB
has traded since 1932 and is a great place to find
obscure CDs or vinyl. It's also good for second-hand
music books and DVDs, and vintage sheet music.

Egg Records
3 Wilson Street, Newtown (9550 6056,
www.eggrecords.com.au). CityRail Newtown.
Open 10am-6.30pm Mon-Wed, Fri, Sat; 10am-
7pm Thur; 11am-5pm Sun. **Credit** AmEx, DC,
MC, V. **Map** p334.

Space.

Collectibles, rarities, film memorabilia and a constantly changing range of new and second-hand CDs and vinyl make this a cornucopia for the discerning music enthusiast. Get in the mood for some sweet, sweet music by flipping through the second-hand racks.

Fish Records
261 King Street, between Church &
Mary Streets, Newtown (9557 3074,
www.fishrecords.com.au). CityRail Newtown.
Open 9am-9.45pm Mon-Sat; 9.30am-9pm Sun.
Credit AmEx, MC, V. **Map** p334.
Next to the Dendy cinema, this branch of Fish stocks mostly Top 40 and dance music, with a good soundtrack section. The 350 George Street and QVB branches focus on classical music.
Other locations throughout the city.

★ Red Eye
66 King Street, between George & York Streets,
CBD (9299 4233, www.redeye.com.au). CityRail
Wynyard. **Open** 9am-6pm Mon-Wed, Fri; 9am-9pm Thur; 9am-5pm Sat; 11am-5pm Sun. **Credit**
AmEx, MC, V. **Map** p327 E6.
The biggest of the indie shops, Red Eye has an excellent range of Australian bands and labels, as well as a good selection of imports. There's also second-hand merchandise at this outlet, but it's the Pitt Street branch that specialises in second-hand. You can also buy tickets for gigs here.
Other location 370 Pitt Street, CBD (9262 9755).
▶ *Some of Sydney's greatest bands, such as the Beasts of Bourbon, have been shepherded to infamy by the Red Eye label. See p309 for more information.*

TITLE
499 Crown Street, Surry Hills (9699 5222,
www.titlespace.com). Bus 333, 352, 378, 380.
Open 9am-6pm Mon-Wed, Fri, Sat; 9am-8pm
Thur; 11am-6pm Sun. **Credit** AmEx, DC, MC, V.
Map p329 G10.
With a filing 'system' designed to encourage chance discoveries, you're bound to find something enticing among the handpicked selection of cult DVDs, books and music.

OP SHOPS

Op (for 'opportunity') shops are second-hand shops, the Australian version of the UK's charity shops and the US's thrift stores.

St Vincent de Paul
292 Oxford Street, between Elizabeth &
Underwood Streets, Paddington (9360 4151,
www.vinnies.org.au). Bus 333, 352, 378, 380.
Open 9.30am-6pm Mon, Tue; 9.30am-8pm
Wed-Sat; 10am-6pm Sun. **Credit** MC, V.
Map p332 K10.

The proceeds of these shops – fondly known as 'St Vinnie's' – go to the St Vincent de Paul hospitals and help towards the generally unsung charity work done by this Catholic organisation. This branch specialises in clothes and, thanks to the quality of the stock, turnover is quick. Look out for current-season fashion and designer labels.
Other locations throughout the city.

★ Salvos Store St Peters
7 Bellevue Street, off Princes Highway, St Peters
(9519 1513). CityRail St Peters. **Open** 8.30am-3.30pm Mon-Fri; 8.30am-1.45pm Sat. **Credit**
AmEx, DC, MC, V.
More department store than humble op shop, this warehouse-size emporium holds racks of clothes, enough furniture to fill an apartment block, plus old computers, a good collection of records and cut-price household goods. Proceeds go to the Salvation Army ('Salvos') – huge in Australia.
Other locations throughout the city.

SPORTS & FITNESS

For surf- and swimwear, *see p206.*

Kathmandu
Shop 35, Town Hall Arcade, corner of Kent
& Bathurst Streets, CBD (9261 8901,
www.kathmandu.com.au). CityRail Town
Hall/Monorail Galeries Victoria. **Open** 9am-5.30pm Mon-Wed, Fri; 9am-8.30pm Thur; 9am-5pm Sat; 10am-4pm Sun. **Credit** AmEx, MC, V.
Map p329 E7.
'Live the dream, ski it, sail it, run it, climb it, surf it, walk it, paddle it, explore it, skate it': that's the motto, and this shop means it. It has everything in here: the gear, the clothes, the gadgets.

Paddy Pallin
507 Kent Street, at Bathurst Street, CBD
(9264 2685, www.paddypallin.com.au). CityRail
Town Hall/Monorail Galeries Victoria. **Open**
9am-5.30pm Mon-Wed; 9am-9pm Thur; 9am-6pm
Fri; 9am-5pm Sat; 10am-5pm Sun. **Credit** AmEx,
DC, MC, V. **Map** p329 E7.
Bushwalker Paddy opened his first shop in the 1930s, selling lightweight camping and walking gear. The mini national chain is still going strong, with the shops stocking everything that the modern-day backpacker might want.

TRAVEL AGENTS

The reliable chains **Flight Centre** (66 King Street, between York & George Streets, CBD, 9262 6644, 13 3133, www.flightcentre.com.au) and **STA Travel** (855 George Street, at Harris Street, Haymarket, 9212 1255, www.statravel.com.au) have branches throughout the city.

CONSUME

Arts & Entertainment

Chinese Laundry. *See p225.*

Calendar

Sydney's events calendar makes the city a festival wonderland.

Sydney's festivals represent the city's multi-faceted personality. From the paper dragons of Chinese New Year to the dancing boys of the Gay & Lesbian Mardi Gras to the indoor sports spectacles of Writers Festival and the Sydney Film Festival and the tall sails of the Sydney Hobart Yacht Race, old and new traditions sit cheek by jowl and the party spirit reigns. Many events are free and these tend to command huge crowds. But with every suburb now holding its own festival, there are plenty of events that attract smaller, more manageable audiences.

SPRING

★ Festival of the Winds

Bondi Beach (8362 3400, www.waverley.nsw.gov. au). CityRail Bondi Junction then bus 381, 382, 380, 333/bus 222, 380, 333. **Date** 2nd Sun in Sept. **Map** p334.

Australia's largest free kite-flying festival is staged outside the Bondi Pavilion on Bondi Beach and in the park behind the sands, attracting up to 50,000 people and hundreds of kites of all shapes and sizes. The competitions are only open to kite club members, but there are plenty of other activities for beginners and non-kiters, including kite-making lessons, live music and masses of stuff for kids.

Sydney Running Festival

www.sydneyrunningfestival.org. **Date** Sun, mid Sept.

First held in 2001 and incorporating the Sydney Marathon, the Running Festival is the only community event that closes the Sydney Harbour Bridge. It comprises four road races – the marathon, a half-marathon, a 9km (5.6 mile) Bridge Run and the most recent addition, a family fun run of 4km (2.5 miles). Entry is open to all, though you have to apply in advance and pay an entry fee.

★ Art & About

Various venues (www.cityofsydney.nsw.gov. au/artandabout). **Date** Late Sept-Oct.

For three weeks in October the parks, squares, streets and shopping centres of the city become the canvas for events, exhibitions and workshops showcasing local artists both established and emerging. There's fashion, photography, ice sculpture, flower arrangements and more.

Crave Sydney

Various venues (www.gfm.smh.com.au). **Date** Oct.

A multi-tiered umbrella festival that has replaced Good Food Month, Crave Sydney offers an international food festival of chef showcases, gourmand events and night markets in Hyde Park. The centrepiece of this banquet is arguably Breakfast on the Bridge, in which 6000 Sydneysiders picnic on freshly-laid turf across eight lanes of the closed Harbour Bridge.

Manly International Jazz Festival

Manly (9976 1400, www.manly.nsw.gov.au/ manlyjazz). Ferry Manly. **Date** Oct. **Map** p334.

Australia's largest and longest-running community jazz festival attracts crowds of over 20,000. Local and international artists play on the outdoor stages set along the Corso, the beach and the council forecourt opposite Manly Wharf. Along with roving bands, there are more than 60 free performances from noon till sunset, as well as indoor sessions (for which you'll have to pay) going into the night.

FREE Riverbeats Live

Parramatta (8839 3311, www.riverbeats.com.au). Rivercat Parramatta. **Date** Nov. **Map** p321.

Sydney's western suburb of Parramatta comes alive with Riverbeats, an annual celebration held on and around the banks of the Parramatta River between Wilde and Lennox Bridges. There are music performances and public sculpture displays plus a Carp Fish Out to rid the River of its giant gilled pests. The highlight is Loy Krathong, a Thai water festival in which hundreds of tiny leaf boats carrying candles are launched to carry away bad luck, sins and suffering.

Sleaze Ball

Entertainment Quarter, Driver Avenue, Moore Park (9568 8600, www.mardigras.org.au). Bus 339, 373, 374, 376, 377, 393, 395, 396. **Date** 1st Sat, Oct. **Map** p332 J12.

A spectacular and, of course, very sleazy dance party organised as a fund-raiser for gay Sydney's main event, Mardi Gras (*see p220*). There's a hot new theme each year to inspire wild costumes and shows. Sleaze kick-starts the gay summer party season. For more information, *see p248*.

★ FREE Sculpture by the Sea

Along the cliff walk from Bondi to Tamarama (8399 0233, www.sculpturebythesea.com). CityRail Bondi Junction then bus 381, 382, 380, 333/bus 222, 380, 333. **Date** 1st 3wks in Nov. **Map** p334.

This must surely be one of the world's most spectacular locations for an art event. For three weeks, Australia's largest free outdoor exhibition of contemporary sculpture shows off over 100 works by local and overseas artists along the coastal cliff walk from Bondi Beach to Tamarama Beach. Alongside the outdoor event, 'Sculpture Inside' exhibits smaller works by selected artists at the Bondi Pavilion Gallery and the Tamarama Surf Life Saving Club.

FREE Newtown Festival

Camperdown Memorial Park, corner of Lennox & Australia Streets, Newtown (9519 2509, www.newtowncentre.org). CityRail Newtown. **Date** Sun in mid Nov. **Map** p334.

This free festival boasts a dog show like no other ('Celebrity Look-a-Like', anyone?). If you're not into the pooches there's plenty of other stuff going on, with music, workshops, food and activities for kids. The festival runs from 10am to 6pm.

Glebe Street Fair

Glebe Point Road, from Parramatta Road to Bridge Road, Glebe (9281 0024, www.glebestreet fair.com.au). LightRail Glebe/bus 370, 431, 432, 433, 434. **Date** 3rd Sun in Nov. **Map** p328 A8.

Sydney's longest-running street festival takes over Glebe Point Road as traffic gives way to food stalls, wine-tasting booths, arts and craft stalls, clowns, stilt-walkers and music stages. Foley Park is devoted to children's activities. Expect crowds of around 100,000. The fair runs from 10am to 5pm.

SUMMER

Carols in the Domain

The Domain, Mrs Macquarie's Road, Royal Botanic Gardens, CBD (www.carolsinthe domain.com). CityRail Circular Quay or Martin Place/ferry Circular Quay. **Date** wk before Christmas. **Map** p327 G/H5.

In case you were worried that Christmas wouldn't be Christmas in all the heat, you can join the 100,000 who fill the Domain for an evening of traditional car-

ols by candlelight. The crowds are kept in tune by a 150-strong choir and a chorus of local and celebs, and the evening is sealed by a firework display.

Christmas Day on Bondi Beach

Bondi Beach. CityRail Bondi Junction then bus 333, 380, 381, 382/bus 222, 333, 380. **Date** 25 Dec. **Map** p334.

Thousands of travellers from around the world (especially Brits) gather on Bondi Beach each year for an impromptu party, some with their own sofa and Christmas tree. Since the council introduced an alcohol ban on the beach a few years ago, this traditional festivity has become more of a family affair and the backpacker crowd instead heads to the Bondi Pavilion for an all-day dance party.

Sydney Hobart Yacht Race

Sydney Harbour (8292 7800, www.cyca.com.au). **Date** 26 Dec.

Hundreds of keen yachtsmen and supporters turn out to watch the spectacular lunchtime start of this notoriously gruelling race to Hobart. The best viewing areas are coastal cliff spots around the harbour, such as Bradleys Head, Chowder Bay and Georges Heights on the west, Vaucluse Point, South Head and the Gap on the east, and North Head in the north.

★ FREE New Year's Eve Fireworks

Sydney Harbour & Darling Harbour (9265 9757, www.cityofsydney.nsw.gov.au/nye). **Date** 9pm & midnight 31 Dec.

When it comes to pyrotechnic experiences, New Year's Eve in Sydney is in a league of its own. Each year the stakes to be the best in the world are raised, and each year Sydney usually wins. After a day of public spectacles, there are two fireworks displays, one at 9pm for families and then the midnight extravaganza. For ideas of where to watch them, *see p221* **Look up.**

★ Sydney Festival

Various venues (8248 6500, www.sydneyfestival. org.au). **Date** Jan.

Launched in 1976 to celebrate the city and bring people into the CBD, the festival now includes venues in Parramatta. This is Sydney's major cultural event: held in the three weeks leading up to Australia Day (26 January) and it's a feast of dance, theatre, visual arts, opera and music, with performances from homegrown and international superstars. Ticketed events are supplemented by an impressive free outdoor programme, including Festival First Night, which has in past years seen huge concerts by Brian Wilson, Grace Jones and Al Green in the Domain.

Australia Day

Various venues (9513 2000, www.australia day.com.au). **Date** 26 Jan.

Festivities take place all over the city (and the rest of Australia) in this annual celebration of European

ARTS & ENTERTAINMENT

settlement in Australia. Events focus around Hyde Park, the Rocks and Darling Harbour, with music, food, kids' entertainment and plenty of flag-waving. The day ends with fireworks over Darling Harbour.

FREE Ferrython
Sydney Harbour (www.sydneyfestival.org.au). **Date** 26 Jan.
Thousands of spectators watch four of Sydney's catamaran ferries race for the title of Ferry Champion, with the Harbour Bridge as the finishing line. The race, from 11am, is a traditional part of the Sydney Festival's Australia Day celebrations (*see p219*), and is followed by a prize for best-dressed ferry. Good viewpoints are Milsons Point, McMahons Point, the Botanic Gardens and Mrs Macquarie's Chair.

FREE Chinese New Year
Chinatown, Haymarket (9265 9333, www.city ofsydney.nsw.gov.au). CityRail Central/LightRail Capitol Square/Central. **Date** varies, usually end Jan/early Feb. **Map** p329 F9.
Now the biggest CNY celebrations outside China itself, Sydney has really amped this festival in recent years. Unsurprisingly, Chinatown hosts much of the action over its 15-day span. There are firecrackers galore, markets, a colourful Twilight Parade through the centre of town and dragon-boat racing on Darling Harbour on the final weekend.

AUTUMN

FREE Gay & Lesbian Mardi Gras
Various venues (9568 8600, www.mardigras. org.au). **Date** Feb; ends 1st Sat in Mar.
Sydney's gay, lesbian and transgender community swells with the arrival of thousands of international visitors, who join in an extravaganza of shows, exhibitions, plays, art, film and sport. The finale is the parade, which sees marching boys and girls shimmy and strut their stuff along the 'Golden Mile' from Hyde Park down Oxford Street to the party venue at the Entertainment Quarter. *See also p244.*

★ Royal Easter Show
Sydney Showground, Sydney Olympic Park, Homebush Bay (9704 1111, www.eastershow. com.au). CityRail Olympic Park. **Date** from Thur before Good Fri.
A Sydney institution: for two weeks rural Australia is packaged up for the urbanites and attracts over a million visitors. There are competitions galore – not just livestock prizes and sheepdog trials, but also contests for bees, alpacas, rats and mice, not to mention the popular women's wood-chopping contest.

FREE Anzac Day March
Along George Street from Martin Place to Hyde Park. CityRail Circular Quay, Martin Place, Town Hall or Wynyard/ferry Circular Quay. **Date** 25 Apr. **Map** (Martin Place) p327 F5–p329 F7.

Sydneysiders pay their respects to the Australian and New Zealand troops killed at Gallipoli and in other wars by turning out in their thousands to watch the parade of veterans and Defence Force bands. A public holiday, the day starts with a dawn service at the Martin Place Cenotaph followed at 9am by a march along George Street and a 12.30pm service at the Anzac Memorial in Hyde Park. There are dawn services throughout Sydney and Australia.

Sydney Writers' Festival
Various venues (9252 7729, www.swf.org.au). **Date** mid-late May.
From highbrow to pulp, fact to fiction, writers from around the world as well as home-grown talents come together for a week of debate and discussion. This is Sydney's biggest literary event, with readings, workshops and the chance to meet authors. Some events are free, but all require booking.

WINTER

Sydney Film Festival
Various venues (9318 0999, www.sydneyfilm festival.org). **Date** 2 wks in June.
Featuring new and independent as well as mainstream movies, this filmfest aims to please all with cinema from Australia and beyond. In 2008, the festival became part of an official international competition circuit, with 12 films from around the globe competing for a cash prize. For more details, *see p234.*

Sydney Alpine Winter Festival
Various venues in the CBD and at Bondi Beach (www.winterfestival.com/sydney). **Date** 24 June-25 July.
New since 2009, this five-week freeze-fest sees the historic forecourt of St Mary's Cathedral iced over into a skating rink. Folks glide around and stop for hot totties and delicious Euro-styled food. In 2010, festivities extended to Bondi where another rink was installed and markets built around the perimeter.

Biennale of Sydney
Various venues (9368 1411, www.biennaleof sydney.com). **Date** June-Sept, even-numbered years only.
Each festival explores a specific subject or theme through the works of Australian and international artists. Alongside what is claimed to be 'the southern hemisphere's largest collection of contemporary art' there are seminars, talks and screenings.

City to Surf Fun Run
From corner of Park & College Streets to Bondi Beach (1 800 555 514, www.city2surf.sunherald. com.au). **Date** mid Aug.
This 14km (8.7-mile) community fun run starts near Hyde Park and ends at Bondi Beach. Around 60,000 runners participate, mostly amateur joggers and walkers, with at least one chicken suit guaranteed.

Look Up

Where to watch the New Year fireworks.

One event draws more eyes to Sydney than any other. Here's where to check the pyrotechnics on New Year's Eve:

Bicentennial Park
Federal Road, Glebe; access via Chapman Road.
There are waterside seats to be had here along the industrial side of the harbour. Food is for sale, but load up on alcohol before you go because there's none there.

Blues Point Reserve
Blues Point Road, McMahons Point; access via Blues Point Road. **Map** p327 E1.
A superb site with dress circle views of the fireworks and the Opera House. The road is closed to cars and the capacity is small, but don't be deterred. Alcohol is for sale only.

Bradfield Park
Alfred Street South, Milsons Point; access via Broughton Street or Alfred Street South. **Map** p327 F1.
If you can't get into Blues Point Reserve, try neighbouring Bradfield Park. There's room for 50,000 and the slope of the hill makes viewing good for all. You can't bring alcohol, but booze and food are for sale on site.

Cockatoo Island
Junction of the Parramatta & Lane Cove Rivers. **Map** p325.
The former shipyard, reformatory and jail is now open to campers for the big night. Reserve one of 475 sites, bring along a tent and perch in prime position for both western and city fireworks. There's no BYO alcohol but it's available for sale on the island.

Cremorne Point Reserve
Milson Road, Cremorne; access via Milson Road.

One of Sydney's most spectacular vantage points, the leafy setting of Cremorne is great for families. There's room for 1,000 and food on sale but booze is banned.

Embarkation Park
Victoria Street, Potts Point; access via Victoria Street or Cowper Wharf Road. **Map** p330 J5.
In Kings Cross, this is the place to catch the fireworks. It's heavily policed and you can't bring your own alcohol nor buy it there but there are food stalls. Come early.

Illoura Reserve
Peacock Point, Weston Street, East Balmain; access via Weston Street or Darling Street. **Map** p326 C3.
Stake your spot mid-afternoon in this pretty park. Expect 3,000 others to join you and don't come by car – public transport is great here. Food is for sale; BYOB.

McKell Park
Darling Point Road, Darling Point; access via park gate on Darling Point Road or Darling Point Wharf. **Map** p331 M5.
Cocktails at dusk followed by champagne and canapés is the civilised way to watch the fireworks for 500 in the know.

Mrs Macquarie's Point
Mrs Macquarie's Road, the Domain; access via Art Gallery Road. **Map** p330 J3.
The grand dame of vantage points – with some 19,000 fellow revellers. There's no BYO, strictly no glass; food and alcohol are for sale only and there's plenty of police.

North Head
North Head Scenic Drive, Manly; access on foot via North Head Scenic Drive. **Map** p334.
Manly-ites make the trek to the Head rather than the city. Be prepared for a hike in the dark; bring a torch and something to sit on.

Sydney Opera House
Bennelong Point, Circular Quay; access via Macquarie Street. **Map** p327 G3.
First time? Then join the milling throngs of around 12,000 hugging the sails of the Opera House. There's no doubt you'll get an in-your-face view, but be prepared for a tight squeeze.

ARTS & ENTERTAINMENT

Children

Big blue fun for the little ones.

Sydney is a natural wonderland for kids and local 'grommets' (an Aussie surfing term for ankle-biters) have no trouble making their own fun. At most of the city's beaches there are myriad coves and rock pools to explore on foot or by boat or canoe. And the cornucopia of gardens, parks and bushland all team with wildlife, walks and rangers to guide you. In fact, there's very little in the city that's not open to children, which makes it family holiday heaven.

For full information on children's activities, pick up a copy of *Time Out*'s monthly magazine or log onto timeout.com/sydney.

BEACHES

BEACHES

Beaches both with and without surf co-exist at **Manly** (*see p101* and *p122*), which also has pleasant walks and plenty of cheap places to eat as well as an **Oceanworld Manly** (*see p104*) full of sharks, turtles and amazing marine life.

North of here there are great playgrounds at **North Steyne** and **Queenscliff** while south along Fairy Bower, the waterfront pathway will lead you to a paddling pool and safe swimming at **Shelly Beach** (*see p122*); older kids may even like to take a surf lesson (*see p261*) and families should keep their eyes peeled for the residenty colony of Little Penguins. The surf at **Bondi Beach** (*see p119*) is usually too strong and crowded for little ones, but there's a natural rock pool and playgrounds at the north end, and lots of space for inline skating. At the south end is a challenging skateboarders' ramp.

South of Bondi, sheltered **Bronte Beach** (*see p120*) has a large park with barbecue facilities, a fantastic playground and a superb fish and chip shop, Fishy Bite (491 Bronte Rd, 9387 7956). While the sea is too dangerous here for youngsters, there's a great natural 'bogey hole' rock pool that was once a fertility pond for the Gadigal tribes and which today fills up at high tide and hosts darting schools of translucent fish. Next door, **Clovelly Beach** (*see p120*) is one of the safest and most tranquil in Sydney, with lots of colourful fish awaiting snorkellers. Look out for Bluey their famously curious and child-friendly blue groper. On land there are barbecue pavilions, a playground, rock pools and surrounding grassy cliffs for the perfect picnic.

Balmoral Beach (*see p119*) on the North Shore is also good for picnics, and you can sip a drink in the café while the kids enjoy the playground or swim in a netted area. Further south, just before Maroubra, you'll find **Mahon Pool**, which boasts a rock platform filled with starfish, sea anemones and crabs.

Of the northern beaches, the best are **Dee Why Beach**, with its cool playground and host of child-friendly eateries, and **Collaroy Beach** (*see p122*), which boasts a paddling pool, large playground and barbecue facilities. Secluded **Clareville Beach** (*see p105*) is a safe swimming beach on the Pittwater (western) side of the peninsula; the water's too shallow for adults, but is ideal for little kids.

MUSEUMS

As well as animal skeletons, the **Australian Museum** (*see p58*) has interactive exhibits, a Kids' Island, an indoor play and discovery area for under-sixes plus a pricey but amazing Behind-the-Scenes tour for over-12s. The **Australian National Maritime Museum** (*see p68*) has a playground, plus various ships to be explored and the **Powerhouse Museum** (*see p68*) has regular exhibitions and interactive spaces. The **Ian Thorpe Aquatic Centre** (*see p260*) is adjacent if it's hot and you fancy cooling the brood off with a swim.

PARKS & PLAYGROUNDS

For wet and wild adventures without the beach, head to **Manly Waterworks** (corner of West

ARTS & ENTERTAINMENT

Esplanade and Commonwealth Parade, 9949 1088, www.manlywaterworks.com); sluicing down the gullet of the Insane Earthworm is an experience never to be forgotten.

Darling Harbour (*see p66*) is touristy, but has lots for kids of all ages. There's a giant playground at Tumbalong Park, conveniently surrounded by cafés, and a fun water play area, paddle-boats and a merry-go-round – not to mention the **Sydney Aquarium** (*see p69*), an **IMAX** cinema (*see p232*) and **Sydney Wildlife World** (*see p69*). At weekends and during school holidays, you'll see lots of street entertainers and perhaps an open-air concert or dusk firework display. Look for the whale watching fleets that gather at nearby Cockle Bay – so adept at tracking these gentle behemoths, they will guarantee you a whale sighting.

For older children, lovely **Centennial Park** (*see p77*) is big and buzzy: inline skates, bikes and pedal cars can be hired from **Centennial Park Cycles** (*see p298*) at Hamilton and Grand Drives, and for horseriders there's the **Centennial Parklands Equestrian Centre** (*see p260*). Alternatively, find a shady spot, lay down your picnic rug and let the kids run riot feeding bread to the native geese, turtles, giant carp and eels that call the ponds home.

SERVICES

Dial an Angel
1300 721 111. **Open** *Phone enquiries* 8.30am-8.30pm daily. **Credit** AmEx, MC, V.
24-hour nanny or babysitting service.

WILDLIFE

Shark fans should head to **Sydney Aquarium** (*see p69*) and **Oceanworld Manly** (*see p104*). Both offer close encounters with sharks and stingrays, as well as hands-on experiences with starfish and sea urchins. Oceanworld Manly also has an interactive 'Dangerous Australian Animals' show and sleepover nights for kids. Sydney Aquarium offers an incredible range of marine life, including fairy penguins and the celebrated dugong duo, Pig and Wuru.

Harbourside, **Taronga Zoo** (*see p99*) has an incredible array of both native Australian and exotic animals on show. The most scenic way to get there is by ferry – from the dock you can catch a cable car up the hill to the zoo and work your way back down to the ferry.

Over the Bridge in Kirribilli you'll find **Luna Park** (*see p97*), the famous fun park perched right on the harbour which celebrated 75 years of thrilling Syd kids in 2010.

For more home-grown creatures, head west to **Featherdale Wildlife Park** (*see p112*) near Blacktown, where kids can hand-feed a

> **INSIDE TRACK**
> **SNUGGLEPOT & CUDDLEPIE**
>
> Snugglepot & Cuddlepie are two of Australian literature's most cherished characters and Nutcote, the former home of author May Gibbs, is a lovingly tended shrine to the woman who brought these gumnut babies and their Banksia Men pursuers to life.
> *5 Wallaringa Avenue, Neutral Bay (www.maygibbs.com.au).* **Open** 11am-3pm Wed-Sun. **Admission** $3-$17.

wallaby, kangaroo or emu and have their photo taken with a koala. More koala cuddling is on offer at the **Koala Park Sanctuary** (*see below*). A colony of flapping fruit bats inhabits the spacious **Royal Botanic Gardens** (*see p55*) on the harbour – it's also an ideal picnic spot and kids love the tour by 'trackless train'.

If you want to get out into the bush, there are several easy walks in and around Sydney, in particular at **Berry Island Reserve** (*see p100*), where you'll find a short track with informative plaques about the area's Aboriginal heritage. **Manly Dam Reserve**, off King Street, Manly Vale (catch a bus from Wynyard or Manly Wharf), has easy and very scenic walks, and you can swim safely. The **NSW National Parks & Wildlife Service** runs Discovery walks, talks and tours for children (1300 361 967, www.nationalparks.nsw.gov.au).

Australian Reptile Park4
Gosford exit of Sydney-Newcastle Freeway, Somersby (4340 1022, www.reptilepark.com.au). CityRail Gosford then 10min taxi ride. **Open** 9am-5pm daily. **Admission** $24.50; $17 reductions; $12.50 3-15s; $64 family of four; free under-3s. **Credit** AmEx, MC, V.
An hour's drive north of Sydney lives this collection of cold-blooded critters, creepy-crawlies and native animals including koalas, echidnas, wombats and Tasmanian devils. There are lots of noisy, colourful birds too. Interactive exhibits include Spider World and the Lost World of Reptiles.

Koala Park Sanctuary
84 Castle Hill Road, West Pennant Hills (9484 3141, www.koalaparksanctuary.com.au). CityRail Pennant Hills then bus 632, 636. **Open** 9am-5pm daily. **Admission** $19; $9 reductions; free under-4s. **Credit** AmEx, DC, MC, V.
Koalas are Australia's cutest animal, and who wouldn't want to cuddle one? The main attractions are joined here by emus, kangaroos, echidnas, dingoes and wombats, plus ten acres of lush rainforest, eucalyptus groves and native gardens to explore.

ARTS & ENTERTAINMENT

Clubs

Don't let up till the sun does.

There was a time when Sydney's clubs struggled to fill their biggest nights despite a wealth of gimmicks, but not any more. Whether it's venues like **Home** (*see p226*) and **Arq Sydney** (*see p224*), or seedy late-night haunts such as **Club 77** (*see p225*), Sydney's club scene is alive and thriving, with a wealth of local and international DJs filling their stages on a regular basis.

This return to former glories can be laid squarely at the feet of Fuzzy, a dance outfit that specialises in annual outdoor events. The festival format has exploded and this once niche outfit for serious clubbers has revived the dance music scene with a word-of-mouth buzz that's had a knock-on effect few would have predicted. As a result, there's been a boom in venues working hard to keep their crowds content – including **Ivy** (*see p227*) and **Chinese Laundry** (*see p225*) – and rising young talent like **Good God** (*see p226*).

BARS & CLUBS

Arq Sydney
16 Flinders Street, between Oxford & Taylor Streets, Darlinghurst (9380 8700, www.arqsydney.com.au). Bus 311, 333, 352, 373, 377, 378, 380, 392, 394, 396. **Open** 9pm-late Thur-Sun. **Admission** (after 10pm) $5-$25 Fri-Sun. **No credit cards. Map** p329 H9.
The quintessential gay club par excellence bumps and grinds with wild abandon, bolstered by a regular influx of big-name local talent to pump it up. The main action takes place over two levels, with a flesh-friendly vibe throughout. Have a huge bender on the weekend or sit on the floor on Thursday nights and take in a free drag show themed around the likes of Beyoncé and Lady Gaga.

ArtHouse Hotel
275 Pitt Street, between Park & Market Streets, CBD (9284 1200, www.thearthousehotel.com.au). CityRail St James or Town Hall/Monorail Galeries Victoria. **Open** 11am-late Mon-Wed; 11am-1am Thur; 11am-3am Fri; 5pm-6am Sat. **Admission** Free-$30. **Credit** AmEx, DC, MC, V. **Map** p329 F7.
On the weekend, this former 19th-century school of art – which has also been a chapel and a theatre in its day – transforms into a heaving nightclub. With dubstep, hip hop, jungle and techno nights often taking place, it's best to check its website to see exactly what kind of party you're getting yourself into. For something a little more subdued, there are always the weekly life drawing classes in the Attic Bar.

★ Beach Road Hotel
71 Beach Road, Bondi Beach (9130 7247, www.beachroadbondi.com.au). CityRail Bondi Junction then bus 380, 381, 333/bus 380, 333. **Open** 10am-11pm Mon, Tue; 10am-midnight Wed-Fri; 9am-midnight Sat; 10am-10pm Sun. **Admission** free. **Credit** MC, V. **Map** p334.
The Beach Road serves all the eastern suburbs' indie needs and is more quintessentially Bondi than most of the suburb's other venues. Immense in scale, this one-stop pub has something for most people. Hipsters, students and trashbags find solace upstairs at the Rex, a cavernous band room offering an often impressive line-up of DJs and Australian indie bands most nights of the week, many for free. It even comes to life of a Sunday night with free bands, DJs and hoards of punters who just aren't ready to give up the weekend.

Cargo Bar
52-60 The Promenade, King Street Wharf, Darling Harbour (9262 1777, www.cargobar.com.au). CityRail Wynyard and Town Hall/ferry Darling Harbour/Monorail Darling Park/bus 412, 413. **Open** 11am-late daily. *DJs* 8pm-late Thur-Sun. **Credit** AmEx, DC, MC, V. **Map** p326 D6.

Cargo is a bar most of the time, but as the sun sets over the harbour, the music, a blend of piano house and top 40 hits, is turned up. On a Friday it attracts a lot of corporates looking to loosen their ties after a long week, and keen to take a turn on the dancefloor.

Chinese Laundry

Corner of Sussex Street & King Street, CBD (8295 9950, www.merivale.com.au). CityRail Town Hall or Wynyard. **Open** 10pm-4am Fri; 9pm-4am Sat. **Admission** $15-$20 Fri; $15-$25 Sat. **Credit** AmEx, DC, MC, V. **Map** p327 E6.

One of Sydney's biggest and most respected clubs, the Laundry has a top-notch sound system and has attracted heavyweight internationals James Holden, Gui Boratto and Sasha. The outdoor dance floor is a summer clubbing staple. The team behind Laundry is serious about dance music and also run the popular Good Vibrations Festival in February. *Photo p225.*

Civic Underground

388 Pitt Street, CBD (8080 7000, www.civichotel. com.au). CityRail Town Hall. **Open** 10pm-5am Fri, Sat. **Admission** $10-$25. **No credit cards**. **Map** p329 F8.

Sydney is finally starting to gain some cred in the late-night clubbing stakes. Despite recent tighten ups in late-night licensing, a few venues are putting on the kind of nights that would make our European counterparts proud. With possibly the city's best sound system, this small, underground club attracts big internationals for all night techno, deep house and filthy electro parties.

★ Club 77

77 William Street, between Crown & Yurong Streets, East Sydney (9361 3387). CityRail Kings Cross. **Open** 8pm-late Thur-Sun. **Admission** free-$20. **Credit** AmEx, DC, MC, V. **Map** p329 G7.

Once a favoured haunt of the city's goth and fetish community, Club 77 is now well and truly on the beaten track thanks to Sydney's Bang Gang DJ collective. The 7s are still a fave haunt of art school kids, rockabilly enthusiasts and the odd laced-up and leathered reveller, but now attracts a large mainstream club kid crowd.

After Midnight

Sunrise nigh and still hungry for action? Buckle up!

Bada Bing

70 Darlinghurst Road, Kings Cross (9356 2442). **Open** to 6am.
With regular DJs, Thugs and Hoes themed nights, a mixed crowd and the occasional nude bath extravaganza, come and enjoy the sexy show or just carry on the party.

Crystal Boudoir

Crystal Bar, GPO, 1 Martin Place (9229 7799). **Open** to 2am Sat.
OK, so the clothing doesn't really come off, but you won't even care – these scantily clad dancers deliver plenty of thrills as they offer up naughty burlesque moves at this weekly event.

Men's Gallery

92 Pitt Street (9232 1800).
Open to 3am Fri, Sat.
Swap your Aussie dollars for MG dollars and prepare to be entertained as these ladies strut their stuff on tabletops or in one of the 15 private rooms.

Minx

72 Pitt Street (1300 789 798). **Open** to 2am.
This swanky CBD strip joint serves up nude entertainment to tickle the fancy of both gents and ladies along with dishes and cocktails to tickle their taste buds.

Porky's

77 Darlingurst Road, Kings Cross (9357 7120). **Open** 24hrs daily.
A Sydney landmark, this grimy little joint is the real deal oozing sleaze and girls galore – just keep your hands to yourself, especially when it comes to the peanuts; it's no fun being chucked out of a strip joint.

Crystal Boudoir.

How To Get Around After Midnight

If you don't have a broomstick, use these to get home.

Buses
Sydney Buses run late in all directions to compensate for the railway closures, so if you're stranded in the city, head to Town Hall and jump on an 'all nighter'.

Trains
The last train usually leaves around midnight and services don't start again until 4.30am. During this period Night Ride Bus services take over, departing from Town Hall Station on George St (near Woolworths).

Taxi
Beware the 3am changeover time! Around this time of night it can be near impossible to find a driver willing to pick you up unless you're headed in their direction. If things are

looking particularly dire, head to one of the secure taxi ranks or try calling: Taxis Combined: 13 3300; Silver Service Taxis: 133 100; Legion Cabs: 13 1451

Stranded...
Armed with an iPhone but without a way of getting home? Get your hands on the TripView app, which can tell you the next departing bus, train or ferry from anywhere in Sydney, with the option to search directly by route or just by suburb if you're lost. It's free, but if you're going to be using it a lot, we recommend downloading the full version for $2.49, which saves all your routes and travel information for easily accessible convenience. Remember you may incur roaming charges.

ARTS & ENTERTAINMENT

Exchange Hotel
34-44 Oxford Street, between Riley & Liverpool Streets, Darlinghurst (9360 1375, www. exchangehotel.biz). CityRail Museum/bus 311, 333, 352, 373, 377, 378, 380, 392, 394, 396. **Open** 9pm-late. **Admission** free-$30. **Credit** DC, MC, V. **Map** p329 G8.
Home to several of the city's favourite venues, the Exchange is the seedy after-party joint for anyone and everyone. At Q bar there's a dance floor that swirls with funk and house, Spectrum boasts a consistently impressive live music line-up, Phoenix, an underground indie lair, has a killer sound system and an up-for-anything crowd and 34B is home to the best burlesque acts in town. The only downside is deciding which to visit first.

Forum
122 Lang Road, Moore Park (8117 6700, www.forumsydney.com.au). **Open** 7pm-1am Mon-Thur, Sun; 7pm-2am Fri, Sat. **Admission** varies. **No credit cards. Map** p332 J12.
One of the better additions to Sydney's venue circuit in recent times, The Forum has great sound, a great set up and a great vibe. It has attracted everyone from Orbital and Autechre to the Kaiser Chiefs and Ghostface Killah and is a hit with older clubbers looking for more than sticky dance floors and a party pash.

Good God
55 Liverpool Street, CBD (9267 3787, www.good godgoodgod.com). CityRail Town Hall. **Open** 5pm-1am Wed; 5pm-2am Thur; 5pm-5am Fri; 8pm-5am Sat. **Admission** $5-$30. **No credit cards. Map** p329 F8.

This alternative fixture started life as Good Good Small Club, a dungeon at the rear of a very shabby Spanish restaurant. The restaurant went under, Good God spread out and got a makeover and the rest is clubbing history. The club now has popular indie, retro, tech and hip hop nights on rotation and gets its fare share of big names too. If it's cool enough for Karen O, it's cool enough for you.

Home
Cockle Bay Wharf, Darling Harbour (9266 0600, www.homesydney.com). CityRail Town Hall/ Monorail Darling Park/ferry Darling Harbour. **Open** 9pm-6am Fri, Sat. **Admission** varies. **No credit cards. Map** p328 D7.
Home is one of Sydney's few old-school, large-scale clubbing experiences. It sprawls over three levels and four bars, with chill-out areas, space-age lighting and a great view over Darling Harbour. On Fridays, expect everything from deep house to trance and drum 'n' bass at Sublime, Sydney's longest-running club night and live bands and DJs play nu-rave, acid house and techno at the club's Oh My! parties. Home Terrace also hosts the city's best after-hours party, Spice, which will keep you moving well into the day with deep house and electro from 4am on Sundays.

Hugo's
33 Bayswater Road, Kings Cross (9357 4411, www.hugos.com.au). CityRail Kings Cross. **Open** 8pm-3am Thur-Sun. **Admission** free-$20. **Credit** AmEx, MC, V. **Map** p330 J7.
Sitting just off the Kings Cross strip, Hugo's is a hipster's paradise. The weekend begins on Thursdays at Hugo's and doesn't stop till the wee hours of

Monday morning. We recommend Sneaky Sundays for a true taste of the city's fashion and clubbing scene. Famed local acts Sneaky Sound System and Bang Gang man the decks and entry, cocktails and pizzas are all $5.

Ivy

330 George Street, CBD (9240 3000, www.merivale.com). CityRail Wynyard. **Open** 11am-late Mon-Fri; 6pm-late Sat. **Admission** $15-$25. **Credit** AmEx, MC, V. **Map** p327 E5.

Merivale, Sydney's clubbing juggernaut, built this answer to Soho house a few years back. Costing a mammoth $160 million, the complex features 13 individual venues including the super exclusive rooftop pool club, stylish cocktail bar and pick-up hot spot Ivy Lounge and Changeroom, the city's most popular hetero pseudo-sex club (wallflowers take note: don't make direct eye contact).

★ Oxford Art Factory

38-46 Oxford Street, at Pelican Street, Darlinghurst (9332 3711, www.oxfordart factory.com). Bus 373, 377, 378, 380, 382, 391, 394, 396. **Open** 9pm-late Thur-Sun. **Admission** (after 10pm) $10 Fri, Sun; $20 Sat. **No credit cards. Map** p329 G8.

A sparkling star on the performance scene, Oxford Art Factory has hosted a cavalcade of local up-and-comers and impressive internationals. The two rooms host socialites and punters, divided by a drawing room and two bars. It's well decorated and interesting, and the lighting's great and most importantly it gives scenesters somewhere to go when they get a new haircut.

Chinese Laundry. *See p225.*

Oxford Hotel

134 Oxford Street, Darlinghurst (9331 3467, www.theoxfordhotel.com.au). Bus 311, 333, 352, 373, 377, 378, 380, 392, 394, 396. **Open** 10am-4am Sun-Thur; 10am-6am Fri, Sat. **No credit cards. Map** p329 H9.

An institution of the strip, the Oxford is everything a good gay bar should be. Spread over three levels, the Oxford is a heaving nightclub (Gilligan's), sophisticated lounge bar (Supper Club) and late night dive bar (Main Bar). Sit on the deck for an afternoon drink and watch the strip go by, or head underground to see the most glamorous of Sydney's GLBT community cut loose at the monthly Gay Bash parties.

Sugarmill

33-37 Darlinghurst Road, Kings Cross (9368 7333, www.sugarmill.com.au). CityRail Kings Cross. **Open** *Sugarmill* 10am-5am daily. *Kit and Kaboodle* 7pm-5am Tue; 8pm-5am Wed, Thur; 6pm-5am Fri, 5.30pm-5am Sat. **Admission** free-$20. **Credit** AmEx, MC, V. **Map** p330 J7.

The sleaze of Kings Cross has slowly, but surely been giving way to the schmooze of style. At the Sugarmill fat leather booths meet plastic bucket seats in a room that looks like what it is – a former bank. Inside you'll find high ceilings, marble everything and a really good-looking crowd. Head upstairs to Kit and Kaboodle (*see p189*) for cocktails, great local and international DJs and an art fix courtesy of the Absolut Stairwell Gallery.

Tank

3 Bridge Lane, off Bridge Street, between George & Pitt Streets, CBD (9240 3000, www.merivale. com). CityRail Circular Quay or Wynyard/ferry Circular Quay. **Open** 10pm-6am Fri, Sat. **Admission** $15-$30. **Credit** AmEx, DC, MC, V. **Map** p327 F4.

This über-club is all about house music. Tank's more chilled out Friday nights are generally over shadowed by bigger names on Saturdays when clubbers may be treated to the likes of Digweed and Layo & Bushwacka. With an impressive sound system and serious rave lighting, Tank offers the quintessential clubbing experience.

★ White Revolver

Corner of Curlewis Street & Campbell Parade, Bondi (www.whiterevolver.com). **Open** see website for opening times. **Admission** free. **No credit cards. Map** p334.

The Sydney set love a secret and exclusive club and White Revolver is no exception. Hidden in the Basement of Bondi favourite Cream Tangerine, Revolver has a door policy that you'll need to blag or bluff your way around, but once in you'll be partying with all the soap stars, models and local gangsters you can handle.

ARTS & ENTERTAINMENT

Film

The Emerald city shines bright on its silver screens…

In Sydney, going to the movies is almost as popular as going surfing, having a barbecue or watching the Test series. Locals love the silver screen, and observe with pride the success of many Sydney actors in international movies. The list is formidable and growing all the time: to the familiar names of Russell Crowe, Cate Blanchett, Nicole Kidman, Hugh Jackman, Geoffrey Rush, Toni Collette, Rose Byrne, Naomi Watts and Hugo Weaving, add Sam Worthington (*Avatar*), Abbie Cornish (*Sucker Punch*), Xavier Samuel (*The Twilight Saga: Eclipse*), Mia Wasikowska (*Alice in Wonderland*), Joel Edgerton (*The Thing*) and Rachael Taylor (*Transformers*), to name a few. The fact that Oscar winners Cate Blanchett and Geoffrey Rush frequently appear on stage at the Sydney Theatre Company and Belvoir generates a lot of excitement around town.

THE LOCAL SCENE

The prognosis for local filmmaking is good too. After many years in the doldrums, Australian films are starting to attract Australian audiences again. Baz Luhrmann's ambitious epic *Australia* was a huge hit in its country of origin, grossing well over $30 million. In 2009, the made-in-Sydney, set-in-China-and-Texas *Mao's Last Dancer* took a whopping $15 million. The biggest Australian film of 2010, the youth-oriented action film *Tomorrow, When the War Began*, grossed $11 million, while the indigenous-themed musical *Bran Nue Dae* surprised everyone by taking nearly $8 million. Thoughtful World War I drama *Beneath Hill 60* did well with $3.5 million, while knockabout comedy *Wog Boy 2* raked in a healthy $5 million.

But perhaps the most exciting Australian film of recent times was made in Melbourne by Sydney writer-director David Michôd, a former editor of movie industry magazine *Inside Film*. *Animal Kingdom* is a powerful crime drama that won rave reviews worldwide (especially for a chilling performance by veteran Sydney actress Jacki Weaver) and earned nearly $5 million in cinemas.

The evidence suggests that local audiences aren't turned off by locally made films – just by badly made ones. That said, mainstream Hollywood blockbusters remain the core of Sydney's filmgoing diet, with stars pouring in to appear at premières to push the lucrative Australian box office.

Reflecting this boom is the nature of cinema-going itself. Watching movies outdoors has become a Sydney passion, with the successful **OpenAir Cinema** (*see p233*) and **Moonlight Cinema** (*see p233*) leading the fray. Indoors, where once there was a series of independent cinemas dotted about town, now there are very few. Inevitably bowing to the teen-targeted multiplexes, the heritage-listed **Ritz Cinema Randwick** (*see p230*) and **Hayden Orpheum Picture Palace** (*see p231*) both screen mainstream fare. But despite the homogenisation, Sydney has a healthy appetite for art-house cinema, found at the **Palace**, **Dendy** and **Chauvel** theatres. And the giant theatres offer a luxurious touch, with **Hoyts EQ**'s La Premiere (*see p230*) and **Event Cinemas Bondi Junction**'s Gold Class options (*see p229*) available at a price.

Film festivals are an important part of Sydney's screen culture. In addition to the annual **Sydney Film Festival** (*see p234*) there are festivals dedicated to short films as well as more than a dozen annual festivals dedicated to the cinemas of specific countries, including France, Germany, Spain, Italy, Japan, Korea and Russia.

ARTS & ENTERTAINMENT

TICKETS AND INFORMATION

First-run movies open on Thursdays, with around four premières a week. Unless it's a blockbuster, you can usually get a ticket with no problem. Prices are around $16 to $18 for adults ($18 to $22 for 3D movies), with reductions for children, senior citizens, students and the unemployed. Public holidays usually involve a $1 'surcharge', while Monday and Tuesday are traditionally bargain nights, when tickets are reduced to as little as $8. The major chains – **Hoyts**, **Event Cinemas**, **Greater Union**, **Palace** and **Dendy** – have websites with screening times, plus there are cinema ads in the entertainment sections of the *Sydney Morning Herald* and *Daily Telegraph*. Screen times are also available on the **Cinema Information Line** (1 902 263 456, premium-rate).

CINEMAS

First-run

The multiplexes typically offer Hollywood blockbusters and kids' movies. Christmas, September school holidays and the Easter long weekend are key periods for distributors, who often hold back movies for that all-important opening weekend at these times.

Event Cinemas Bondi Junction

Westfield Bondi Junction, Level 7 & 8, 500 Oxford Street, Bondi Junction (9300 1500, www.greaterunion.com.au). CityRail Bondi Junction/bus 333, 352, 378, 380. **Screens** 11. **Tickets** $16; $7-$12.50 reductions; $9 Tue. **Credit** AmEx, DC, MC, V. **Map** p333 P11.
This ultra-modern complex has cheery staff, digital surround sound, comfy seating, its own bar, a 'fine dining' food court right on its doorstep and harbour views to boot. Programmes feature a mix of blockbusters and the mainstream end of art-house. There's free parking in the Westfield car parks for up to two hours, but do factor in the half hour it takes to find a spot here. The Gold Class option ($25-$36), similar to Hoyts EQ's La Premiere (*see p230*), offers plush armchairs that recline until you're almost horizontal, a separate lounge and food and drink on demand.

Event Cinemas George Street

505-525 George Street, between Bathurst & Liverpool Streets, CBD (9273 7431, www.event cinemas.com.au). CityRail Town Hall/Monorail World Square. **Screens** 17. **Tickets** $17.50; $13-$15 reductions; $10.50 Tue. **Credit** AmEx, DC, MC, V. **Map** p329 E7.
This sprawling cinema complex shows virtually every new commercial movie release as soon as it opens. Located in the heart of George Street's garish entertainment strip, it attracts throngs of noisy kids and can get a little edgy at night, so guard your valuables. The state-of-the-art auditoria with digital surround sound and comfy (if rather narrow) seats are especially popular with teens and out-of-towners, as you'll see from the queues.

Hoyts Broadway

Broadway Shopping Centre, Bay Street, at Greek Street, Glebe (9211 1911, www.hoyts.com.au). Bus

Kernels of Filmmaking Wisdom

There's nothing corny about Sydney's 'pop'ular culture.

If there is any doubt that Sydney is a town of film lovers then the success of **Popcorn Taxi** should lay that to rest. Every month this award-winning independent film event holds a screening of an upcoming movie or classic film followed by live interviews with key creative personnel, giving an insight into the filmmaking process. Since 1999, Popcorn Taxi has hosted around 500 events, including on-stage appearances by George Miller, Dennis Hopper, Baz Luhrmann, Gillian Armstrong, Wim Wenders, Tim Robbins, Danny Boyle, Phillip Noyce, Roger Corman, Richard Linklater, Ewan McGregor, Karen Allen, Ang Lee and Quentin Tarantino.

Screenings are usually held at Event Cinemas Bondi Junction (*see p229*), although sometimes the State Theatre (*see p272*) is used, along with the Roxy Hotel in

Parramatta (as for the *Mad Max* cast and crew reunion in 2010).

As for highlights, creative director Chris Murray cites an onstage interview with movie legend Jerry Lewis in 2009. 'In this age of everybody downloading things or watching films at home on their widescreen TVs, I would hope that we've made going to the cinema an event again,' Murray says. 'It's about engaging an audience to be genuinely excited to share a cinema experience and to be able to interact with it. To have a screening of *Raiders of the Lost Ark* and then have one of the stars walk on stage – there's a genuine excitement and you just can't fake that.'

To find out about upcoming screenings, visit www.popcorntaxi.com.au, and subscribe to the email newsletter.

Rosemount Bar, **Hayden Orpheum Picture Palace**.

370, 412, 432, 434. **Screens** 12. **Tickets** $17.50; $13-$15 reductions; $11 Tue ($10 reductions). **Credit** AmEx, DC, MC, V. **Map** p328 C9.

Situated on top of a major shopping centre, this huge complex (the largest auditorium has 379 seats) often wilts under the pressure of sheer numbers, particularly at weekends when the rowdy teen crowd descends. Three of the theatres are 'CinemaxX' standard, with high-backed seats, perfect sight lines, super-large screens and digital surround sound. As with the Palace chain's 'Babes in Arms' events, 'Mums and Bubs' sessions for movie-craving carers and their infants run twice a month.

★ Hoyts EQ

Bent Street, Entertainment Quarter, Driver Avenue, Moore Park (9332 1300, www.hoyts. com.au). Bus 355, 371, 372, 391, 392, 393, 394, 395, 396, 397, 399, 890. **Screens** 12. **Tickets** $17.50; $10.50-$18 reductions; $11 Tue ($10 reductions). *La Premiere* $32 ($24 seat only); $20 Tue. **Credit** AmEx, DC, MC, V. **Map** p332 K12.

Located in the Entertainment Quarter, part of the Fox Studios complex, this vast pseudo-retro cinema boasts huge screens, stadium seating (total capacity 3,000) and smart facilities, and is a refreshing change from the pushing, shoving and traffic-choked thoroughfare of George Street. A classy upgrade package,

popular with first-time daters, is La Premiere: for twice the cost of a usual ticket you get a cosy, two-person sofa with unobstructed views, plus free soft drinks, tea, coffee, snacks, hot food and popcorn in the La Premiere lounge. There's also booze to buy, which you can take in with you, and single seats for those not in a couple.

Manly Cinemas

25/43-45 East Esplanade, opposite Manly Wharf, Manly (9977 0644, www.manlycinemas.com. au). Ferry Manly. **Screens** 2. **Tickets** $15; $10-$14 reductions. $10 Tue. **No credit cards**. **Map** p334.

This modest two-screener opposite the wharf features quality art-house flicks and selected mainstream movies, and is a second home to Manly's many culture vultures. There's stadium seating, a recently upgraded sound system and fresh juice on sale in the foyer.

► *Hugos Manly (see p101) is a great place on the wharf for a bite before a film.*

★ Ritz Cinema Randwick

43-47 St Paul's Street, at Avoca Street, Randwick (9399 5722, www.ritzcinema.com.au). Bus 302, 373, 376, 377. **Screens** 6. **Tickets** $13; $8-$11 reductions; $7 Tue. **Credit** MC, V.

With a distinctive art deco design, which has now been restored to its former 1930s glory, and an impressive sound system, the six-screen Ritz is both a local landmark and an excellent venue for catching the latest mainstream releases. Signs explain the regulations – no alcohol, bare feet, smoking or skateboards – which make sense if you hit the place in the afternoon after school's out. In the evening, the place attracts a different crowd, including film geeks who frequent the cinema for its great acoustics and old-fashioned flair. Upstairs, the inimitable Bar Ritz boasts a marble bar and balcony – perfect for pre- and post-film drinks.

Art house

Both the **Dendy** and **Palace** cinema chains have great-value membership schemes, which are worth the investment if you plan to go to the cinema regularly.

Chauvel

Paddington Town Hall, corner of Oxford Street & Oatley Road, Paddington (9361 5398, www. chauvelcinema.net.au). Bus 333, 352, 378, 380. **Screens** 2. **Tickets** $16; $8.50-$14 reductions; $10.50 Mon. **Credit** AmEx, DC, MC, V. **Map** p332 J10.
Named after the Australian film pioneer Charles Chauvel – of *Jedda* fame – this much-loved local cinema is now part of the Palace chain and has taken up the slack from the recent closure of the Palace Academy down the road. Its proscenium arch brings true grandeur to the art of film and the staff really know their stuff. There are Cinemateque and late-night cult movie screenings.

Cinema Paris

Bent Street, Entertainment Quarter, Driver Avenue, Moore Park (9332 1633, www.hoyts. com.au). Bus 355, 371, 372, 391, 392, 393, 394, 395, 396, 397, 399, 890. **Screens** 4. **Tickets** $17.50; $10.50-$15 reductions; $11 Tue. **Credit** AmEx, DC, MC, V. **Map** p332 K12.
An unassuming art-house cinema within Fox Studios' Entertainment Quarter, with a total seating capacity of 600. The Paris also hosts several film festivals, including the Bollywood Film Festival.

Dendy Newtown

261-263 King Street, between Mary & Church Streets, Newtown (9550 5699, www.dendy.com. au). CityRail Newtown. **Screens** 4. **Tickets** $16; $9.50-$13.50 reductions; $10 Tue ($8 reduction). **Credit** AmEx, DC, MC, V. **Map** p334.
Matching its Opera Quays sister (*see below*) for style if not setting, the Dendy Newtown offers quality first releases, 562 super-comfortable seats, big screens, Dolby digital surround sound and a bar. There's free parking for filmgoers in the Lennox Street car park behind the cinema

Dendy Opera Quays

2 East Circular Quay, Circular Quay, CBD (9247 3800, www.dendy.com.au). CityRail/ferry Circular Quay. **Screens** 3. **Tickets** $16; $9.50-$13.50 reductions; $10 Tue ($8 reductions). **Credit** AmEx, DC, MC, V. **Map** p327 G3.
A stone's throw from the Opera House, with great views to the Harbour Bridge, this luxurious complex (with a total capacity of 579) usually offers a mix of middlebrow and art-house fare, and is fully licensed. There's also disabled access to all screens.

Govinda's

112 Darlinghurst Road, between William & Hardie Streets, Darlinghurst (9380 5155, www.govindas.com.au). CityRail Kings Cross. **Screens** 1. **Tickets** $13.90; $29.80 with meal. **Credit** AmEx, MC, V. **Map** p330 J8.
Adored by its twenty- and thirtysomething regulars, this Krishna-operated restaurant-cum-quality art-house cinema is a must-visit film experience. After you've loaded up on the generous vegetarian buffet, sit (or lie) back on the cushions and bean bags and enjoy arty films, documentaries and classics in 35mm. You can watch and not eat, but diners are given entry preference and since there are only 65 seats in the cinema – roughly half the restaurant's capacity – it's best to buy your ticket early.

★ Hayden Orpheum Picture Palace

380 Military Road, between Winnie & Macpherson Streets, Cremorne (9908 4344, www.orpheum.com.au). Bus 143, 144, 151, 228, 229, 230, 243, 246, 247, 257. **Screens** 6. **Tickets** $17.50; $10.50-$15 reductions; $8.50-$11.50 Tue. **Credit** MC, V.
Without doubt the grandest cinema in Sydney, Cremorne's art deco picture palace is a stunning step back in time. Built in 1935 by George Kenworthy, the top theatrical architect of the period, today's version is even glitzier than the original thanks to a $2.5-million restoration some years back by owner and local TV celeb Mike Walsh. Each of the six auditoria has its own colour scheme and decor, but the 744-seat Orpheum is the true star of the show. It even has a genuine Wurlitzer cinema organ, which rises out of a stage pit on weekend evenings complete with flashing lights and a grinning organist. Expect a mix of mainstream US, British and Australian fare, with some art-house, special presentations and the occasional cabaret show.

Palace Norton Street Cinemas

99 Norton Street, between Marion Street & Parramatta Road, Leichhardt (9550 0122, www.palacecinemas.com.au). Bus 435, 436, 437, 438, 440, 445, L38, L40. **Screens** 4. **Tickets** $18; $9-$14 reductions; $10.50 Mon ($8.50 reductions). **Credit** AmEx, DC, MC, V.
Located in the heart of Little Italy, the sleek and stylish Norton Street Cinema is the cream of the Palace

ARTS & ENTERTAINMENT

chain. The air-conditioning keeps you cool, the seats are plush and comfortable, and the sound and sight lines are uniformly excellent. There's not much else you could ask for from the fabric of a cinema. You'll find an intelligent mix of offbeat Hollywood releases, foreign movies and Australian art-house fare. The 'Babes in Arms' sessions on Thursday mornings are popular: the lights are turned up, the sound down and breastfeeding is everywhere.

★ Palace Verona Cinema

17 Oxford Street, at Verona Street, Paddington (9360 6099, www.palacecinemas.com.au). Bus 333, 352, 378, 380. **Screens** 4. **Tickets** $18; $9-$14 reductions; $10.50 Mon ($8.50 reductions). **Credit** AmEx, DC, MC, V. **Map** p332 H9.

The modern Verona is the eastern-suburbs equivalent to Norton Street, and Paddington's intellectuals, gays and art-house crowds attend with glee. The four screens are on the small side and the seats aren't quite as soft as you'd expect, but the movies are an enticing blend of quirky commercial, sexy foreign and Australian.

IMAX

IMAX Sydney

31 Wheat Road, southern end of Darling Harbour (9281 3300, www.imax.com.au). CityRail Town Hall/ferry Darling Harbour/ Monorail or LightRail Convention. **Tickets** $19.50-$28.50; $15-$24.50 reductions; $47-$81 family. **Credit** AmEx, MC, V. **Map** p327 E6.

The giant, eye-shaped IMAX theatre sticks out on the water in touristy Darling Harbour. The 540-seat theatre claims to have the world's largest screen, some eight storeys high, and shows around 12 films a day. Expect a mixed bag of 2D and 3D affairs, with documentaries too. Hardly essential viewing, although the sheer impact of seeing a film on a giant screen makes it a worthy stop for the uninitiated.

Open-air

Given the climate, it's hardly surprising that Sydneysiders flock outdoors whenever they can. Open-air screenings are a firm fixture on the summer social calendar, with three main inner-city offerings: a picnic-on-the-grass affair in Centennial Park, a similar set-up in North Sydney Oval (with seats and cover if desired) and a sensational harbourside experience in the Domain. All make for a great night out. You should be aware, though, that weather permitting is a relative concept here and screenings are usually cancelled only in gale-force conditions. You may have to pay booking fees on top of the prices quoted below.

Bondi Openair

Bondi Pavilion, Queen Elizabeth Drive, Bondi Beach (9130 1235, www.bondiopenair.com.au). CityRail Bondi Junction then bus 333, 380, 381, 382/bus 222, 333, 380. **Tickets** $13.90- $18. **Credit** AmEx, MC, V. **Map** p334. **Dates** Jan-Feb.

Like the beach that hosts it, Bondi Openair cinema is wonderfully unpredictable and offers myriad

And the Oz-car Goes To...

Australia's most prestigious film festival returns to Sydney.

Australia's answer to the Oscars is the **Australian Film Institute Awards**. The annual prizes have been given out since the very infancy of the local industry in 1958, and winners of the best film award include *My Brilliant Career, Breaker Morant, Gallipoli, Strictly Ballroom, The Piano, Muriel's Wedding, Shine, Lantana* and *Samson and Delilah*. Broadcast on TV since 1997, the AFI Awards were held in Melbourne from 2001 to 2010, but in 2011 will finally return to Sydney to be handed out at the Sydney Opera House.

Ambassador for the awards, Cate Blanchett, said 'It's apt and true to the nature of the film industry that this ceremony moves around the country,' while New South Wales premier Kristine Keneally declared, 'Together we'll put the AFI on an

international stage.' The NSW government has agreed to host the event until 2014, with an option to extend.

The AFIs are voted for by members of the institute; but there is an alternative to the awards that has been held in Sydney since 1999, and which allows the public to pick their own winners. The Inside Film (IF) Awards are run by the eponymous magazine. Filmgoers rate Australian films with a score from 1 to 5 and winners are determined by the overall average score, not by the number of scores received, which make the IF Awards accessible even to Australian films that do not get a commercial cinema release. More than 200,000 ratings are recorded every year and anyone can vote. Visit www.ifawards.com for more information, or to have your say.

Palace Verona Cinema.

forms of entertainment. Outside the beautiful Bondi Pavilion the bar offers a local DJ and bands plus drinks and dinner near the ocean. When it's time for the main feature, grab a bean bag and head to the lawn or sit in the amphitheatre – and all this with the ocean roaring in the background.

Moonlight Cinema
Belvedere Amphitheatre, Centennial Park, Woollahra (1300 511 908, www.moonlight. com.au). Bus 333, 378, 380. **Tickets** $15-$17; $13-$15 reductions. **Credit** AmEx, DC, MC, V. **Map** p333 N11. **Dates** early Dec-mid Mar.
The nationwide Moonlight's programme focuses heavily on current and recent mainstream releases, with customary classics *Grease* and *Breakfast at Tiffany's* (on Valentine's Day) popular fixtures. Films kick off at sunset and entry is via Woollahra Gate (Oxford Street) only. Bring a picnic, cushions and insect repellent, and arrive early. Limited Gold Grass tickets (at $32 a pop) guarantee a prime spot, a 'bean bed' and a glass of wine.

★ OpenAir Cinema
Mrs Macquarie's Chair, The Domain, CBD (1300 366 649, www.stgeorge.com.au/openair). CityRail Circular Quay or Martin Place/ferry Circular Quay. **Tickets** $23-25; $22-$23 reductions. **Credit** AmEx, DC, MC, V. **Map** p330 J3. **Dates** early Jan-mid Feb.
This is the ultimate outdoor movie-going experience, with the Harbour Bridge and Opera House twinkling in the background. You get several Sydney premières of mainstream movies, as well

as a pick of current and classic fare. Films start at 8.30pm but the gates open at 6.30pm – as do the stylish on-site bar and restaurant. Capacity is around 1,700. *Photo p234.*

Starlight Cinema
North Sydney Oval, Miller Street, North Sydney (1300 438 849, www.starlightcinema.com.au). CityRail North Sydney. **Tickets** $18-$20; $10-$18 reductions. **Credit** AmEx, DC, MC, V. **Dates** mid Jan-mid Mar.
The Starlight has a similar mix of movies to its Moonlight equivalent in Centennial Park, but with seating and covers if the weather turns nasty. There's an on-site bar and food, with waiter service and deckchairs for an additional fee. Screenings are also held at the Leichhardt Oval.

FESTIVALS

Flickerfest
Bondi Pavilion, Bondi Beach, NSW 2026 (9365 6888, www.flickerfest.com.au). CityRail Bondi Junction then bus 333, 380, 381, 382/bus 222, 333, 380. **Tickets** $13-$15. **Credit** MC, V. **Map** p334. **Date** early Jan.
Running for nine days after the New Year madness has subsided, Flickerfest is the only short-film festival in Australia to be recognised by the American Academy of Motion Picture Arts and Sciences as an Oscar-qualifying event. As a result, it's not only a serious event on the world film calendar, it's also one of few forums in which local short-film-makers can directly compare their work with international fare.

Mardi Gras Film Festival & queerDOC Festival

Information *Queer Screen, PO Box 1081, Darlinghurst, NSW 2010 (9332 4938, www. queerscreen.com.au)*. **Date** *Mardi Gras* Feb; *queerDOC* Sept.

Part of Sydney's month-long gay and lesbian jamboree, the Dendy Newtown (*see p231*) and other venues. In September, Queer Screen also puts on the queerDOC festival, the world's first dedicated entirely to queer documentaries.

▶ *For more on the Mardi Gras festival, see p244* **Gay & Lesbian**.

Sydney Film Festival

Information *Suite 102, 59 Marlborough Street, Surry Hills, NSW 2010 (9318 0999, sff.org.au)*. **Date** early June.

A slick, high-profile, intensive two-week orgy of international and Australian film (with up to 150 movies screened), opening on the Queen's Birthday weekend in early June. Regular highlights include major retrospectives and meet-the-film-maker forums, and the main venues are the grand State Theatre (*see p272*) and the Dendy Opera Quays (*see p231*). From 2008, the festival has included an official competition, with 12 films from around the world selected to compete for a cash prize of $60,000.

Sydney Underground Film Festival

Information *P.O. Box 202, Summer Hill NSW 2130 (9797 9428, www.suff.com.au)*. **Date** Sept.

A three-day festival held in the inner west, SUFF champions experimental, outrageous and politically inflammatory shorts, features and documentaries from around the world. Screenings range from trendy, underground work to bigger leftfield films – if you're interested in alternative cinema you shouldn't miss this.

Tropfest

Information *62-64 Riley Street, East Sydney, NSW 2010 (9368 0434, www.tropfest.com.au)*. **Date** Sun in late Feb.

Instigated by actor-turned-director John Polson (*Mission: Impossible II, Swimfan, Hide and Seek*), this free outdoor festival of short films is held every February, and was originally held at Polson's old hangout, the Tropicana café in Darlinghurst (*see p179*). The films are simulcast on giant screens in the Domain to an audience that runs into the tens of thousands, and also to other cities around Australia. The festival is heavily frequented by actors, directors and writers, and its judging panel usually includes A-list celebs who are working in town: Samuel L Jackson, Russell Crowe and John Woo have all performed judging duties in the past. All films are under seven minutes, made specially for the festival and have to contain a reference to the year's Tropfest Signature Item (past items have included a bubble, an umbrella, a kiss, a coffee bean and dice).

World of Women Film Festival

Chauvel Cinema, 249 Oxford Street, Paddington (9357 1490, www.wift.org). **Date** Oct, biennial.

Women in Film & Television (WIFT), a non-profit outfit committed to improving the lot of women in film, organises this festival of short and feature-length work by new and established female talents.

OpenAir Cinema. *See p233*.

Galleries

Sydney's art scene is a canvas forever ripe for reinvention.

How exactly do the seemingly countless art galleries in Sydney survive? The answer, quite simply, is that the art world is thriving here. Not only are artists' works snapped up by locals; public buildings, restaurants, cafés and hotels are also keen to fill their walls with the work of homegrown talents. Patrons range from serious collectors to those who save up for a piece of original art, and others who just walk past and like the look of something. It helps that prices aren't as steep as in Europe – yet – but big hitters like John Olsen, Sidney Nolan and Brett Whiteley still fetch huge sums.

WHERE AND WHEN

The city's gallery heartland is **Paddington**, where scores of spaces offer schmoozy opening nights and exhibitions that regularly feature the best in Australian contemporary art. This is the place to get a snapshot of what's driving the visual arts scene. In one afternoon you could see top-notch work by the likes of subversive photographer Tracey Moffatt at **Roslyn Oxley9 Gallery**, cutting-edge new media at **Sarah Cottier Gallery**, a diverse selection of Aboriginal art at **Coo-ee Aboriginal Art Gallery** and an engaging local or international showing at the **Australian Centre for Photography** (for all, *see p238*).

Not that the city's art scene is restricted to the eastern suburbs. Just south of the CBD, the increasingly gentrified suburb of **Waterloo** shines brightly on the art radar. That's thanks mainly to converted warehouse complex **2 Danks Street** (*see p240*), home to several important galleries. The city centre also has its share of venues: you can see shows from likely future stars at the **Mori Gallery** (*see p236*) or sample established artists (and free drawing classes) at drinking spot-cum-exhibition space the **Arthouse Hotel** (*see p236*).

Although art remains a fashionable pursuit among Sydney's most trend-conscious (and affluent) citizens, some of the scene's most vital components are free. High-profile exhibitions that meld Sydney's fabled natural beauty with local artistic talent are the most reliable crowd-pullers. Perhaps most alluring is **Sculpture by the Sea** (*see p219*), a massively popular event held each November in which artworks are displayed along the stretch of coast between Bondi and Tamarama Beaches. **Art & About** (*see p218*), held in October, has several outdoor components, including a series of oversized photographs documenting local life set amid the fig trees in Hyde Park, while Art Month Sydney in March is a festival of talks, tours and events taking place in galleries across the city.

Look out too for the annual Archibald Prize at the **Art Gallery of New South Wales** (*see p58*), with the winner usually announced in late March. This portraiture competition is as entertaining for the fierce division of opinion it sparks as for the always varied works on show. Nor should you miss the general collections at the Art Gallery of NSW or Sydney's other major public gallery, the **Museum of Contemporary Art** (*see p56*).

For an excellent round-up of what's on, grab a copy of *Art Almanac* ($4, published 11 times a year, www.art-almanac.com.au) or *Art Gallery Guide Australia* ($5, published bi-monthly, www.artguide.com.au). The latter has a useful calendar of gallery openings and events. Both are available at bookshops, galleries and newsagents, as is the quarterly journal *Art & Australia* ($28.50, www.artaustralia.com), which takes a more in-depth look at visual arts news and exhibitions.

Many galleries are shut on Mondays, and for some time between Christmas and New Year, so call before you set out. Admission is free unless otherwise stated.

Urban Uprising.

CENTRAL SYDNEY

★ Arthouse Hotel
275 Pitt Street, between Park & Market Streets, CBD (9284 1200, www.thearthousehotel.com.au). CityRail St James or Town Hall/Monorail Galeries Victoria. **Open** 11am-1am Mon-Thur; 11am-3am Fri; 5pm-6am Sat. **Credit** AmEx, DC, MC, V. **Map** p329 F7.

This popular Sydney watering hole also doubles as an art gallery, holding about 30 shows each year. Aboriginal artist Fran Dunn is just one of the intriguing artists to have exhibited here and a permanent collection includes the work of Shona Wilson, Guy Hawson and many others. If you fancy an art lesson with your aperitif, there are free life drawing classes each Monday from 6.30pm; the model is supplied, but bring your own materials.

Birrung Gallery
134 William Street, between Bourke & Forbes Streets, Woolloomooloo (9550 9964, www.worldvision.com.au/birrung). Bus 324, 325, 326, 327. **Open** 10am-5.30pm Tue-Fri; 11am-5pm Sat. **Credit** AmEx, MC, V. **Map** p330 H7.

Birrung Gallery is a World Vision initiative to raise funds for indigenous communities, especially in the areas of employment, education and leadership. Its diverse Aboriginal art offerings include works in fibre from Arnhem Land, Western Deserts paintings and various pieces from artists living on the Tiwi Islands, off Australia's north coast near Darwin.

Legge Gallery
183 Regent Street, between Boundary & Margaret Streets, Redfern (9319 3340, www.leggegallery. com). CityRail Redfern. **Open** 11am-6pm Tue-Sat. Closed mid Dec-early Feb. **Credit** MC, V.

Contemporary Australian painting, sculpture and ceramics make up Legge Gallery's diverse collection. The mix of young and established artists who have exhibited here include abstract painter John Bartley and Annette Iggulden, of Softshoe Sojourn fame.

King Street Gallery on William
117 William Street, Darlinghurst (9360 9727, www.kingstreetgallery.com.au). Bus 325, 326, 389, 461, 480, 485. **Open** 10am-6pm Tue-Sat. **Map** p330 H6.

In operation for nearly 30 years, the respected King Street Gallery relocated to William Street in 2007. Its roster of well-known artists includes multiple award-winners Elisabeth Cummings, Idris Murphy, Jenny Sages, and Wendy Sharpe.

Liverpool Street Gallery
243A Liverpool Street, between Riley & Crown Streets, East Sydney (8353 7799, www.liverpool streetgallery.com.au). CityRail Museum. **Open** 10am-6pm Tue-Sat. **Credit** AmEx, DC, MC, V. **Map** p329 G8.

Behind its impressive glass façade, Liverpool Street Gallery showcases a diversity of Australian contemporary artists alongside modern international works. Painting – whether abstract, realist or figurative – predominates but you might also find sculpture, works on paper and photography.

Martin Browne Fine Art
57-59 Macleay Street, at Challis Avenue, Potts Point (9331 7997, www.martinbrownefineart. com). CityRail Kings Cross/bus 311. **Open** 11am-6pm Tue-Sun. **Credit** MC, V. **Map** p330 J6.

This building is a landmark of Bohemian Kings Cross and one-time residence of iconic Australian artists including Brett Whiteley and Martin Sharp. Its eye-catching yellow paintwork is said to represent Van Gogh's unrealised ambition of having a home for artistic expression. Today, it offers a strong selection of new work by emerging artists as well as curated exhibitions over two floors.

Mori Gallery
168 Day Street, between Bathurst & Liverpool Streets, CBD (9283 2903). CityRail Town Hall/Monorail Chinatown. **Open** 11am-6pm Wed-Sat. **No credit cards. Map** p329 E7.

ARTS & ENTERTAINMENT

Stephen Mori's gallery shows an eclectic mix of works from established young Australian names, including Jenny Bell, Giles Alexander and conceptual artist Alana Hunt. He has also shown a talent for exhibiting an interesting selection of art by impressive 'unknowns' over the years, including new media as well as more traditional offerings.

Object Gallery
417 Bourke Street, between Campbell and Albion Streets, Surry Hills (9361 4511, www.object.com. au). Bus 311, 333, 352, 373, 377, 378, 380, 392, 394, 396. **Open** 11am-5pm Tue-Fri; 10am-5pm Sat, Sun. **Credit** AmEx, DC, MC, V. **Map** p329 G9
This gallery used to be in the Queen Victoria Building (*see p196*), but it seems much more suited to its new home in the edgy St Margarets development on Bourke Street. Downstairs is a great little shop, called Collect (*see p212*), selling collectible glass and ceramics, while upstairs Object passionately supports innovative craft and design, and uses its space to raise awareness of the wealth of artistic talent both at home and overseas.

Ray Hughes Gallery
270 Devonshire Street, between Bourke & Crown Streets, Surry Hills (9698 3200, www.rayhughes gallery.com). Bus 301, 302, 303, 352. **Open** 10am-6pm Tue-Sat. Closed 2wks after Christmas. **Credit** MC, V. **Map** p329 G11.
A colourful character on the Sydney art scene and former subject of the controversial Archibald portraiture competition held each year (entries always generate heated argument), Ray Hughes shows leading contemporary Australian and Chinese artists in his inner-city gallery. Names to look out for include landscape artist Joe Furlonger, Chinese painter Li Jin and Scottish ceramicist Stephen Bird.

Robin Gibson Gallery
278 Liverpool Street, between Forbes & Darley Streets, Darlinghurst (9331 6692, www.robin gibson.net). CityRail Kings Cross. **Open** 11am-6pm Tue-Sat. **Credit** MC, V. **Map** p329 H8.
In an atmospheric three-storey Georgian sandstone house, Robin Gibson Gallery is known for varied, mainly Australian exhibitions that strike a balance between contemporary and traditional styles. The late sculptor Clement Meadmore and emerging Australian painters Gina Bruce and Catherine Fox feature on the long list of artists shown.

★ Urban Uprising
314 Crown Street, Darlinghurst (9331 6614, www.urbanuprising.com.au). Bus 311, 333, 352, 373, 377, 378, 380, 392, 394, 396. **Open** noon-6pm Mon-Wed, Fri, Sat; noon-7pm Thur; 1-5pm Sun. **Credit** AmEx, MC, V. **Map** p329 G9.
The growing taste for graffiti art among Sydney collectors is reflected by the success of galleries such as this one, where prints by major international urban artists including Banksy, Shepard Fairey and Pure Evil are sold. Shows by Sydney and Melbourne artists are also held here.

Watters Gallery
109 Riley Street, at Stanley Lane, East Sydney (9331 2556, www.wattersgallery.com). CityRail Museum. **Open** 10am-5pm Tue, Sat; 10am-7pm Wed-Fri. Closed mid Dec-early Jan. **Credit** AmEx, DC, MC, V. **Map** p329 G7.
Established in 1964, this Sydney institution maintains a loyal following among some of Australia's most significant artists. Among the notables are late sculptor Robert Klippel, figurative painter Vicki Varvaressos and Australia's great, recently deceased surrealist painter James Gleeson. Another Watters regular is Chris O'Doherty (aka Reg Mombassa) whose colourful, politicised images fuse fashion and art.

EASTERN SUBURBS
Australian Art Print Network
68 Oxford Street, between Crown & Riley Streets, Darlinghurst (9332 1722, www.aboriginalart prints.com.au). Bus 311, 352, 371, 377, 378, 380, 392, 394, 396, 397, 399. **Open** 10am-6pm Mon-Fri; 11am-5pm Sat. **Credit** AmEx, DC, MC, V. **Map** p329 G8.
Director Michael Kershaw says that his collection of limited-edition Aboriginal and Torres Strait Islander prints is probably the largest in the world. A number of the country's best indigenous artists are represented here, among them Kimberley legend Rover Thomas and urban artist Sally Morgan.

ARTS & ENTERTAINMENT

Australian Art Print Network.

Galleries

Australian Centre for Photography
257 Oxford Street, between Ormond & William Streets, Paddington (9332 1455, www.acp.org. au). Bus 333, 352, 378, 380. **Open** noon-7pm Tue-Fri; 10am-6pm Sat, Sun. **Credit** AmEx, MC, V. **Map** p332 K10.
Impressive local and international photography and new media feature in the ACP gallery; innovative video works are an increasingly regular highlight. Aspiring photographers can enrol in the centre's various courses and hone their skills in its digital suite or darkroom. ACP also publishes the informative *Photofile* magazine.

Blender Gallery
16 Elizabeth Street, between Oxford & Underwood Streets, Paddington (9380 7080, www.blendercom.au). Bus 333, 352, 378, 380. **Open** 11am-6pm Tue-Fri; 10am-6pm Sat. **Credit** MC, V. **Map** p332 L10.
Expect mainly photography and, less regularly, sculpture, painting and mixed media over two floors in a converted Paddington terraced house. The annual exhibition of photography finalists in the national Walkley journalism awards is a highlight and there are new shows every three to four weeks.

Coo-ee Aboriginal Art Gallery
31 Lamrock Avenue, at Chambers Avenue, Bondi Beach (9300 9233, www.cooeeart.com.au). CityRail Bondi Junction then bus 333, 380, 381, 382/bus 333, 380. **Open** 10am-5pm Tue-Sat. **Credit** AmEx, MC, V. **Map** p334.
This highly regarded Aboriginal art gallery has been around for almost 30 years. It specialises in quality artworks from indigenous communities in the Northern Territory, Western Australia and the Torres Strait Islands.

Eva Breuer Art Dealer
83 Moncur Street, between Queen Street & Jersey Road, Woollahra (9362 0297, www.evabreuerartdealer.com.au). Bus 352, 378, 380, 389. **Open** 10am-6pm Tue-Fri; 10am-5pm Sat. **Credit** AmEx, MC, V. **Map** p333 M10.
High-end 20th- and 21st-century Australian art is the focus here, with an emphasis on paintings by such home-grown greats as Arthur Boyd and Sidney Nolan. Its varied programme includes solo shows and arresting thematic exhibitions.

Rex Irwin Art Dealer
1st Floor, 38 Queen Street, between Oxford Street & Halls Lane, Woollahra (9363 3212, www.rexirwin.com). Bus 333, 378, 380, 389. **Open** 11am-5.30pm Tue-Sat; also by appointment. Closed mid Dec-early Feb. **Credit** MC, V. **Map** p332 L11.
This compact gallery represents several of Australian art's leading names, including landscape artist Nicholas Harding and painter Peter Booth.

The gallery also deals in pieces by important Australian artists such as ceramicist Prue Venables, as well as European works including British figurative painting and prints and drawings by Picasso.

★ Roslyn Oxley9 Gallery
8 Soudan Lane, off Hampden Street, Paddington (9331 1919, www.roslynoxley9.com. au). CityRail Edgecliff then 5min walk or bus 389. **Open** 10am-6pm Tue-Fri; 11am-6pm Sat. Closed Christmas-late Jan. **Credit** AmEx, MC, V. **Map** p332 L9.
Top-flight Australian artists including renowned photographer Bill Henson feature, as do sculptor James Angus, indigenous photographer Destiny Deacon and installation artist Lindy Lee. Big-name internationals such as Tracey Emin have also shown here, and the gallery encourages offshore talent.

Sarah Cottier Gallery
3 Neild Avenue, corner of Gosbell Street, Paddington (9356 3305, www.sarahcottier gallery.com). CityRail Kings Cross/bus 389. **Open** 11am-5pm Wed-Sat. **Credit** AmEx, MC, V. **Map** p330 K8.
Nestled in a quiet, leafy part of Paddington, the relatively new Sarah Cottier Gallery showcases work by hip young Australian artists including Gemma Smith, Tony Schwensen and Julie Fragar.

Sherman Contemporary Art Foundation
16-20 Goodhope Street, Paddington (9311 1112, www.sherman-scaf.org.au). Bus 389, 380. **Open** 11am-5pm Wed-Sat. Closed mid Dec-late Feb. **Credit** AmEx, MC, V. **Map** p332 K9.
For 21 years Sherman Galleries launched the careers of important artists including Tim Storrier, Mike Parr and Janet Laurence. But in April 2008 the gallery ceased trading and transformed into a not-for-profit organisation, Sherman Contemporary Art Foundation (SCAF), championing research, education and exhibitions of contemporary art from Australia, the Asia-Pacific and the Middle East.

Stills Gallery
36 Gosbell Street, between Boundary Street & Neild Avenue, Paddington (9331 7775, www.stillsgallery.com.au). Bus 324, 325, 326, 327. **Open** 11am-6pm Tue-Sat. Closed mid Dec-Jan. **Credit** AmEx, MC, V. **Map** p330 K8.
This large, bright exhibition space shows leading contemporary Australian photographers and some installation and video works. Represented artists include the noted photojournalist Narelle Autio, Trent Parke and Petrina Hicks. Every five weeks sees a Saturday discussion by the artist on show.

Tim Olsen Gallery
63 Jersey Road, at Caledonia Street, Woollahra (9327 3922, www.timolsengallery.com). Bus 333, 352, 378, 380. **Open** 10am-6pm

A Wonderland of Chinese Art

A new gallery brings new art to Sydney.

Since the turn of the 21st century, Chinese contemporary art has been among the hottest commodities in the international art market, fetching record prices while amazing audiences with its scale and ambition. In August 2009, an extraordinary new gallery opened its doors in Chippendale, designed to showcase a private Australian collection of recent Chinese art. The **White Rabbit Collection** (30 Balfour Street, Chippendale, 8399 2867, www.whiterabbitcollection.org) occupies a state-of-the-art, four-floor building, refurbished from an old knitting factory at a cost of $10 million. It's the project of Judith Neilson, wife of billionaire fund manager Kerr Neilson, who began collecting Chinese art in 1999 and now possesses one of the largest collections in the world.

'The size and nature of the collection make White Rabbit unique in Australia,' says the gallery's manager, Paris Neilson. 'The fact we aren't beholden to anyone for funding gives us enormous freedom in selecting and displaying the art.'

Exhibits range from painting, drawing and photography to outlandish, large-scale sculptural works. Chen Wenling's 'Valiant Struggle No 11' (2006) is a good example: a full-sized red car with a tongue protruding out of its bonnet ten metres into the air, from which dangles a life-size golden sow and two figures hanging onto it for dear life. It's a grotesque and spectacular comment on China's new prosperity.

Open from 10am until 6pm, Thursday to Sunday, the free gallery's exhibitions are changed every six months. White Rabbit boasts a library, hosts Chinese cultural events and even has a Chinese tea room. Visiting Sydney to look at Chinese art may sound like a strange idea, but no one who drops by White Rabbit goes away unimpressed.

'What we'd like to be is an additional cultural space to the Art Gallery of NSW and the Museum of Contemporary Art,' explains Paris Neilson, and it looks like they've succeeded: even AGNSW's director (and Chinese art expert) Edmund Capon, has given White Rabbit his stamp of approval. 'This is an amazing glimpse across the vivid plains of contemporary Chinese art,' Capon says.

White Rabbit Collection.

ARTS & ENTERTAINMENT

Mon-Fri; 10am-5pm Sat; noon-5pm Sun. **Credit** AmEx, MC, V. **Map** p332 L10. John Olsen, now in his 80s, is one of Australia's most revered painters – and he's still going strong. His work, along with a Who's Who of great and up-and-coming contemporary Australian artists, is on show (and for sale) at this new two-floor space, recently relocated from around the corner in Paddington. The gallery is run by Tim Olsen, John's son, whose sister Louise is a member of Dinosaur Designs (*see p212*).

INNER WEST

Aboriginal & Pacific Art Gallery
2 Danks Street, at Young Street, Waterloo (9699 2211, www.2danksstreet.com.au). Bus 301, 302, 303, 304, 339, 343. **Open** 11am-5pm Tue-Sat. Closed mid Dec-mid Feb. **Credit** AmEx, MC, V. Under the direction of long-time indigenous art specialist Gabriella Roy, this gallery shows traditional and contemporary Aboriginal works, specialising in Arnhem Land barks and carvings. The gallery represents major artists including Kitty Kantilla, Kay Lindjuwanga and Spider Snell.

Annandale Galleries
110 Trafalgar Street, at Booth Street, Annandale (9552 1699, www.annandalegalleries.com.au). Bus 370, 470. **Open** 11am-5pm Tue-Sat. Closed mid Dec-mid Feb. **Credit** MC, V. Australian abstract painter Guy Warren and overseas artists such as Leon Kossoff and William Kentridge are some of the names to look out for. The

Tim Olsen Gallery. *See p238.*

gallery also has a strong selection of Aboriginal work, and pieces by the likes of Chagall and Miró.

Boomalli Aboriginal Artists' Co-op
55-59 Flood Street, between Marion & Myrtle Streets, Leichhardt (9560 2541, www.boomalli. org.au). Bus 436, 437, 438, 470. **Open** 11am-4pm Wed-Sun. **Credit** AmEx, DC, MC, V. Boomalli's focus on contemporary urban Aboriginal art sets it apart from most indigenous galleries, which tend to prefer regional works. The gallery has associations or past links with many of Australia's foremost indigenous artists, including Jeffrey Samuels and Bronwyn Bancroft.

Grantpirrie
86 George Street, Redfern (9699 9033, www.grant pirrie.com). CityRail Redfern. **Open** 10am-6pm Tue-Fri; 11am-5pm Sat. **Credit** AmEx, MC, V. This cutting-edge commercial gallery represents local avant-garde painters Michael Zavros and Ben Quilty as well as cross-media artist Hossein Valamanesh. There are three gallery spaces on the premises and three shows occurring at any one time.

★ NG Art Gallery
3 Little Queen Street, Chippendale (9318 2992, www.ngart.com.au). CityRail Central. **Open** 11am-10pm Tue-Fri; 9am-10pm Sat. **Credit** AmEx, MC, V. Young and mid-career artists including Susan O'Doherty, Jane Gillings and Johnny Romeo exhibit in this first-floor gallery in the burgeoning inner-city art district of Chippendale. Downstairs boasts the lively Mission Restaurant and Bar.

2 Danks Street
2 Danks Street, at Young Street, Waterloo (www.2danksstreet.com.au). Bus 301, 302, 303, 304, 339, 343. **Open** 11am-6pm Tue-Sat. Closed mid Dec-Feb. **Credit** MC, V. In a traditionally industrial but increasingly residential (and upwardly mobile) inner-city suburb, this former warehouse boasts seven permanent galleries and three spaces devoted to temporary shows. These include Aboriginal and Pacific Art, Utopia Art Sydney, the international Conny Dietzschold Gallery and the Brenda May Gallery, which shows modern, often experimental work in a variety of media.

Utopia Art Sydney
2 Danks Street, at Young Street, Waterloo (9699 2900, www.2danksstreet.com.au). Bus 301, 302, 303, 304, 339, 343. **Open** 10am-5pm Tue-Sat. Closed mid Dec-mid Jan. **Credit** AmEx, MC, V. Utopia Art Sydney promotes Aboriginal artists from the Northern Territory, along with work by non-Aboriginal artists including sculptor Marea Gazzard and the gallery's owner Christopher Hodges. Emily Kame Kngwarreye is among the leading indigenous artists regularly shown here.

Gay & Lesbian

Welcome to the gay capital of the southern hemisphere.

Sydney is one of the most vibrant and most open queer destinations on the map. It's also one of the safest. What the city lacks in same-sex marriage reform it makes up for with an out and proud queer culture that's welcoming to outsiders, and one that offers many diversely bent scenes right across the city and its fringes.

While most visitors will head straight for the city's famous **Oxford Street** precinct, there are plenty of other places to go searching for some action, be it of the gentle evening out variety or a date with sleaze heaven.

WHERE THE ACTION IS

Darlinghurst (or Darling-it-hurts, as the locals call it) is the queerest neck of the woods and includes the internationally renowned Oxford Street where most of the city's GLBTI bars and clubs can be found.

Many of the clubs on the strip have been serving up cock-sucking cowboys and screaming orgasms for close to 30 years and counting. Poor press may have plagued Oxford Street during the last few years as some more undesirable clubs opened up beside their queer counterparts, resulting in homophobic violence. Thankfully, like a bad smell, these clubs soon lost their lustre, closed shop and the strip again feels as gay as a Liza remix album.

A hop, (camp) skip and a jump away from Darlinghurst lies **Surry Hills**. This inner city suburb has recently enjoyed a well-deserved renaissance as the mayor's small bar bill allowed for a number of quaint wine bars to open within its lanes and back streets. **Crown Street** is always abuzz with foodies on the prowl for Sydney's next great plate and art lovers who frequent local small galleries like Urban Uprising and Outre Gallery (both on Crown Street). While most of the bars on Crown Street are not exclusively gay, no one is going to so much as blink at any man-on-man action that unfolds in this 'hood.

Potts Point and **Kings Cross** are two more inner city suburbs that have more than a smear of queer to their names. While Kings Cross is Sydney's infamous red light district you can always see local gay boys meandering through the streets on their way to work, the gym or the

sauna. Some fabulous shopping can be found on **McCleay Street** in Potts Point as well as gorgeous architecture found in the art deco and Georgian inspired apartment buildings in **Springfield Avenue**.

The Inner West houses popular queer 'hoods such as **Newtown**, **Erskinville** and **Enmore**. While these unusual names sound more like sexually transmitted diseases than suburbs, they boast a distinctly left-of-centre charm. This precinct is popular with artists, students and an awesome array of dykes. Erskinville is home to the **Imperial Hotel**, where many scenes from *Priscilla, Queen of the Desert* were shot and where most of Sydney's old-school drag royalty got their first big break. This iconic hotel is considered Sydney's first home of drag. After being closed for a massive renovation that

---

Cheap Entry

Get more for less.

Kingsteam - Quick Facial
Whatever you are studying, you can get some action on a student's budget with Kingsteam's (1st Floor, 38-42 Oxford Street, Darlinghurst, 9360 3431) student or gym members' discount: $15 entry.

Sydney City Steam - Buddy Pass
Bring a pal, lover or some random you met on the way, and get yourselves in to Sydney City Steam (*see p249*) as a tag team for just $20.

ARTS & ENTERTAINMENT

lasted three years, the Imperial opened again in September 2010, revealing an impressive nip'n'tuck to the gay community. Right beside Newtown train station you'll find the **Bank Hotel** which never fails to pull in a great catch of local lesbians and alternative gay boys, particularly on a Sunday afternoon as most Aussie queers have a total disregard for the phrase 'school night'.

But gay Sydney's scene extends far beyond the pubs and clubs. There are lots of community groups covering every possible leisure activity, political bent, social cause or medical issue. For a full listing of the groups on offer, check out the website of the oldest-running gay community publication, the *Sydney Star Observer*, at www.ssonet.com.au. You'll also find up-to-date listings at www.samesame.com.au.

PROTECTION

Homosexuals and transgender people in NSW are legally protected against discrimination, as are those living with HIV or AIDS. Same-sex sex is legal (the age of consent is 16 for everyone) and the state government recognises same-sex partnerships. Homophobia exists everywhere and Sydney is no exception. While homophobic violence does occur, it is regularly monitored by the Anti Violence Project. The Surry Hills Police station is your nearest port of call in an emergency when in the inner city. In an emergency, dial 000.

Colombian Hotel.

WHERE TO STAY

It can safely be said that any 'international' hotel in Sydney (glass front, big lobby, expensive cocktails) will be gay-friendly. And a large number of staff at any of these places will also be 'family', so you should have no hassles. If you want the full ghetto-accommodation experience, check before arriving with the US-run **International Gay & Lesbian Travel Association** (www.iglta.org). Other good online sites for travel to and within Australia, including lists of friendly accommodation, are **Gay Australia Guide** (www.gayaustralia guide.com) and **Gay & Lesbian Tourism Australia** (www.galta.com.au).

SAFE SEX

Safe sex is a way of life here – and while a decade of safe-sex campaigns has hugely reduced the incidence of new infection, the dangers are still out there. The Aids Council of NSW is the government department in the fore front of the HIV/AIDS awareness issue and spearheads a number of exciting and engaging projects that inspire the local community and beyond to play safe (www.acon.org.au). *See also p302* **STDs, HIV & AIDS**.

INFORMATION

For the latest on what's happening, ask the friendly staff at the **Bookshop Darlinghurst** (*see p199*). Alternatively, check the queer press, available in gay outlets, bottle shops, music venues, newsagents and cinemas around town. The city's two free weekly gay newspapers, *Sydney Star Observer* and *SX*, have full, up-to-the-minute 'what's on' and venue guides. Dykes will find the free monthly news magazine *Lesbians on the Loose* (www.lotl.com) and new *Cherrie* magazine (www.cherrie.e-p.net.au) required reading.

For gay community groups, helplines and support networks, *see p301*. Before your arrival in Oz subscribe to *Time Out Sydney*'s Gay and Lesbian monthly newsletter at www.timeoutsydney.com.au/gaylesbian.

NIGHTLIFE
Bars & pubs

Bank Hotel
324 King Street, between Newman & Wilson Streets, Newtown (8568 1900, www.bankhotel. com.au). CityRail Newtown. **Open** 10am-late daily. **Credit** AmEx, MC, V. **Map** p334.
Already one of Newtown's most popular pubs, the Bank recently underwent a multi-million dollar

Cruising Sydney's Sex Venues

The ins and outs of cruising.

Ken's At Kensington – Sauna
See p249.
High The steam room. Bring some VO5 Hot Oil and a mud mask and give yourself a little treatment while being 'treated'.
Low The Dark Room. There's a reason it's not lit like the Sydney Cricket Ground, so make like Helen Keller and feel for a pretty face before you head south.
Etiquette Always play nice. Even if a Ray Martin look-alike grabs your arse, a discreet 'I'm fine, thanks' is nicer than 'Bugger off!'
Happy Hour Feeling peckish around lunchtime? Kens has a $13 entry fee between 11am and 3pm Monday to Friday. With spa, pool, sauna and steam room amenities, that's the cheapest day spa with extras in town.

Bodyline Spa & Sauna – Wet cruising
See p249.
High For many, it's just a hop, skip and hump away from home.
Low The showers. Throw Cher and Meryl Streep in there and you've got Silkwood.
Etiquette Try not to trip over a threesome and break a hip. It makes for an awkward insurance claim.

Happy Hour Weekdays are popular when it comes to cruising. Bodyline swings the doors open Monday to Thursday between noon and 7pm for $16. Students score well too with $12 entry daily.

HeadQuarters on Crown – Dry cruising
See p249.
High Staying clothed. Dry cruising is perfect for hiding spare tyres, full-body psoriasis and humpbacks.
Low Nasty surprises. You may not know what you are undressing until it's too late.
Etiquette Shush! HQ is a virtual library when it comes to silence, so zip your lip if you want any action.
Happy Hour For the best discounted booty call, get down to HQ Monday to Friday between 7am and 7pm, with entry only $10.

Pleasure Chest - Video booths
161 Oxford Street, Darlinghurst (9332 2667).
High With the sex shop upstairs, toys and porn are always at hand.
Low Lost, drunk clubbing girls trying to break into your video booth.
Etiquette Wipe down afterwards.

ARTS & ENTERTAINMENT

facelift. It draws a smattering of gays and lesbians throughout the week, but traditionally gets overrun with grrrls on Sunday nights. The three-level venue includes great outdoor areas, casual bars, a quality cocktail lounge and DJs at night. Also try the superb in-house (but outdoor) Thai restaurant.

Colombian Hotel
117-123 Oxford Street, at Crown Street, Darlinghurst (9360 2151). Bus 311, 333, 352, 373, 377, 378, 380, 392, 394, 396. **Open** 9am-6am daily. **Credit** AmEx, MC, V. **Map** p329 G8.
More gay pubs should be like this. Inside are two levels of fun, both decorated in an 'art deco meets Aztec' design theme that succeeds against all the odds. The ground-floor bar opens on to the street, and is excellent for people-watching, while the upstairs cocktail bar is more sedate, although boogie fever breaks out later on Friday and Saturday nights. Both floors get crowded pec-to-pec on weekends.

★ Imperial Hotel
35 Erskineville Road, at Union Street, Erskineville (9519 9899, www.theimperialhotel. com.au). CityRail Erskineville or Newtown. **Open** noon-late daily. **Map** p334.

The Imperial is featured at the beginning of the film *Priscilla, Queen of the Desert* and the pub has honoured this by staging a succession of rude but hilarious Priscilla drag shows. After a three-year facelift the Imperial Hotel has removed her bandages to reveal the Inner West's largest GLBTI venue and features a drag showroom, a public bar and a tiered dance room where a pumpin' great crowd can be found on Friday and Saturday nights.

Oxford Hotel
134 Oxford Street, at Taylor Square, Darlinghurst (9331 3467, www.theoxford hotel.com.au). Bus 311, 333, 352, 373, 377, 378, 380, 392, 394, 396. **Open** *Main bar* 24hrs daily. *Basement bar* 10pm-10am Fri, Sat. *Will & Toby's* 7pm-late Wed-Sun. *Polo Lounge* 6pm-3am Tue-Sun. **Credit** AmEx, MC, V. **Map** p329 H8.
A mainstay of the 'Golden Mile' for about as long as anyone can remember, the Oxford has undergone a few changes in recent years. The ground-floor pub used to be dark and cloistered, but renovations and additions have opened it up considerably. A wooden veranda now enables outdoor drinking over Taylor Square, which is lovely in the warmer months. But the best things about the place haven't changed: the

main space is still virtually a 24-hour bar, and an almost universally gay male venue. Upstairs levels have two sophisticated and rather ritzy lounge bars, with live entertainment and a superb cocktail list.

Slide

41 Oxford Street, between Crown & Bourke Streets, Darlinghurst (8915 1899, www.slide. com.au). Bus 311, 333, 352, 373, 377, 378, 380, 392, 394, 396. **Open** 7pm-3am Wed-Sun. **Credit** AmEx, MC, V. **Map** p329 G8.

Undoubtedly one of the hottest spots in town, the very slick bar/restaurant/club Slide opened its doors at the end of 2005. New gay bars in Sydney can be a risky venture, but Slide has found its niche as a more upmarket gay watering hole. French chef and venue manager Marc Kuzma (who is also drag queen Claire de Lune) oversees the popular El Circo

on Sunday nights, where guests enjoy a nine-course tasting menu for $90 while watching amazing performances. Most weeknights are open for a dinner and show experience where guests can see some of Sydney's most interesting and entertaining jazz, soul and cabaret performers at their best. Visitors are also welcome to pay to see the show only. On Friday and Saturday nights, Slide becomes a bar and club that promises a league of funky yet polished queers who like to boogie in the surrounds of a classy club.

Sly Fox

199 Enmore Road, between Cambridge Street & Stanmore Road, Enmore (9557 1016). Bus 423, 426, 428. **Open** 10am-4am Mon-Thur; 10am-6am Fri, Sat; 9am-midnight Sun. **No credit cards**.

From the outside, the Sly Fox looks like an average spit-and-sawdust Aussie pub, but get past security

Hoorah for the Mardi Gras!

How to get the most from Sydney's gay party.

You'd have to be living under a rock not to know that Sydney is host to the world's largest GLBTI parade with the annual Sydney Gay and Lesbian Mardi Gras parade and party. The parade route runs from the lower end of Oxford street to Flinders Street and contains hundreds of floats and thousands of participants chanting, singing and dancing away their message of freedom and liberation for the hundreds of thousands in the crowd there to cheer them on. This stand-out event pulls in bent punters from every nook of the globe as well as celebs including George Michael, Margaret Cho, Amanda Lepore and a myriad of other queer and queer-loving A-listers. When the five-hour Parade winds up, the post-parade party kicks off at the Entertainment Quarter. This 12-hour dance fest unfurls across a variety of venues within the former showgrounds, with regular spectacular performances staged throughout the night. By far the biggest queer party in the southern hemisphere, if not the world.

WHAT AND WHEN

The Mardi Gras festival takes place over three or four weeks, ending on the last weekend in February or the first weekend

in March (dates move a little so check at the time). Although it's the parade and party on the final Saturday that get the publicity, it's worth joining the locals at as many of the pre-parade events as you can fit in.

Things kick off with the Festival Launch (usually on a Saturday): many bring a picnic and make a night of it. Entertainment comes in the form of speeches and a few snippets from Mardi Gras festival shows. Other celebrations include the Mardi Gras Film Festival (*see p234*), art exhibitions, themed parties and nightly cabaret and stage shows in venues all over Sydney. The Fair Day in Victoria Park, Camperdown (held on the Sunday a fortnight before the final weekend), attracts more than 60,000 people and features an excellent high-camp pet show.

The parade itself begins at sunset. It starts at the corner of Hyde Park and Whitlam Square, heads up Oxford Street to Flinders Street and finishes at the party venue, the Entertainment Quarter in Moore Park. Crowds have been estimated at anything up to half a million. Many stake out their territory at least six hours before the parade starts, while hotels and restaurants along the route sell seats at and you'll find one of Sydney's hottest bars. It's a queer and alternative venue, mostly inhabited by lesbians. Wednesday night, known as Queer Central, is the big event, with lesbians and gay men. You'll find dancing, pool, competitions, lots of drag shows and well-known DJ Sveta on the decks. This is the home of Sydney's drag king scene, so expect some wild acts.

Clubs

Arq Sydney

16 Flinders Street, between Oxford & Taylor Streets, Darlinghurst (9380 8700, www.arqsydney.com.au). Bus 311, 333, 352, 373, 377, 378, 380, 392, 394, 396. **Open** 9pm-late Thur-Sun. **No credit cards. Map** p329 H9.
Arq is the busiest club on the Sydney scene, and the first port of call for many a gay tourist. Its big nights

are Saturday and Sunday, when it draws a very Oxford Street crowd of bare-chested pretty boys. With two levels and a mezzanine walkway, it holds around 900 people when full – and it always is at weekends. Head for the upper floor for sensational lighting and uptempo house and trance music, delivered via an ultra-crisp sound system; the lower floor is more chilled, with lounges, pool tables and more funky music. Shows are a speciality, whether drag or song and dance numbers from pop stars (both aspiring and actual). The club goes into overdrive on long weekends, and its recovery parties are hugely popular. Look out for the Fomo foam parties in summer.

Midnight Shift

85 Oxford Street, between Riley & Crown Streets, Darlinghurst (9360 4319, www.themidnight shift.com). CityRail Museum/bus 311, 333, 352,

Mardi Gras.

ticket-only cocktail parties. Another comfortable option is the Bobby Goldsmith 'Glamstand', which seats several thousand (for tickets and information, visit www.bgf.org.au or call 9283 8666); all proceeds go to assist men, women and children living in poverty with HIV/AIDS.

After the parade comes the party. Attracting some 17,000 revellers, it features top DJs and performers whose identities are usually kept secret right until the night (don't expect Kylie, though: she hasn't come for years). As well as the crammed dance halls and outrageous drag shows, there are plenty of places in the Entertainment Quarter complex for drinking, eating and chilling out.

There's also a hefty medical presence, just in case things go wrong.

INFORMATION AND TICKETS

To keep abreast of what's going on, contact New Mardi Gras (9568 8600, www.mardi gras.org.au) or get the excellent free programme, available from January from gay-friendly venues around Oxford Street and Newtown. You'll need to book accommodation and tickets (at least for the major events) months ahead. Tickets for the main party are available from mid December and can sell out quickly, so buy them before you arrive in Sydney if possible (13 2849, www.ticketek.com.au). For more information go to www.mardigrasparty.org.au/party.

Gurlesque.

Phoenix is an underground club that has enjoyed a variety of incarnations over the years. This small club, famous for its low ceiling and industrial furnishings hosts a number of regular and occasional club nights. Currently monthly club night Sweat takes the lead as one of the better gigs that pulls in a hot, sweaty and sexy crowd of guys looking to cruise hard men on the dancefloor on the first Saturday of the month. Regular club nights includes Phoenix Rising – a day club that starts at 5am and keeps a Friday night crowd pumping well into Saturday afternoon with its dirty beats and slightly hedonistic vibe and Loose Ends a Sunday night clubbing gig that appeals to the alternative gay scene who prefer Visage to Kylie.

Stonewall Hotel
175 Oxford Street, between Taylor Square & Crown Street, Darlinghurst (9360 1963, www.stonewallhotel.com). Bus 311, 333, 352, 373, 377, 378, 380, 392, 394, 396. **Open** 9.30am-5am Mon-Fri; 9.30am-7am Sat, Sun. **No credit cards. Map** p329 G9.
A large, three-level pub and dance venue, much loved and always busy. The crowd tends towards younger gay men (think tiny tank tops and Justin Bieber haircuts) and those who fancy them. The street-level bar has a chatty, pub-style atmosphere, with drag shows, the occasional talent quest, a small dancefloor and sexy male dancers on the bar on weekends. Tuesday night's queer Karaoke is a must do! Upstairs there are two lounge areas with more bars; it's a bit like partying in somebody's living room. The hotel also hosts various events, launches and parties during Gay Pride Week in June.

Taxi Club
40-42 Flinders Street, between Taylor & Short Streets, Darlinghurst (9331 4256, www.the taxiclub.com). Bus 311, 333, 352, 373, 377, 378, 380, 392, 394, 396. **Open** 10am-2am Mon-Thur; 10am-6am Fri-Sun. **No credit cards. Map** p329 H9.
When everything else is closed on a weekend, and desperation strikes, never fear – there's always the Taxi. It provides the cheapest drinks in queer Sydney and is open until 6am at the weekend. Which is why it's a favourite with both drag queens – who stop here after a night's work – and some extremely intoxicated out-of-towners. There's also a restaurant and café on the ground floor, a gaming room, a TV area and lounge on the first floor, and a small dancefloor above that. It's a members' club, but you can get temporary membership on the door for free.

373, 377, 378, 380, 392, 394, 396. **Open** *Video Bar* noon-late Mon-Fri; 2pm-late Sat, Sun. *Club* 11pm-late Fri, Sat. **No credit cards. Map** p329 G8.
Another Sydney legend is the Midnight Shift. This classic establishment has two levels, however the street level bar seems to be where all the action is at. This dance club and bar is very popular with Sydney's diverse and always energetic queer Asian community, and as such, pulls in a thick crowd of the men who love them. Relaxed, warm and friendly, the Midnight Shift is attitude free and features two main bars, pool tables and a generous dancefloor where video pop hits run wild.

Palms on Oxford
124 Oxford Street, at Taylor Square, Darlinghurst (9357 4166). Bus 311, 333, 352, 373, 377, 378, 380, 392, 394, 396. **Open** 8pm-midnight Thur; 8pm-3am Fri, Sat. **No credit cards. Map** p329 H8.
It's unassuming and basic but always fun. Palms makes feature of 'cheap' with its low budget sound system, tacky dancefloor and '80s lighting, but there is always a smile on everyone's face at this popular little nook of a club. The sounds spinning off the decks are as camp as a purse full of rainbows so if you don't like Donna Summer, Kylie, or Steps remixes, girlfriend probably oughta go someplace else. Palms is a great night out with not a whiff of attitude to be found.

★ Phoenix Bar
34-44 Oxford Street, between Riley & Liverpool Streets, Darlinghurst (9331 1936, www.exchange hotel.biz). CityRail Museum/bus 311, 333, 352, 373, 377. **Open** check website for details. **Credit** phone for details. **Map** p329 G8.

Dance parties

This city loves a good dance party. Whether it's during Mardi Gras season or outside of it, small to large dance parties are a way of life for Sydney queers. Most parties are regularly patrolled by police using sniffer dogs as drug use of any kind is a criminal offence in all states across Australia, so party people be warned. Outside of the fun police, dance party culture is alive and well right across this town and a great place to meet the locals or pick up some Aussie trade.

★ Bad Dog

www.baddog.net.au. Also check local gay press. Organised by a group of DJs and artists dismayed by the stodgy sameness of Sydney's gay clubs, the Bad Dog events, which happen every few months, are a refreshing alternative to the norm. The venues tend to be away from the Oxford Street Golden Mile, while the parties are renowned for drawing a crowd that's high on friendliness and low on attitude.

DTPM

This event, held at Tank Nightclub (3 Bridge Lane, CBD, 9420 3000), is an offshoot of London's famed DTPM (or Delirium Tremens Post Meridien). The venue is built into the site of an old tank stream, with exposed brick walls and remnants of its former state. The resident DJ is Alan Thompson, the main spinner at the now-defunct London club for over a decade, and the long weekend events are packed with a fun up-for-it crowd spread out over two rooms of house and electro. Tickets from www.fag-tag.com.au and www.samesame.com.au.

Fag Tag

www.fagtag.com.au.
A much-needed innovation on the party scene, Fag Tag has a simple premise: each party sees a horde of lesbians and gay men descend on an otherwise straight venue and claim it for a night. But this is no guerrilla act: the venues are in on the joke, which means there's little risk of trouble from surprised regulars. Venues that have been Fag Tagged in the past few years include the Opera Bar at Circular Quay and the Eastern Hotel in Bondi Junction. Details of events are announced about two weeks ahead, so keep an eye on the website.

Gurlesque

www.gurlesque.com.
Eight years old and showing no signs of maturity (thank goodness), the Gurlesque strip shows continues to pack out venues and leave the dykes of Sydney gasping for more. Formed by dancers who were tired of stripping for men and wanted to 'give it to the girls', the Gurlesque events encourage all women to explore and interpret the art of striptease. The results, they say, have ranged 'from hilarious comedy and drag to seriously sexy, in-your-face pussy strutting'. With stunning costumes (just waiting to come off), raunchy routines and music from DJ Sveta, Gurlesque has truly brought something unique and unrivalled to the girls' scene. The girls perform at a number of different venues, so check the website or the local gay press for details.

Inquisition

Entertainment Quarter, Driver Avenue, Moore Park (9319 2309, www.sydneyleatherpride. org). Bus 355, 339, 373, 374, 376, 377.
Map p332 J12.
Held in May, Inquisition brings the annual Leather Pride Week to its climax. Festivities usually include an art exhibition, workshops, the Love Muscle

Sleaze Ball. *See p248.*

competition and Darlinghurst's Forbes Street Fair, but Inquisition is the party for punters of all kinds to fly their fetish flag for a night. Some die-hards have decried the influx of 'leather tourists' at the event, but it remains gay Sydney's premier fetish party, with a music policy that runs to the harder side of house, and some spectacular floor shows.

★ Sleaze Ball

Entertainment Quarter, Driver Avenue, Moore Park (9568 8600, www.mardigras.org.au). Bus 339, 355, 373, 374, 376, 377. **Map** p332 J12.
As the second biggest party on queer Sydney's calendar this 29-year-old costume party signifies gay liberation in Sydney as it came about during a time of great change. A Mardi Gras fundraiser, Sleaze Ball is held on the Saturday night of the October long weekend. Each year, Sleaze Ball's theme is announced a few months ahead of the date so that punters can get thinking about how much or how little they will dress up. Previous themes have included Zirkus, The Villain's Lair, Game On, and Decadence. A huge line-up of DJ's and special local and international performers make up this mainstay event. *Photo p247.*

Toybox

www.toyboxparty.com.au. Also check local gay press.
'Daytime is playtime!' That's the motto of the phenomenally successful Toybox parties, which have attracted many thousands of buff party boys and girls since 2003. Held every few months in various venues, the parties start in the early afternoon and continue until late. Several have taken place at Luna Park as a recovery event after the Mardi Gras and Sleaze Ball parties, leading some of the faithful to abandon the main event and devote their

---

A Thoroughly Gay Day

Sex is as much in the mind as the body. Feed yours.

SEXY SHOPPING

Sydney has almost as many sex shops as it has Turkish *pide* takeaway joints. The underground stores dotted through the CBD and suburban retail strips are lined with enough designer dildos, varying vibrators and faux fists to amuse a nation of porn stars. Among Sydney's best adult stores is the **Toolshed Oxford Street** (191 Oxford Street, Darlinghurst, 9360 1100, www.toolshed.com.au), which sells creative and imaginative objects destined for the orifice of your choice.

'We want people to feel able to ask us anything,' says store manager Kevin Vailey. 'Our range is as eclectic as our customer base, which keeps things interesting.'

SULTRY STYLING

Leather fetish culture is a universal admiration for all things leather and kinky, and the purveyors of the city's sexiest leather and fetish wear are the boys at **Sax Fetish** (110A Oxford Street, Darlinghurst, 9331 6105, www.saxfetish.com). This delightful den caters for both newbies and old hands at the fetish game and carries some seriously sexy wear from studded harnesses, chaps and codpieces for the boys, through to latex leggings, rubber skirts and chrome bras for the gals. Don't be fooled by the fetish stereotype though; the store attracts a diverse clientele ranging from plumbers and chippies through, to kindergarten teachers and high court judges.

LUSCIOUS LITERATURE

From hunky bear calendars through to saucy lesbian erotica, the **Bookshop Darlinghurst** (207 Oxford Street, Darlinghurst, 9331 1103, www.the bookshop.com.au) (*see p199*), in, er, Darlinghurst, has been stocking its shelves with some of the sexiest queer literature available, including rare imports. Aside from stocking a steamy array of books, the Bookshop has a great porn section that has proved to be a popular cruising zone with queer bookworms.

RUDE FOOD

When it comes to appetites, sex and food are often found on the same menu. Darlinghurst's **Slide Bar** (41 Oxford Street, Darlinghurst, 8915 1899, www.slide. com.au) has been pulling sexy serving suggestions out of the bedroom and on to the dinner plate through its ever-popular degustation menu, El Circo.

'We have created a very European feel to the venue,' says manager and brain behind the El Circo concept, Marc Kuzma. 'Now, after two successful years, El Circo is taking a more sexy turn.' By mixing sensual dishes such as boxed Mexican crab tortilla, filled with spicy guacamole, blue swimmer crab and topped with tomato salsa with live entertainment including an erotic silhouette performance by burlesque performer Miss Elouise Sauer, Slide's Sunday night sitting is the perfect pre-shag dinner date.

energies to Toybox instead. Renowned for their awesome lighting, superior sound quality and high production values all round, these parties are a very hot ticket in gay Sydney right now.

GYMS

As in all large gay cities worthy of that mantle, there is a thriving culture of the body in Sydney. Below are two gyms popular with gay men and lesbians; also try Bayswater Fitness (58 Kippax Street, Surry Hills, 9211 2799, www.bayswaterfitness.com.au).

City Gym Health & Fitness Centre
107-113 Crown Street, between William & Stanley Streets, East Sydney (9360 6247, www.citygym.com.au). CityRail Kings Cross/ bus 323, 324, 325, 389. **Open** 5am-midnight Mon-Fri; 6am-10pm Sat; 8am-10pm Sun. **Admission** $25 (day), $79 (week), $95 (month). **Credit** AmEx, MC, V. **Map** p329 G8.
A legendary venue, popular with gay men and the serious bodybuilding crowd. Full fitness facilities, an extensive programme of classes and, for the men, a notoriously cruisey changing area (with steam room).

Gold's Gym
Level 1/58 Kippax Street, Surry Hills 2010. (9211 2799, www.goldsgym.com). CityRail Museum. **Open** 5.30am-9pm Mon-Fri; 7am-8pm Sat; 8am-6pm Sun. **Admission** $19 (day). **Credit** AmEx, DC, MC, V. **Map** p329 G8.
A very busy franchise of the global gym brand, with a huge gay and lesbian clientele. Classes, solarium, massage and all the usual workout facilities are on offer... with fringe benefits for members.

SAUNAS & SEX CLUBS

When it comes to getting it on, Sydneysiders are anything but shy. The city has a number of great sex-on-premises venues both wet and dry, and while there is plenty of action any night of the week, Sydney is big on shielding up. As the saying goes 'if it's not on, it's not on'. Most venues have signed up to a code of practice organised by the AIDS Council, meaning they distribute free condoms and lube to customers so they can come and come again. Over-18s only.

Bodyline Spa & Sauna
10 Taylor Street, at Flinders Street, Darlinghurst (9360 1006, www.bodylinesydney.com). Bus 311, 333, 352, 373, 377, 378, 380, 392, 394, 396. **Open** noon-7am Mon-Thur; 24hrs noon Fri-7am Mon. **Admission** $23; $16 gym members Mon-Thur; $12 reductions. **Credit** AmEx, DC, MC, V.

Established in 1991, Bodyline was the first lawfully established sex-on-premises gay venue in NSW, and is still gay-owned and -operated. It has a huge spa, steam room and sauna on the lower ground floor; a coffee lounge and cinema on the ground floor; private rooms and a video room on the first floor; and a great sun deck on the second floor. It's kept very clean and tends to attract the buff party crowd from many of the nearby nightclubs, including Arq.

HeadQuarters on Crown
273 Crown Street, at Campbell Street, Darlinghurst (9331 6217, www.headquarters.com.au). Bus 311, 333, 352, 373, 377, 378, 380, 392, 394, 396. **Open** 24hrs daily. **Admission** 7pm-7am Mon-Thur $16; 7am-7pm Mon-Fri $10; Fri 7pm-Mon 7am $18. **Credit** AmEx, MC, V. **Map** p329 G9.
Sprawling over three large levels, HeadQuarters specialises in 'fantasy play areas' including a pig pen, a jail room and enough mazes to get (happily) lost in. It holds frequent fetish nights (including leather, Speedo and footy shorts parties), as well as the occasional all-nude evening. There's a coffee lounge and full air-con – thank goodness.

Ken's at Kensington
83 Anzac Parade, opposite Ascot Street, Kensington (9662 1359, www.kensat kensington.com.au). Bus 391, 392, 393, 394, 395, 396, 397, 399. **Open** 11am-6am Mon-Thur; 24hrs 11am Fri-6am Mon. **Admission** $19; $13 11am-3pm Mon-Fri. **No credit cards**.
Ken's is Sydney's answer to New York's infamous Continental Baths and has been putting smiles on men's faces for over 30 years. This wet cruising venue has a spa, and steam room and sauna, where group action runs wild. The upper level features a chill-out cinema, a gym and a few private booths with glory holes for the shier types. Friday's 'Buck Naked' nude nights are extremely popular, and Sunday nights are always spilling over with fellas who want a happy ending to the weekend. Without a doubt the most popular sauna in Sydney.

Sydney City Steam
357 Sussex Street, at Liverpool Street, CBD (9267 6766, www.sydneycitysteam.com.au). CityRail Town Hall. **Open** 10am-6pm Mon-Thur; 24 hours 10am Fri-6am Mon. **Admission** $20; $17 reductions; $13 10am-2pm Mon-Fri. **No credit cards**. **Map** p329 E8.
Gay-owned and -run, and located in the heart of Chinatown, Sydney City Steam features four floors of action. The crowd is mainly Asian and mature men, so if you are looking for buff, beefy gym types this is not the place for you. Sydney City Steam is very clean, and modern but has no distinct vibe. Facilities include a spa, steam room, sauna, two cinema spaces, various 'fantasy rooms', and a coffee shop and internet kiosk.

ARTS & ENTERTAINMENT

Music

Sydney hits all the right notes.

Music is the lifeblood of the harbour city. It's had its challenges over the years, from the gentrification of the inner city replacing sweaty venues with fancy townhouses through to the rise (and, thankfully, fall) of poker machines, but nothing has stopped Sydney from being one of the greatest places to make and experience music.

In fact, Sydney is unique among world-class music cities. Most of the great musical centres have weather that encourages people to huddle inside and create art – London, New York, and even Melbourne – Sydney offers great music and a superb climate. Whether you wish to take in the ambience of the magnificent **Sydney Opera House** (*see below*) or cram into a sweaty gig at the Annandale, absorb high culture at the **State Theatre** (*see p254*) or hear some steamy jazz at the **Basement** (*see p255*), Sydney's got it all.

CLASSICAL & OPERA

Sydney's flourishing classical music scene is broader than just the internationally admired Vladimir Askhenazy conducting in the **Sydney Opera House**. Sydney's very enthusiastic classical crowd flock to concerts – especially when they're laid on in an outdoor picnic-style setting. The **Sydney Festival** (*see p219*) alleviates post-Christmas blues by running musical events throughout January – including the Sydney Symphony's free Symphony in the Domain. The other main outdoor event, also free, is Opera Australia's Mazda Opera (www.opera-australia.org.au) in the Domain, on a Saturday near the end of January. The mainstream orchestral and carol-singing sit-ins in the Domain pack in tens of thousands of families every year, although connoisseurs steer clear of such mainstream fare, which tends to favour well-worn classics.

Venues

The **Eugene Goossens Hall** (ABC Centre, 700 Harris Street, 8333 5790, www.abc.net.au) – named after the British composer and conductor who first suggested the idea of the Opera House back in 1954, and housed in the ABC headquarters in Ultimo – is often used by smaller ensembles playing contemporary music. **Sydney Town Hall** (*see p65*) also showcases contemporary music, plus free organ recitals, the Sydney Youth Orchestras, and Sydney Festival events. A guide to church music can be found in the *SMH*'s Metro section; free lunchtime concerts are held weekly at St James', St Stephen's Uniting Church, and **St Andrew's Cathedral** (*see p64*). The Historic Houses Trust of NSW offers classical and jazz concerts in the ballroom at **Government House** (*see p59*).

★ City Recital Hall Angel Place

2 Angel Place, near Martin Place, CBD (admin 9231 9000, box office 8256 2222, www.cityrecitalhall.com). CityRail Martin Place or Wynyard. **Open** *Box office* 9am-5pm Mon-Fri; 3hr 30min before show Sat, Sun. **Tickets** free-$90. **Credit** AmEx, MC, V. **Map** p327 F5.

The 1,238-seat City Recital Hall in the centre of the CBD gives Sydney's orchestras room to roam, as well as hosting international names (including one David Helfgott). Created via a deal with the AMP Corporation, the three-level, shoebox-shaped hall has a colour scheme borrowed from a Latvian Baroque church (soft grey, soothing aubergine and twinkles of gold) and the architecture and acoustics have been designed for both chamber orchestras and solo performers.

Sydney Opera House

Bennelong Point, Circular Quay (box office 9250 7777, admin 9250 7111, www.sydneyopera

house.com). CityRail/ferry Circular Quay. **Open** *Box office* 9am-8.30pm Mon-Sat; 2hrs before show Sun. **Tickets** *Opera Theatre* $70-$250; $70-$195 reductions. *Concert Hall* prices vary. *Drama Theatre and Playhouse* $35-$80; $30-$60 reductions. *Studio* $25-$50; $25-$40 reductions. **Credit** AmEx, DC, MC, V. **Map** p327 G3.

The largest shell of the Sydney icon houses the 2,700-seat Concert Hall (although it was first intended for opera productions). Thanks to its purpose-built acoustics, symphonic music can be heard with a full, rich and mellow tone. Eighteen adjustable acrylic rings (aka the 'doughnuts') are suspended above the orchestra platform to reflect some of the sound back to the musicians. The hall also has the largest mechanical tracker-action organ in the world, with 10,154 pipes. The smaller, 1,500-seat Opera Theatre is used by Opera Australia, but its small pit and stage are a tight fit for grand opera. The Studio (capacity 350) showcases anything from rap to percussion bands and spoken-word shows. The Utzon Room hosts small ensembles and the Baby's Proms. *See also p255, p257 and p36* **Profile**.

Orchestras & groups

Australian Brandenburg Orchestra

9328 7581, www.brandenburg.com.au.

Australia's first period-instrument group – Baroque and classical periods, that is – has played to sell-out audiences from Tokyo to Germany. Formed by artistic director Paul Dyer in 1990, the orchestra now puts on regular seasons at the City Recital Hall. Its concerts are fashionable events – rich mixes of visual and musical experience.

Australian Chamber Orchestra

8274 3800, www.aco.com.au.

Under the flamboyant artistic directorship of high-profile violinist Richard Tognetti, the ACO has been praised as one of the most exciting classical ensembles worldwide. Formed in 1975, the Sydney-based touring orchestra is relatively youthful, and Tognetti's programming is always provocative. He likes to mix periods, offer rarely heard works and blend period-instrument soloists with contemporary instruments. The results are invariably startling.

★ Musica Viva

8394 6666, www.musicaviva.com.au.

Musica Viva is the world's largest chamber music organisation, touring Australian and international groups around the country. The outfit, which turned 65 in 2010, arranges performances in a wide range of styles from classical to world music. A roll-call of the world's best ensembles, including the Emerson, Jerusalem and Tokyo Quartets and violinist Gidon Kremer and his band, have all appeared on its impressive calendar.

Opera Australia

Opera Centre, 480 Elizabeth Street, between Devonshire & Belvoir Streets, Surry Hills (box office 9318 8200, tours 9318 8330, www.opera-australia.org.au). CityRail/LightRail Central. **Open** *Box office* 9am-5pm Mon-Fri. **Tours** 10am, 11am, 2pm Mon-Fri. **Tickets** *Shows* $55-$245. *Tours* $15 incl tea; 11am tour $35 incl lunch. **Credit** AmEx, MC, V. **Map** p329 F11.

Australia may be far from the great European opera houses, but the country's divas have been disproportionately represented in the ranks of global opera stars, among them Nellie Melba, Joan Hammond, the late Joan Sutherland, Elizabeth Whitehouse and Yvonne Kenny. And Opera Australia has the third-largest programme (after Covent Garden and the Vienna Staatsoper) of the world's opera companies. It performs in the Opera Theatre of the Sydney Opera House for seven months of the year; from April to May and November to December, it ups sticks to Melbourne.

Visitors can go behind the scenes at OA's fascinating headquarters in Surry Hills. Tours (which must be booked about two weeks ahead) take in the costume, millinery and wig-making departments.

Sydney Symphony

8215 4600, www.sydneysymphony.com.au.

Under the artistic directorship of Vladimir Ashkenazy since 2009, the Sydney Symphony continues to be the flagship of a network of Australian state capital city orchestras. Established in 1932 as a radio broadcasting orchestra, it has grown into the biggest and best in the country, attracting the finest soloists from Australia and abroad. The orchestra presents more than 140 events a year.

Other ensembles

Look out for the **Sydney Philharmonia Choirs** (9251 2024, www.sydneyphilharmonia.com.au), which has been going strong for nine decades and stages several big concerts each year of choral works famous and obscure. A capella outfit the **Song Company** (8272 9500, www.songcompany.com.au), Australia's premier vocal ensemble, perform early operas and oratorios. The **Sydney Chamber Choir** (1300 661 738, www.sydneychamberchoir.org) specialises in Renaissance music as well as works from contemporary Australian composers. Pianist Kathryn Selby is the artistic director of **Selby & Friends** (9969 7039, www.selbyandfriends.com.au) whose core ensemble is popular piano group **TrioZ**.

ROCK & POP

The genesis of Australian pub rock – and the scene that gave birth to every great Australian artist, from Johnny O'Keefe to Powderfinger –

was the rise of feminism. No, really. Most of the great Australian pubs were built in the early decades of the 20th century. These cornerstones of Australian life were built with a saloon bar or lounge area where women – too delicate to tolerate the rough'n'tumble atmosphere of the front bar – could enjoy a drink in private with their sensibilities un-offended. During the 1950s and early '60s, however, women were drifting into the front bar and pubs were starting to fill with teenagers who wanted to be entertained, and starting to wonder what to do with their increasingly superfluous saloon bars. It's unknown who was the first far-sighted publican to say 'eh, let's stick a band in there', but whoever they were, they started a cultural movement that's still going strong today.

The live scene has ebbed and flowed over the decades, and while Melbourne possibly has the greater claim on being Australia's premier music city, Sydney's been no slouch: while internationally it's probably best known for

spawning Johnny O'Keefe, the Easybeats, Rick Springfield, AC/DC, INXS and Midnight Oil (and Silverchair were born 150-odd kilometres north-east in Newcastle), it's had a rich and storied history as the home town of decades of stars: Col Joye, the Atlantics, Rose Tattoo, Icehouse, Divinyls, X , Noiseworks, Radio Birdman, The Reels, Air Supply, Human Nature, The Sunnyboys, Celibate Rifles, Natalie Imbruglia, the Whitlams, Youth Group, Sarah Blasko and, perhaps most excitingly, the Wiggles are all products of Sydney's fertile creative scene.

It's also been a place to try something new: Billy Thorpe became a star here after stints in Brisbane and Melbourne, the Hoodoo Gurus was formed by former members of Perth punks the Hitmen, while Ed Kuepper formed the Laughing Clowns here after quitting the Saints and moving from London. Bands like the Church and the Hummingbirds were quick to leave Canberra for the brighter lights of the bigger city. It's been an inspirational place for

Death to the POPE

Bringing back live music.

No, this isn't the outline of a *Da Vinci Code*-style thriller: it's the single biggest change to the live music scene in Sydney, and it's already having a major, positive impact. The Place of Public Entertainment (POPE) laws were taken off the books in New South Wales in 2009 thanks to a campaign led by local musician John Wardle. In broad terms, the change has removed many of the barriers that might have prevented a venue from staging live music. No longer must extra security be hired, fire exits added, or expensive, complicated applications for live music licenses made. Essentially, the law is this: will having live music completely alter the way your venue/restaurant/bar/pub does its business? No? Then off you go.

It sounds like a small thing, but it's had huge consequences. Bars and restaurants

are employing live performers, and legendary venues that had given up the ghost have returned (such as the **Town Hall Hotel** (826 King Street, Newtown, www.townhallhotel.com.au) and the **Newtown RSL** (52 Enmore Road, Newtown, 02 9557 5044 www.atnewtown.com.au). But what's changed the most – and what is likely to have a major effect on the music of Sydney in the coming years – is the return of jazz and singer/songwriters.

The rise in acoustic performance makes sense given that the new venues are generally too small for louder bands. The jazz resurgence is a bit more of a surprise, and tied in with the 'small bar revolution'. Sydney's campaign for more small bars in laneways and sidestreets was modelled on Melbourne's experience, with one interesting difference: because the timing coincided broadly with the changes to the POPE laws, live music became part of the small bar scene. **Low** (302 Crown Street Darlinghurst, www.low302.com.au) in Surry Hills was an early adopter of live jazz, while **505** (*see p257*) went the other way and used the small bar momentum to make the leap from illegal live room to legit venue/bar/restaurant. It might be early days, but the Australian jazz revolution seems to be around the corner – and coming from Sydney.

505.

songwriters too: James Reyne wrote Australian Crawl's masterpiece 'Reckless' after gazing over Sydney Harbour, and many of Paul Kelly's best-loved songs have been inspired by his time in Sydney, though not always entirely affectionately ('From St Kilda to Kings Cross', 'Randwick Bells', 'Darling It Hurts'). Adelaide immigrants Cold Chisel decamped to Sydney and ended up celebrating it in song (most notably on 'Breakfast at Sweethearts', named after a Kings Cross café), and Tim Rogers found poetry under the Glebe Point Bridge in You Am I's 'Purple Sneakers'.

The rise of poker machines in the 1990s, accompanied by increasingly-restrictive licensing laws, threatened to spell the end of Sydney's rich musical heritage. However, the laws were changed in 2009, pokies began to vanish into back corners and a new crop of young artists emerged: Angus & Julia Stone, Art vs Science, Sparkadia, PVT and Cassette Kids are some of the most high-profile products of the Sydney scene, while the Holidays and Cloud Control are from the surprisingly fertile environment of the nearby Blue Mountains. Of course, that couldn't have happened without the venues that kept the faith in the bleak times, and the new blood that took advantage of the changes – all of which you can read about in the following pages.

Sydney is also home to many music festivals. All of the big touring fests have a Sydney stop – **Big Day Out** (www.bigdayout.com), **Good Vibrations** (www.gvf.com.au), **Future Music Festival** (www.futuremusicfestival.com.au), **St Jerome's Laneway Festival** (www.lanewayfestival.com.au), **Soundwave** www.soundwavefestival.com) and **Parklife** (www.parklife.com.au) all make stops in the big city – and there are some traditional Sydney-only events, such as the annual **Homebake** (www.homebake.com.au) all-Australasian concert in the Domain in November, Bondi Beach's New Years Day celebration **Field Day** (www.fuzzy.com.au), and the artist-curated **Vivid Festival** (www.vivid.sydney.com) at the Opera House. The annual **Sydney Festival** (*see p219*) traditionally has a strong musical component, and if you fancy travelling out of Sydney to camp out for a few days of music there's the **Peats Ridge Festival** (www.peatsridgefestival.com.au) over New Years and the **Playground Weekender** (www.playgroundweekender.com.au) around February at Wisemans Ferry.

As the nation's largest city it's to be expected that Sydney would have a major influence on the development of the Australian music scene – and it has always been the centre of the Australian music industry, with every major label's head office and most of the larger indie

labels and booking agencies based here, including the recording industry's peak body, ARIA (who also hold the annual music awards).

Radio is also vital to the lifeblood of Sydney's local scene. The national youth broadcaster **Triple J** (105.7) is based in Sydney, but the key stations to listen to for what's going on at ground level are the excellent community stations **FBi** (94.5 FM) and **2SER** (107.3 FM), both of which are staffed by enthusiastic volunteers.

Major venues

Sydney's generally the most important stop for any international touring act. Many tours will be 'east coast only' (Sydney, Melbourne, Brisbane), plugging the gap between the New Zealand visit and the Japanese leg of the world tour. These are the venues those big acts play: the stadiums, the big theatres, the largest clubs. Tickets generally sell quickly in the first day, but then tail off so it's always worth checking, even if you're sure such-and-such would be a sell-out. And remember: you'll need ID to drink, so bring your passport to the bar.

Acer Arena

Olympic Boulevard, at Edwin Flack Avenue, Sydney Olympic Park, Homebush Bay (08765 4321, www.acerarena.com.au). CityRail Olympic Park/RiverCat Homebush Bay then bus 401. **Tickets** vary. **Credit** AmEx, DC, MC, V.
Built for the 2000 Olympics, the Acer Arena (previously called the Sydney SuperDome) boasts a whopping 21,000-seat capacity. It's where the biggest shows play, and extra services from Lidcombe to the Olympic Park are generally put on when events are taking place. While the venue houses everything from monster truck and extreme sports showcases to motivational speaker appearances, it's mainly used for gigs by arena-filling international acts, although it's also held many significant moments in Australian music including Powderfinger's final Sydney show.

Big Top

Luna Park, Milsons Point (9033 7600, www.bigtopsydney.com). CityRail/ferry Milsons Point. **Tickets** vary. **Credit** AmEx, MC, V.
Sitting in the middle of Luna Park is what amounts to a mighty shed called the Big Top. That might sound like a negative description, but it's actually the venue's great strength since it means that the venue can accommodate everything from festival shows to metal bands and big indies: Pixies played their first Sydney show there, while the likes of Nine Inch Nails and My Chemical Romance also graced its stage. It's been regularly used as a venue since 2004 and has the undeniable advantage of being one of the few venues adjacent to a rollercoaster.

ARTS & ENTERTAINMENT

★ Enmore Theatre

118-132 Enmore Road, between Simmons
& Reiby Streets, Newtown (9550 3666,
www.enmoretheatre.com.au). CityRail Newtown.
Tickets vary. **Credit** AmEx, MC, V. **Map** p334.
It's possibly Sydney's best known venue, not to say
the most loved. The art deco theatre was built in
1908 and has operated as a venue continuously since
its 1920 remodelling (and is listed in the Heritage
Buildings Register, which is remarkable for an
active venue). The 1,600-seat theatre plays host to
large national and international bands and stand-up
acts, as a glance at the poster-covered walls of the
street-level snug bar will demonstrate.

Factory Theatre

105 Victoria Road, Enmore (9550 3666, www.
factorytheatre.com.au). CityRail Newtown then
bus 423, 426. **Tickets** vary. **Credit** MC, V.
Since opening in December 2006, this custom-built
venue has fired up the scene with shows by local and
international musicians, plus dance, cabaret and film
events. Since 2009, it's been the hub of the annual
Sydney Comedy Festival, a role its also has for the
Sydney Fringe Festival thanks to its large main
room, good-sized courtyard/bar area and rabbit warren of small-to-medium sized spaces

★ The Forum

207/122 Lang Road, Moore Park (8117 6700,
www.forumsydney.com.au). Bus 339, 373, 374,
376, 377, 393, 395, 396. **Tickets** vary. **Credit**
AmEx, MC, V.
It's the Hordern's little brother, sitting across the road
from it in the Entertainment Quarter, but the great
sound system, sunken dancefloor and three tiers of
viewing (with bars on each) makes it a great band
venue, as well as a very popular venue for touring
DJs and club nights. The gents at the Forum also
boasts arguably the best urinal in any Sydney venue,
with a gentle waterfall running down the wall.

Gaelic Club

64 Devonshire Street, between Chalmers &
Elizabeth Streets, Surry Hills (9211 1687,
www.thegaelicclub.com). CityRail/LightRail
Central. **Tickets** $20-$80. **Credit** AmEx, MC, V.
The Gaelic's long been a bit of a funny one: despite
having one of the better live rooms in Sydney and
being a key venue in the 1990s, it was woefully
underused for much of the following decade.
However it appears to have gotten its mojo back
with a healthy roster of big local and touring acts –
and if the balcony's open, grab a drink and head up
there: the sightlines are astonishing.

Hordern Pavilion

Driver Avenue, Moore Park (9921 5333,
www.playbillvenues.com.au). Bus 339, 373, 374,
376, 377, 393, 395, 396. **Tickets** vary. **Credit**
AmEx, DC, MC, V. **Map** p332 J12.
Despite looking like an airline hanger with raked
seating, the Hordern has surprisingly good sightlines and sound. It's where many big acts play, and
lots of dance events take place here too, as many of
the more DJ-oriented festivals base themselves
around Moore Park with the Hordern as their headline centrepiece. If an act's in the upper echelons of
a festival's line up, chances are they'll be doing their
headline sideshow here.

★ The Metro

624 George Street, at Central Street, CBD (9550
3666, www.metrotheatre.com.au). CityRail Town
Hall/Monorail World Square. **Box office** 9am-
6pm Mon-Fri; 10am-4pm Sat. **Tickets** $20-$150.
Credit MC, V. **Map** p329 E7.
Technically, it's been the Virgin Mobile Metro since
a sponsorship deal was struck in 2008, but the
changes to the venue have been few and superficial
at press time: it's still the key venue of the CBD, it's
where damn near everyone has (or will) play, it
boasts one of the city's best live rooms in terms of
sightlines, sound quality and atmosphere (with bars
at the back and sides, very conveniently) and a small
sub-venue (the Lair) for smaller events.

State Theatre

49 Market Street, between Pitt & George Streets,
CBD (9373 6852, www.statetheatre.com.au).
CityRail St James or Town Hall/Monorail City
Centre. **Tickets** $40-$250. **Credit** AmEx, MC, V.
Map p327 F6.
State Theatre performers tend to the more heritage
end of the spectrum – performers that suit a seated
audience paying rapt attention rather than a boozy
general admission crowd. It's also a gorgeous building, mixing rococo and art deco with playful abandon, and is more often used for recitals and theatrical
performances than gigs – but there are still plenty
of music and comedy acts who get to perform on that
gorgeous stage each year.

Sydney Entertainment Centre

35 Harbour Street, between Hay & Pier Streets,
Darling Harbour (9320 4200, www.sydentcent.
com.au). CityRail Central or Town Hall/Monorail/
LightRail Paddy's Markets. **Tickets** vary.
Credit AmEx, DC, MC, V. **Map** p329 E8.
The 12,500 capacity EntCent has had its share of
controversy since opening its doors in 1983, primarily due to its location in the much-sought-after
Haymarket area between Chinatown and Darling
Harbour, where the Sydney City Council would like
to put something more lucrative: a shopping complex, say, or a conference centre. One day the venue
will lose the fight, but for the time being it's home
to the acts whose acts clash with Acer Arena: big
ticket names, often playing multiple shows (Pink's
multi-show 2008 stand seemed set to turn into a residency). It's not the most charming of venues, but it
does get the job done.

Enmore Theatre.

★ Sydney Opera House

For listings *see p250*.

Once upon a time the Opera House was home only to the highbrow, but now the only Sydney venue that can genuinely be called 'iconic' plays host to a wide range of performers in all of its venues. The Concert Hall is still home to the class acts (although its also where many of the performers for the Vivid festival perform, meaning that the unexpected likes of Battles, Melt Banana and Ladytron have played that stage), while the Opera Theatre is still mainly for orchestral, theatrical and operatic seasons. Down a level and the Studio has become home for everything from rock to cabaret, and the Drama Theatre is increasingly popular as a venue for comedy. *See also p250, p257* and *p36* **Profile**.

Pubs & clubs

Sydney's pub scene took a major hit in the '90s when band rooms were gutted to make room for pokies, but things have been on the up since the restrictive Place of Public Entertainment (POPE) laws were scrapped in 2008 (*see p252* **Death to the POPE**). Many of these venues are the ones that weathered the hard times, but new spaces have opened in recent times and more pubs are adding live music to their entertainment mix – so here's hoping that Sydney's about to recapture her '80s reputation as a live music town, not to mention developing the next wave of great Australian talent. All of these venues are licensed, so you'll need to be over 18 and have photo ID for entry unless the performance specifies that it's All Ages. Keep your passport with you.

★ Annandale Hotel

Corner of Parramatta Road & Nelson Street, Annandale (9550 1078, www.annandalehotel. com.au). Bus 413, 435, 436, 437, 438, 440, 461, 483. **Open** 11am-10pm Mon, Tue, Sun; 11am-midnight Wed-Sat. **Tickets** $10-$30. **Credit** MC, V.

It's down to the tireless work of publican brothers Dan and Matt Rule that the Annandale soldiers on, one of the few sticky carpet venues left. The music-loving siblings kept the live music flag flying when it would have been so much easier to make the place a bistro (though it actually has a decent Thai bistro out the back). Big locals, medium-sized nationals and smaller internationals play most nights, and with a bar along the wall and a grunt-heavy sound system, there are few better venues around.

The Basement

29 Reiby Place, off Pitt Street, Circular Quay (9251 2797, www.thebasement.com.au). CityRail/ferry Circular Quay. **Open** 7.30pm-1am daily. **Tickets** $15-$100. **Credit** AmEx, MC, V.

It's most often cited as a jazz and blues venue, but the Basement is a favourite stop for any act that wants to play to an audience that actually listens – making it a favourite with acoustic performers. With tables (and table service) on the sunken floor and decent sightlines around the bar, it can get pretty crowded in the below-ground venue, and once that room's full it doesn't take long to become pretty darn hot and humid. Still, it all adds to the ambience.

Lansdowne Hotel

2-6 City Road, at Broadway, Chippendale (9211 2325, www.myspace.com/lansdownehotel). Bus 370, 422, 423, 426, 428. **Open** 10am-midnight, Mon-Wed, Sun; 10am-2am Thur-Sat. **Tickets** free. **Credit** AmEx, MC, V. **Map** p328 C10.

The Lando is a throwback to the times when Sunday meant seeing live music in Sydney. Bands tend to be locals and the odd interstate visitor hawking their debut CD, but the atmosphere's great, the bistro upstairs is cheap 'n' cheerful, and entry is always completely free. That's reason enough to get along.

Notes Live

75 Enmore Road, Newtown (9557 5111, notes live.net.au). CityRail Newtown. **Open** 6pm-midnight Tue-Sun. **Tickets** $10-$60. **Credit** MC, V. **Map** p334.

In a former function centre on Enmore Road is one of Sydney's newer venues, with an in-house restaurant and strong commitment to artists of a more grown-up flavour. While bands certainly play the 300 capacity room, many of the nights are given over to established singer-songwriters – performers like Ian Moss, Diesel and Deborah Conway have filled the place, while former Tea Party mainman Jeff Martin damn near calls it home. To some extent, it's picked up the mantle of the Vanguard since its transformation to a more theatrical venue.

★ Oxford Art Factory

38-46 Oxford Street, Darlinghurst (9332 3711, www.oxfordartfactory.com). Bus 311, 371, 373, 377, 378, 380, 392, 394, 396, 397, 399, 890, X39. **Tickets** $5-$70. **Map** p329 G8.

The Oxford Street venue seemed a pretty risky proposition in a strip better known for nightclubs than venues, but it's proved itself with a steady mix of cult internationals, big locals, CD launches, label nights, art exhibitions and more, with hopes to expand its slate of events even further in future. It also looks great, with its brushed concrete industrial look making a sly nod to legendary Manchester nightclub the Haçienda (owned by Factory records – geddit?). They also do a great line in house cocktails, which are well worth your attention.

★ Red Rattler

6 Faversham Street, Marrickville (02 9655 1044, www.redrattler.org). CityRail Newtown then bus 423, 426. **Tickets** $5-$40. **No credit cards.**

Marrickville's industrial past has made for a number of short-lived (and technically illegal) venues in empty warehouse spaces – the Pitz and Quirkz had short, colourful lives in the suburb's backstreets – but the Rattler is totally legit, run by a collective of queer artists as a venue and art space. With a 200 capacity room filled with overstuffed couches and mismatched furniture (and a bar that serves it's own 'Rat's Piss' microbrew) the place gives off the vibe of the coolest share house you ever wished you could live in, with the added bonus of great Australian (and, increasingly, international) bands, solo performers, cabaret and drama.

Sandringham Hotel

387 King Street, between Holt & Goddard Streets, Newtown (9557 1254, www.sando.com. au). CityRail Newtown. **Open** 10am-midnight Mon-Wed, Sun; 10am-1am Thur-Sat. **Tickets** $5-$25. **No credit cards. Map** p334.

The Sando's a Newtown institution and one of the few venues in the neighbourhood that kept the faith when pokies and draconian licensing laws were killing the live scene. The upstairs live room (refurbished in 2009) is home to the bands and the front bar is home to blues jams and acoustic acts most nights of the week. And the meals are pretty decent too, as is the beer garden out the back.

Spectrum

Exchange Hotel, 34-44 Oxford Street, between Riley & Liverpool Streets, Darlinghurst (9331 1936, www.pashpresents.com). Bus 311, 371, 373, 377, 378, 380, 392, 394, 396, 397, 399, 890, X39. **Open** 8pm-2am Wed-Sat. **Tickets** $5-$30. **Credit** AmEx, MC, V. **Map** p329 G8.

The Exchange Hotel has many rooms – 34B, Vegas, Q Bar – but Spectrum is its main live venue. It's got a reputation as the indiest of indie rooms, where the next generation of up-and-comers (and, to be fair, down-and-goners) join multi-band bills in a room with a good stage, a decent PA, and genuinely terrifying toilets. It's also a nightclub with a regularly-rotating range of club nights, mainly when the bands finish around 11pm.

Supper Club

Lvl 1, 134 Oxford Street, Darlinghurst (9331 3467, www.poloandsupper.com.au). Bus 311, 371, 373, 377, 378, 380, 392, 394, 396, 397, 399, 890, X39. **Open** 7pm-late Wed-Sun. **Tickets** $5-$50. **Credit** AmEx, MC, V. **Map** p329 H8.

The 220-capacity Supper Club lends itself to a variety of uses, from cabaret to burlesque, but it's a big favourite with bands who want to enjoy an intimate atmosphere while packing 'em in. A sunken dancefloor lets the punters get up close and personal while allowing those at the bar to see what's going on – and the glitzy decor gives it a certain panache in comparison with the sticky carpet live venues.

The Vanguard

42 King Street, between Queen & Fitzroy Streets, Newtown (9557 7992, www.thevanguard.com. au). Bus 352, 370, 422, 423, 426, 428. **Tickets** $10-$70. **Credit** MC, V. **Map** p334.

It's a beautiful venue – think 1920s bordello and you're on the right track – which explains why the Vanguard has been moving away from its once regular fare of acoustic acts and blues performers and gravitating towards an entertainment mix that includes more cabaret and burlesque. There's still plenty of music though, and the meal deals are well worth examining.

JAZZ

Until recently, jazz fans in Sydney found themselves becalmed in a cult music backwater with only a handful of dedicated venues and individuals keeping the faith and the genre accommodated largely as a sideline in multipurpose venues. However, it has now moved further into the mainstream. More and more of today's music stars are coming not from sweaty pub stages but universities: rising chart stars Kate Miller-Heidke and Megan Washington are alumni from Brisbane's Conservatorium of Music, for example. The relaxing of the restrictions around live music has coincided with an explosion in the number of small bars and venues that don't work for rock but perfect for something a bit more subtle.

Sydney is also home to an increasing number of multi-day jazz festivals. The **Darling Harbour Jazz & Blues Festival** (www. darlingharbour.com) normally takes place over the Queen's Birthday long weekend in June, the **Manly Jazz Festival** (www.manly.nsw.gov. au) happens in early October over the Labor Day long weekend, and the **Newtown Jazz Festival** (www.thevanguard.com.au) in 2010 has events in January and July.

There are two key organisations without which the Sydney scene would have withered and died. **Jazzgroove** (www.jazzgroove.com) has long been instrumental in keeping Sydney's jazz community furnished with gigs and the **Sydney Improvised Music Association**, aka SIMA (www.sima.org.au) is dedicated to providing an environment that encourages experimentation and musical exploration.

Hotel bars and suburban pubs provide background jazz, and Mascot Airport Terminal now plays host to the Montreux Jazz Café if you need a fix pre- or post-flight, but if you're in Sydney and want to get your jazz on these five venues should be your highest priorities.

★ 505
Corner of Cleveland Street & Perry Street, Surry Hills www.venue505.com). CityRail/ LightRail Central. **Open** 7.30pm-midnight Mon-Sat. **Tickets** $10-$15. **No credit cards**.
There were stories about this room somewhere in Surry Hills where, on a Monday night, you bought a bottle from the nearby takeaway, ascended a signless stairwell and watched live jazz. Of course, sooner or later word would get around (though it took five years to happen, which speaks volumes for the quality of the neighbours) – but unlike most illegal venue owners the team behind 505 decided to go straight, moving the venue and opening it as a bar and restaurant with live jazz, blues, world and roots music six nights a week. Aside from their own aesthetic they've provided a home to fellow travellers like the Jazzgroove Association, who run the Tuesday night programme.

The Basement
29 Reiby Place, off Pitt Street, Circular Quay (9251 2797, www.thebasement.com.au). CityRail/ferry Circular Quay. **Tickets** $15-$100. **Credit** AmEx, MC, V. **Map** p327 F4.
Sure, plenty of acts play the Basement – but, as the below-street-level vibe and walls covered in posters and photos of the likes of Miles Davis make clear, at its heart the Basement is all about jazz. Many acts choose to record their live DVD or album here, not least because the sound system's well-tuned, the sightlines are good (with a sunken dancefloor/dining area and bars to the back and side) and because it attracts the sort of audience who like to listen to good music. You won't need your jacket, though: it gets pretty warm, especially in summer.

★ Sound Lounge
Cnr City Road & Cleveland Street, Chippendale (9351 7940, www.sima.org.au). Bus 370, 422, 423, 426, 428. **Tickets** $10-$30. **Credit** AmEx, MC, V. **Map** p328 C11.
The influence of SIMA on the development of Sydney's scene cannot be understated: as a breeding ground for new artists and as a meeting place for national and international performers, the Sydney Improvised Music Association has both nurtured the existing scene while remaining dedicated to expanding the brief. Its home venue, the Sound Lounge in the Seymour Centre, is one of the most acoustically superb rooms in Sydney and is a frequent home for Sydney's jazz elite: Tina Harrod, Mike Nock and the Catholics are some of the regular performers you'll find there.

Sydney Opera House
For listings, *see p250.*
Sydney's centre of culture has always been dedicated to jazz. It's where the big names play, and the Concert Hall stage is one of the best-sounding on the planet. It sounds even better now, actually, with the arrival of an exquisite new Steinway piano. There are also regular jazz and funk performers playing for drinkers and diners at the Opera Bar, which may not have quite the acoustics of the Concert Hall, but wins hands down for the Sydney Harbour view. *See also p250, p255* and *p36* **Profile**.

The Vanguard
42 King Street, between Queen & Fitzroy Streets, Newtown (9557 7992, www.thevanguard. com.au). Bus 352, 370, 422, 423, 426, 428. **Tickets** $10-$70. **Credit** MC, V.
The Vanguard's long been a welcome home for jazz, as well as blues, with a solid line up of touring acts and local favourites. Like the Basement, it's a favourite for those who like to enjoy an entire evening out with a meal and some good quality bottles, although it also has a more experimental side with cabaret-jazz-burlesque nights becoming increasingly popular.

ARTS & ENTERTAINMENT

Sport & Fitness

Sweating in a field or spectating from afar, Sydney is built for action.

Sport is part of Sydney's soul – since convict days, the city has been geared to getting ahead of the next guy. Sweat is currency in Sydney and it has the champions to prove it. With such an abundance of open space, it's easy for the visitor to get active and embrace adrenaline as part of their daily menu. And if you don't like sport, the safest thing to do is to fake it. Australians respect anyone who 'has a go'. Skill is secondary to spirit for Sydneysiders, and win, lose or draw, it won't be long before even the least sporty visitor is won over by their enthusiasm and the the variety of action on offer.

ACTIVE SPORTS

Canoeing & kayaking

Sydney's most spectacular sports arenas are its waterways and there's no fresher, flexible or more original way to take in the city's jewel than from water level. For as little as $20 an hour you can hire a canoe from **Sydney Harbour Kayaks** (9960 4389, www.sydney harbourkayaks.com) in Mosman. At weekends, the company runs four-hour guided eco tours of Middle Harbour ($99 per person).

Down south, **Bundeena Kayaks** (9544 5294, www.bundeenakayaks.com.au) offers a superb kayaking experience around the coves, coasts and old pirate grottoes of Sydney's Royal National Park. If you feel up to braving the choppier waters of the Pacific, head north to **C-Kayak Australia** (4324 2867, www.kayaktours.com.au), which is based an hour out of Sydney in West Gosford.

For an overview of paddling opportunities in the state's lakes, rivers and ocean waters, contact **New South Wales Canoeing** (8116 9730, www.nswcanoe.org.au).

Climbing

The areas surrounding the city, especially the Blue Mountains and Hunter Valley, provide plenty of natural resources for rock climbing, abseiling and canyoning. **Outward Bound Australia** (1800 267 999, www.outwardbound.org.au) is a good port of call for the novice, and the **Australian School of Mountaineering** (4782 2014, www.asmguides.com) caters for all

levels. The latter is based in the Blue Mountains, a wilderness of canyons, plateaus and sandstone cliffs, and visits the Snowy Mountains in winter for ice-climbing trips.

Experts might want to go and talk the talk in **Paddy Pallin** (8799 2430, 1800 805398, www.paddypallin.com.au), a gear shop in the CBD. The **Edge Adventure Centre** (Hudson Avenue, Castle Hill, 9899 8228, www.edge-adventure.com.au) is a good indoor centre, with climb heights up to 18.5 metres (61 feet). You'll also find climbing walls at **Climb Fit** (4/12 Frederick Street, St Leonards, 9436 4600, www.climbfit.com.au) and **City Crag** at the back of Mountain Designs (499 Kent Street, CBD, 9267 3822, www.mountaindesigns.com).

If you want to combine climbing with a range of other adventurous sports, **Bush Sports** (9630 2222, www.bushsports.com.au) tackles the lot, including climbing, abseiling, canyoning, rafting and caving, as well as survival programmes and treasure hunts.

Cycling

First things first: cycle helmets are compulsory in Sydney, and bottled water is a must. The good news, bikers, is the city is embracing cycling with gusto, with 200 kilometres (125 miles) of dedicated cycleways and bike paths rolling out all over town. A great starting point is the **City of Sydney website** (www.cityof sydney.nsw.gov.au/cycling), where lots of great urban bike trails and traffic tips can be found. Similarly, the recreational and commuter bike group **Bicycle NSW** (Level 5, 822 George Street, 9218 5400, www.bicyclensw.org.au) has sound advice for novices and veterans alike. Competitive cyclists can speak to **Cycling NSW** (9738 5850, www.nsw.cycling.org.au) for the best information on local clubs, rides and racing, while off-roaders should approach **BMX NSW** (6367 5277, www.bmxnsw.com.au) for the latest on BMX facilities, tracks and events.

If you're after social riding with a social conscience then hook up with your local BUG (Bicycle User Group) and kick carbon emissions to the curb. Like *Time Out* magazines around the world, *Time Out Sydney* has been a passionate advocate for the two-wheel revolution and its site features heaps of great social rides with café, restaurant and gallery stops along the way (www.timeout.com/sydney).

Fishing

If it involves water, Australians love it. But as befits modern times, it ain't as easy as simply 'wetting a line' any more. Sydney anglers now need a recreational fishing licence ($6 for three days, $12 for one month, $30 for one year, $75 for three years) and must keep the receipt on them for proof of payment. You can do this at fishing shops and clubs, by phoning 1300 369 365 or online at www.dpi.nsw.gov.au/fisheries.

Once the licence is sorted you'll find a few suggested fishing spots on the government website above, or call the helpline on 1300 550 474. Better yet, get chatting with the staff at your

kayak

INSIDE TRACK
FISHING FOREWARNED

Fishing might be Australia's most popular sport but it's also the most dangerous by far – 23 people were killed between July 2009 and July 2010, most male and the majority non-English speaking anglers who ignored signage and didn't wear safety gear. Check the tides, abide by signage, wear a life vest and never turn your back on the sea!

local angling shop, they may let you in on a sneaky secret – the guys at **Compleat Angler** in the CBD (3rd Floor, Dymocks Building, 428 George Street, 9241 2080, www.compleatangler. com.au) are among the most generous for local expertise and demonstrations.

For a dawn-to-midday session out in the harbour, try **Fishabout Tours** (9451 5420, www.fishnet.com.au/fishabout_tours), which runs tours of Sydney Harbour and Hawkesbury River. Prices range from $540 for one person to $195 each for four. Boat, licence, equipment, hot and cold snacks, and drinks are included.

At certain times in autumn and spring, big-game fishing is an option. A charter with Botany Bay-based sea dog Captain John Wright of **Game & Sport Fishing Charters** (0414 542548, www.gamefisher.com) offers a thrilling day fishing marlin, tuna, shark and other big ocean fish. Prices for up to six people range from $1,500 for game fishing and $1,200 for sport fishing. No licence is required.

Golf

Many of Sydney's plenitude of golf courses are private, but public courses near the CBD include the gorgeous **Moore Park Golf Course** (Cleveland Street, 9663 1064, www.mooreparkgolf.com.au). Green fees range from $45 to $50 for 18 holes. Club hire costs $40, lessons are around $60 per half-hour, and the course also has a three-level driving range where buckets of balls are cheap as chips.

Also central is the south-eastern suburbs' **Eastlake Golf Club** in Kingsford (Gardeners Road, 9663 1374, www.eastlakegolfclub. com.au), where it's $38-$42 for 18 holes, club hire is $28, and lessons $50 for half an hour. The **Bondi Golf Course** (5 Military Road North Bondi, 9130 3170, www.bondigolf.com. au) is set bang on the cliffs (and atop several Aboriginal rock engravings) and provides nine charming holes in a spectacular setting. For more courses contact the **NSW Golf Association** (9505 9105, www.nswga.com.au).

ARTS & ENTERTAINMENT

Gyms & sports centres

Blessed as it is with sun and space, Sydney is home to lots of gyms, sports centres and fitness outlets.

Whether it's working the weights, cruising in cardio or attacking a circuit, Sydney gyms have it all. The ubiquitous **Fitness First** (9762 1600, 1300 557 799, www.fitnessfirst.com.au) has among the cheapest facilities and branches all over the city. Membership (valid in any branch the world over) starts at $15 a week, while one-off visits cost $22.

Cook & Phillip Park

4 College Street, at William Street, CBD (9326 0444, www.cookandphillip.com.au). CityRail Museum or St James. **Open** 6am-10pm Mon-Fri; 7am-8pm Sat, Sun. **Admission** *All facilities* $16; $8.50 reductions. *Pool only* $6; $4.40 reductions. **Credit** AmEx, MC, V. **Map** p329 G7.

This well-equipped, centrally located aquatic and fitness centre has a 50m heated indoor swimming pool, a leisure pool with wave machine, hydrotherapy pools, basketball courts and a good gym, with physiotherapy also available. It hosts various classes and team sports; the aqua aerobics classes are especially popular.

► *For gyms popular with gay men and women, see p249.*

Ian Thorpe Aquatic Centre

458 Harris Street, Ultimo (9518 7220, www.itac.org.au). CityRail Central/LightRail Convention/Monorail Convention. **Open** 6am-9pm Mon-Fri (gym till 10pm); 6am-8pm Sat, Sun. **Admission** *All facilities* $16; $8.50 reductions. *Pool only* $6; $3.70-$4.40 reductions; $15 family. **Credit** AmEx, MC, V. **Map** p328 D8.

This $40 million facility, which opened at the end of 2007, provides the residents of Ultimo with a fantastic sports centre. There are three indoor pools (one Olympic-sized), lots of Aquatic Education services, a spin and fitness studio with classes galore, and steam, sauna and spa. There's even parking on site. Oh, and it's all housed in a fabulous Harry Seidler-designer white wave-form building

Hang-gliding, skydiving & paragliding

If you're hankering for an adrenalin rush, take to the skies with **Sydney Hang Gliding Centre** (4294 4294, www.hanggliding.com.au) where flights start at $220.

Beginners get the thrill of skydiving in tandem with an instructor at **Adrenalin Club** (1300 791 793, 8755 3100, www.adrenalin.com.au). It costs from $275-$325. **Sydney Skydiving Centre** (1800 805 997, 9791 9155, www.sydneyskydivers.com.au) also offers a pulse-racing accelerated free-fall (AFF) course. Prices start at $430, including gear hire, training and membership.

If jumping off a cliff with only a parachute and an instructor for company sounds like fun to you, **Sydney Paragliding Centre** (4294 9065, www.sydneyparagliding.com) offers tandem adventures from $195, about an hour out of the city.

Horse riding

Horseplay can be found in the old Sydney Showgrounds in Centennial Park. The **Centennial Parklands Equestrian Centre** (114-120 Lang Road, next to the Entertainment Quarter, 9332 2809, www.centennialstables.com.au) runs the site and offers lessons to novice or experienced riders of all ages. Prices start at $70, while simple rides in the park along the 3.6km (2.2 mile) bridleway cost $100 per hour.

Rollerblading (in-line skating)

You won't walk far along the promenades at Manly and Bondi beaches without seeing Rollerbladers. Centennial Park, with its flat roads and moderate traffic, also attracts more than its fair share of multi-wheeled pedestrians, and **Rollerblading Sydney** (0411 872 022 www.rollerbladingsydney.com.au) hires out blades plus safety gear for $25 an hour or $35 a weekend and arranges lessons ($55 adults, $45 children). Skates can also be hired from some surf shops at the beaches. Try **Skater HQ** at Manly (2/49 North Steyne, Manly, 9976 3833, www.skaterhq.com.au).

Sailing

Sailing, fishing, houseboats, charter boats, tall ships trips, function boat hire – you name it, if it's nautical, Sydney embraces it. But if the Manly ferry's too tame for your adventurous blood, the **Pacific Sailing School** (9326 2399, www.pacificsailingschool.com.au) in Rushcutters Bay is one of many schools in the Sydney Harbour, Middle Harbour and Port Hacking areas who can teach you the ropes (literally). **Eastsail** (9327 1166, www.eastsail.com.au), also based in Rushcutters Bay, makes available courses in crewing and sailing: courses cost $645 each, with discounts for group bookings. The nationwide company **Ausail** (1300 135 632, 9960 5451, www.ausail.com.au) also gives lessons, as well as luxury yacht charters.

For more information, including details of companies and locations, get in touch with **Yachting New South Wales** (8116 9800, www.nsw.yachting.org.au) or check out the

Australian Charter Guide Directory
(9818 8640, www.charterguide.com.au).

Scuba diving

The Great Barrier Reef may be a few thousand kilometres north, but the diving opportunities around Sydney are almost as magnificent with lots of reefs, coves and bays presenting a glorious array of marine life – including non-threatening sharks, wobbegongs, sting rays, blue gropers, and the native weedy seadragons – sponge gardens and shipwrecks.

One of the most experienced diving companies in Australia, **Pro Dive** (1800 820 820/9255 0300, www.prodive.com.au), has scuba centres throughout town. It organises day trips and scuba holidays, and its PADI Open Water Certification (which qualifies you to dive almost anywhere in the world) includes classroom theory, pool skills training and ocean dives, and costs $395 per person. The linked outfits **Dive Centre Manly** (10 Belgrave Street, 9977 4355, www.divesydney.com) and **Dive Centre Bondi** (192 Bondi Road, 9369 3855, www.dive bondi.com.au) also have a variety of courses for everyone, from beginners to advanced.

For other snorkelling opportunities at Sydney's beaches, *see p117.*

Surfing

Surfing is as integral to Sydney life as slaking your thirst with a cool drink after taking a dip in the Big Blue. **Manly**, **Dee Why** and **Freshwater** have good waves for beginners, while **Bondi**, **Bronte**, **Cronulla** and any of the northern beaches tend to attract the more confident wave-riders. Most beaches have a surf

---

INSIDE TRACK TOP SPORTS

Although football (aka 'soccer') has enjoyed a big resurgence since Australia's brave showings at the 2006 and 2010 World Cups and the establishment of the national A League competition in 2005-06, 'footy' here generally refers to Sydney's real game of choice, rugby league. Rugby union still commands big crowds in the Super 15 and Test arena but it has nowhere near the grassroots popularity of league. In fact, the code's only real rival for the city's affection is Australian Rules Football, the national sport, which soared locally when the Sydney Swans won the 2005 premiership. Aussie rules is set to spike further when the Greater Western Sydney team debuts in 2016

---

lifesaving club to help you stay out of trouble and you can hire surfboards and body boards for around $15 an hour.

If you've never stood up on a board before, consider having lessons. Matt Grainger at **Manly Surf School** (9977 6977, www.manly surfschool.com) has 25 years' experience and charges adults $60 ($50 children) for a lesson or $130 for four-day kids' camps. **Let's Go Surfing** in Bondi (128 Ramsgate Avenue, 9365 1800, www.letsgosurfing.com.au), charges $175 for a 90-minute private lesson and hires boards for as little as $20 per hour. **Long Reef Surf** in Collaroy (1012 Pittwater Road, 9982 4829, www. longreefsailboards.com.au) gives lessons too.

For the latest information about surfing conditions, go to www.coastalwatch.com or www.realsurf.com.au.

Swimming

THE SEA
The ocean is part of Sydney's lifeblood and the city's fortunes ebb and flow on the tidal flows of its Big Blue. If you haven't taken a dip, you haven't tasted and felt the city. As iconic as the beaches themselves are the brave souls who protect them – professional surf lifeguards and the trained volunteers who make up the red-and-yellow capped lifesavers. Always swim between the red and yellow flags, follow the beach patrol's directions and signposting and raise your hand if you get into difficulty. Different sections of beaches are marked for swimming each day but try never to swim alone and avoid dips at dusk and dawn for fear of interludes with the 'men in grey suits' – aka sharks.

OCEAN/HARBOUR POOLS
If you fancy sea water without the hostility of waves, try one of Sydney's tidal swimming pools. North Bondi has two small paddling pools, while south Bondi has the lane-marked Icebergs pool, famous for the winter exploits of the Speedo-clad elderly men who have for years braved freezing waters on Sunday mornings. Wylie's Baths in Coogee is the best preserved of the seaside pools, and there are also women-only baths about 200 metres south of Wylie's. You'll also find pools at Collaroy, Bronte, Cronulla, Palm Beach and Dee Why beaches, all of which get jammed in the summer. Some harbour beaches, including Clontarf, Balmoral, Nielsen Park and Double Bay, have enclosed swimming areas.

PUBLIC POOLS
One of the many grand sporting venues that graced Sydney for the 2000 Olympics is the **Sydney International Aquatic Centre** (*see p263*), a fantastic facility with wonderful play

ARTS & ENTERTAINMENT

ARTS & ENTERTAINMENT

areas for kids, which is open to the public when there isn't a competition on.

In town, there are Olympic-sized pools at the **Ian Thorpe Aquatic Centre** (*see p260*) and **Cook & Phillip Park** (*see p260*). Two splendidly sited outdoor pools are the **North Sydney Olympic Pool** (*see p98*), beneath the northern end of the Harbour Bridge at Milsons Point, and the **Andrew (Boy) Charlton Pool** (*see p58*) by the Botanic Gardens. For more on the history of Boy Charlton Pool, *see p58* **Inside Track**. The **NSW Swimming Association** (9763 5833, www.nswswimming. com.au) has information about other pools throughout Sydney.

Tennis

Tennis has a great history in Australia, and while the fortunes of its tennis players have diminished since the glory years of the 1950s, '60s and '70s, you'll never be court short if you want a hit.

Sydney's public tennis courts are usually run by local councils and charge anything between $12 and $30 an hour. Ever keen to promote the sport, **Tennis NSW** (9763 7644, www.tennis. com.au) will happily advise on courts in your area. The website has a facility that allows you to search for a partner, coach, club or racquet hire.

Turning the Tide

Sydney's love for sport (and danger) is clear on its beaches.

With over a century's history patrolling Sydney's often beautiful and occasionally brutal coastline, **Surf Life Saving Australia** (SLSA) represents all that is great about Australia's volunteer culture. However, it's also come to show how the city has changed politically and socially. Until 1980, the clubs were a bastion of macho Anglo Saxon male dominance, teeming with square-shouldered, barrel-chested, bronzed warrior embodiments of top-to-toe fitness launching themselves fearlessly into the waves, while the womenfolk sat on the beach clutching towels and dabbing themselves with bronzing olive oils.

But then a quiet revolution began. Women were permitted to take their place alongside men at all the 303 surf lifesaving clubs across the nation, training for their bronze medallion – a running, swimming, rescuing and resuscitation mini-marathon – to join today's 34,000-strong service of full and active SLSA beach patrollers. Today, women make up 41 per cent of the SLSA's 111,000-plus members, while Nippers Clubs (which train kids aged 5-14 to brave the waves safely) boast a 49 per cent female membership.

Nor is it just the male/female ratio that has shifted. Recognising the need for greater awareness in non-English speaking circles, SLSA clubs have actively recruited members from differing ethnic and cultural backgrounds, the goal being to produce a team of volunteers truly representing Australia's multicultural society.

Under the programme, 22 Lebanese, Palestinian, Syrian, Egyptian and Libyan men and women aged 14 to 40 signed up.

One Muslim girl, Mecca Laalaa from Cronulla, made international headlines by patrolling in a 'burquini'. This revolutionary piece of swimwear – created for the SLSA by a local fashion designer – was a two-piece lycra suit that covered all, with a natty hood for the hair. And just to prove the inclusion doesn't stop there, gay SLSA members are now regular marchers in Sydney's annual Gay & Lesbian Mardi Gras Parade.

Maybe it's unsurprising that in a country that's as obssessed with the beach as Australia, lifesaving should be a part of a lot of peoples' lives, but what is amazing is how much cash is saved by the authorities: $1.5 billion a year in wages from having SLSA volunteers dedicated to 'vigilance and service'. For information and events, contact **Surf Life Saving NSW** (9984 7188, www.surflifesaving.com.au). Want to serve Sydney? Join the SLSA!

Waterskiing

Wisemans Ferry Water Sports (River Road, Wisemans Ferry, 4566 4544, www.skischool.com.au) operates out of the NSW Water Ski Federation Ski Grounds, and is 75 minutes drive north of Sydney. Lessons cost $180 an hour, which includes coaching and the use of skis and wetsuits. There is also a ski gate charge of $5.50 per person per day to enter the ski grounds. If you want to make a night (or two) of it, accommodation is available in the ski grounds in cabins or camping at an extra cost.

Wakeboarding

Imagine skateboarding on the water and you're close to the rush that is wakeboarding. With lessons, you'll be carving and shredding your way through the water of Sydney in no time. **Black Diamond Wakeboarding School** (Koveda Holiday Park, River Road, Wisemans Ferry, 02 4566 4511, www.blackdiamondwakeboarding.com.au) will give you a taste with one-day lessons from $240 or a five-day course from $1,345. Experienced wakeboarders should head down to the Georges River in Southern Sydney for flat waters that are perfectly suited for an afternoon wake session.

SPECTATOR SPORTS

Venues

Since the 2000 Olympics, Homebush Bay has been Sydney's centre of gravity for top-level spectator sport. **Sydney Olympic Park** (*see below*) comprises a cluster of venues for both national and local sporting events. **ANZ Stadium** (*see p262*), the focal point of the park, is its pride and joy, with a crowd capacity of 83,500 people.

The **Sydney Olympic Park Visitor Centre** (1 Showground Road, 9714 7888, www.sydneyolympicpark.com.au) has details of all the venues. Its website is a cyber shrine to sport in Sydney, well worth checking out.

TICKETS

Ticketek (13 2849, www.ticketek.com) is the main outlet for most sporting events in Sydney, including those held at any of the Olympic venues at Homebush Bay, but **Ticketmaster** (13 6100, www.ticketmaster.com.au) also sells tickets for many fixtures. Both charge booking fees. You can sometimes buy tickets at the venue on the day, often for cash only.

ANZ Stadium

Olympic Boulevard, Sydney Olympic Park, Homebush Bay (8765 2000, guided tours 8765 2300, www.anzstadium.com.au). CityRail Olympic Park/RiverCat Sydney Olympic Park then bus 401.

ANZ plays host to some of the world's greatest musical acts on tour and, every week of every year, the biggest sporting clashes in Sydney, with rugby league, Aussie rules, cricket and soccer all vying to ply their trade on Sydney's greatest sporting stage. To see ANZ during the annual State of Origin or Bledisloe Cup clashes is to see Sydney's love of sport writ large. The stadium really is a must for sports fans; for information on tours, *see p111* **Sydney Olympic Park**.

Sydney Cricket Ground (SCG) & Sydney Football Stadium (SFS)

Driver Avenue, Moore Park (1800 801 155, 9360 6601, tours 1300 724737, www.sydneycricketground.com.au). Bus 372, 373, 374. **Tours** 10am, 1pm Mon-Fri; 10am Sat. **Tickets** $25; $17 reductions; $65 family. Book ahead for a one-and-half hour tour.

The SCG, Sydney's most beloved sporting coliseum, has come a long way in its 135-year-plus history. The land that began as sand hills and swamplands – prime hunting and fishing territory for the Gadigal tribes has since borne witness to some of Australia's most amazing sporting feats not to mention performances from the Rolling Stones, Michael Jackson and Madonna.

Sydney International Aquatic Centre

Olympic Boulevard, Sydney Olympic Park, Homebush Bay (9752 3666, www.sydneyaquaticcentre.com.au). CityRail Olympic Park/RiverCat Sydney Olympic Park then bus 401. **Open** 5am-9pm Mon-Fri; 6am-8pm Sat, Sun. *Tours* on request only. **Admission** *Swim & spa* $6.40; $4.40-$5 reductions; $20 family. *Swim & gym* $13; $9.30 reductions. *Tours* $3 self-tour, phone for group guided tours. **Credit** MC, V.

Having hosted the pool events during the Olympics, the Centre is still home to high-quality international meets and inter-school competitions.

Sydney International Athletics Centre

Edwin Flack Avenue, Sydney Olympic Park, Homebush Bay (9752 3444, www.sydneyathleticcentre.com.au). CityRail Olympic Park/RiverCat Sydney Olympic Park then bus 401. **Open** Visits 3-8pm Mon-Fri; 8am-1pm Sat; 9am-1pm Sun.

Sydney Olympic Park Sports Centre

Olympic Boulevard, Sydney Olympic Park, Homebush Bay (9763 0111, www.sportscentre.com.au). CityRail Olympic Park/RiverCat Sydney Olympic Park then bus 401. **Open** visits 7.30am-10.30pm daily.

ARTS & ENTERTAINMENT

Pub Talk

Where to watch the game.

Although there's a vast array of natural sports amphitheatres inland and off-shore and a fleet of big stadiums dotted all over the city, Sydney's watering holes are where much of the real action happens; in fact, you'll struggle to find a pub in Sydney without a television screen. Before the game, after it, and as an alternative to being there, the bars, pubs and clubs of the city and its suburbs are soundtracked by the passionate banter of sports fans following cricket, football, golf, and all manner of racing, much of it segueing into mad gambling at the nearby TAB betting outlets.

In the CBD, the latest and greatest is **York 75** (Hotel CBD, Level 2, York 75 CBD, 8297 7020 www.york75.com) which offers a new breed of sports bar with leather booths, table service and 20 big screens.

Cheers Bar (561 George Street, 9261 8313, www.cheersbar.com.au) and **Jacksons on George** (176 George Street, 9247 2727, www.jacksonsongeorge.com.au) have more humble environs but no less liquid passion for sports fans, no matter the brand of footy on view. At Bondi Beach is expat favourite **Hotel Bondi** (178 Campbell Parade, 9310 3271, www.hotelbondi.com.au) while the **Dolphin Hotel** (412 Crown Street, 9331 4800, www.dolphinhotel.com.au) in Surry Hills is huge with Rugby Union fans. And for really homesick footy fans, there are a number of local supporters' clubs for British Premier League teams, including Arsenal's Ozarsenal (www.ozarsenal.com), the Manchester United Supporters Club of NSW (www.manutdnsw.com) and Ozspurs (www.ozspurs.com).

It hosted tae kwon do and table tennis during the 2000 Olympics and now is home to various indoor spectator sports including gymnastics, soccer, badminton, volleyball, hockey and martial arts. For more information and full details on events and activities, check out the website.

Sydney Olympic Park Tennis Centre

Rod Laver Drive, Sydney Olympic Park, Homebush Bay (9764 1999, www.sydneyolympicpark.com.au). CityRail Olympic Park/RiverCat Sydney Olympic Park then bus 401.
The Olympic Park Tennis Centre provides world-class tennis courts, for hire and competition. Home of the annual Medibank International (lead up event to the Australian Open), Sydney Olympic Park Tennis Centre gives enthusiastic amateurs the opportunity to play on high quality surfaces. Casual courts are available for hire at $22 per court, per hour (02 9024 7628, www.soptennis.com.au).

Athletics

Athletics has been quick out of the blocks, with its popularity growing since the 2000 Olympics. The **Sydney International Athletics Centre** (*see p263*) is home to various major events, including trials for Commonwealth and Olympic Games. Contact **Athletics Australia** (03 9820 3511, www.athletics.org.au) or, for competition within the state, **Athletics NSW** (9746 1122, www.nswathletics.org.au).

Aussie rules

Forget its sanctioned warfare image abroad – this hybrid of soccer, rugby and Gaelic football is a thrilling sport, involving great athleticism, strength and tactical prowess, and it's better appreciated at the game rather than on TV.

The sport was innvented in Melbourne around 1858. The local team, the **Sydney Swans** (9339 9123, www.sydneyswans.com.au), were founded in 1982 and were starved of success (but not controversy) until 2005, when the Swans (aka 'the Bloods' for their red-and-white uniforms) won the AFL premiership flag in spectacular fashion. The unconverted quickly turned fanatical, and today, the Swans regularly sells out the 42,000-seat Sydney Cricket Ground with their family-based fan base. Big games are at the huge ANZ stadium (*see p262*). The season runs February to September.

Baseball

Baseball has a small but stoical scene in Sydney, with most areas having a team in the state's 'Major League'. The season runs September to February, with games on Wednesday and Thursday evenings and Sunday afternoons. Women's games are on Friday nights, and there is also a beginners' league and under-18s competition. **NSW Baseball League** (9675 6872, www.nsw.baseball.com.au) has details, or for more general information about the sport in Australia, visit www.baseball.com.au.

Basketball

Basketball has fought for a foothold in the crowded Sydney sport scene, but the fiscal dilemmas of its teams, the Sydney Kings and (now-defunct) Western Sydney Razorbacks, have stymied its progress in the Harbour City. Nonetheless, the **National Basketball League** (www.nbl.com.au) is an exciting mix of hot young Australian talent, and ex-NBA stars. Despite a rocky few years the **Sydney Kings** (9281 1777, www.sydneykings.com.au) are now back, and ready to reclaim their crown as the NBL's top team. The Kings play at the Sydney Entertainment Centre (*see p254*), and the season runs September to February, with tickets starting at around $10. For more information about the sport, contact the **NSW Basketball Association** (8765 8555, www.nswbasketball.net.au).

Cricket

Australian cricket has been hit for six lately, the once-indomitable team of the '90s slipping down the world rankings since 2005. England even regained the Ashes in 2009. The England tour to Australia in late 2010 is keenly anticipated, with two evenly matched teams fighting it out on Australian soil, where the home side remains formidable. The performance of the baggy greens will set the tone for Australian cricket in the next decade.

During the summer months, cricket enjoys a stranglehold on the sporting calendar, for spectators and participants. If there's an international match on, a trip to the famous **Sydney Cricket Ground** (*see p263*) is a must. Matches involving Australia at the SCG are viewed – both live and on Channel Nine – with an almost religious obsession, and the highlight of the cricketing calendar is the Sydney Test, played over five days against a touring side in the first week of January. A handful of one-dayers follow, most at the SCG under lights, but the quicker form of cricket is also slated for the larger ANZ Stadium in the near future. As it has around the world, T20 (Twenty20) games, where the batting is big and the bowling is lethal, draws huge after-work crowds to suburban grounds and major stadiums alike. Getting tickets for the bigger matches can be difficult, but local games don't usually sell out. For information on matches, phone the SCG or visit www.baggygreen.com.au.

Hardcore fans craving the thwack of leather on willow can always catch the **NSW Blues** season between October and March in the interstate Weetbix Sheffield Shield competition. The early March final, should NSW reach it, always takes place in Sydney. The Blues also play in the high energy KFC Twenty20 Big Bash at ANZ. Meanwhile, hundreds of fields around Sydney host cricket matches of all levels on summer Saturdays. **Cricket NSW** (9339 0999, www.cricketnsw.com.au) has information on fixtures and venues and welcomes amateurs keen for a game.

Golf

The jewel in the crown of Australian golf is the **Australian Open**, a prestigious tournament that takes place at The Lakes (www.thelakes golfclub.com.au) in Sydney during December. Many international stars jet in to try their hand at the purse on offer. Tee up some tickets at www.golfaustralia.org.au

Greyhound racing

Wentworth Park Greyhound Track
Wentworth Park Road, Glebe (9552 1799, www.wentworthparksport.com.au). LightRail Wentworth Park. **Open** 6-11pm Mon, Sat. **Admission** $6. **No credit cards**. **Map** p328 C8. Ten races each Saturday and Monday night starting at around 7.30pm.

Horse racing

There are race meetings in Sydney every Saturday as well as several midweek events. The **Australian Jockey Club** (9663 8400, www.ajc.org.au) runs meets at Royal Randwick, flanking Centennial Park at its southern edge, and in the southern suburbs at Warwick Farm. The **Sydney Turf Club** (9930 4000, www.theraces.com.au), meanwhile, organises programmes at Rosehill Gardens in Parramatta and in Canterbury Park to the south. Admission is $7-$12 ($4 reductions), $20-$30 for major races, with under-18s free. Evening racing is a regular

---

INSIDE TRACK
VICTOR TRUMPER

Over 93 years after he died, Victor Trumper's name lives on in the new Sydney Cricket Ground grandstand. Born in Surry Hills, 'Vic' once batted for six consecutive weeks in the schoolyard of Crown Street High without being dismissed. He hit the first century before lunch in a Test and the first triple century by an Aussie in England. But it was his generosity as a man that made him truly heroic. His premature death halted the nation and drew the largest funeral crowd in Sydney history.

INSIDE TRACK
SYDNEY CRICKET GROUND

As a cricket ground, the SCG hosted Don Bradman's world record 452 not out in 1930 and the very first one-day cricket match under lights in 1978. As a football field, it squeezed in 78,056 people for St George v South Sydney in 1965, and shook to the rafters in 1996 when Tony Lockett kicked the Sydney Swans into their first Grand Final in over six decades. In between it has hosted the Empire Games, A-League soccer and even Highland Dancing knees-ups. Today, it is the active home ground of the NSW Blues cricket team in summer and the Sydney Swans AFL squad through winter and, all year round, the spiritual home to Sydney rugby league and rugby union... and all Sydney sports lovers.

weekday fixture at Canterbury from October to March and makes a fantastic night out.

Major milestones on the Sydney racing calendar include the Australian Jockey Club's four-day carnival every Easter, which includes the down-under versions of Doncaster Day and Derby Day, and features $10 million in prize money. Other huge events are the Golden Slipper at Rosehill, usually held a week before Derby Day, and the Spring Carnival at Randwick.

If you're in town on the first Tuesday of November be prepared for Melbourne Cup fever. Famously titled 'the race that stops a nation,' the Melbourne Cup is a true spectacle of Australian sport and the richest horse race in the world. Duck into any Sydney pub, or squeeze into Randwick Racecourse to behold the punters in a frenzy. Many people take the afternoon off work, and there's a party atmosphere all over town.

Canterbury Park Racecourse *King Street, Canterbury (9930 4000). CityRail Canterbury then shuttle bus or bus 428.*
Rosehill Gardens Racecourse *Grand Avenue, Rosehill (9930 4000). CityRail Rosehill/RiverCat Parramatta then shuttle bus.*
Royal Randwick Racecourse *Alison Road, Randwick (9663 8400). Bus 372, 373, 374, 376, 377, 391, 392, 393, 394, 395, 396, 397, 399.*
Warwick Farm Racecourse *Hume Highway, Warwick Farm (9602 6199). CityRail Warwick Farm then shuttle bus.*

Rugby league

In Sydney, rugby league is the biggest of all the permutations of 'football'. Australia's domestic

league, run by the **National Rugby League** (9339 8500, www.nrl.com.au), starts in late-February and culminates in a four-week finals series at the **Sydney Football Stadium** (*see p263*) and **ANZ Stadium** (*see p262*) in October. Sydney's passion for Rugby League is unmatched, and the 2010 triumph of the long-suffering **St George Dragons** has given the state bragging rights. Adult tickets can cost over $100 for a prime seat, but average around $20.

Other big matches to look out for include the State of Origin series, where New South Wales takes on Queensland, and NRL players return to their home province for a 'state versus state, mate versus mate' derby which has to be seen to be believed. To find out about the international tours of the **Kangaroos**, Australia's national team, contact the **Australian Rugby League** (9232 7566, www.australianrugbyleague.com.au).

SYDNEY TEAMS
Bulldogs *9789 2922, www.bulldogs.com.au.*
Cronulla-Sutherland Sharks *9523 0222, www.sharks.com.au.*
Manly-Warringah Sea Eagles *9970 3000, www.mightyeagles.com.*
Parramatta Eels *8843 0300, www.parraeels.com.au.*
Penrith Panthers *4720 5555, http://penrith.panthers.com.au.*
St George Illawarra Dragons *9587 1966, www.dragons.com.au.*
South Sydney Rabbitohs *8306 9900, www.rabbitohs.com.au.*
Sydney Roosters *8063 3800, www.sydneyroosters.com.au.*
Wests Tigers *8741 3300, www.weststigers.com.au.*

Rugby union

The 'game they play in heaven' has long been viewed as the playground of the privileged. But in recent years, the once-amateur Union has enjoyed a surge, thanks to World Cup victories in 1991 and 1999 and the country's successful hosting of the Rugby World Cup itself in 2003.

The **Super 15** (www.superxv.com) competition pitches provincial teams from all across Australia, New Zealand and South Africa against each other. It runs from February to May, and involves a handful of home matches for the **NSW Waratahs** (www.waratahs.rugby.com.au) at the **Sydney Football Stadium** (*see p263*).

The national side, the **Wallabies**, play occasional test or tri-nation matches at the Sydney Football Stadium or ANZ Stadium (*see p262*). More information is available from the **Australian Rugby Union** (8005 5555, www.rugby.com.au).

Surfing

Competitive surfing is a serious business in Sydney, and coastal comps pack beaches state wide, ranging from local inter-club meetings to junior tournaments to professional events involving the world's best surfers. Whether you're looking to see Slater, Parkinson or Fanning shred, or after some up and comers, you'll find what you're looking for.

For more information contact the sport's governing body, **Surfing NSW** (6674 9888, www.surfingaustralia.com.au) for information on events and locations.

Swimming

Sydney is famously full of breathtaking places to have a dip, and swimming is also a massive spectator sport. Several World Cup swim meets take place in the city, and the **Sydney International Aquatic Centre** (*see p263*) in the Homebush Bay Olympic Park is the venue for most of the major local events.

A more alien spectacle to non-locals are the local beach swims, in which up to 500 local and international competitors embark on one- to three-kilometre swims in the ocean from different beaches around Sydney.

More details of all competitions are available from the **NSW Swimming Association** (9763 5833, www.nswswimming.com.au).

Tennis

The Medibank International (www.medibank international.com.au) tennis tournament is held at the **Sydney Olympic Park Tennis Centre** (*see p264*) in Homebush Bay. The Medibank International attracts top seeds looking to prepare for the Australian Open Series, and is the perfect opportunity to see world class tennis in Sydney. The tournament takes usually takes place during weeks two and three of January.

For upcoming tournaments being held in the city, contact **Tennis NSW** (1800 153040, www.tennisnsw.com.au).

Rusty's Rabbitohs

Rabbit-proof offensive.

It's quite the tale. First there's the name, the story of which is classic Sydney. Around the time of the club's foundation in 1908, South Sydney Rabbitoh's working-class players earned extra money before games by hawking rabbits around using the traditional cry of 'Rabbitoh!'. The blood and fur clung to the jerseys they wore in the big game later that afternoon and carried a grim aroma that rivals loathed.

Then there's the record: they've won more premierships than any other club in Australian rugby league... but just not for a long, long time. Yet that's all about to change, according to the Rabbitohs' Oscar-winning owner Russell Crowe.

Crowe bought the battling Bunnies in 2006. As a boy he'd snuck under the fence to watch his heroes play. As a child he made his acting debut on TV wearing their famous red and green jersey. And as a star on the rise in Hollywood he donated ever-bigger chunks of change to prop them up as they lurched from one disaster to another. But after 25 years watching his beloved Rabbitohs deliver their fans nothing but heartbreak, the Gladiator himself stepped in, took the reins and set about steering the 102-year-old club to what he hopes will be a new era of prosperity.

The changes that Crowe brought in at the club were as much social as sporting. He removed poker machines and sacked the team's cheergirls to win back families and women to the fanbase. The players decked out in Armani suits after Crowe inked a deal with Giorgio himself and, most importantly, he set about wooing high-profile star players to the club's roster, imposing a 'no dickheads' credo to recruitment. He was hands-on to the max, even drawing on his big screen braggadocio to fire up his charges before a game by reading them a fractured fable from a tome he commissioned called *The Book of Feuds*, detailing the historical ills done to the club by their opponents.

Five years in and South Sydney is yet to win that elusive premiership they've pined for since 1971. But they've improved immeasurably, on-field and off. Once the most impoverished of clubs – News Limited expelled them from the competition in 2000 but public rallies and prolonged court marshalling saw them returned in 2002 – as of 2010 the Rabbitohs' membership was the highest in the NRL. Today, the streets of Sydney are awash with cars proudly displaying bumper stickers bearing the white rabbit.

ARTS & ENTERTAINMENT

Theatre, Dance & Comedy

Sydney board-walkers are taking their theatre worldwide.

The megawatt star power of wife-and-husband team Cate Blanchett and Andrew Upton has turned the **Sydney Theatre Company** into a world-ranked player. The stars they've attracted, and the work they've commissioned, have even threatened to supplant sport as Sydney's number one spectator pursuit.

Dance in Sydney is also on the brink of a cultural revolution, with some offerings drawing on ancient traditions (**Bangarra**) and others firmly steeped in the here and now (**Force Majeure**). And, with fresh young artistic director Rafael Bonachela heading up the **Sydney Dance Company**, Sydney stages are seeing plenty of action.

But it's not all serious. Go to any comedy festival in the world and chances are that there'll be a horde of Australians in the line-up. Sydneysiders love to laugh, and the city's comics are the nation's best stand-ups.

INFORMATION AND TICKETS

For detailed information about what's happening on stages in Sydney, check the 'Performing Arts' section of *Time Out Sydney*'s monthly magazine or the *Spectrum* supplement in Saturday's *Sydney Morning Herald*.

In general, tickets bought directly from theatre box offices are cheapest and many theatres sell discounted tickets on certain nights. For some shows, you can use a booking agency such as **Ticketek** (13 2849, www.ticketek.com.au), **Ticketmaster** (13 6100, www.ticketmaster.com.au) or **MCA Ticketing** (1300 306776, www.mca-tix.com.au), though all charge booking fees.

THEATRE

Companies

Australian Theatre for Young People
9270 2400, www.atyp.com.au.
ATYP is primarily devoted to the nurturing and training of young people, staging mostly new and

contemporary work starring aspiring thesps. There may be a whiff of star-factory fantasy about it, but the company has extended its reputation for putting on worthwhile work for the young and young at heart. It's based within the arts precinct at Walsh Bay and performances take place in venues all over Sydney – many at Fort Street Primary School in the Rocks. Nicole Kidman is its patron and film director Baz Luhrmann its ambassador – both trod the boards with the company as children.

Bell Shakespeare Company
8298 9000, www.bellshakespeare.com.au.
In 1970, actor-director John Bell founded the Nimrod company, widely regarded as spearheading the Australian theatre revival of that decade in Sydney. Today, he devotes his energies to the Bell Shakespeare Company, whose unofficial motto is 'Shakespeare with an Australian accent'. The company, which celebrated its 20th anniversary in 2010, is known for its innovative, utterly comprehensible and intelligent remountings of the canon (not limited to Shakespeare), with Bell himself often directing or acting. Based in Sydney, with regular seasons at the Opera House, Bell productions also tour to regional Australia and other capital cities.

★ Belvoir

9698 3344, www.belvoir.com.au.

Belvoir, under the artistic leadership of designer Ralph Myers since 2010, specialises in bold readings of the classics and new Australian plays, with a strong history of exploring indigenous voices and the Aboriginal experience in contemporary Australia. Many of the country's best actors and directors have created their strongest work in collaboration with the company – think Geoffrey Rush, Cate Blanchett, Deborah Mailman and Richard Roxburgh. The company's home is the once shabby but now entirely respectable Belvoir Street Theatre (*see below*).

Ensemble Theatre Company

9929 8877, www.ensemble.com.au.

Founded in 1958 by American Hayes Gordon, the Ensemble is the oldest surviving professional theatre company in NSW. Sandra Bates is the artistic director, a role she's held for more than 20 years. The company manages without government funding, though it treads a fine line between cosseting and challenging the legion of loyal subscribers on whom it depends. Among its usual highlights is a combination of new plays and seasoned classics, and it has become the theatre of choice for new work from playwright David Williamson. It has its own theatre on the water in Kirribilli (*see p270*).

Griffin Theatre Company

9332 1052, www.griffintheatre.com.au.

One of the essential engines of Sydney's theatre scene, Griffin is the city's only company solely dedicated to nurturing, developing and performing new Australian work. Founded in 1978 and under the artistic direction of Sam Strong since 2010, this not-for-profit venture produces four to six shows a year at the Stables (*see p272*). It also tours its highly regarded Playwright's Residency programme. Hit films *Lantana* and *The Boys* started their lives as plays here.

New Theatre

9519 3403, http://newtheatre.org.au.

Established back in 1932 as a workers' theatre, the New – like Newtown, the once working-class inner-city suburb in which it resides – has changed a lot over the decades. Although it's still committed to political and socially enquiring work, the company has moved away from simplistic agit-prop and now has a wide remit ranging across classics, neglected Australian repertoire, contemporary European and American work, gay theatre and musicals performed on its stage in King Street (*see p270*). Technically amateur (the actors are all unpaid), the New is at its best when mounting large-cast classics that are no longer considered economically viable anywhere else.

★ Sydney Theatre Company (STC)

9250 1700, www.sydneytheatre.com.au.
See *p271* **The Reign of Cate and Andrew**.

Belvoir.

► *For news of Cate Blanchett's 'greening' of the STC's Wharf complex see p32* **Sydney Today**.

Urban Theatre Projects

9707 2111, www.urbantheatre.com.au.

Urban Theatre Projects' mission is to work with Sydney's diverse cultures to make challenging and relevant contemporary theatre. Based in western Sydney (Bankstown), its work is produced through collaboration between artists and local residents, with a focus on storytelling, geographical identity and multimedia. UTP can be found performing in warehouses, railway stations, schools, shopping centres, town squares, private homes and buses. Sometimes they even perform in theatres.

Venues

The plush, 1,200-seat **Theatre Royal** in the CBD (MLC Centre, King Street, 9224 8444) once hosted major productions on a regular basis, but, thanks to having Sydney's least capacious foyer and the perennial rumble from nearby undergound trains, it's only used sparingly. It does, however, see some brief action around Sydney Festival time. The **National Institute of Dramatic Art** (215 Anzac Parade, Kensington, 9697 7600, www.nida.edu.au), Australia's most eminent drama school – and the alma mater of Mel Gibson, Cate Blanchett and several thousand people you've never heard of – also puts on shows throughout the year, including more-than-satisfactory work from its graduating classes.

Belvoir Street Theatre

25 Belvoir Street, at Clisdell Street, Surry Hills (9699 3444, www.belvoir.com.au).

CityRail/LightRail Central. **Box office** 9.30am-6pm Mon, Tue; 9.30am-7.30pm Wed-Sat; 2.30-6pm Sun. **Tickets** *Upstairs* $57. *Downstairs* $24-$32. **Credit** AmEx, MC, V. **Map** p329 F11.
This one-time tomato sauce factory is now owned by Belvoir (*see p269*), a non-profit consortium of performers, actors, writers and their supporters. Belvoir stages productions in its intimate 350-seat Upstairs Theatre and its somewhat more intimate 80-seat Downstairs Theatre, attracting Sydney's most discerning and loyal theatregoers.

Capitol Theatre

13 Campbell Street, between Pitt & George Streets, Haymarket (ticketmaster1300 723 038, admin 9320 5000, www.capitoltheatre.com.au). CityRail Central/LightRail Capitol Square. **Box office** 9am-5pm Mon-Fri. **Tickets** $79-$180. Production prices vary. **Credit** AmEx, DC, MC, V. **Map** p329 E8.
Completed in 1893, the interior of the Capitol (originally known as the Hippodrome) was designed by an American theatre specialist to create the illusion of sitting outdoors under the stars. Like most illusions, it generally fails. Once reduced to being a too-big porn cinema and then nearly derelict for years, the Capitol was expensively and extensively restored just as the fashion for gargantuan musicals peaked. It's thoroughly kitsch, and the perfect venue for such long-running shows as *The Lion King*, *Billy Elliot* and *Wicked*.

Darlinghurst Theatre

19 Greenknowe Avenue, at Baroda Street, Elizabeth Bay (8356 9987, www.darlinghurst theatre.com). CityRail Kings Cross/bus 311. **Box office** 6pm on performance days. *Phone bookings* 9.30am-5.30pm Mon-Fri. **Tickets** $20-$37. **Credit** (phone bookings only) AmEx, MC, V. **Map** p330 J6.
The 111-seat Darlinghurst Theatre (not actually in Darlinghurst) is located on the edge of Kings Cross, and has comfortable, individually sponsored seats (with name-plates – which semi-famous actor will you sit on tonight?) and excellent sight lines. It's one of Sydney's best-value theatres, with Darlinghurst Theatre Company co-producing a variety of new work and updated classics in collaboration with a range of local and touring companies. At the time of writing, Darlinghurst Theatre Company is finalising plans to make a new home in the Burton Street Tabernacle (actually in Darlinghurst). They're due to set up shop there in September 2012.

Ensemble Theatre

78 McDougall Street, at Willoughby Street, Kirribilli (9929 0644, www.ensemble.com.au). CityRail Milsons Point/ferry Kirribilli. **Box office** 9.30am-4.30pm Mon; 9.30am-7.30pm Tue-Sat; 1.30-4.30pm Sun. **Tickets** $46-$62; from $22 reductions. **Credit** AmEx, DC, MC, V.

Hayes Gordon transformed an old boathouse into Sydney's first in-the-round space in the 1950s, but the theatre has since recovered from the fickle whims of offshore trendiness. The company (*see p269*) is now consistently commendable. Run by Sandra Bates since 1986, it has one of Sydney's most scenic foyers and a house style of producing honest, no-nonsense work.

Lyric Theatre

Star City Casino, 80 Pyrmont Street, between Jones Bay Road & Union Street, Pyrmont (9777 9000, bookings 1300 795267, www.starcity.com.au). LightRail Star City/ferry Darling Harbour/bus 443. **Box office** 9am-5pm Mon-Sat; 11am-5pm Sun; later on show days. **Tickets** prices vary. **Credit** AmEx, DC, MC, V. **Map** p326 C6.
The Lyric is a state-of-the-art theatre that, like the Capitol, is generally the home of big budget musicals (think *Cats* and *West Side Story*) and spectacular all-ages theatre. Sightlines are good and there are bars and restaurants aplenty in the complex – and you can try your luck in the casino afterwards.

New Theatre

542 King Street, between Angel & Knight Streets, Newtown (9519 3403, bookings 1300 306776, www.ramin.com.au/online/newtheatre). CityRail Newtown or St Peters/bus 308, 370, 422. **Box office** 10am-6pm Mon-Fri; & 1hr before show. **Tickets** $28; $22 reductions. **Credit** (phone bookings only) MC, V. **Map** p334.
An intimate 160-seater on the calmer end of King Street, home to the New Theatre (*see p269*), Australia's most committed continuously producing company. Cheap as chips and more nourishing, the New is one of Sydney's best, and best-value, theatre options.

Old Fitzroy Theatre

129 Dowling Street, at Cathedral Street, Woolloomooloo (9380 5553, bookings 1300 438849, www.oldfitzroy.com.au/theatre.html). CityRail Kings Cross/bus 200. **Box office** from 6.30pm on show days. **Tickets** $20-$28; $34 beer/laksa/show. **Credit** MC, V. **Map** p330 H7.
Founded in 1997 by a desperately hip yet talented collective of Sydney actors called the Tamarama Rock Surfers Theatre Company, and located under an old backpacker's pub, the Fitz has a reputation for hosting bleeding-edge work, new talent and whatever's currently hip, hot or happening. It hosts up to 12 main productions a year and also puts on the work of visiting companies. Book a 'beer, laksa and show' ticket and pick up the first two an hour before the third. *Photo p272*.
▶ *The Old Fitzroy hosts thirsty thesps in its bar and restaurant. See p191*.

Parramatta Riverside Theatres

Corner of Church & Market Streets, Parramatta (8839 3399, www.riversideparramatta.com.au).

ARTS & ENTERTAINMENT

The Reign of Cate and Andrew

The star duo prove critics wrong.

Not everyone was a fan of the decision to appoint Cate Blanchett and Andrew Upton artistic directors of the **Sydney Theatre Company** in 2007 – but the duo have silenced critics in glorious fashion. They've led the company from strength to strength and, more than that, have shaken up the Sydney theatre scene as a whole.

A crucial part of the success of the company has been harnessing the power of celebrity. STC has brought and continues to bring a wealth of big-name talent to Sydney theatre audiences including, of course, Blanchett herself. During her tenure as artistic director (in between the odd film project), Blanchett has trod the boards in the eight-hour Shakespearean epic *War of the Roses*, as Blanche DuBois in *A Streetcar Named Desire* and in Anton Chekhov's *Uncle Vanya*. The Blanchett-starring 2011 production of *Gross und Klein* will likely be no different.

But it's not just Blanchett bringing star quality to the STC. *A Streetcar Named Desire* also starred Joel Edgerton, and Blanchett was just one member of *Uncle Vanya*'s all-star cast – it included John Bell, Hugo Weaving, Richard Roxburgh and Jacki

Weaver. William Hurt starred in the Upton-directed production of *Long Day's Journey into Night*, Philip Seymour Hoffman (a close friend of Blanchett and Upton) directed Brendan Cowell in *True West* and, in 2011, Bryan Brown and Colin Friels will be duking it out in a new Australian play, Ross Mueller's *ZEBRA!*

Blanchett and Upton have also fostered international relationships. After successful runs in Sydney, *A Streetcar Named Desire* dazzled audiences in Washington and New York, while *Long Day's Journey into Night* travelled to Portland, Oregon. Likewise, *Gross und Klein* is set to tour Europe in 2012. Fortunately for Sydney theatregoers, the STC is importing as well as exporting. They brought Sydney the must-see theatrical event of 2010, Chicago-based Steppenwolf Theatre's acclaimed production of *August: Osage County*, and, similarly, will be bringing Abbey Theatre's *Terminus* to the Opera House 2011.

The happy result is that Sydneysiders who wouldn't normally brave the theatre are packing out houses – and there's every indication that things will only get more exciting in future.

ARTS & ENTERTAINMENT

Andrew **Upton** and Cate **Blanchett**.

ARTS & ENTERTAINMENT

CityRail/RiverCat Parramatta. **Box office** 9am-5pm Mon-Fri; 9.30am-1pm Sat; & 1hr before show.**Tickets** $15-$50. Production prices vary. **Credit** AmEx, MC, V.

This Bicentennial project is a council-mandated but difficult multi-theatre complex, perched beside a dried-up patch of the Parramatta River. It gets shows touring from around Australia, including inner Sydney venues such as STC, Griffin and Ensemble, and hosts the annual Big Laugh Comedy Festival early in the year.

Performance Space

245 Wilson Street, Eveleigh (8571 9111, bookings 1300 723 038, www.performancespace.com.au). CityRail Redfern or Macdonaldtown. **Box office** 10am-6pm Mon-Fri; & 1hr before show. **Tickets** $20-$25; $15 reductions. **Credit** MC, V. **Map** p328 B12.

Part of the increasingly vibrant and happening Carriageworks complex, the Performance Space is contemporary and funky and has the only foyer in Sydney where banging on about 'post-performative practice' won't earn you instant derision. With a strong focus on experimental performance and installations, the P Space remains the finest escape from the stultification of the mainstream.

Seymour Centre

Corner of City Road & Cleveland Street, Chippendale (box office 9351 7940, admin 9351 7944, www.seymour.usyd.edu.au). Bus 370, 422, 423, 426, 428. **Box office** 9am-6pm Mon-Fri; 11am-3pm Sat; & 2hrs before show. **Tickets** $10-$60. **Credit** AmEx, MC, V. **Map** p328 C11.

The Seymour showcases a grab-bag of productions in three different theatres including family entertainment, university revues, dance, musicals and, in past years, Belvoir and Ensemble shows too large for their regular homes. The York Theatre, designed with Tyrone Guthrie's open-stage model in mind,

can feel too open, while the Downstairs Theatre can feel like a classroom, but the outdoor barbecue gets a welcome work-out prior to many a performance.

▶ Stables Theatre

10 Nimrod Street, at Craigend Street, Kings Cross (8002 4772, bookings 1300 306776, www.griffintheatre.com.au). CityRail Kings Cross. **Box office** (in person) 1hr before show. **Tickets** *Griffin productions* $26-$57. Production prices vary. **Credit** AmEx, DC, MC, V. **Map** p330 J8.

Renovated and spruced up in 2010, this former stables seats a closely packed audience of 120, with audience members on busy nights sometimes left to sit on cushions on the stairs. It is home to the Griffin Theatre Company (*see p269*) – New Oz is the house style – who are well on the way to turning the site into a creative hub for artists and audiences alike.

State Theatre

49 Market Street, between Pitt & George Streets, CBD (admin 9373 6852, bookings 1300 139 588, www.statetheatre.com.au). CityRail St James or Town Hall/Monorail City Centre. **Box office** (in person) 9am-5pm Mon-Fri; & until 8pm on show days. **Tickets** $50-$135. Production prices vary. **Credit** AmEx, DC, MC, V. **Map** p327 F6.

Designed at the dawn of talking pictures, the impossibly over-the-top State is Australia's only example of true rococo. All plaster and all fake, the State mainly hosts concerts but does occasionally host theatre productions that couldn't find a better venue. It's a good cinema and average sit-down music venue, but not great for live theatre.

▶ Sydney Opera House

Bennelong Point, Circular Quay (box office 9250 7777, www.sydneyoperahouse.com). CityRail/ferry Circular Quay. **Box office** 9am-8.30pm Mon-Sat; & 2hrs before show Sun. **Tickets** *Opera Theatre* $70-$250; $70-$195 reductions. *Concert Hall* prices

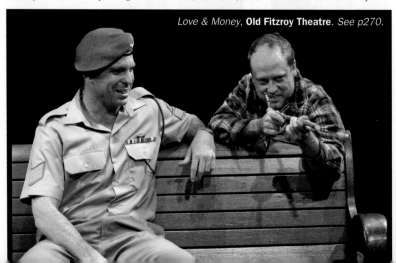

Love & Money, **Old Fitzroy Theatre.** *See p270.*

vary. *Drama Theatre & Playhouse* $35-$80; $30-$60 reductions. Studio $25-$50; $25-$40 reductions. **Credit** AmEx, DC, MC, V. **Map** p327 G3.

Danish architect Jørn Utzon's difficult child, the Opera House is a wonderful piece of sculpture masquerading as a functional arts venue. Despite the fact that it's best appreciated from the outside, experiencing the weirdness of Sydney's best-known built icon is a must. In addition to the Opera Theatre and the larger Concert Hall, it contains three theatre spaces: the Drama Theatre (notoriously widescreen and distant), the smaller Playhouse (mid-sized) and the Studio (a late attempt to reclaim the funk). Regardless of the building's drawbacks, the work is up there with Sydney's best, with the STC (*see p269*) and Bell Shakespeare (*see p268*) making regular appearances, Sydney Festival productions popping in annually and a spate of excellent touring shows throughout the year. For music, *see p251*.

▶ *See p38* **Architecture** *for the inside story on the tragedy and triumph behind the Opera House.*

Sydney Theatre

22 Hickson Road, opposite Pier 6/7, Walsh Bay (9250 1777, www.sydneytheatre.com.au). CityRail/ferry Circular Quay then 15min walk. **Box office** 9am-8.30pm Mon-Sat; 3-5.30pm Sun (show days only). **Tickets** $25-$70. Production prices vary. **Credit** AmEx, MC, V. **Map** p327 E3.

The lavish and relatively new Sydney Theatre represents the city's longstanding lust for a quality theatre space. The nigh-on-900-seater theatre is programmed by the STC (*see p269*) so it doesn't depend on the whims of commercial producers. It often features good drama and good dance (courtesy of the Sydney Dance Company), though its seating plan makes skipping out before interval a nightmare. Also on site is the Hickson Road Bistro, offering pre- and post-dining, drinks and coffee. It's fairly out-of-the-way, so it may help to think of the walk through the Rocks and under the Bridge as part of a great night out.

Wharf Theatres

Pier 4/5, Hickson Road, Walsh Bay (9250 1777, www.sydneytheatre.com.au). CityRail/ferry Circular Quay then 15min walk. **Box office** 9am-7pm Mon; 9am-8.30pm Tue-Fri; 11am-8.30pm Sat; 2hrs before performance Sun. **Tickets** $48-$79; $42-$67 reductions (not Fri, Sat). Production prices vary. **Credit** AmEx, MC, V. **Map** p327 E2.

The Wharf Theatres is a converted wharf and warehouse on the western side of the Harbour Bridge, near the Sydney Theatre (*see p273*). Surrounded by ever more swanky residential redevelopment, it houses the STC's (*see p269*) artistic, managerial and production staff, rehearsal space and a lovely restaurant, as well as two theatres, Wharf 1 and Wharf 2. The Sydney Dance Company (*see p273*), Australian Theatre for Young People (*see p268*) and Bangarra Dance Theatre (*see p273*) also perform here.

DANCE

Led by artistic director Kate Champion, **Force Majeure** (8571 9084, www.forcemajeure.com.au) has carved a niche for itself with a unique blend of dance, theatre, music and multimedia, while Gideon Obazarnek's **Chunky Move** (03 9645 5188, www.chunkymove.com), based in Melbourne but touring Sydney often, indulge in some genre-bending on their own, drawing heavily on technology. Both companies are worth checking out.

Australian Ballet

9669 2700, 1300 369741, www.australianballet.com.au.

Australia's national ballet company is based in Melbourne but their productions regularly grace the stage of the Sydney Opera House (*see p273*). With a repertoire that combines the contemporary and the classical, the company draws on Australian and international choreographers – the inventive and imaginative choreography of dance colossus Graeme Murphy (formerly artistic director of the Sydney Dance Company) being a particular highlight. Australian Ballet and Opera Australia (*see p251*) are the only taxpayer-propped companies that aren't required to program new Australian work.

★ Bangarra Dance Theatre

9251 5333, www.bangarra.com.au.

Australia's leading contemporary indigenous dance company, Bangarra has been artistically directed by Stephen Page since 1991. Its value is in its mix of contemporary style with ancient Aboriginal traditions of storytelling through movement. Consistently popular, Bangarra regularly tours the world and remains one of Australia's only distinctive arts exports. A unique experience.

▶ *The history of the indigenous people of Sydney is fascinating but also, often tragic. See p16* **The Other History**.

Sydney Dance Company

9221 4811, www.sydneydance.com.au.

With the appointment of new artistic director and self-described 'movement junkie' Rafael Bonachela in 2009, the Sydney Dance Company continues its commitment to bringing contemporary dance – from Australian as well as international choreographers

ARTS & ENTERTAINMENT

ARTS & ENTERTAINMENT

– to wide audiences. That's not to say that they dumb down – the company is renowned for exciting and challenging work that is both highly visual and highly emotional.

COMEDY

Australia has always loved its comedy and – despite the relatively small population – there are some major regional variations, which can be broadly summed up as 'Sydney style' and 'Melbourne style'.

In Melbourne, the comedy tradition is more theatrical: there were dedicated comedy clubs in the city and comedy developed as its own art form with a very specific, comedy-savvy audience. In Sydney, comedy developed as part of the entertainment mix in RSLs and pubs, jostling for space alongside bands, strippers and meat raffles. As a result of their different early environments, two distinctive modes of comedy performance developed. Melbourne comics are more likely than Sydney comics to perform in character and deliver monologue-style pieces, as befits their theatrical heritage. Sydney comics, on the other hand, are more often solo stand-ups, delivering quick-fire gags – the legacy of distracting a rowdy audience in a noisy venue.

The **Sydney Comedy Festival** (www.sydneycomedyfest.co.au) has been running annually from mid-April since 2005. While it's not quite the size of Melbourne's annual event, it has been growing steadily, attracting headliners of the calibre of Dylan Moran, Ross Noble, Steven Wright, Henry Rollins, Julian Clary, Tom Green, Steve Coogan, Danny Bhoy and Pablo Francisco.

Comedy Store

The Entertainment Quarter, 207/122 Lang Road, Moore Park, 9357 1419, www.comedy store.com.au). Bus 339, 373, 374, 376, 377, 393, 395, 396. **Shows** 8.30pm Tue-Sat. **Tickets** $10-$40. **Credit** AmEx, DC, MC, V. **Map** p332 J12.
The Comedy Store has settled into offering a solid five nights of comedy a week, generally one- or two-week seasons of touring international comics and solid Australian headliners with two or three support acts. It's the home of the NSW heats for Triple J's Raw Comedy contest and also stages showcase multi-comic bills. The Store can be a little tricky to find in the Entertainment Quarter, but if you head along the parking garage toward the cinemas you should be fine.

Laugh Garage

60 Park Street, at Elizabeth Street, CBD (9264 1161, www.thelaughgarage.com). CityRail Museum. **Shows** 8.30pm Tue-Sat. **Tickets** $10-$40. **Credit** AmEx, MC, V. **Map** p329 F7.

Run by respected local comic Darren Sanders, the Laugh Garage boasts that it's the only comedy club in the CBD – and it's right. It's also the only one that's underground, in the classic NYC comedy club tradition, complete with the spotlight-against-a-red-curtain stage setup. While other clubs will sometimes mix it up with sketch nights or cabaret, the Laugh Garage offers meat-and-potatoes stand up from solid performers: experienced locals and smaller touring acts, generally doing Thursday to Saturday. Light meals are available.

Roxbury Hotel

182 St Johns Road, Glebe (9692 0822, www. roxbury.com.au). Bus 431, 431, 436, 438. **Shows** 8pm Wed. **Tickets** $10-$30. **Credit** AmEx, MC, V. **Map** p328 A9.
Comedy at this Glebe pub is a labour of love, run by much-loved local comedy enthusiast and, latterly, performer Kathryn Bendall and her family. Comedy on the Rox is the regular Wednesday night event with a headliner, an MC and a few supports, but for about five months a year it's also the heats for the Quest for the Best open mic competition. While sometimes hit-and-miss the calibre tends to be on the high side, and the grand final is inevitably a sell-out.

The Friend in Hand

58 Cowper Street, Glebe (9660 2326, www. friendinhand.com.au). Bus 431, 431, 436, 438. **Shows** 8.30pm Thur. **Tickets** $10-$15. **No credit cards**. **Map** p328 B9.
It only has comedy once a week, but Mic in Hand is the must-see Sydney open mic night. Every week around ten newcomers will try their luck upstairs at the Friend in Hand, with an experienced MC and a headline act which is often a big name trying out new material ahead of a tour or festival. The room fills early, with couches and chairs scattered around, and the audience is notoriously comedy-savvy and encouraging. As a performer it's one of the best rooms in Sydney – as a punter it's a great way to see the newest acts on the circuit.

Star Bar

600 George Street, between Bathurst Street & Liverpool Street, CBD (9267 7827, www. starbar.com.au). Cityrail Town Hall. **Shows** 8pm Fri, Sat. **Tickets** $10-$20. **Credit** AmEx, MC, V. **Map** p329 E7.
It's hidden in the back of a bustling CBD bar in the George Street entertainment precinct (close to the Metro and the Event Cinema complex), but once you've negotiated your way through the after-work throng you'll find an odd little custom-built comedy theatre, complete with armrest buttons for voting in the weekly Comedy Court every Friday night, where an experienced MC marshals a group of hopefuls trying their luck. Saturdays the voting stops, but the Quick Comedy still promises multiple comics doing short, punchy sets.

Escapes & Excursions

Three Sisters in the Blue Mountains. *See p278.*

1000s of
things to do…

TIME OUT GUIDES
WRITTEN BY
LOCAL EXPERTS
visit timeout.com/shop

Escapes & Excursions

Go wild in the country.

Escaping Sydney's urban sprawl only takes a couple of hours' drive in any direction. Inland, to the west are the World Heritage-listed **Blue Mountains** (*see below*), with breathtaking views across deep valleys, sheer cliffs, waterfalls and bushland. To the north is **Hunter Valley** (*see p283*), famous for its wineries, while a trip south leads to the historic villages of the **Southern Highlands** (*see p291*). Beautiful beaches, rainforests and national parks can be found up and down the coast, with plenty to see along the way.

INFORMATION

CountryLink (central reservations 13 2232, www.countrylink.info) operates trains and coaches in NSW, around Canberra, and in Queensland and Victoria. Visit its website for details of its good-value multi-day train and tour packages to destinations in NSW.

For general information on areas around Sydney, visit the **Sydney Visitor Centre** (*see p307*). **Tourism New South Wales** (9931 1111, www.tourism.nsw.gov.au) will direct you to a regional tourist office.

Heading West

BLUE MOUNTAINS

A mere two hours west of the CBD, the **Blue Mountains** are one of Australia's most popular natural playgrounds and a must-visit for any tourist. This spectacular wilderness covers over 10,000 square kilometres (almost 4,000 square miles) of breathtakingly beautiful and rugged country: in 2000, the **Blue Mountains National Park**, which covers nearly 2,500 square kilometres (965 square miles), was grouped together with six other nearby national parks to form the **Greater Blue Mountains World Heritage Area**. Most of it is so isolated from Sydney's urban sprawl to the east that it could hide a species

of tree, the Wollemi pine, that was thought to have been extinct for 150 million years.

The Blue Mountains – in reality a maze of plateaus and dramatic gorges – are part of the Great Dividing Range, which separates the eastern seaboard and its cities from Australia's rural and desert heart. They only look blue from a distance, due to sunlight refracting through the eucalyptus oil that evaporates from the bush's legion of gum trees.

For decades after the first settlers arrived in Sydney, the Blue Mountains were thought to be impassable – but the very future of the colony depended on breaking through the dense bush and bridging its gaping canyons. With no sheep tracks to follow and river paths ending in crashing waterfalls, it took until 1813 before its secrets were finally unlocked and farmers had access to the sprawling fertile land beyond. Today, the area is easily traversed by rail and car (thanks to the efforts of a group of prisoners who were offered pardons if they could complete the first road in a matter of months – they did).

The administrative region called the City of the Blue Mountains is a narrow strip of townships and villages snaking its way along a high plateau between vast tracts of virginal bush. The townships are usually deliberately picturesque, full of twee 'Olde Wares' shops and pricey 'Devonshire' teas. Lavishly restored cottages nestle amid English cold-climate gardens, though some residents are radically embracing native flora, often to the discomfort of older locals who like their traditional conifers, rose beds and topiary hedges.

With nature the area's star attraction, the best way to explore is by taking one or several of the numerous well-signposted and maintained bushwalks. These range from hour-long quickies to camping treks of several days' duration. Good advice on walks can be found at the **Blue Mountains Information Centre** (*see p281*). More adventurous types can enjoy rock climbing, abseiling and the thrill of riding mountain bikes in actual mountains.

Almost all Sydney-based tour companies offer a one-day bus trip for a quick look around, but the better (and cheaper) option is to catch a CityRail train from Sydney's Central Station. Trains depart hourly every day, and take around two hours to reach the upper mountains.

While most townships have their own bush trails, the centre of the action lies in the adjoining townships of **Katoomba** and **Leura**. One easy sightseeing option is the **Blue Mountains Explorer Bus** (4782 1866,1300 300915, www.explorerbus.com.au). It's a double-decker (for some reason painted in the livery of a red London bus) departing just across from Katoomba train station 12 times a day between 9.45am and 4.15pm ($33, $28-$16.50 reductions, $82.50 family). It stops at

Blue Mountains National Park.
See p277.

30 resorts, galleries, tea rooms and general scenic attractions around Katoomba and Leura. You can get off and on as often as you like, and tickets are valid for up to seven days. CityRail also offers a combined train-plus-Explorer-bus ticket.

Katoomba is the most popular township for visitors thanks to its proximity to attractions such as the **Three Sisters** rock formation near Echo Point and **Scenic World** (*see p279*), where a range of gravity-defying vehicles grant spectacular views as you travel over and into the Jamison Valley. If you've got some time, descend the precipitous 841-step **Giant Staircase** next to the Sisters (only the genuinely athletic or masochistic should attempt to climb up it), and then do the two-and-a-half-hour easy walk through the Jamison Valley to the foot of the Scenic Railway for a sweat-free, mechanised ascent.

Katoomba is home to the Blue Mountains City Council, three pubs, a swathe of cafés and plenty of writers, artists and poets of steeply varying quality. Its chief built attractions are the 1880s **Carrington Hotel** (*see p279*), a popular wedding venue, and the intimate and terribly 'heritage' **Paragon Café** (65 Katoomba Street, 4782 2928). There are also some excellent second-hand bookshops. The three best for dusty bibliophiles are **Brian's Books** (44 Katoomba Street, 4782 5115), **Mr Pickwicks** (86 Katoomba Street, 4782 7598) and **Blue Mountains Books** (92 Katoomba Street, 4782 6700).

Linked to Katoomba by bus, train, a panoramic cliff drive or a half-hour walk is Leura, with its more upmarket guesthouses, vastly smarter shops and manicured gardens. In local parlance, if Katoomba is Mount Penrith, then Leura is Mount Paddington. One of the world's chintz capitals, Leura is a delight for all lovers of knick-knacks, baubles and ornamental flummery.

Further into the mountains beyond Katoomba, the **Hydro Majestic Hotel** (*see p279*) in Medlow Bath is popular for pricey coffee with an expansive view. Rather more down to earth is the village of **Mount Victoria**, the starting point for many more fine mountain hikes.

On the northern side of the mountains, off the Bells Line of Road above the Grose Valley, is the quintessentially transplanted English hamlet of **Mount Wilson**. This charming village is best visited in spring or autumn, when some house-proud locals open their gardens for your viewing pleasure and herbaceous envy. It's also notable for **Withycombe** (corner of the Avenue and Church Avenue), the house where the parents of Australia's only Nobel literature laureate,

Blue Mountains.

Patrick White, lived for a time. For more natural splendour, try the hushed and majestic remnant rainforest grandiloquently named the **Cathedral of Ferns**.

Also in the area are the magnificent **Mount Tomah Botanic Gardens** (4567 2154, www.rbgsyd.nsw.gov.au), which showcase cool-climate plants from around the world. A range of guided and self-guided tours – including bushwalks – is available, but bookings (call 4567 2154) are essential.

You'll need to travel to the south-western edge of the Blue Mountains to reach the other main attraction in the area: the **Jenolan Caves** (1300 763 311, www.jenolancaves.org.au). A tangled series of extraordinary underground limestone caverns, complete with stalagmites and stalactites, within a large and peaceful nature reserve, they're open 9am to 5pm daily. The caverns come in two flavours – easy guided tours with walkways and steps, and various adventure caves requiring helmets, overalls and climbing (from $60). If you're less adventurous, take a tour of the Lucas Cave ($23, $16 reductions, $59 family).

Scenic World

Corner of Cliff & Violet Streets, Katoomba (4782 2699, www.scenicworld.com.au). **Open** 9am-5pm daily. **Tickets** *Skyway return trip* $16; $8 children; $40 family. *Cableway & Railway return trip* $19; $10 children; $48 family. **Credit** AmEx, DC, MC, V.
Views and vertigo are the main features of this collection of tourist transports. The Scenic Skyway – a cable-car system over the Jamison Valley – was renovated a few years ago. The new cars have glass floors, so now you can see it really is a long way down – 270m (890ft), in fact. The Scenic Railway features an old coal train reinvented as the world's steepest rail incline, which takes you down into the rainforested valley – as does the Scenic Cableway, another cable car ride. There's a 2km (1.25-mile) boardwalk between the lower Railway and Cableway stations, so you can go down on one and back on the other.

Where to stay & eat

Blue Mountains YHA

207 Katoomba Street, Katoomba (4782 1416, www.yha.com.au). **Rates** $26-$29 dorm; $73-$82 double; $104-$116 family. **Credit** MC, V.
The Blue Mountains outpost of the YHA empire is an excellent modern hostel in a historic 1930s art deco building right in the centre of Katoomba.

Carrington Hotel

15-47 Katoomba Street, Katoomba (4782 1111, www.thecarrington.com.au). **Rates** from $119 B&B. **Credit** AmEx, DC, MC, V.
A gorgeous, rambling, old-style resort hotel with lots of antiques and oodles of 19th-century charm. Cocktails on the balcony are a must.

Hydro Majestic Hotel

Great Western Highway, Medlow Bath (4788 1002, www.hydromajestic.com.au). **Rates** from $210 midweek; $280 weekend. **Credit** AmEx, DC, MC, V.

Bags packed, milk cancelled, house raised on stilts.

You've packed the suntan lotion, the snorkel set, the stay-pressed shirts. Just one more thing left to do – your bit for climate change. In some of the world's poorest countries, changing weather patterns are destroying lives.

You can help people to deal with the extreme effects of climate change. Raising houses in flood-prone regions is just one life-saving solution.

**Climate change costs lives.
Give £5 and let's sort it *Here & Now***

www.oxfam.org.uk/climate-change

Be Humankind Ⓧ Oxfar

An upmarket, beautifully restored historic hotel with astonishing views and a Victorian feel, once famous for its spa cures, hence the 'Hydro'. Even if you're not staying at the Hydro, it's worth a visit for its tea and scones.

Jenolan Caves House
Jenolan Caves (1300 763311, www.jenolancavesresort.com.au). **Rates** B&B plus dinner per person from $85 midweek; $110 weekend. **Credit** AmEx, DC, MC, V.
Inside the caves complex, this dark, wood-panelled hotel with roaring fires has the feel of a grand English country house. Next door, the Gatehouse Jenolan offers four-bed dorms for $30 a head.

Lilianfels Blue Mountains
Lilianfels Avenue, Echo Point, Katoomba (4780 1200, www.lilianfels.com.au). **Rates** $389-$705 deluxe; $679-$995 executive suite. **Credit** AmEx, DC, MC, V.
This five-star pile perched just above Echo Point is the poshest accommodation in the heart of the mountains, with two famed restaurants (Darleys, serving Mod Oz cuisine, and Tre Sorelle, serving Italian) plus great views.

Wolgan Valley Resort & Spa
2600 Wolgan Rd, Newnes, (02 9290 9733, www.emirateshotelsresorts.com). **Rates** from $1950. **Credit** AmEx, DC, JCB, MC, V.
Perhaps Australia's finest regional property, Wolgan Valley Resort & Spa, owned by Emirates, is highlighted by not just its stunning location deep in the Wolgan Valley, but the luxuriously appointed villas and all-inclusive price tag. The degustation restaurant menu changes daily and features only the finest local produce.

Getting there

By car
Springwood, Faulconbridge, Wentworth Falls, Leura, Katoomba & Mount Victoria Take Great Western Highway (Route 32) and/or Western Motorway (Route 4). It's 109km (68 miles) from Sydney to Katoomba – about 2hrs.
Kurrajong & Mount Tomah Take Great Western Highway (Route 32) or Western Motorway (Route 4); turn off to Richmond via Blacktown; then Bells Line of Road (Route 40). Mount Wilson is 6km (3.75 miles) off Bells Line of Road.
Jenolan Caves Take Great Western Highway (Route 32) via Katoomba and Mount Victoria; then turn south at Hartley; it's another 46km (29 miles) to the caves.

By train
Trains depart hourly from Central Station. It's about 2hrs to Katoomba.

Tourist information

Also check out the websites www.katoomba-nsw.com and www.bluemts.com.au.

Blue Mountains Information Centre
Echo Point Road, Katoomba (1300 653408, www.visitbluemountains.com.au). **Open** 9am-5pm daily.

Heading North
HAWKESBURY RIVER

If you've ever wondered what the west coast of Scotland would look like without the rain, mist and midges, head to **Hawkesbury River**. It's like Argyll with sunshine. Skirting the outer edges of Australia's biggest city for much of its length, the great greenish-brown giant licks over 1,000 kilometres (620 miles) of foreshore as it curls first north-east and then, from Wisemans Ferry, south-east towards the sea, emptying into an estuary at Broken Bay. The river's fjord-like saltwater creeks and inlets are ideal for exploring by boat, and houseboating holidays are popular.

The town of **Windsor** retains many of its original buildings, as well as its waterwheel and charm. Among the stalwarts is the oldest inn in Australia still being used for its original purpose (the Macquarie Arms, built in 1815), Australia's oldest courthouse (1822), St Matthew's Anglican Church, built by convict labour from a design by convict architect Francis Greenway (also in 1822), and the oldest Catholic primary school still in use (1836). Also of note is John Tebbutt's house and observatory, with its outsized telescope.

It's worth taking a cruise with **Hawkesbury Valley Heritage Discovery Tours** (4577 6882), as you'll get the enthusiastic low-down on the area's history from a local guide.

Within easy reach of Windsor, there's more colonial architecture at **Richmond**, a tree-lined garden town whose railway station dates back to 1822, and Ebenezer, with Australia's oldest church (on Coromandel Road, built 1809).

The Hawkesbury's change of course is marked by an S-bend at **Wisemans Ferry**, another of the river's historic villages. It has Australia's oldest ferry service, which still runs 24 hours a day (and is one of the few remaining free rides in New South Wales). On the far side of the ferry is a section of the convict-built Great Northern Road, once 264 kilometres (164 miles) long, which shows just what sweat and toil really mean.

Up the road in the Macdonald River Valley, in the secluded hamlet of **St Albans**, is another colonial inn, the **Settlers Arms** (1 Wharf Street, 4568 2111). A couple of kilometres from here, in the Old Cemetery on Settlers Road, lies the grave of William Douglas, a First Fleeter who died in 1838. Rumours also suggest that St Albans was Windsor magistrates' preferred venue for illicit nooky over the years.

The lower reaches of the Hawkesbury are its most spectacular, with steep-sided forested banks and creeks branching off its wide sweep. Near the end of **Berowra Creek** (west of the Pacific Highway), at the foot of two deep, bush-covered hills, is beautiful **Berowra Waters**. There's not much here apart from a small car ferry, a cluster of bobbing boats and a few restaurants offering fine cuisine (including Hawkesbury oysters). Much of the remainder of the river, as it makes its way to the sea, is equally tranquil – notably the slender fingers of water that make up **Cowan Creek** (east of the Pacific Highway). It's here, in the sweeping expanse of the **Ku-ring-gai Chase National Park**, that many people choose to cruise or moor for a spot of fishing.

If you haven't got time for houseboating, Australia's last **riverboat postman** may be the answer. The four-hour cruise from Brooklyn allows you to participate in the delivery of mail while taking in the scenery – an inside view that few see. The boat leaves Brooklyn Wharf at 9.30am weekdays, excluding public holidays: for details call 9985 7566.

Otherwise, you could hike from Berowra railway station down to Berowra Waters along a fascinating, well-marked bush track (part of the Great North Walk). A round trip takes about four hours.

Where to stay & eat

Able Hawkesbury Houseboats
3008 River Road, Wisemans Ferry (1800 024979, 4566 4308, www.hawkesburyhouseboats.com.au). **Rates** from $530 (2 days, 1 night) midweek. **Credit** MC, V.
Choose from seven different sizes of boat, from 26ft up to 52ft in length. Facilities are wide-ranging, and include shower, toilet, fridge, TV, barbecue, cutlery and crockery.

Berowra Waters Fish Café
199 Bay Road, Berowra Waters (9456 4665). **Open** 9am-8pm Mon-Sat; 8.30am-7pm Sun. **Main courses** $11-$17. **Credit** MC, V.
A great setting with views across the water. Serves fish and chips in various guises. BYO.

Court House Retreat
19 Upper Macdonald Road, St Albans (4568 2042, www.courthousestalbans.com.au). **Rates** from $160. **Credit** MC, V.

B&B accommodation in a historic sandstone building that once housed a courtroom, police station and lock-up. Booking essential.

Retreat at Wisemans
5564 Old Northern Road, Wisemans Ferry (4566 4422, www.wisemans.com.au). **Rates** from $120. **Credit** AmEx, DC, MC, V.
Comfortable rooms with views of the golf course or river. The Riverbend Restaurant, serving Mod Oz food, is recommended (about $36 for two courses).

Ripples Houseboat Hire
87 Brooklyn Road, Brooklyn (9985 5534, www.ripples.com.au). **Rates** from $500 for 2 nights midweek. **Credit** MC, V.
Two kinds of boat, sleeping up to four or ten.

Getting there

By car
Richmond & Windsor It's 59km (37 miles) from Sydney to Windsor, and the journey takes 60-90mins.
Via Hornsby Pacific Highway (Route 83) to Hornsby; Galston Road; then Pitt Town Road.
Via Pennant Hills Epping Road (Route 2) to Pennant Hills; then Route 40.
Via Parramatta Western Motorway (Route 4) to Parramatta; then Route 40.
Wisemans Ferry & St Albans Pacific Highway (Route 83) to Hornsby; Galston Road; then Old Northern Road.
Berowra Waters Pacific Highway (Route 83); 12km (7 miles) north of Hornsby, Berowra turn-off signed. The Brooklyn turn-off is 12km (7 miles) further north.

By train
Richmond & Windsor There's a regular train service to Windsor and the upper Hawkesbury River area on the Richmond line (via Blacktown) from Central Station. Journey time is around 1hr.
Berowra Waters The main Sydney-Newcastle line from Central Station goes to Berowra Waters (via Berowra Station) and Brooklyn (via Hawkesbury River Station). The trip takes about 40mins (not all trains stop at both stations).

By bus
For details of bus and coach services to the Hawkesbury region, contact the local tourist office (see below) or CountryLink NSW (13 2232, www.countrylink.info).

Tourist information

Hawkesbury River
Tourist Information Centre
5 Bridge Street, Brooklyn (9985 7064). **Open** 9am-5pm Mon-Fri; 9am-4pm Sat; 11am-3pm Sun.

Tourism Hawkesbury
Ham Common, Windsor Road, Clarendon (4578 0233, www.hawkesburytourism.com.au). **Open** 9am-5pm Mon-Fri; 9am-4pm Sat, Sun.

HUNTER VALLEY

The second-most visited region in New South Wales after the Blue Mountains is the state's main wine-growing region – and that is the reason to visit. The area around the main town of **Pokolbin**, two hours north of Sydney, boasts more than 75 wineries (from the smallest boutiques to the big boys, such as Lindemans), which offer tastings and cellar-door sales of wine ranging from semillon and shiraz to buttery chardonnays. Mingled among the vineyards are award-winning restaurants and luxury hotels, but there are plenty of cheaper options too.

While such wine-based indulgence has put the Hunter firmly on the tourist map, the area's personality is, in contrast, also bound up with coal mining. The very waterway from which the region gets its name was originally known as the Coal River (it was renamed in 1797 after the then NSW governor, John Hunter), and the founder of the Hunter's wine-making industry, Scottish civil engineer James Busby, arrived in Australia in 1824 partly to oversee coal-mining activities in nearby Newcastle. But while the Hunter Valley once boasted the largest shaft mine in the southern hemisphere, which held the world record for coal production in an eight-

hour shift (Richmond Main Colliery, now a museum and open irregularly), all but two of its mines have now closed.

The wine industry sprouted from humble beginnings in the 1830s, but has fared rather better. The original vines were cuttings taken from France and pre-dated the phylloxera disease that tainted European wine. Thus Australian grapes are now claimed to be more authentic than modern-day French wines, which use roots from American vines. Seeing out the tough 19th century, then the Depression of the 1930s and later fighting off competition from other antipodean wine regions, such as South Australia, the Hunter made it to the 1970s wine rush and ever since then it has done little but flourish.

Despite its small area – the main vineyard district north of the town of **Cessnock** is only a few kilometres square – the sheer number of wineries in the Lower Hunter Valley can present the wine tourist with a problem: where to start? Inevitably, familiarity leads many to the bigger, more established vineyards – which is a good way of gaining an insight into wine-growing traditions. Large family companies in Pokolbin, such as **Tyrrell's** (Broke Road, 4993 7000) and **Tulloch** (Glen Elgin Estate, DeBeyers Road, 4998 7580) have been producing wine in the area for more than a century, while at **Lindemans** (McDonalds Road, 4998 7684) – in existence for 150 years – there's a museum exhibiting old wine-making equipment. Other big wineries, such as

Enjoy the Ride

Different ways to explore Hunter Valley.

Perhaps it's people's reluctance to mix drinking wine and driving, but there are many unusual ways to take in – and get to – the Hunter Valley.

Rather than spend two hours stuck in a car on the freeway, you can now skip the traffic and fly up in an amphibious aircraft with **Sydney Seaplanes** (1300 732752/ 9388 1978, www.sydneyseaplanes. com.au). Departing from Rose Bay, the seaplane takes off over Sydney Harbour and then traces the coast past the northern beaches and Central Coast, before landing at Cessnock Airport, where you can be met by a tour bus or hire a car.

Balloon Aloft (1800 028568/4938 1955, www.balloonaloft.com) offers hot-air balloon rides for people staying overnight; rendezvous are an hour before dawn, though, so best not to sample too much of

the local drop the night before. The relaxing flight takes in the spectacular landscape of vineyards, rivers, forests and the rolling hills of the valley, followed by a champagne reception back on land.

For a slower place, travel in style by horse and carriage. **Hunter Valley Wine & Dine Carriages** (0410 515358, www.huntervalleycarriages.com.au) can pick you up from your hotel and tailor a tour of wineries and somewhere for lunch. Tours are also available in a chauffeur-driven Cadillac with **Hunter Valley Cadillac Tours** (4996 4059, www.cadillactours.com.au).

Or if you're feeling guilty about all the wine and cheese you've consumed, then hire a bicycle and burn off some of those calories. Contact **Hunter Valley Cycling** for hire or tours (0418 281480, www.huntervalleycycling.com.au).

Hunter Valley. *See p283.*

Wyndham Estate (Hermitage Road, 4998 7412), on the banks of the Hunter River itself and Australia's oldest continually operating winery, and **McGuigan Simeon** (corner of Broke and McDonalds Roads, 4998 7402), offer full on-site facilities, including galleries, museums, restaurants and cafés.

But it would be a shame to miss out on the smaller enterprises. Places such as **Oakvale** (set against the Brokenback Range, Broke Road, 4998 7520) and Petersons (Mount View Road, 4990 1704) offer the time and space for a more individual tasting experience. Many of these boutique wineries are set within picturesque surroundings. **Hungerford Hill** (Broke Road, 4998 7666) – formerly housed in a beautiful tiny converted church, and recently moved into a new landmark designer building – has some of the best 'stickies' (dessert wines and rich ports) in the area. The grounds of **Pepper Tree Wines** (Halls Road, 4998 7539) incorporate a former convent – the area's swishest guesthouse (*see p285*) – which was moved lock, stock and barrel to the Hunter for the purpose. Further afield, in Lovedale, the **Wandin Valley Estate** (Wilderness Road, 4930 7317) offers accommodation in villas, and has its own cricket ground. Talking of which, have a look at **Brokenwood** (McDonalds Road, 4998 7559) to enjoy its always cracking Cricket Pitch and Graveyard wines. And yes, they do both come from vines grown on cricket pitches and graveyards.

Look out for the vintages that were produced during 1988, 2000 and 2003: these were the best

years in the Hunter Valley for decades.

Since the Hunter is reasonably flat and compact, and the wineries never far apart, it's a good place to ditch four-wheel transport. Bikes are available from some guesthouses for a small charge, while **Grapemobile** (4991 2339/0418 404 039) hires out bikes and also runs enjoyable day and overnight cycling and walking tours of the wineries from Cessnock. Finally, if you're not high enough already, see the regimented rows of vines from above with a sunrise balloon flight: try **Balloon Aloft** (*see p283* **Enjoy the Ride**) – prices vary based on the number of people and the season.

BARRINGTON TOPS

Although it's less than an hour's drive north of the Hunter Valley, the Barrington Tops is as different from the wine-growing district as it's possible to be. A national park with a world heritage listing, its upper slopes are thick with subtropical rainforest containing thousand-year-old trees, clean mountain streams and abundant wildlife. With its swimming holes, camping and bushwalking, the Barrington Tops is a domain for outdoor enthusiasts. The area can also be explored with mechanical help: try eco-specialist **Bush Track Tours** (0419 650 600, www.bushtracktours.com). Further south are green hillocks and greener valleys, the sort of landscape that insists you jump out of bed straight on to the back of a horse or a mountain bike. If you have your own transport and three or four days to spare, you might consider visiting the triangle of attractions in this area – the Hunter Valley, Barrington Tops and Port Stephens. An excellent and unique place to base yourself is the award-winning **Eaglereach Wilderness Resort** (Summer Hill Road, Vacy, 4938 8233, www.eaglereach.com.au). Perched on a mountain top, you have vistas in all directions from your luxury log cabin (from $250 per night) set in 400 hectares (1,000 acres) of raw bushland. Despite the luxury, nature is on your doorstep – expect to see kangaroos at your window and giant lizards in the front yard.

Wine tours

While many vineyards offer tastings at the cellar door, the local cops rightly take exception to drink-driving, so the best idea may be to take an organised tour. You can travel in old-fashioned style in a horse-drawn carriage: **Pokolbin Horse Coaches** (4998 7189, 0408 161133) offer regular tours and can custom-design a tour (minimum four) to suit your needs. The **Hunter Valley Wine Country Visitor Centre** (*see p286*) has details of other outfits.

Activity Tours Australia

9904 5730, www.activitytours.com.au. **Rates** (with lunch) $100; $94 reductions. Day trips from Sydney to the Hunter Valley, taking in five wineries, a tour to see how wine is made and a cheese factory. Maximum 19 people.

Hunter Vineyard Tours

4991 1659, www.huntervineyardtours.com.au. **Rates** from $55; $80 with lunch. Full-day tour in 12- or 22-seat buses, taking in five wineries (lunch optional) in the Cessnock area. Pick-up from local hotels.

Trekabout Tours

4990 8277, www.hunterweb.com.au/trekabout. **Rates** $45 half day (Mon-Fri only); $55 full day. Half- or full-day winery tours for up to six people. The shorter tour visits four to five wineries. Pick-up is from hotels in the Cessnock/Pokolbin area.

Where to stay & eat

Most Hunter Valley guesthouses won't take bookings for less than two nights, especially over weekends. Rates drop considerably midweek. There are more – and cheaper – hotels and motels in Cessnock.

Barringtons Country Retreat

1941 Chichester Dam Road, 15mins drive from Dungog, Barrington Tops (4995 9269, www.thebarringtons.com.au). **Rates** (minimum 2 nights) from $120. **Credit** MC, V.

If you like to flirt with rural surroundings safe in the knowledge that all modern comforts are reasonably close at hand, try this place. Log cabins overlooking the valley, spa baths and imaginative cooking at moderate rates.

Casuarina Restaurant & Country Inn

Hermitage Road, Pokolbin, Hunter Valley (4998 7888, www.casuarinainn.com.au). **Rates** (suite) $185 weekdays; $310 weekend. **Credit** AmEx, DC, MC, V.
Over-the-top themed suites are the thing here: choose between the Moulin Rouge, Casablanca, the French Bordello, Susie Wong's, Italian Bordello, Love Boat, Palais Royale, Out of Africa and, finally, Casanova's Loft. Plus a pool, tennis court and a pretty good Mediterranean-style restaurant.

Peppers Convent Guest House

Grounds of Pepper Tree Wines, Halls Road, Pokolbin (4993 8999, www.peppers.com.au). **Rates** (double) from $328 Mon-Thur, Sun; from $792 Fri, Sat. **Credit** AmEx, DC, MC, V.
The ultimate indulgence, with lots of antiques and surrounding vineyards. One of the country's classiest restaurants, Robert's, is also here.

Tallawanta Lodge

Hunter Valley Gardens, next to McGuigan Winery, corner of Broke Road & McDonalds Road, Pokolbin (4998 4000, www.hvg.com.au). **Rates** (B&B) from $334 Mon-Thur, Sun; $848 weekend 2-night stay. **Credit** AmEx, DC, MC, V.
A pleasant place to lay your head, right in the heart of the wine area. The associated Harrigan's Irish Pub also has decent rooms from $251.

Wandin Valley Estate

Wilderness Road, Lovedale (4930 7317, www.wandinvalley.com.au). **Rates** from $175. **Credit** AmEx, DC, MC, V.
Winery accommodation in six self-contained, well-appointed villas and studios just five minutes from Pokolbin. Great restaurant too.

Getting there

By car
Lower Hunter Valley Sydney-to-Newcastle Freeway (Route 1) to Freemans Interchange; then turn off to Cessnock (Route 82). Alternatively, leave Route 1 at Calga; head through Central Mangrove towards Wollombi; then turn off to Cessnock (Route 132). Journey time: 2hrs. The main wine-growing district around Pokolbin and Rothbury is about 12km (7 miles) north-west of Cessnock.
Barrington Tops The journey takes about 3hrs. Direct route Sydney-to-Newcastle Freeway (F3/Route 1) to Maitland turn-off on New England Highway (Route 15); Paterson Road;

Take a Tour

Get high, get wet, go wild.

Plenty of tour operators run interesting and entertaining day trips in and around the Blue Mountains. Some tours start in Sydney, while others leave from Katoomba. The following outfits are recommended:

Australian School of Mountaineering
4782 2014, www.asmguides.com.
Prices phone for details.
Based in Katoomba, ASM has provided outdoor training and guiding for more than two decades. It runs a range of canyoning, rock climbing and abseiling trips.

Fantastic Aussie Tours
4782 1866, 1300 300915, www.fantastic-aussie-tours.com.au. **Prices** from $70.
A day tour to Jenolan Caves from Katoomba, with cave entrance. Cheaper tickets are offered for bushwalkers who just want a bus service to the caves.

High 'n' Wild
4782 6224, www.high-n-wild.com.au.
Prices from $99.
This Katoomba-based adventure outfit runs canyoning expeditions involving swimming, wading and squeezing through tight spaces, as well as other outdoor fun options

including bushwalking, ice climbing, mountain biking and abseiling. It also offers snow- and ice-climbing courses.

Oz Trek Adventure Tours
9666 4262, www.oztrek.com.au.
Prices $55.
A packed day trip from Sydney includes a visit to the Olympic site at Homebush, a tour of the major Blue Mountain sites and a one- to two-hour bushwalk.

Visitours
9499 5444, www.visitours.com.au.
Prices from $83.
The Blue Mountains tour from Sydney also includes a stop at Wentworth Falls and Scenic World, where you can ride the world's steepest railway. Learn about Aboriginal culture and rock engravings.

Wonderbus
9630 0529, 1300 556357,
www.wonderbus.com.au. **Prices** from $89.
A range of tours to the Blue Mountains, including a day trip from Sydney that involves three hours of bushwalking and covers most of the area's main sites, such as the Three Sisters and a local winery.

then turn right for Dungog approx 5km (3 miles) beyond Paterson.
Via Hunter Valley Follow signs from Cessnock to Maitland (via Kurri Kurri), then as above.

By train
Dungog, just south of Barrington Tops, is served by a few daily trains from Sydney (journey time just over 3hrs) via Newcastle (90mins). Some guesthouses will pick up from Dungog.

By bus
Rover Coaches (4990 1699, www.rovercoaches.com.au) runs a daily service to the Hunter Valley from Sydney (departing at 8.30am, returning at 7.15pm), plus day and weekend tours of the region; call for departure points.

Tourist information

Gloucester Visitor Information Centre
27 Denison Street, Gloucester (6558 1408, www.gloucester.org.au). **Open** 8.30am-5pm Mon-Fri; 8.30am-3pm Sat, Sun.
For information on the Barrington Tops.

Hunter Valley Wine Country Visitor Centre
455 Wine Country Drive, Pokolbin (4990 0900, www.winecountry.com.au). **Open** 9am-5pm Mon-Fri; 9.30am-5pm Sat; 9.30am-3.30pm Sun.

PORT STEPHENS

The third point in a triangle of northern attractions that includes the Hunter Valley and Barrington Tops, Port Stephens Bay is a beautiful stretch of water most famous for its whale and dolphin cruises. Two pods of dolphins – around 70 individuals – inhabit the bay, and your chances of getting up close to them are very high. Whales come into the calmer waters of the bay on their migration route from Antarctica.

The main town in the area is **Nelson Bay**, on the northern bank of the harbour, where you'll find hotels, restaurants and takeaways.

Several operators run good dolphin- and whale-watching tours. Highly recommended is a cruise on **Imagine** (5104 Nelson Bay Road, Nelson Bay, 4984 9000, www.imaginecruises.

com.au), a luxury catamaran operated out of Nelson Bay Marina by Frank Future and Yves Papin. All year except June and July they offer a daily two-hour dolphin trip departing at 10.30am ($22, $14-$20 reductions), and a range of longer cruises departing from d'Albora Marina. There's a boom net on board, which is lowered over the edge for thrill-seekers to lie in and get really close to the dolphins. They also operate humpback whale cruises from June to mid November. You can also go looking for dolphins in a kayak with **Ocean Planet** (4342 2222, www.kayaktours.com.au).

Another option for nature lovers is a visit to the **Tomaree National Park** (4984 8200, www.nationalparks.nsw.gov.au) on the southern shore of the inner harbour. Here, you can see low-flying pelicans skidding in to land on the water, and there's a large breeding colony of koalas at Lemon Tree Passage. And if you have access to a 4WD, you can't miss **Stockton Beach**, a 32-kilometre (19-mile) expanse of sand starting at Anna Bay, where you can drive through the waves or even take a shot at dune-bashing over the towering silica hills (providing you have someone to help tow you out when you get stuck – or overturn).

Also worth a visit is **Fighter World** (Medowie Road, Williamtown, 4965 1810, www.fighterworld.com.au, $7, $5 reductions, $20 family). An offshoot of the RAAF Williamtown airbase, it celebrates Australia's fighter-plane history with a wide variety of exhibits and aircraft.

Where to stay & eat

Peppers Anchorage Port Stephens

Corlette Point Road, Corlette (4984 2555, www.peppers.com.au). **Rates** from $285 midweek (minimum 2 nights). **Credit** AmEx, DC, MC, V.
This is a top-class resort right on the water. Private balconies offer sweeping views across the bay.

Port Stephens Motor Lodge

44 Mangus Street, Nelson Bay (4981 3366). **Rates** $80-$155. **Credit** AmEx, DC, MC, V.
A motel-like place located a short stroll from the main township. There's also a swimming pool.

Salamander Shores

147 Soldiers Point Road, Soldiers Point (4982 7210, www.salamandershores.com). **Rates** from $149 midweek. **Credit** AmEx, DC, MC, V.
A pleasant hotel featuring lovely rooms with sea views, a pretty garden and a good restaurant.

Getting there

By car

Take Sydney-to-Newcastle Freeway (F3/Route 1); it's a 2.5hr drive.

Kiama. *See p289.*

Jervis Bay.

By train
CityRail trains run almost hourly from Central Station to Newcastle. Buses connect with the trains for transfers to Port Stephens.

By bus
Port Stephens Coaches (1800 045949, 4982 2940, www.pscoaches.com.au) runs a daily service to Nelson Bay, departing Eddy Avenue, Central Station, Sydney, at 2pm. It leaves Nelson Bay for the return trip daily at 9am. The journey takes 3.5hrs.

Tourist information

Port Stephens Visitor Information Centre
Victoria Parade, Nelson Bay (4980 6900, www.portstephens.org.au). **Open** 9am-5pm daily.

Heading South
SOUTH COAST

According to most of the people who live there, particularly residents of the Shoalhaven region (which stretches 160 kilometres/100 miles south of the town of Berry), this is the area of New South Wales that has it all: wilderness galore, including large tracts of national park and state forest; beaches so long and white they make Bondi look like a house party at a sewage dump; some of the cleanest, clearest water in Australia; a bay 82 times the size of Sydney Harbour, with pods of crowd-pleasing dolphins; easy access to magnificent mountain vistas; heritage and antiques; 'surfing' kangaroos at Pebbly Beach, just to the south of Ulladulla; and the best fish and chips in the country at Bermagui (head for the marina and just follow the seagulls).

If you're driving from Sydney along the Princes Highway (Route 1), take a quick detour towards Stanwell Park and drive along Hargrave Road between Coalcliff and Clifton to marvel at the spectacular **Sea Cliff Bridge**, which twists and turns as it hugs the rocky coastline below and the ragged cliffs at your side. Back on the Princes Highway and beyond the Royal National Park, the first region you encounter is Illawarra, the administrative centre of which is the city of **Wollongong**. It's perhaps unfair to view Wollongong as one of the two ugly sisters on either side of Sydney (the other being Newcastle), but as you approach its smoking industrial surroundings it's hard not to.

The road then begins to slide prettily between the coast on one side and the beginnings of the Southern Highlands on the

other (Illawarra comes from an Aboriginal word meaning 'between the high place and the sea'). The first seaside town worthy of a stop is **Kiama** *(photo p287)*. The town's main attraction is the **Blow Hole**, which spurts spray up to 60 metres (200 feet) into the air from a slatey, crenellated outcrop next to a comparatively tranquil harbour. Also by the harbour is a fresh fish market, while on the way into town there's a block of 1885 quarrymen's cottages that have been renovated and turned into restaurants and craft shops. On the way out, don't miss the wonderful sign 'Stan Crap – Funeral Director'.

Kiama is a good base for exploring the subtropical **Minnamurra Rainforest**, the **Carrington Falls** and nearby **Seven Mile Beach**, an undeniably impressive caramel arc, backed by a hinterland of fir trees.

An alternative base is the tree-lined inland town of **Berry**, a little further south. It's an entertaining hybrid of hick town and quaint yuppie heaven, where earthy locals mix with weekending Sydneysiders in search of antiques and fine dining. The former are catered for by a couple of daggy pubs, while many of the latter bed down at the **Bunyip Inn Guest House** *(see p290)*.

JERVIS BAY
Undoubtedly the Shoalhaven region's greatest attraction, and the one that drives normally restrained commentators to reach for their superlatives, is Jervis Bay. A huge place, it encompasses the wonderful **Booderee National Park** and 56 kilometres (34 miles) of shoreline. It also has a history of close shaves. First, in 1770, Captain Cook sailed straight past it on the way towards Botany Bay, recording it only as 'low-lying wetlands' and missing entirely its deep, wide natural harbour (which made it an ideal alternative to Sydney as fulcrum for the new colony). Later, this ecologically sensitive beauty spot was mooted as a possible port for Canberra and the ACT. And in 1975, Murrays Beach, at the tip of the national park, was chosen as a site for a nuclear reactor (a project thankfully defeated by public protest).

These narrow escapes and a fortuitous lack of population growth around Jervis Bay mean that this coastal area remains one of the most undisturbed and beautiful in Australia. Divers testify to the clarity of its waters; swimmers are sometimes literally dazzled by the whiteness of its sands (Hyams Beach is said to be the whitest in the world). It's not just popular with people: among its regularly visiting sea and bird life are fur seals, giant rays, whales (southern right, pilot and killer), sharks, sea eagles, penguins and many, many more.

A good way to get a feel for Jervis Bay and meet its resident bottlenose dolphins is to hook up with **Dolphin Watch Cruises** (50 Owen Street, Huskisson, 4441 6311, www.dolphinwatch.com.au), which also runs whale cruises. **Huskisson**, the launching point for the cruises, is one of six villages on the shores of the bay. It's got a couple of accommodation options, a dive shop – **Deep6Diving** (64 Owen Street, 4441 5255, www.deep6divingjervisbay.com.au) – wonderful fish and chips, and a pub with a bistro, the **Husky Pub** (4441 5001) on Owen Street. Just south of Jervis Bay there is excellent sailing, snorkelling and swimming at St George's Basin, and fishing at **Sussex Inlet**.

You could stay in Huskisson, but it's worth bringing a tent to get a proper feel for the Booderee National Park (admission $10 per vehicle per day), which is jointly managed by the local Aboriginal community. The best place to camp is at **Caves Beach**, where you wake up to the calls of birds and eastern grey kangaroos. **Green Patch** has more dirt than grass, but better facilities and can accommodate camper vans as well. The Christmas/New Year period sees a ballot for places. Book through the park's visitor centre (*see below*).

ULLADULLA

Despite all the stunning scenery around Jervis Bay, it can be worth venturing further south to the sleepy fishing town of Ulladulla for somewhere to stay. Ulladulla's protected harbour may not quite recall Sicily, but the town has a sizeable Italian fishing community (guaranteeing decent local pizzas and pasta), and the **Blessing of the Fleet** is an annual event on Easter Sunday. From here it's easy to access wilderness areas to the west and further south – **Budawang** and **Murramarang National Parks** – plus yet more expansive beaches, such as **Pebbly Beach** (which is actually sandy) with its resident kangaroos.

Where to stay & eat

Bunyip Inn Guest House

122 Queen Street, Berry (4464 2064). **Rates** from $120 midweek, $140 weekend. **Credit** AmEx, DC, MC, V.
A National Trust-classified former bank with 13 individually styled rooms, one with a four-poster bed. There's also a swimming pool.

Huskisson Beach Tourist Resort

Beach Street, Huskisson (4441 5142, www.huskissonbeachtouristresort.com.au). **Rates** from $30 camping; from $85 cabin. **Credit** MC, V.
This resort offers various cabins (including self-catering ones) as well as plenty of camping spots right opposite the beach. There's a pool too.

Jervis Bay Guest House

1 Beach Street, Huskisson (4441 7658, www.jervisbayguesthouse.com.au). **Rates** from $145. **Credit** AmEx, DC, MC, V.
This four-and-a-half-star guesthouse opposite a beach has just four rooms, with balconies overlooking the sea and the sunrise, and is a short walk to the shops and restaurants in Huskisson. All this makes it very popular, so book well ahead.

Ulladulla Guest House

39 Burrill Street, Ulladulla (1800 700905, 4455 1796, www.guesthouse.com.au). **Rates** from $248. **Credit** AmEx, DC, MC, V.
A popular five-star option with great service and ten lovely rooms. It also has self-catering units, a pretty saltwater pool, sauna, hot tub, small gym, art gallery and an excellent French restaurant. A variety of in-room massages is available.

Getting there

By car

Take Princes Highway (Route 1). Allow at least 2hrs to Jervis Bay, 3hrs to Ulladulla and slightly longer to Pebbly Beach.

By train

There are regular trains from Central Station to Wollongong, Kiama, Gerringong, Berry and Bomaderry (for Nowra and Ulladulla), via the South Coast line, changing trains at Dapto. It's 3hrs to Bomaderry; from there a limited coach service operated by Premier Bus Services (13 3410/4423 5233, www.premierms.com.au) continues on through Nowra as far as Ulladulla.

By bus

Interstate coaches travelling the Princes Highway between Sydney and Melbourne stop at many of the towns mentioned above. There are also local bus and coach services along the coast. Contact the local tourist offices for more details.

Tourist information

Booderee National Park Visitor Centre

Jervis Bay Road, Jervis Bay (4443 0977, www.environment.gov.au/parks/booderee). **Open** 9am-4pm daily.

Shoalhaven Tourist Centre

Corner of Princes Highway & Pleasant Way, Nowra (1300 662808, 4421 0778, www.shoalhaven.nsw.gov.au/region). **Open** 9am-5pm daily.

Ulladulla Visitors Centre

Princes Highway, Civic Centre, Ulladulla (4455 1269). **Open** 10am-6pm Mon-Fri; 9am-5pm Sat, Sun.

Morton National Park.

Tourism Kiama
Blowhole Point, Kiama (1300 654262,
4232 3322, www.kiama.com.au). **Open**
9am-5pm daily.

SOUTHERN HIGHLANDS

The Southern Highlands, known by wealthy
19th-century Sydneysiders as the 'sanatorium
of the south' for its cool climes and fresh air,
has recently experienced something of a
renaissance as a tourist destination. It's easy
to see why – just a two-and-a-half-hour train
ride from Sydney, the area has well-preserved
villages such as Berrima (founded 1831), fading
stately homes such as Ranelagh House in
Robertson and a range of cosy accommodation,
all set in a gently undulating landscape so easy
on the eye that it evokes a different country
(even before the area was first settled, Governor
Macquarie said it reminded him of England).

There's some truth to the local saying that
the Southern Highlands are mostly for 'the
newly-weds and the nearly-deads', but there is
something here for most tastes: the highlands
encompass tropical and subtropical rainforest,
the second-largest falls in NSW and the edge
of Morton National Park.

Of the many pleasant approaches by car,
two leading from the main coastal road (Princes
Highway) stand out. The first is to take the
Illawarra Highway (from Albion Park) through
Macquarie Pass National Park; the second

is to take the tourist drive from just beyond
Berry. The route from Berry – rising, bending
and finally dropping towards the **Kangaroo
Valley** – is often romantically thick with mist,
but on even a partly clear day it affords
luscious views of the countryside.

Kangaroo Valley Village, despite its iron
roofs and sandstone-pillared Hampden Bridge
(built in 1897), is a little disappointing, but the
walking and camping nearby are excellent, as
are canoeing and kayaking on the **Kangaroo
River** (contact Kangaroo Valley Tourist Park
near the bridge, 1300 559977/4465 1310,
www.holidayhaven.com.au/kangaroovalley).

Leaving Kangaroo Valley, the road rises and
twists once more before leading to the **Fitzroy
Falls**. A short saunter from the impressive
Fitzroy Falls Visitor Centre (4887 7270,
open 9am-5.30pm daily) and you are amid
scenery that's as Australian as Paul Hogan.
There are five falls in the vicinity, but Fitzroy
is the nearest and biggest, plummeting 81
metres (266 feet) into Yarunga Valley. Take
any of the walks around the falls and you
could encounter 48 species of gum tree, lyre
birds and possibly a wombat.

Another way of exploring the top end of
underrated **Morton National Park** is to
use the town of **Bundanoon** as a base for
bushwalking and cycling. Bundanoon, which
means 'a place of deep gullies', is as Scottish in
flavour as its name sounds. Every year in the
week after Easter the town transforms itself

into Brigadoon for a highland gathering, featuring traditional games, Scottish dancing and street parades. Bundanoon was also once known as the honeymoon centre of the Southern Highlands – in its heyday it had 51 guesthouses – but these days the bedsprings rarely squeak, as it has largely fallen out of fashion.

Slightly north of the forgettable town of Moss Vale is **Berrima**, considered Australia's finest example of an 1830s village. This is the town the railways forgot, so many of its early buildings remain in pristine condition. A highlight is the 1838 neo-classical **Court House** (corner of Wilshire and Argyle Street, 4877 1505, www.berrimacourthouse.org.au) with its sandstone portico and curved wooden doorways. Don't miss the reconstruction of the 1843 trial of the adulterous Lucretia Dunkley and her lover: particularly good is the judge's sentencing of the pair for the murder of her dull husband. Other historic buildings include **Harper's Mansion** and Australia's oldest continually licensed hotel, the **Surveyor General Inn** (*see right*), both built in 1834.

An unexpected delight on the long road to Bowral is **Berkelouw's Book Barn** (Old Hume Highway, 4877 1370, open 9.30am-5pm daily), containing some 200,000 second-hand books. Bowral itself is attractive enough, especially during the spring Tulip Festival, but its biggest claim to fame is as the town that gave Australian cricket the late **Donald Bradman** – arguably the greatest sportsman of all time. The great man is honoured in the **Bradman Museum** (St Jude Street, 4862 1247, www.bradman.org.au, open 10am-5pm daily, $8.50, $4-$7 reductions, $22 family) on the edge of the lush Bradman Oval, opposite the old Bradman home. If cricket doesn't captivate you, then take a trip up **Mount Gibraltar**, overlooking the surrounding countryside, and the view surely will.

About 60 kilometres (37 miles) west of the town of Mittagong (via part-dirt road), the mysterious and beautiful **Wombeyan Caves** feature a number of unique encrustations and deposits. You can take a guided tour, and there's on-site accommodation and camping: contact the **Wombeyan Caves Visitor Centre** (Wombeyan Caves Road, Taralga, 4843 5976, www.jenolancaves.org.au, open 8.30am-5.30pm daily) for details.

Destined to become the area's most famous village, and all because of a talking pig, is the sleepy hollow of **Robertson**, where the film *Babe* was shot. Almost the entire cast is on the breakfast menu at **Ranelagh House** (*see right*). On the way back to Sydney, be sure to take the road out of Robertson to the Princes Highway for some spectacular sea views as you twist and turn your way down the hillside.

Where to stay & eat

Briars Country Lodge & Inn
Moss Vale Road, Bowral (4868 3566, www. briars.com.au). **Rates** from $120 midweek; $190 weekend. **Credit** AmEx, DC, MC, V.
A country retreat with 30 garden suites set in beautiful parkland. Adjacent to the lodge is the Georgian Briars Inn (c.1845), which has a true country atmosphere, with cosy bars and bistro food.

Bundanoon Hotel
Erith Street, Bundanoon (4883 6005, www.bundanoonhotel.com.au). **Rates** (per person) $65-$80. **Credit** AmEx, DC, MC, V.
This creaky old hotel boasts a wonderful billiards table and the occasional poetry reading.

Ranelagh House Guesthouse
Illawarra Highway, Robertson (4885 1111, www.ranelagh-house.com.au). **Rates** (per person) from $70 weekend B&B. **Credit** AmEx, MC, V.
The best place in the area to take a leisurely cream tea. It also offers a 'country-style' lunch and has a good dinner menu.

Surveyor General Inn
Old Hume Highway, Berrima (4877 1226, www.highlandsnsw.com.au/surveyorgeneral). **Rates** from $80 weekend. **Credit** AmEx, MC, V.
The rooms are simple, with brass beds and a shared bathroom, but the inn oozes historical charm.

Getting there

By car
The inland route (120km/75 miles) via Hume Highway (Route 31) takes just under 2hrs. The coastal route is via Princes Highway (Route 60); then turn inland on Illawarra Highway (Route 48) by Albion Park. It's slightly longer (130km/80 miles) and slightly slower (just over 2hrs).

By train
Trains to the Southern Highlands depart from Sydney's Central Station every day. Most stop at Mittagong, Bowral, Moss Vale and Bundanoon. The journey takes about 2.5hrs.

By bus
Several bus companies serve the Southern Highlands area, among them Priors Scenic Express (1800 816234, 4472 4040) and Greyhound (13 2030, www.greyhound.com.au).

Tourist information

Tourism Southern Highlands
62-70 Main Street, Mittagong (1300 657559, 4871 2888, www.southern-highlands.com.au). **Open** 9am-5pm Mon-Fri; 9am-4pm Sat, Sun.

Directory

Getting Around

ARRIVING & LEAVING

By air

Sydney Airport (9667 9111, www.sydneyairport.com.au) is on the northern shoreline of Botany Bay, nine kilometres (six miles) south-east of the city centre. Opened in 1920, it's one of the oldest continuously operating airports in the world. Since a swanky upgrade for the 2000 Olympics and another upgrade of the domestic terminal in 2005, it's now among the world's best – and quite proud of it.

There are three terminals: **T1** is for all international flights on all airlines and for QF (Qantas) flights 001-399; **T2** is a domestic terminal for Tiger, Virgin Blue, Regional Express, Jetstar, OzJet, Aeropelican, Air Link and QF flights 1600 and above (10 million passengers pass through T2 every year and a $20 million upgrade is planned for 2011); **T3** is the Qantas terminal for QF domestic flights 400-1599.

The international terminal is a great place to shop, with more than 120 outlets ranging from ordinary duty-free stores and international designer showcases to Aussie gear such as Done Art & Design, Between the Flags, Swim by Beach Culture and RM Williams, plus souvenir outlets selling Aboriginal artefacts and kitsch mementos. And there's more to come with future upgrades expanding the departures level by 7300 square metres and a host of new food and beverage and retail outlets planned for 2011.

Getting to and from the airport

Built for the Olympics, the **Airport Link** rail service (131 500, www.airportlink.com.au) between Sydney Airport and Central Station runs an efficient service every ten minutes from both international and domestic terminals and trip between T1 and T2/3 takes two minutes, runs from 5am–12am and costs $5. The line is a spur of the green CityRail line, so serves all the main inner-city interchanges. It takes ten minutes to reach Central Station from the domestic terminals and 13 minutes from the international one. Trains run from 5.19am to 11.45pm Monday to Friday and from 5.06am to 11.43am Saturday and Sunday. A single fare from the international terminal to Central Station costs $15.80; $10.40 reductions daily. It's $15; $10 reductions, daily from the domestic terminals. GatePass fares are also available from CityRail stations and give you until 4pm the next day to complete your journey. GatePass fares are $11.80; $8.40 reductions.

Bus-wise, the **KST Sydney Airporter** (9666 9988, www.kst.com.au) shuttle runs a door-to-door service to all hotels, major apartment blocks and backpacker joints in the city, Darling Harbour and Kings Cross. A single costs $14 ($23 return) on the day or you can book online for $12.60 ($20.70 return) Look for the white buses with a blue and red logo outside 'The Meeting Point' outside T1 and at 'The Horseshoe' outside both T2 and T3. Book three hours in advance for hotel pick-ups and give yourself plenty of time to get to the airport, as the shuttle will take twice as long as a taxi.

Each terminal has its own sheltered taxi rank, with supervisors in peak hours to ensure a smooth and hassle-free flow of **taxis**. You never have to wait for long, even in the vast sheep-pen-style queuing system of the international terminal, where 190 vehicles are on call. If you have any special needs – wheelchair access, child seats or an extra-large vehicle – go to the front of the queue and tell the supervisor, who will call you a specially fitted taxi. It takes about 25 minutes to get into the city, depending on the traffic and time of day, and costs around $40.

The main car rental companies all have desks at the airport.

Airlines: International

Around 40 airlines operate regular flights into Sydney, including:
Air Canada
1300 655767, www.aircanada.com
Air New Zealand
13 2476,
www.airnewzealand.com.au
British Airways
1300 767177,
www.britishairways.com
Cathay Pacific
13 1747, www.cathaypacific.com
Emirates
1300 303777, www.emirates.com
Garuda Indonesia
1300 365330, www.garuda-indonesia.com
JAL (Japan Airlines)
9272 1111, www.jal.co.jp
Malaysia Airlines
13 2627, www.malaysiaairlines.com
Qantas
13 1313, www.qantas.com.au
Singapore Airlines
13 1011, www.singaporeair.com
Thai Airways
1300 651960, www.thaiair.com
United Airlines
13 1777, www.united.com
Virgin Atlantic
1300 727340, www.virgin-atlantic.com

Airlines: Domestic

Aeropelican
13 1313, www.aeropelican.com.au
Jetstar
13 1538, www.jetstar.com.au
OzJet
1300 737000, www.ozjet.com.au
Qantas
13 1313, www.qantas.com.au
Regional Express (Rex)
13 1713,
www.regionalexpress.com.au
Tiger
www.tigerairways.com
Virgin Blue
13 6789, www.virginblue.com.au

By bus

Lots of bus companies operate throughout Australia; they all use the **Sydney Coach Terminal** located in Central Station as their main pick-up and drop-off point. National carrier Greyhound (1300 473946, from abroad +61 2 9212 1500, www.greyhound.com.au), transports more than a million passengers a year.

By rail

The State Rail Authority's **CountryLink** (reservations 13 2232, www.countrylink.info) operates out of Central Station with extensive user-friendly services to all main NSW and interstate destinations.

By sea

International cruise liners, including the QE2, dock at the **Overseas International Passenger Terminal** located on the west side of Circular Quay, or in Darling Harbour.

PUBLIC TRANSPORT

To get around Sydney you'll probably use a combination of trains, ferries, buses and maybe the 'airborne' Monorail or the chic LightRail streetcars aka trams. As well as the Sydney Buses network (run by the State Transit Authority, STA), there are CityRail trains and Sydney Ferries. The other transport services are privately run and therefore generally more expensive. The centre of Sydney is so small that if you're in a large group, it's often cheaper to pool for a taxi. Look for Sydney's new (and clearly-marked) network of bike lanes if you're on two wheels.

Transport Infoline

13 1500, www.myzone.nsw.gov.au. Phone enquiries 6am-10pm daily. A great, consumer-friendly phone line and website offering timetable, ticket and fare information for STA buses, Sydney Ferries and CityRail, plus timetabling (only) for cross-city private bus services.

Fares & tickets

There are several combination travel passes covering the government-run transit system, and they're worth buying if you plan extensive use of public transport. Since 18 April 2010, a new fare structure called **MyZone** has made travelling on Sydney public transport much easier. MyZone tickerts are accepted on the entire CityRail, State Transit and Sydney ferries network, as well as private bus services and some private ferries too.

MyMulti 1,2 & 3

MyMulti tickets give you unlimited travel in one of three zones and unlimited bus and ferry travel across Greater Sydney. These tickets are available as a weekly, monthly, quarterly or yearly tickets. To find the right MyMulti ticket for you, check www.cityrail.info or ask at any train station or bus information kiosk (where you can also buy them). Newsagents displaying a MyMulti Ticket Stop sign, and

ticket offices or vending machines at Circular Quay and Manly also sell passes. Please note these passes cannot be used on the STA premium Sydney Explorer and Bondi Explorer bus services, Sydney Ferry harbour cruises, JetCats or private buses.

SydneyPass

This one is specifically aimed at tourists. Unlimited travel on selected CityRail trains, buses (including premium services such as the Explorer buses) and ferries (including premium services such as JetCats and cruises). Valid for any three, five or seven days within an eight-day period. A three-day pass costs $116 ($58 reductions, $290 family); for a five-day pass it's $152 ($76 reductions, $380 family); and $172 ($86 reductions, $430 family) for a seven-day pass.

MyMulti Day Pass

Perfect for one-day shopping binges or exploring Sydney's tourist attractions, the MyMulti Day Pass is an all-in-one ticket that gives you unlimited travel on buses, ferries and CityRail trains throughout Greater Sydney until 4am – but not on the Explorer buses or JetCats. It costs $20 ($10 reductions) and is available from station ticket offices, TransitShops, Sydney ferries ticket offices and selected 7-Eleven stores, newsagencies and convenience stores.

Family Funday Sunday

A new innovation and a hugely popular one, the Funday Sunday pass works like this: for $2.50 per person, your family can enjoy CityRail tyrain services, StateTransit and private buses and all regular Sydney ferries service. They can be purchased at ticket vending machines and station ticket offices, on board buses, at Sydney Ferries ticket booths and selected newsagents, 7-Elevens and convenience stores.

Buses

Buses are slow but fairly frequent, and offer a better way of seeing the city than the CityRail trains, which operate underground within the centre. Buses are the only option for transport to popular areas such as Bondi Beach, Coogee and the northern beaches (beyond Manly), which aren't served by either train or ferry. Sydney is divided into sections, with each section equivalent to 1.6km. Sections are

marked on all route maps and are shown on some bus stop signs. The minimum adult fare is $2 ($1 reductions) for 1-2 sections and the maximum is $4.30 ($2.10 reductions) for 6+ sections

The bus driver will not stop unless you hold out your arm to request a ride. If you're in the suburbs you'll probably be able to pay the driver in small change (big notes=big grimace) or validate your MyBus pass in the green machines at the door.

The bus route numbers give you an idea of where they go. Buses **131-193** service Manly and the northern beaches; **200-296** the lower north shore (including Taronga Zoo) and the northern suburbs; **300-400** the eastern suburbs (including Bondi, Paddington, Darlinghurst and Sydney Airport); **401-500** the inner south and inner west suburbs, including Balmain, Leichhardt, Newtown and Homebush; and **501-629** the north-west including Parramatta and Chatswood. In general, the **100s** and **200s** start near Wynyard Station and the **300s-600s** can be found around Circular Quay.

Bus numbers starting with an 'X' are express services, which travel between the suburbs and major centres on the way into the city. Stops are marked 'Express'. Limited-stop or 'L' services operate on some of the longer routes to provide faster trips to and from the city (mainly for commuters).

Buses in the central and inner suburbs run pretty much all night, but services from central Sydney to the northern beaches stop around midnight until 4.30am. **Nightride** buses operate hourly services to outer suburban train stations after the trains have stopped running until 5am and cost $3.70 ($1.90 reductions for up to three sections and $7.50 ($3.70 reductions) for 7+ sections.

STA also runs the tourist-oriented **Sydney Explorer** and **Bondi Explorer** bus services. For full details of both these, and private bus tours, *see p295*.

CityRail

CityRail (www.cityrail.info) is the passenger rail service covering the greater Sydney region and the sister company to CountryLink, covering country and long-distance routes within NSW). The sleek, double-decker silver trains run underground on the central

DIRECTORY

DIRECTORY

City Circle loop – Central, Town Hall, Wynyard, Circular Quay, St James and Museum stations – and overground to the suburbs (both Central and Town Hall stations provide connections to all the suburban lines). Although certainly quicker than the bus, trains are not as frequent as many would like and waits of 15 minutes, even in peak time, are not uncommon. For one of the best rides in Sydney, take the train from the city to the north shore – it crosses the Harbour Bridge and the views are spectacular.

MyTrain tickets can be bought at ticket offices or vending machines at rail stations. Expect huge queues in rush hour and top-of-the-card prices. A single ticket anywhere on the City Circle costs $23.30 ($1.60 reductions); an off-peak return costs $4.40 ($2.20 reductions).

For more details on CityRail services, call the **Transport Infoline** (*see p295*) or visit www.cityrail.info. For a map of the CityRail city network, *see p336*.

Ferries

No trip to Sydney would be complete without clambering aboard one of the picture-postcard green-and-yellow ferries that ply the harbour and are used daily by hundreds of commuters. They're not only cute, they're useful, too. All ferries depart from Circular Quay ferry terminal, where **Sydney Ferries** operates from wharves 2 to 5. These stately vessels are a great way to explore the harbour: there's plenty of room to take pictures from the outdoor decks or just to sit in the sun and enjoy the ride. Ticket prices vary, but a single from Circular Quay to destinations within the Inner Harbour (under 9km) costs $5.30 ($2.60 reductions) and $6.60 ($3.30 reductions) for trips beyond 9km. Tickets are sold at ticket offices and vending machines at Circular Quay and Manly. Tickets for Inner Harbour services can also be purchased on board. For a map of the ferry system, *see p335*. For a rundown of the best sightseeing rides *see p45* and for unorthodox waterborne explorations *see p47* **Wet and Wild**.

Sydney Ferries Information Centre
Opposite Wharf 4, Circular Quay (13 1500, www.sydneyferries.info). CityRail/ferry Circular Quay. **Open** 6.45am-6.15pm Mon-Sat; 7.15am-6.15pm Sun. **Map** p327 F4.

JetCats

JetCats – sleek, fast catamarans – once operated services to Manly but the service wound up in 2008, because although the journey took 15 minutes, as opposed to 30 minutes on an ordinary ferry, the JetCats cost three times as much to run and were 'characterised by poor reliability and highly fluctuating availability', according to an inquiry. Two private ferry operators, Bass & Flinders and Sydney Fast Ferries were persisting with the service privately despite losing government endorsement.

Metro LightRail

Having once run the biggest and most successful (and sustainable) tram service in the world, Sydney finally caved to public demand and welcomed back its streetcars in 1997. Trams were taken out of service in the early 1960s, but the privately run Metro LightRail, operated by Veolia Transport Sydney (which is also in charge of the Metro Monorail), now provides a slick 14-station service from Central Station via Darling Harbour, Pyrmont and Star City casino to the inner west. It's useful for visiting Darling Harbour, Paddy's Market, Sydney Fish Market, Glebe and the Powerhouse Museum. In 2010, the government announced a $500 million expansion of the light rail system with up to 20 new stations and 10km of new track planned – 5.6km from Lilyfield to Dulwich Hill and 4.1km from Haymarket to Circular Quay via Barangaroo.

Trams today operate 24 hours a day, seven days a week, between Central and Star City stations, and from 6am to 11pm Monday to Thursday and Sunday, 6am to midnight Friday and Saturday, from Central all the way out to Lilyfield in the west. Trams run about every ten to 15 minutes from 6am to 11pm, and every 30 minutes outside these hours. The line is divided into two zones. Single tickets for zone 1 cost $3.40 ($2.20 reductions), and tickets for both zones cost $4.40 ($3.40 reductions). A Day Pass offers unlimited trips for $9 while a MetroConnect offers seven days of monorail and light rail travel for $30. Tickets are available from Central Station or on board the train.

For more information, call 8584 5288 or see the website www.metrolightrail.com.au.

Metro Monorail

Sydneysiders are not great fans of the noisy aerial monorail that runs anti-clockwise around the CBD at first-floor office level – blame *The Simpsons* who mercilessly lampooned the towns who succumbed to such tacky visions of the future – but it's often the first thing tourists notice and does provide a fun, novelty ride between Darling Harbour, Chinatown and the city centre. It runs every three to five minutes, 7am to 10pm Monday to Thursday, 7am to midnight Friday and Saturday, 8am to 10pm Sunday.

The seven-station loop costs $4.90 (free under-fives) whether you go one stop or all the way. A Monorail Day Pass ($9.50) offers a full day of unlimited travel, plus some discounts on museum admissions while a Family Monorail Day Pass is $23. Tickets can be bought at station ticket offices or vending machines. For more details, call 8584 5288 or visit www.metromonorail.com.au.

TAXIS

It's quite easy to flag down a taxi in Sydney and there are many taxi ranks in the city centre, including ones at Central, Wynyard and Circular Quay. Staff in a restaurant or bar will also call a taxi for you. A yellow light indicates the cab is free, and it's common to travel in the front passenger seat alongside the driver. Drivers will often ask which of two routes you want to follow, or if you mind if they take a longer route to avoid traffic. But there are swags who don't know where they're going and will stop to check the map; if this happens, make sure they turn off the meter. Tipping is not expected, but passengers sometimes round up the bill and, for all the griping about Sydney cabbies that goes on, they are one of the few drivers in the world who'll 'round-down' fares for convenience sake.

The standard fare is $1.99 per kilometre from 6am to 10pm (add an extra $1.20 per km from 10pm to 6am), plus a $3.30 booking fee and, if relevant, a $2.20 telephone booking fee. If a cab takes you across the Bridge, the maximum $4 toll (less during off-peak hours) will be added to the fare, even if you travelled via the toll-free northbound route.

If you've left something behind in a cab, see **Lost Property**, *p301*.

Taxi companies

Legion Cabs
13 1451, www.legioncabs.com.au
Premier Cabs
13 1017, www.premiercabs.com.au
RSL Cabs
9581 1111
St George Cabs
13 2166, www.stgeorgecabs.com.au
Silver Service Taxis
13 3100, www.silverservice.com.au
Sydney's popular luxury taxi
service; amazingly, the same price
as a regular taxi, but often hard to
book.
Taxis Combined Services
13 3300,
www.taxiscombined.com.au
Zero200
Wheelchair Accessible Taxis
Service 8332 0200,
www.zero200.com.au

Water taxis

Great fun, but expensive. The
cost usually depends on the time of
day and the number of passengers,
but the fare for two from Circular
Quay to Doyles fish restaurant at
Watsons Bay, which takes ten to 12
minutes, is anywhere from $60-$95.
The outfits below accept all major
credit cards, and can be chartered
for harbour cruises.

Beach Hopper Water Taxis
0412 400990, 1300 306676,
www.watertaxi.net.au.
If you want to be dropped off at a
beach – literally on to the sand –
call Sydney's only beach-landing
water taxi service. It also operates a
summer 'Beach Safari' service: for
$35 per person per day, you can hop
on and off at any number of
harbour beaches on its run.

Water Taxis Combined
9555 8888,
www.watertaxis.com.au.
This company can pick you up
from almost any wharf, jetty or
pontoon provided there is enough
water depth, and, in the case of
private property, there is
permission from the owner.
The limousine taxis take up to
20 passengers.

Yellow Water Taxis
9299 0199,
www.yellowwatertaxis.com.au
Claiming to be 'Australia's most
experienced water taxi operator',
Yellow offer instant quotes online
and guarantees cheaper prices
than its competitors and that it
will beat any rival written quote if

challenged. They can carry up to 16
passengers and on their standard
craft but their 'maxi-taxi' carries 28.

DRIVING

Driving in Sydney can be hair-
raising, not so much because of
congestion (Sydneysiders may
complain, but it's not at all bad for a
major city), but primarily because
of the fast and furious attitude of
locals – this is not a city backward
in coming forward.
   Under Australian law, most
visitors can drive for as long as
they like on their domestic driving
licence without the need for any
additional authorisation. A resident
must apply for an Australian
driving licence after three months,
which involves a written test. You
must always carry your driving
licence and your passport when in
charge of a vehicle; if the licence is
not in English, you need to take an
English translation as well as the
original licence.
   Driving is on the left. The general
speed limit in cities and towns is
60kph (38mph), but many local and
suburban roads have a 50kph
(30mph) limit and in 2010 plans
were announced to reduce speed
limits to 40kph in the CBD's high
pedestrian areas. The maximum
speed on highways is 110kph
(60mph), and 110kph (70mph) on
motorways and freeways. Speed
cameras are numerous and there
are heavy penalties for speeding.
The legal blood alcohol limit is 0.05
per cent for experienced drivers,
zero for provisional or learner
drivers. Seat belts are mandatory
and baby capsules or child seats
must be used for all children.

Fuel stations

Petrol stations are fairly plentiful,
and easy to find on main roads,
although you won't find so many
in central Sydney. At the time of
writing, the cost of petrol (regular
unleaded) was $1.40 per litre
although an hour out of Sydney it
can fall as low as 96c per litre. Try
www.motormouth.com.au to find
the cheapest fuel in your
neighbourhood.

Parking

In central Sydney parking is a pain
and not recommended. In some
suburbs, such as tree-lined
Paddington, the quality of the road
surface is poor, and narrow one-
way streets with parking on both

sides compound the problem. Then
there's the hyper-vigilant parking
inspectors ('Brown Bombers' to
locals on account of their quick
descent and staid uniforms). Note
that you must park in the same
direction as the traffic on your side
of the road and display tickets on
your dashboard. Many street
meters now accept credit cards.
   Rates at city-centre car parks
range from $16 to $23 for one hour,
with $20 to $62 the day rate. 'Early
Bird' special rates often apply if
you park before 9am and leave after
3.30pm. Look under 'Parking
Stations' in the *Yellow Pages* for
more car parks.

Secure Parking
*60 Elizabeth Street, CBD (9233
2445, www.secureparking.com.au).*
Open 7am-10.30pm Mon-Thur;
7am-midnight Fri; 8am-midnight
Sat; 8.30am-6pm Sun. **Credit**
AmEx, DC, MC, V. **Map** p327 F6.
Other locations 2 Market Street,
CBD (9283 1383; 1 Martin Place,
entrance on Pitt Street, CBD (9231
4933).

**Wilson Parking –
Cinema Centre**
*521 Kent Street, between Bathurst
& Liverpool Streets, CBD (9264
5867, www.wilsonparking.com.au).*
Open 24hrs daily. **Credit** AmEx,
DC, MC, V. **Map** p329 E7.
Other locations CitiGroup Centre,
2 Park Street, CBD (9261 4710); St
Martin's Tower, entrance on
Clarence Street, CBD (9261 5568).

Tolls

The toll for the Harbour Bridge and
Tunnel varies between a maximum
charge of $4 for cars heading south
(free for northbound cars) at peak-
hour and as low as $2.50 (off-peak).
The toll for the 'eastern distributor'
is $4.50 for northbound cars
travelling into the city, free for
those heading out or south. The
Cross-City Tunnel (www.
crosscity.com.au) running west to
east opened in 2005 to ease
congestion in the CBD, but has
proved much less popular than
expected because of the toll fees –
exclusively electronic and still
considered extortionate for a trip of
just over two kilometres. The toll
fee depends on the size of your
vehicle, most pay $4.41 for the
Eastbound Tunnel (Darling
Harbour to Eastern Distributor Exit
or Rushcutters Bay), $4.41 for the
Westbound Tunnel (Rushcutters
Bay to Darling Harbour) and $2.08

DIRECTORY

for Sir John Young Crescent Exit (from the East). For vehicles with a height exceeding 2.8m, or length exceeding 12.5m, it's $8.82 (Eastbound and Westbound) and $4.16 for Sir John Young Crescent.

Vehicle hire

Most of the major car rental firms are situated on William Street in Kings Cross, and also have outlets at Sydney Airport. Rates vary almost hourly and all offer discounted deals. What's given below is the rate for the cheapest hire car available for a one-day period quoted on a given day. Rates drop if the car is hired for a longer period. More outfits are listed in the *Yellow Pages* under 'Car &/or Minibus Rental'. Those offering ultra-cheap deals should be approached with caution, though: always read the small print before you sign.

You will need to show a current driver's licence and probably your passport. Credit cards are the preferred method of payment and are nearly always asked for to cover insurance costs, even if you do eventually pay by cash or travellers' cheque. A few firms will rent to 18-year-olds, but usually you have to be over 21 and hold a full driving licence to rent a car in NSW. If you're under 25, you'll probably have to pay an extra daily surcharge, and insurance excesses will be higher.

Avis
200 William Street, at Dowling Street, Kings Cross (9357 2000, www.avis.com.au). CityRail Kings Cross. **Open** 7.30am-6pm Mon-Thur, Sat, Sun; 7.30am-7pm Fri. Rates (unlimited km) from $48/day. **Credit** AmEx, DC, MC, V. **Map** p329 H7.
Other locations Central Reservations (13 6333, 9353 9000); Sydney Airport (8374 2847).

Budget
93 William Street, at Crown Street, Kings Cross (8255 9600, www.budget.com.au). CityRail Kings Cross. **Open** 7.30am-6pm daily. Rates (unlimited km) from $38/day. **Credit** AmEx, DC, MC, V. **Map** p329 G7.
Other locations Central Reservations (1300 362 848, 9353 9399); Sydney Airport (9207 9165).

Hertz
Corner of William & Riley Streets, Kings Cross (9360 6621,

www.hertz.com.au). CityRail Kings Cross. **Open** 7.30am-6pm daily. Rates (unlimited km) from $39/day. **Credit** AmEx, DC, MC, V. **Map** p329 G8.
Other locations Central Reservations (13 3039); Sydney Airport (9669 2444).

Red Spot
Hyde Park Plaza, 38 College Street, at Oxford Street, Sydney (1300 668810, 9356 8333, www.redspotrentals.com.au). CityRail Museum. **Open** 8am-5pm Mon-Thur; 8am-6pm Fri; 8am-noon Sat, Sun. Rates (unlimited) $35/day. **Credit** AmEx, DC, MC, V. **Map** p329 G8.
Other locations Sydney Airport (9352 7466, 9317 2233).

Thrifty
75 William Street, at Riley Street, Kings Cross (8374 6177, www.thrifty.com.au). CityRail Kings Cross. **Open** 7.30am-6pm daily. Rates (unlimited km) from $40.50/day. **Credit** AmEx, DC, MC, V. **Map** p329 G7.
Other locations Central Reservations (1300 367227); Sydney Airport (1300 367227).

CYCLING

Sydney's steep hills, narrow streets and chaotic CBD make cycling a challenge, even for the most experienced of cycle couriers. But, gradients aside, that's all changed recently, as councils have introduced cycleways and exclusive bike lanes to the city centre and CBD fringe. Both Centennial Park and Manly offer safe cycle tracks and there's a fantastic junior track (replete with traffic lights) at Sydney Park in St Peters.

Helmets are compulsory for all cyclists in Sydney, including children carried as passengers. During the day, a bicycle must have at least one working brake and a bell or horn. At night, you'll need, in addition, a white light at the front and a red light at the rear, plus a red rear reflector. There are lots of other road rules, and you are well advised to respect them, as bicycles are considered to be vehicles so rule breaking incurs heavy fines. For full details, go to cityofsydney. nsw.gov.au/cycling or check out *Time Out* magazine's recent series of bicycle features at www.timeout.com/sydney.

Cycle nuts are becoming increasingly vocal in Sydney and with good reason – the Bike Plan

2010 network of arterial cycleways now spans over 200 kilometres (125 miles) and is growing apace with the boom in hipster bike shops (many centred on the Clarence Street strip in the CBD). The City of Sydney provides 'Cycleways' maps for the Sydney metropolitan area and also free cycling courses with bike maintenance classes and cycling in the city confidence sessions. View them online at cityofsydney.nsw.gov.au/cycling or call 9265 9333.

Centennial Park Cycles
50 Clovelly Road, between Avoca & Earls Streets, Randwick (9398 5027, www.cyclehire.com.au). Bus 339, X39. **Open** 8.30am-5.30pm daily. Rates mountain bikes from $12/hr; children's bikes from $10/hr. **Credit** AmEx, MC, V. **Map** p333 N14.
Family-run, Sydney's largest cycle and in-line skate hire shop has been in operation for more than 30 years. They have it all here, from tandems to tricycles, pedal cars and scooters. They also provide a bicycle pick-up and delivery service. Credit card details and photo ID are required to hire equipment.

Manly Cycle Centre
36 Pittwater Road, at Denison Street, Manly (9977 1189). Ferry Manly. **Open** 9am-6pm Mon-Sat; 10am-5pm Sun. Rates $15/hr; $35/day. **Credit** AmEx, MC, V. **Map** p334.
Located a block from Manly Beach, this full-service bike shop hires out front-suspension mountain bikes, and even jogging pushchairs for the ultra-fit mums and dads out there. Credit card details and photo ID are necessary.

WALKING

Walking is often the most practical – and enjoyable – way of getting around central areas, though there can be long waits at pedestrian lights. There are a number of marked scenic walks that you can follow: enquire at the Sydney Visitor Centre (*see p306*) for details. Some harbour and beachside walks are detailed in the Sightseeing chapters. For central Sydney street maps, *see p326*. To buy street maps, travel guides and national park walking guides, visit Map World (*see p200*) or Dymocks (*see p199*); most newsagents stock Sydney street guides and travel guides.

Resources A-Z

TRAVEL ADVICE

For up-to-date information on travel to a specific country – including the latest on safety and security, health issues, local laws and customs – contact your home country government's department of foreign affairs. Most have websites with useful advice for would-be travellers.

AUSTRALIA
www.smartraveller.gov.au

CANADA
www.voyage.gc.ca

NEW ZEALAND
www.safetravel.govt.nz

REPUBLIC OF IRELAND
foreignaffairs.gov.ie

UK
www.fco.gov.uk/travel

USA
www.state.gov/travel

ADDRESSES

Addresses begin with the apartment or unit number, if any, followed by the street number, followed by the street name. For example, Apartment 5, 50 Sun Street would be written as 5/50 Sun Street. This is followed by the locality and then by the state or territory and postcode – for instance, Paddington, NSW 2021. Postcodes cover a much larger area than their UK equivalents. Many residents and businesses have post office box numbers instead of personalised addresses.

AGE RESTRICTIONS

It is legal to buy and consume alcohol at 18. A learner's driving licence can be applied for at 16. A driving test can be taken at age 17, and if passed, drivers must then show a provisional 'P' plate (red P for one year, green P for two years), before being eligible for a full driving licence. Both gays and heterosexuals can have sex at 16 in NSW (though be warned, laws vary from state to state). It is illegal to sell cigarettes to anyone under 18, but there is no legal minimum age for smoking.

BUSINESS

Conventions & conferences

Sydney Convention & Exhibition Centre
Darling Harbour (9282 5000, www.scec.com.au). Ferry Darling Harbour/Monorail/LightRail Convention. **Map** p328 D7.
This integrated convention and exhibition centre has 30 meeting rooms and six exhibition halls, plus two business centres, inhouse catering and audio-visual services, 24-hour security and parking for more than 900 cars.

Couriers & shippers

Australia Post (13 1318, www.auspost.com.au) has national and international courier services: Messenger Post Courier is the national service, while Express Courier International (ECI) dispatches to more than 180 countries. Other services you could try include **Allied Express** (13 1373, www.alliedexpress.com.au) and **DHL Worldwide Express** (13 1406, www.dhl.com.au).

Office hire & business services

The multinational **FedEx Kinko's** chain (www.kinkos.net.au) has several branches around Sydney, some of which are open round the clock for internet access, self-service computers, photocopying and printing. The company also offers commercial shipping.

Servcorp
Level 17, BNP Centre, 60 Castlereagh Street, between King Street & Martin Place, CBD (1300 847 863, 9220 3663, www.servcorp.com.au). CityRail Martin Place. **Open** 8.30am-5.30pm Mon-Fri. **Credit** AmEx, DC, MC, V. **Map** p327 F6.
Servcorp offers office space in CBD and North Sydney for one-to 15-person companies with full business services (minimum lease one month) – and it claims to be cheaper than a secretary. Geared up to cater for foreign clients, with a multilingual support team. It also provides 'virtual' receptionists and business addresses.

Secretarial services

AW Secretarial Services
Suite 3, Level 5, 32 York Street, between King & Market Streets, CBD (9262 6812). CityRail Town Hall. **Open** 8.30am-5pm Mon-Fri. **Credit** MC, V. **Map** p327 E6.
For word processing, CVs and spreadsheets.

Translators & interpreters

Commercial Translation Centre
Level 20, 99 Walker Street, North Sydney (9954 4376, www.ctc4. com). CityRail North Sydney. **Open** 9am-5pm Mon-Fri. **Credit** MC, V.
The worldwide CTC has 80 linguistic staff with languages that include Japanese, Mandarin, Korean, Thai, Malay, French, German, Spanish, Dutch and Swedish.

Useful organisations

Australian Stock Exchange
20 Bridge Street, CBD (13 1279, 9338 0000, www.asx.com.au). CityRail Wynyard or Circular Quay. **Open** 10am-4.30pm Mon-Fri. **Map** p327 F4.

Australian Taxation Office
100 Market Street, CBD (13 2861, www.ato.gov.au). CityRail St James. **Open** 8.30am-4.45pm Mon-Fri. **Map** p327 F6.

State Chamber of Commerce
Level 12, 83 Clarence Street, CBD (1300 137 153, www.thechamber.com.au). CityRail Wynyard. **Open** 9am-5pm Mon-Fri. **Map** p327 E6.

DIRECTORY

CONSUMER

The excellent and practical website of the **NSW Office of Fair Trading** offers advice for consumers on how to avoid 'shady characters, scams and rip-offs' and for businesses on how to do the right thing by its customers. The excellent **Traveller Consumer Helpline** (1300 552001 www.travelhelp @fairtrading.nsw.gov.au) provides a rapid response (including access to translators) for travellers who experience unfair employment schemes, problems with accommodation or car rental, faulty goods or overcharging.

NSW Office of Fair Trading
1 Fitzwilliam Street, Parramatta (13 3220, www.fairtrading.nsw.gov.au). Ferry/CityRail Parramatta. **Open** 8.30am-5pm Mon-Fri.

CUSTOMS

Before landing on Australian soil you will be given an immigration form to fill out, as well as customs and agriculture declaration forms. You will pass through either the Green (nothing to declare) channel or the Red (something to declare) channel. Your baggage may be examined by Customs, regardless of which channel you use.

Anyone aged 18 years or over can bring in $900 worth of duty-free goods ($450 for under-18s), 2.25 litres of alcohol and 250 cigarettes or 250 grams of other tobacco products. You must declare amounts of $10,000 or more. Visitors can bring items such as computers into Australia duty-free, provided Customs is satisfied that these items are intended to be taken away again on departure.

UK Customs & Excise (www.hmce.gov.uk) allows travellers aged 18 and over returning from outside the EU to bring home £390 worth of gifts and goods, 200 cigarettes or 250 grams of tobacco, one litre of spirits or two litres of fortified wine, 60ml perfume and 250ml toilet water.

US Customs (www.customs.ustreas.gov) allows Americans to return from trips to Australia with goods valued up to US$800.

Quarantine

You must declare all food, plant cuttings, seeds, nuts or anything made from wood, plant or animal material that you bring into Australia. This includes many souvenirs and airline food. If you don't, you could face an on-the-spot fine of $220, or prosecution and fines of $66,000. Sniffer dogs will hunt out the tiniest morsel as they roam the airport with their handlers.

Quarantine officers use high-tech X-ray machines to check your luggage. Quarantine bins are provided at the airport for you to ditch any food and plants you may have about you before you reach immigration. Check the website of the **Australian Quarantine & Inspection Service** (www. daffa.gov.au) for details.

Australia also has quite strict laws prohibiting and restricting the export of native animals and plants, and items deemed 'moveable cultural heritage'. These include birds and their eggs, fish, reptiles, insects, plants, seeds, fossils and rock art. Products made from protected wildlife, such as hard corals and giant clam shells, are not allowed to be taken out of the country. If in doubt, check with the **Department of the Environment & Heritage** (6274 1111, www.deh.gov.au).

If you need to carry medicine for yourself in or out of the country, it is advisable to have a prescription or doctor's letter. Penalties for carrying illicit drugs in Australia are severe and could result in a jail term. Check the **Customs National Information Line** (1300 363263, www. customs.gov.au).

DISABLED

It was not until 1992 that building regulations required that provisions be made for disabled people, so some older venues do not have disabled access. Restaurants tend to be better, as most of them are equipped with ramps.

New transport standards will require that people with disabilities have access to most public transport within 20 years. For the time being, many Sydney streets are far from wheelchair-friendly. Constant construction upheavals and the city's hills aside, the standard of pavement surfaces in the inner suburbs leaves a lot to be desired. Poor street lighting compounds the problem.

For more information, check out the excellent website of the **Disability Information**

Resource (www.accessibility. com.au), which provides details on wheelchair access throughout the city, from music venues and restaurants to museums and public toilets. Or contact the following:

Information on Disability & Education Awareness Services (IDEAS)
Suite 208, 35 Buckingham Street, Surry Hills (1800 029904, 9657 1796, www.ideas.org.au). **Open** 8.30am-4.30pm Mon-Fri. **Map** p329 F10.
Provides information and referral on all disabilities for the whole of NSW and has a great, up-to-date database on eastern suburbs services.

Spinal Cord Injuries Australia
9661 8855, www.scia.org.au. This organisation provides consumer-based support and rehabilitation services to help people with physical disabilities participate fully in society. Phone/internet enquiries only.

State Library of NSW Disability Information
State Library of NSW, corner of Macquarie Street & Cahill Expressway, CBD (9273 1583, www.sl.nsw.gov.au/access). **Open** Phone enquiries 9am-5pm Mon-Fri. **Map** p327 G5.
A helpful information line that offers a great starting point for disabled visitors.

DRUGS

Cannabis and harder drugs are illegal in Australia, but that hasn't prevented a significant drug culture – and problem – from developing. High-volume imports from Asia ensure cheap and dangerously pure strains of heroin arrive on the streets, while cannabis, ecstasy, cocaine and ice (crystal meth) are the chosen poisons of the city's youth.

Kings Cross is the epicentre of drug dealing in Sydney and has been the target of a clean-up campaign by the local government. The future of the 'shooting gallery' safe injection room in the area hangs in the balance, as nay-sayers and project supporters argue over its success rates. Still, come nightfall it's not uncommon for addicts to shoot up on the streets, in the parks and even on beaches. Needle disposal bins are everywhere. *See also p302* Helplines.

ELECTRICITY

The Australian domestic electricity supply is 230-240V, 50Hz AC. UK appliances work with a basic plug adaptor, but US 110V appliances need a transformer as well. The plug is Australasia specific.

EMBASSIES & CONSULATES

Canada
Level 5, Quay West Building, 111 Harrington Street, at Essex Street, CBD (9364 3000, visa information 9364 3050, www.canada.org.au). CityRail/ferry Circular Quay. **Open** 8.30am-4.30pm Mon-Fri. **Map** p327 E4.

Ireland
Level 26, 1 Market Street, CBD (9264 9635, www.dfa.ie). CityRail Town Hall. **Open** 10am-1pm, 2.30-4pm Mon-Fri. **Map** p327 E6.

New Zealand
Level 10, 55 Hunter Street, at Castlereagh Street, CBD (8256 2000/pm). CityRail Martin Place or Wynyard. **Open** 9am-12.30pm, 1.30-5pm Mon-Fri. **Map** p327 F5.

South Africa
Rhodes Place, State Circle, Canberra (6272 7300, www. sahc.org.au). **Open** 8.30am-1pm, 1.45pm-5pm Mon-Fri.

United Kingdom
Level 16, The Gateway, 1 Macquarie Place, at Bridge Street, CBD (9247 7521, www.britaus.net). CityRail/ferry Circular Quay. **Open** *Phone* 9am-5pm Mon-Fri. *Counter* 10am-12.30pm, 1.30pm-4pm Mon-Fri. **Map** p327 F4.

USA
Level 59, MLC Centre 19-29 Martin Place, CBD (9373 9200, http://sydney.usconsulate.gov/ sydney). CityRail Martin Place. **Open** *Phone* 8am-5pm Mon-Fri. *Counter* 8am-11.30am Mon-Fri. **Map** p327 F5.

EMERGENCIES

For the fire brigade, police or ambulance, dial **000**. It's a free call from any phone. From a mobile phone, call **112** – which allows your location to be pinpointed.

For hospitals, see below Health. For other emergency numbers, *see p302* Helplines. You can contact the Poisons Information Centre (open 24 hours daily) at 13 1126.

GAY & LESBIAN

The quickest way to find gay-related information is via weekly newspapers *Sydney Star Observer* (www.ssonet.com.au), the boysy *SX* (www.evolutionpublishing.com.au/s xnews), or, for women, the excellent monthly mag *Lesbians on the Loose* (www.lotl.com). All are available free from newsagents, clubs and bars all over town.

For the Gay & Lesbian chapter, covering the entertainment scene, *see p241.*

Help & information

For information on STDs, HIV & AIDS, *see p302.*

Gay & Lesbian Counselling Service of NSW
8594 9596 www.glcsnsw.org.au. **Open** 5.30pm-10.30pm daily. Information and phone counselling.

Gay & Lesbian Tourism Australia
0414 446401, www.galta.com.au. A non-profit organisation dedicated to the welfare of gay and lesbian travellers in Australia.

HEALTH

The universal government healthcare system, Medicare Australia, has a reciprocal agreement with Finland, Italy, Malta, the Netherlands, New Zealand, Norway, Republic of Ireland, Sweden and the UK, entitling residents of those countries to get necessary medical and hospital treatment for free. This agreement does not cover all eventualities (for example, ambulance fees or dental costs), and only applies to public hospitals and casualty departments.

If you have travel insurance, check the small print to see whether you need to register with Medicare before making a claim; if not, or if you don't have insurance, you can claim a Medicare rebate by taking your passport and visa, together with the medical bill, to any Medicare centre.

For more information, phone or write to the information service below. *See also p302* Doctors and Prescriptions.

Medicare Information Service
Postal address: PO Box 9822, Sydney, NSW 2001 (13 2011, www.medicareaustralia.gov.au).

Open Phone enquiries 9am-4.30pm Mon-Fri.

Accident & emergency

In an emergency, call 000 for an ambulance.

Prince of Wales Hospital
Barker Street, Randwick (9382 2222). Bus 373, 374.

Royal North Shore Hospital
Pacific Highway, St Leonards (9926 7111). CityRail St Leonards.

Royal Prince Alfred Hospital
Missenden Road, Camperdown (9515 6111). Bus 412.

St Vincent's Public Hospital
Corner of Burton & Victoria Streets, Darlinghurst (8382 1111). CityRail Kings Cross/bus 333, 378, 380.

Complementary medicine

Australians are very open to complementary medicine and treatments; indeed, many conventional doctors take a holistic approach and combine mainstream treatments with complementary care. Look in the *Yellow Pages* under 'Alternative Health Services' for hundreds of practitioners.

Australian Natural Therapists Association
1800 817577, www.anta.com.au.

Australian Traditional-Medicine Society
Postal address: PO Box 1027, Meadowbank, NSW 2114 (9809 6800, www.atms.com.au).

Contraception & abortion

FPA Health (Family Planning Association)
Clinics and advice: 1300 658886, www.fpahealth.org.au. **Open** 9am-5.30pm Mon-Fri.

Marie Stopes International
1800 003707, www.mariestopes.com.au. **Open** 8am-9pm Mon-Fri; 9am-2pm Sat.

Dentists

Dental treatment is not covered by Medicare, and therefore not by the reciprocal agreement *(see left)*. In the absence of medical insurance be prepared for hefty fees. Check the Yellow Pages for listings, though it's a good idea to ask locals or hotel

DIRECTORY

staff to recommend a dentist they know and trust.

Doctors

For listings of doctors, see the *Yellow Pages* under 'Medical Practitioners'. If your home country is covered under the reciprocal Medicare agreement, and your visit is for immediately necessary treatment, you can claim a refund from Medicare. Try to get to one of the increasingly rare 'bulk billing' medical practices, where your trip will be free. Otherwise you will only get back a proportion of the fee, which must be claimed in person.

Hospitals

Hospitals are listed in the White Pages at the front of the phone book in the 'Emergency, Health & Help' section, with a location map. For hospitals with 24-hour A&E, *see p301* Accident & emergency.

Opticians

See p212.

Pharmacies

Standard opening times for chemists are 9am to 5.30pm Monday to Friday, and usually 9am to 5.30pm Saturday, 10am to 5pm Sunday (though weekend opening times depend on the area). Many convenience stores and supermarkets stock over-the-counter drugs. *See also p214.*

Prescriptions

In Australia, prescription costs vary depending on the drugs being prescribed. On the Pharmaceutical Benefits Scheme (PBS) you shouldn't have to pay too much – but to get the price you must have a Medicare card or temporary Medicare card, available to visitors from nations with a reciprocal health care agreement from any Medicare office, with your passport and visa.

STDs, HIV & AIDS

AIDS Council of NSW (ACON)
9 Commonwealth Street, Surry Hills (1800 063060, 9206 2000, www.acon.org.au). CityRail Museum. **Open** 10am-6pm Mon-Fri. **Map** p329 F9.
ACON offers information, advice and support.

HIV/AIDS Information
9332 9600, www.sesahs. nsw.gov.au/albionstcentre. **Open** 8am-7pm Mon-Fri; 10am-6pm Sat. Statewide information service.

Sydney Sexual Health Centre
Sydney Hospital, 8 Macquarie Street, opposite Martin Place, CBD (1800 451624, 9382 7440). CityRail Martin Place. **Open** *Phone enquiries* 9.30am-6pm Mon-Fri. *Clinic* 10am-6pm Mon, Tue, Thur, Fri; 2-6pm Wed. **Map** p327 G5/6.
Government-funded clinic aimed at young people at risk, gay men and sex workers.

HELPLINES

Alcohol & Drug Information Service
1800 422599, 9361 8000. **Open** 24hrs daily.
Crisis counselling, information, assessment and referrals.

Alcoholics Anonymous
9387 7788, www.alcoholics anonymous.org.au. **Open** 24hrs daily.
Manned by volunteers who are recovering alcoholics.

Child Abuse Line
13 2111, www.community. nsw.gov.au. **Open** 24hrs daily.
For immediate help, advice and action involving children at risk.

Domestic Violence Line
1800 200526. **Open** 24hrs daily.
Call 000 if in immediate danger, otherwise this service offers expert counselling and advice.

Gamblers Counselling Service
9951 5566, G-Line 1800 633635, www.wesleymission.org.au. **Open** 9am-5pm Mon-Fri. G-Line 24hrs daily.
A face-to-face counselling service plus 24-hour telephone helpline.

Kids Helpline
1800 551800, www.kidshelp. com.au. **Open** 24hrs daily.
Confidential support for children and young people aged five to 18. Counsellors available by email or for real-time web counselling.

Law Access
1300 888529, www.lawaccess. nsw.gov.au. **Open** 9am-5pm Mon-Fri.
Advice and information on all on legal issues.

Lifeline
13 1114. **Open** 24hrs daily.
Help for people in crisis.

Rape Crisis Centre
1800 424017, 9819 7357. **Open** 24hrs daily.
Rape counselling over the phone.

Salvation Army Salvo Care Line
1300 363622. **Open** 24hrs daily.
Help for anyone in crisis or contemplating suicide.

INSURANCE

Getting some travel insurance is advisable, especially if you're aiming to stay in backpacker hostels, where thefts are common. Australia has reciprocal health care agreements with many countries; *see p301* Health.

INTERNET

Cybercafés are everywhere in Sydney. Most backpacker hotels have internet links, and most libraries will provide access.

LANGUAGE

Despite the country's history, contemporary vernacular Australian owes more to US English than the UK variety and the mongrel tongue that has emerged from the hybrid is 'Strine'. Words that have a peculiarly Australian flavour include: arvo (afternoon); bludger (scrounger, as in 'dole bludger'); daggy (nerdy or goofy); daks (trousers); doona (duvet); dunny (lavatory/loo/toilet); and thongs (flip-flops, not G-strings) as spoken by sheilas (ladies) or blokes (gents). Take special care when talking about your roots (root means shag/bonk/sexual encounter while 'I'm rooted' can imply extreme weariness or a dire situation – more so than your ancestry or the streaks in your hair). You will probably hear 'G'day, mate' and 'Fair dinkum', but often said with a knowing wink. *See p19,* How to Speak Convict: An A-Z, for more bonza exaples of Strine, each more beaut than the last.

LEFT LUGGAGE

There are left-luggage lockers for hire in the international terminal of **Sydney Airport** (call 9667 0926 for information). They cost $11 per bag for up to 24 hours.

LEGAL HELP

For embassies and consulates, *see* p301. For information on the Law Access service, see above Helplines.

LOST PROPERTY

For belongings lost on State Transit public transport, try phoning the main STA switchboard on 9245 5777, or 9379 341 for CityRail and CountryLink. For the Monorail and LightRail, phone 9285 5600. If you've left something behind in a cab, phone the relevant taxi company. For property lost on the street, contact the police on 9281 0000. For items lost at the airport, phone 9667 9583 or contact the relevant airline direct.

MEDIA

Magazines

Time Out Sydney magazine has a fantastic feel for the pulse of the city – its food and drink section is revered by both diners and chefs and its entertainment listings and local features draw huge traffic online. The magazine launched in 2007 and is going strong, with *Time Out Melbourne* planned for 2011. *Time Out Sydney* comes out on the first or last Wednesday of the month and is sold in all major newsagents and many bookshops. Check out the website as well at www.timeoutsydney.com.au or subscribe to the weekly newsletter at www.timeoutsydney.com.au/ newsletter.

Newspapers: dailies

Sydney has two local papers, the broadsheet *Sydney Morning Herald* (www.smh.com.au, owned by Fairfax) and the tabloid *Daily Telegraph* (http://daily telegraph.news.com.au, News International, owned by Rupert Murdoch). The *SMH* is an institution with an ego to match. Local stories prevail, with solid coverage of politics and events, but beware the comment columns.

The *Daily Telegraph* is a true tabloid, with plenty of scandal splashes and bitchy celebrity news in its 'Sydney Confidential' spread.

News International also produces a freebie newspaper, *MX* (www. mxnet.com.au), handed out at CityRail stations Monday to Friday. The two national newspapers, the *Australian* (www.theaustralian. news.com.au, Murdoch) and the

Australian Financial Review (http://afr.com, Fairfax), are both based in Sydney, and carry that bias in their coverage. The *Australian* has been trying to shake out its starchiness, but the result has been a rather bizarre mish-mash of armchair trendiness and what could be called a kind of 'gentle conservatism'. The *Review* offers excellent news coverage, plus business and politics.

Newspapers: weekend

The Saturday *Sydney Morning Herald* is a vast publication, mainly due to a surfeit of classified advertisements. The *Saturday Telegraph* is not as thick, but still has its fair share of supplements. The *Australian* aspires to stylish minimalism, with a slick, svelte weekend broadsheet on Saturday, accompanied by a print-heavy magazine. On Sundays, there is Fairfax's tabloid *Sun-Herald*, designed to compete with the popular *Sunday Telegraph*.

Radio

AM stations
NewsRadio (ABC) 630 AM
Rolling news service with strong international content and daytime coverage of parliament.
Radio National (ABC) 576 AM
Intelligent, provocative talk shows, arts and current affairs.
Radio 2GB 873 AM
Veteran talk show radio station that feeds off local whingeing, humorous tirades and chatty hosts.
SBS Radio 1107 AM
Ethnic, multilingual programmes for Sydney's diverse communities.
2BL (ABC) 702 AM
The Australian Broadcasting Corporation's popular and 2nd largest (after 2GB) talk station features non-commercial, non-ranting, reasonably intelligent banter and news.
2CH 1170 AM
Easy, yawn, listening.
2KY 1017 AM
Racing, racing and more racing.
2UE 954 AM
The place for controversial talkback shows.

FM stations
ABC Classic FM 92.9 FM
Classical music for non-purists, and some cool jazz.
MIX 106.5 FM
Celine Dion, Phil Collins, the Spice Girls – oh, and is that Lionel Ritchie?

FBi 94.5 FM
Take a side-step from the mainstream and discover the groovin' underground.
Nova 96.9 FM
This relative newcomer is young, brash and cheeky.
SBS Radio 97.7 FM
Special-interest ethnic programming.
Triple J 105.7 FM
Well respected as the station most devoted to the discovery and spread of new music.
2DAY 104.1 FM
Made its name by taking women seriously. And the listeners flocked. Funny, that.
2000FM 98.5 FM
Ethnic specialist with community-driven shows.
2MMM (Triple M) 104.9 FM
Rock, ads and then more rock.
Vega 95.3 FM
Sydney's newest radio station, launched in 2005, targeting the baby-boomers with talk and music.
WSFM 101.7 FM
Classic hits from the 1960s to '80s, every one a singalong.

Television

The government-funded TV and radio networks are **ABC** (Australian Broadcasting Corporation) and **SBS** (Special Broadcasting Service). ABC has strong links with the BBC and tends to get first dibs on new BBC series while maintaining a strong raft of homegrown shows. Its strengths are documentaries and current affairs and comedy considered too edgy for their commercial rivals. Recent Aussie international hits *Kath & Kim* and *Summer Heights High* both debuted on ABC before being picked up in global broadcasting deals. In 2010, ABC launched its long-awaited 24 hour news channel **ABC News 24**. SBS has a remit to support multicultural programming and is woefully underfunded, a dollar dearth it has of late supplemented with advertising. It features foreign films (subtitled), has good world news at 6.30pm every night and is renowned for its documentaries, many from independent Australian producers. It's also where you'll find comprehensive European football coverage and many HBO series such as *Mad Men*, *Big Love*, *Oz* and *Flight of the Conchords*, all considered too risqué for the commercial networks. The other three networks – **Seven**, **Nine** and **Ten** – are commercial and, for the

DIRECTORY

most part, populist, featuring a large dose of US TV, heaps of local lifestyle shows and ads seemingly every five minutes.

MONEY

In 1966, Australia relinquished the old country's pounds, shillings and pence for the Australian dollar ($) and cent (c). Paper money comes in $100, $50, $20, $10 and $5 denominations. Coins come in bronze $2 and $1 pieces, and silver 50c, 20c, 10c and 5c pieces.

ATMs

There are 24-hour ATMs all over town – outside banks, and increasingly in pubs, bottle shops and convenience stores. Most also accept debit cards linked to international networks such as Visa Debit, which will charge for withdrawals.

Some ATMs accept credit cards – check the card logos displayed. Be aware that withdrawing money on your credit card usually incurs interest, starting immediately.

Banks

The banks below have branches throughout the city. All are open 9.30am to 4pm Monday to Thursday, and 9.30am to 5pm Friday.

ANZ

97 Castlereagh Street, CBD (13 1314, www.anz.com). CityRail St James. **Map** p327 F6.

Commonwealth Bank of Australia

48 Martin Place, CBD (13 2221, www.commbank.com.au). CityRail Martin Place. **Map** p327 F5.

National Australia Bank

75 Elizabeth Street, CBD (13 2265, www.national.com.au). CityRail Martin Place. **Map** p327 F6.

Westpac

60 Martin Place, CBD (13 2032, www.westpac.com.au). CityRail Martin Place. **Map** p327 F/G5.

Bureaux de change

American Express

105 Pitt Street, between Martin Place & Hunter Street, CBD (1300 139060, www.americanexpress. com/australia). CityRail Wynyard. **Open** 9am-5pm Mon-Fri. **Map** p327 F5.
Other locations throughout the city.

Travelex

Queen Victoria Building, 455 George Street, between Market & Druitt Streets, CBD (9264 1267, www.travelex.com). CityRail Town Hall. **Open** 9am-6pm Mon-Fri; 10am-3pm Sat. **Map** p327 E6.
Other locations throughout the city.

Credit cards

MasterCard (MC), Visa and American Express (AmEx) are widely accepted. You can also use credit cards to get cash from any bank (take your passport), and some ATMs. To report lost or stolen cards, call (free) these 24-hour numbers:

American Express 1300 132639
Diners Club 1300 360060
MasterCard 1800 120113
Visa 1300 651089

Tax & tax refunds

A ten per cent GST (Goods & Services Tax) is charged on some goods, food and services, including accommodation, and is included in the display price. Tourists can reclaim it on selected goods when they leave the country by using the **Tourist Refund Scheme** (TRS). This scheme applies only to goods you carry as hand luggage or wear on to the aircraft or ship when you leave.

The refund can be claimed on goods costing a total of $300 or above (including GST) bought from one shop no more than 30 days before you leave. You can buy several lower-priced items from the same shop, either in one go or at different times, provided you've spent at least $300 total within the 30-day period. And you can reclaim tax for items bought from any number of shops, as long you've spent at least $300 in each one.

To claim a refund, you must get a tax invoice from the shop or shops in question. You then claim your refund at a TRS booth, after passport control. Here you'll need to show the goods, the tax invoices, your passport and boarding pass. Refunds can be paid to a credit card, taking five business days.

Full details are on the Australian Customs website, www.customs. gov.au – click on 'travellers'.

NATURAL HAZARDS

With a dangerously thin ozone layer, the sun is Sydney's biggest natural hazard. The best way to

avoid it is to 'slip, slap, slop' – slip on a T-shirt, slap on a hat, and slop on some sun-cream, preferably SPF 30 or higher.

Australia's array of mini-creatures is legendary. And Sydney, being temperate and humid, is the perfect breeding ground for all things cold-blooded or with six or more legs. Most bugs, arachnids and reptiles are completely harmless, and most tend to bother residents rather than visitors in built-up areas, but there are a few nasties to look out for. The following are the critters you should be aware of.

Spiders

While many different types of spider tend to congregate in Sydney, there are two with a potentially fatal bite – the Sydney funnel web and the redback. The funnel web is a nasty, aggressive creature native to the Sydney bush. Black, sparsely haired and much-feared (despite not adding to its death toll of 13 since anti-venom was introduced in 1981), it lives in holes in the ground. Unlike most spiders, males are the more deadly of the species. If bitten, apply pressure and immobilise the wounded area, using a splint if possible, and get to a hospital (or dial 000) immediately. The redback, which is smaller and black with a red stripe on its pea-sized body, lives mainly outside, where it is one of two species in which the male actively assists the female in sexual cannibalism. Apply ice if bitten and seek immediate medical help.

Snakes

Five of the ten most dangerous snakes in the world are said to live in Australia, with names like King brown, Taipan and Tiger. Most are more scared of you than you are of them, but a couple can be aggressive if cornered – so play it safe: always wear boots when hiking through the bush, don't put your hands in any holes or crevices, and watch where you're walking. If someone with you is bitten, assume that the snake is venomous. Wrap the limb tightly, attach a splint and keep the victim still and calm, then seek immediate medical help. Snake bites will not cause immediate death and antivenom is usually available from medical services.

Cockroaches

They say the 'cockie' would be the only thing to survive a nuclear holocaust – whether or not this is true, Sydneysiders will try anything short of napalm to wipe them out. Despite being nasty, the cockroaches (which seem to grow to the size of frogs during summer – perhaps a response to the chemical warfare being waged against them) are harmless.

Flies and mosquitoes

Flies and mozzies are a fact of Aussie life, but besides imparting an itchy bump (mozzies) and an irritable disposition (flies), they're not dangerous. There are also a couple of flies that bite, such as the march fly – but their bite is not poisonous, just a tad painful. Some people can experience nasty allergic reactions to bites – if this is you, try prescribed or over-the-counter antihistamines (ask the pharmacist for advice). Personal repellents, such as Aeroguard or Rid, tend to be fairly effective, or you can buy coils to burn outdoors, or repelling candles. Mosquito nets and screens are a good idea in summer.

Bushland brutes

If you plan to fit in a little bushwalking anywhere on Australia's east coast, there are a couple of creatures you need to watch out for besides snakes. Ticks are very dangerous, if not removed immediately, as they excrete a toxin that can cause paralysis or, in extreme cases, even death. So each day after bushwalking check your body for lumps and bumps – they tend to like hairy areas, skin creases and ears – and slowly pull or twist any ticks out with sharp-pointed tweezers. Leeches are common bushland suckers – literally. However, they aren't dangerous and can easily be persuaded to let go by applying salt or heat.

OPENING HOURS

Shops are usually open from 8.30am or 9am to 5pm or 6pm Monday to Saturday, and from 10am or 11am to 4pm or 5pm Sunday. Thursday is late-night opening (usually until 9pm). Some shops close at noon on Saturdays. Banks are usually open from 9.30am to 4pm Monday to Thursday, until 5pm on Friday, and closed at the weekend.

POLICE

To report an emergency, dial **000**. If it is not an emergency, call the police at **13 1444**. The **City**

Central Police Station is at 192 Day Street, CBD (9265 6499). More info at www.police.nsw.gov.au.

POSTAL SERVICES

Australia Post (13 1318, www.auspost.com.au) says about 90 per cent of letters within the metropolitan area arrive the next business day. Post is delivered once a day Monday to Friday, with no delivery on Saturdays or Sundays. Post to Europe takes four to ten days. Stamps for postcards to Europe and the USA cost $1.45; for letters it's $2.20 (up to 50 grams), and international aerogrammes cost 95c. Letters within Australia cost from 60c to $2.60 and $4.60 for express post.

Most post office branches open from 9am to 5pm Monday to Friday, but the GPO Martin Place branch is also open on Saturdays. Stamps can also be bought at some newsagents and general stores. Suburban post offices will receive post for you; otherwise have it sent Poste Restante (general delivery) to GPO Sydney, NSW 2000 – and collect it from the address below. .

General Post Office

1 Martin Place, CBD (9244 3713). CityRail Martin Place or Wynyard. **Open** 8.15am-5.30pm Mon-Fri; 10am-2pm Sat. **Map** p327 F5/6.

Poste Restante

Level 2, Hunter Connection Building, 310 George Street, CBD (13 1318). CityRail Martin Place or Wynyard. **Open** 9am-5pm Mon-Fri. **Map** p327 F5.

RELIGION

Have a look in the *Yellow Pages* under 'Churches, Mosques and Temples' for places of worship.

SAFETY & SECURITY

Sydney is a fairly safe city, although car theft, vandalism and burglary are on the increase. That said, you will frequently read about drug-related shootings, and racial tension has heightened since the Bali bombings and the riots on Cronulla Beach in 2005. And while the stereotype of hot-blooded Aussie males ending an alcohol-fuelled evening with a pub brawl is not the norm, it's not entirely unknown either – so steer clear of drunk rednecks at closing time.

In an emergency, dial **000**.

SMOKING

Smoking is banned on public transport and in cafés, restaurants and many enclosed spaces, such as theatres, shopping malls and community centres. Smoking in pubs and clubs is now completely banned. There are fines for tossing cigarette butts out of car windows.

STUDY

Anyone can apply to study in Australia, but you must obtain a student visa before starting a course.

For more details, visit the Department of Immigration's website at www.immi.gov.au. You'll only be granted a student visa if you're signing up for a full-time registered course.

UNIVERSITIES

University of NSW

Postal address: University of NSW, Sydney, NSW 2052 (9385 1000, www.unsw.edu.au). Location: Anzac Parade, Kensington. Bus 302, 303, 391, 392, 393, 394, 395, 396, 397, 399, 400, 410, 890, L94. The UNSW is one of the leading teaching and research universities in Australia. Almost 9,000 of its 40,000 students are foreign.

University of Sydney

Postal address: University of Sydney, NSW 2006 (9351 2222, www.usyd.edu.au). Location: City Road, Darlington, & Parramatta Road, Camperdown. City Road entrance: bus 422, 423, 426, 428/Parramatta Road entrance: bus 412, 413, 435, 436, 437, 438, 440, 461, 480. Australia's first uni has around 46,000 students, of whom nearly 9,000 are international.

Macquarie University

Postal address: Macquarie University, NSW 2109 (9850 7111, www.mq.edu.au). Location: Balaclava Road, North Ryde. Bus 288, 292. Macquarie has more than 30,000 students, around 9,000 of them from overseas. The university is set in bushland north of Sydney, offering a rural alternative to city unis.

TELEPHONES

Dialling & codes

The country code for Australia is **61**; the area code for NSW,

DIRECTORY

including Sydney, is **02**. You never need to dial the 02 from within the state. Numbers beginning 1800 are free when dialled within Australia; numbers beginning 13 or 1300 are charged at a 25c flat fee.

Making a call

To make an international call, dial an international access code – either **0011** or **0018**, or + on a mobile – followed by the country code, area code (usually omitting any initial 0), and then the number.

The different international access codes have different pricing systems. Telstra, the dominant Australian phone company, offers a choice of 0011 Minutes or 0018 Half Hours. The 0011 calls are for shorter chats, charged per second. The 0018 calls are for a long chat and you'll know exactly how much your call will cost up front. Warning beeps tell you when your half-hour is almost up.

The country code for the UK is **44**, for New Zealand **64**, for the USA **1**, for the Republic of Ireland **353** and for South Africa **27**.

Standard local calls are untimed flat-fee calls between standard fixed telephone services within a local service area. To check if local call charges apply, call 13 2200.

STD calls (national long-distance calls) are charged according to their distance, time and day, plus a fee. Each call starts with five pip tones.

Public phones

There are still a few public phones dotted around the city, as well as in bars, cafés, railway stations and post offices. You can also make long-distance and international calls at many internet cafés. Most public phones accept coins ($1, 50c, 20c, 10c). Some also accept major credit cards. Cheap international phonecards are available from newsagents.

Directory enquiries

Dial **1223** to find a number within Australia, and **1225** for international directory enquiries.

Operator services

For operator-assisted national or international calls, phone **1234**.

Mobile phones

Australia's mobile phone network operates on dual-band 900/1800

MHz (megahertz). This means that if you're coming from the UK you should be able to use your own mobile phone – but that's not as simple as it sounds.

If you keep your UK SIM card in the phone, when you arrive your phone will register itself with a local network with which your UK service provider has an agreement. If you want to use this facility, check with your service provider before you go, as you may need to set your phone up to work abroad. This is the easiest method, but it can be potentially very expensive: calling numbers in Australia will cost the same as calling back to the UK – a lot – and you'll have to pay to receive calls as well as to make them.

Another simple option is to to buy or rent a phone. Plenty of Sydney companies offer competitive mobile phone rentals with local networks, for a minimum of three days, billed to your credit card. Or you could just buy or rent a SIM card for an Australian network and put it in your UK phone (and top it up as required). However, your phone may have been 'locked' so that it works only with your UK service provider's SIM card. You're entitled to get the phone unlocked, and the service provider has to give you an unlocking code – for free – if you ask for it. Once you've unlocked your phone you can put any SIM card in it. In practice, service providers tend not to make this easy, and the process can be fraught with difficulties. Alternatively, any mobile phone repair shop will do it, for about $40. If you're in Sydney for a year or more, you could get a phone or SIM card on a billed package. To get this kind of plan – usually 12 months minimum – you'll need an Australian credit rating, and it takes six months to get one.

To investigate further, look under 'Mobile Telephones & Accessories' in the *Yellow Pages* or try these places:

Paddington Phones
241 Commonwealth Street, at Foveaux Street, Surry Hills (9281 8044, www.paddingtonphones. com.au). CityRail Central. **Open** 9am-5.30pm Mon-Fri. **Map** p329 F9. Rentals, pre-paid and fixed-term deals are all available.

Vodafone Rentals
Arrivals Hall, T1 International Terminal, Sydney Airport (9700

8086, www.vodafone.com.au). **Open** 6.30am-9pm daily. Rent or buy a phone or SIM card as soon as you arrive. **Other locations** 333 George Street (8753 3324); Westfield Bondi Junction (8753 3302).

TICKETS

You can book tickets for all major venues (music, theatre, dance and so on) through agencies **Ticketek** (13 2849, www.ticketek.com.au) and **Ticketmaster** (13 6100, www.ticketmaster.com.au). Also try **MCA Ticketing** (1300 306776, www.mca-tix.com) or **Moshtix** (1300 438849, www.moshtix. com.au). All charge booking fees.

TIME

New South Wales operates on **Eastern Standard Time** (GMT plus 10 hours). Between October and March, Daylight Saving Time comes into operation, and the clocks go forward one hour. Australia has three time zones – the others are Western Standard Time (GMT plus 8 hours) and Central Standard Time (GMT plus 9.5 hours). Confusingly, Queensland doesn't recognise Daylight Saving Time.

TIPPING

Tipping is appreciated but not usually expected in restaurants and cafés, where ten per cent is the norm. Locals tend not to tip in taxis.

TOILETS

There are plenty of free, well-maintained public lavatories in Sydney – in department stores, shopping centres, rail stations, beaches and parks. It is frowned upon to use the toilet in a bar if you're not also buying a drink. And a note for women: Sydney's sewage pipes are a lot narrower and so more prone to blockage than most of those elsewhere, and tampons and sanitary towels can easily block them up. Always use a bin instead!

TOURIST INFORMATION

As well as the visitor centres below, the City of Sydney's website – at www.cityofsydney.nsw.gov.au – and Tourism NSW's site – at www.visitnsw.com.au – have lots of useful information. If you plan to travel elsewhere in the country, Australia's official website –

AVERAGE CLIMATE

Month	Temperature (°C/°F)	Rainfall mm/in
January	19-26/66-79	89/3.5
February	19-26/66-79	102/4
March	17-25/63-76	127/5
April	15-22/58-72	135/5.3
May	11-19/52-67	127/5
June	9-17/49-61	117/4.6
July	8-16/49-61	117/4.6
August	9-18/49-63	76/3
September	11-20/52-66	74/2.9
October	13-22/56-72	71/2.8
November	16-24/61-75	74/2.9
December	17-25/63-77	74/2.9

www.australia.com – is packed with helpful ideas and information.

Sydney Visitor Centre
Level 2, corner of Argyle & Playfair Road, The Rocks (9240 8788, 1800 067676, www.sydneyvisitor centre.com). CityRail/ferry Circular Quay. **Open** 9.30am-5.30pm daily. **Map** p327 F3.
Other locations *33 Wheat Road, Darling Harbour (9240 8788). Ferry Darling Harbour/City Rail Town Hall/Monorail Darling Park.* **Open** 9.30am-5.30pm daily. **Map** p328 D7.
This is the main official information resource, with two city-centre locations – in the Rocks and in Darling Harbour.

Cadman's Cottage/ Sydney Harbour National Park Information Centre
110 George Street, between Argyle Street & Mill Lane, The Rocks (9247 5033, www.nationalparks. nsw.gov.au). CityRail/ferry Circular Quay. **Open** 9.30am-4.30pm Mon-Fri; 10am-4.30pm Sat, Sun. **Map** p327 F3.

Manly Visitor & Information Centre
Manly Wharf, Manly (9976 1430, www.manlytourism.com). Ferry Manly. **Open** 9am-5pm Mon-Fri; 10am-4pm Sat, Sun (5pm summer). **Map** p334.

Parramatta Heritage & Visitor Information Centre
346A Church Street, next to Lennox Bridge, Parramatta (8839 3311, www.parracity.nsw.gov.au). CityRail/ferry Parramatta then 10mins walk. **Open** 9am-5pm daily.

VISAS & IMMIGRATION

All travellers, including children – except for Australian and New Zealand citizens – must have a visa or an **ETA** (Electronic Travel Authority) to enter Australia. An ETA is sufficient for tourists from EC countries – including the UK and Ireland, except holders of GBN (British National Overseas) passports – the USA, Canada and Japan (but not South Africa), who are intending to stay for up to three months.
ETAs, available for straightforward tourist and business trips, are the simplest to arrange: your travel agent or airline or a commercial visa service can arrange one on the spot if you give them details or a copy/fax of your passport (no photo or ticket is required). You don't need a stamp in your passport: ETAs are confirmed electronically at your port of entry. Alternatively, you can apply for an ETA online via www.eta.immi.gov.au. The service costs $20, and you can be approved for entry in less than 30 seconds.
If your entry requirements are more complex or you want to stay longer than three months, you will probably need a non-ETA visa, which you apply for by post or in person to the relevant office in advance of your trip. For up-to-date information and details of the nearest overseas office where visa applications can be made, check www.immi.gov.au. For details on working visas, see below Working in Sydney.

WEIGHTS & MEASURES

Australia uses the metric system.

WHEN TO GO

Sydney has a moderate climate, with warm to hot summers, cool winters and rainfall all year round.
Spring brings blossoming flowers and clear blue skies, with temperatures warm enough to shed the woollies, especially when the sun shines. In summer, Sydneysiders live in shorts. In January and February, the sun bakes the city, and temperatures can top 30°C (90°F) – and even go over 40°C (104°F). In autumn, the city is swept by strong winds, while winter mornings and nights mean low temperatures that can – but rarely do – dip down to 6°C (43°F). Winter daily maximums tend to hover between 14°C (57°F) and 18°C (64°F), and on occasion snow falls in the Blue Mountains.

NSW public holidays

New Year's Day (1 January); **Australia Day** (26 January); **Good Friday**; **Easter Monday**; **Anzac Day** (25 April); the **Queen's Birthday** (2nd Monday in June); **August Bank Holiday** (1st Monday in August); **Labour Day** (1st Monday in October); **Christmas Day** (25 December); and **Boxing Day** (26 December).

WORKING IN SYDNEY

If you want to work while you're staying in Sydney, you'll need to have a visa that allows this. **The Working Holiday Program** provides opportunities for people aged 18 to 30 from some countries (including Belgium, Canada, Republic of Cyprus, Denmark, Estonia, Finland, France, Germany, Hong Kong, Republic of Ireland, Italy, Japan, Republic of Korea, Malta, Netherlands, Norway, Sweden, Taiwan and the UK) to holiday in Australia and supplement their funds through incidental employment. The visa allows a stay of up to 12 months from the date of first entry to Australia, regardless of whether or not you spend the whole time in Australia. You are allowed to do any kind of work of a temporary or casual nature, but you cannot work for more than three months with any one employer.
Working holiday visas can be obtained by making an application on the internet at www.immi.gov.au, or by lodging a written application at an overseas visa office.
If you do not fit the working visa mould, you may still be able to work if you are sponsored by a company or if you apply for residency. Be warned though, the latter option is complex, expensive and takes a great deal of time.

DIRECTORY

Further Reference

BOOKS

Non-fiction

Birmingham, John *Leviathan*
Sydney's dark, seductive
underbelly laid bare by the nation's
pre-eminent gonzo author.
Carey, Peter *30 Days in Sydney:
A Wildly Distorted Account*
Dual Booker Prize winner and ex-
Balmain resident returns to Sydney
after 17 years in NYC to pen a love
letter told through many characters.
Clark, Manning *A History of
Australia*
Six-volume history, with sympathy
for the underdog.
Dalton, Robin *Aunts Up the
Cross*
Dalton's affectionate memoir of life
in Sydney's most raffish locale,
Kings Cross.
Doyle, Peter *City of Shadows*
Mesmerising police mug-shots from
1920s to 1950s Sydney tell of Sin
City's desperate years and the
insolence of the underdog.
Drewe, Philip *Sydney Opera
House*
An incisive and intellectual
examination of Utzon's building.
Dupain, Max & Rex *Inside
Sydney*
Max Dupain's 1920s and '30s
photographs reflected Sydney's
emergence as a modern city.
Facey, Albert *A Fortunate Life*
Successful autobiography tracing
Facey's life from Outback
orphanage to Gallipoli, the
Depression and beyond.
Falconer, Delia *Sydney*
A sultry, unflinching and violently
loving paean to Sydney – sexy,
gaudy, golden but full of
melancholic rot and humour.
Foster, David & others
Crossing the Blue Mountains
Accounts of journeys into the
interior from Sydney, including that
of Darwin in 1836.
Gill, Alan *Orphans of the Storm*
Shocking true story of the
thousands of people who came to
Australia in the 20th century as
child migrants.
*Gregory's Sydney Compact Street
Directory*
A bit of a brick, but the best guide
to Sydney's streets you'll find.
Halliday, James *Australia Wine
Companion*

Good to take on a tour of vineyards.
**Hooke, Huon & Kyte-Powell,
Ralph** *The Penguin Good
Australian Wine Guide*
This long-running annual guide to
the Australian wine industry is
aimed mostly at enthusiasts, but
accessible to beginners as well.
Hughes, Robert *The Fatal Shore*
Epic tale of brutal early convict life;
made into a TV series.
Hughes Turnbull, Lucy *Sydney,
Biography of a City*
Authoritative tome from way back
to now. Good reference material.
James, Clive *Unreliable Memoirs*
Achingly funny memoir of 'the Kid
from Kogarah's' Sydney childhood
by Britain's favourite Aussie.
Keneally, Thomas *The
Commonwealth of Thieves*
History of the colony in the time of
the first three fleets.
Moorhouse, Geoffrey *Sydney*
A fresh look at the city's history by
a distinguished travel writer.
Morgan, Sally *My Place*
Bestselling autobiography of an
Aboriginal woman from Western
Australia.
O'Brien, Siobhan *A Life by
Design: The Art and Lives of
Florence Broadhurst*
The mysterious death and
extraordinary life of the Sydney
socialite and wallpaper queen.
Pilger, John *A Secret Country*
Passionately critical account of
Australia by the expat journalist.
Tench, Watkin *Complete Account
of the Settlement of Port Jackson*
The diary kept by the heroic Tench
was Sydney's first bio: part thriller,
travelogue and comedy.
Walsh, Kate *The Changing Face
of Australia*
A pictorial chronology of a century
of immigration, underlining the
shift towards a multiculture.
Wheatley, Nadia *The Life and
Myth of Charmian Clift*
Well-crafted biography of one of
Australia's best writers.
Writer, Larry *Razor*
Sydney's badlands from the 1920s
to the 1950s, as controlled by two
opposing but equally colourful
madams, brought vividly to life.

Fiction

Carey, Peter *Bliss; Illywhacker;
Oscar and Lucinda; The True*

History of the Kelly Gang; Theft
Booker Prize-winning novelist
whose *Bliss* (later a film and, in
2010, an opera) captures Sydney's
charged sexuality.
Courtenay, Bryce *Brother Fish;
Whitethorn*
Australia's bestselling writer,
though he doesn't always stick to
Oz-related subject matter.
Drewe, Robert *The Bodysurfers*
Brilliant collection of short stories
captures the sex, swelter and gaudy
kink of Sydney through
interchanging eyes.
Franklin, Miles *My Brilliant
Career*
Famous 1901 novel about a rural
woman who refuses to conform.
Gibbs, May *Snugglepot and
Cuddlepie*
Most famous of Gibbs's children's
books about the gumnut babies.
Grenville, Kate *The Secret River;
The Lieutenant*
Local author's acclaimed trilogy of
Sydney as the final – and the first –
frontier for black and white
relations.
Keneally, Thomas *Bring Larks
and Heroes; The Chant of Jimmy
Blacksmith*
Two novels about oppression – of
convicts in the former, Aboriginal
people in the latter.
Lawson, Henry *Joe Wilson and
His Mates*
Collection of short stories about
mateship and larrikinism by the
first Australian writer to be given a
state funeral (in 1922).
Lindsay, Norman *The Magic
Pudding*
Splendidly roguish children's tale –
as Australian as a book can get.
Made into a so-so movie.
Nowra, Louis *Ice*
Two ambitious British
entrepreneurs tow an iceberg to
Sydney in the 1920s with
transformative effects on the city.
Park, Ruth *The Harp in the
South; Poor Man's Orange*
Tales of inner-city struggle, written
in the 1940s. Park also wrote the
wonderful children's book *The
Muddle-Headed Wombat*.
Porter, Dorothy *The Monkey's
Mask*
Sydney-born poet who reinvented
the verse novel with this mesmeric
tale of a lesbian detective who falls
for her suspect.

Slessor, Kenneth *Selected Poems*
The quintessential Sydney poet, famed for his haunting epic 'Five Bells'
White, Patrick *Voss; Tree of Man*
The triumphs and travails of Sydney suburbia colliding with the wild Australia at its doorstep by Sydney's Nobel Prize winner.
Winton, Tim *Cloudstreet; That Eye, the Sky; In the Winter Dark*
The best novels from a twice winner of the Miles Franklin literary award.

Travel

Bryson, Bill *Down Under*
Amusing travel writer Bryson dissects the Aussie character and explores the brown land.
Dale, David *The 100 Things Everyone Needs to Know about Australia*
Essential background reading: covers everything from Vegemite to Malcolm Fraser's trousers.
Jacobson, Howard *In the Land of Oz*
Parodic account of Jacobson's travels down under.

FILM

The Adventures of Priscilla, Queen of the Desert (Stephan Elliott, 1994)
Terence Stamp joins Guy Pearce and Hugo Weaving in high heels for this gritty high camp tale of Sydney drag queens on tour.
Blue Murder (Michael Jenkins, 1995)
Banned for over a decade in NSW, this explosive tele-movie tells of Sydney's blurring of cop and crim and 'the best force money could buy'.
Candy (Neil Armfield, 2006)
Heath Ledger is mesmerising as the cocky heroin addict also in love with the beautiful Candy (Abbie Cornish). Set in Sydney and Melbourne it's a depressing and deeply affecting tale, made even more poignant in the light of Ledger's death in 2008.
Cedar Boys (Serhat Caradee, 2009)
Restless Lebanese youths collide with suburban white girls in an artfully directed drug heist thriller.
Dirty Deeds (David Caesar, 2002)
Set in '60s Sydney, this rollicking crime tale tells of the Mafia's arrival in Kings Cross. Stars John Goodman, Bryan Brown, Toni Collette and Sam Neill.
Finding Nemo (Andrew Stanton & Lee Unkrich, 2003)
Pixar family favourite finds two

fish searching for a clownfish in Sydney Harbour. Bill Hunter stars as the dentist.
Godzilla: Final Wars (Ryuhei Kitamura, 2004)
For his 50th birthday, Godzilla battles a series of monsters across Sydney, decimating downtown Haymarket and blowing up the Sydney Opera House.
Lantana (Ray Lawrence, 2001)
AFI award-winning thriller about marriage and relationships, set in Sydney. Stars Aussie actors Geoffrey Rush, Kerry Armstrong and Anthony LaPaglia.
The Last Wave (Peter Weir, 1977)
Hometown director Peter Weir's spine-tingling tale of a white lawyer haunted by mystical Aboriginal influences.
Little Fish (Rowan Woods, 2005)
A look at Sydney's underworld of drug dealing and addicts in Cabramatta starring Cate Blanchett.
Looking for Alibrandi (Kate Woods, 2000)
An Italian-Australian battles with her identity in Sydney's western suburbs. Pia Miranda and Anthony LaPaglia excel.
Moulin Rouge! (Baz Luhrmann, 2001)
OTT love story from local boy Baz Luhrmann, filmed at Sydney's Fox Studios starring north shore's Nicole Kidman.
Muriel's Wedding (PJ Hogan, 1994)
Toni Collette plays a young woman stifled by the tropics but liberated by Sydney's lunatic fringe.
Newsfront (Phillip Noyce, 1978)
A beautifully told and deftly written tale of rival news teams in 1950s Sydney battling to shoot the best newsreel.
Sirens (John Duigan, 1994)
Notable for featuring Elle McPherson and Portia De Rossi in the nuddy, Sirens follows hedonist painter Norman Lindsay and a clergyman (Hugh Grant).
Stone (Sandy Harbutt, 1974)
A trashy, brutal bikesploitation B-movie filmed at Middle Head and beloved by Quentin Tarantino
The Sum of Us (Geoff Burton & Kevin Dowling, 1994)
A youthful Russell Crowe plays a gay plumber looking for love in Sydney's inner-west.
Two Hands (Gregor Jordan, 1999)
Panania boy Bryan Brown plays an underworld Sydney crime boss, with Heath Ledger as the hapless lad who's entangled in his world.
X Men: Origins (Gavin Hood, 1999)
Sydney boy Hugh Jackman brings the X-Men franchise to Sydney's Cockatoo Island.

MUSIC

AC/DC Australia's greatest rock export. New album: *Black Ice*.
Beasts of Bourbon Revered Surry Hills-sired supergroup. Classic opus? *The Low Road*.
Blasko, Sarah This Sydney songbird won the ARIA for 'Best Female Vocalist' in 2009. Latest album: *As Day Follows Night*.
Cave, Nick Enigmatic, brooding vocalist from the Bad Seeds.
Crowded House The beautifully balladeering Neil Finn-led trio.
Easybeats, The Australia's first international rock stars.
Empire of the Sun Chart-topping duo fronted by Luke Steele.
Divinyls, The Punchy vintage rock outfit fronted by satanic schoolgirl Chrissie Amphlett.
Hirschfelder, David One of Australia's most successful modern composers.
Hoodoo Gurus One of Australia's great singles bands, going strong 30 years after forming in Sydney.
INXS Michael Hutchence, fronted this globally successful outfit until his death in 1997.
Keyes, Perry Sydney's gutter laureate of song. New opus: *Johnny Ray's Downtown*.
Kelly, Paul A Melbourne troubadour who came of age in Sydney, Kelly's paeons to the city include 'Randwick Bells' and 'From St Kilda to Kings Cross'.
Mess Hall Two Sydney boys on a mission to make unholy blues.
Midnight Oil Northern beaches boys turned international rock stars. The band split in 2002 so that frontman Peter Garrett could concentrate on politics – he's now Minister for Youth in the federal government.
Pnau An electronic dance duo whose fourth album is being mentored by Elton John.
Presets, The A DJ duo who met at the Sydney Conservatorium of Music, their 2008 *Apocalypso* album won them a string of awards.
Silverchair The Newcastle trio attracted a huge following with *Diorama* in 2002. Frontman Daniel Johns's struggle with arthritis in that year turned them into a studio outfit.
Wiggles, The The super-successful Sydney-born 'Fab Four of kid rock'.
Wolfmother Grammy award-winning rockers from Erskineville.
You Am I Definitive mod-rockers still going strong two decades on. Their *Hourly Daily* album captures Sydney like no other.

DIRECTORY

Content Index

INDEX

INDEX

Venue Index

INDEX

INDEX

Street Index

STREET INDEX

Advertisers' Index

Please refer to the relevant pages for contact details.

INDEX

Maps

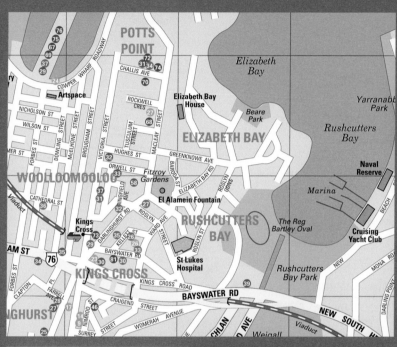

Area name .... PADDINGTON

Major sight or landmark ....

Park ....

Hospital/university ....

CityRail station ....

Monorail station .... ○

LightRail station .... □

Steps ....

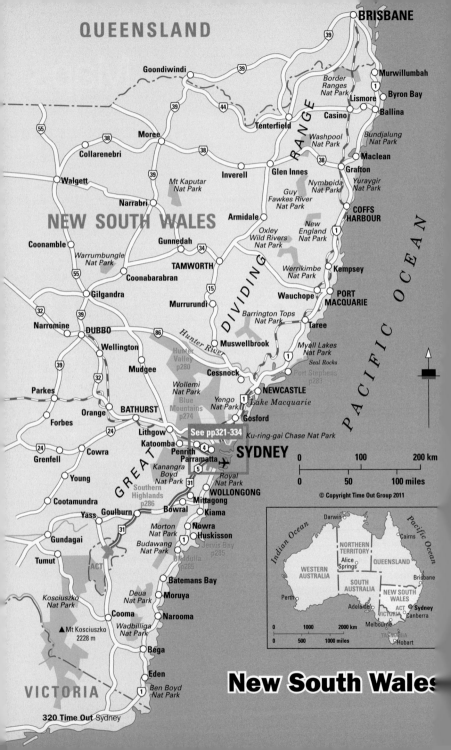

New South Wales

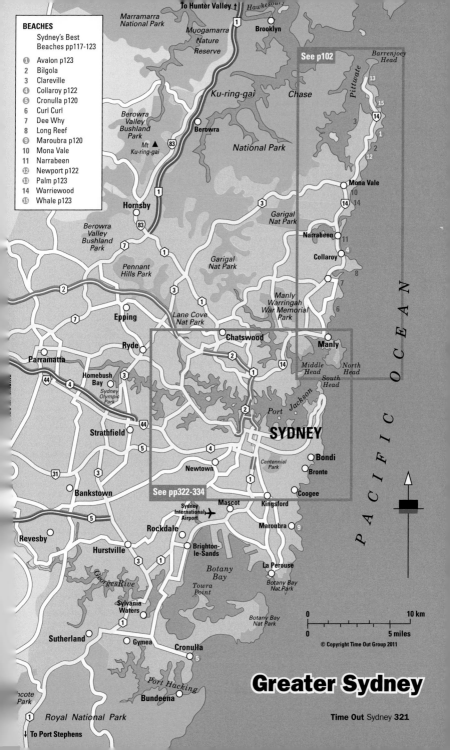

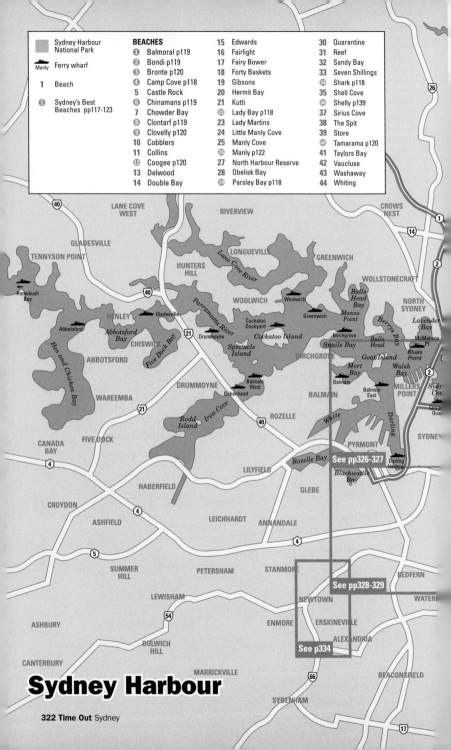

BEACHES

- ① Balmoral p119
- ② Bondi p119
- ③ Bronte p120
- ④ Camp Cove p118
- 5 Castle Rock
- ⑤ Chinamans p119
- 7 Chowder Bay
- ⑧ Clontarf p119
- ⑨ Clovelly p120
- 10 Cobblers
- 11 Collins
- ⑫ Coogee p120
- 13 Delwood
- 14 Double Bay
- 15 Edwards
- 16 Fairlight
- 17 Fairy Bower
- 18 Forty Baskets
- 19 Gibsons
- 20 Hermit Bay
- 21 Kutti
- ㉒ Lady Bay p118
- 23 Lady Martins
- 24 Little Manly Cove
- 25 Manly Cove
- ㉖ Manly p122
- 27 North Harbour Reserve
- 28 Obelisk Bay
- ㉙ Parsley Bay p118
- 30 Quarantine
- 31 Reef
- 32 Sandy Bay
- 33 Seven Shillings
- ㉞ Shark p118
- 35 Shell Cove
- ㉟ Shelly p139
- 37 Sirius Cove
- 38 The Spit
- 39 Store
- ㊵ Tamarama p120
- 41 Taylors Bay
- 42 Vaucluse
- 43 Washaway
- 44 Whiting

Sydney Harbour National Park

Manly Ferry wharf

1 Beach

① Sydney's Best Beaches pp117-123

See pp326-327

See pp328-329

See p334

Sydney Harbour

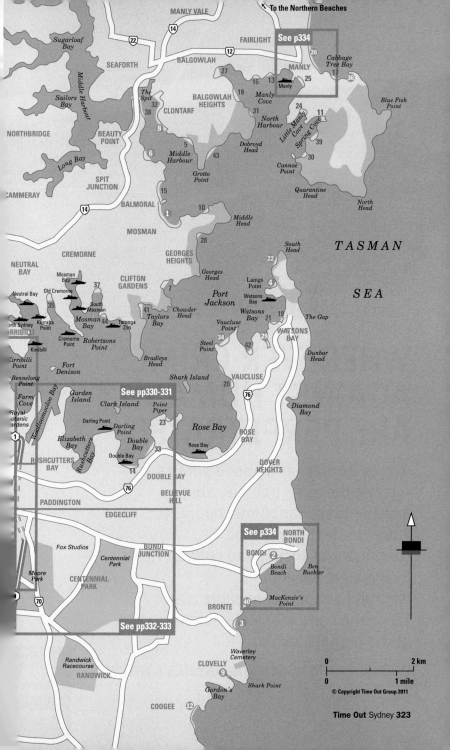

To the Northern Beaches

MANLY VALE
FAIRLIGHT
See p334

22
12
14

SEAFORTH
BALGOWLAH
26
Cabbage Tree Bay

MANLY
27
16 13
25
17
36
Manly

Sugarloaf Bay
Sailors Bay
Middle Harbour

The Spit
32
38
CLONTARF
BALGOWLAH HEIGHTS
18
31
Manly Cove
North Harbour
24
11

Blue Fish Point

8
5
Little Manly Cove
Spring Cove
39

NORTHBRIDGE
BEAUTY POINT
6
Middle Harbour
43
Dobroyd Head
Cannae Point
30

Long Bay
15
Grotto Point
Quarantine Head
North Head

SPIT JUNCTION
BALMORAL
1
10
Middle Head

CAMMERAY
14
MOSMAN
28

CREMORNE
GEORGES HEIGHTS
South Head
TASMAN

NEUTRAL BAY
CLIFTON GARDENS
Georges Head
22
4

Mosman Bay
37
7
Laings Point
Watsons Bay
SEA

Neutral Bay
35
Old Cremorne
South Mosman
41
Taylors Bay
Chowder Head
Watsons Bay
21 19
The Gap

Kurraba Point
Mosman Bay
44
Taronga Zoo
Vaucluse Point
34
29
WATSONS BAY

North Sydney
Cremorne Point
Robertsons Point
Bradleys Head
42
Dunbar Head

Kirribilli
KIRRIBILLI
Port Jackson

Kirribilli Point
Fort Denison
Shark Island
Steel Point
VAUCLUSE

Bennelong Point
Woolloomooloo Bay
Garden Island
20
76

Farm Cove
See pp330-331
Clark Island
Point Piper
Diamond Bay

Royal Botanic Gardens
1
Darling Point
23
Rose Bay

Elizabeth Bay
Darling Point
Double Bay
ROSE BAY
DOVER HEIGHTS

Rushcutters Bay
Double Bay
33
Rose Bay

RUSHCUTTERS BAY
14
DOUBLE BAY

76
BELLEVUE HILL

PADDINGTON
EDGECLIFF

See p334
NORTH BONDI

Fox Studios
BONDI JUNCTION
BONDI
2

Centennial Park
Bondi Beach
Ben Buckler

Moore Park
CENTENNIAL PARK
MacKenzie's Point

70
40

BRONTE
3

Randwick Racecourse
Waverley Cemetery

RANDWICK
CLOVELLY
9

Gordon's Bay
Shark Point

COOGEE
12

0 ____ 2 km
0 ____ 1 mile

© Copyright Time Out Group 2011

N

WHEREVER CRIMES AGAINST HUMANITY ARE PERPETRATED.

Across borders and above politics.
Against the most heinous abuses
and the most dangerous oppressors.
From conduct in wartime
to economic, social, and cultural rights.
Everywhere we go,
we build an unimpeachable case
for change and advocate action
at the highest levels.

HUMAN RIGHTS WATCH TYRANNY HAS A WITNESS

WWW.HRW.ORG

HUMA
RIGH
WAT

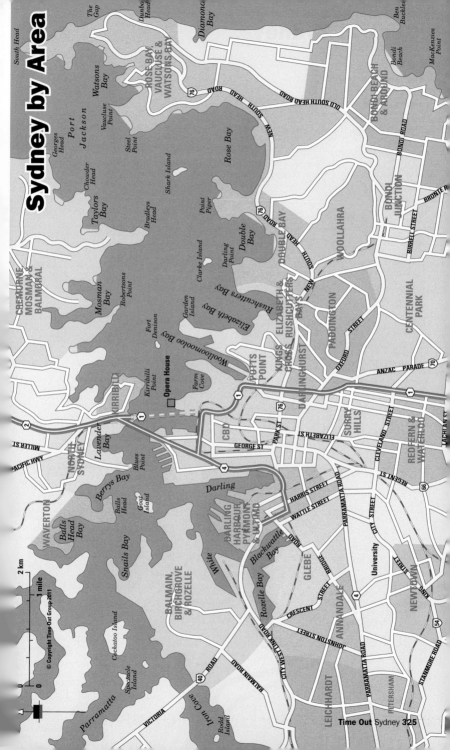

Sydney by Area

South Head

The Gap

Dunbar Head

Diamond Bay

Ben Buckler

MacKenzies Point

Bondi Beach

ROSE BAY, VAUCLUSE & WATSONS BAY

Watsons Bay

Port Jackson

Georges Head

Vaucluse Point

Steel Point

Chowder Head

Taylors Bay

Bradleys Head

Shark Island

Rose Bay

BONDI BEACH & AROUND

Bond Road

BONDI JUNCTION

Point Piper

BRONTE

BIRRELL STREET

Double Bay

Clarke Island

Darling Point

DOUBLE BAY

WOOLLAHRA

CREMORNE, MOSMAN & BALMORAL

Mosman Bay

Robertsons Point

Garden Island

Elizabeth Bay

Rushcutters Bay

CENTENNIAL PARK

PADDINGTON

OXFORD STREET

Fort Denison

Woolloomooloo Bay

KINGS CROSS

ELIZABETH & RUSHCUTTERS BAYS

DARLINGHURST

Kirribilli Point

KIRRIBILLI

Opera House

Farm Cove

POTTS POINT

ANZAC PARADE

Lavender Bay

NORTH SYDNEY

PACIFIC HWY

MILLER ST

Blues Point

GEORGE ST

CBD

PARK ST

ELIZABETH ST

SURRY HILLS

CLEVELAND STREET

REDFERN & WATERLOO

LACHLAN ST

REGENT ST

Berrys Bay

Balls Head

Goat Island

Darling

HARRIS STREET

CITY STREET

WAVERTON

Balls Head Bay

Snails Bay

White

DARLING HARBOUR, PYRMONT & ULTIMO

WATTLE STREET

PARRAMATTA ROAD

University

Blackwattle Bay

GLEBE

ANNANDALE

NEWTOWN

KING STREET

Cockatoo Island

BALMAIN, BIRCHGROVE & ROZELLE

Rozelle Bay

CRESCENT

JOHNSTON STREET

STANMORE ROAD

Spectacle Island

CITY WEST LINK ROAD

BALMAIN ROAD

LEICHHARDT

PARRAMATTA ROAD

PETERSHAM

Parramatta

Iron Cove

VICTORIA

Rodd Island

2 km

1 mile

© Copyright Time Out Group 2011

Central Sydney

❶ Hotels pp126-147
❶ Restaurants pp148-175
❶ Cafés pp176-183
❶ Bars & Pubs pp184-193

© Copyright Time Out Group 2011

400 m
400 yds

WHARF ROAD
YEEND ST

Goat Island

Balmain
Wharf

Mort Bay

Millers
Point

CAMPBELL ST
WATERVIEW ST
COLGATE AVE
THE AVE
DUKE STREET
NICHOLSON STREET
GALLIMORE AVE
JOHNSTON ST
WESTON ST
LITTLE NICHOLSON ST

Balmain East
Wharf

Harbour
Control
Tower

BETTINGTON
ST

94
DARLING STREET
GLADSTONE STREET
JUBILEE PLACE
GRAFTON ST

BALMAIN

Peacock
Point

Johnstons Bay

Pyrmont Point
Park

Jones Bay
Wharf

Jones Bay

Pyrmont Bay

Overseas
Pasenger
Terminal

ROZELLE

39

PYRMONT

PIRRAMA ROAD

Darling
Harbour

BOWMAN STREET
John Street
Square
LR
JOHN STREET
HARRIS STREET
PYRMONT STREET
36
LR
Star
City
Star
City
22
LR
Australian National
Maritime Museum

King Street
Wharf

Sydney
Aquarium

SAUNDERS STREET
MILLER STREET
LR
Pyrmont
Bay
LR
Pymont
Bridge

Darl
Pe

Blackwattle Bay

40
38

40
UNION STREET
PYRMONT BRIDGE RD
Fish
Markets
ADA PLACE
BULWARA ROAD
BUNN ST
PYRMONT ST
Harbourside
MURRAY ST
DARLING DRIVE
24
M
Harbourside

Cock
Bay W

See
p328

Convention
LR
23
M
Cockle Ba

Convention Cent

A   B   C   D

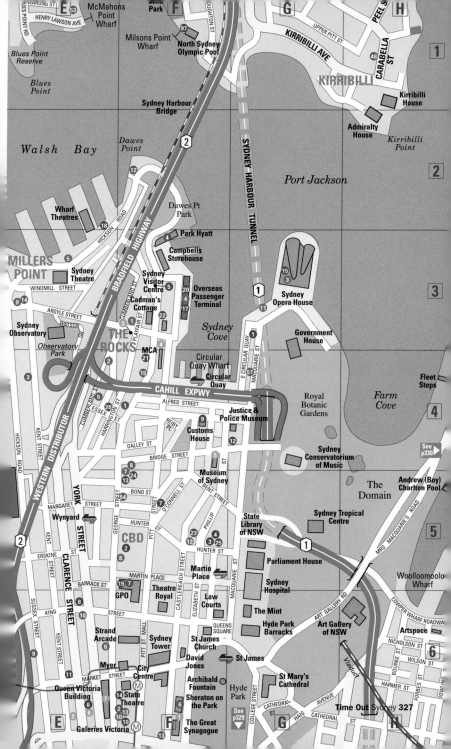

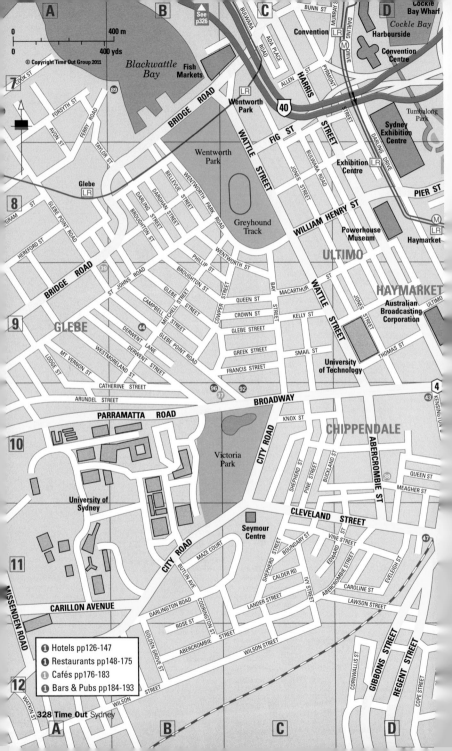

Legend

① Hotels pp126-147
① Restaurants pp148-175
① Cafés pp176-183
① Bars & Pubs pp184-193

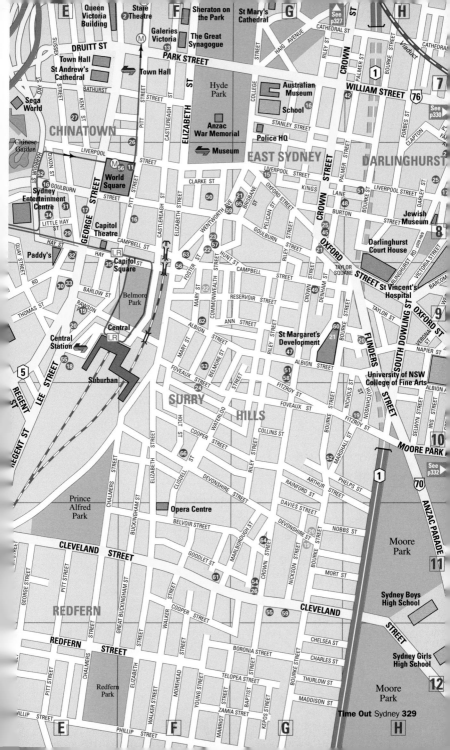

E

Queen
Victoria
Building

State
Theatre

F

Sheraton on
the Park

St Mary's
Cathedral

G

See
p327

CATHEDRAL ST

CROWN

BOURKE STREET

H

Viaduct

CATHEDRAL

DRUITT ST

Galeries
Victoria

The Great
Synagogue

HAIG AVENUE

PALMER STREET

RILEY STREET

1

7

Town Hall

PARK STREET

St Andrew's
Cathedral

Town Hall

BATHURST

PITT STREET

STREET

CASTLEREAGH

ELIZABETH

STREET

STREET

Hyde
Park

COLLEGE

STREET

Australian
Museum

School

STANLEY STREET

WILLIAM STREET

76

See
p330

FORBES ST

CLAPTON

Sega
World

CHINATOWN

27

Chinese
Garden

52

16

GOULBURN
STREET

31

GEORGE STREET

17

29

Paddy's

HAY ST

32

30

33

20

LIVERPOOL

STREET

56 11

World
Square

PITT

16

Capitol
Theatre

LITTLE HAY
ST

LR

HAY

35

Capitol
Square

BARLOW ST

RAWSON
15

26

ST

34

Sydney
Entertainment
Centre

STREET

Anzac
War Memorial

Museum

CLARKE ST

50

WENTWORTH AVE

21

59

Police HQ

EAST SYDNEY

LIVERPOOL STREET

15

BRISBANE
ST

OXFORD STREET

PELICAN ST

KINGS

CROWN

STREET

PALMER

STREET

LANE

51

48

BURTON

25

45

OXFORD

21

STREET

TAYLOR
SQUARE

60
21

DARLINGHURST

25

17

Jewish
Museum

8

Darlinghurst
Court House

DARLINGHURST RD

VICTORIA STREET

9

St Vincent's
Hospital

BARCOM

WE

CASTLEREAGH

STREET

ELIZABETH

STREET

63

22

FOSTER

56

ST

GOULBURN

RILEY

STREET

CROWN

STREET

DENHAM

STREET

23

57

HUNT ST

CAMPBELL

ST

22

COMMONWEALTH

MARY ST

ALBION

62

ANN

STREET

Belmore
Park

Central

Central
Station

LR

55

18

Suburban

5

REGENT ST

LEE

STREET

THOMAS ST

QUAY STREET
RD

RESERVOIR

STREET

STREET

49

60
21

FLINDERS STREET

St Margaret's
Development

47

ALBION

51

58

TAYLOR STREET

SOUTH DOWLING ST

20

University of NSW
College of Fine Arts

OXFORD ST

VERONA ST

NAPIER ST

ALBION

IRIS

SELWYN

STREET

10

MOORE PARK

See
p332

FITZROY ST

SURRY

HOLT

ST

COOPER

ST

66

ST

53

FOVEAUX

24

ST

BELMORE ST

MARY ST

FOVEAUX

STREET

HILLS

WATERLOO

STREET

COLLINS

STREET

FITZROY ST

BOURKE

STREET

19

NICHOLS ST

NICHOLSON ST

52

MARSHALL ST

PHELPS ST

1

70

ANZAC PARADE

STREET

Moore
Park

11

Prince
Alfred
Park

CLEVELAND

STREET

Opera Centre

BELVOIR STREET

CHALMERS

STREET

BUCKINGHAM STREET

GREAT BUCKINGHAM STREET

ELIZABETH

STREET

GOODLET ST

MARLBOROUGH ST

DEVONSHIRE

STREET

CLISDELL

STREET

RILEY

ST

RAINFORD ST

DAVIES STREET

20

19

NOBBS ST

ARTHUR

STREET

MORT ST

CROWN

STREET

NICKSON ST

BOURKE

STREET

Moore
Park

Sydney Boys
High School

REDFERN

GEORGE STREET

PITT STREET

REDFERN

STREET

Redfern
Park

CHALMERS

ELIZABETH

STREET

WALKER STREET

64

61

54
26

COOPER

STREET

55

59

CLEVELAND

CHELSEA ST

BORONIA STREET

CHARLES ST

THURLOW ST

BOURKE STREET

STREET

Sydney Girls
High School

12

Moore
Park

PHILLIP

STREET

PITT

STREET

MOREHEAD

YOUNG STREET

BAPTIST

TELOPEA STREET

ZAMIA STREET

MARRIOTT

KEPOS STREET

PHILLIP

STREET

E

F

G

H

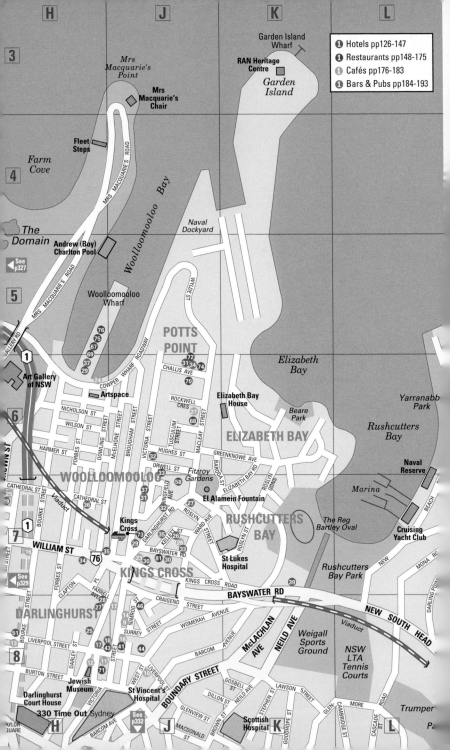

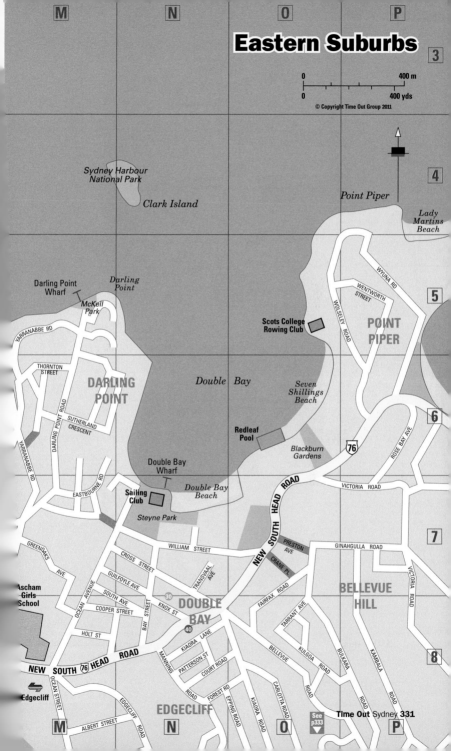

0   400 m
0   400 yds
© Copyright Time Out Group 2011

M   **N**   **O**   **P**

3

4

5

6

7

8

Sydney Harbour National Park

Clark Island

Point Piper

Lady Martins Beach

Darling Point Wharf

Darling Point

McKell Park

Scots College Rowing Club

POINT PIPER

WYUNA RD

WENTWORTH STREET

WOLSELEY ROAD

ROSE BAY AVE

YARRANABBE RD

THORNTON STREET

DARLING POINT

Double Bay

Seven Shillings Beach

DARLING POINT ROAD

SUTHERLAND CRESCENT

YARRANABBE ROAD

EASTBOURNE RD

Redleaf Pool

Blackburn Gardens

76

VICTORIA ROAD

Double Bay Wharf

Sailing Club

Double Bay Beach

NEW SOUTH HEAD ROAD

Steyne Park

WILLIAM STREET

PRESTON AVE

GINAHGULLA ROAD

VICTORIA ROAD

CROSS STREET

TRANSVAAL AVE

CRANE PL

GREENOAKS AVE

GUILFOYLE AVE

OCEAN AVENUE

SOUTH AVE

COOPER STREET

30

KNOX ST

BAY STREET

DOUBLE BAY

FAIRFAX ROAD

TARRANT AVE

BELLEVUE HILL

VICTORIA ROAD

Ascham Girls School

HOLT ST

40

KIAORA LANE

MANNING ROAD

PATTERSON ST

COURT ROAD

BELLEVUE ROAD

KULGOA ROAD

BULKARA ROAD

KAMBALA ROAD

NEW SOUTH 76 HEAD ROAD

OCEAN STREET

EDGECLIFF ROAD

ALBERT STREET

EDGECLIFF

FOREST RD

EPPING ROAD

KIAORA ROAD

CARLOTTA ROAD

Edgecliff

See p333 ▼

Time Out Sydney **331**

M   **N**   **O**   **P**

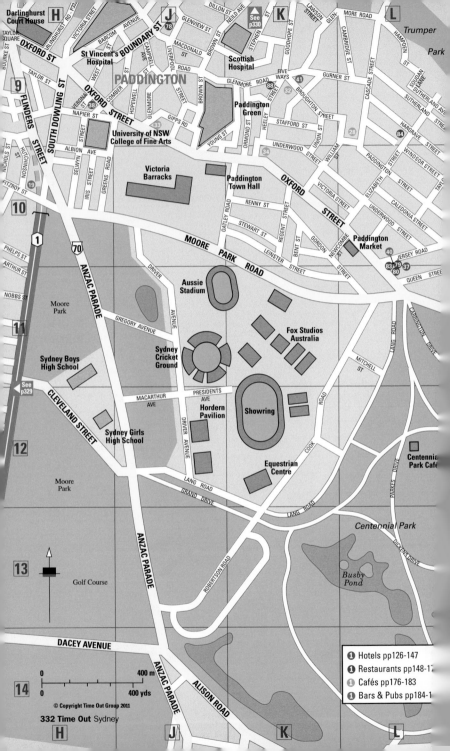

332 Time Out Sydney

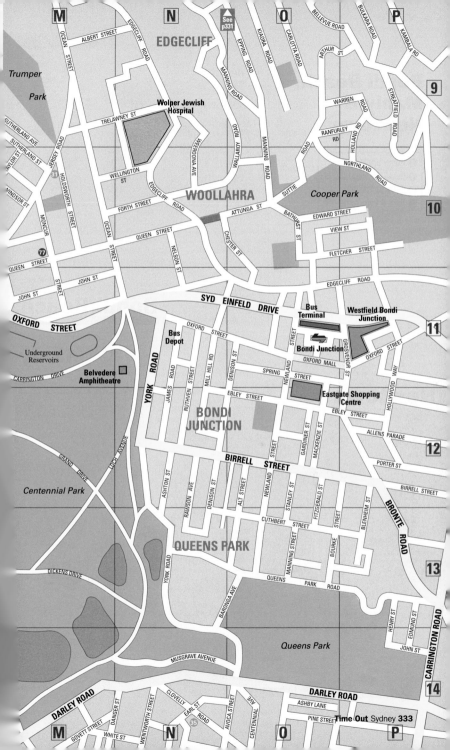

Bondi Beach, Manly & Newtown

- ❶ Hotels pp126-147
- ❶ Restaurants pp148-175
- ❶ Cafés pp176-183
- ❶ Bars & Pubs pp184-193

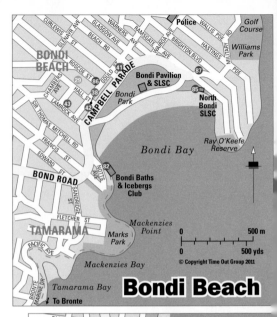

Bondi Beach

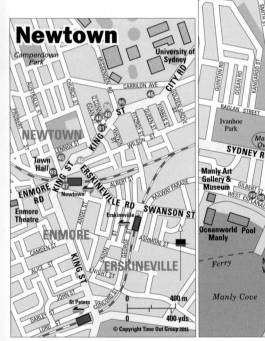

Newtown

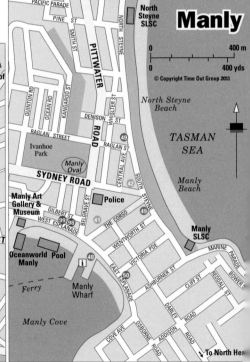

Manly

Network Map

Sydney Ferries

Parramatta
Charles St

Rydalmere
John St ♿

Meadowbank
Bowden St

Bayview Park
Burwood Rd ♿

Kissing Point
Kissing Point Rd ♿

Sydney Olympic Park
Burroway Rd ♿

Cabarita
Cabarita Pl ♿

Abbotsford
Great North Rd ♿

Chiswick
Blandford Dr ♿

Huntleys Point
Huntleys Point Rd

Drummoyne
Wolseley St

Cockatoo Island

Woolwich
Valentia St ♿

Greenwich
Mitchell St

Birchgrove
Louisa Rd

Balmain West
Elliott St

Balmain
Thames St

Balmain East
Darling St

Pyrmont Bay
(Casino/Maritime Museum)
(No wheelchair access at very low tide) ♿

Darling Harbour
Terminal ♿

McMahons
Point
Henry Lawson Ave

Milsons Point /
Luna Park
Alfred St South

Kirribilli
Holbrook Ave

North Sydney
High St

Neutral Bay
Hayes St ♿

Kurraba
Point
Kurraba Rd

Mosman Bay ♿
Avenue Rd

Old Cremorne
Green St

South Mosman
Musgrave St

Cremorne Point ♿
Milson Rd

Taronga Zoo ♿
Athol Wharf Rd

Manly
Terminal ♿

Watsons Bay
Military Rd

Rose Bay
Lyne Park

Double Bay
Bay St

Darling Point ♿
McKell Park (Stops Mon–Fri only)

Garden Island ♿
Naval Heritage Centre

Circular Quay Ferry Terminal

Wharf **2** ♿

Wharf **3** ♿

Wharf **4** ♿

Wharf **5** ♿

▲ N

Services:

— Darling Harbour / Balmain East
— Parramatta River
— Woolwich / Balmain
— Neutral Bay

| | |
|—|—|
| Mosman |
| Rose Bay / Watsons Bay |
| Manly |
| Taronga Zoo |

Key:

∞ Multiple services stop at this wharf

♿ Wheelchair access
(ramp grade varies depending on tide)

⋯ Saturday, Sunday and Public holiday
(Woolwich / Balmain Route only)

(!) Monday to Sunday after 7.30pm,
all services from wharves 2 and 5
will depart from Wharf 4.

Transport
NSW | Sydney Ferries

© Copyright Sydney Ferries October 2010

Includes South West rail link - under construction

Sydney suburban train lines

- Eastern Suburbs & Illawarra Line
- Bankstown Line
- Inner West Line
- Cumberland Line
- Airport & East Hills Line ✈
- South Line
- North Shore and Western Line
- Northern Line
- Carlingford Line
- Olympic Park Sprint and special event services

Tram line

- Lilyfield Line

Operated by Metro Light Rail. Separate fares apply.

Transport interchanges

- Interchange between CityRail services
- Bus (including bus transitways)
- Ferry wharf near station
- Monorail stop near station
- Tram
- Sydney Airport
- Coach
- Car park near station

Stations with wheelchair access

- Wheelchair access (staffed for all train services)
- Wheelchair access (not staffed for all train services)
- Assisted access (may be accessible with staff assistance)

Station access fee applies at these stations

N

NSW GOVERNMENT | Transport CityRail

www.cityrail.info
Transport info 131 500

To CityRail's Newcastle & Central Coast Line and Hunter Line

To CityRail's Blue Mountains Line

To CityRail's South Coast Line

To CityRail's Southern Highlands Line

Some Southern Highlands services operate directly to and from Central.

South West rail link under construction